CASTLES
OF BRITAIN AND
IRELAND

CASTLES
OF BRITAIN AND
IRELAND

THE ULTIMATE REFERENCE BOOK
WITH OVER 1,350 GAZETTEER ENTRIES

PLANTAGENET SOMERSET FRY

LONDON NEW YORK SYDNEY TORONTO

A DAVID & CHARLES BOOK

PHOTOGRAPHS BY
DAVID LYONS

Text Copyright © Plantagenet Somerset Fry 1980, 1990, 1996
Photography Copyright © David Lyons 1996
Artworks by Richard Maguire and David Dawson, © David & Charles 1996

First published in the UK in 1996
This edition published 1996 by BCA by arrangement with David & Charles

CN 8807

Parts of this book were first published in 1980 as *The David & Charles Book of Castles*
and revised in 1990 as *Castles of the British Isles.*

Plantagenet Somerset Fry has asserted his right to be identified as author of
this work in accordance with the Copyright, Designs and Patents Act, 1988.

A catalogue record for this book is available from the British Library.

ISBN 0 7153 0242 6

Book design by Paul Cooper
and printed in Italy by New Interlitho Italia SpA
for David & Charles
Brunel House   Newton Abbot   Devon

Page 1: Dundrum (see page 92)
Page 2: Rochester (see page 36)

Contents

Acknowledgements 6

Introduction 7

1 What is a Castle? 9

2 Timber and Earth Castles 15

3 The First Stone Castles 22

4 Building Castles 35

5 Attack and Defence 41

6 Gunpowder and Firearms 56

7 Castles in Wales 60

8 Border Castles 68

9 Castles in Scotland 73

10 Castles in Ireland 86

11 Life in a Medieval Castle 104

12 Later Castles in England and Wales 108

13 The End of the Castle 111

Gazetteer

Introduction to the Gazetteer 116

England 119

Ireland 192

Scotland 238

Wales 297

County Listing 325

Glossary 330

Bibliography 331

Index 333

Acknowledgements

In the Bibliography I have acknowledged the very considerable help afforded to my research assistants and myself, for the original 1980 edition and for this new enlarged edition, by many government departments, agencies, university and city libraries, local authorities, and private organisations and individuals. I remain very grateful to Geoffrey Kelly and Richard Slaughter, both at the University of East Anglia when the original work was done. They helped prodigiously with examining thousands of journals, chronicles, documents, reports etc in England and Wales. Charlotte Sellar did likewise in Scotland. For the new edition I owe a debt to many people for individual aspects of Irish castles (included for the first time), in particular to Dr C.T. Cairns, Kenneth Wiggins, several of the staff of the Office of Public Works in Eire who gave much help at individual sites, and to Glory Chenery for coordinating the Irish studies.

For the first edition I had essential help from Scotland's Ordnance Survey and from the Department of Map Studies at Edinburgh University, which I went to again for the new edition. I owe a renewed debt to the staff of the University Library at Cambridge, in particular to the Map Room. I am also very grateful to the Ordnance Survey in Dublin. I have been consistently encouraged for some twenty years by a huge number of people interested in, or involved with, castles of Britain and Ireland, a list too long to set out, but I believe they know how much I owe them all.

My neighbours, Maureen and Michael Stephenson, at very short notice and with the highest skill and enthusiasm, produced the revised text and the new work on Ireland in diskette and print-out form, and I am extremely grateful to them both.

I am also most grateful to the Society of Authors, who generously gave me a grant from the Authors' Foundation to help with my expenses in the Irish research.

Whatever virtues this work has, they are greatly enhanced by the fine drawings and plans of English, Welsh and Scottish castles by the artist Richard Maguire, and of Ireland by the artist David Dawson, and I acknowledge the high quality of their work with great gratitude.

PLANTAGENET SOMERSET FRY   Suffolk 1996

PHOTOGRAPHIC CREDITS

Athenry p195, *Cahir* p97, Roscrea p234: Office of Public Works, Dublin

King John's, Limerick p224: Shannon Development

Windsor: right of centre is the huge cylindrical shell enclosure, which surrounds a slightly oval great tower, about 31 metres (100 ft) in diameter.

Introduction

Why another book on castles? The reader may well ask. What is there left to say that has not already been written in the seemingly endless succession of books on the subject? And indeed, apart from details of recent excavations at several castle sites – and one can reckon that there will be about a dozen interesting discoveries every 10 years – the subject may seem to have been all but exhausted. Yet it has not.

Throughout Western Europe there is a growing interest in castles, their architecture, the economics of building them, their roles in medieval society, their influence on events, and their influence on each other. There is even a learned journal devoted to 'castellology', called *Château Gaillard*, which is named after the famous French castle of that name, built by Richard the Lionheart on a rock overlooking the Seine. And there are the books and monographs that continue to appear. These may be divided into two kinds: the academic studies, all of which are essential reading for anyone interested in castles beyond the point of an afternoon out visiting one; and the more popular surveys, which attempt to encapsulate in one volume the complex subject of castles and what people used them for. There will always be a need for both sorts. I believe there is also room for a fresh look at castles which bridges the gap between the serious study and the popular survey, and projects in perhaps simpler terms the latest thinking about castles based upon the most recent investigations. And there is room for a one-volume gazetteer of the castles of Great Britain and Ireland, whether they be extensive, palatial stone buildings or long-neglected earth mounds with or without stone remnants.

There is a tendency in popular studies of castles to perpetuate some of the theories and assumptions of earlier works. One can, for example, still read of the notion that there was a tidy progression in the development of medieval castle-building: square great towers (wrongly called 'keeps') were followed by polygonal great towers, which in turn advanced to cylindrical great towers. Yet this view has been disposed of for some time (see Chapter 3). Another oft-repeated contention is that the role of the castle declined because

A view of the north-west front of Tolquhon, with its two semi-cylindrical towers on the gatehouse. Note the triple opening gunports at chest level in the twin towers, covering the entrance.

of the introduction of gunpowder and artillery, but this overlooks the long period (more than three centuries) after these innovations, during which castles remained for most of the time manifestly important. It also ascribes to early artillery an effectiveness that it certainly did not possess. Indeed several medieval castles withstood months of intermittent artillery attack during the Civil War (notably Raglan and Donnington) and are still standing to prove it. These and other assumptions merit discussion, for alternative views add greatly to the overall fascination of castles and their development.

The first third of this book is directed to wards an understanding of castle design and building, of the materials used, and of the role castles played in medieval society. It proposes no new theories and it reveals few startling discoveries. But the most interesting research results of recent years are discussed in some detail.

The first part is followed by the gazetteer, which is arranged in alphabetical order in England, Ireland, Scotland and Wales. It contains a full list of over 1,350 castles and sites that have any significance. It is comprehensive within the limits of the definition of a castle which is given on p. 9, and it covers a building period of about 600 years, from 1066 to about 1650. The gazetteer is probably the first of its kind to deal with the castles in all four countries in one volume. Excluded are the later seventeenth- and eighteenth-century baronial houses in Scotland and Ireland, which might have afforded some protection against siege but which were not normally designed for that purpose. Likewise, English and Welsh great houses which are (or were) called 'castle' but which were not fortified are omitted.

This is a source book of information about castles and castle sites, the result of visiting over 1,000 sites over the past few years and of studying the considerable literature on the subject, from the earliest medieval texts (in translation) to the most recently published books and papers. In several instances I have been able to examine and discuss findings yet to be written up, and it is a privilege to be allowed to include digests of these. Within the compass of the book it is not possible to include everything, but there is enough to whet the appetite of castle enthusiasts to take up the search for more, and to join the ranks of those many painstaking and enthusiastic local historians and archaeologists who have done so much for castle history, without whose work no book like this could be written.

Trim is the largest Anglo-Norman castle in all Ireland, its great tower standing inside a huge stone enclosure with many flanking towers and two gateways. The great tower was erected on an earlier motte in c.1200.

1
What is a Castle?

Buildings are generally designed and constructed for a single purpose. The cathedral, the house, the factory, the office block, the barn, the hotel, the theatre – even the lighthouse, the prison and the public convenience – each is designed basically to fulfil one function. Looking back in history it was the same: the temple, the villa, the arena, the pyramid and the palace were all single-purpose buildings.

The exception was the castle. From the beginning, when it appeared as a structure in the years following the break-up of the empire of Charlemagne and the resulting collapse of the authority of central government in Western Europe in the ninth century, the castle was built for two separate but interdependent purposes. It was a home for its owner, where he could shelter his family and dependants and entertain his guests, and at the same time a structure strong enough to keep unwanted people out and from which he could attack his neighbouring or more distant enemies or rivals. In short, it was a properly fortified residence. And since the castle was introduced at a time when society was becoming dominated by the mounted knight in armour and by his superiors – the lords, counts, dukes and kings, in ascending order – whom he served and to whom he owed allegiance, we should add the word 'military' to our definition. Thus, the castle was a properly fortified military residence, which is as exact a definition as can be given.

The stereotyped idea of a castle is generally one of a palatial complex of many towers, great and small, some clustered together, others standing alone: thick, tall, battlemented walls interspersed with numerous turrets and a huge gatehouse or two; drawbridges with screeching chains; a vast dining hall; dark corridors; grim dungeons where prisoners eked out their days in a losing battle with rats, hunger and diseases; a chapel and a courtyard; and a plethora of portcullises and heavily iron-studded gates at every point where men came in or went out. This is the familiar picture, fostered by the imaginations of some medieval artists, Victorian illustrators and twentieth-century cinema set designers. The great majority of castles, however, were much less complex and glamorous than that. Palatial castles were expensive to build and very few people throughout the Middle Ages could afford them. And yet each castle, however complex or simple, was an intensely individual structure, reflecting the mixture of basic military needs for defensive and offensive capability with the more personal residential demands of the owner, and it is this, more than anything else, that makes castles so fascinating.

Our definition embraces many thousands of castles, in a great variety of shapes and sizes, which, during a period of 800–900 years, appeared all over Western Europe (as well as those in Eastern Europe and the Levant). More than 5000 were built in Britain and Ireland and all were of two fundamental designs – the fortified great tower and the fortified enclosure and, in numerous instances, combinations of the two. These design types and their variations are discussed in Chapter 3, but we should identify the two basic forms. The great tower, *magna turris* as it is called in medieval documents, is the right phrase for that vertical structure, generally though not always taller than its maximum width, which is nowadays commonly called a 'keep'. 'Keep' is a misleading word: it was not used in English documents until the sixteenth

An artist's drawing of the castle of Saumur, on the Loire in France. This castle was begun in the eleventh century but its appearance here is as it was drawn in the fourteenth-century Trés Riches Heures du Duc de Berry.

century, and it will not be used in this book. The great tower was a fortified house, with two, three, four, five or even six storeys. It was square, rectangular, triangular, cylindrical, polygonal, or D-ended in plan. It had thick walls, battlemented parapets at the top, well protected entrances, narrow windows (though there were exceptions) and it generally, although not always, stood on a sloping plinth. It was built of wood, stone, or sometimes both, or later of brick. If it was made of wood, it was almost certainly part of a motte castle (*see* Chapter 2). If it was stone or brick, it stood inside a surrounding wall with a gateway and with or without turrets along the wall, or it was built as part of the surrounding wall.

It was extremely rare for a great tower not to be inside a walled enclosure of some kind, whereas the fortified enclosure was always constructed as a complete castle

without having a great tower. In these instances, and they were many and varied, the quarters that would otherwise be in a great tower were in alternative buildings inside the enclosure, such as a chapel, dining hall, chambers and guardrooms, which would be ranged together or separately along the inside of the wall or free-standing in the courtyard. Most castles with great towers would also have additional buildings in the enclosure. Enclosure castles were provided with a gateway or a larger version of the gateway, the gatehouse of which in some cases was as big as a great tower (cf., Tonbridge, Dunstanburgh). Although the great tower inside an enclosure was the last line of defence under siege, since defenders of the castle retired to it once they had been dislodged from the parapets on the wall, it should not be thought that enclosure castles without great towers were not capable of offering stout resistance. Many were provided with specially strong towers or turrets along the wall, each of which could be fought for, inch by inch, tower by tower, before surrender. Two excellent examples of such enclosure castles are Framlingham and Conwy (qq.v.).

It used to be thought that the first castles were all built of wood, either on mounds of earth (motte castles) or on more level ground, and that stone castles followed as a form of improvement and as more permanent structures. Stone castles were certainly longer lasting, but it is now clear that castles of wood and castles of stone were built at the same time, in Britain and in Europe, although in Britain the great majority of the 200 or so castles built between 1066 and about 1100 were wooden. What largely determined the choice of material was how quickly the castle was needed and what was available locally. Wooden castles in Britain (whose characteristics are described in Chapter 2) were often built of oak. In the eleventh century this tree was plentiful and widely distributed, and of its many species, green oak was especially suitable for buildings. Green oak was easy to work, and if cut down after about 30 years' growth, it was ready to be made into planks and posts to be cut and shaped without a lot of trimming and wastage. Other woods were also used.

Stone castles were generally built from the nearest supply of stone, and in Britain, as in Europe, the geological map provides a fascinating variety of types of rock which produce stone for building. Among the most instantly recognisable types of stone for castle building are flint, red sandstone, yellow sandstone, carstone, ragstone, limestone and granite. A fine limestone produced at Caen in Normandy was also used in several British castles, although bringing it across the Channel to the site was an expensive operation. Later, in the fifteenth century, some castles were built of brick, often made locally. This may seem too soft a material for fortification, but this is not always so and one or two brick-built castles were involved in sieges or attacked with guns.

The castle was the product of feudalism, the system whereby a lord and his vassals had a contract, the former to provide protection and to lease land to the latter in return for services of one kind or another, in particular military service. In the chaos that followed the break-up of central government in the countries of Western Europe in the ninth century, accelerated as it was by Viking invasions, there emerged a new unit of society, the estate or domain, which was controlled by a king, a lord or the church, and which became a self-reliant and self-sufficient community. The estate was based on land, not as a mere possession so much as a food-producing unit. The controllers retained some of the land for themselves and employed people to work on it, generally under conditions of slavery; the remainder was leased to tenants to work for themselves in return for payment in kind, that is, a proportion of the produce.

Some controllers, particularly the kings, owned several estates, some bordering on each other and others scattered, and they employed people to manage them and collect the produce from the fields. Because it was so difficult to move goods about the countryside in those times, controllers found it more satisfactory to visit their estates and live off their produce for short periods rather than have everything brought to a central point. Where controllers were kings (rulers of large areas) or powerful counts (eg Counts of Anjou), they were often accompanied on these visits by a retinue of officials to assist with the variety of necessary business such as the administration of justice, taxation and estate matters. As Maurice Keen put it, government became peripatetic. But in doing so, it yielded much of its authority to the lords at the next level in the social structure, for they had the advantage of permanent residence in their domains. They had their own domain laws and were responsible for maintaining order. They swore allegiance to the king or to their senior counts but often ignored their authority. William, Duke of Normandy, for example, was so powerful that his overlord, the King of France, was afraid of him.

The lords became petty kings in their domains and had private armies to defend them against the attacks of neighbours and rivals. But private armies had to be paid for, fed, clothed and equipped, and lords expected their tenants who were, after all, protected by the armies, to contribute to these expenses. Gradually, tenants surrendered many rights and freedoms as the price of continued security. In effect they, and in due course their

children after them, came to be bound to the land for their lives. For the lords the system was useful for continuity in the working of the estates.

There was another class of men, neither great lords nor tenants: they were the professional fighting men. They were bound to the king or the lords by oaths of loyalty to fight for them, usually on horseback, to assist them in any enterprises they might undertake. In return they were protected by the king or lords in the latter's courts, they were given help to maintain their horses, equipment, weapons and armour, and they might be granted land to run as income-producing farms or allotted the revenues of existing estates. These vassals, as they were called, were very important members of the communities. Sometimes they were appointed as local governors by the king, and later as governors of greater regions, counties as they were known (from the Latin *comes*), who collected taxes, presided over local courts and led local levies of troops in war. They were called upon to protect their neighbourhoods when these were threatened by invasion, particularly during the long years of the Viking raids in Western Europe (c.780–c.1100).

Very gradually, a new kind of aristocracy developed, a military caste, and it was strengthened when it became hereditary. When a vassal died his son took over. He became the king's man, as the saying went, with an oath of fealty to the king, promising to serve faithfully for life. In return he was given a fee (Latin, *feudum*), that is, the rights and revenues that his father had enjoyed. It is from this that the term feudal is derived. The feudal system was not, however, foolproof, and vassals could not always be depended upon to remain loyal. They could be won over by other, more powerful, lords ready to give them a better deal. Or they could rebel in order to set themselves up as great lords. They were the men with weapons, horses and training for war, and the initiative was generally on their side. Only a powerful king, duke or count could control them and some even failed to do this effectively. The warring between lords and vassals, and also between lords and their superiors, was to become a more or less permanent feature of the European scene for nearly half a millennium, from the beginning of the eleventh century right through to the mid-fifteenth.

This warfare was sometimes waged in the open, that is, pitched battles between mounted knights and foot soldiery on both sides, but it was more often waged around the power base of the lord, his properly fortified military residence. This brings us back to the castle to whose definition we must now add one final phrase. The castle was the properly fortified military residence of a lord, and by lord we include king, duke, count and certain kinds of knight. A lord required a fortified residence for his own and his family's comfort and protection, to shelter his dependants in time of war and to provide barracks for his knights and their horses, together with the blacksmiths, armourers, carpenters and other needed craftsmen. He also required headquarters from which to administer his estates, and here the nature and size of the castle played a vital role. The castle dominated the landscape. It was the visual expression of his authority over the land he controlled. His tenants and their workers could feel some security under the shadow of the building, as it were, and some of his potential enemies might be overawed by it or, at least, encouraged to think twice before attacking it.

The extent of the lord's control, moreover, could be measured by how far he and his knights could ride to battle, fight and return to the castle in one operation, thought to have averaged about 10 miles each way. In other words, he who held the castle controlled the land around it. The principal objective of a lord at war was not only to keep things that way but also to take the castle of his enemy, if he could, for that would greatly increase his power and wealth, since he would also win the lands that went with it – subject, of course, to the permission of his overlord that he might enjoy his prize. The possession of castles, therefore, was as crucial to maintaining power as having a well disciplined private army of armoured knights. This was recognised by most of the kings, dukes and counts in the tenth and eleventh centuries (and later, too), and by none more than the Dukes of Normandy. Castles evolved in Western Europe as an integral part of the development of feudalism at least two centuries before William, Duke of Normandy, landed on the south coast of England late in September 1066. When castles did finally come to Britain they were grafted on to the landscape by force. They were entirely foreign structures, and to the Anglo-Saxons, the Welsh, and finally the Scots and the Irish, they were strange, alien and terrifying.

The role of the castle in Europe often went beyond our basic definition, such as a toll station for a mountain pass, or an arsenal or a watch-tower. But whatever function they performed, they were the most important secular buildings in medieval Western Europe (and to some extent in Eastern Europe as well). Apart from ordinary homes, they were probably the most numerous, too. Authoritative estimates range from over 10,000 in Germany, as many in France, several thousand in Spain, about 1000 in what is now Belgium, and eventually well over 5000 in Britain and Ireland. The map on p.17 relates solely to motte castles in Britain between about 1066 and the early thirteenth century. It would have been hard to

travel 10 miles in most areas without seeing one.

The earliest fortifications in Europe in the ninth and tenth centuries were enclosures surrounded by ditches and earthwork ramparts, with timber buildings inside. They were essentially defensive and were often built in a hurry to escape the Viking raids or to protect communities threatened by marauding robbers and brigands. As the Viking raids became more frequent and more wide-ranging, the need for fortifications increased. This coincided with the growth of the feudal idea of society. Small areas of land were coming under the control of powerful lords (and larger areas under greater lords, or kings) which they ruled from fortified enclosures and, in due course, castles which became symbols of their authority as well as practical signs of it. Castles evolved from these community-protecting enclosures into more personal residences intended chiefly for housing lords, their families and most necessary dependants, such as servants, armed knights and sometimes bodyguards.

William Anderson (in *Castles of Europe*) has suggested a possible evolution from a fortified site at the Husterknupp on the River Erft in Western Germany where excavations indicated as follows: an assemblage of buildings for domestic use, with stables for horses and stores for weapons, surrounded by a tall and thick timber palisade (a). Sometimes sites were chosen in a loop of a river or stream. The lord and his dependants lived within them, safe – or at least safer – from attacks by Vikings, marauders or greedy neighbours. As the power of the lord grew, because of the increasing need for a protector, he began to separate himself from his dependants who were becoming more firmly bound to him. This is shown by a change in design. The enclosure split into two, with palisading round both halves, the lord's half being on slightly higher ground, i.e. a platform (b). The new form then evolved into the motte-and-bailey castle in which the lord's quarters were piled one on top of the other inside a wooden tower on a mound (c). It seems likely that many European castles followed this sort of pattern, but in time, the last stage, a real castle according to our definition, probably began to be built from scratch in the late tenth century, particularly in France where it was used as an offensive weapon in the imposition of feudalism. By then some towers in stage (c) were being built of stone, not timber. Certainly, when the Conqueror came to England in 1066, he and his Normans knew all about the construction of stage (c) castles in both materials – and indeed in a mix of the two – and the Bayeux Tapestry depicts several examples of timber castles already raised in Normandy by him or with his permission, or by his adversaries. It also portrays the first motte-and-bailey castle he built in England, by the shore at Hastings.

The Normans originated from Viking settlers in north-west France. Under their leader Rollo they established a colony around the mouth of the Seine, with a capital at Rouen, in the early 900s. Rollo was obliged to acknowledge Charles the Simple, King of France, as his overlord, but the Viking raids of the previous century had so fragmented France that royal authority was impossible to enforce. Rollo and his successors, first Counts of Rouen and later Dukes of Normandy, built up their power base over the years through the medium of feudalism and by the use of castles. Wooden castles were built in Rollo's time (not on mounds of earth but simple palisaded enclosures), but his grandson Richard I (942–96) introduced stone castles, notably at Rouen where, some time in the 970s or 980s, he built a fortress-palace that contained a great tower of stone. At Ivry, near Evreux, his half-brother Ralph held a castle which the twelfth-century chronicler Ordericus Vitalis described as huge and strongly fortified. According to another chronicler, it was sited on top of a hill overlooking the town. Ordericus added that the builder was put to death after finishing the work, so that he could not repeat his skills on behalf of anyone else! Other castles built in Normandy between about 1000 and the 1030s included Falaise, Cherbourg, Tillières and Cherrueix. Falaise (probably the place where William, Duke of Normandy, was conceived and born of a love affair between his father, known as Robert the Devil, and Arlette, a tanner's daughter), received a great tower in the time of William. It was rebuilt by his youngest son, Henry I.

The Dukes of Normandy encountered the same difficulties in maintaining their authority as other dukes and counts. The vassal lords they appointed to police the various sub-divisions of land could not always be relied upon to keep their oaths of loyalty. In times of danger from outside, particularly from Anjou or even from the kings of France, or of civil war, vassals sometimes forgot their feudal obligations and pursued private quarrels, besieging each other's castles and even building new ones to add to their power. Technically they were not allowed to build a castle without leave from their dukes; control of castle-building had been instituted as early as the mid-ninth century when Charles the Bald (823–77), King of France, banned the construction of fortifications without royal permission and had, in 864, actually ordered 'castles and fortifications and enclosures' raised without leave to be demolished. The rule was upheld in Normandy, but illegal (sometimes known as adulterine) castles were built, nonetheless, and by the time of the death of Robert, Duke

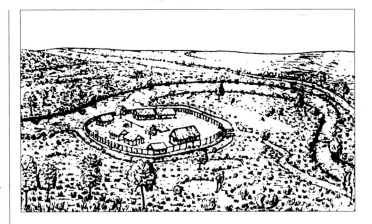

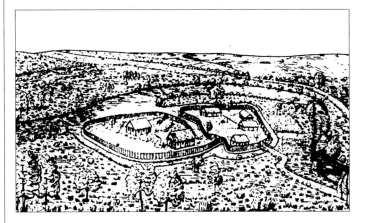

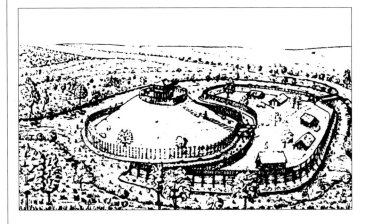

Sequence of stages of the fortified site of Husterknupp, on the River Erft in West Germany. From top to bottom: (a) Domestic enclosure with wooden wall, sited in a loop of the river. (b) The enclosure is divided, both parts having a wooden wall, the enclosure on the left slightly higher than the other, as it is the residence of the head of the community, and (c) the enclosure now occupied by a feudal lord. The enclosure is dominated by his wooden fortress-residence on top of an earth mound.

of Normandy, in 1035, there were almost as many castles in private hands as those which belonged to the duke or to a lord loyal to him. At Robert's death the position was aggravated because he had named his bastard son William, not yet ten years old, as his heir. William was not acceptable to many of the duke's vassals and there was a fresh flurry of illegal castle-building. 'They raised earthwork enclosures throughout many districts and built themselves very safe castles', was how the chronicler William of Jumièges (who died c.1090) put it.

For 10 years the Duchy of Normandy was in a state of anarchy. Then, in 1047, William, barely 20 years old but already hardened by his war-ridden environment, met and crushed a coalition of vassals at the Battle of Val-des-Dunes. This was a battle in the open and he triumphed through the superior skill and horsemanship of his loyal armed knights and by his leadership. In the same year he began the siege of the castle at Brionne and brought it down the next year. These two events were not the end of his troubles, but they marked the end of the anarchy, a fact decisively confirmed when William ordered the destruction of many of the adulterine castles.

For the next 18 years, William warred incessantly to stabilise his duchy. He fought against his own vassals, against Anjou and even against the Vikings, notwithstanding that he was of Viking descent himself. He fought in the open field, he besieged and took his enemy's castles and, according to the records, he won every battle and every castle he invested. By 1065 he had become the foremost warrior and one of the most experienced castle-builders in Europe. He had developed feudalism in Normandy to such an extent that all his knights were bound to give him up to 40 days' service each year, which more or less guaranteed him a standing army in battle order throughout the year. Most of his lords had sworn oaths of allegiance to him (they had by now stopped worrying about whether he was legitimate or not) and few were prepared to break them. His long run of success and his gifts of leadership won him a respect offered to few men in those times.

But the Viking spirit was essentially restless, adventurous and warlike. William, his male relatives and his lords were unable to settle down and enjoy what they had. They felt an irresistible urge to move on, to seek new lands to conquer and bring under the Norman concept of feudalism; so in the middle of the eleventh century, they fanned outwards from Normandy, south into Italy under Robert Guiscard and north-west into England under William himself. William picked a quarrel with Harold II, King of the English, who had refused to continue the pro-Norman policies of his predecessor Edward the Confessor (who surrounded himself with Norman lords for friends), and in 1066 he embarked upon the only successful invasion of England ever to take place in the thousand years following the time of Ethelred II (the Unready). In return for their military assistance in the form of men, arms, horses and money, William offered his land-hungry lords large areas of England in which to settle and construct new feudal lordships, once the Anglo-Saxons had been overcome and dispossessed.

William planned the invasion with consummate skill and carried it out with remarkable daring. Using a force of about 7000 men, he launched his attack against a nation of more than 1,000,000 people. His weapons were the mailed knight on horseback and the motte-and-bailey castle. He intended to impose upon England a revised form of feudalism which had as its principal obligation the allegiance of every man in the kingdom to the king first, and to his immediate overlord, or superior tenant, a tardy second. It would be easier to enforce this revision in a newly conquered land, and the danger of over-mighty lords threatening to break up the new order could be greatly reduced by allotting to the lords their lands in separated estates. If they wanted to rebel, they would not be able to assemble all their knights and troops without running the gauntlet of crossing the king's land, or lands belonging to other lords whose support, or even acquiescence, could not necessarily be counted upon.

William had rebellions on his hands in Normandy now and again during the remainder of his rule (1066–87) but, except for those led by Waltheof and Hereward, Anglo-Saxons who refused to recognise the Norman Conquest, there were no rebellions in England. Under a strong king, William's system worked. It was greatly facilitated by his keeping control of all castles built by himself or by permission. This was the beginning of the system of licensing castles in England, although it was not formalised until the thirteenth century. Castles acted not only as offensive structures in the consolidation of William's conquest and settlement; they were also administrative centres for the king and his lords in the business of getting the feudal system to work. For either use they had to be built in a hurry, and it is easier to understand the nature of castle-building if it is remembered that the great majority of castles were raised under great pressure. The first two, at Pevensey and at Hastings, were probably built inside a fortnight. They had to be, for when William landed at Pevensey at the end of September 1066, his adversary, Harold II, was marching down from his recent victory against Harald Hardraada, King of Norway, at Stamford Bridge in Yorkshire and would reach the Sussex coast within that time.

2
Timber and Earth Castles

William the Conqueror and his Norman lords and knights built the first castles in Britain expressly as military stronghold-cum-residences from which to police their newly conquered lands. They built them of stone (with or without timber) or of earth and timber, and the majority of the earliest castles were of this latter type. These consisted of a huge, flat-topped mound of earth (motte) surmounted with a tall wooden tower, with an irregularly shaped enclosure (bailey) at one side of the tower (or in some cases surrounding it), the whole encircled by a deep ditch. The top of the motte and the perimeter of the bailey were enclosed by timber palisading. These castles, which for convenience we will henceforth call motte castles, were erected in their hundreds between 1066 and about 1200 (and a few even later). The most prominent remains of a great many of them, the mottes, can still be seen throughout England and Wales, here and there in Scotland and there are hundreds in Ireland, too. They are as a rule instantly recognisable. A few examples which can be seen unadorned in towns or villages include Thetford (Norfolk), Pleshey (Essex), Hawick (Borders), Naas (Co. Kildare) and Nobber (Co. Meath), and in the countryside at Hallaton (Leicestershire),

Hen Domen (Powys) and Dromore (Co. Down). There are also many more, bearing the remains of later stonework additions, such as Carisbrooke (Isle of Wight), Clifford's Tower (York), Clough, Co. Down and the two mottes at Lewes (Sussex).

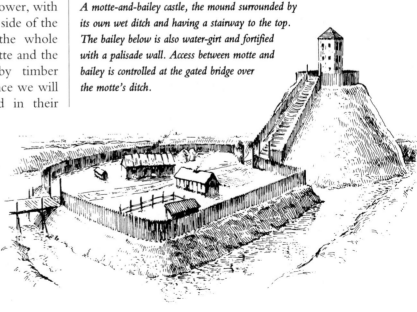

A motte-and-bailey castle, the mound surrounded by its own wet ditch and having a stairway to the top. The bailey below is also water-girt and fortified with a palisade wall. Access between motte and bailey is controlled at the gated bridge over the motte's ditch.

Clifford's Tower (York): the thirteenth-century quatrefoil-plan great tower was built on an eleventh-century motte. The forebuilding is in the centre.

At the time of the Conquest the Continental feudal system was not operating in Britain. In Scotland, Wales and Ireland society was to some degree clannish and none of the countries had strong central government. In England, the Anglo-Saxons were more united, but they had no need for instruments of military repression such as armies of mailed and mounted knights or exclusive fortresses, and there were no Anglo-Saxon castles. The three castles in Herefordshire – Ewias Harold, Hereford and Richard's Castle – suggested in the *Anglo-Saxon Chronicle* and believed by later historians to have been built by Norman friends of Edward the Confessor in the 1050s, cannot be substantiated. Such experience as the Anglo-Saxons had of defensive earthworks and fortifications was confined to their *burhs*, towns that were

strengthened with walls and ramparts, in which whole communities sought protection from Viking raids.

When the Conqueror arrived on the coast at Pevensey, late in September 1066, one of his first acts was to have an enclosure castle built on the spot, inside the old Roman fort of the Saxon shore. The castle went up with great speed. The construction work was done largely by Anglo-Saxons pressed into service as diggers, as is graphically shown on the Bayeux Tapestry which illustrates William's building of a motte castle at Hastings a week or so later. This was *before* the great battle which was fought on 14 October. The castle was a sign of things to come.

The Anglo-Saxon army was overwhelmed and the king, Harold II, slain. Even if Harold had had a castle nearby, it would probably not have made any difference to the outcome. But the fact that there were no Anglo-Saxon castles anywhere in England did have a decisive effect upon Anglo-Saxon resistance to the conquerors.

Building the motte castle at Hastings — an artist's impression of the original panel on the Bayeux Tapestry. The castle was raised on the shore before the battle which William of Normandy won so decisively.

Ordericus Vitalis reckoned that they did not stand a chance against the Norman knights and William's conquest was certainly swift and thorough. By the end of 1066 he had been crowned King of England at Westminster Abbey, work had been started on two, possibly three, motte castles in London, and the Anglo-Saxon earthworks at Dover had been reconstructed. Work had probably begun on several other motte castles as well, including Wallingford and Winchester.

In the next 20 years the Conqueror built, or gave his lords leave to erect, nearly 100 motte castles upon the landscape of England. By 1100, his successor, William Rufus, and his lords, had pushed the number over 200, and these included many in east and south Wales. Probably twice as many again were raised and in use by about 1150, and this does not include the first stone castles that were being built on a smaller numerical scale. Motte castles had also begun to be erected in Scotland by Norman associates of the Kings of Scotland, Edgar, Alexander I and David I. It is worth considering these figures and what they meant to the native inhabitants of Britain. In Ireland, over 340 motte castles were raised by the Anglo-Normans during the first century or so of their colonising, c.1170–c.1300, and though there are many records of Irish attacks on – and destruction of – these castles, indicating a much greater degree of resistance to Norman hegemony than in England and Wales, the concentration of mottes must have had a generally depressing effect upon the Irish (*see* map, p. 18).

Until the first of the stone great towers were completed in the last years of the eleventh century and the first cathedrals and abbeys went up, these motte castles were the biggest buildings ever seen in this country since Roman times. Many of them, particularly those in East Anglia, could be seen from great distances. They dwarfed the houses nearby: the smallest mottes were at

least 30.5 metres (100 ft) across the base, though the average was much greater, at between 61–76 metres (200–250 ft) (as at Ongar, Pleshey, Lewes, Berkhamsted, York *et al*). With their wooden towers, motte castles were anything from about 21.3–36.5 metres (70–120 ft) tall – Thetford may have been 42.7 metres (140 ft). The top of the motte at Berkhamsted was large enough to contain several houses, on which Thomas Becket, later Archbishop of Canterbury, spent money in 1157–8. More than 100 houses were demolished in Norwich to make room for the motte castle put up in the early part of the Conqueror's reign. To many of the simpler town and country folk in England, motte castles were objects of terror. But they were meant to be, for the conquerors had them built to frighten the Anglo-Saxons into submission and keep them subjugated. To emphasise the

The distribution of motte castles in Great Britain (after D.F. Renn).

MOTTES
Extant Examples, 1973

0   60m

The distribution of motte castles in Ireland. (After Glasscock, R.E., Mottes in Ireland, *Château-Gaillard, 7, 1975). County boundaries removed. Question marks indicate possible sites of mottes.*

point, the Normans compelled the Anglo-Saxons to do most of the building work.

The keynotes of William's invasion and conquest were speed and ruthlessness, which of course create terror. They were the equivalent of Nazi *Blitzkrieg* methods. Motte castles were wanted in a hurry. Some were actually completed for occupation purposes inside a fortnight (Hastings, York, Dover). But this was only possible by deploying – 'employing' implied there would be payment for the work – large gangs of men, and William had a vast pool of labour to draw upon in England. Before the Conquest, English kings had a right, called *burh-bot*, to direct workers from their normal jobs into building fortifications for the *burhs*. The men were helping to protect themselves and their compatriots, and they probably received pay. The Conqueror, on the other hand, was forcing men to work on private fortresses which were, with bitter irony, being raised in order to

suppress them. According to the first volume of *The History of the King's Works*, 'Burh-bot became castelwerke'. Labour gangs were rounded up from the nearest towns and, where necessary, from further afield. To build a motte castle at Ely (now visible as Cherry Hill), William took men from Bedfordshire and Huntingdonshire as well as from Cambridgeshire. He also expropriated land from the Abbot of Ely for the site.

It has been suggested that William had a preconceived overall strategic plan for castle-building in England. This is unlikely, for he could not have known the geography well enough. Moreover, an overall plan was not necessary. His army of mail-clad mounted knights, supported by archers of high skill, was the most formidable in Western Europe. Even the King of France, the overlord of Normandy, was afraid of them. William was confident that he would be able to establish his bridgehead in Sussex, take the English by surprise, and win in any confrontation with the forces of the English king. So it happened, and with his army of only 7000 men he swiftly overran a nation of over 1,000,000 people. He could afford to work out the castle-building programme as he went along. It would follow certain tactical requirements.

William divided the programme into two spheres. He would build a number of castles himself with Anglo-Saxon labour directed by Norman captains, at sites at or near key points in England. He would also allow his followers to build castles in those pockets of land he had decided to award them for their part in his victory. They too would use Anglo-Saxon labour. But their castles were to be held only with his specific permission: what he gave he could always take away. Practically all castles built in his reign, and in that of Rufus, were sited on or near important routes of communication across the country. They were near river crossings (Hereford, Cambridge, Bedford, Shrewsbury); they guarded harbours (Dover, Newcastle, Rochester); they protected the coasts from foreign attack (Bramber, Arundel, Lewes); they were built on elevated land to dominate extensive areas of countryside (Carisbrooke, Ely, Windsor), or to overawe towns (York, Lincoln, Winchester, Norwich). They were always near a water supply of some kind. The need for them was often dictated at short notice. Ely Castle, for example, was erected to deal with the last embers of resistance to Norman rule following the surrender of Hereward the Wake. Durham Castle was built to house a garrison for the Bishop of Durham to call out in the event of invasion from Scotland, which the King expected following his recent expedition across the River Forth.

In general, motte castles conformed more or less to a

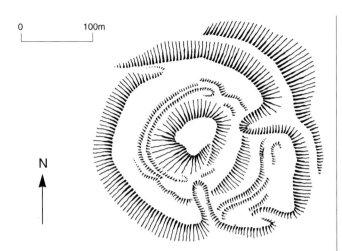

Montacute: plan of the eleventh-century motte castle (after Ella S. Armitage). The high oval motte is still visible today.

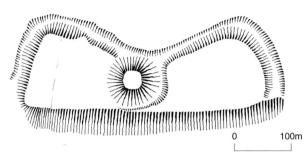

Windsor: ground plan of the original motte castle as it was in the Conqueror's time, long before the splendid buildings were raised.

basic plan. The motte stood astride or next to an edge of the bailey. There were, however, many variations of the plan. In some cases the motte was inside the bailey, as at Montacute and Oxford. At Lewes and Lincoln there were two mottes astride the edges of one bailey. At Windsor there were two baileys, one each side of the motte, and one at a lower level than the other – still the basic plan today. Mottes and baileys were constructed in a variety of shapes. Mottes ranged in height from about 7.6–9.1 metres (25–30 ft) (Hawick) to over 24.4 metres (80 ft) (Thetford). The size of a bailey might be anything from 0.8–4 hectares (2–10 acres) or so, but would generally be such that it could be covered at all points within bowshot from the tower. Indeed, each castle was a unique structure; no two of the several hundred erected were exactly alike.

The construction of a motte castle followed much the same procedure everywhere, depending upon the geography of the site. Some mottes were adapted from natural hill or rock structures. Others were raised artificially by excavating earth from a notional ring on level ground and heaping it upwards inside the ring, which in turn became roughly a V-shaped ditch. If the ditch was to be water-holding, known as a wet ditch, the depth below the water line would not be more than a few feet. Mud and water make good obstacles in themselves. Generally, more earth and other materials were needed than were thrown up from the scooping, and they would have to be brought from elsewhere. Materials included stones (flint and rock), gravel, chalk, clay, loam and sand. Some mottes were built on top of existing earthworks, burial mounds and even buildings. One of the motte castles at York was raised over a crouched burial ground (in which corpses were buried in a foetal position); and Thetford was erected over part of an Iron Age hill-fort. Cambridge was put up on an Anglo-Saxon graveyard. The two mottes at Lewes contained squarish blocks of

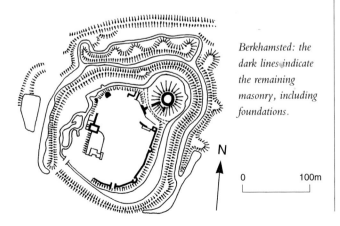

Berkhamsted: the dark lines indicate the remaining masonry, including foundations.

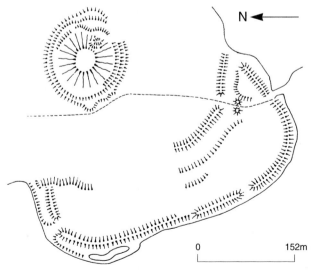

Skipsea: the motte was separated from the bailey by marshes.

chalk and these may have come from earlier buildings. Lincoln and Norwich were raised on the remains of demolished streets.

The digging gangs, probably containing 100 or more labourers, closely supervised by armed Norman soldiers, worked all day. At this rate an average motte could be raised within two to three weeks (York took eight days). The timberwork and the bailey probably needed another month or so, unless prefabricated components were used. When the motte was complete the top was flattened down, and in some instances covered with a hardcore of stone and earth. A palisade of timber planks with sharpened points was malleted into the top around its perimeter, reaching about 2.1–2.4 metres (7–8 ft) high. Some planks were cut to provide slits for observation and for firing bows. And in the centre of the motte a large wooden tower was built.

The tower was the focal point of the castle. It acted as a watch-tower, not only over the area around the castle but also over the bailey itself, in case of revolt in the garrison. It is thought that Anglo-Saxons were recruited to strengthen garrisons where there were not enough Norman troops, and subject people employed by their conquerors can seldom be relied upon for long. The tower was the last line of defence in time of siege, when those of the garrison that had managed to retreat to the top of the motte withdrew inside and shut the door against the besiegers. It was also intended to be a residence for the castle owner.

This raises an interesting point: were these towers fit to be occupied for more than a few days or weeks at a time? Since the earlier motte castles in England and Wales were designed chiefly to play a military role as a base from which Norman troops could police a district, their towers would have been very simple. They had the same accommodation as that of an ordinary grange or manor-house of the time, that is, kitchen and stores at one end, main dining/living room in the centre and owner's sleeping quarters at the other end. Turn this horizontal accommodation vertically on to the kitchen end and you arrive at a tower, three storeys high, with the rooms in the same order, bedroom at the top. Quarters for horses, cattle and other livestock, workshops for blacksmith and armourer, even perhaps a small chapel, all these would have been erected in the bailey, itself well protected by a high palisade all round the edge. Outside this was a ditch as deep and wide as the motte ditch, and wet wherever water could be let in from local springs, river or stream, or in some cases from the sea. Access from the bailey to the motte was by bridge or causeway over the separating ditch or, if there was no separating ditch, through a simple gateway, and then up a flight of steps to the gate in the palisade at the summit of the motte. The motte which can still be seen at Hawick has been provided with a modern step-way that conveys a lifelike idea of a medieval flight of steps.

It is conventional wisdom to accept that timber towers built on newly thrown-up mottes were constructed of logs or planks hammered at one end into the summit vertically, with horizontal timberwork playing a secondary role. There is, however, a case for accepting that towers were built from logs laid horizontally, one resting upon the one underneath which has a rounded groove along its top in which the upper log rests. These logs interlocked the corners at right angles with those of the wall(s) into which they were mortised. The ramming down of four walls made up from vertical components into relatively unconsolidated earth mounds, even if they were made of layers of different material, gravel, sand, stone, mud etc, must have been extremely difficult to carry out and must also have resulted in considerable instability in the positions into which they were forced. Resting the timbers horizontally, even if one on top of the other, and anchoring them together at their extremities will not have put anything like the same sort of strain on newly heaped up earth, but on the contrary would disperse the weight of the tower around the summit. This method of timber construction has been practised for centuries on a colossal scale in Scandinavia, Russia and parts of East Europe, introduced largely by the Vikings from the ninth century onwards. It would not be surprising if William of Normandy brought such techniques to England – he was himself of Viking descent (*see* references in Bibliography).

Like their stone successors, motte castles had an offensive/defensive role, and kings and lords knew very well that there was a good chance they would be put to the test of siege. A motte castle's wooden parts were naturally vulnerable to fire, although it should not be forgotten that thick logs or planks of timber take much longer to burn to the point of collapse than walls of lath and plaster. Castle owners guarded against possible attempts during sieges to burn down their bailey walls and motte towers by draping them with wet hides or regularly splashing them with buckets of water. This was easier to do in the bailey which was near water level if it was surrounded by a wet ditch, but the tower was further away. Contemporary writers often refer to individual castles being burned down. The towers were probably destroyed by fire, which was started by flaming bolts from bows or from siege catapults employed by men on the other side of the bailey bank. But if the besiegers were unable to get the woodwork alight then they would attack the motte directly.

Standing at the base of the great motte at Thetford today, it is difficult to imagine how any medieval army could successfully besiege the tower on the summit. Beneath a top layer of chalk rubble, the mound was earth. One morning of heavy rain would render the sides like an ice rink, sheer and unscalable. Unless the timber flight of steps, which rose at 45 degrees to a height of 24.4 metres (80 ft), could be captured the besiegers would have had to crawl up the slippery sides, metre by metre, hammering wooden stakes into the earth and using these to tie ropes with which to hoist themselves up, one stake at a time – a sitting target for the garrison on top, which could pelt them with all manner of missiles, especially the sharp, cutting and very heavy flintstones with which the Thetford terrain bristles. Many attackers would be pushed down or would slither into the castle's huge moat, so it was necessary to start out with a force of several times the size of the castle garrison (which would probably be between 50 and 100).

Other ways open to the investing army were to try to cut off supplies to the garrison, especially water, and starve them into surrender, or to bring up siege engines like mangonels and, later on, trebuchets (*see* Chapter 5) and assault the motte wall and tower with a heavy barrage of big stone balls. Even if the assailants succeeded in capturing the steps and breaking into the palisade gateway, that would involve the greater part of the force, which would leave the rear part of the motte uncovered and so allow defenders to abandon the tower, let themselves down on ropes to the ground, and then slink off to rafts and boats waiting on the River Ouse nearby, and so escape.

During the unsettled years of King Stephen's reign (1135–54), castles were built in considerable numbers, generally without leave, by various barons and knights who used the absence of firm rule as an opportunity to settle old scores, indulge in territorial aggrandisement and generally earn the well used sobriquet 'the turbulent baronage'. The Anglo-Saxon Chronicle bemoaned the state of the country thus: 'For every great man built him castles and held them against the King; and they filled the whole land with these castles. They sorely burdened the unhappy people of the country with forced labour on the castles; and when the castles were built, they filled them with devils and wicked men.' When Henry II (Plantagenet) became King in 1154, he brought some order to England with speed and vigour. One of his policies was to demolish as many of these adulterine castles as he could, as well as many of those that had been licensed. The first years of his reign saw the destruction of several hundred. More were pulled down after the failure of a revolt in 1173–4, organised against the King by his son, Prince Henry, and supported by many powerful barons. One castle to go was Thetford.

Motte castles continued to be built right into the thirteenth century, although the number diminished. The first stone castles, meanwhile, had been going up in England and Wales since about 1070–80. Among these were stonework fortifications or buildings grafted on to motte castles, for example at Farnham, Berkeley, Berkhamsted, Guildford, Totnes, Bristol, Newcastle, Clonmacnoise, Co. Offaly, and Clough, Co. Down. The extent to which a motte castle could be converted to stone was limited, however, and in the next chapter it will become clear that many stone castles in Britain were built from scratch, even if in some instances they occupied motte castle sites.

In addition to motte castles, the Normans also built a much smaller number of timber and earth enclosure castles, called (unhelpfully) by some specialists 'ring-works' (*see* especially Castles in Ireland, pp. 89–91). These were constructed by raising a platform of earth, in one of a variety of shapes, cutting a ditch round its perimeter and creating an outside rampart from the earth, and erecting round the platform a palisade. Inside would be built timber structures for various needs. The owner would have a residential building, generally single-storey with pitched roof, a separate dining-hall building which might double as administrative quarters, a separate chapel, separate kitchen, and buildings for other needs (stables, workshops, stores, additional accommodation etc). There would be a gateway or a wooden gate-tower, occasionally two. Many of these enclosure castles were later converted to stonework. A good early example was Eynsford in Kent (q.v.), begun in timber in the eleventh century and which received its first stonework c.1100.

3

The First Stone Castles

The Normans imposed an alien ruling class upon English society, dominating the countryside with their motte castles. The speed with which they were erected, the overpowering heights which many of them reached and the huge numbers that were built, were all decisive psychological factors in the Norman success. But as in Normandy, Anjou and elsewhere in Europe, the new feudalism was not maintained solely by the use of motte castles. The Normans intended their dominion in England to be permanent, and their ruthless, practical genius required expression in something more durable than mounds of earth topped with buildings of timber. So they grafted their experience of stone castle-building upon the landscape of England, and within 10 years or so of the Conquest the first stone castles were under construction. We know for certain of the beginnings of the White Tower of London (c.1078), of Colchester (c.1076) and of Chepstow (c.1067–71). Work also began at Pevensey, Rochester, Richmond (Yorkshire), Peveril, Brough and others in the 1080s or 1090s.

What kind of stone castles did the Normans build in England and in those parts of Wales they overran and in which they settled? It is tempting to slot them into neat categories over and above the two fundamental types mentioned in Chapter 1, namely, the fortified great tower and the fortified enclosure. But it really cannot be done.

Very few castles were built in one operation (however long it took) and without later additions, alterations or improvements. Many had several building periods, spread over two, three or even four centuries, which would have meant that their categories changed probably as many times.

Let us look at some of the earliest. In London in about 1078, William I started a huge, rectangular great tower, 36 x 32.6 metres (118 x 107 ft), with an apsidal extension

at one end, which eventually rose to a height of 27.4 metres (90 ft). This was the White Tower. At Colchester, probably a year or two before, he authorised an even larger rectangular great tower, 46 x 33.5 metres (151 x 110 ft) on the same plan, of much the same height, also with an apsidal extension. At Chepstow, beside the River Wye, William allowed one of his principal lords, William FitzOsbern, to construct an oblong tower which was probably meant to be a hall but which was to be fortified (and later enlarged). This was between 1067–71. At Rochester, possibly just before William's death and certainly within a year or two of it, work began on a stonework enclosure near the River Medway, within which, later in the 1120s, a rectangular great tower 34.4 metres (113 ft) tall – 38.1 metres (125 ft) with its corner

The great tower at Colchester was the first in England and became the largest in all Britain and Ireland.

turrets – was raised. In the late 1090s William's son, William Rufus, authorised the erection of a walled enclosure at Eynsford in Kent which was never to have a great tower at all. Rufus also allowed an enclosure to be built at Brough in Westmoreland, while the Peveril family was granted leave to build at Peveril in Derbyshire some time in the 1080s. And at Richmond in Yorkshire, in a superbly commanding position over the valley of the Swale, Alan the Red, who held the estate from 1071 to 1089, was given leave to start on his castle; before he died nearly the whole triangular enclosure of stone had been built. Each of these structures was different from the next, even at these early stages. The differences were to become more marked as additions and improvements were made. The White Tower at London, for example, became the central feature of an extensive and complex

(Opposite) Chepstow was the first stone castle to be begun in the British Isles, c.1067–71. In the foreground are the thirteenth-century great gatehouse (right) and Marten's Tower (left).

A general view of Richmond, with the early twelfth-century great tower at the rear. The eleventh-century Scolland's Hall is on the right.

stone castle of concentric walls with towers and turrets and gates, while Colchester great tower remained almost in isolation, surrounded only by existing Roman and freshly dug Norman earthworks, some of which were later replaced by stone walling with towers and gates. Colchester never grew into the kind of complex that the Tower of London became.

It is easy to see that we cannot classify Norman stone castles meaningfully. Each was a unique structure, the brain-child of a master mason who tailored it to the chosen site. In these early castle-building days, these masons were improvisers, practical men who learned their craft by experience and who did not have the architectural disciplines often ascribed to them. There were no manuals for them to study, so far as we know, and no contemporary plans have been found. As a rule masons were locally hired craftsmen who visited one or two castles nearby and learned something from them, but who in the end did what the country builder does today, that is, discussed the overall idea with his client, made a number of suggestions to fit his requirements, probably pointed out what could not be done, and then got on with the job.

Later in the twelfth century, named masons working on royal castles appear in official records like the Pipe Rolls, although generally the entries relate to what they were paid. It is interesting to find some masons working on several castles, for that is evidence of their experience, suggesting they could be among the most practised master masons in the castle-building business. But it is too early for them to have become the kind of sophisticated military architects we shall encounter in the later thirteenth century, like Master James of St George, whose design skills were triumphantly displayed in the Edwardian castles in Wales and the Savoyard castles in east France, west Switzerland and north-west Italy. Experienced as the eleventh- and twelfth-century masons were, they built castles for their employers to on-the-spot assessments and requirements. In the 1170s, for example, Richard of Wolviston worked at Norham and at Bowes, and possibly at Durham, too, but despite some similarities, Norham great tower and Bowes great tower were not the result of a master-plan adjustable to both sites. The differences were too great.

As the eleventh century gave way to the twelfth, other stone castles began to go up in many more parts of England, notably Ludlow, Norwich, Canterbury, and more were started in the first decades of the 1100s by, or with the permission of, Henry I and Stephen, the best known of which (not in chronological order) were Hedingham, Portchester (inside a Roman fort), Corfe, Ogmore, Bramber, Castle Rising, New Buckenham,

Goodrich, Carisbrooke, Kenilworth and two that have since vanished, Bristol and Gloucester. Most of these castles had a great tower as the central feature, the home of the lord (or, in the case of a royal castle, of the king's governor or castellan), in which he and his family and closest associates and dependants lived, to which they retired in time of siege, accompanied by anyone else within the castle walls, especially if the gates or the walls were successfully breached. It is appropriate now to look at great towers.

In Chapter 1, the categories of great towers were listed as rectangular, square, polygonal, triangular, cylindrical and D-ended. The first stone great towers in England were mostly but not all rectilinear (that is, rectangular or square). These towers can be classified in four categories:

1 Rectangular where the height was greater than the horizontal dimension (Rochester and Hedingham).

2 Rectangular where the height was less than the longer horizontal dimension (Norwich, Castle Rising).
3 Square where the height was greater than the width (Appleby, Guildford).
4 Cuboid, notably Dover, 29 metres tall, 29.3 x 29.9 metres wide (95 ft tall, 96 x 98 ft wide), and Bamburgh.

Rectilinear great towers have thick walls, generally at least 3–3.6 metres (10–12 ft), thicker at the corners, and in some cases, such as Dover, as much as 6 metres (20 ft). Walls were built of rubble and mortar and faced with better-quality masonry, or built straight from cut stone blocks whose outer surfaces were smoothed and squared. They rose from a splayed (or battered) plinth (but

The Norman great tower of c.1120–30 is to the left of this view of Portchester. The outer enclosing walls are chiefly remnants of the Roman coastal fort of the third century.

occasionally, as at Richmond and Goodrich, there was no battered plinth), which provided defenders with an oblique surface on which to throw down missiles from the battlements at the top, or through slits in the wooden hoarding or holes in stone machicolation, confident that these would bounce into the faces of besiegers. Many towers incorporated shallow pilaster buttresses along the outer wall faces and at corners for strengthening. In some later castles, a latrine shaft was incorporated in the pilaster buttress. Some corner buttresses were so proud of the wall line that they are more rightly known as buttress turrets, such as at Kenilworth. The corners of some rectilinear great towers were reinforced with fine-cut ashlar quoins keyed into the otherwise rubble coursing of the walls, as at Colchester, Guildford and many more. At Middleham you can see a good example not only of rubble masonry walls faced with better quality stonework (where the latter has come away in some places, probably taken for another later building) but also how the quoins were keyed into the masonry at the corners. Norwich great tower was restored during the nineteenth century more or less to resemble its original appearance in the twelfth century, and this provides a good idea of the high quality of stonework of which Norman castle-builders were capable.

Walls generally contained a variety of small rooms, such as chambers, garderobes (latrines whose exits issued out on to the wall exterior or down a shaft to emerge at or near ground level into the surrounding ditch – Orford is a good example), devotional chapels, guardrooms, stores, small kitchens and bedrooms. The great tower walls at Castle Sween in Argyll, however, contained very few chambers. At Hedingham, and at other great towers, the upper level of the two-storeyed great hall has a mural passage all the way round, like the triforium of an abbey or cathedral, which passes through the window bays at that level and joins up at the spiral staircase in the north-west corner turret. In many great towers the well is situated in one of the corner turrets and, as in the case of Dover, the well-head was raised to the floors above the basement, serving each floor.

Window openings in great tower walls were generally small on the outside, although splayed on the inner walls to let in more light and so help to funnel out smoke from interior fires. The distribution of windows and loopholes (thin apertures of varying shapes through which arrows could be shot outwards with some protection from retaliation – see the drawing below) was often irregular, and there were fewer at lower level than on high. Many of the two-storeyed great halls in these towers had no windows except at top level, with only loopholes at

lower levels, or perhaps nothing at all. Great towers with particularly scant window provision include Brough, Brougham, Guildford, Middleham, Newcastle, Richmond and the cylindrical Conisbrough, but there are great towers with a more generous window area at Corfe, Rochester and Scarborough.

As a rule there was only one point of entry to a great tower, namely, through a doorway generally placed at first-floor level, which was reached by a flight or flights

Part of a projecting garderobe above the southern ditch at Harlech, built by Master James of St George. It is similar to a pair of his design at the castle of La Batiaz, near Saillon in Switzerland.

Part of a mural passage round the top half of a two-storey great hall in a great tower, such as at Hedingham and Castle Rising.

of steps. In most great towers the steps were wholly or certainly in part covered by a special structure built over them against the wall. This was the forebuilding, and among those that have survived are some of interesting design, notably Castle Rising which has a decidedly ecclesiastical look with its blind arcading; Newcastle which is two-storeyed, has two turrets that are battlemented and occupies the whole of the east wall width; Dover which wraps right round the corner of the great tower; and Rochester which is four-storeyed. Forebuildings are often keyed into the wall, especially if they were constructed at the same time, but sometimes one would be added as an afterthought and was more in the manner of a 'lean-to', as at Hedingham where it has

(Opposite) The great tower of Castle Rising and, on its west side, the forebuilding with blind arcade decoration.

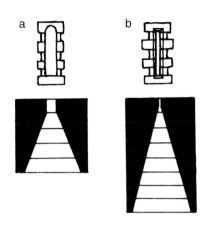

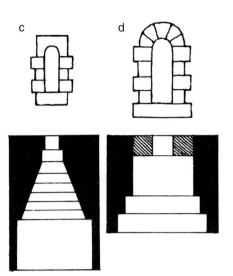

The two figures on the left show windows in the basement storey of (a) Chepstow great tower and (b) Skenfrith. The two on the right show the elevation and plan of window openings at (c) Colchester Great Hall and (d) Canterbury (reconstructed from ruins).

since disappeared. The line of the roof of the forebuilding can be seen on the wall, and it does not appear to have been keyed in. Indeed, the entrance door to the great tower was protected by its own portcullis. Some forebuildings, including Rochester, contained a chapel at one level, generally over the level of the doorway into the tower, and at Dover there were two chapels.

The various storeys of great towers were reached by staircases whose arrangement differed from castle to castle. Most great towers had spiral staircases built into the corner turrets, rising clockwise or anti-clockwise, continuously in one corner all the way up or, in some instances, rising at alternate corners floor by floor, so that besiegers who had broken in had to fight their way

The arcaded cross-wall at Rochester great tower. The well shaft rises up the centre turret.

towers are rare. They have been described by some authorities as a development — indeed, an improvement — upon rectilinear great towers, but of course they are not. None of those that have survived appears to provide any advantages not offered by rectilinear great towers. None incorporates the variety of rooms in their walls that one finds in so many rectilinear great towers. Only Orford Castle in Suffolk whose design is multangular (polygonal with three equidistantly placed square-plan buttress turrets in the circumference — *see* plan on p. 168) offers sizeable accommodation in the walls and buttresses. Orford is a unique structure with no parallel in Britain and therefore in no sense any kind of 'transitional' great tower, whatever that phrase might mean.

Two possible reasons for building polygonal great towers such as Odiham, Chilham or Tickhill (qq.v.) have been conjectured. One is that the builders intended them to be completely cylindrical but ran into difficulties in construction. This is disposed of by the fact that builders had for some time been erecting both church and castle

Orford: the uniquely shaped multangular great tower built by Henry II is in much the same condition now as it was in the mid-twelfth century.

across each floor before being able to get to the next. Some towers had straight flights of stairs, as at Richmond and Bamburgh.

It will be seen that the interior features of great towers were often planned with care and thought to take into account the dual fortress/residence role, and to allow for the fact that in time of siege the complement of people inside might be swelled several times over. It was said of Coucy great tower in France that 1000 people could be accommodated in such circumstances. Most towers were divided internally down the middle or a little off-centre (like Rochester and Duffield) by a cross-wall, sometimes at every floor level. This cross-wall might be a solid wall, a huge flying arch, an arcade of arches or wide pillars and spaces. It served several purposes: it strengthened the tower; it enabled floor joists and beams to be cut to about half the length that would be required to extend the entire tower width and so reduced the need to find huge trees for long timbers; and it provided an additional obstacle for besiegers who had broken in and were fighting their way gradually up the tower (as at Rochester in 1215), although a flying arch would be no obstacle.

Polygonal towers or turrets placed in enclosing walls or as part of gatehouses are quite common in Britain. The Romans had employed this shape, but polygonal great

(Above) Ashby de la Zouch: in the centre of this view is the ruined rectangular great tower (the Hastings Tower) built during the later fifteenth century.

(Right) New Buckenham, showing the stub of the earliest English cylindrical great tower (built in the 1140s), with what is left of the cross-wall. The tower may have been as tall as 20–21.5 metres (65–70 ft).

cylindrical towers. The other and perhaps more acceptable explanation is that they were the personal preference, for unspecified reasons, of the owner – King John, in the case of Odiham. Certainly, the hexagonal great tower built at Raglan (much later, in the fifteenth century, q.v.) was the choice of the owner, Sir William ap Thomas, and his son, Sir William Herbert, who made the six-sided shape a feature of other parts of the castle including the gatehouse, the closet tower, the kitchen tower and the end of the long gallery.

If the polygonal great tower was not a tidy or logical step in the development of great tower design, nor was the cylindrical great tower the next stage after that. Cylindrical great towers were not superior to rectilinear great towers. The chronological progression theory, namely, that cylindrical great towers did not appear in Britain until the rectangular great tower had been established but found wanting, does not hold. Rectilinear great towers continued to be built for nearly five centuries (the Hastings Tower at Ashby de la Zouch, c.1470) and so cannot be said to have been outdated. The earliest cylindrical great tower in Britain so far datable with any precision is that at New Buckenham in Norfolk (q.v.). This was built in the 1140s, at much the same time as the early and uncompromisingly rectilinear great towers of Hedingham, Norwich and Rising. Indeed, it was built for the same man as Rising, namely, William d'Albini, Earl of Sussex, who married the widow of Henry I. Two of the earliest great towers in Britain, London and Colchester, had round (apsidal) extensions at one end. Numerous round church towers (particularly in East Anglia) were raised before square-plan church towers. There were many cylindrical great towers built in France in the eleventh century concurrently with rectangular ones. Comparatively few cylindrical great towers were ever built in Britain, which does not say much for their 'superiority'.

It is clear that cylindrical great towers, like polygonal great towers, were styles of buildings concurrent with rectilinear towers. The decision whether to build square or polygonal or round depended upon factors such as the type of stone material available, whether ashlar quoins and dressing could be afforded, how quickly the tower was needed, and so forth. Clearly, too, there was an element of what was fashionable, and everybody knows that what is fashionable is by no means necessarily an improvement on what has gone before. The tower was to be the owner's home as well as his fortress and if he was wealthy or influential he would wish to impress: a rectilinear great tower was on the whole more imposing than a cylindrical great tower.

There is another point. A number of the great towers in the Welsh Border castles, like Bronllys, Longtown, Tretower (inside a shell enclosure) and Skenfrith (qq.v.), all raised in the last years of the twelfth and first years of the thirteenth century, are cylindrical, while the towers in the Border district between England and Scotland, built

in the thirteenth and fourteenth centuries, are rectilinear, notably Aydon, Belsay, Chipchase and Prudhoe (qq.v.). Clearly we are confronted with examples of regional preference. In Ireland, in the first 250 years or so of castle building (c.1170–c.1420), the number of castles with cylindrical great towers can almost be counted on the fingers of two hands. In the early fifteenth century, when the construction of tower-house castles began in earnest and on a wide scale throughout Ireland, over 95 per cent of the 3000 or so tower-houses raised between c.1420 and c.1650 were rectangular or square in plan.

We have looked in some detail at the nature of great towers of the years c.1070–1200, since they predominated in castle works of the period. Every one of them, except Bowes in Yorkshire (built between 1171 and 1187), is part of a castle containing other buildings. Normally, these consisted of an enclosing curtain wall with mural towers or turrets, a gateway or larger gatehouse, and other buildings set up inside the enclosure, leaning against the curtain or standing free. Orford, for example, now consisting only of its multangular great tower, was once a substantial stone enclosure with wall towers and gatehouse surrounding the great tower. Pembroke great tower stands inside an inner enclosure that is part of a larger enclosure, with various other structures in the curtain and standing free. The castle owner could not get everything into a great tower, certainly not his horses and cattle which were best protected inside the enclosure. If the great tower was to be a residence and a last line of defence, it needed additional protection, so a high and thick enclosing wall was built with a walkway and battlemented parapet around the top, mural towers (square, round or polygonal) and a gatehouse for covering every angle and area of the wall. The art of keeping besiegers away from great towers was to build as many obstacles as possible between them and the tower, compelling them to fight for each one, be it ditch or rampart, turret or gatehouse, in the hope that these would either drag out the siege long enough for a relieving force to raise it, or that so many besiegers would be killed or wounded before the time came for the final assault on the tower that it might be abandoned.

Another type of castle built in Britain from the earlier half of the twelfth century, and mainly in that century, too, was the shell enclosure. This is the term used to describe a motte castle that, later in its history, has had the wooden parts wholly or partly converted to stonework, especially on the motte summit. The palisade round the flattened top of the motte was removed and a stone wall erected. The wall was given a gateway. In some cases,

A view of the large Border enclosure castle at Prudhoe.

wing walls were built down the motte slopes to meet the bailey wall which was also converted to stone. This is well demonstrated at Pickering and Berkhamsted. Inside the stone enclosure at the top – the shell – one of two plans was followed. Either, as at Restormel, a series of buildings was put round the inside of the wall, using it as the fourth side; or, as at Launceston and Tretower, a central tower was built to contain similar quarters but stacked one on top of the other. The tower was often a cylindrical one, but not always so (Farnham and Totnes were rectangular). The outer wall of the shell was topped with a battlemented parapet which was reached by steps, sometimes sited next to the gateway.

There were many variations of the shell enclosure. At Berkeley (q.v.) and Farnham the motte was revetted with stonework; at Farnham the foundations of a rectangular great tower, about 15.2 metres (50 ft) square with thick walls, were found near the top inside the shell enclosure which had substantial rectangular buttresses. At Carisbrooke and Cardiff the shell enclosure was polygonal; at Castle Acre the motte was recently

An aerial view of the early thirteenth-century oval shell enclosure at Restormel, built on an earlier motte. The gatehouse is beside the staircase, near the top of this photograph.

The thirteenth-century tower at Tretower was raised within the stone shell enclosure of high walling.

(Left) In the background of this view of Castle Acre is the late eleventh-century motte castle, which received first a stone hall building (the remains of which are visible in the mound) and then a stone shell enclosure around it. The hall was later modified into a great tower.

(Below left) Rothesay was attacked by Vikings in the thirteenth century.

period; the earliest were in the times of William I and II, including parts of Eynsford and parts of Richmond before the great tower, and embracing Framlingham, c.1200, Beeston, c.1225, Barnwell, c.1265, the sophisticated Conwy, 1280s, Caernarfon, c.1283–c.1323 (which for all its magnificence is only an enclosure with flanking towers); and continuing through the fourteenth century to Bolton, c.1379, and Bodiam, c.1386, and even to Thornbury, c.1510, possibly the last medieval castle to be built in England. Many enclosure castles were built in Ireland after 1400.

Some enclosures were built round a bailey of a motte castle previously having a wooden palisade wall, or on a new site on low or high ground, or even adapting an earlier site of something else, such as a Roman fort or an Anglo-Saxon *burh*. Some enclosures, like Eynsford, began with a simple stone wall built in a ring, inside which various buildings were raised, in stone or wood, at the same time or later. Most enclosures were fortified outside by ditching and ramparts. The ditch was sometimes a wet one, that is, supplied with water generally to a level deeper than a man's height, provided from nearby springs, a lake or river or, in a few cases, the sea. Some ditches were dry, in which case they might be lined with

Framlingham is a good example of an enclosure castle with many flanking towers (in this case, 13). Most of the towers are many metres (feet) taller than the 13.5 metres (44 ft) high walls.

excavated and found to contain the lower parts of a seemingly massive rectangular great tower; at Restormel there was a courtyard inside the compartmented shell; and at Rothesay in Bute, Scotland, one of the only shell enclosures in Scotland, round towers were added to the circumference of the shell for extra protection, and later a large gatehouse was built that had the appearance of a great tower. Other shell enclosure gateways were substantial; Restormel's was two-storeyed and presented a formidable challenge to the besieger.

If we stick to the two basic stone castle types, the shell enclosure castle belongs to the category of fortified enclosure type. We are also left with a considerable number of other castles built during the Middle Ages, and these must be put with the enclosure type as well.

The fortified stone enclosure was a fortress capable of offering resistance to attackers or intruders and of providing a satisfactory residence for a lord and his dependants in a variety of buildings assembled inside. Numerous enclosures, sometimes – and not very helpfully – called castles of *enceinte*, were built over a long

A view of the west front of Bolton, a later fourteenth-century quadrangular enclosure castle, in Wensleydale.

clay or with stone slabs, although the recently discovered ditch thus lined at Bedford was probably wet. Many enclosures were further fortified at the time of construction, or later, by building towers or turrets, cylindrical, square, D-ended or polygonal, in the walling, either as an integral part or 'tacked on'.

Some were complete towers, some were open-backed like Framlingham. In most of these, temporary back walls of timber were inserted at each level in times of danger or attack. The towers were inserted along the circumference or at the extremities where two stretches of wall met, as at Inverlochy. Some were raised standing free from the wall. Some enclosures, like Eynsford, had no towers or turrets, except a gateway or gate-tower, and relied upon their position, the walling thickness, and the ditch and rampart defences outside. The walling is generally called the curtain wall because it hangs, so to speak, between the towers. A quick look at Framlingham from any angle, with its 13 rectilinear flanking towers and gateway (in most cases several feet taller than the high curtain), shows the curtain effect very well. Curtains were usually battlemented and had a parapet along the inside near the top reached by ascending a tower or, more rarely, an outside staircase.

In the Middle Ages there were at least two criteria by which a castle was judged to be fortified. In early Norman times, when permission was given to build a castle, it meant that the structure, wooden or stone, was allowed to be surrounded wholly or partly by ditching and ramparts where the distance from the bottom of the ditch to the top of the rampart was equal to the distance an average digger could throw a spadeful of earth (from a ditch base to a rampart top) in one go, that is, about 7.6–9.1 metres (25–30 ft). Later, licences were granted to build 'in stone or lime' and to 'crenellate', that is, to construct along the top of the curtain and round the tops of towers, battlements of merlons (solid rectilinear projections) and crenels or embrasures (gaps in between), as at Framlingham (*see* p.32). Numerous licences to crenellate were granted by the kings over the centuries, and these are generally indicated in the gazetteer where known.

Enclosures did become increasingly interesting as they acquired improvements or

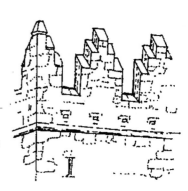

A number of tower-houses in Ireland have merlons that are stepped, as in the drawing, a style also used in a variety of mainland British church towers.

In the foreground of this view of Goodrich is one of the double-enclosure corner towers equipped with a spur base for added strength. Behind can be seen the early great tower, built in the twelfth century.

Looking down on Ludlow's enclosure with towers, which stands on the hill in Ludlow town, with parts of the town in the background (see plan, p. 160).

alterations. The enclosure at Rochester developed into a castle with one of the biggest rectangular great towers in Britain (which was besieged and taken in 1216, an event documented, *see* Chapter 5). The enclosure at Ludlow was begun in the very late eleventh century, and over succeeding centuries acquired a unique range of buildings including a gatehouse whose entrance was subsequently blocked up to make the building a great tower (*see also* Dunstanburgh). The enclosure at Caernarfon was built in two main stages and became one of the most sophisticated defensive structures in Europe (one gateway had five portcullises in series). The enclosures at Goodrich were built up over the thirteenth and fourteenth centuries, long after the original great tower had been erected on the rocky outcrop overlooking the Wye. There were many smaller enclosure castles of varying shapes and construction, each different from the next, and they are included in the gazetteer. All of them fulfil the dual role of the castle, and enjoyed, or endured, a variety of fortunes.

4

Building Castles

In Chapter 2 we saw that motte castles could be erected in a few weeks. Stone castle construction, however, was a very different matter and generally took years, despite the fact that most stone castles were wanted in a hurry. D.F. Renn estimated that the annual building rate on a great tower was about 3 metres (10 ft) of elevation, allowing for weather, stopping work in winter or if funds ran out. Scarborough, some 27.4 metres (90 ft) tall, took ten years (1158–68). This 3-metre average applies to great towers. In the same period, work on other parts of the castle must have been done simultaneously, such as constructing the curtain with towers (if any), raising the gateway or gatehouse and so forth. At Orford, for example, it is thought that the whole castle, great tower and surrounding enclosure with its smaller (rectangular?) towers and gate went up in seven or eight years, the tower itself in two years. The time may seem lengthy, but the medieval builder had no mechanical aids except the pulley-wheel crane and the wheelbarrow, and stone cutting and dressing had to be done by hand.

Every stone castle posed a veritable catalogue of problems, some of which had to be dealt with in advance and which could not be solved merely by riding roughshod over the feelings of local people. Early in the Norman occupation, the conqueror-lords steamrollered their way through towns and countryside to clear sites for castles and pressed Anglo-Saxons into forced labour. But in the time of Henry I, who introduced a new spirit of co-operation between Norman and Anglo-Saxon (setting an example by marrying the daughter of an Anglo-Saxon princess), proper formalities were observed. Some sites were paid for, some were exchanged, and there are even instances of compensation being paid for intrusion upon neighbouring land, such as at Gloucester. It is interesting to look at the various problems, for it is still a matter of some wonder how well the medieval builder coped with them, particularly in the construction of the great tower type of castle.

Some stone great tower castles were superimposed upon motte castles because the site had proved advantageous. Others were built on new sites, generally selected for their strategic position *vis-à-vis* the lands of neighbours as well as suitability for controlling their own lands, and for the nearness to water sources. There were other important questions for the builders to consider. Could stone be quarried on the site, or nearby, and was it suitable or too soft? If not, where was the nearest quarry? Did it belong to the king or the Church? Most quarries were royal or ecclesiastical property. How much would the stone cost? Where was the nearest waterway for transporting the stone and other materials? Water transport was much cheaper than land cartage, and it was quicker. Many of the best quarries, such as Barnack in Northamptonshire, were close to navigable rivers. How easy would it be to find enough masons and assistants to extract stone (by hammering iron wedges into the layers in the stone beds) and to cut by saw or split the lumps into appropriate shapes and sizes, and to dress (smooth) them? What sort of rubble was available nearby? Were there any Roman remains, such as tiles and brick segments? At Colchester great tower, both brick and dressed stones were taken from the extensive ruins of the old Roman town at Camulodunum and used in the masonry, and can be seen in many parts of the tower, notably in some of the steps of the great stairs. The owner and builder of a castle might also have considered whether he wanted to obtain a supply of the cream-yellow limestone quarried at Caen in Normandy, generally reckoned the best of its kind, to make the ashlar quoins and other features such as arch heads, keystones, window mullions and lintels, loopholes and battlement tops.

While masons were attending to the stone supply problems, carpenters and joiners were worrying about timber availability. Was there a source close to the site and were the trees big enough to produce the lengths of beam and plank? In some cases owners contracted to buy the wood from a supplier; in others they would buy a stretch of forest with the appropriate trees. Oak in one or other of its many species was preferred. Wood was also needed for burning to make charcoal for blacksmiths.

There were other materials wanted in quantity: lead for the tower roofs and water pipes; iron for a multitude of requirements; sand and lime for mortar (cement). All

had to be acquired and transported to the site. Details of this kind today would be skilfully estimated down to the last nail, and the operations supervised by one or other of a building team of architect, quantity surveyor, consulting engineer and services engineer, but in those times there were no such disciplines. Estimating had to be guesswork.

Once the material supply problem was satisfactorily in hand, the building gangs were recruited, or pressed into service, generally from the immediate neighbourhood. However, in the case of the castles of Edward I in Wales, the authorities found they had to recruit from English counties, from Norfolk to Devonshire, because they could not depend upon loyal service from the Welsh whom they had just overcome. In early Norman days men were not generally paid, but as Norman and Anglo-Saxon began to edge towards a better relationship, castle owners started to pay wages. Pay was not standard, except in so far as it was low everywhere. In the late thirteenth century we read of diggers, carpenters and masons being offered bonuses for good work – and docked wages for absenteeism – but these were the country men recruited for work on the Edwardian castles in Wales. A site supervisor, or *custos operationum,* at Builth could earn 12d a day in 1277 and a master mason 7½d a day in 1278. Piecework was also done: at Flint, in 1280, masons were paid 1d or 1¼d per stone for cutting and dressing. Diggers were paid 3d a day at Rhuddlan. At Deal in 1539, a number of labourers on the site of the coastal fort being built at the order of Henry VIII went on strike because of low wages: they were only paid 6d – and some even 5d – a day. The differentials of the thirteenth century seem much the same as today: thus the head of a building team on a large project would generally expect to earn about 3½ to 4 times the basic wage (without overtime) of the builder's labourer.

Work on a castle site began with a careful scrutiny of the ground. If it was an existing motte site, the owner would have known about its earth content and whether there was rock or not. If it was a new site, this would have to be discovered. The presence of rock meant that possibly the great tower could be built on rock foundations. If so, the rock was flattened by gangs of men chipping it away with iron cold chisels, and the plinth of the tower was laid down. If the ground was soft, deep trenches were cut, a yard or two wider than the intended thickness of wall, and filled with an assortment of rubble, stone and timber – a kind of hardcore – which was

Rochester: the great tower of the 1120s–30s, with the forebuilding on the left, was built of Kentish ragstone with ashlar corners.

A medieval picture of building a wall (redrawn by R. Maguire).

there with horizontal poles, called put-logs, let into the masonry already built. These put-logs slotted into put-log holes, and many great towers (such as Hedingham) today bear the patterns of rows of put-log holes. In most cases they were horizontal lines. A more sophisticated system was used during the building of some of the Edwardian Welsh castles of the late thirteenth century, where helicoidal, or inclined scaffold paths, about 35–40 degrees from the horizontal, supported ramps for hauling or winching materials, notably at Harlech gatehouse. This system appears to have been a speciality of Master James of St George, the Savoyard master-mason. Whether the ramp for a wheelbarrow was more efficient than the pulley wheel and basket is a moot point.

Great tower walls rose in a vertical straight line (although at Oxford the walls tapered inwards with offsets

Hedingham: one of the best-known rectangular great towers in England is almost all that is left of the powerful medieval castle of the Earls of Oxford. The great tower was built in the mid-twelfth century.

rammed down. The plinth was laid on these foundations. In many great towers, plinths were battered, that is, they sloped outwards and downwards for structural strength and for ricocheting missiles; though some led straight downwards, such as at Richmond. Then the first levels of wall were put together above the plinth.

In some castles the walls consisted of an inner 'skin' of an aggregate of rubble, old brick, pebbles and almost anything else hard, held together by a tough mortar of sand and lime which set as hard as rock, sometimes prepared by creating a trough of wooden planks between which the aggregate was poured. The method may have been learned by the Normans from the Saracen castle-builders in Spain of the tenth century who used *tapia*, a mix of pebbles and cement poured between boards and left to dry in the sun. A fine example of a castle built of this material is at Banos de la Encina. The aggregate skin was generally clad, in England, with an outer skin of dressed stone, and the corners of the towers were set with quoins of dressed stone which tied in with both skins. In some castles, such as Rochester, the walls were all rubble (Rochester was Kentish ragstone) with corners of ashlar. At Middleham great tower you can see stretches along the wall faces that are stripped of the outer skin, and part of the corners where the quoins have disappeared, leaving the inner rubble skin exposed. At Baconsthorpe, the quoins in the corners of the great flint-built rectangular gatehouse were deliberately taken out to provide for a later building nearby.

As the first courses of wall went up, scaffolding became necessary to continue to work. Long poles held together with rope were erected, anchored here and

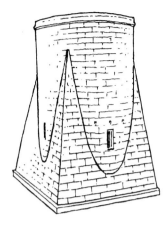

A cylindrical tower rising from a spur base. This type of tower fortification first appeared in British castles during the late twelfth century.

fires and from slops thrown out of windows and loops, it would not have remained clean for long. It was a preservative for the stone, and it is also held that medieval builders thought it helped to fireproof the castle.

The building operations we have outlined applied to great towers. They were much the same for gatehouses and gatehouse-towers, chapels and halls. Put-log holes can be seen in many smaller curtain wall towers and in gatehouses, such as at Tonbridge. In some of the Edwardian castles, the put-log holes are also in helicoidal pattern on the smaller towers and gatehouses. At Goodrich the three early fourteenth-century cylindrical towers in the inner quadrangle enclosure stand on a square base with spurs up the tower sides, an alternative to a battered plinth. This type of support was particularly appropriate for structures on sheer cliff faces, like the Constable's Gate at Dover.

Since castles were residences as well as fortresses, we should not be surprised to find them having many domestic features. Internally, many had fireplaces, some of considerable decorative attractiveness and elaboration, from the simple thirteenth-century sloping ashlar hood on corbels and columns at Tretower great tower, to the massive 6-metre (20-ft) wide pillar-supported hood at the great hall at Linlithgow. Windows in great towers and halls are endlessly fascinating in variety. Loopholes (arrow slits) are likewise varied. We have mentioned the chapels in the forebuilding at Dover. At Castle Rising the chapel is next to the great chamber, at its east end. At Conisbrough the chapel, hexagonal in plan, projects into one of the wedge-shaped buttresses. At Colchester and the White Tower of London, the chapels are in the apsidal ends in the east wall. Numerous great towers had kitchens in the wall thicknesses, or in the basement, or at the top – perhaps a better place, so that the cooking smells could get out without affecting the occupants. At Orford there were two kitchens, one at ground- and one at first-floor level.

spaced out in the height), either solid or hollow with passages here and there, and in the greatest of the towers, chambers and staircases until they reached the desired height whereupon they were topped with the wall-walk and parapet and given the outer protective battlements. Many towers had corners which were in effect corner turrets, and these rose higher than the four walls with their battlements. Corner turrets contained the spiral

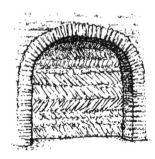

(Left) A wall fireplace in the King's Gate at Caernarfon. (Right) A fireplace in Colchester's great tower. Note the Norman herringbone masonry.

staircases and also rooms, and they acted as buttresses. Some great towers had one corner turret of slightly greater dimensions than the other three.

When the walls were completed they might be coated with plaster and whitewashed, or whitewashed directly on the stonework. Occasionally, the plastering was made to look like coursing of large stone blocks (as may be seen on many Georgian or nineteenth-century town buildings), by means of thin lines etched into the wet plasterwork. The great tower at London is called the White Tower because of the whitewashing it received in the thirteenth century. Whitewashing was not simply decorative; indeed, with the smoke and dirt given out by

What did all this castle building cost? A great deal of work has been done on the costing of building works on castles in the Middle Ages, particularly those in royal hands, and the costs to private owners other than kings must have been much the same. Expenditure for many royal castles is well documented, and sums looked at in relation to the total income of the kings in a year are startling. We may take the position over the period c.1155–1215, namely, the reigns of Henry II and his sons Richard I and John. It is reckoned that the king's annual income from taxes and rents was not much more than £10,000. It is also estimated that none of his lords was worth more than about one-twelfth of that £10,000, and

This view of Newcastle shows the great tower of 1173–84, built by the same mason, Mauricius, who constructed the massive great tower at Dover (1180–9) Note the powerful forebuilding.

that the average knight could indeed live comfortably on £20 a year.

If the king's annual income was about £10,000, then from the evidence in the Pipe Rolls of the Exchequer, he seems to have spent a significant percentage of it on castle works, from new structures like Orford, to new parts at Dover, Newcastle and so forth, to repairs and upkeep on many others. *The History of the King's Works* considers the outlay on castles to have been the biggest single item of expenditure in all three reigns. Orford cost about £1400 in seven years, Dover had nearly £7000 spent on it in nine, Newcastle cost £1000 in ten years and Bowes £600 in seventeen years. *King's Works* estimates that about £780 a year was spent on castles by the Crown throughout the period 1155–1215, or a total of over

Corfe: the ruins of the twelfth-century great tower are near the top of the hill on which the mound of the eleventh century was raised. To the right are the ruins of King John's expensive 'gloriette'.

£46,000 – about 7–8 per cent of the total income the Crown received over the 60-year period. Interestingly, while Henry II spent some £21,000 on about 90 castles, the great majority of the expenses were on less than 30 castles. In John's reign, £17,000 was spent in 15 years, the lion's share being on only 10 castles: over £500 on Hanley, Horston, Lancaster and Norham; over £1000 on Corfe, Dover, Kenilworth, Knaresborough and Odiham (his polygonal great tower castle); and over £2000 on Scarborough. A graph of his expenditure over the 15 years would show an acceleration towards the latter end, in both new works and repairs, and this has been taken as an indication of the growing tension between Henry II and his feudal lords at home, and the growing danger of invasion from abroad (Dover, Southampton and other castles in south-east England are recorded to have received the main attention).

If we turn now to the expenditure of the three Edwards (I, II, III) in Wales from 1277 to 1330, the figures for which many writers on castles quote with relish, the sums involved are centred on ten new castles (Aberystwyth, Beaumaris, Builth, Caernarfon, Conwy, Flint, Harlech, Hope, Rhuddlan and Ruthin), with renovations to three Welsh-originated castles (Castell y Bere, Criccieth and Dolwyddelan). Aberystwyth (£3885), Beaumaris (£14,444), Builth (£1666), Caernarfon (£19,892), Conwy (£14,248), Flint (£8951), Harlech (£6224), and Rhuddlan (£9292) give an idea of the sort of money these kings were laying out. These sums are the minimum, as they do not include absolutely everything, but they are near enough for us to stand back in some wonder, more so when it is learned that some of the castles actually began to decay almost before they were finished, that Caernarfon took more than a quarter of a century to complete entirely, and that Beaumaris was never completed nor was it ever involved in any warlike event.

Beaumaris, an almost perfectly symmetrical concentric castle, was begun in 1295 by Edward I on the southern coast of Anglesey but was never finished, even after 35 years.

5
Attack and Defence

In the last chapter we looked at the construction of stone castle buildings. The emphasis was on the builders providing those amenities which they and their employers agreed could be included within the confines of the site, the availability of materials and the cash limits. There was one more factor of crucial importance. What were they going to do to the buildings to help keep intruders out, to make it difficult for a siege to succeed, and at the same time enable troops within to sally forth on to the offensive with the minimum of difficulty? It is appropriate to look first at the means with which besiegers could break into a castle and eventually compel its garrison to surrender.

In the Middle Ages, besieging a castle was not as a rule a sudden or surprise operation. The king or lord who set out against the castle of a rebel, or a rival, announced his intentions sometimes by letter demanding the surrender of the castle on pain of having a barrage of artillery hurled at it, sometimes by sending a delegation under the safe conduct of a white flag to make his demands to representatives sent out of the castle to 'parley', that is, to discuss the matter. Occasionally, the king or lord would arrive outside the castle walls himself and have a herald or crier call out for surrender. If no surrender was forthcoming – and medieval lords were fearless and impetuous men who loved a fight, and who placed the

honour of throwing down a challenge and of accepting one very high on the list of virtues – then both sides withdrew to prepare for siege.

The besieging army usually arrived in the neighbourhood of the castle with its siege equipment ready, its ammunition accumulated and stacked up. In the case of the siege of Bedford in 1224, Henry III issued the order for surrender, heard that it was rejected, and had to

A thirteenth-century picture of a siege (redrawn by R. Maguire).

gather up his men and munitions very quickly from all over the country to prosecute the assault. How should a besieging army attack and what siege equipment did it employ?

Assuming that the castle about to be besieged was a fortified great tower inside a fortified enclosure with flanking towers and a gatehouse, the principal points of attack were the gatehouse, with its wooden gates that could be set alight and burned or more simply battered down; the walls, which could either be broken through by battering or have holes made in them by undermining the foundations, which could be scaled by ladders or whose parapets could be fought for and captured by means of belfries filled with fighting men; and the great tower, which could be invaded once a corner had been successfully undermined by sappers and a way through to the interior opened up. In addition, the inside of the enclosure and the top of the great tower could be subjected to barrages of missiles of one kind or another from several kinds of siege-engine positioned outside and some distance away. Barrages would reduce the numbers of effective defenders within the enclosure and would help to demoralise the garrison generally. They would also damage the walls of the great tower. The weaponry available to besiegers, certainly by the eleventh century in Europe and by the close of that century in Britain, were the battering ram, the *terebra*, the *ballista*, the mangonel – and, a little later, an improvement on the mangonel, the trebuchet. In addition, attackers had a variety of mobile protective shields and platforms such as the penthouse, the 'cat', the mantlet and the belfry. And they had scaling ladders as well.

The ram was a long pole with an iron-cased head. It was suspended from ropes or chains within a wooden-framed structure on wheels and covered on its sides, known as a penthouse. It was wheeled up to the wall and driven against it again and again. To do so it was necessary first to fill in the ditch in front of the castle curtain to make a bridge, and all manner of things were used to close that trench, including on a few occasions corpses of humans and animals. To protect the men operating the ram in their wooden framework, a gabled structure was fitted over the frame, called a *testudo*. The *terebra* was a smaller pole with a sharp iron point, and it was used to pick holes in the masonry of the lowest parts of the walls, and this, too, was covered with a smaller penthouse, sometimes known as a 'cat' or a 'sow'.

The *ballista* was a special device for firing iron shafts and javelins. It was much like a huge cross-bow and was remarkably accurate. It was meant for picking off individual defenders along the walls. The mangonel, and its successor, the trebuchet, were engines for discharging stone balls or metal balls, rotting animal carcasses or even lumps of the deadly Greek fire, lobbing them over the top of the wall. The mangonel worked on the principle of torsion. A pivoted arm ending in a cup (or a sling) was held by a twist of ropes that stretched between posts. The arm was pulled down against the torsion and the missile put into the cup. When it was released, the arm swung up and over, hurling its projectile in a trajectory to take it over the enemy wall. Mangonels were often sited some way from the walls, behind a rapidly heaped up earth rampart. The trebuchet worked on the principle of the unequal counterpoise arm. A pivoted arm ending in a cup or sling was counterbalanced at the other end by a weight greater than the missile. The counterweight could be slid along to adjust the swing. When let go, the weight swung down and brought the cup up and over, discharging the missile generally with greater force than a mangonel, and with more accuracy because its range could be adjusted by sliding the counterweight along the arm. Trebuchets appeared in Western Europe in the twelfth century.

The principal missiles were stone balls, sometimes quickly fashioned by masons on site (as at Bedford, and a pile of stone balls can be seen at Pevensey). These were very effective against masonry if they scored direct hits. Greek fire, the liquid akin to the napalm of the twentieth century, made from a type of naphtha and used since its

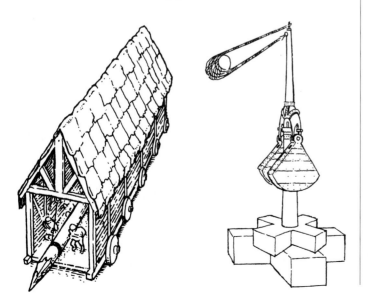

(Far left) A battering ram being operated under the protection of a penthouse, otherwise known as a cat.

(Left) A trebuchet in full swing.

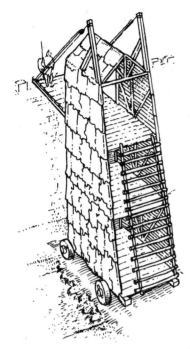

A belfry dragged close to a castle wall. The side of the top storey is let down to allow troops to rush to the wall-head. Belfries were also called siege-towers.

discovery by the Egyptian chemist Callinikos c.650, was more devastating. It is known to have been used by Edward I at the siege of Stirling in 1297. The effectiveness of rotting animal carcasses was limited to producing temporary nausea among those immediately disarrayed when the carcasses landed on the ground and split open, disgorging everything in a disgusting mess.

The belfry was a movable timber tower three or four storeys tall, with step-ladders between floors, the whole apparatus on wheels. It carried besiegers on each floor. On the top floor a drawbridge hinged so that when the belfry was hauled up to a castle wall, the flap could be lowered to provide a platform for the men inside to surge forwards onto the wall walk and engage the defenders in hand-to-hand fighting. As the first ranks of the besiegers ran across the platform, other men clambered up the belfry ladders to support them. A belfry was easy to build, for it consisted of tree trunks that did not have to be stripped or planed. Those used in Philip Augustus' siege of Château Gaillard in 1204 were constructed of trees cut down and their branches removed. Occasionally, a belfry was used to move a small siege-engine close to the walls. Henry I built his belfries several feet taller than the walls of Pontaudemer Castle when he laid siege to it in 1123, so that archers and stone-throwers could direct their fire down into the enclosure.

The other protective structure used for a variety of exposed and dangerous tasks was the mantlet, a sloping screen made of timber or wickerwork panels on wheels. One of the activities of a mantlet was to protect a gang of

men approaching a castle's wooden gates in the gatehouse to set them on fire with burning tow arrow tips. Another was to protect miners chipping away at the foundations of a curtain wall or the wall of a flanking tower in order to cut open a hole which could then be propped up with logs. These were burned and, when they collapsed, the masonry (hopefully) came down with the charred timber. This was done successfully at Château Gaillard: it was also done at Rochester in 1215.

In the war between King John and the barons, which broke out after Magna Carta was sealed (1215), the King's castle at Rochester was taken over. John demanded its return but this was refused. So he set out to take it by siege, and within days he had broken into the city and positioned an array of siege-engines directed against the castle. A preliminary barrage of fire was started on the south part of the bailey wall. Part of the wall was brought down, and some of his men got into the castle, driving the defenders into the great tower, their last refuge. The King decided to undermine the great tower, ordered 'as many picks as you are able' to be sent to him by the sheriffs of Canterbury, and prepared to excavate. A mine shaft was dug and a tunnel driven towards the tower's south-west corner. Some days later, the sappers reached underneath the corner foundations and set up a frame of beams and props. The King then sent an urgent call to Hubert de Burgh, telling him to despatch 'with all speed, forty of the fattest pigs of the sort least good for eating, to bring fire to the tower'. The animal carcasses duly arrived and were packed within the frame under the tower. They were set alight and burned steadily. After a time the supports collapsed and the corner of the tower fell away, leaving a huge gaping hole into the tower basement. The King's men rushed in, chased the defenders behind the cross-wall and fought them floor by floor to the top until surrender. The siege had taken nearly two months. Other mining stories are mentioned in the gazetteer, under Bedford (*see* pp. 124–25), Dover (*see* pp.

Mine shaft: sappers about to set fire to a series of props in a mine tunnel under the corner of a great tower. This is how the corner of Rochester great tower was brought down in 1215.

141–43), Dryslwyn (*see* p. 309), and St Andrew's (*see* pp. 288–89).

There is no doubt that in siege operations the attackers had the lion's share of the advantage – certainly in the first two centuries of castle history in Britain. Naturally, when designing and building castles, the works' supervisors considered the defensive fortifications above everything else, but they were limited in what they could provide against attack. The answer to stone balls hurled by mangonels or trebuchets at curtain or tower walls was thicker masonry. Between 3–3.6 metres (10–12 ft) of well mortared blocks or tightly compacted rubble with cement (with or without ashlar dressing) could normally withstand even the largest stone ball which the best trebuchet was capable of hurling, and many great towers (but rather fewer curtains) had 3–3.6-metre thick walls, and some even more substantial than that (such as parts of Dover, 6 metres [20 ft] and Duffield, 5.5 metres [18 ft]); of course, thicker walls took longer to yield to battering rams or *terebrae*. But the problem of warding off missiles sent over the tops of walls could only be solved by raising the heights of the walls. Framlingham has a 12.2-metre (40-ft) tall curtain, which was higher than average. But higher walls could be overcome by improving the range and trajectory of siege-engines, and better mangonels were produced. The trebuchet was introduced, quite possibly for this purpose. The answer lay rather in arranging things so that the besieger could not get close enough to give his siege engines their maximum fire-power.

We have seen that a regular technique for bringing down walls was to undermine them. How could a gang of enemy sappers be prevented from tunnelling through to the foundations of a great tower? One answer was provided at Kenilworth, where the corner buttress turrets were made excessively thick, almost twice as thick as the tower walls in between. Another answer was to dig a very deep and wide moat round the tower, which could not be tunnelled through, but that meant taking up a large amount of otherwise valuable space inside the enclosure. A third was to sink a countermine. Here, the defender, having detected or guessed the direction in which the attacking miners were tunnelling, bored down through the basement floor, or through the open ground outside the tower, in the opposite direction, hopefully to meet somewhere along the way underground. This happened at St Andrews in 1546, although the tunnels met at a point underground where one was about 1.8 metres (6 ft) above the other – and this was in the rock on which the castle stood. You can crawl along the two tunnels today and see the join, stepping from the higher tunnel to the

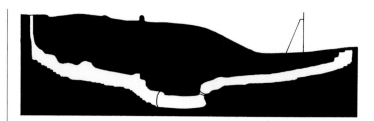

St Andrews: mine and countermine.

lower by means of an iron ladder. The St Andrews' tunnels, incidentally, effectively dispose of the theory that castles built on rock foundations could not be undermined by tunnelling.

Other devices for fighting off besiegers and their armoury were beams with forked heads to deflect battering rams, poles with forked heads to push scaling ladders away from the walls and sacks stuffed with feathers, wool and rope ends lowered down from the parapet to deaden the blows of a battering ram.

There were several features that builders could incorporate in castles for defending them. One was hoarding, or brattices. This was a wooden gallery around the top part of a curtain wall or tower wall supported on horizontal posts let into the masonry. The gallery was protected on its outer side with timber panelling, with slits for observation, and provided with a sloping timber roof. The floor, also of timber, was slatted to allow defenders to drop missiles or liquids on to attackers. To prevent the timber being set alight, wet hides were hung on the front walls and draped over the sloping roof. Hoarding was vulnerable to stones, however, and a few carefully aimed balls could smash a hole in it, breaking the continuity of the structure and causing it to collapse. In later centuries, this wooden hoarding was incorporated in a stone form and called machicolation (*see* Glossary). Another feature, more specifically to deal with attackers' attempts to fire the gates, was the inclusion in the ceiling of the passage in the gateway or gatehouse of a series of holes which

Medieval timber hoarding at the wall-head. This type of defence preceded stone machicolation.

The great castle at Warwick has several major features. In the centre is the 40-metre (128 ft) tall Guy's tower, which has fine machicolations all round below the battlements.

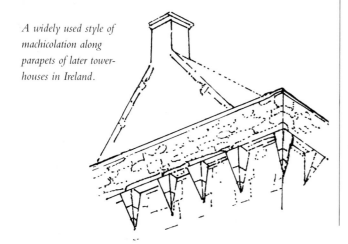

A widely used style of machicolation along parapets of later tower-houses in Ireland.

were situated in the floor of the room over the passage. Generally known as murder-holes, because it is commonly said that they were used for pouring boiling liquids or molten lead on to any attackers who had managed to get through the gates, they were more probably used for pouring cold water on to wooden gates that had been set alight.

Perhaps the two most famous defensive features of a

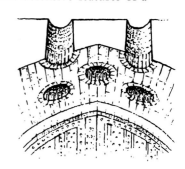

Section of the ceiling of a castle gateway with murder-holes.

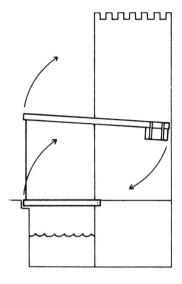

Probably the earliest type of mechanical drawbridge. The top beam pivots in the centre and is weighted at one end, inside the tower. When that end is lowered, the other end (outside) rises, lifting by means of chains the outer end of the platform across the moat in front of the gate.

castle, however, were the drawbridge and portcullises. The drawbridge worked like a see-saw, pivoting in the centre with heavy weights at one end. Then the catches were released, the weights pulled one end down and the bridge part, which straddled the moat, swung upright across the gates of the entrance to the gateway passage. Alternatively, the bridge was lifted and lowered by chains which were turned inside the gatehouse. The portcullis was a grille of wood or iron, or wood lined with iron on its outer faces. It was set in deep grooves. Some castles were provided with numerous portcullises: at Caernarfon, the King's Gate alone had six. It is not difficult to imagine the palaver associated with admitting someone who had a bona fide invitation to visit the castle.

Nearly all castles had a parapet along the top of the curtain wall, round the flanking towers (if there were any) and the gatehouse. The top of the great tower was invariably battlemented. Indeed, as we have seen, what determined whether a stone fortress-residence was fortified

A portcullis.

was the existence of battlements, or crenellation. When Bedford Castle was partially demolished after the 1224 siege, Henry III ordered that the bailey walls should be reduced in height and not have any battlements. Castles were also provided with arrow slits, or loopholes, in many parts of the buildings, at all levels. These were narrow openings, usually vertical, splayed inwards to give the archer room to shoot without fear of retaliation. There was a variety of arrow-slit shapes, and a tour of several castles will generally give an interesting range of local preferences, from the simple vertical loop, anything from 0.9 to 2.7

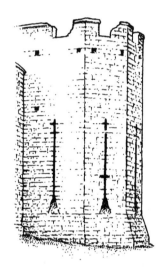

Fish-tail arrow slits at Grey Mare's Tail Tower on the east wall of Warkworth's inner bailey.

(Below) Some types of arrow-loop. (Left to right) Skenfrith (fish-tail bottom), Trematon (crosslet with fish-tail bottom), Manorbier (top crosslet with fish-tail bottom) and Pembroke (slit with rectangular oillet).

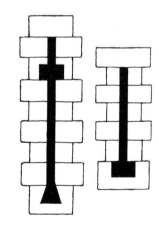
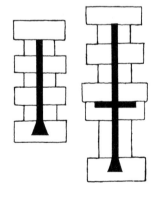

metres (1 to 3 yards) long and 3.7 to 10.1 cm (1½–4 in) wide (*see* those at Brougham, Dover, Newcastle), to loops with round holes at top, middle and bottom (Trematon), loops with a horizontal cross loop in the middle (Berkeley), loops with holes at top and bottom and at each end of a horizontal cross loop (Kenilworth), and loops with one vertical and two horizontal cross loops. Arrow slits are often found in walls near, or even in the corners of towers where there is a spiral staircase or a platform for archers, in

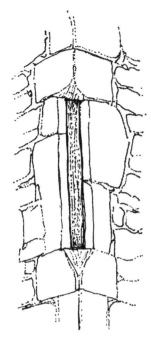

the merlons of the battlements, in wall chambers and even where one of the wedge-shaped buttresses at Conisbrough joins with the cylindrical wall of the great tower. At Dover, the Avranches Tower in the outer curtain, a polygonal flanking tower perched on a cliff edge, has rows of arrow slits behind which are fighting galleries.

In his attempt to build a castle from which he could be sure to exclude all unwanted people, a castle owner naturally aimed at making his castle impregnable. This is a term used at some time or other to describe many interesting and sophisticated military fortress-residences that did in fact fall to siege or stratagem. In the thirteenth and fourteenth century, the offensive/defensive role of British castles appears to have become more pronounced, and this was a step toward achieving that elusive 'impregnability'. One of two lines of defence turned over to the offensive would have a better chance of keeping people out of a castle than starting on the defensive from the outer ramparts inwards. This may have been the thinking behind the growing practice of building an outer ring of fortifications around an inner fortress (of

tower encircled by curtain, or of curtain with flanking towers), and indeed of adding a third 'ring' outside that, which is the principle of concentric fortification.

The idea stemmed from Byzantium and the Near East. The walls of Constantinople built by Emperor Theodosius II between 410–47 were raised on the following plan: an inner wall about 12.2 metres (40 ft) tall and an outer wall about 9.1 metres (30 ft) tall were erected parallel, separated by about 4.6 metres (15 ft). Each wall had protruding towers at regular intervals. In front of this composition was a moat bridged only at the points where the five main gates were situated. There was a parapet between the walls which could only be reached by staircases inside the towers, which themselves were massively built to support the weight of artillery such as machines for hurling big stones and for discharging Greek fire. The higher wall provided scope for a line of archers to fire their arrows over the heads of another line of archers along the lower wall. This also enabled offensive troops from the lower wall to descend and go out through passages into the foreground and thence into the battlefield, while being covered by the higher wall archers. There is something in the fact that, between the 400s and 1204 (the disastrous year when the Crusaders of the Fourth Crusade attacked the great city), no one had succeeded in breaching these walls.

The lessons of the apparent impregnability of

Dover possesses the finest great tower in the British Isles. It is cuboid, 30 x 29.5 metres (98 x 96 ft) and 29 metres (95 ft) tall, with walls that are 6.5 metres (21 ft) thick in places at ground level. It is part of a splendid concentric castle which has just about everything the castle enthusiast could want to see.

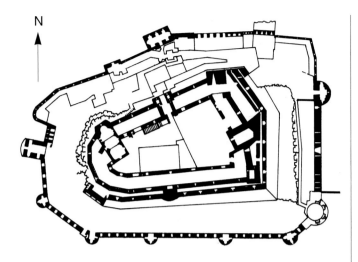

Constantinople were grafted by the Crusaders on to a number of castles that they built between 1100 and about 1300 in the Near East, notably those in Syria at Sahyun, Markab and the much-mentioned and possibly overpraised Krak des Chevaliers. The principles of concentric design were applied throughout Europe, and reached Britain probably through returning Crusader knights, possibly soon after the Second Crusade (1147–9). It is difficult to resist the wish to believe that Henry II, one of the greatest castle-builders, worked out the concentric idea for himself and was not influenced by the Near East when he ordered the works at Dover. There, the great tower was surrounded by an inner curtain with flanking towers and gateways, and that was surrounded

(Above) Krak des Chevaliers, Syria: ground plan of this mainly twelfth- and thirteenth-century Crusader castle. It will readily be seen as a fine concentric plan (after Muller-Wiener, via Anderson).

The Tower of London: the White Tower (c.1078–90s), the first main structure of the famous castle, stands behind the southern stretches of outer and inner curtains (see plan, p. 186).

by a substantial section of outer curtain also with flanking towers, and with steep, scarped cliffs outside. This work was completed by Henry's death in 1189. Dover was probably the first castle in Britain to become concentric, although it was a concentricity from improvement, not from scratch. The Tower of London began to receive its concentric form in the reign of Henry III, but it was not until the 1270s that the first concentric castle was built in Britain from new, and then it was in Wales and not England – the remarkable Caerphilly, still regarded by some authorities as the greatest castle in the British Isles.

The concentric principle in Britain, as far as entirely new castles were concerned, was embodied in an inner quadrangle of high curtain walls and flanking towers (generally cylindrical) at the four corners. Two opposite walls were usually dominated by huge twin-towered gatehouses, although in some castles there was only one. Encircling the inner quadrangle was a second quadrangle, lower in height but with towers along the perimeter, or not, as in the cases of Harlech and Caerphilly. The distance between the quadrangles was only a matter of yards and this allowed the defenders on the battlemented inner quadrangle walls to fire over the heads of their fellows who were raking the assailants from the lower quadrangle walls. The lower defenders could also go over to the offensive and sally forth to attack a besieging army, confident that the inner defence could take care of itself.

This was the plan at Caerphilly, which was surrounded entirely by an artificial moat and lake complex. It was also the plan at Harlech, built in the period 1283–90 and sited high on a rock above what was the estuary of the Dwyryd River, although the outer lower wall was only a few feet above the ground and contained no flanking towers. At Caerphilly, too, the lower outer wall was only a few feet tall with no towers. And it was the plan, triumphantly displayed at Beaumaris, built between 1295 and 1330, but never completed. Among other concentric castles raised in the later thirteenth century and early fourteenth century were Rhuddlan and Kidwelly in Wales, and Caerlaverock in Scotland. The appearance of the concentric castle in thirteenth-century Britain is often but inaccurately described as the apogee of military fortification in medieval Britain, but only a handful of new concentric castles were built and an equally small number of other castles were improved to concentric 'status'. It was an extremely expensive undertaking, and only the Crown and the very richest nobles could afford it. And yet castles were still required and they still needed to be as capture-proof as possible.

In the late twelfth century another feature was introduced to the castle scene, the gatehouse. Previously, gateways to enclosure castles were simple and small, like the single tower pierced by a passage with a chamber over it at Exeter (c.1068), or the hardly complicated version of the same at Framlingham (c.1200). Then at Dover we see the beginning of a larger idea, a pair of flanking towers placed one each side of the entrance to the inner bailey by a doorway through the curtain wall, near enough for both to cover the entrance (King's Gate and also at the opposite end of the inner bailey, Palace Gate). These towers are rectangular. The idea develops a little later into the gateway in which the towers are closer together to form an integral structure where they are joined by a roofed passage over the arch which they protect, and which contains residential accommodation, such as at Beeston (c.1220–30); Rockingham (1280–90), lit on the exterior only by arrow slits; St Briavels (1292–3); Llanstephan (c.1280); and Skipton. The idea is still further enlarged at Tonbridge (c.1275), at the great Edwardian

Caerphilly: general plan of the castle. At the north-west is the suggested site of the Roman fort. At the north-east is the north lake, bordered on the east side by the north platform, and at the south is the south lake, bordered on the east by the south platform. An outer moat runs north to south in front of the platforms on the east side. At the west (centre) is the western outwork separated from the main castle block by an inner moat. The main castle block is concentric in plan, with two twin-towered gatehouses on the west and two on the east. The inner enclosure wall of the block is of the first period, c.1268–71.

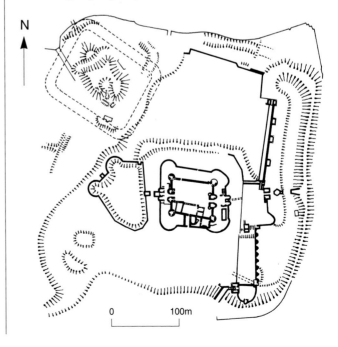

Caerphilly was the first concentric castle build from scratch in Britain. It was constructed in three main phases between c.1267 and c.1327, becoming concentric as early as the 1270s.

castles of Harlech, Flint and Beaumaris, and the de Clare castle, Caerphilly, where the structures are so vast that we can call them gatehouse-towers or great gatehouse-towers (but *not* keep gatehouses), and which have gates, machicolation (in some cases), portcullises, murder-holes, drawbridges, and suites of sumptuous accommodation. Tonbridge, for example, has what was described in *Archaeologia Cantiana* as a noble apartment in the upper storey measuring 15.8 x 8.5 x 4.6 metres (52 x 28 x 15 ft). By this time the gatehouses had often become the central point of the castle and the strongest features, as at Tonbridge and Dunstanburgh (c.1313–25). They drew the main attention of the attackers in the same way as did the great towers. Some were cylindrical-towered, but many were square or polygonal.

In the fourteenth century and afterwards, some gatehouse-towers were converted into great towers by blocking up the entrances and building alternative ways into the enclosure. This happened at Dunstanburgh, Ludlow, Llanstephan, Lea (Co. Laois) and several others. It was partly as a result of the inconvenience endured by people using the gatehouse as a residence within the castle. The heavy and complicated machinery needed to operate several portcullises and a drawbridge took up a lot of space in the gatehouse. At Harlech, for example, a portcullis actually operated from a chapel, while at Tonbridge and Dunstanburgh the great hall was sited on the second floor, at some inconvenience. At Tonbridge, too, the noise of the gate and portcullis closing must have been frightful: two portcullises were provided, one at each end of the entrance, as well as a pair of gates and portcullises over entrances to the side lodges and even to wall-walks.

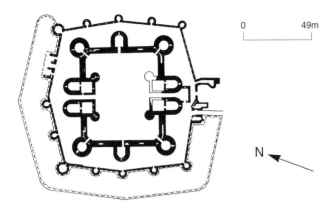

Beaumaris: the plan is almost perfectly concentric.

A good many castles had large gatehouses and some of them were unusually elaborate. At Denbigh, the gatehouse is the star feature of the formidable enclosure castle with curtain wall and flanking polygonal and cylindrical towers. It consisted of three large polygonal towers, each over 12.2 metres (40 ft) across, clustered in a triangle. The order of obstacle to an intruder was first to cross the drawbridge covering the approach to the entrance passage which was flanked by two of the towers,

and joined across the top of the passage. Then he had to get through an outer portcullis and gate, and an inner portcullis and another gate, running the gauntlet of murder-holes in the passage ceiling. Once through, he entered a roughly octagonal chamber with vaulted roof, and ahead was the third tower, bigger than the others and joined to them on the sides of the octagonal chamber by thick-walled linking buildings. At the right of the chamber was a passage into the main courtyard of the castle, but this was protected by yet another portcullis, while passage to it was observed through spy-holes situated in the walls.

To make it more difficult, and certainly more hazardous, for assailants to head for the gatehouse, many castles were given an arrangement of walls projecting outwards from the gatehouse, sometimes at right-angles, sometimes at more acute angles and rounded on the way, which terminated in another gateway with or without towers, guarded by a portcullis and perhaps another drawbridge. This was the barbican, or outwork, which was generally unroofed. There was a wall-walk along

A view of Kidwelly, showing the south-west gatehouse (left) in the outer enclosure of this concentric castle.

The late thirteenth-century, twin-cylindrical-towered gatehouse at Rockingham, with only narrow loops for windows.

each of the walls protected by a battlemented parapet. Defenders could stand along the parapets and shower their opponents with arrows and missiles.

Barbicans appear first in later twelfth-century castles, the one at Dover being among the earliest. They were simple structures for the most part, although the barbican built at Goodrich in the early fourteenth century was quite elaborate, ending in a half-moon tower-like structure with walls several feet thick and with a gateway at right-angles to the gate passage that led into the half-moon from another side. Interesting barbicans can still be seen at Warwick, Conwy, Chepstow, Sandal and Cahir, Co. Tipperary.

It might seem to the twentieth-century castle enthusiast that the castle had reached the point of impregnability. But medieval military builders were not so sanguine and they continued to look for ways to improve defences, such as higher walls, greater distances between outer walls and the ditches and banks outside, and more towers along the curtains. They also developed the employment of water defences, using natural sources, diverting rivers, manufacturing dams and creating artificial lakes.

The earliest castle-builders of Europe appreciated the value of surrounding castles with wet ditches, that is, moats which were more or less permanently supplied with water from springs or nearby rivers. The motte castle at the Husterknupp (*see* Chapter 1) in western Germany had been developed from a fortified farmstead lying in marshy ground, and by stage (c) was almost

completely surrounded by water which was provided by what appears to have been a natural and gradual rise in the water level of the district. Many of the first motte castles in Britain were sited on river banks or near rivers, or on land which had natural springs. Berkhamsted motte castle was almost totally surrounded by water from its first years, fed by springs. Skipsea motte castle was sited in a mere which separated the motte from its bailey. Clavering, one of the very earliest Norman castles, had moats fed by the River Stort, and Rothesay, one of the very few shell enclosures in Scotland, stood like an island in a surrounding moat fed by a stream from a nearby loch. And a good many castles have ditches today that are dry and tidily sown with grass but which were wet in the active military-residential role, for the Normans and early Plantagenets (and the lords whom they allowed to build castles) generally provided their greater fortresses with wet moats most of, if not all, the way round.

Two major castles in Britain which may be classified as water-castles or lake-fortresses (along with their other classifications) are Kenilworth in Warwickshire and Caerphilly in Wales. In both cases the use of extensive areas of water was deliberately integrated into the overall plans as a major defensive feature, and they were worked out according to the topography of the sites.

Caerphilly has already been mentioned in relation to its concentric form. Its water defences were additional fortifications, and they rested principally upon the creation of two large lakes. The south lake with its moats

The great gatehouse-tower at Tonbridge was built by Gilbert de Clare (builder of Caerphilly Castle in Wales).

Dunstanburgh: the early fourteenth-century great gatehouse in the centre was converted into a great tower about half a century later.

encircling three sides of the inner fortress was fed from a stream of the Nant-y-Gledyr. To the north of the inner fortress was raised a scarped bank curved at its two ends.

This view of Denbigh shows all that remains of the three-towered, triangular-plan gatehouse and its complex defensive mechanisms.

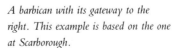

The western end leads into a hornwork, or separate earthwork island, revetted with stone and encircled by the water from the south lake. The east end joins at right-angles to a stone platform (the north platform) raised above water level and screened with a curtain wall, polygonal towers and a gatehouse at the north end. This arrangement formed a north lake whose levels could be controlled by sluices. In the same straight line, but veering slightly to the south-east, a south platform was erected with a curtain and a close row of projecting buttresses. This contained tunnels and sluices that regulated the flow of water from the south lake behind, into the ditches in front. Between the two fortified platforms is a third 'hook-shaped' platform with curtain but no towers or buttresses (the central platform), at the northern end of which is the main entrance to the castle, and

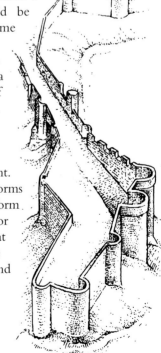

A barbican with its gateway to the right. This example is based on the one at Scarborough.

A general view of Kenilworth, a great castle of the twelfth and thirteenth centuries. The great tower, of massive proportions, is on the right.

this entrance gate joins with the north platform. The 289.6-metre (950-ft) long continuous platform was in the nature of a barbican, acting as a huge dam. The inner fortress is thus an island site, protected on all sides by lakes whose levels could be controlled by the defenders.

At Kenilworth, the original castle of the twelfth century was a polygonal enclosure whose ends led into a massive rectangular great tower of mid-twelfth-century construction and, in King John's reign, was circled by an outer enclosure with flanking towers and many pilaster buttresses. His son, Henry III, granted Kenilworth to his brother-in-law, Simon de Montfort, who was almost certainly responsible for the elaborate water defences which were to figure so dramatically in the great siege of Kenilworth in 1266. Basically, the castle of Simon de Montfort was artificially surrounded by water from springs south of the castle flowing into the low ground

around it by means of a 122-metre (400-ft) long mole, or dam, topped by a double wall with gatehouse at each end, projecting from the south-east of the outer curtain. In effect, the 'island' site stood in a large lake, called the Great Mere, which covered the south and west sides and fed a moat round the north and north-east sides leading into a lower mere on the east side, north of the mole.

During the siege, which was conducted by Prince Edward, Henry's eldest son, against supporters of Simon de Montfort (who had fought the King and lost at Evesham in 1265), barges were brought by road from Chester in order to launch a water-borne assault on the castle from the Great Mere. The attack was beaten off by the defenders, probably by a combination of missiles from siege-engines in the castle enclosure and concentrated fire from archers along the south wall which had been erected by King John.

There were many other castles with important water defences, and among them was Bodiam in Sussex. Bodiam Castle was built in one complete operation in the 1380s in a huge rectangular lake artificially created and fed by the River Rother. The water defences are interesting. In front of the main gatehouse to the north is a causeway out to a second gate and thence to an octagonal island platform in the lake. Today, this is connected to the north bank of the 'mainland' by a second causeway probably built in the seventeenth century. In the 1380s, however, no second causeway was provided at that point. Instead, there was a long bridge from the octagon westwards to the west bank. An introducing force therefore had to expose its flank to everything that the defenders wanted to hurl at it, including fire through the gatehouse gun-ports. The rear postern had a bridge projecting across the southern part of the lake to a harbour which was specially cut in the River Rother; in the fourteenth century the river was navigable at that point.

Moats were of course effective obstacles against besiegers, whether dry or filled with water, and the greater part of the 1350 or so castles in the gazetteer in this book were provided with ditching and ramparts of some kind. It is pleasing to record that some which were originally wet moats, but which dried up over the centuries, have been cleared out and refilled in the present century, as at Berkhamsted, to reveal the castles more in their medieval state. The presence of a drawbridge does not always indicate a wet moat, for it was necessary to be able to bridge a dry moat as well. And a stone-lined ditch does not necessarily indicate a dry moat. Bedford Castle has a stone-lined moat which appears from recent excavations to have led directly into the river, and so must have been part-filled if not wholly filled with water. Wet moats made undermining walls of towers or gatehouses behind them practically impossible, but there was nothing to stop an attacking army getting across the moat to the stretch between it and the walls (called the berm) and, under cover of a penthouse, boring underneath the foundations of a wall. Medieval castle owners probably echoed the belief in the effectiveness of a moat that Shakespeare puts into the last soliloquy of John of Gaunt (*Richard II*, II.i.) when he says: 'This precious stone set in the silver sea, which serves it in the office of a wall, or as a moat defensive to a house…'

Built by Sir Edward Dalyngrygge, Bodiam stands in an artificial lake fed from the River Rother.

6

Gunpowder and Firearms

In the middle of the thirteenth century the English-born scientific experimentalist and philosopher Roger Bacon (c.1214–90) discovered how to make gunpowder. Although gunpowder had been known and used by the Chinese for centuries, the secret had not reached the West, and Bacon's discovery was quite independent. It may be presumed he did not try to hide his work, and by the end of the century it was being manufactured and used all over the Continent, quite often with unpredictable and dangerous results.

The first suggestion of gunpowder's possible use in castle siege warfare in Britain was in Edward I's reign (1272–1307). He may have employed it in his siege of Stirling Castle in Scotland in 1304. This said, it would be quite wrong to deduce that the arrival of gunpowder in medieval artillery materially changed siege operations or caused any decline of the use of the castle as a fortress-residence. There is a mass of evidence to the contrary. Any decline in the use of the castle (with more than one building) as a fortress-residence was due when it did come to changes in medieval society. By the early fifteenth century, these kinds of castle were becoming less desirable because powerful men had begun to build beautiful but much less fortified homes instead (*see* pp. 108–10). Some castles were not even wanted unless they could be modernised, and this could sometimes mean

reducing their defensiveness. The decline also coincided with an increasing tendency to fight battles in the open field, where the opponents represented larger sectors of the kingdoms, duchies or counties involved in the hostilities. There is another point. If there was any decline, it was more than balanced by a widespread expansion in Scotland and Ireland in the demand for the single stone tower-house of several storeys, with protective stone wall, and many thousands of these were built between about 1300 and 1700 (*see* Chapter 9 and Chapter 10).

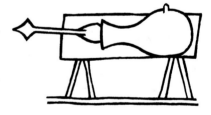

A drawing of a cannon taken from one of the earliest known pictures of this firearm, c.1327.

The siege of Stirling Castle is now thought to have been superintended by Master James of St George, by then an old man of nearly 70. It is mentioned in medieval accounts, and in one there is an order by the king for a supply of sulphur and saltpetre to be sent up from York. To what use these two constituents of gunpowder were put we are not told but, since charcoal, the third constituent, would have been obtainable near the castle, we may infer some explosive device. Once account states that fire was hurled into the castle, but this could have been Greek fire (see Chapter 5). For more tangible evidence of any form of gun we have to wait until the 1320s when, in a manuscript now at Christ Church, Oxford, there appears a picture of a rudimentary cannon. This shows a table on which lies a huge, presumably iron, bulb-shaped vessel with narrow neck and wide mouth, and it is discharging a bolt, or heavy arrow. An operator stands to the right behind the bulk, holding what looks like a long bar which may be red hot, to ignite the gunpowder. The arrow head is hard up against a pillar of an entrance into a battlemented tower. The implication is obvious: it is a type of gun or cannon. The word 'gun', or 'gonne' as it occasionally appears in contemporary manuscripts, is probably derived from mangonel.

The picture probably represents the earliest type of cannon, and it may be one used by Edward III in about 1327 in his first clash with the Scots. A later historian, John Barbour (c.1316–96), refers to 'crakys of wer', the Lowland Scottish phrase for cannon or gun, used by Edward in this war. It is also said that cannon was used at Crécy in 1346. These early guns were probably still discharging bolts and not shot.

Progress towards a useful type of cannon was in fact very slow. Up to the middle of the fourteenth century, guns had to be breech-loaded. They were no more effective than cross-bows or longbows and much less accurate. Barrels had to be cleaned after every firing, which meant time had to be allowed for the barrel to cool down. That could be up to an hour. Guns were difficult and costly to make and to move around. They were easily captured by a defending force that sallied out of a castle to attack besiegers. Many cannons blew up in the faces of those firing them, as much the result of faulty manufacture of the gun as of clumsy handling of the gunpowder charge. James II of Scotland (1437–60), an enlightened monarch and one perhaps too deeply interested in pyrotechnics, 'did stand near the gunners when the artillery discharged [at the siege of Roxburgh Castle]: his thigh bone was dung in two with the piece of a misformed gun that brake in shooting, by which he was stricken to the ground and died hastily…' (quoted from the *Historie and Cronicles of Scotland* by Robert Lindsay of Pitscottie).

The principal value of early cannons was more psychological than destructive. Opponents may at first have been demoralised by gunfire, and there were instances when surrender was followed by the first shot or two. The garrison at Berwick yielded to Henry IV's first gunshots in a siege during 1405. Certainly, opponents' horses would have been thoroughly frightened and would have bolted. On the other hand, there is a record of two cannons firing over 400 shots at the siege of Ypres, in 1383, and not one person being injured. But the longer-term potential

A copy of a medieval sketch of a hand-gun in operation.

of gunpowder and guns must have been appreciated, for military engineers clearly determined to press on with the dangerous and expensive business of developing them.

In the fifteenth century new types of gun and improvements to existing types emerged. Among these were hand-guns, although the earliest of these were cumbersome and manifestly awkward to use (see picture). Engineers also discovered that the muzzle velocity of a gun would be increased if the bore was reduced. Cannons were made smaller. One experiment was a number of small hand-guns clustered together and fixed to a carriage, with charges in each barrel. These would be lit by the swift movement of a taper across every touch-hole. Cannons were also made with longer barrels. In the middle of the century we see the introduction of very large guns, on the whole better made than their predecessors, although they were still pretty unsafe for their users.

The great Ottoman Sultan, Mohammed II, who captured Constantinople by siege in 1453 and thus altered the course of European history, used the largest cannon the world had hitherto seen. Two years later, there appeared in Scotland at the siege of Threave Castle, the famous 'Mons Meg', an 'iron murderer' which can still be seen at Edinburgh Castle. The cannon is about 4 metres (13 ft) long, and it was manufactured from long, flat hammered iron bars girded by hoops, the normal way to make gun barrels at the time. The barrel bore was 51 cm (20 in), and if properly loaded and charged with about 47.6 kg (105 lb) of powder and set at an angle of about 15 degrees, it could fire an iron ball over 1280 metres (1400 yd). Mons Meg was made in Flanders, probably at Malines, which was rendered as Mollance in Scottish dialect (from which Munce or Mons). Meg is short for Marjory or Margaret, a name sometimes given to guns. Mons Meg exploded in 1680 when used to fire a salute for the birthday of James, Duke of York, who was the brother of Charles II, and later James II (VII of Scotland). The gun was left unrepaired until 1829.

The first gun made in Britain was probably one fabricated in 1474 for James III (1460–88). An early instance of Scottish home-produced guns in use at a siege was at Dumbarton in 1489, when the next king, James IV (1488–1513), successfully brought the castle's owner, Lord Darnley, to his knees. The King also employed Mons Meg at this siege.

The first English gun does not appear to have been made before the time of Henry VIII, who acquired a special interest in ordnance. By this time there had been significant improvements in gun-making, not least gun barrels of non-ferrous metals such as brass. These could be cast instead of made in strips. By the 1530s guns were being made in sizes and in ranges: a culverin was a cannon that normally fired a ball from 6.8–8.2 kg (15–18 lb) in weight, a distance of 1.6–2.4 km (1–1½ miles), although hand-culverins of much shorter range, using smaller shot, are also mentioned. A saker was smaller than a culverin and fired a 2.7-kg (6-lb) ball up to about 1.6 km. A demi-cannon shot balls that weighed 12.2–14.5 kg (27–32 lb). A falcon was a very small cannon that fired a 0.9-kg (2-lb) shot about 1.6 km, and a falconet was even smaller, shooting a 0.4-kg (1-lb) ball rather less distance. These guns were usually mounted on two wheels, except for the hand-guns. Of course, there were others, and the names given above were sometimes applied to guns of different size and range.

Guns could be mobilised to attack castles. As the ranges were far greater than those of mangonels and trebuchets (which are believed to have discharged missiles over little more than 457.2 metres [500 yards]), they could be positioned much further away from the castle, out of range of any retaliatory fire, until the first defenders

This view of Ravenscraig shows the great tower (left) on the north-west. In the centre, in front of the southern end of the great tower, are the remains of an artillery platform facing inland.

began to use guns in response. Guns inside castles were positioned at ground level inside inner or outer baileys, or on platforms at wall-walk level, or on the tops of towers, or even on turrets specially built for them (notably, the coastal fortresses). Guns at ground level could be elevated high enough to shoot over the wall top, although the exercise was a hazardous one. Guns on wall tops could be dipped to fire outwards into the thick of a besieging army but that was also dangerous – and superfluous if the ball had rolled out of the barrel before the charge was fired.

Artillery was seldom a dominating weapon in British castle sieges until the seventeenth century. Bamburgh was besieged in 1464 by the great 'Kingmaker', Richard Neville, Earl of Warwick, when he used two enormous cannons like Mons Meg, and the castle was almost battered into surrender. But this was an unusual occurrence. Machiavelli (1469–1527), the wily Florentine statesman and author of *The Prince* (a manual of dictatorship), had no time for gunpowder artillery and said as much in the 1520s. Fauchet, writing in the 1600s, stated that cannons were used only by cowardly people. But used they were, although it is clear that their value in sieges was, at times, hotly debated. Cross-bows and longbows were still widely in use at this time: James V of Scotland (1513–42) is known to have preferred the bow to the gun.

So far as castle designers were concerned, few alterations were made in any castles before the mid-fifteenth century in response to artillery. In England and Wales, the main and one of the only adjustments was the insertion of gun-loops, or gun-ports. Existing arrow slits

Some castle gun-ports: (left to right) Herstmonceux (crosslet with separated port at bottom), Ravenscraig (inverted keyhole with large opening), Tillycairn (inverted keyhole with top crosslet), and Leslie (slit with wide-mouth port).

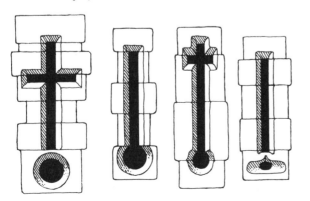

Noltland, Orkney: note the almost total absence of window openings along the walls.

were altered to cater for hand-guns or very small culverins. At Bodiam, for example, the oillets (round openings out of the bottom end of straight arrow slits) were adapted for hand-guns. At some other castles, such as Kirby Muxloe, a round opening was inserted, spaced apart, below an arrow slit. At many castles, special gun-ports were built in, as at Raglan and Caister. These were splayed on both horizontal sides or all round, outside and sometimes internally too; that is, the opening converged inwards from both faces of the wall, creating an 'X' in plan. This allowed the maximum sweep from side to side for the guns. But many castles did not have gun-ports, notably three big fortresses built in Scotland in the first half of the fifteenth century – Borthwick, Comlongon and Elphinstone.

But indifference to artillery was not universal in Britain. At Ravenscraig in Fife, Scotland, there was built the first castle specifically designed for defence by firearms. This interesting structure was begun in the spring of 1460 by the advanced-thinking James II for his wife, Mary of Gueldres, only a few months before his untimely death at the siege of Roxburgh on 3 August, and is described in the gazetteer on p. 287.

Another castle in Scotland that almost bristles with gun-ports is Noltland, on Westray in Orkney. This is a Z-plan castle whose end towers are square-plan upon a central rectangular block. The exterior wall surfaces of the castle are equipped with over 70 gun-ports at several levels and of two kinds – rectangular and unsplayed, and oval with splays.

In the sixteenth century the majority of new Scottish tower-houses were given gun-ports at various levels. Designers were fond of inserting them at or near entrances (Claypotts and Tolquhon are interesting examples). Older castle buildings were adapted to take gun-ports, such as at Caerlaverock. And the artillery-fortification of tower-houses and other forms of castle in Scotland continued into the seventeenth century, and in a few cases into the eighteenth. Corgarff in Aberdeenshire began as a rectangular tower-house of the mid-sixteenth century. In 1746–7 it was occupied by Hanoverian troops as a base for policing the area after the collapse of the second Jacobite Rising at Culloden in 1746. The tower was then surrounded by a star-shaped curtain wall with numerous gun-ports, of tall vertical shape intended for muskets.

Perhaps the damage done to Borthwick Castle in Midlothian by the artillery of Cromwell in 1650 demonstrates as well as anything the limited influence of guns in castle warfare. Today the east wall of the massive tower contains a large gash in the 4.6-metre (15-ft) thick masonry (which has been partly patched up). The owner, Lord Borthwick, surrendered rather than have further damage done, but it is clear that Cromwell would have been hard put to reduce the tower to a heap of stone (as is implied in his threat contained in a surviving letter to Borthwick and quoted on p. 244).

Borthwick's massive tower-house has machicolated parapets. Note also the very limited window openings.

7

Castles in Wales

When we look at the castles in Wales, we may be tempted to see them largely as those remarkable structures erected in the late thirteenth century by Edward I, or by powerful lords with his permission, as part of his invasion, conquest and suppression of the country in the years 1277–83 and thereafter. We may also be tempted to accept the notion that these castles represent the apogee of military architecture in Britain. But that is to suggest that everything which came before was but a lead-up to these castles, and that everything which followed was in the nature of a decline. This is not the case. Edwardian castles are more properly considered outside the general stream of British castle history, and they ought to be viewed for what they are, what they were built for, and finally, for what happened to them.

Their plans and construction were part of a single, exclusive programme initiated by Edward to make short shrift of the Welsh in a vigorous campaign and to impose his dominion over them. Wales was to be absorbed. The programme began and virtually ended with him. It was not repeated by him in his attempts to conquer Scotland (if Caerlaverock was intended to be a castle on the Welsh scale, it was a lone one, and not part of any programme – and there is argument as to how much of it was Edwardian-inspired in any case). It was not imitated by

any succeeding monarch in Britain: the only comparison that could be advanced is the programme of coastal fortification initiated by Henry VIII in the invasion scare of 1538–43, and these fortresses were entirely defensive structures. Within half a century some of the new castles in Wales were already in a state of decay and requiring considerable attention.

The Edwardian programme was gigantic by the standards of the time, and it involved men, materials and money on an unprecedented scale. Ten new castles were to be built, at Aberystwyth, Beaumaris, Builth, Caernarfon, Conwy, Flint, Harlech, Hope, Rhuddlan and Ruthin. The majority were to be major works, in some cases associated with town fortifications. Work was also to be undertaken on four new 'lordship' castles, Chirk, Denbigh, Hawarden and Holt, on three originally Welsh-built but captured castles, Castell-y-Bere, Criccieth and Dolwyddelan. We shall be looking at the figures applying to the first ten; details of the work on the others will be found in the gazetteer.

The vast programme cost nearly £80,000 in the years 1277–1304, and another £15,000 were spent between 1304 and 1330. It involved a major exercise in recruitment and impressment of labour from all over England. The map on p. 61, reproduced from the *History of the King's Works* vol. I, shows the areas from which craftsmen and labourers were drafted to Wales for these works, via two gathering points, Bristol and Chester. In round figures, about 150 masons, 400 carpenters, 1000 diggers and 8000 woodcutters for clearing were raised by one means or another in 1282–3. Most counties contributed, from Norfolk to Hampshire, Northumberland to Warwickshire. Those who assembled at Bristol were taken by ship to the south Wales coast and then travelled to the site at Aberystwyth. At Beaumaris, 3500 or so men were employed on the castle in the summer of 1295 – a figure equal to about 15 per cent of the total number of men employed in trade or commerce in London at the time. At Harlech, 1000 men were at work in 1286.

The impressment of workmen for the 'King's works' in north Wales, 1282–3. It will be noticed that none of the labour forces came from Wales. Some English gangs were taken by ship from Bristol to Carmarthenshire and then by land northwards.

	Movement of labour, May–June 1282
	Movement of labour, 1283
	Gathering points
	Carpenters
	Diggers
	Masons
	Counties so marked also provided some 1600 woodcutters (coupiateres), mainly for clearing tracks and passes
	New castles under construction

In the centre of this view of Rhuddlan is one of the two twin-cylindrical-towered gatehouses in the inner enclosure of this concentric castle, built by Master James of St George in 1277–82.

Although the craftsmen and workers were paid, they were also conscripted, that is, they were drafted for the jobs. In Professor Allen Brown's phrase, 'this was direction of labour'. And the military was employed to guard contingents of men travelling to Chester and Bristol. One batch of men coming from Yorkshire to work at Flint and Rhuddlan was guarded by sergeants who were paid 7½d a day in case the men should abscond. Bonuses were paid for fast work, in kind rather than in cash, but wages were docked for absenteeism.

The purpose of the castles was to terrify the Welsh into submission, to frighten those already defeated so that they would not rise, and to provide the Welsh with a permanent reminder of who was master of their land. Stage One, from 1277–82, was to include new castles at Rhuddlan, Flint and Aberystwyth, and renovations at Builth. It is thought that the scale of the works at Flint

and Rhuddlan (where the River Clwyd was diverted more than 3.2 km (2 miles) off course so that there would be uninterrupted access to and from the sea) alarmed the Welsh in north Wales enough to initiate the 1282 campaign in which they were finally crushed and their great prince, Llywelyn the Last (1246–82), killed. This victory prompted Edward I to embark on Stage Two of his programme – Caernarfon, Conwy, Harlech, Beaumaris, Hope and Ruthin.

The remains of the great tower (foreground) at Flint.

Harlech: the great gatehouse in the inner walling of this famous concentric castle, built by Master James of St George (1283–90).

The sites of the Edwardian castles were well chosen. They were not all new sites: there had been a motte castle at Caernarfon and a stone structure at Builth. All except Builth were by or very close to the sea which guaranteed access, and which meant that they could all be supplied with men, weapons and food if they were attacked by Welsh forces from the landward side, as happened at Caernarfon in 1294–5.

Of the new works, four were concentric, built so from scratch: Aberystwyth and Rhuddlan (lozenge-shaped-plan), Harlech (slightly rhomboidal) and Beaumaris (almost square). Conwy and Caernarfon were curtain enclosures with flanking towers and gatehouse, like Framlingham in concept but vastly more sophisticated. Flint was an enclosure with corner towers and a huge cylindrical great tower outside the south-east corner separated by a moat; in fact, like a motte-and-bailey castle in plan. Hope and Ruthin were enclosures

with towers, and so on, and Builth a motte castle with later shell enclosure (or possibly great tower: the documents of the time say *magna turris*).

The programme may well have been ignored in most parts of England (except the homes of the men drafted to Wales) to whom Wales was a distant land of men speaking a foreign tongue, but it was real enough to the men of Wales, and on several occasions they rose to attack the structures as they went up, pulling them down or burning them. Notably, Caernarfon was severely damaged in 1294 and 1295 by Prince Madog ap Llywelyn.

Edward's programme required a mastermind to superintend the works involved. The King was a ruler with grandiose ideas not only of uniting the component parts of Britain into one kingdom, but also of ensuring that future generations should forever see monuments to his power. He chose one of the foremost castle-builders of Western Europe, Master James of St George, who may be regarded as combining the abilities and functions of master mason, designer and military engineer. Magister Jacobus Ingeniator, or Magister Jacobus Le Mazun, appears first in British records in 1277–8. He had been working on castles in Savoy, in particular at Yverdon, Chillon and Saillon, and appears in records in Turin as Magistri Jacobi Cementarii and Jaquetto de Sancto Jorio (George). Dr A.J. Taylor examined Saillon Castle in the 1950s and found architectural parallels with Harlech and Conwy. He also examined the castle at St Georges d'Esperanche in the Viennois, south-east of Lyon, and found parallels with the plan of Conwy and details comparable with Harlech. One was a garderobe shaft at St Georges which was almost the same as the one beside the north-west tower at Harlech.

Master James, therefore, arrived in Wales fully experienced as a castle designer, mason and engineer, and was appointed Master of the King's Works, probably in 1282, for which he was to receive 3 shillings a day, plus

A splendid view of Conwy, a great enclosure castle with massive flanking round towers – eight in all – built in only four years (1283–7).

a pension of 1s 6d a day for his wife, who gloried in the name of Ambrosia, should she survive him. It is clear that he more than pleased his employer, for preferments of one kind and another followed, and he seems to have been on the royal payroll up to his death c.1309. For example, he was appointed Constable at Harlech, 1290–3, was granted an estate in 1295, and worked for Edward from 1298 to 1305 in Scotland on several fortification projects, particularly Linlithgow and possibly Caerlaverock.

The age of the specialist military architect-engineer had arrived in Britain at this time. Men like Master James and his colleague, Master Robert of Beverley (who made the Tower of London concentric, fortified Goodrich and improved Windsor and Rochester) and no doubt others of whom we lack details so far, were in a different category from those builders of the twelfth century whom we met in Chapter 3. These thirteenth-century men had benefited from the important rediscovery of

The powerful Welsh enclosure castle of Castell-y-Bere is built below Cadair Idris in North Wales.

A huge and sophisticated enclosure castle with massive flanking towers and gatehouses, Caernarfon was begun in 1283. The castle was attacked more than once during building operations by angry Welsh national forces.

Greek sciences, in particular geometry, and this enabled them to visit a site and assess its possibilities, envisage a structure thereon as a whole and say what was possible and what was not. That is not to say that their buildings were without mistakes: they erred, like their predecessors – and like their colleagues on the cathedrals (Ely, York, Peterborough *et al*) – and often had to change direction as the work went on. It is thought that mason-engineers made wooden models of the structures they proposed to build (some were made as presents for royal children) and they may also have committed schemes to paper, although such plans have not survived for castles. They worked with the leaders of the other disciplines, such as master carpenters and probably ironsmiths, in a team, and did not interfere with them. It is unlikely that they exerted the supervisory role that the architects of today take for granted.

The Edwardian castles are described under their entries in the gazetteer, but one or two points that are common to many of them may be mentioned here. We have seen, in the chapter on the first stone castles, that

few castles were built and finished in one operation or series of operations. Among the few are some of these Welsh castles: Aberystwyth (1277–89), Harlech (1283–90), Rhuddlan (1277–82), Flint (1277–85), Conwy (1283–9), Caernarfon (1283–1327) and Beaumaris (1295–c.1330, unfinished). They were planned and constructed as single and enormous units. Nothing of importance was added as an afterthought and no major rebuilding was done to improve the fortification. Four of them were built after the conquest and absorption of Wales and were therefore not aggressively offensive structures so much as administrative centres, police headquarters as it were, terror weapons, buildings from which to emerge only in times of civilian disturbance.

They were lived in, not by monarchs or their families (except in rare circumstances and for extremely short periods), but by constables and officials, and so they differ somewhat from the private military fortress-residence role of other castles. Additionally, five of them were built in association with towns which were fortified with walls and turrets at the same time, in the hope that castle and town would work together to make the new order in Wales function as smoothly as possible. They have been compared with *bastides*, a type of town built by lords in southern France to protect their feudal borders, when the townsfolk were expected to contribute to the lord's purse and help to defend his interests in return for mercantile privileges. In a subtle way the arrangement in Wales was to create pockets of loyal, or at least passive, people among a population that was hostile. And architecturally, of course, the castles have several features in common, notably (except for Flint) the great gatehouse which was a substitute for the great tower. The gatehouse in the Edwardian and lordship castles reached a high level of sophistication in defensiveness as well as strength in construction. At Rhuddlan and Beaumaris, Master James incorporated two massive gatehouses at opposite ends of the inner enclosure. And at Denbigh, a lordship castle, the great gatehouse was one of the most elaborate of its kind anywhere in Europe.

Readers may by now have wondered where the massive and splendid concentric castle at Caerphilly fits into this picture of works in Wales. It was not a royal castle, although it belonged to a man who had exceptional wealth and wielded considerable power, Gilbert de Clare, who was Lord of Glamorgan, this being a semi-independent province about one-quarter the size of Wales. Caerphilly was started by de Clare in 1268. What gave him the idea of building Caerphilly on the concentric plan, and much like the later Harlech and

Beaumaris as it turned out? And what influence, if any, did his plan have on Master James of St George? It is possible we may have the answer before the end of the present century, but for the moment the questions remain unanswered and open.

Although much space has been given to the Edwardian fortresses of the late thirteenth century, it should not be thought that the Welsh were unable to build their own castles or find a use for fortification. They felt the heavy hand of the Normans only a few years after the Conquest of 1066, but unlike the Anglo-Saxons they determined to maintain resistance for as long as possible. They were helped by their natural geography: the Normans were at first more interested in the low-lying territories of Wales. The Welsh, therefore, were able to learn about castle-building and to put it into practice.

Soon after the Conquest, three powerful, bullying,

Dolwyddelan: the birthplace of Llywelyn the Great. The rectangular tower was built in the later twelfth century.

war-happy robber-barons, Hugh d'Avranches, Lord of Chester, Roger of Montgomery, Lord of the Lands of Shropshire and William FitzOsbern, Earl of Hereford and Master of the Wye Valley, launched a three-pronged invasion of Wales, taking the difficulties of Offa's Dyke, the Brecon Hills and the Black Mountains in their stride and establishing a firm foothold in a substantial part of the ancient land of the Cymru. Motte castles were raised with astonishing swiftness over wide areas, namely at Clifford, Monmouth, Chepstow, Montgomery, Degannwy, Radnor, Brecon, Cardiff and also at many more. By the end of the eleventh century, the Normans were settled in the west, the south and in some of the north-east, leaving only the centre and the mountainous north-west in Welsh hands. And they had started to build in stone at Chepstow and elsewhere.

The Welsh were taken aback by the Norman invasion and their brutal and grandiose military engineering, and at first made only sporadic attempts to fight back. Newly erected Norman mottes were besieged and sometimes taken, building works in stone were interrupted by lightning raids of Welsh warriors who pulled down the walls and set fire to the wooden parts, as at Cardiff, Laugharne and Llandovery (where the castle was said to have been seized before the mortar had dried between the stone blocks). Then, in the middle of the twelfth century, the Welsh recovered their poise and their national spirit was rekindled under strong leaders like Owain Gwynedd and Llewelyn the Great. Their attacks on Norman castles and towns were stepped up, they were better organised and on the whole more successful in their outcome. Henry II had tried but failed to reassert English power in the south-east and west, and the Welsh had taken the fullest advantage of the difficulties between his son, John, and his grandson, Henry III, and their factious barons, which resulted in civil wars in both reigns. The Welsh did not have the technical capacity to assault the tough, well built fortresses still in English hands, such as Chepstow, Cilgerran and Pembroke, but they could and did build castles of their own, especially in the north.

Castell-y-Bere, near Dolgellau, under the slopes of Cadair Idris, had an irregular curtain with towers, one of them a sizeable rectangular tower, and the castle was able to withstand siege. Dolbadarn, an unusual boomerang-shaped enclosure, had a large cylindrical great tower which is 12.2 metres (40 ft) high today, and had other towers and buildings. Dolwyddelan, the birthplace of Llewelyn the Great, was a three-storeyed rectangular great tower with an entrance protected by one of the few forebuildings put up by Welsh masons. Criccieth, a

This view of Ewloe shows the square trunk of the D-plan great tower, which sits in the middle of a stone enclosure flanked on the west by an outer bailey.

triangular enclosure on a mound over the sea, had two rectangular towers. There were others, such as Dolforwyn in Montgomeryshire and Ewloe in Flintshire, both built as acts of defiance of the English by Llewelyn the Last.

But these castles were mostly sited on rocky outcrops in mountainous countryside, and they were intended much more for the defensive purposes of the princes struggling for independence or playing military 'hide-and-seek' with the English. When the conquest of Wales was completed (in the 1280s) by Edward I, and English rule established in fact as well as in law, some of these Welsh structures were allowed to decay, if not actually encouraged to fall down. Dolbadarn was stripped of its timber for the new Caernarfon Castle and others were used as quarries for their stone. Others were remodelled for English use, as we have seen.

8

Border Castles

If the need for castles began to diminish generally in England and Wales in the fourteenth century, there was one area where, on the contrary, it grew. That was the border district between England and Scotland which for centuries, after the Scots had won their War of Independence under Robert Bruce, was the scene of warfare and looting, and destruction of crops, farms and houses by raiders on both sides. It was also the scene for many better organised invasions, counter-invasions and also 'punitive' expeditions which employed armies, siege-engines (where needed) and all the other paraphernalia of medieval warfare.

Principally we are concerned here with great castles, and smaller fortified tower-houses all known as peles (but we are not including the smaller, fortified, more horizontal houses known as bastles) on the English side in Northumberland whose northern boundaries make up about three-quarters of the whole border. There are more than 200 of them, although not all are of medieval origin. (Bastles had two, or less frequently three storeys, generally with only slits for ventilation and light, the ground floor reserved for livestock which were brought inside during trouble, the first floor given to

accommodating the owner and his family, and others to whom he might offer refuge.)

The word 'pele' comes from the Latin *palus*, a stake, which was used in the building of a palisade round a tower. Pele-towers probably began as wooden towers, like motte castles. They were generally three-storeyed

Bamburgh is a castle of many periods of construction.

with substantial walls, small and with few windows (*see* Vicar's Pele, Corbridge), although the visitor will find two- and four-storeyed peles. Nearly all the peles and bastles are fourteenth-century or later. Some were built on the remains of older castles, including motte castle sites.

The third fortified structure in Northumberland is the castle proper, and both principal types – great tower with enclosure, and enclosure with flanking towers, gatehouse, and so on – are found. Some were begun soon after the Norman Conquest. Bamburgh was started on a rocky hill beside the sea during the Conqueror's reign by Robert de Mowbray, Earl of Northumberland.

Other great castles of Northumberland which were begun in the eleventh and twelfth centuries, to which we may add some in Durham and Cumberland, were Alnwick (c.1100), Carlisle (c.1092), Durham (c.1072), Norham (c.1120), Newcastle upon Tyne (c.1080), Prudhoe (c.1170s) and Warkworth (c.1140), and these were to be added to in subsequent centuries, so that some, like Alnwick, ended up by being palatial as well as military. In the thirteenth to fifteenth centuries several medium-sized castles were raised, including Aydon, Belsay, Bothal,

Bywell, Chillingham, Chipchase, Edlingham, Etal, Ford (all in Northumberland), Cockermouth in Cumberland, Raby in Durham and Sizergh in Westmoreland (*see* entries in gazetteer). Some of these began as towers, great or pele, and were subsequently enlarged.

There is an interesting point about the small peles of Northumberland and Cumberland: they were diminutive, and were only effective against the kind of small-scale, although tiresome, raiding carried out by the Scots – and of course the Scots had their own small tower-houses as protection against equally irritating English raiding. And yet the peles were modelled on great towers and were in a sense miniature versions of them. The parapet at the Vicar's Pele at Corbridge was no less in proportion to the size of the rest of the tower than was Newcastle's. Many of the larger towers had additional bartizans and turrets, and some had machicolation as well, as at Featherstone and Chipchase.

Why was there this emphasis on vertical building in Northumberland? The answer is that the great tower, the tower-house and the pele are all examples of a horizontal residence being up-ended and fortified for security reasons. Even when in the later fourteenth and fifteenth centuries there was more prosperity and more people were able to build themselves fine residences, there was always the need to fortify and protect against marauders.

Alnwick: much of this Border castle is restored fourteenth-century work, with later buildings added to improve the domestic role.

Warkworth: the multangular great tower, built on the mid-twelfth-century motte, is similar in plan to those at Trim, Co. Meath, and Castle Rushen, Isle of Man.

It is also possible that there was some influence from the Scottish preference for building upwards rather than sideways, manifest not only in their numerous tower-houses great and small, but also in many of their private homes, and in towns that one could expect normally to be out of danger. The pele-tower was the least complicated and least expensive way for a landowner to provide himself with a private residence incorporating military, that is, defensive and offensive, characteristics. Many pele-towers even dispensed with stone stairs, and merely had a wooden step-ladder leading from the higher level to the ground, which could be lifted out of reach of raiders at a moment's notice. Some pele-towers have no doorway or staircase inside between the ground floor and the quarters above. Also, some ground-floor chambers were vaulted to prevent fire. Thus peles were very often built with as much thought as their greater counterparts.

It has been said that the essential military character of many northern towers and pele-towers is the reason for not displaying any great variety of layout, decorative effect or architectural interest, such as one finds in the greater castles and fortified houses of the rest of England of the same period. This view is not really tenable. A closer look at any six Northumberland or Cumberland towers would reveal many details of individual character in one that are not repeated in the other five, which of course is part of the fascination of castles in general – each one is different somewhere. Chipchase Tower, for example, has four storeys, with turrets on the four corners, each rising from corbelled courses, with a short projecting wing at the south-east end up the whole height. The entrance to the tower was in this wing at first-floor level, and it was defended by a portcullis. The top storey was a great chamber or hall, with an adjacent kitchen screened off at one time. The chapel is in the wall masonry on the third floor. Edlingham Tower once had a forebuilding on the west wall which has now disappeared. Vicar's Pele, Corbridge, has its entrance on the ground floor and this was defended by an iron yett. It has straight flights of stairs in the wall thickness, and bold parapets round the top. The tower is roofed with a gable. Yet another example is Cocklaw Tower, which has a postern opening from the main chamber at second-floor level, about 5.5 metres (18 ft) from the ground. This was accessible only by ladder or rope.

Many Northumberland peles were surrounded by a simple enclosing stone wall called a barmkin. As a rule the barmkin was not fortified by any flanking towers or gatehouse, and the gateway was little more than a break in the masonry, or an arched doorway. The barmkin was intended for penning livestock in time of trouble. Presumably the prime animals were shepherded into the ground-floor area of the tower, where a tower had such an area allotted. This was not normally the case with the greater towers.

There were exceptions to the vertical building preference. Haughton Castle was more a fortified hall-house, of two storeys at first, but with a later addition of another two floors with turrets at the top corners. Aydon was a substantial rectilinear block in cruciform plan, two storeys high, with four main room areas on each floor. The higher floor was reached by means of an external open staircase.

Watching over these smaller castles and towers in the Border country, as it were, stood the great castles – Alnwick, Bamburgh, Carlisle, Durham, Norham, Newcastle, Prudhoe and Warkworth. Owned and improved over the years by the Crown or by powerful magnates such as the Percys, they were among the greatest fortresses in the land. Two of them, Carlisle and Norham, had particularly tempestuous histories.

Carlisle is a great tower inside a triangular curtain with buttresses and gatehouse attached to a larger bailey also enclosed on all but one side by a stone curtain wall with flanking towers. The last side was a long stretch of man-cut ditch and bank. It began as an earthwork castle erected by William II c.1092. It was taken by the Scottish

The substantial great tower at Norham, built by the bishop of Durham in the mid- to late twelfth century, was about 27.5 metres (90 ft) tall.

king, David I, in the 1140s and he started the stone great tower. Carlisle was returned to Henry II in 1157. Besieged in 1174 by William the Lion, King of Scotland, with a huge army, it held out for three months. It was successfully besieged and taken by Alexander II, King of Scotland, in 1216. Returned to Henry III a year later, it was in a sorry state after Alexander's attentions and it continued to decay. Then in 1285–90, Edward I rescued the castle and greatly improved it. Carlisle was besieged by Robert Bruce soon after his victory at Bannockburn in 1314; he had used catapults for hurling large stones, and then tried to assault it from on high with a belfry, but this became stuck in the mud on the far side of the moat. The castle was besieged twice by the Scots in Richard II's reign but it did not fall. And it was besieged again in the Civil War by Leslie, the Scottish general and ally of the English Parliamentary cause. The garrison is said to have been reduced to eating rats, linseed meal and dogs.

Norham, at the north-east end of the border, has a great tower inside a roughly D-shaped inner enclosure of stone (whose north-east and south-east sides form two sides of the great tower), with a deep moat round the enclosure. This is situated in the north corner of a much larger outer stone enclosure with flanking towers of various shapes, D-ended, square and even one with a pointed edge, and with a gatehouse. This outer enclosure is also surrounded by a moat and bank. The great tower was the first stone building, 25.6 x 18.3 metres (84 x 60 ft), eventually reaching to about 27.4 metres (90 ft) tall, with walls from 3.3–4.3 metres (11–14 ft) thick. It was raised between 1160 and 1174. Norham was besieged in 1214 by Alexander II of Scotland for six weeks, but without success. Robert Bruce tried three times (1318, 1319 and 1322) to take Norham by siege, using the latest siege-engines (which were presumably new developments of the trebuchet). He failed each time, but then in 1327 he was successful. Norham was returned to England under the ensuing peace treaty.

For more than a century Norham remained unassaulted and the castle was gradually repaired and enlarged. Then, during the Wars of the Roses, Norham, held by the Yorkists for a time, was besieged in 1463 by the Lancastrians. It was relieved by the great Kingmaker, Richard Neville, Earl of Warwick, the foremost Yorkist general. But in 1464 the garrison defected to the Lancastrians. The next major siege was in 1513 by James IV, King of Scotland, in the short war with England. James used the famous cannon Mons Meg and others and smashed down large masses of the great tower and the castle walls, barbican and other towers. The state of the great tower today is largely the result of that particular battering. The garrison surrendered. It was of no value to James, however, for he and the flower of his nobles and knights were cut down and killed at the grievous Battle of Flodden in the same year. Afterwards, Norham was returned again to English hands.

9
Castles in Scotland

In Scotland, castles were introduced not by force but by choice, by Scottish kings who were influenced by Norman ideas, and by Norman lords whom the kings welcomed into Scotland and to whom they gave lands (in many cases with permission to build castles). The kings were in effect implementing the introduction of feudalism into parts of Scotland, predominantly into the Lowlands and up the north-east to Moray and Nairn.

The first castles in Scotland, therefore, were mainly motte castles, and between about 1100 and about 1250 more than 200 were raised. The most notable remains today are those at Duffus (Grampian), Mote of Urr (Dumfries and Galloway), Bass of Inverurie and Doune of Invernochty (Grampian), Hawick (Borders) and Dunscaith (Highland), some of which later received stonework. These castles were constructed in the same way as the English motte castles and played much the same role, for while the kings of Scotland and their lords were 'feudalists', their subjects were not so receptive to the new order and had, therefore, to learn. Scottish castles had additional roles, to act as fortresses for the defence of the country against attack from England (a very real and continuous danger) and also against continued Viking

incursions up to the middle of the thirteenth century.

Motte castles were raised in south-west Scotland in some quantity, as the map in Chapter 2 indicates. They were also built north of the Forth in a north-easterly sweep from the Clyde, up the fertile Midland Valley into Aberdeenshire, Morayshire and Nairnshire. The Bass of Inverurie was raised c.1180 and rose to at least 18.3 metres (60 ft) tall before its wooden tower was built upon the summit. It is a handsome monument today, although its top has no buildings. At Hawick, the motte was very

Bass of Inverurie: an aerial view of this late twelfth-century motte.

Castle Sween is the oldest stone castle in Scotland.

a projection on the east wall containing a straight flight of stairs and acting as a kind of forebuilding. This tower was built in about 1300. At a later (unknown) date, the north-west corner fractured away from the rest of the tower and slid down the motte, coming to rest in the position it occupies today. The Mote of Annan, raised in the early twelfth century, was 15.2 metres (50 ft) tall and separated from its bailey by a deep ditch. The motte at Selkirk was developed upon a natural mound in the early 1100s and also had a wide and deep ditch around it.

As in England and Wales, stone castles began to be built in Scotland at much the same time as the earth-and-timber motte castles. Probably the earliest (for none has yet established an earlier claim) was Castle Sween. This interesting structure remains to a substantial extent what

much smaller, and probably supported no more than a watch-tower. Today, it has a flight of steps up the slope which gives a good idea of how the summit would have been approached in its time as a castle. (The stone steps up the motte to the quatrefoil stone great tower at Clifford's in York give a similar impression.) At Duffus, near Elgin, the motte, raised in about 1150, was given a rectangular, stone great tower upon a splayed plinth, with

The design of Kildrummy, an early enclosure castle with towers, has French influence (see plan, p. 277).

Dirleton, showing the south donjon (left), with the forework of the entrance next to it.

it was when erected on the shore of Loch Sween in South Knapdale, Strathclyde. The date of the castle cannot be given precisely, but it is reckoned to be late eleventh or early twelfth century, which suggests a structure put up under Norman influence (probably by permission of one of the Scottish kings), and this is supported by its pilaster buttresses, a Norman feature.

If Sween was the first stone castle in Scotland others were soon to follow, and they emerged in the main

Doune of Invernochty is a motte castle that later received a shell enclosure, of which only traces remain.

The first buildings at Bothwell, one of Scotland's greatest castles, were constructed under French influence.

patterns with which we are already familiar in England and Wales: the great tower and the curtain enclosure with flanking towers and other buildings inside. Sween's successors include the enclosure types Kiessimul (twelfth/thirteenth century) on the Isle of Barra in the Outer Hebrides; Mingary (thirteenth-century beginnings) in the Ardnamurchan peninsula, Highland; Dunstaffnage (early thirteenth-century beginnings) in Strathclyde; Tioram (early thirteenth-century beginnings) in Moidart, Highland; and Skipness (thirteenth-century beginnings) in Kintyre, Strathclyde.

Many more of these simpler enclosure castles were built in the twelfth and thirteenth centuries, and displayed individual variations: Roy in Highland, with a square projecting tower on one angle; Kinclaven in Tayside, with projecting corner towers (now vanished); and Kincardine, with ranges of buildings constructed against three sides. Enclosure castles of greater elaboration and dating to the thirteenth century include Kildrummy in Grampian, Dirleton in Lothian, and Inverlochy in Highland. Dated to about 1270–80, Inverlochy is an almost square-plan curtain enclosure, with walls nearly

Drum: particular points of interest are the rounded corners of the parapet and the top part of the great tower.

metres (10 ft) thick and 9.1 metres (30 ft) tall.

The other kind of castle, the shell enclosure, is a rarity in Scotland. The best known is Rothesay, in Bute. Rothesay's shell curtain wall is almost circular, and it was raised probably in the late twelfth century on a flat-topped motte of earlier date (the first half of the twelfth century). Two other mottes that received shell enclosures are the great Peel of Lumphanan (Grampian) and the Doune of Invernochty, although neither has much more to show today than low stretches of walling. The motte at Lumphanan appears to have been part natural, part artificial. The Doune has a little more surviving stonework than the Peel. It is a huge motte with a summit area of 76 x 36.5 metres (250 x 120 ft), which is

Caerlaverock: this view shows the formidable gatehouse of this unique triangular-plan castle. The original gatehouse stonework is thirteenth century, but the machicolations were constructed in the fifteenth.

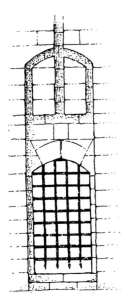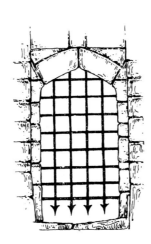

Two examples of yetts. The one on the left has a recess above for the mechanism of the drawbridge in front.

over 18.3 metres (60 ft) tall from the ground level of the motte. Both mottes had extensive earthworks with relatively sophisticated water defences.

These castle patterns take us to the end of the thirteenth century. Two outstanding castles remain to be mentioned: Bothwell in Strathclyde, a great tower castle which is attached to a powerfully defended curtain wall enclosure with flanking towers and twin-towered gatehouse, like Flint Castle in some respects; and Caerlaverock, a triangular-plan high-walled enclosure castle with large corner towers and a huge twin-cylindrical-towered gatehouse, unlike any castle this side of the English Channel or North Sea.

We may single out one or two of their more vital features. Bothwell has been described as 'among the foremost secular structures of the Middle Ages in Scotland', and its cylindrical great tower (of which only one half remains standing) has been called 'the grandest and most accomplished piece of medieval secular architecture in Scotland' (Simpson). The second comment seems a trifle exaggerated, when such monuments as Borthwick Castle or Stirling Castle's great hall are considered, but there is no doubt that the great tower must have created a sensation when it was completed. Some 24.4 metres (80 ft) tall, 20 metres (65 ft) in diameter, with 4.6-metre (15-ft) thick walls, it had four storeys, the lower two vaulted, and some rooms, passages and even garderobe chambers in the wall

thicknesses were also vaulted. Built of a gentle-hued red freestone ashlar, the great tower – or 'donjon' as it is generally known in Bothwell's case – was intended to be a fortress-residence, as its accommodation (storage basement, owner's hall, garrison's quarters and lord's private quarters at the top) and its fortifications (thick walls, fighting deck at top, separate wide moat) attest. The castle was slighted by the Scots after their great victory at Bannockburn in 1314, as a result of Robert Bruce's policy of neutralising castles once held by the English in the War of Independence, where they were likely to be strategically valuable to the English again in the event of renewed hostilities. It was captured by Edward III during his campaign against the Scots in 1336 and partly repaired for English use, but was retaken by the Scots in 1337 and again dismantled. These two slightings have made the history of the buildings, certainly in the fourteenth century, difficult to determine. It is of interest to mention that Bothwell's donjon bore resemblances to the massive cylindrical great tower at Coucy in France, now demolished (in 1916; *see also* Kildrummy). Coucy Castle had been built by Enguerrand de Coucy in the period 1225–40, and Enguerrand's daughter Marie married Alexander II of Scotland (1214–49).

The dating of Caerlaverock is problematic. The better argument is for c.1280–90, which means it was Scottish-built as a fortress with which to protect the north Solway coast and its hinterland against English attack. The alternative suggestion is c.1290–1300, built by Edward I once he had taken control of Scotland after the fall of Balliol and intended as a bridgehead for English forces to

Loch Leven: one of the earliest tower-houses in Scotland.

advance into south-west Scotland in the event of trouble. But Caerlaverock was besieged in 1300 by the old English king and captured, an event celebrated in a ballad by the scholar, Walter of Exeter, an extract of whose description of the castle is quoted in the gazetteer entry. There is no record of it having been taken away from the English by the Scots earlier, and so on balance we may attribute its construction to the Scots and to the period before the Edwardian aggression.

The dominating feature of Caerlaverock is its massive twin-cylindrical-towered gatehouse standing on a rock outcrop in low, marsh-girt land. It became a gatehouse tower later in its history, but even in the first building stage it must have been an imposing structure (and in much-damaged state today it is still impressive), with a tall, narrow entrance passage overwhelmed by the two

The fifteenth-century tower-house at Affleck, showing one square corner turret on the parapet.

flanking towers which were bridged by a vaulted hall approachable only from a staircase behind in the courtyard. The gatehouse admittedly bears resemblances to some of those built in the great Welsh castles – Beaumaris, Rhuddlan and Caerphilly, the first two of which were the work of Master James of St George. But this is not necessarily evidence that he had any hand in the Caerlaverock work, as has been mooted. Moreover, twin-cylindrical-towered gatehouses were, by c.1280, already fairly common in Europe (cf. Angers, Carcassonne, Avila) and were also being erected in castles throughout England, Wales and Ireland, in one form or another.

The fourteenth century saw the emergence of the Scottish tower-house. It was a basic form of tower that was developed over the next three centuries with many interesting variations, and probably about 700 of them were raised in nearly every part of Scotland. From the early 1330s, the Scots chose to build vertically, and the first tower-houses were extremely well put together. The survival of so many tower-houses, albeit in most cases their walls only, testifies to this high constructional skill. Tower-houses completely dominated Scottish castle-building. Castles like Kildrummy and Bothwell were no longer built, but this by no means implies that the need for fortified residences had diminished. On the contrary, it was to become more pressing. The fact that the War of Independence had been won and King Robert I (Bruce) was later recognised (posthumously) by the Pope as king of the independent kingdom of Scotland, did not remove the English threat. Nor did the check to English ambitions materially affect Scotland's feudal organisation.

There were other reasons for continuing to raise fortress-residences. The lords in the Highlands, the clan chiefs, continued to menace the kingdom's stability and order. The Douglases, who dominated large tracts of southern Scotland, were reluctant to make a bid for the Scottish throne, but at the same time did not like the Stewart succession of 1371, and for nearly a century did what they could to subvert it. But the continuing need for kings and lords to protect themselves, their families and dependants and to watch over their lands was gradually leavened with a growing desire for more comfortable living. This became more apparent in Scottish tower-houses of the fifteenth and sixteenth centuries, and in many cases they became almost palatial, yet without losing their defensibility.

Numerous tower-houses were given walls many feet thick: the average was 1.8–2.1 metres (6–7 ft), which is about three times the average thickness of house walls today. The towers had battlemented parapets (like Drum)

The early to mid-fifteenth-century great tower-house at Comlongon is one of the largest in Scotland.

or parapets protected by toughened corbelled turrets on the corners overlooking them, or both. Some parapets projected outwards, proudly supported by corbelling (Old Dundas). Many were surrounded at the time, or later, by stone curtains which in Scotland are known as barmkins, and these were often tall.

Tower-houses were also surrounded by ditches and banks, the moats sometimes being fed from nearby streams or rivers, with drawbridges across them leading to and from gateways. From the last decades of the fifteenth century onwards a few tower-houses began to be equipped with gun-ports for small cannons and other artillery. But great towers like those at Borthwick, Comlongon, Drum, Elphinstone, Hallforest and Threave did not have them. After about 1500, tower-houses were equipped with a variety of loops for small guns, oillets at the bottom of the loops, wide-mouth ports, fan-tail openings and so forth, which were inserted in new structures and in earlier buildings alike.

Most early tower-houses had the entrance on the first floor, reached by a stone staircase or wooden stairway, or even a simple ladder, their basements having no access to the first floor except by a single hatch in the ceiling. Most entrances were protected by an iron yett, an open-work grille of interlacing iron bars that acted like a portcullis. Some could be raised and lowered, others swung open and shut on hinges. Chambers with spy-holes were built into wall thicknesses from which to look out into great halls, some of them in fireplace flues (such as

Elphinstone). Walls were fitted with channels, one end of which issued secretly into a chamber, the other opened into a second room, perhaps on another floor, enabling an eavesdropper to hear what was going on in the room at the other end, a medieval form of 'bugging'. These were called luggies, and there were luggies at Affleck, Elphinstone and many others.

Considerable attention was also given to staircases in Scottish tower-houses and many were constructed with some ingenuity. The earlier towers had spirals in one corner in the wall thickness, although some had straight mural flights. They were not designed so much for the easy use of the owner as to deter intruders. The flights did not always all go up the same corner, which meant that intruders and occupants had to cross the floor to reach another flight, as in some English great towers. In some castles, flights crossed over other flights. In others, spiral flights led from the ground to the parapet without opening into intervening floors, which were reached by a second set of flights nearby but not easily seen. Some tower-houses had straight flights as well as spirals, such as Elphinstone. Some had false storeys and unexpected changes of floor levels to baffle intruders.

The desire for more residential space and accommodation (kitchens, servants' rooms, guest rooms and so forth) was met with similar attention and ingenuity of design. Plain, rectangular tower-houses like Crichton (the earliest building), Comlongon, Cumbrae, Drum, Elphinstone, Hallforest, Loch Leven and Threave, and

A powerfully built Douglas castle, Threave was reinforced in the fifteenth century by an artillery wall with turrets.

(Opposite) Craigievar: a fine example of a stepped L-plan tower-house, which is seven storeys tall.

The substantial long, rectangular tower-house at Elcho has extra, smaller towers on three corners and two more along one wall.

many more, built over the years c.1300–c.1450 (Drum was a little before 1300), were well provided with chambers, closets and stairs within the wall thicknesses. Before the end of the fourteenth century the first rectangular tower-houses with extending wings had been built, erected as one unit. These were the L-plan tower-houses – a rectangular tower-house block with a short wing, usually of square plan, projecting from one side, generally one of the longer sides. These wings are sometimes called jambs, but we shall continue to use the term wing. The purpose of the wing was to incorporate private apartments and stairs that could be separate from the main block whose storeys generally consisted of one main large room, or hall, in some cases screened off near one end, in others more solidly walled off. A good example is Affleck in Angus (*see* gazetteer pp. 238–39). The wing also enabled the tower to have a well-protected entrance on the ground floor (which was additionally more convenient from a residential viewpoint). The angle, called the re-entrant, could easily be defended by covering fire from both main block and wing. Later, many L-plan towers had gun-ports inserted adjacent to the entrance. This re-entrant door arrangement was a feature of most L-plan tower-houses.

Most of the fourteenth- and fifteenth-century tower-houses, L-plan and plain, were not large and not the sort of size we came to expect in twelfth-century English great towers. They averaged between 9.1–12.2 metres (30–40 ft) square or rectangular, rising to 12.2–18.3 metres (40–60 ft) tall (with some large exceptions). Each was an individual structure built by a master mason in charge of a gang of craftsmen, stonemasons, carpenters, ironsmiths, plasterers, glaziers, diggers and (doubtless) apprentices and men-of-all-work. The tower-houses were not built from sets of drawings obtained from a central Ministry of Fortification and Building, or a Department of Works, although some castles for the kings were built under the aegis of a governmental organisation of royal works. Tower-houses were put up on well-chosen sites and tailored to fit them by men who had building in their blood, masons who undoubtedly worked on neighbouring castles and took ideas from one to the next, enlarging their experience and increasing their ingenuity as they went, like the Bell family of masons in Aberdeenshire in the latter half of the sixteenth century. To an extent, their designs will have been governed by the amount of money available to pay for

works. Licences to build often spelled out the basic fortifications allowed, which were regarded as the standard equipment, as it were: walls, ditches, iron gates and parapets and turrets at the top of the tower. Loops and gun-ports were not specified in the licence, but presumably were embraced in the general phrasing along the lines of 'warlike apparatus necessary for its defence' quoted by S.H. Cruden.

Two tower-houses of the end period perhaps represent the apogee of the tower-house in its simple but nonetheless formidable shape. They are Borthwick in Lothian and Comlongon in Dumfries and Galloway, and

The late sixteenth-century Z-plan tower-house at Claypotts is in very good condition.

The late sixteenth-century, Z-plan tower-house at Glenbuchat has diagonally opposite square towers.

are among the strongest castles ever built in Scotland. Borthwick, begun in 1430 by the first Lord Borthwick, is a rectangular tower-house with two wings off one longer wall (the space between being very small). The horizontal dimensions are 22.9 x 20.7 metres (75 x 68 ft), and the massive tower rises to over 30.5 metres (100 ft) tall. The walls are 3–4.3 metres (10–14 ft) thick, except for the two short facing inner sides of the wings. The tower is a labyrinth of staircases, passages and wall chambers, some of considerable spaciousness. It was enclosed by a barmkin with a large cylindrical tower at the south-west corner and a gatehouse, probably of early sixteenth-century construction. Comlongon, seat of the Earls of Mansfield (still), is a massive square-plan tower-house of c.1440, whose thick walls are honeycombed with chambers, garderobes, stairs and, at ground level, dungeons, as at Elphinstone. The basement is vaulted, and the great hall has two fireplaces: the second fireplace (in a recess) acted as a cooking range for the kitchen in the recess, which would have been screened off.

We have seen that, apart from the castles in the Border counties of England, particularly Northumberland and Cumberland, the military uses of English and Welsh castles came to an end in the early sixteenth century, to be revived in the Civil War (1640s) and for a few years after. It was not the case in Scotland – indeed, their military role became more important. The sixteenth century in Scotland saw the gradual watering down of the

Auld Alliance with France, which coincided with growing aggression on the part of England. Three times in a generation Scottish armies were badly defeated by the English, at Flodden Field (1513) where James IV and the flower of his nobles were slain, Solway Moss (1542), news of which hastened James V's death a few days later, and Pinkie (1547), together with many lesser but still damaging skirmishes and invasions, including the notorious 'rough wooing' of 1544–6, when Edinburgh was burnt.

Internal conditions were not helped by the fact that three times in the century the kingdom passed from a dead or deposed monarch to a successor in infancy: James V succeeded James IV in 1513, aged one; Mary, Queen of Scots succeeded James V in 1542, aged one week; James VI succeeded Mary, Queen of Scots in 1567, aged one year. Years of minority rule, when one faction after another jockeyed, intrigued and even murdered to gain power, re-created the sort of anarchy England had endured in Stephen's reign, and this entailed lords fortifying castles and attacking those of their rivals. Little wonder that in so uncertain and dangerous an age, leading men, and lesser lairds and rich merchants too, chose to shut themselves in strong, tall, ill-lit fortresses of stone, at a time when their contemporaries in England were building themselves horizontal residences chiefly of brick, with tall, wide windows and without a gun-port to be seen anywhere. Building activity slowed down in the decades after the disaster of Flodden, but a fresh impetus was experienced with the troubles of the time of Mary, Queen of Scots.

Stirling: on the left is the King's Old Building with, near the centre, one end of the 'Lion's Den' and Palace Block.

Edinburgh, seen from Princes Street Gardens.

In Scotland, gunpowder was monopolised by the Crown, although the system did not always succeed in preventing factious lords obtaining and using it. Ravenscraig in Fife was the first castle in Scotland – indeed, in Britain – to be designed specifically for systematic defence by guns (*see* Chapter 6 and in the gazetteer). It was commissioned by the pyrotechnic enthusiast, James II, in 1460. By that time, an artillery wall had already been added to Threave Castle, not by the king but by the Douglas family which owned it. But cannon was not regarded as a major war weapon until the sixteenth century, by which time a variety of smaller guns, including hand-guns, had come into use, and the Crown was unable to exercise much control over possession and employment of them. This is reflected in the appearance of small gun-ports in a variety of styles in numerous castles: the inverted keyhole at Affleck and others; the loop with crosslet at top and oillet at bottom (Towie Barclay and others); the dumb-bell (Rowallan);

the wide-mouth port (inserted later at Caerlaverock, built in new at Noltland, Claypotts, *inter alia*); and at Tolquhon, two rows of three ports beside the gateway.

The sixteenth century also witnessed new shapes of tower-houses, notably the stepped L-plan, the Z-plan and the rectangular tower with various wings added to its sides. The stepped L-plan was an L-plan with an additional square (or occasionally semi-cylindrical) wing in the re-entrant, housing the entrance and a staircase, as at Craigievar; at Greenknowe Tower the step was a semi-cylindrical turret. The tower with wings added haphazardly round the sides varied individually every time: Elcho has a square tower on the south-west corner, a smaller square tower on the north-west corner and a cylindrical tower on the north-east corner, with a fourth tower, cylindrical with staircase, on the north wall. McLellans has two steps in the re-entrant and a square tower positioned on the south-west corner, with separate spiral staircase.

The Z-plan castle was a unique style of fortified residence. A rectangular tower block was augmented with two wing towers, at diagonally opposite ends of the block. Each wing, equipped with gun-ports and/or shot-holes, covered two faces of the block which in turn, similarly equipped, could cover the wings, so that it was impossible to attack the castle from any direction without coming into the field of fire. The wing towers were square in plan (Noltland, Glenbuchat) or cylindrical (Claypotts, Kilcoy), or one of each (Tolquhon – a modified Z-plan, and Midmar). The first Z-plan was built late in the fifteenth century, but the period usually associated with them is the second half of the sixteenth and early years of the seventeenth centuries. Over sixty Z-plan castles were built in Scotland, a good many of which have survived. Two of the most interesting are Claypotts, with its wide-mouth gun-ports, one inserted right by the entrance, at chest level; and Noltland, with over 70 gun-ports, arranged in tiers along every wall round the whole castle.

The two most famous castles in Scotland are Edinburgh and Stirling. Both stand on mighty basalt rock mounds, nearly 91.4 metres (300 ft) high above the

The impressive east front of the great palace-fortress of Linlithgow. The round-headed arch in the centre of the façade is the 'Old Entrie'.

ground below (Edinburgh 82.3 metres [270 ft], Stirling 76 metres [250 ft]), dominating the countryside around them for miles, each visible from the other on a clear day. Their strategic positions speak for themselves. Stirling in particular guards the principal routes into the Highlands. Both have today an extensive range of buildings clumped together on their summits, in Stirling's case dating from the fifteenth century, and in Edinburgh's a chapel dating from the early twelfth century, a tower of the fourteenth century, and the rest also dating from the fifteenth century. They were always royal fortresses, even in the days of timber and earth: Edinburgh was the fortified residence of Malcolm III Ceanmor, and Stirling the fortified residence of Malcolm's son, Alexander I, who died there in 1124. And, of course, Edinburgh Castle is guardian of Scotland's capital, and has been ever since the city was officially established as the capital by James III. Neither of them falls into any of the castle types we have outlined; they are royal palace-fortresses which have assumed their present form over a long period, due to special requirements, many of them over and above military needs. They have had lavished on them the finest skills available to Scotland at the times concerned, notably the great hall at Stirling (built by James III's favourite, the

Cawdor: in the centre of a palatial rectangle of buildings stands the original fifteenth-century rectangular great tower (above).

courtier and architect, Robert Cochrane, who was hanged at Lauder Brig by Archibald 'Bell-the-Cat' Douglas, Earl of Angus, in 1482).

Two more palace-fortresses may be considered alongside Edinburgh and Stirling, and they are Falkland and Linlithgow. Falkland, owned by Her Majesty the Queen and administered by the National Trust of Scotland, was begun by James II and considerably extended by James IV and V, so that it became a courtyard castle with a tower-house-cum-gateway flanked by two huge cylindrical towers with battlemented parapets. Linlithgow, now roofless but with most of its

walls standing, is a splendid quadrangular castle building (of fourteenth- to seventeenth-century work), one of whose principal features is the great hall on the eastern range, with walls about 3 metres (10 ft) thick, sandwiched between two massive corner towers, and containing at its southern end what has been described as the finest fireplace of its kind in Scotland.

In the seventeenth century new structures were built, some of them castles in the right sense, such as Craigievar (stepped L-plan, 1625–6), Coxton (rectangular tower-house, 1644) and Leslie (stepped L-plan, 1661). Many others were magnificent-looking mansions, in some cases built round earlier more military structures, like Cawdor, a practice already followed in the previous century, as at Glamis, Crathes, Midmar, Tolquhon and Aberdour, among others. Some of these mansions were highly ornamented, with tall, pointed turrets, rows of oriel windows, false machicolations, excessive and non-military battlementing, mansion-type windows, ornate entrance arches and window voussoirs, pediments and so forth. They certainly adorn the building scene of Scotland and enhance towns and countryside alike, but they are not fortified residences. 'This house was not a Tower … and had neither Fosse nor Barmkin-wall about it, nor Battling, but was only an ordinary house …' The quotation is taken from a summary of a legal case which arose in 1630, and it is an appropriate comment on these ornate mansions, as well as a pertinent definition of a castle in Scotland.

'A rambling assemblage of ruins of several periods', this is Aberdour seen from the north-east.

10
Castles in Ireland

The history of castles in Ireland centres on two things. One is that in the period from about 1170 to 1700 we are talking about over 3000 castles. The other is that of this total, the great majority were built by people other than the Irish. Even to this day, the numerous remains of towers and walls scattered all over the Irish countryside, north and south, are often regarded as symbols of foreign dominion – which of course is what they were, in precisely the same way as the first Norman castles represented the imposition of a new order by an alien aristocracy upon Anglo-Saxon England, and the Edwardian castles in Wales were a brutal demonstration of a half-mad king's obsession with conquering and ruling all Britain.

The castle enthusiast will not find many of the 3000 in good condition today, or well cared for. A great many are derelict piles, isolated in fields, next door to farm buildings, perched on rocks over the sea or on cliffs beside rivers, or squashed incongruously between more modern buildings in the middle of towns, sticking up like sore thumbs in the gardens of houses great and small, and so on. Some have been restored, modernised, embellished and altered out of all recognition. Yet there are more than enough remains amply to illustrate every period, every style, every shape and every geographical vantage point that one could want to find in a general survey of the history of castles in Ireland.

The study of castles in Ireland opens up problems in the study of castles throughout the British Isles that may not be widely acknowledged at present. Of all the useful works on castles in Britain and Ireland that are available (*see* Bibliography), few deal with Ireland, despite the fact that there are more castles there than in England, Wales and Scotland put together. Very few books on English, Welsh and/or Scottish castles, moreover, refer to contemporary, earlier or later structures in Ireland, or draw attention to similarities or differences. One interesting challenge to received castle knowledge concerns Roscommon Castle, Co. Roscommon, and its 'lookalike', Harlech in North Wales. Harlech is said to have been built to a new design by Master James of St George, Edward I's principal castle-builder in Wales, who built it between 1283 and 1290. The plan of this enclosure castle, with large round towers on the four corners and a huge, twin-round-towered gatehouse in one wall between two towers, in many respects follows the plan of Roscommon. Now, work on Roscommon was begun at least three years earlier than on Harlech. Did Master James have anything at all to do with it? Did he ever see it? No evidence has yet been found that he ever visited Ireland, although we do know a great deal about his career and movements in mainland Britain

between c.1280 and the early 1300s.

There are other challenges, such as the appearance in Ireland in the early and mid-thirteenth century of rectangular great towers with four round corner towers (eg Ferns, Co. Wexford; Carlow, Co. Carlow; Lea, Co. Laois; and Terryglass, Co. Tipperary) a century before similar types were being built in mainland Britain. It is clear that the whole history of castle-building in the British Isles is due for a major re-think and revision, and that the castles in Ireland cannot take a back seat for much longer.

The concept of the properly fortified military residence of a king or feudal lord was not relevant to Irish society, nor was its need understood before the twelfth century. If any of the Irish kings had any ambitions to act like feudal lords in the manner of William the Conqueror and his lords in England, there is no evidence of any anxiety to build castles all over the place. The records point only to a handful of structures that might be classed as castles which were erected in the early decades of the twelfth century, and only one of them, Athlone, was built by an Irish king, Toirrdelbach Ua Conchobair, King of Connacht (1120–56), who claimed also to be *ard rí* (High King of Ireland). It was probably an enclosure surrounded

Roscommon is a quadrangular-plan enclosure castle with round corner towers and a twin-cylindrical-towered gatehouse on the east wall (left).

A view of the principal remains of the early thirteenth-century rectangular great tower at Carlow, with its round corner turrets. This photograph shows the western wall.

Carrickfergus was probably the first stone castle to be begun in Ireland. The great tower was started in the early 1190s. In about 1200 the castle was taken over by King John, and it remained a Crown property and administrative headquarters until 1928.

by a rampart, that is, a ring-fort. The other six, Ballinasloe, Galway, Collooney, Cuileanntrach, Tuam and Ferns are unattributed. Of these so-called 'castles', all were built between about 1124 and 1166, all were attacked, burned or pulled down, some more than once, some time between those dates.

Between 1166, when Toirrdelbach's son, Ruadrí, assumed the title *ard rí* after defeating Muirchertach Mac Lochlainn (*ard rí*, 1156–66), and 1171, the year that England's Henry II set sail for Ireland with an army, a number of things happened that were to begin a transformation of Ireland. One was the erection of the first Anglo-Norman castles. How did the Normans ever get to Ireland in the first place?

In 1166, Diarmait Mac Murchada, King of Leinster,

was driven out of his kingdom by the forces of an alliance between Ruadrí, Tigernán Ua Ruairk (King of Bréifne) and the Ostmen of Dublin. He took the unprecedented step of seeking help from a foreign king, Henry II, who had some years earlier been granted by Pope Adrian IV the right to hold Ireland but who had done nothing to assert it. Henry responded by letting Diarmait recruit help from among the Anglo-Norman lords in south-west Wales, the obvious place since it was closest to the Irish coast. After some failures, Diarmait succeeded in enlisting Richard FitzGilbert de Clare, Anglo-Norman Earl of Pembroke, known in history as Strongbow, who accepted in return the offer of Diarmait's daughter, Aiofa, as a bride. In May 1170 Strongbow sent an advance party of some 90 men under his brother-in-law, Raymond FitzGilbert Le Gros, who landed at Baginbun Point, Co. Wexford, where they constructed a base protected by a double rampart and ditch fortification – the first Anglo-Norman military construction in Ireland. Three months later, Strongbow himself, with 200 knights and 1000 archers, landed near Waterford, then an important Viking port-town, on 23 August. Two days later, he attacked and captured the town. When news of that reached Diarmait, who was at Ferns in Co. Wexford, he set off for Waterford with his daughter Aiofa, and she and Strongbow were married in Waterford cathedral. Strongbow led his force against Dublin, then held by the Viking Ostmen. The town fell – and the Anglo-Normans thereby established a major foothold in Ireland, in its principal town.

The next spring Diarmait died, and Strongbow claimed the throne of Leinster by right through his wife. This did not suit the people of Leinster who wanted Diarmait's nephew, nor was it approved by Ruadrí, the *ard rí*, or by his colleagues. And the Ostmen did not want it, either. A large army of some 30,000 men was thereupon assembled and it surrounded Dublin, hoping to compel Strongbow to yield. After a few weeks, Strongbow managed to get a detachment of 600 well armed mounted knights, foot-soldiers and archers out of the town, and they got behind the huge army and attacked in the rear. The Irish force, fighting on foot, was no match for the mounted knights, the medieval equivalent of tanks, and it was routed.

News of Strongbow's victory reached Henry II, already concerned about the growing power of the Anglo-Normans in Ireland. He summoned Strongbow to court to demand renewal of his oath of fealty, which Strongbow gave. The king then decided – reluctantly, it is now thought – to visit Ireland in person to assert his overlordship and to demand fealty from the Irish kings. With a force of some 500 knights and 3000 archers and foot-soldiers, together with portable wooden towers, siege-engines and much weaponry, Henry embarked on 16 October 1171 in some 400 ships from Milford Haven and landed at Crook, near Waterford, entering the town the next day. His aim was to impress, not to fight war or ravage the countryside, and his very presence did just this. Several of the Irish kings submitted, as did Strongbow (again), along with other Anglo-Norman lords who had already begun to carve out for themselves huge feudal territories. The king proceeded to Dublin where he set up a royal base, holding court there for the next few months. In February 1172, the Irish bishops and senior clergy, who were at a synod at Cashel, also submitted.

In March, hearing of a conspiracy by his eldest son, Prince Henry, to rebel, Henry decided to return to England and left on 17 April. He put the Anglo-Norman lord, Hugh de Lacy, in control as justiciar over those parts of Ireland of which he was overlord, partly to counterbalance the power of Strongbow whom he did not entirely trust.

In the short period between Strongbow's arrival at Waterford and the king's expedition, a few motte-and-bailey castles and some enclosure castles were raised on or near the east coast of Ireland, but there is not much information on numbers or locations. Two timber and earth castles that appear to date from this period are Carrick, near Wexford, and Dublin. It is after the departure of the king that castle-building began in earnest. Documents, annals and other written records of the time or soon after provide much information about the early buildings. Among the most useful sources are two works by Giraldus Cambrensis (Gerald of Wales), namely, *Topographica Hibernica* and *Expugnatio Hibernica*. The latter was written in 1189 and it provides more than the former. Gerald accompanied Henry's youngest son, John (later, King John) on his period in Ireland as the king's viceroy in the 1180s. This second work is an account of Strongbow's campaign, of Henry's expedition and of the immediate results. It has many fascinating details, including material about the first castles built (and in many cases attacked, and even destroyed) in the first two decades of English overlordship. These descriptions and their locations have been exhaustively examined by castle historians and archaeologists, and we now have a fair picture of Anglo-Norman castle-building in Ireland from the 1170s up to the early thirteenth century, by which time the first stone castles were already being constructed. Among the early stone castles were

Knockgraffon is one of the largest motte castles in Ireland. A small stonework structure was added later, on the east of the bailey (left).

A view of the ruins of Clonmacnois, some of which are of stone buildings that were raised upon the original thirteenth-century earth-and-timber enclosure castle.

Carrickfergus, Co. Antrim, Carlingford, Co. Louth and Trim, Co. Meath.

The Anglo-Normans built their castles on high ground to dominate the immediate neighbourhood, or on frontiers such as in Westmeath (on the west edge of which the River Shannon was the eastern boundary of Connacht), or on lower ground to protect river crossings. As well as raising new buildings, they also built on existing Irish ring-forts (defended farmsteads) which were quite suitable, and on prehistoric mounds and barrows (the now famous megalithic burial mound at Knowth, Co. Louth, was chosen for conversion to a motte castle in about 1175). The Anglo-Normans built both motte castles and enclosure castles, although far more of the former. The procedures for building motte castles and enclosure castles of timber and earth were much the same as for the similar castles in England and parts of Wales built in the first century of Norman occupation, although to what extent the Anglo-Norman colonisers in Ireland pressed the Irish into work on the castles is not known.

The colonisers had one advantage over their forbears. There was a wealth of accumulated experience at various levels to draw on, and many models in England and Wales to copy. But there were also disadvantages. To judge from the lists of the early castles that were burnt or otherwise destroyed in their early days (according to Gerald of Wales and others), the Irish gave their new overlords far more trouble than the demoralised Anglo-Saxons had given in the days of the Conqueror and his

two sons. Despite this, a considerable number of timber and earth castles were raised in the first six decades of the colonisation, from c.1170 to c.1230. R.E. Glasscock in *Mottes in Ireland*, published in *Château Gaillard*, Vol. VII, 1975, pp. 95–110, listed some 340 surviving mottes (184 in Leinster, 128 in Ulster, 24 in Munster and only 4 in Connacht), based on map and site examinations. T.B. Barry (in his *Archaeology of Mediaeval Ireland*, Routledge, 1987, pp. 52–53) published a map and list of enclosure castles of much the same period, amounting to 45, which brings the total to just under 400. Current thinking is that the total should perhaps be higher. Immediately noticeable is the great preponderance of sites in the eastern half of Ireland, in which the early colonisers largely confined their estate-carving to the counties around Dublin.

Looking first at the motte castles, they were either dug in the manner of the English mottes (*see* pp. 19–20) or they were produced by first building a ring-bank (roughly, a circular rampart of packed-down earth) and then carting earth from outside and shovelling it into the 'dish' made by the bank, until it was high enough, as for example, at Lorrha, Co. Tipperary. Another technique was to superimpose a mound in this way upon an existing Irish ring-fort, raising the height of the ring-fort bank, as at Rathmullan, Co. Down. This conversion of ring-forts into motte castles took place at a number of sites.

Several motte summits have been examined in Ireland and an interesting variety of weapons, coins, iron objects and pottery fragments have been found, but on the whole, evidence for structures on the top has been scanty. Traces of palisading have been detected at, for example, Dromore and Clough, both in Co. Down, the latter a most rewarding site generally (surviving stone tower remains, a later addition to the stone tower, later still wall fragments, among them). The dearth of evidence of timberwork could be because the wooden towers on the

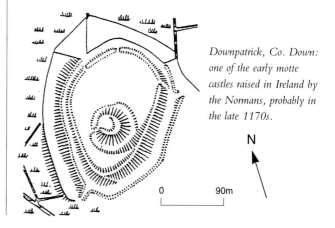

Downpatrick, Co. Down: one of the early motte castles raised in Ireland by the Normans, probably in the late 1170s.

N

0   90m

summit were often built in the Scandinavian/Russian manner, with the walls constructed from horizontal logs laid one of top of the other, much like early European log cabins in North America, stave churches in Norway, buildings of all kinds in early Novgorod and Kiev, and so forth. It is clear that such structures would not leave traces of continuous or regular post-holing. Whatever processes were employed, many sites continued to be occupied by buildings and used well into the fourteenth century, even if occupation was not continuous. There are many surviving mottes listed in the gazetteer, and among some of the more interesting are Downpatrick, Co. Down, Nobber, Co. Meath, Knockgraffon, Co. Tipperary, Naas, Co. Kildare, Kilbeg, Co. Meath, and Louth, Co. Louth. Some were later built upon in stone, such as Castleknock, Co. Dublin, Clough, Co. Down, Clonmacnois, Co. Offaly and Shanid, Co. Limerick.

With regard to the timber-and-earth enclosure castles in Ireland, these are, like their English and Welsh counterparts, described by some authorities – not very helpfully – as 'ring-works'. The term is easily confused with the ring-fort, which is similar to look at but which in Ireland is pre-Norman and therefore not castellar. Using the term in Ireland is particularly unfelicitous since the Irish had for centuries before 1170 been building defended farmsteads (or ring-forts), and continued to do so after the arrival of Henry II. We shall use the term 'enclosure castles', as in England, Wales and Scotland. T.B. Barry's list shows 45 surviving enclosures, but he believes the figure ought actually to be nearer to 100 or so. Future excavation work may help to locate a few more. Some enclosures were Anglo-Norman rebuilds or developments of earlier Irish ring-forts. One was Beal Boru (Killaloe), Co. Clare. The majority of the list seem, however, to be Anglo-Norman originals. Some were later converted to stonework, or built on or around or adjacent to, and among these are the enclosures that formed the beginnings of some of the greatest of all the stone castles in Ireland, such as Trim, Co. Meath, Adare, Co. Limerick, Rinndoun, Co. Roscommon, and Ferns, Co. Wexford.

In recent years there has been much excavation work on Anglo-Norman enclosure castles, and on new and adaptations of ring-forts. At Castleventry, Co. Cork, and Castletobin, Co. Kilkenny, foundations of a gate-tower were uncovered, and at Castlemore Barrett, Co. Cork, remains of a hall-tower were found in the enclosure, dated about 1250. This examination work continues, although restricted through lack of funds, as with most archaeological projects anywhere these days. Meanwhile, work is also being undertaken to assess the extent to which the Irish themselves continued to build ring-forts after the arrival of the Anglo-Normans, particularly in areas not immediately of interest to the colonisers, principally further west.

Moving from timber-and-earth castles, we should look at the beginnings of castles in stonework. While the very earliest stonework castle built in Ireland is not established absolutely beyond doubt, the best candidate so far are the Phase 1 buildings of Carrickfergus, Co. Antrim, 1178–95, on the northern shore of Lough Belfast (*see* gazetteer, pp. 202–03). This phase included the polygonal stone enclosure known as the Inner Ward, with buildings inside, in particular the first storeys of the first great tower in Ireland. Other major stone castles whose main parts were completed in the last decade of the twelfth century or the first quarter of the thirteenth century were Trim, Co. Meath; Adare, Co. Limerick;

The cylindrical great tower at Nenagh is one of the earliest in Ireland and was built up to the storey below the arcade of vertical openings in c.1200 by Theobald Walter. The top level, with its arcade and parapet with stepped merlons on top, is a nineteenth-century addition.

Dunamase: the remains of the original rectangular great tower built on this rock outcrop are among the ruins seen on the summit. The castle was begun by William Marshal in the early thirteenth century.

The round great tower at Dundrum was probably started in c.1227, when the castle was granted by the king to Hugh de Lacy.

Maynooth, Co. Kildare; Nenagh, Co. Tipperary; Dundrum, Co. Down; Carlingford, Co. Louth; Dunamase, Co. Laois; Athlone, Co. Westmeath; King John's, Co. Limerick; Shanid, Co. Limerick; Carlow, Co. Carlow; Terryglass, Co. Tipperary; and Kilkenny and Dublin. Of these a great tower was the main feature of Trim (square with square projection in the centre of each side); Adare (square with projecting pilasters at east and west end walls); Maynooth (rectangular, with pilaster buttresses); Nenagh (cylindrical); Dundrum (cylindrical); Dunamase (rectangular); Athlone (polygonal); Shanid (multangular); and Carlow and Terryglass (rectangular with four round corner towers). The most interesting point about these early great towers in Ireland is that we have square, rectangular, polygonal and cylindrical great towers all being built at much the same time. If further support were needed to giving up the belief that there was a tidy progression from square/rectangular to polygonal and then to cylindrical shapes, here it is.

The second period of stone castle building is roughly the second quarter of the thirteenth century to the beginning of the fourteenth. Many stone structures were put up in this time, mostly without great towers, and among the main features we see are extensive stone enclosures, double enclosures, great gatehouses, enclosures with four or more corner towers or turrets in addition to gatehouses, the enclosures being of an almost limitless variety of shapes. Meanwhile, motte castles and enclosure castles of timber and earth continued to be built, attacked, destroyed and re-built, and many lasted much longer than their English and Welsh counterparts.

Principal stone castles include Castle Roche, Co. Louth; Glanworth, Co. Cork; Greencastle, Co. Down; Greencastle, Co. Donegal; Lea Castle, Co. Laois; Roscrea, Co. Tipperary; Ballymote, Co. Sligo; Ballymoon, Co. Carlow; Roscommon, Co. Roscommon; Rinndoun, Co. Roscommon; Ballintober, Co. Roscommon; Dunluce, Co. Antrim; Quin, Co. Clare; Liscarrol, Co. Cork; and Swords, Co. Dublin. These and many others are described in the gazetteer. Ballintober is thought to have been built not by the Anglo-Normans but by the Irish, probably the O'Connors, the ruling family in Connacht. It is not

unlike the Anglo-Norman Roscommon, some 16 km (10 miles) away and of slightly earlier date. Ballymoon, a square enclosure with a rectilinear gate-tower and two other small, square-plan wall-towers, appears not to have been completed, nor was it ever lived in. Quin was abandoned and later became absorbed in a new friary built round it. The castle plan can be seen more clearly from the air. Swords was an archbishop's castle and so not as defensive as the others. Inside its courtyard are the remains of the original motte. Castle Roche began as a great tower in the mid-thirteenth century, built at the request of the widow of a knight; the rest of the work surrounding the great tower (which is now ruined) was by her son.

After the first decade of the fourteenth century, larger castle-building in Ireland appears to have slowed down, and remained desultory for the rest of the century. A start was also made on the first of a new type of smaller castle, the tower-house, otherwise know as a 'fortalice', for which there is evidence of government support for private individuals wishing to build them. We return to these shortly, but first we need to see why there was a slow-down in the larger works. The reasons must largely

Maynooth: the huge rectangular great tower (left) of c.1210 and, next to it, the three-storeyed gatehouse with its rounded arch.

Lea: only ruins remain of this once extensive and fascinating castle, which endured a stormy, destructive history. The tall ruins are of the original mid-thirteenth-century, rectangular great tower with round corner turrets, like those at Carlow, Ferns and Terryglass.

be connected with the history of the time. First, the reign of the weak but sensitive and artistic Edward II (1307–27) was bedevilled by unrest and open rebellion by his relatives. The devastating defeat of the English at the battle of Bannockburn in 1314 by the Scots under Robert Bruce, the greatest military event in Scotland's history, demoralised huge sections of the English nobility and was felt even in Ireland among the Anglo-Normans. Edward Bruce, Robert's brother, took advantage of this situation to launch an invasion of Norman Ireland in order to throw the Anglo-Normans out. It was not in the end successful, but an exceptionally large number of Anglo-Norman castles were besieged, captured, slighted, recovered and otherwise involved. The campaign damaged the country generally and brought famine to

One of the two north polygonal corner towers of Ballintober. This was converted into a tower-house in the early seventeenth century.

some parts, and acute shortages everywhere.

Then in 1349–50, Ireland, like most of the rest of Europe, was ravaged by the Black Death, which reduced the population by one-third or more. It respected no class divisions: nobles, landowners, even kings were as vulnerable as the ordinary townsman or peasant. It struck Europe soon after the invasion of France by Edward III of England who claimed the throne of France. In 1346, he won a spectacular victory over the French at Crécy, and in 1356 his son, the Black Prince, won another, at Poitiers. Four years later, the two kingdoms reached agreement as to who should rule where in France. This military activity, together with the severe disruption caused by the Black Death, detached Edward and his principal lords from their commitments in Ireland, and this continued for the rest of the century. It coincided with a Gaelic resurgence and the Irish recovered appreciable parts of their country, including taking many castles and generally, although not always, rendering them useless. Not surprisingly, relatively few castles were built in Ireland in the century, and most of those were actually raised by Irish lords. Among castles either started from scratch or which received major renovation or extensions were Harry Avery's, Co. Tyrone; Ballyloughan, Co. Carlow; Carrigogunnel, Co. Limerick; Glenogra, Co. Limerick; and Buncrana, Co. Donegal.

Soon after the beginning of the fifteenth century, there was something of a revival in castle building, and this was to be more or less continuous for more than a century and a half. Some of the work was limited to repair or enlargement but the main output was the construction in almost every part of Ireland of the relatively new single-towered fortified residence, the tower-house (or fortalice), mentioned briefly above (see p. 93). There are huge numbers of these still standing today, in the most varied states of repair, while the sites of many that have since disappeared are known. Received opinion, based largely on important work by C.T. Cairns, suggests we are talking about 3,000 or more such structures in Ireland, dating from the first years of the fifteenth century. These tower-houses, with some exceptions, are just what the phrase says – residential structures which are fortified, which would protect the inhabitants against assault in the long period of raids, civil strife, quarrels between clans, and so forth. They were built by Anglo-Norman (later, Anglo-Irish) and Gaelic Irish alike, not only by landowners and others with feudal power but also by richer, more influential members of the rising merchant class. The surviving examples are by far the most numerous representatives of the buildings of their period. Not much is known about a great many –

' ...from the south [it] looks like a tremendous battleship forever moving down the Shannon... ' – a description of Carrigogunnel from H.G. Leask's Irish Castles.

although several external features are instantly recognisable – and where there is a history, it is often that of the family or families that owned them. H.G. Leask says that if a tower-house survives today in good condition (unless it has been renovated in recent times) it generally means the history is uneventful, and we can accept that. Conversely, ruined examples – and there are many, many of these – must suggest unhappy stories. Many were slighted in the time of Cromwell or later in the century, in the war between William III and the exiled James II (1689–91) and its aftermath, and they were never repaired or occupied again. Yet they remain in their damaged state in huge numbers for us to see. Before sketching the background and the principal features of these tower-houses, a passing look should be taken at a small class of castles of the period c.1400 to c.1500, which are much larger and more substantial than the tower-houses.

Perhaps the most interesting of these larger castles are Askeaton, Co. Limerick; Blarney, Co. Cork; Bunratty, Co. Clare; Cahir, Co. Tipperary; Carrigafoyle, Co. Kerry; Dunsoghly, Co. Dublin; and Fiddaun, Co. Galway. The dominant feature of all of them is a great tower, much larger than the average contemporary tower-house and more akin to the early great towers of the thirteenth century. The towers, incidentally, are all rectilinear. Some are conversions of earlier buildings (Askeaton's was once a thirteenth-century hall, Cahir's once a thirteenth-century gate-tower). All these castles such quantity all over Ireland. We have seen that a few were raised as far back as the start of the fourteenth century, when they were still fortified residences of feudal lords. These would all have been enclosed by a strong stone-built wall, known in Ireland as a bawn, and some would have had strong gateways or gate-towers. The towers themselves would have been smaller versions of the earlier great tower but with thinner walls, less accommodation inside, lower ceilings in some cases. This early version of the tower-house had a few parallels in England (although nothing like to the same extent) and more so in Scotland, but not many date-proven examples survive. It is the fifteenth century – and the following two – which provide us with such a catalogue of

Blarney: the famous Blarney Stone is incorporated in part of the prominent machicolated parapet.

One of the largest tower-houses in Ireland, Bunratty is also among the best preserved.

are described in detail in the gazetteer.

When we consider the tower-houses, of which there are so many hundreds of extant examples, we should divide them roughly into the straight vertically dominant single-tower type, and the more horizontally emphasised strong-house which was either a single structure built in one operation, or a compound building of tower-house with subsequently added range on one or both sides to give it horizontal prominence and, incidentally, to provide space for much extra accommodation. Looking at the vertical type first, it is this type that can be seen in

Cahir: the great Butler castle. The gate into the outer ward can be seen on the left. Behind the wall, in the centre, is the great tower, which is in the inner ward.

specimens, and we can only summarise here the principal features which figure in the great majority of them. There are features such as gun-ports that do not appear until the sixteenth century, although it is quite impossible to be precise about dates of introduction.

The tower generally had between three and six storeys. In many cases the top storey was an attic storey squeezed between two gables, and some of these were added after the main construction work. The tower was of square or rectangular plan or, very occasionally, cylindrical (Newtown, Co. Clare), and on the whole was not more than 9.1 x 12.2 metres (30 x 40 ft), more frequently less. One or more of the storeys was vaulted, not always in any set order: at Clara, Co. Kilkenny, it was the fourth storey (or third floor); at Rathmacknee, the second storey (first floor); and at Newtown, Co. Clare, both ground floor and second floor had domed vaults.

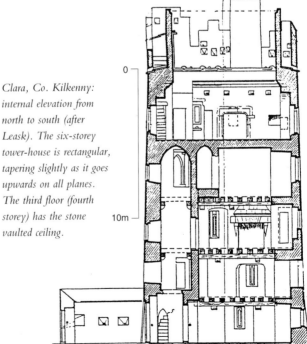

Clara, Co. Kilkenny: internal elevation from north to south (after Leask). The six-storey tower-house is rectangular, tapering slightly as it goes upwards on all planes. The third floor (fourth storey) has the stone vaulted ceiling.

0

10m

Vaulting, by the way, was generally achieved in the tower-houses of Ireland by using matting of woven wickerwork or basketwork. This meant that almost any curve could be fabricated in the ceiling and done so without the more expensive timber procedures followed by Anglo-Norman builders in earlier times. Trusses of wood were erected closely together and then covered with the willow rods woven into mats which were curved to the required shape. A thick coat of mortar was applied to the matting and the stone blocks for the arch were pressed in, with more cement being worked in or grouted from above. When the whole edifice had set hard, the timber was removed, but the wickerwork was usually left in place, to be plastered over later. There are several tower-house vaults today where traces of the matting can still be seen, as at Narrow Water, Co. Down and Athclare, Co. Louth.

The wall thickness of tower-houses was generally 1.8 x 2.4 metres (6–8 ft), although of course there were both thinner and thicker examples. Nor were the walls always of uniform thickness, particularly when one

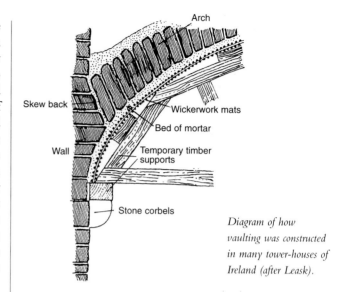

Diagram of how vaulting was constructed in many tower-houses of Ireland (after Leask).

shorter wall contained the staircase and/or small chambers or garderobes (as at Claregalway, Co. Galway). The entrance to the tower-house was generally at ground floor and led to the first flight of stairs upwards, whether spiral or straight. At Termon, Co. Donegal, you had to find a wooden stairway to the beginning of the proper staircase on the first floor.

The order of the apartments going upwards was not the same for every building. Some tower-houses had the main hall at the top, as at Burnchurch, Co. Kilkenny. Inside the tower-house there were fireplaces on some but not all floors, and many were of fine architectural form. Some were inserted later than the date of building the tower. The window openings were of a great variety of styles, narrow loop, wider with window seats inside, double-lighted with square or round heads and, in later stronghouses, groups of mullioned windows. There were garderobes in the wall thickness (with outside shoots at various levels, such as ground floor at Audley's, Co. Down). Staircases were either straight flights in the wall thickness (Carrigaphooca, Co. Cork and Buncrana, Co. Donegal) or spirals in one corner (hundreds of examples).

Among the external features which almost all the towers had were parapets round the wall tops, enclosing gabled roofing where present, battlemented either with plain merlons and embrasures or more often with stepped merlons in what is sometimes called Irish style (but you can see this style round church towers in many places in England). The outside of the parapet often carried

Clara: the fifteenth-century, six-storeyed tower-house still has many of its original floor beams. Its walled courtyard, in the foreground, was built in the seventeenth century.

Narrow Water: the sixteenth-century tower-house at the top of Carlingford Lough is surrounded by its quadrilateral bawn. The castle has recently been restored.

Rectilinear box machicolation on the angle where the parapets join at the top of the tower. This one is at Coolhull, Co. Wexford.

machicolation in some form or other: individual rectilinear boxes positioned in vertical line with the tower entrance, to protect it (as at Narrow Water, Co. Down and Slade, Co. Wexford), or a row of openings between corbels along one or more walls or just parts of walls (as at Pallas, Co. Galway and Ballyvaghan, Co. Clare), or rectilinear corner boxes (Castle Matrix, Co. Limerick and Derryhivenny Castle, Co. Galway), or rounded corner boxes – sometimes called bartizans –

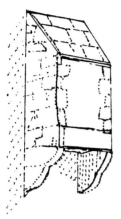

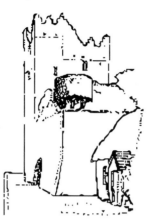

Rounded corner box machicolation, on a corner of the bawn of Rathmacknee, Co. Wexford.

Single rectangular machicolation box high up on tower wall to protect the entrance below.

(Gleninagh, Co. Clare and Rathmacknee, Co. Wexford), or polygonal corner boxes as at Shrule, Co. Mayo. Some towers had rectilinear machicolation boxes (single or double) projecting from the wall, not at parapet level but lower down, either wrapped round a corner (Ballymalis, Co. Kerry and Aughnanure, Co. Galway) or just on its own along the wall (Lisdoonvarna, Co. Clare). After the arrival of more reliable firearms, small cannon and so forth, gun-ports of various shapes and sizes were inserted

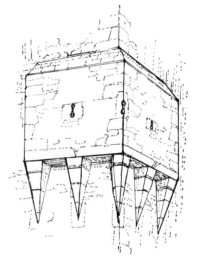

Rectilinear corner machicolation box round the join of adjacent walls below parapet level, as at Ballymalis, Co. Kerry.

in walls at all levels, sometimes as part of older loops, sometimes fresh insertions in walling.

One version of the tower-house had a small-diameter round turret at one corner of the tower, which contained the staircase. An early version of this was Donore, Co. Meath (about 1430). This may have been, incidentally, one of a number of smaller tower-houses built in the fifteenth century known as £10 castles. Leask explains that these result from a statute of Henry VI of 1429: 'It is agreed … that every liege-man of our Lord the King of the said counties (Dublin, Meath, Kildare and Louth …) who chooses to build a castle or tower sufficiently embattled or fortified within the next ten years, to wit, twenty feet in length sixteen feet in width and forty feet in height or more, that the Commons of the said counties shall pay to the said person to build the said castle or tower ten pounds by way of subsidy.'

The round extension in one

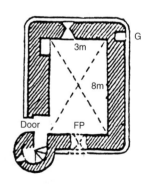

Donore, Co. Meath, which may have been one of the £10 castles of Henry VI's reign. G = garderobe. FP = fireplace.

The six-storeyed tower-house of Aughnanure.

corner persisted throughout the fifteenth and sixteenth centuries, and two examples out of many are Athgoe, Co. Dublin and Termon, Co. Donegal. In many of these tower-houses, whether the £10 type or not, the staircase turret was rectilinear, often simply a projection of one wall, as at Roodstown, Co. Louth (which also has a smaller projection on the diagonally opposite corner). Among those with rectilinear projections are Dunmahon, Co. Louth (two); Kilclief, Co. Down (two); Jordan's, Ardglass, Co. Down (two); and Gleninagh, Co. Clare (one). Some are also known as L-plan towers. Another variety of tower-house was what in Scotland is called the Z-plan, namely, a rectilinear tower core with two diagonally opposed corner turrets (one with staircase), such as Claypotts in Tayside (*see* pp. 250–51). Irish examples include Burt, Co. Donegal and Lisclogher, Co. Meath. While a great majority of the single-building tower-houses of the fifteenth to seventeenth centuries are rectilinear, there were some cylindrical examples. Among these are Newtown, Co. Clare, which is a five-storey round tower standing on a square spur base, and Ballynahow and Synone, both in Co. Tipperary.

The more horizontal stronghouse was either a fortified residence or a semi-fortified one. Some of them had parts reaching five storeys. They are all of the last quarter of the sixteenth century to the middle of the seventeenth century. Some are classified also as plantation castles, that is, stronghouses built by English or Scottish settlers (or planters) who began to make inroads in Ireland with home government encouragement, towards the end of Elizabeth I's reign and into the reigns of James I and Charles I. Most were large, mansion-type buildings, with mullioned windows, tall chimneys and tall gables

The two corner turrets on the east wall of Kilclief are linked by an arch at the top, with space between it and the wall forming machicolation to guard the entrance below.

(Burncourt had 28 gables), with turrets on corners and over main entrances, in case of attack. Many have survived, some in reasonable condition, some dilapidated or quite ruinous. Many were badly knocked about in the Civil War and afterwards in the time of Cromwell's and his successors' suppressions.

We have mentioned that many were built new as complete stronghouses in one operation (such as Kanturk, Co. Cork – early 1600s; Coppinger's, Co. Cork – 1620s–1640; and Burncourt, Co. Tipperary, 1640s). Others started off as large tower-houses of the fifteenth or very early sixteenth century, and then after an interval received extensions on one or both sides of the tower much later on, usually in the seventeenth century (for example, Loughmoe, Co. Tipperary, tower-house of fifteenth century, extension of four storeys, early seventeenth century; Donegal, tower-house of late fifteenth century, extension of 1620s). One style favoured by many builders was the square or rectangular stronghouse, three- or four-storeyed, with large, defensive corner towers equipped with gun-ports, machicolations of a sort, occasionally loops instead of windows. These corner turrets were rectilinear (nearly always about square) such as Portumna, Co. Galway (1609–18); Burncourt, Co. Tipperary (1640s); and Monkstown, Co. Cork (1630s); or rectilinear with acute angle spur-shaped outermost corners, as at Raphoe, Co. Donegal (1630s); Rathfarnham, Co. Dublin (1580s); and

Burt, Co. Donegal: a Z-plan tower-house with diagonally opposed round turrets. G = garderobe. FP = fireplace.

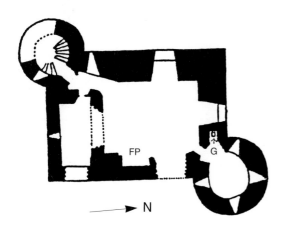

Manorhamilton, Co. Leitrim (1630s). Variations on these basic schemes, where towers were placed along the longer walls or projecting singly out of one corner, not four, occur at Ardtermon, Co. Sligo; Mallow, Co. Cork; and Athlumley, Co. Meath. At Monea, Co. Fermanagh, the stronghouse has two stout round towers close in line at one shorter end only of the rectangular core. This was built by a Scottish owner in the years c.1615–20 and there is much to see today.

The last three named castles were among the dozens of castles and stronghouses in Ireland which were heavily involved in the wars of the 1640s and the occupation of Ireland by Cromwell afterwards, and a good number were besieged, damaged, taken, and some even retaken. After the relative peace and quiet of the reign of Charles II, castles in Ireland endured another period of war involvement, when the exiled James II tried – and failed – to get his throne back by warring with his son-in-law William of Orange (William III) in 1689–91. Among the larger castles which were besieged and captured in that campaign were Athlone, Westmeath; Ballymote, Sligo;

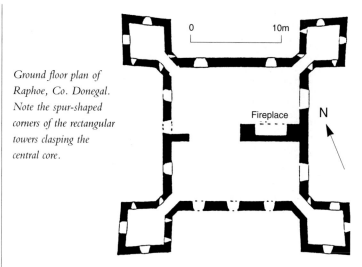

Ground floor plan of Raphoe, Co. Donegal. Note the spur-shaped corners of the rectangular towers clasping the central core.

Carrickfergus, Antrim; Carrigogunnel, Limerick; Doe, Donegal; Limerick; and Nenagh, Tipperary. A few castles also played roles during the United Irish Rising of 1798, and even during the Anglo-Irish War of 1919–21. Today, a number of castles have been restored with very great skill and care by the Office of Public Works, and those at Athenry (Galway), Portumna (Galway), Roscrea (Tipperary), Cahir (Tipperary), Donegal, Parke's

Built in the mid-seventeenth century and gutted by fire a few years later, Burncourt has never been restored.

There were five storeys in each of the four towers clasping the core of the stronghouse at Monkstown. Each had a powerful corner machicolation box on the outer corner.

(Right) Twin round towers front the western end of the rectangular tower-house at Monea, which is nearly 18.5 metres (60 ft) long. The towers have squared caps supported by corbelling.

(Leitrim) and Aughnanure (Galway) are all well worth a detailed visit. Other authorities and individuals have also carried out impressive restorations, and they, too, should be seen. The serious student of castles will also benefit from exploring the many hundreds of surviving castles, tower-houses and stronghouses, whatever their condition.

11

Life in a Medieval Castle

Although a castle was a private fortified military residence belonging to a king or a lord, there could often be a good many people living or staying in it. In time of peace it was the owner's home or, in the case of kings and some great lords, one of many homes. He would generally be accompanied by his wife and children, and perhaps one or two aged relatives, and would be attended by a staff of people, clerks, servants, grooms and craftsmen. He might have important guests, and they would have their families and servants. And in the case of a lord-owner, he might be favoured with a visit from the king which as a rule meant that the royal family would be accompanied by a retinue of servants and bodyguards, many of whom would fetch up at the host castle some days in advance to ensure that everything was properly prepared for the royal visit. The castle had, therefore, to be able to cater for the needs not only of the owner, his family and immediate servants, but also for substantial and short-notice increases in occupants. It is as well to understand this when wandering over the remains of castles, for many of them appear to be too small to have accommodated more than a dozen or two people in any comfort.

In time of war, that is, siege or preparation for expected siege, more people would be brought into a castle than normal. Lords were not as a rule heads of communities and they tended to keep themselves and their families to

themselves, but when a hostile army was approaching they would be moved by policy, if not by sympathy, to invite local villagers, farm workers and others into the greater security offered by their castles. Those invited would be expected to bring with them as much as they could in the way of food and armaments (if they owned any) for, once a siege had begun, supplies from outside were usually cut off. However, castles sited by the sea or on estuaries could always receive supplies by ship. Castle owners did sometimes have the forethought to get in enough stores to use in emergencies, as at Lancaster in 1215 and Bedford in 1224, but there was not often much time for an owner to stock up for a prolonged siege because it was obviously not possible to determine how long a siege would last. Nor was it easy to find supplies locally if the owner of the castle was in

Winchester: the great hall.

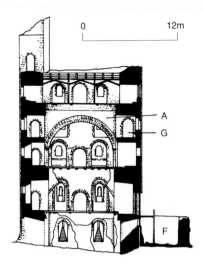

Hedingham: section through elevation of great tower (after W.D. Simpson). A = flying arch cross wall on second-floor level. F = remains of forebuilding. G = gallery of second floor.

open rebellion against the king. To supply such a man would probably result in an arrest for high treason when the siege was over.

Whatever the number of people in a castle at one time, the routine from daybreak to dusk remained much the same at the end of the Middle Ages as it had been at the beginning of the Norman occupation of England. The principal apartment in a castle was the great hall. This might be a separate structure as at Winchester, or the main part of a great tower, generally taking up two storeys without an intervening floor, as at Hedingham and many others. Here, the owner and his wife occupied one end of it as a bedroom, curtained off from the rest of the hall, or in better castles partitioned off in stone or timber, the walls perhaps being decorated with paintings or hung with tapestries. This partitioned area was the solar. The lord rose at daybreak and dressed himself, or allowed a young son of a neighbouring or friendly lord, who was learning to become a squire or a knight, to help. The other occupants of the tower slept on benches or straw along the walls, and they joined the lord for the first meal, for in a medieval castle lords and household lived together and this precluded most of the ordinary privacies we now take for granted.

The lord, his family and a few chosen guests sat at a top table which stretched across one end of the hall. This was generally a solid, rectangular table whose legs could be removed so as to store the table in much less space. A second and perhaps a third table of the trestle kind was put up at right-angles in the centre, to form a 'T', and this arm was occupied by the rest of the household. There they waited to be served. The first meal, however, was little more than bread and ale, or wine for the lord if it could be obtained. Once this was over, the tables were cleared, the trestles removed and the great hall became an administration office. Here, the business of the day – financial and legal, complaints, petitions, grants – was discussed, rents paid, disputes brought for arbitration, sometimes even courts held. If it were in time of siege, this period was reduced to a minimum or abandoned altogether, for the life of those in the castle had to be given over to resisting the assault by all means available. In time of peace, once the business was done, the lord could go down to the bailey yard to look at the horses, he might talk to the knights, squires and soldiers, watch them and the archers and cross-bowmen practising their skills and, in the years after the introduction of firearms, could, if he wanted, study the techniques of loading and manoeuvring artillery pieces.

The main meal of the day was lunch and this was prepared for the lord by about midday, sometimes earlier, for the day had begun long before our twentieth-century 7.30–8.30 a.m. start. It was a much more elaborate meal. The trestles were brought out again, throne-like chairs were provided for the lord and his wife at top table, while everybody else sat on benches. The movable chair with a back was late in reaching England, although it had been in use in Wales probably since the tenth century. Tables were given cloths, each place had a special mat, and bread rolls were set down beside them. The lord and his family had silver and earthenware utensils, the household had cruder pottery, horn or wood. In some castles the food was cooked in a kitchen in the tower, on the same level (perhaps in a mural chamber) as the top storey which enabled the fumes to rise without affecting those in the castle, or in the lower levels. In these circumstances, there was a chance that cooked food arrived hot. In others, the kitchens were part of separate buildings outside so the food had to be brought across the enclosure from the kitchens to the great hall, and then it could arrive tepid and unappetising.

The menu for a medieval lunch embraced meat, boiled or roasted, or more exotic fowl like pigeon or heron or partridge. Medieval man did not have potatoes, but his vegetables were much the same as ours, and he enjoyed salads and herbs. There was butter and cheese, bread and fruits. And there was wine, perhaps from Gascony or Burgundy, and ale from local small breweries or even brewed in the castle. And in case anyone wanted it, there was always water from the castle well.

The only implements on the tables were knives. Diners hacked pieces off meat joints which might be roasted on a spit over a fire in the hall (whose smoke went up the chimney if there was one but into the hall itself if there was not), and they ate with their fingers. Alternatively, they had meat or fish (according to the day of the week) put into bread baps or flat cakes and brought in to them. Meat and fowl bones were thrown to the floor which was often covered with rushes or straw. These were changed regularly but dogs wandered about the rushes looking for scraps. We may look at a simple menu regularly enjoyed by the Percys, perhaps at Alnwick, in the fourteenth century: 'For my lord and lady a loaf of bread in trenchers [cut in slices and used as

Beginning as an eleventh-century motte castle, Arundel has developed over the centuries, with many restorations.

plates], a quart of beer or a quart of wine, two pieces of salt fish, herring or sprats.' While the business of eating and drinking was going on, the lord and his guests might be 'gladded with lutes and harps ... mirth of song and of instruments of music ...'. Henry III once organised a tremendous banquet at Gloucester for friends: 5000 chickens, 1100 partridge, hares and rabbits, 10,000 eels, 36 swans, 34 peacocks and 90 boars were laid on. Kings paid a lot of attention to their food and the cooking of it. King John had new kitchens built at Ludgershall early in the thirteenth century, specifying that they had to have ovens capable of accommodating two or three whole oxen for roasting at one go.

Men and women must eat, and they must also get rid of waste products. How did the castle occupant manage? Castle towers and halls contained garderobes or latrines. These were no modern water closets but small mural chambers with a simple hole in the floor or in a stone platform raised 0.6 metres (2 ft) or so from the ground, which connected with a drain shaft built into the wall thickness, or in a special pilaster on the outer wall. These led down to the moat at the bottom or into cesspools. Sometimes there were arrangements to flush the effluent away but these were not as a rule so elaborate or so carefully planned as at many of

the contemporary abbeys, notably Fountains in Yorkshire. Despite efforts to site them discreetly at the end of a narrow passage in a wall reached via a right- or left-hand turn, it is not hard to imagine how the malodorousness of these garderobes offended. Some could be flushed by water from conduits from the tower water supply (as at Caernarfon and Dover) but most were dealt with by servants with buckets. Some garderobes were so noisome that the kings objected strongly. Henry III complained about the garderobes at Marlborough and the Tower of London, and once ordered one to be re-sited even if it cost £100. At Winchester, however, a garderobe had a ventilation shaft, and at Middleham a special turret with three floors of garderobes was built, cut off from the main great tower.

After his midday meal, the lord and his friends would probably go hunting or take some other vigorous exercise, riding perhaps, or even taking part in the military drills and practices in the bailey. Men hunted deer and boar through the forests, none more so than many of the kings, especially the Conqueror, who set aside huge tracts of forest land for his exclusive use, and his son, William Rufus, who was accidentally shot while out hunting in the New Forest. Men also enjoyed hawking with hooded falcons. While they were out, the household servants attended to various domestic chores, got ready the meal that the lord and guests would eat when they returned and prepared some food for the next day. The hunters would return in the early evening and perhaps want to bathe. This they did in wooden tubs, behind curtains, with warm water brought to them. Then the last meal of the day followed, lighter than the midday meal. They might wander into the castle garden if it was a warm summer evening and the castle had one. At Arundel, Henry II was especially attached to the garden outside his royal apartments.

In the Middle Ages religion played a far greater part in men's lives than today. The Normans, for example, were on the whole a brutal, temperamental and aggressive race of people who acted in an unChristian-like manner for the greater part of their lives. And yet their belief in God and in the possibility of a happy afterlife was dominant, and it was reflected in their cathedral- and church-building, and in the way many of them left their money to religious foundations, and in their habit of seeking remission for their sins by funding good works. We should not be surprised, therefore, to find that most castles in England and Wales had a chapel, and some had two, and that there was usually a resident chaplain on the lord's household staff. Each morning Mass would be taken by the chaplain for the lord and his household. Some of the chapels in castles that have survived seem more like small churches, notably the Chapel of St John in the Tower of London.

We have laid some stress upon the fact that a castle was a lord's home. But of the thousands of castles that remain in one condition or another, scattered about the countryside of Britain and Ireland, there are very few that give one any feeling that they could have been comfortable places to live in. Perhaps, indeed, they were not so. And yet for feudal lords there was no alternative to living in buildings of this kind. They lived in an era of warfare, between nations, between lords, between kings and rebel lords, and they had perforce to organise their lives around a permanent capability for defending themselves. A feudal lord might inhabit a castle for a lifetime without actually undergoing a siege or even being threatened, but how could he know he would never be attacked? His building, therefore, had to be a combination of fortress and residence, and generally it had to be fortress first. That meant sacrificing much in the way of softer surroundings. There were wooden floors in great towers, but builders often inserted vaulted stone ceilings to cut down the danger from spreading fire. Staircases had to be stone, and the almost incessant tramp of people up and down them must have been very noisy. Doors were heavy and doubtless creaked and squeaked on their hinges, and one can imagine a tower reverberating right through with the bang of the main door where the forebuilding joined the tower proper. Then, lords kept prisoners for various

reasons. Some were held with freedom to walk about under careful watch and slept probably as comfortably as a lord's guest or servant. Others were treated much more harshly. They were confined in ground-floor chambers with only an arrow slit as a window, or in oubliettes, dungeons reached only through an opening in the ceiling, where they were likely to be forgotten (hence the name of the cell, which comes from the French verb *oublier*, meaning 'to forget'). Even the hardest of captors could not have remained totally unmoved by the cries of prisoners thus incarcerated.

In time, lords moved out of their great towers and into more spacious building ranges inside the castle walls, and with that improvement in their environment the quality of life advanced. But as soon as there was danger from an enemy assault, or in times of civil war in the land, lords and their household had to be prepared to go back into the stronger towers (or gatehouse-towers) and rough it once more. There was a step forward in comfortable living when the Bodiam-type of quadrangular fortified manor-house began to be built in the fourteenth century, while in the fifteenth century, more attention still was paid to the residential aspects in the construction of new castles and the improvement of old. At Raglan, begun c.1431, the inner area was divided into two parts, the Pitched Stone Court and the Fountain Court, which looked like the square of a medieval city. There were terraces, open staircases, long buildings with handsome doors and mullioned, stained-glass windows, the whole surrounded by a powerfully fortified enclosure with a very thick outer wall, corner and median towers, and protected by ditching and a substantial hexagonal great tower surrounded by its own enclosure and ditch.

Today, some castles built in medieval times but later enlarged and modernised are serving as residences of the highest luxury and sophistication, notably Windsor, Alnwick, parts of the Tower of London, parts of Dover, and much smaller ones such as Penhow; while the owner of Borthwick has made the gaunt, grim, cavernous castle superbly comfortable without altering its medieval construction. But comfort was not the preoccupation of medieval castle-builders on the whole, and we should not take it for granted in their works, but only be gratified when we find it. Owners were moving towards a better balance between military needs and residential comfort in the fifteenth century, but this coincided with the growth in the building of purely residential houses and mansion, and these are outside the scope of this book.

12

Later Castles in England and Wales

While Edward I was squandering a sizeable percentage of the royal revenues on his grandiose castle-building schemes in Wales and his additions to some royal castles in England (notably the Tower of London), other lesser men continued to build or improve castles in both countries, generally with the king's permission and on a smaller scale. The improvements were usually to earlier castles of some strength and defensiveness. The new castles were in some senses borderline candidates for inclusion in the list of front-rank fortress-residences and, despite some impressiveness, particularly in the cases of Bodiam and Bolton, they lacked the inherent powerfulness of, for example, Richmond, Goodrich, Carreg Cennen or Carrickfergus.

Part of this was because these lesser men were building with motives different from their ancestors of the Conqueror's time, and without the pressures that afflicted society during the 'nineteen long winters' of Stephen's reign. Feudalism was not quite dead, but it was dying. Men no longer built castles simply to dominate their lands and frighten the populace: they wanted grand homes with room to spread, to house the possessions they won in wars abroad, bought with money they inherited or made out of better usage of their lands, in particular sheep-rearing and wool production. They still needed protection from enemies, they still feared the possibility of invasion from France, there was always the danger of civil war of some kind, and so they continued to fortify their homes. But it was less and less acceptable to live in a tall tower and share it with family and dependants and servants. It was uncivilised to dine in a room at the corner of which the tower's main staircase was exposed, its users clattering their way up and down. And it was quite intolerable to live in a gatehouse whose portcullis or drawbridge machinery ground its creaking wheels and shafts round and round at the back of the chapel during prayers. From this time, many of the new castles looked different from their predecessors. Principally, they appeared to combine the military function with the residential needs in a single integrated structural form. In doing so, the residential character gradually assumed greater importance as the need for military fortification lessened (although it did not by any means disappear).

Castles continued to be built or improved up to the end of the fifteenth century in England and Wales, and longer still in Scotland and Ireland (*see* Chapters 9 and 10). Such decline as there may have been in the effectiveness of newly built castles was due to the decline of the system that created and fostered castles, namely, feudalism. Feudalism began to break down in the fourteenth century through a number of causes. The Black Death of 1347–50 ravaged Europe and Britain (all parts) and carried off about one-third of the population in Britain, the majority of the dead being the

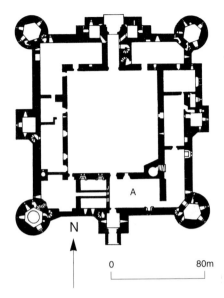

Bodiam: the rectangular ground-floor plan here was for many years believed to be the true shape of the castle but, in 1990, aerial photography revealed that the plan is not quite rectangular but is a parallelogram. A = lord's hall.

tenant and serf classes. This radically changed the labour position and struck at the roots of the relationship between lord and tenant. The wars in France carried off numbers of nobles and their sons and led to confusions of feudal loyalties: more and more tenants were drawn into the spheres of influence of fewer and fewer lords, and the system could not work at all. And the growing need for men on the land reduced the number available for armies abroad, with the result that lords had to employ mercenaries of whatever nationality they could find, and pay them. Some accepted land but more wanted money, at a time when money in the form of minted coins was circulating much more widely than before.

More than 100 new castles of one kind or another were built in England and Wales between Beaumaris (1295–c.1330) and Thornbury (c.1510–20). These were very different from one another in numerous characteristics, bearing in every case the unique and individual whims and preferences of the owner. But they had features in common as well. They were often quadrangular, which was not a new idea, for quadrangular plans had been followed in the twelfth century at Old Sherborne, Windsor and others. They had substantial corner towers, gatehouse on one side, postern on the opposite side, and additional towers or turrets in between the corner towers. The towers and gatehouses were often three-storeyed, or even four-storeyed, but the apartment ranges in between were generally two-storeyed. They stood in lakes or were surrounded by vast moats. In some cases the apartments set aside for the owner were cut off from the rest of the apartments, by walls without doorways, separate staircases or other complicated devices. The received reason for these precautions is that owners were not willing to trust their retainers (who increasingly were mercenaries and so would desert or rebel at the drop of a ducat). But this is perhaps to exaggerate the number of mercenaries a lord might have in his private army, and also

to emphasise the lack of principles in mercenaries as a class.

A typical quadrangular fortress was Bodiam. A licence to build it was granted in 1385 to Sir Edward Dalyngrygge, a knight who had fought in the wars in France. The licence permitted him to strengthen 'with a wall of stone and lime, and crenellate and construct and make into a castle his manor of Bodyham, near the sea, … for the defence of the adjacent country and resistance to our enemies …'. At the time there was serious danger of Kent and Sussex being invaded by the French. The plan of Bodiam was a range of apartments round the inside of what the builders hoped was a square but which was recently discovered (1990) to be slightly rhomboid, with round corner towers, a gatehouse with square turrets and additional square-plan turrets mid-wall. The outer walls were 1.8–2.4 metres (6–8 ft) thick, and the building was two storeys high, although the towers and gatehouse rose to three storeys. The outer walls contained very few windows and were equipped with loops and gun-ports. The gatehouse and the postern gate were machicolated round the parapets. The apartments on the south and east sides and for half the north side (to the gatehouse) formed a complete residential suite of chapel, pantry, kitchen, solar, chamber and hall. Much the same accommodation was provided in the remaining apartments on the west and half of the north sides. The two suites were not connected, and the smaller range (west and north-west) was not connected to the gatehouse. The castle well was sited in the south-west round corner tower, in the main accommodation suite. The south-east round corner tower had a vaulted ceiling in the basement. These arrangements have led some historians to regard the separation of the suites as a deliberate scheme to frustrate possible rebellion and attack on the owner by the retainers (who occupied the smaller range). The well was, for example, kept in the lord's part so that it could not be poisoned. But it seems more likely that the separation was in order to frustrate attack from besiegers or intruders from outside, in just the same way as a great tower in an older castle provided an ultimate refuge for defenders once the gatehouse and/or flanking towers round the

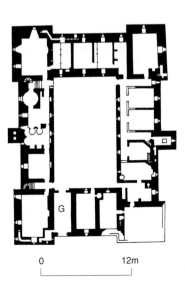

Bolton: plan of the ground floor. G = gatehouse.

The great tower at Tattershall rises to just over 31 metres (100 ft) and is built of bricks manufactured from local clay, dressed with freestone and limestone.

France – it has 17 towers and turrets, arrow slits and gunports, and some of the machicolation was real, while by any standards Tattershall's 31-metre (110-ft) tall tower was a powerfully defensive structure.

The fifteenth century saw the origination of several new castles of strength in England and Wales. They were built by rich and powerful men who were favoured by the kings and granted leave to construct them not so much as war bases but as manifestations of the financial and territorial wealth of their owners. Possibly, some of them were raised in a spirit of competition with one another, or with towns and cities which had for a long time been growing in strength and independence through commercial enterprise. They were certainly solid evidence of wealth and power. Caister was built by Sir John Fastolf, a knight who made his fortune in the wars in France; Tattershall by Ralph Cromwell, a grasping and very able politician who rose to be Treasurer of England (1433–43) with all the perquisites that that entailed; Raglan (with a hexagonal great tower in stone) by an ambitious father-and-son team, Sir William ap Thomas and Sir William Herbert, the fifteenth-century equivalents of property and business tycoons; and of course the stone great tower of Lord Hastings at Ashby de la Zouch, another political parvenu who became in turn mighty, over-mighty and was suddenly executed. These and others of the period give some substance to the phrase quoted for the first time by Sir Edward Coke in 1623 and since oft-repeated, 'an Englishman's home is his castle', an indication that the military first and residential second roles were being reversed.

enclosure had fallen. If Dalyngrygge, for example, was attacked from outside in one suite, he could quite easily go out of one door into the courtyard and walk over to the other suite.

There were several other quadrangular fortresses of the fourteenth century, notably Bolton in Yorkshire built at much the same time, Maxstoke built in the 1340s, and Shirburn in Oxfordshire, c.1380. Most of them were sited in fine lakes which provided excellent defence. The water defences at Bodiam are described in Chapter 5.

Some of the fifteenth-century castles look less military than residential, especially when they are built of brick and not stone, such as Tattershall in Lincolnshire (c.1430–c.1450), Caister in Norfolk (1432–c.1446) and Herstmonceux in Sussex (c.1440). But in many features they were still formidable enough. They were built to impress and to overawe, as well as to accommodate, and undoubtedly to provide shelter in time of civil disturbance, too. Herstmonceux was certainly built to repel raiders from

Raglan: this mid-fifteenth-century castle of three enclosures, one containing the Great Tower of Gwent (left), made use of the hexagonal plan for most towers and turrets.

13

The End of the Castle

Towards the end of the fourteenth century, when the successes of Edward III in the first part of the Hundred Years War had faded into remembrances of past glory and given way to a renewed initiative by France, some castles were built near, if not on, the coast, such as Bodiam, by private individuals with royal permission, in some cases encouragement. These were conceived as fortresses for beating off French or other European raids, for providing bases from which to meet an army that had landed successfully and was marching up the country, and at the same time as fortified homes for their mighty owners. Yet it was not until the late fifteenth century that real co-operation began between the government and an owner who was building or improving a castle on the coast. One early example was Dartmouth in Devon, where the owner was in fact the town council. Built largely between 1481 and 1495, it was the most advanced fortification in England. It was raised round the remains of an earlier fortress built with Edward III's encouragement in the fourteenth century. Dartmouth and a few others were probably the last English or Welsh castles that bore any association with the feudal concept of a castle, and so they mark the beginning of the end of the castle in the two countries.

The real end was brought about by the sensible legislation of Henry VII (1485–1509) who, soon after his defeat of Richard III (1483–85) at Bosworth in 1485, virtually took over the nation's facilities for manufacturing gunpowder, and by statute forbade the maintenance of private armies. This stopped great lords indulging in private wars, using cannon and hand-guns, and brought siege warfare to an end in England and Wales for a century and a half. In effect, Henry dealt the death blow to feudalism.

When the need for castles passed away, the buildings were adapted to new roles, allowed to decay, or were pulled down and the materials used for constructing other buildings or repairing old ones. Many were converted as they stood into more comfortable residences by their owners, or sold to new owners to do likewise. In some cases the alterations were integrated into the existing structure: ranges of domestic buildings were erected against the inside of walls of enclosures, ornate fireplaces were built into walling in towers or halls, and many windows were

Dartmouth: ground-floor plan.

enlarged (which, of course, weakened the walls). In other instances, new free-standing buildings, not associated with the castle as it were, arose within their precincts, such as at Compton and many others. Of the hundreds of castles of one kind and another built in Britain in the Middle Ages and surviving into the sixteenth century, few continued to look as they had in their military heyday. Owners still called them castles, even put in ashlar gun-ports or musket loops, but perhaps – in England and Wales at all events – they did not really envisage their homes ever playing the medieval role again. (It was different in Scotland and Ireland, as we saw in Chapters 9 and 10.)

Over the sixteenth and early seventeenth centuries, castles were to be little more than quaint and picturesque relics of a bygone society. In quite a few instances owners patched them up and attempted to maintain them. Perhaps they even let visitors tramp round them. But in far more numerous cases owners allowed their castles to decay. They became objects of interest to travellers and antiquarians who commented upon them, generally deploring the deterioration and harking back to their better days. The foremost was John Leland (c.1506–52), the London-born antiquary. He spent six years (1536–42) making a detailed tour of England and Wales examining, amongst other things, castles, and he wrote numerous descriptions and comments that are of great interest and value to castle historians.

The Crown had been by far the biggest owner of castles throughout the Middle Ages. When Henry VII won the throne at Bosworth he came into about 40 castles, including Carisbrooke, Carlisle, Dover, London, Nottingham, Portchester, Scarborough and Windsor. As he also took over the principality of Wales he acquired a further string from Conwy to Cardigan, including the great Edwardian fortresses; and as Duke of Lancaster (by virtue of being the heir to the House of Lancaster through his mother, Margaret Beaufort) he could add another collection, notably Bolingbroke, Hertford, Kenilworth, Lancaster, Leicester, Pevensey, Pickering, Pontefract, Tickhill and Tutbury. He even obtained the Duchy of York castles of Conisbrough, Sandal and the Neville ('Kingmaker') castles of Middleham, Warwick and Barnard. And he was owner of Richmond. During his reign he acquired even more: Pembroke, Cardiff, Newport (Monmouthshire) and Tonbridge (then one of the greatest castles in England).

It is not necessary to enlarge upon the Crown's further acquisitions in the time of his son Henry VIII or of his grandchildren Edward VI, Mary I and Elizabeth I. Clearly, the Crown had far more fortresses than it could possibly need or want, and to keep them all in good, or even indifferent, repair for whatever purpose would have been a crushing drain upon the royal funds. What mattered was that practically all the major fortresses in England and Wales were out of private hands and so constituted no danger to the peace of the realm. There was some need for those fortresses on the border between England and Scotland and the royal

The twelfth-century enclosing wall at Conisbrough is dominated by the unusual cylindrical great tower, which is supported by six wedge-shaped buttresses.

This view of Pevensey shows the gatehouse, with the southern tower on the right.

accounts contain details of expenditure on several, some of it high, some of it niggardly (the penny-pinching Elizabeth I refused absolutely to help Hunsdon to repair the very important castle of Norham). These castles included Wark, Berwick, Carlisle (where the twelfth-century great tower was altered to take sixteenth-century guns), Bewcastle (Cumberland) and Harbottle.

The Crown maintained a handful for a variety of more peaceful reasons, notably Pontefract 'to prevent the Ruynes of a Monument of such antiquity and goodly building' (cited in *The History of the King's Works,* vol. 3, p. 289). Chester was a centre of local government and Tutbury was a royal hunting lodge. And of course the Crown maintained London, Windsor, Dover, Portchester and Carisbrooke for defence and for royal palace purposes. Interestingly, Fotheringay in Northamptonshire was meant to be one that received attention. Leland found it in good condition: it was given a face-lift in 1566 for a visit by Elizabeth I (painting

railway stations in the present century has this among many precedents). But when Fotheringay was selected as the location for the trial and eventual execution of Mary, Queen of Scots, in 1586–7, the greater part of it was in poor shape. The walls were low enough to jump over, and the outer gatehouse had decayed to the point of uselessness. Would an attempt to rescue Mary have been successful?

In 1609 the state of the royal and Duchy of Lancaster castles was reviewed by the Exchequer. More than 60 'of his

Cardiff was originally a motte castle, with a later polygonal shell enclosure on the summit.

Donnington Castle: the siege of Donnington Castle lasted from July 1644 to April 1646. The castle had been taken over by Charles I after the outbreak of the Civil War, and in the autumn of 1643 he appointed Colonel John Boys as commander of a garrison of 200 infantry, 25 horses and 4 cannons. Boys fortified the castle with a star-shaped outwork of pointed bulwarks around the stone enclosure with its six flanking towers and its gatehouse. Then he waited. The castle dominated the London to Bath road, near Newbury, and was of strategic value.

In July 1644, Parliament sent 3000 men under General Middleton to besiege the castle. A formal demand for surrender was sent into Colonel Boys, who refused. So Middleton began an assault, using scaling ladders, but this failed, costing him one-tenth of his force. In September, a fresh force under a new commander renewed the siege, using artillery set up on rising ground outside Newbury. For twelve days the cannons thundered across the gently rolling Berkshire hills. Three of the castle's flanking towers were smashed and the curtain wall breached. Boys was again ordered to surrender, and again refused. The next month, yet another Parliamentary army attacked, also with guns, and more than 1000 shots were fired. Still Boys would not yield. Then news arrived that the king was on his way to relieve the defenders, and the Parliamentarians withdrew. The king reached the gallant and exhausted garrison and re-provisioned it.

Soon after this, the Second Battle of Newbury was fought and ended in stalemate. Another assault on the castle followed, under Sir William Waller. Once more, Boys would not yield. In November, the castle was again relieved by the king. A respite followed during the winter, which Boys used to strengthen the earthworks, and in the spring of 1645 he was ready to resist once more. But the Civil War was coming to an end, hastened by the king's defeat at Naseby in June. When, in March 1646, Parliament once more demanded surrender, Boys sent to the king for instructions and was told to shift for himself and get the best terms he could. Boys surrendered in April 1646.

Majestie's decayed castells' were described as decayed, very ruinous or utterly decayed. Among those described as utterly decayed were Beaumaris, Aberystwyth, Conwy, Caernarfon, Ruthin and Rhuddlan. Some of the others in the list were labelled 'utterly ruinated and serve for noe use'. One has to remember that these buildings were examined by agents of the King (James I), presumably to see whether any, and if so which, were suitable for him to occupy or stay at, and that 'decayed' might mean not much more than that windows were broken, damp was coming in, dry rot had eaten at some timbers and so forth.

Quite suddenly, in 1642, castles came into their own again for what was to be their last flourish, their fighting finish as Professor Douglas Simpson called it. The king, Charles I, and Parliament went to war to determine once and for all who was the sovereign power, the monarch or the people, through its elected representatives in the Commons. The king had unwisely left London and raised his standard at Nottingham, abandoning the capital with its vast wealth in the hands of Parliament. We are not concerned with the main progress of the war, since that was fought army-against-army in open battles. But while the leaders on both sides fielded armies of several thousands in an attempt to win decisive victories, there were many much smaller and highly localised campaigns going on concurrently, in which the old castles of England and Wales – and also in Ireland – played the central role. Soon after the outbreak of the war both Royalists and Parliamentarians in all parts of the countryside took them over and repaired them. In many cases the disrepair was so extensive that only parts were rebuilt, parts that could be fortified without much difficulty and which would perhaps stand siege for a time. On the Royalist side, many of the Crown castles and those belonging to lords and knights who were loyal to the king's cause were put into a state of defence and garrisoned. Each was allotted a number of men, between 50 and 300, presumably according to size and to strategic importance.

Geographically, the countryside of England and Wales could be said to have been divided into two parts, so far as the respective sides in the Civil War are concerned: the king drew his support from the west, from Wales and from the North; Parliament was dominant in the east and south. But these areas were not exclusive to one side or the other, and every county had its share of supporters of both. If a Royalist castle was garrisoned by the king's men, Parliamentary supporters attacked it, and vice versa. Both sides lived on the produce of the neighbouring countryside; they plundered the locality if they could not get supplies by asking or by purchasing. On the whole the Royalists behaved marginally worse than the Parliamentarians. They were fighting private wars, sometimes oblivious of what was going on elsewhere, conscious only of doing their bit for their 'party'. This is one reason why many castle sieges went on long after the battles of Marston Moor and Naseby had been fought and the issue decided. Many castles were besieged and captured more than once, alternating between king and Parliament. Sometimes a siege took only a day or two, such as at Nunney or Devizes; others lasted months, such as at Raglan and Denbigh; or well over a year, such as at Pontefract and Donnington.

When the principal Civil War battles had been fought and Parliament triumphed, the victors decided it was time to reduce the Royalist-held castles. Some had been held for years, effectively locking up men in garrisons who would have been better employed in battle for the king. Once he had lost, he advised them to make what terms they could with the Parliamentary armies, although secretly he hoped that as many as possible would hold out and so obstruct the Parliamentarians in the exercise of their new power.

Accounts of several Civil War sieges have survived and they make fascinating reading. One of the longest sieges was that of Donnington Castle in Berkshire, from July 1644 to April 1646. The siege of Donnington may seem to have been an inordinately prolonged business, but this kind of story was enacted at several other sieges, notably at Denbigh, Raglan and Corfe. Pontefract, then one of the most majestic castles in northern England, was besieged three times. Cromwell himself almost despaired of getting the Pontefract garrison to yield. He described it as one of the strongest inland garrisons, well watered, difficult to undermine because every important part of the castle stood on rock. Pontefract fell in the third siege, from mid-1648 to March 1649 and Parliament decided to demolish it. The success of this can be judged by the meagre remains of what was one of the foremost castles of the Middle Ages.

It was not enough to reduce castles in Royalist hands. Parliament was determined to break them up and render them permanently incapable of being used for military purposes again. This process was known as 'slighting' and it was generally carried out with great thoroughness. The idea was not new: Robert Bruce had followed a similar policy in Scotland after his successful campaign to drive out the English. Many castles in England and Wales were ordered by Parliament to be slighted, mostly those that had been held at some time or other during the war by the Royalists. The demolition of Raglan in the summer of 1647 was begun with vigour, but no matter how hard the teams worked, they were unable to destroy it. An account of the slighting was written towards the end of the seventeenth century. In it the writer said that 'The Great Tower [the Yellow Tower of Gwent], after tedious battering the top thereof with pickaxes, was undermined, the weight of it propped with the timber whilst the two sides of the six were cut through:

the timber being burned it fell down in a lump ... After the surrender the country people were summoned into a rendezvous with pickaxes, spades, and shovels to draw the mote [moat] in the hope of wealth ...' (quoted from Raglan Castle by A.J. Taylor). In Ireland, numerous castles taken by Cromwell or his successor commanders after 1650 were slighted. Gazetteer entries record this in several cases.

The subsequent history of the thousands of castles in England, Wales, Scotland and Ireland has been enormously varied. Many have disappeared in town development schemes or under roads, railways and stations, electricity power stations and other public civil engineering works. Many have been left to decay. Many that had deteriorated badly have been carefully restored, some by private owners, but the majority by government environment departments and 'heritage' agencies of England, Wales, Scotland, Northern Ireland and the Republic of Ireland, without whose efforts over many years it would be impossible to provide a fair picture of the castles of Britain and Ireland. Some have been used as quarries for building materials for later, more peaceful, structures. Some were until recently used as prisons. The Tower of London is used for military purposes as well as being open for visitors, and Dover was used for similar purposes until 1958. All of them, from the palatial and extensive Windsor to the single tower-house of Carrigaphooca or the unadorned motte at Thetford, are individual structures with histories that are part of the story of all the lands that make up the British Isles.

Pontefract: looking across from the north to the original motte and the remains of the later great tower built around it. In the foreground are ruins of the kitchen, buttery and other quarters.

Introduction to the Gazetteer

There are over 1,350 entries in the gazetteer, which is probably the most extensive gazetteer of castles in Britain and Ireland ever assembled into one volume. Yet in compiling it one can never satisfy everyone. Something will inevitably be left out: it may even be a glaring omission. If this has happened here, it may have been inadvertent and will hopefully be brought to my notice. If it is not inadvertent, then the reason may lie in the fact that the 'castle' is not in my view a castle within the definition given in Chapter 1.

How is the gazetteer planned? Where possible, the remains of what can be seen today have been outlined, but because of space limitations it has been necessary to highlight some parts and overlook others. For the same reason, historical details and personalities associated with the castles have been kept to a minimum. This is a source book of information which can be used as a pointer to further study of any particular castle or any aspect of design or fortification. It is a gazetteer of structures which, in the great majority of cases, can be seen and explored, and the building details seem to me to be more important. The reader who wants to pursue the historical side can do so without difficulty by searching among documents and publications (see Bibliography).

Those more interested in the buildings, or earthworks, may like to follow a simple suggestion. The entries have been prepared, wherever possible, in such a way that it should be possible to take a piece of paper and draw out a rough plan (in many cases, the basic plan is drawn out accurately and reproduced in the book). From the plan thus sketched out, an idea should emerge of what ground the buildings cover, or covered, and armed with this the site can be explored. Castles in the care of the relevant government departments or agencies in each of the five countries (England, Wales, Scotland, Northern Ireland and the Republic of Ireland) are described in great detail in special handbooks, each of which has a comprehensive site-plan. These booklets are normally obtainable on the site or from HMSO bookshops or any of the HMSO agencies in the UK, and similar facilities exist in the Republic of Ireland.

Of the 1,350 or so castles listed, quite a few have very little to see; they are no more than mounds, or stretches of ditch and bank, or gutted shells of unsafe masonry. Some are interesting, nonetheless, because of what they once were or the position they occupied, or because of some important association. For example, Cambridge

(Opposite) This view of Kanturk shows the early seventeenth-century stronghouse that was never completed. Note the corbelling for an unbuilt machicolated parapet.

Castle has very little except its original mound, and yet if you climb to the summit and look down it is immediately clear what a commanding position it once had over the river, town and countryside below. Again, from the top of Knockgraffon motte in Co. Tipperary, you can see several kilometres round at any point. In its first days it was a centre for the administration of much of Tipperary and elsewhere by the Butler family. Similarly, Aberystwyth Castle in Wales is now little more than an assemblage of ruins, but at one time it was as powerful-looking and impressive as any of the castles built in Wales by Edward I in the late thirteenth century.

It is sometimes easier to read about castles than to visit them. Although the great majority are in ruins, one cannot always just scramble over them and explore the remains. Many are in private ownership and the owners naturally cherish them, even if the remains amount (as many do) to little more than straggling heaps of stone dotted about overgrown earthworks. Some are not open to visitors. Rather more are open, although the owners do not all advertise the fact. Some admit visitors on a regular basis, some on occasional days, and some at special request. Some owners change their arrangements at relatively short notice, while some castles acquire new owners who do likewise. A castle may become unsafe and have to be closed for restoration. Some owners take more of the castle into their own use and close parts to the public. It is therefore best in every case where a castle is privately owned, or appears to be, to check with the owner first before setting out to visit. Guides to stately homes and castles provide advice about accessibility, but details can only ever be accurate at the time the guide goes to press.

Apart from privately owned castles, there are rather more that are in the care of public organisations and these are more easily accessible, although even then one may find a major restoration job in progress and the castle closed for a year, or less, or occasionally even more. The several hundred that are in government care are, as a rule, open throughout the year during the hours of daylight (roughly) or on a regular basis. Some are only accessible between April and October; others are open all year round. They have been looked after, often extensively restored, and made attractive with such skill and care as to put all five countries forever in their governments' debt. Many castles are in the care of local authorities, who maintain them in good repair, and in some cases have landscaped them. Some of these are freely accessible. For others it is necessary to obtain a key or find a curator. Many castles are listed in the relevant telephone directory. Local authority information offices and national and regional tourist boards' main and branch offices and outposts have details of visiting hours for most castles in their areas.

Throughout the gazetteer, the entries are given their Ordnance Survey grid reference numbers, which will help locate them. In England, Scotland and Wales, there are six-figure reference numbers, and in Ireland there are four-figure numbers. The Irish four-figure numbers come from the Ordnance Survey 1:126,720 scale maps.

Beginning as a Norman earthwork castle in the 1090s, Pembroke developed into a powerful stone enclosure of two baileys, dominated by the cylindrical great tower (left) put up by William Marshal, Earl of Pembroke, in c.1200–10.

England

ABINGER Nr Guildford, Surrey
(TQ 114460)
A motte castle built c.1100, this was the subject of extensive excavations in 1947–9, under the direction of Dr Brian Hope Taylor. They revealed post-holes of a wooden tower and also of the surrounding palisade, and of a horizontally placed bridge from the motte to the bailey, across a wet moat that was filled by a local spring. The post-holes of the tower indicate that the tower may have stood on stilts, as it were, to provide a fighting platform underneath the tower ground floor. A gap in the circumference of palisade posts is believed to indicate the gateway at the south-west.

ACTON BURNELL Shropshire
(SJ 534019)
Acton Burnell is known as a castle, but it was really a manor-house whose builder, Robert Burnell, Chancellor of England, obtained a licence to fortify in the 1280s. It is a huge, two-storeyed rectangular tower-hall, now roofless, with smaller (4 metre [13 ft] square) towers on the corners, with a projecting block between the two west towers. It was built of local red sandstone and is more like a palace than a castle although the parapets are in fact battlemented.

ALBERBURY
Nr Shrewsbury, Shropshire
(SJ 358144)
A small thirteenth-century stone enclosure castle, polygonal in plan, containing a rectangular great tower with thick walls, now all in ruins.

ALDFORD Nr Chester, Cheshire
(SJ 419596)
A motte castle was build at Aldford in the twelfth century. Walling erected on the summit of the motte was discovered in recent excavations. Some fragments of stonework round the bailey still survive. The castle overlooked a ford across the Dee.

ALDINGBOURNE Nr Arundel, Sussex
(SU 923048)
One of the castles in Britain (cf. Lydford) where the lowest storey of the stone great tower was enclosed, as it were, inside a mound of earth. The mound can be seen. The tower was square in plan, with a small forebuilding at the south-west. It was built of limestone and flint, which was quarried locally, with dressings of Caen ashlar. Aldingbourne was erected in the mid-twelfth century but is now fragmentary.

ALDINGHAM Lancashire
(SD 278698)
An earthwork enclosure about 36.5 metres (120 ft) square was converted into a motte castle by filling in and raising the height of the enclosure. A further bailey was added. This is unusual: motte castles were generally built from scratch using natural mounds or rising ground or by creating artificial mounds on virgin sites. In the twelfth century the motte seems to have been heightened, which suggests that the first tower was dismantled and a new one built. Excavations in 1968 revealed no remains that can be dated later than the thirteenth century.

ALLINGTON Nr Maidstone, Kent
(TQ 752579)
Today's Allington Castle is an extensive twentieth-century renovation by Sir Martin Conway (later Lord Conway of Allington) of a late thirteenth-century quadrangular structure with square and round towers on corners and mid-wall. The latter had been raised by Stephen of Penchester, under a licence granted by Edward I in 1281, beside the remains of an earlier Norman motte castle of the eleventh century. Allington Castle is sited on the west bank of the Medway river. Some Norman stonework has survived opposite the motte, in the form of some walling in herringbone pattern, which leads into a much later stretch of wall and which may have been part of the bailey wall after its conversion from timber to stone.

Considerable alterations were carried out in the late fifteenth century, converting it to a grander Tudor mansion with large windows, a long gallery, new kitchens and other accommodation ranges. It was burned down c.1600, but the remains patched up as a farmhouse. It is now a Carmelite nunnery.

ALNWICK Northumberland
(NU 187137)
The splendid palatial residence at Alnwick with its towers, gatehouses and high curtain with battlements is the result of centuries of building. Alnwick began as a motte castle of the eleventh century, and in the early twelfth century a polygonal stone shell enclosure was raised on the summit. Stone walling was added to the bailey, and in 1138 the castle was

described as a very well fortified one.

William the Lion, King of Scotland, besieged it in 1172 and again in 1174, but on the second occasion a relieving army surprised him and his principal lords and knights as they rested from the fighting, and captured them. The castle remained a powerful Border fortress throughout the thirteenth century.

Early in the fourteenth century Alnwick was bought from the Bishop of Durham by Henry Percy, ancestor of the great Earls of Northumberland, who then began a major improvement programme. Percy rebuilt the shell enclosure by making it larger with seven semicircular towers round it, in a form that has led it to be called a clustered donjon. The great curtain wall round the central tower was strengthened with several flanking towers, square, rectangular, D-ended and cylindrical. The inner tower and the outer curtain received huge gatehouses and a great barbican. The greater part of the work was done by Percy, his son, grandson and great-grandson, and in magnificence it was hardly less impressive than contemporary royal works at Windsor.

In the fifteenth century, Alnwick was often in the front line of war. Headquarters of the Percys who rebelled against Henry IV in 1404–5, it was besieged and taken by that king. It was attacked during the Wars of the Roses. Subsequently it began to decay, until in the eighteenth century the 1st Duke of Northumberland rebuilt it, employing Robert Adam as architect. The result was not felicitous and it was swept away in the nineteenth century by Anthony Salvin who restored it to its external medieval appearance.

ALTON STAFFORDSHIRE
(SK 074425)
A castle was built on a rocky precipice in the time of Henry II (1154–89). The slopes provided defence to most sides. A ditch was cut into the rock. The remains of a curtain wall on the south side and of two round towers along it have recently been investigated.

ALMONDBURY WEST YORKSHIRE
(SE 152140)
The remains of a twelfth-century motte castle raised upon the site of an Iron Age hill-fort were found in excavations here earlier this century. There is evidence of continued occupation as a castle up to the early part of the thirteenth century.

AMBERLEY NR PULBOROUGH, SUSSEX
(TQ 027132)
Today, Amberley Castle is a much restored structure occupied as a home. It appears to have begun as a stonework enclosure with high curtain walls, towers, hall and gateway, erected in the fourteenth century following a licence to build dated 1377. It was a fortress residence for the Bishops of Chichester. The hall is in ruins, the gateway has been restored and there are stretches of high curtain wall.

ANCROFT NR BERWICK-ON-TWEED, NORTHUMBERLAND
(NV 043437)
Described in the 1540s as a 'little fortress', this interesting tower was constructed in the thirteenth century as an integral part of Ancroft Church, a twelfth-century chapel raised by Holy Island monks. It is three-storeyed above the lower storey of the nave, about 6.7 x 7.9 metres (22 x 26 ft), with a spiral staircase in one corner. The small windows are set in thick walls.

ANSTEY HERTFORDSHIRE
(TL 404330)
Anstey was a motte castle of the late eleventh or early twelfth century. The surviving low motte, about 9.1 metres (30 ft) high, was surrounded by a wet moat of varying width. The motte top is almost 0.1 hectares (¼ acre) in area and it may have contained more buildings than just a tall wooden tower. The castle was strengthened during the Magna Carta war (1215–16) by one of the opponents of King John.

APPLEBY CUMBRIA
(NY 685200)
Beginning as a motte castle probably of early twelfth-century construction, Appleby first became an enclosure castle with a sandstone rubble curtain around the bottom of the motte, inside which was built a square-plan great tower, in about 1170. The great tower rises to about 24.4 metres (80 ft) and has four storeys. The first floor is reached by a spiral staircase in the south-east corner, and the remaining floors by the continuation of this, together with a second staircase in the south-west corner. Unusually for a square great tower, the entrance is not protected by any forebuilding.

Appleby was held for Henry II from 1173–9 and again for the royal family from

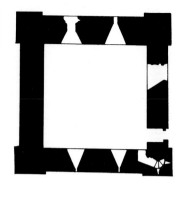

Appleby: plan of the ground floor of the great tower.

0   12m

1190–1203. During the first period it was attacked by William the Lion, King of Scotland, and the constable surrendered without putting up a fight. In 1203 King John granted the castle to Richard de Vipont.

ARDLEY OXFORDSHIRE
(SP 539273)
An oval enclosure with a shallow ditch in Ardley Wood. There are traces of Norman masonry. It has been conjectured that it was an adulterine castle of Stephen's reign, demolished after 1154 on the orders of Henry II.

ARMATHWAITE CUMBRIA
(NY 506459)
Armathwaite is a four-storeyed pele-tower of the fifteenth century, overlooking the Eden river and not far from the Carlisle to Penrith road which was used frequently by the Scots in Border raids.

ARUNDEL SUSSEX
(TQ 019074)
Arundel Castle began as a substantial motte castle, whose motte was 18.3–21.3 metres (60–70 ft) tall, with elevated bailey on each side (a layout similar to that of Windsor Castle), raised on a spur overlooking the Arun river. This was probably built c.1088. About a century later the motte received a shell enclosure with ashlar pilaster buttresses and a battlemented parapet, which was approached through a rounded arch, later replaced by a gate-tower constructed against the shell wall, next to the arch which was filled in. A wing

wall of stone led down the motte slope on one side to a small turret from which a stone curtain continued round the top of the bank of one of the baileys and into the other. This work was mainly of 1176–89, and the king, Henry II, also made a garden for himself, probably the earliest royal garden in an English castle.

From the thirteenth century onwards the castle was held for the most part by the Earls of Arundel, and later the Dukes of Norfolk, and the late medieval structures that emerged were their work.

ASCOT D'OILLY Oxfordshire
(SP 304191)

Ascot d'Oilly is a very interesting castle, consisting of raised ground surrounded by broad ditching. The mound was piled in stages against the lower walls of a great tower as the masonry went up (cf. Aldingbourne). Only traces of the tower remain, and they indicate that it was about 10.7 metres (35 ft) square, with walls 2.4 metres (8 ft) thick. The tower was demolished, probably in 1175–6, and this could have been at the order of Henry II following his suppression of the revolt led by his eldest son, Prince Henry.

ASHBY DE LA ZOUCH Leicestershire
(SK 363167)

Ashby was a Norman hall of twelfth-century beginnings. Over the next three centuries it was extended to become a fair-sized manor-house. In 1464 it was granted by Edward IV to William, Lord Hastings, his Lord Chamberlain, who decided to convert the manor into a castle. In 1474 Edward gave him the necessary licence.

The principal building of Hastings' time was his new great tower (Hastings' Tower). This formidable structure was a fortress-cum-residence of the old kind. It originally reached about 27.4 metres (90 ft) to its semi-octagonal angle turrets. It is rectangular in plan, about 14.3 x 12.5 metres (47 x 41 ft), with a rectangular extension on the north-east side. The main tower was four-storeyed, but there were seven floors in the extension. The tower walls are nearly 2.7 metres (9 ft) thick on the ground floor, which has no windows and only a small door once protected by a portcullis. There was an underground passage from the basement of the tower along to the kitchen building to the west. The tower was placed on the periphery of the castle and not in the centre; this enabled the owners to have a view of the other occupants of the castle.

The most interesting feature of the great tower is that it was rectangular in an age when it is believed, in some quarters, that rectangular towers had long since given way to cylindrical towers (*see* Chapter 3).

ASHLEY Hampshire
(SU 385308)

South of the church are the remnants of an enclosure castle of earthworks, inside which are foundation traces of stonework building. This was approximately rectangular, with a cylindrical turret, probably of the late twelfth/early thirteenth century.

ASHTON KEYNES Wiltshire
(SU 049943)

An earthwork enclosure which had a dry-stone wall along the ramparts. It was probably raised in the time of Stephen.

ASLOCKTON Nottinghamshire
(SK 744402)

A rectangular earthwork enclosure whose moat was fed from a nearby stream, with a low motte, about 4.9 metres (16 ft) high. Nothing of its history is known. Some earthworks remain.

AYDON
Nr Corbridge, Northumberland
(NZ 001663)

Aydon Castle began as a private residence of the late thirteenth century. It was probably built by Robert de Raymes as a two-storeyed home with the solar, dining hall and kitchen on the higher floor. These were reached by an outside staircase. The house had hardly been completed when Raymes felt compelled to fortify it with battlements (he obtained a licence in the first years of the fourteenth century) because of the increasingly unsettled conditions in Northumberland that followed Edward I's illegal assumption of the throne of Scotland and his invasions of Scotland. Raymes then surrounded the house with 'a wall of stone and lime against the king's enemies, the Scots', and this had towers and a deep ditch outside. The precautions were not entirely effective: the Scots captured Aydon Castle in 1315 and took it again in 1346. It was recovered later in the fourteenth century and remained in private ownership until 1975. Substantial parts of the original work survive.

BACONSTHORPE
Nr Holt, Norfolk
(TG 122383)

Without bothering to obtain a licence, the Heydons, an aggressive, self-seeking, middle-class Norfolk family of the fifteenth century, constructed a quadrangular manor-house at Baconsthorpe and fortified it. A deep ditch was excavated round the north, west and south sides and the east side was protected by a lake which fed the ditch. In the middle of the south wall the Heydons erected a substantial three-storeyed rectangular gatehouse largely of flint, faced on the outside with the best East Anglian knapped flintwork, with ashlar quoins. The quadrangle was completed later in the century and it contained several flanking towers, square and cylindrical, and a range of long rooms on the east side. The gatehouse was approached by a drawbridge over the moat. An outer gatehouse was added, some fifty yards away to the south.

John Heydon I, who built the inner gatehouse, was a tough and quarrelsome magnate who survived the dangerous sport of backing first one side, then the other, in the Wars of the Roses (1455–85). Today the castle is in ruins, but is well worth a visit.

BAKEWELL Derbyshire
(SK 221688)

There was a motte castle at Bakewell in the twelfth century. It may have been one of those raised illegally in the time of King Stephen. The motte appears to have been added to an earlier rubble-built ramparted enclosure, possibly square in plan. For a long time it was believed that Bakewell was a *burh* of the time of Edward the Elder (900–24), Alfred the Great's son, but this was disproved by Ella Armitage (*Early Norman Castles of the British Isles* p. 47).

BAMBURGH Northumberland
(NU 184350)

Bamburgh stands on a 45.7-metre (150-ft) tall rock face on the wind-swept Northumbrian coast, one side sheer with the cliff to the shore. Its remaining structures, the residue of a powerful medieval castle, are the last in a line of fortified buildings on the site. Iron Age men, Romans, Anglo-Saxons, even Vikings had built fortifications there. And in 1095, whatever shape the structure was, it was besieged by William II using a siege-castle (a

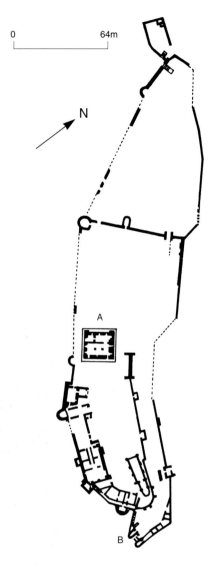

Bamburgh: from a plan of the castle drawn at the end of the nineteenth century. A = great tower. B = great gate.

temporary structure like a belfry) nicknamed Malvoisin – Evil Neighbour – and taken from its holder, Robert de Mowbray. Thereafter, except for a few years, Bamburgh was a royal castle up to the seventeenth century.

The building history of Bamburgh is problematic. The principal structure is the great tower which from a distance looks like Dover's. But it is not like it (except that it is almost cuboid) and it is much smaller: the measurements are 21 x 18.6 x 20 metres (69 x 61 x 65 ft) tall. It has been drastically altered. It has proud clasping buttresses on the corners

and also along the walls, and it has a spiral stair serving all floors in the northern corner. The basement is vaulted and the entrance is at ground-floor level. There is a straight flight of stairs in the wall thickness at ground level.

There are some remains of a curtain wall enclosing the castle, with cylindrical and square towers, and there is a gatehouse on the east side. Again, much of this bears alterations and repairs of later periods. The stonework may have been initiated when the castle was held by Henry, Earl of Huntingdon, a son of David I of Scotland. This was during the chaotic years of Stephen of England, a time when Henry's father captured Carlisle Castle and started work on its great tower (q.v.). The attribution of Bamburgh's great tower to Henry II between c.1160 and c.1170 may relate to continuation of works already begun.

Considerable sums were spent on repairs by King John and King Henry III and, to a lesser extent, by Edward III. It was held on behalf of the Lancastrians in the Wars of the Roses and was besieged twice, in 1462 and 1464. On the second occasion, when the assault was directed by Richard Neville, Earl of Warwick, the great 'Kingmaker', the castle fell after the walls were pounded with artillery. It deteriorated still further until it was rehabilitated by two owners between the mid-eighteenth and early twentieth centuries.

BAMPTON Nr Tiverton, Devon
(SS 959225)

The remains of a motte castle situated beside the River Batham, have been found here. Bampton was a motte castle, probably of the twelfth century. It may have been held against King Stephen.

BAMPTON Oxfordshire
(SP 310031)

A motte castle was raised here by Empress Matilda c.1142, during the reign of her cousin Stephen. The castle was taken by Stephen and slighted. Many years later (c.1315), Aymer de Valence received a licence to fortify the site, then in his possession, and he began a quadrangular enclosure with corner towers and intermediate turrets, with a vaulted gatehouse in one wall. This was a very early quadrangular type of castle of which Bodiam and Bolton, *inter alia*, were later, more celebrated examples (1380s). It lends weight to the belief that quadrilangular castles are of earlier origin in England than once thought.

BANBURY Oxfordshire
(SP 454404)

There is practically nothing to see of Banbury Castle, but it is included because its original formation has been carefully calculated by recent excavation.

The castle was built in the early twelfth century by the Bishop of Lincoln. In the reign of King John, the castle was strengthened (1201–7), according to the Pipe Rolls. Then, some time later in the thirteenth century (or possibly early fourteenth), it was remodelled into a concentric plan, the inner enclosure being a rectangle with one side angled outwards, and the outer enclosure a rectangle. Both curtains were surrounded by ditches and both had corner towers and interval towers.

BARNARD Durham
(NZ 049165)

Barnard overlooks the Tees. Beginning as a small fortified enclosure of the late eleventh or early twelfth century, and belonging to the Baliol family, it developed into a 2.6-hectare

Barnard Castle: note in the north-west corner the cylindrical great tower with a forebuilding. A = inner ward.

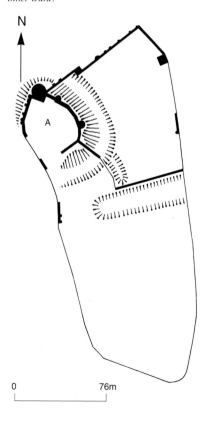

The cylindrical great tower at Barnard is on the left in this view. Part of the rectangular projection beside it is what remains of a forebuilding.

(6½-acre) oblong enclosure (thirteenth and fourteenth centuries). This was divided into four wards: the inner ward inside the smaller stone-walled enclosure, the middle ward to the south, the town ward to the east, and the outer ward which is about equal to the other three put together and most of which is bounded by sheer cliff.

The most interesting feature of Barnard is its cylindrical great tower at the north-west of the inner ward astride the curtain. Built of sandstone blocks which contrast with the rougher masonry of the curtain, it is about 11 metres (36 ft) across and 12.2 metres (40 ft) tall, with a battered plinth, although it was taller in its heyday. Of early thirteenth-century construction, it was raised on the ruins of an even earlier structure. It is unusual for having a forebuilding. To the south-west

of it and projecting from a narrow range of rooms beside it are the remains of a one-storey thirteenth-century great hall.

Barnard was besieged by Alexander II of Scotland in 1216. It was still held by the Baliols, a descendant of whom was John, who became King of Scotland in 1292. When he was deposed in 1296, Barnard passed to the Bishop of Durham, but it was granted c.1300 by Edward I to the Earl of Warwick. It was held for a time by Richard, Duke of Gloucester (later Richard III), through his wife who was the daughter of Richard Neville, Earl of Warwick (the 'Kingmaker'). A white boar (Gloucester's emblem) is carved on a window soffit in the west wall of the inner bailey.

BARNSTAPLE DEVON
(SS 557332)

William the Conqueror had considerable trouble in Devon in the first years of his new order in England: Devonians did not accept the Conquest without a fight. A motte castle

was built here in William's reign by one of his followers, Judhael, who was probably responsible for the clearance of twenty-three houses on the site to make room for it (Domesday). A cylindrical shell enclosure was built round the motte top early in the twelfth century and further improvements were made later in the same century. The motte remains.

BARNWELL
NR OUNDLE, NORTHAMPTONSHIRE
(TL 049853)

There are traces of a possibly twelfth-century motte castle beside the thirteenth-century building that is Barnwell Castle. The stone structure was started c.1265 and is quadrangular, with cylinder towers on the north-east, north-west and south-west corners. On the south-east corner is a twin-towered gatehouse, whose exterior ends are D-ended in shape. The quadrangle walls are of military dimensions: 9.1 metres (30 ft) tall and over 3.6 metres (12 ft) thick. The two northern towers have the unusual feature of

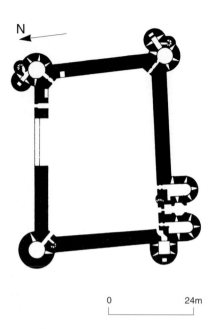

N

0   24m

Barnwell: note the cluster of turrets in the north-east and south-east corners of the enclosure.

their staircases being inside another adjacent round turret, while a third turret, also adjacent, contained the garderobes, providing an irregular trilobe plan for each individual tower. The castle is in a ruinous state and is only open on certain days.

BARWICK-IN-ELMET
WEST YORKSHIRE
(SE 398375)
A motte castle of the twelfth century which contains some stone walling. It was raised in the reign of Stephen and may have been an adulterine castle.

BASING HAMPSHIRE
(SU 663526)
Basing is famous for the role it played in the Civil War. In that time it was a fortified house which was defended valiantly for three years by the Marquess of Winchester, its owner, on behalf of the king. The house stood on the remains of a much earlier structure, an earthwork enclosure with bailey, which had stone additions of the thirteenth and fourteenth centuries.

BEAUDESERT WARWICKSHIRE
(SO 157662)
An earthwork enclosure with a flat-topped oval motte, dating probably from the twelfth

century. Stonework has been found in the enclosure but it is too scanty to suggest any definite shape of a castle that may have been built there.

BEDFORD BEDFORDSHIRE
(TL 053497)
Bedford began as a motte castle of the late eleventh century, near the Ouse which flows through the town. Late in Henry I's or early in Stephen's reign, the castle received important stonework. This included a shell enclosure on the motte. Slightly later, a cylindrical great tower was erected inside. A thirteenth-century drawing of these structures has survived in a manuscript of Matthew Paris's *Chronica Majora*, which also describes the siege of 1224 (*see* caption to this entry).

Bedford Castle: The shell enclosure and great tower at Bedford. This is an adaption of the drawing that appears in the contemporary manuscript of Matthew Paris's Chronica Majora. *The siege of Bedford Castle in 1224 was written up in the* Dunstable Chronicle *and by Matthew Paris in his* Chronica Majora. *It is interesting because it succeeded when the besiegers undermined the walls of a round great tower inside a shell enclosure, and forced a surrender, thus showing that round towers could be undermined as well as rectangular towers.*

The castle was held by Faulkes de Bréauté, a feudal lord who, in 1224, defied the order of Henry III's justices to release a prisoner and pay a fine. Determined to fight the king, he set out westwards to gather military support, leaving the castle in his brother's control. The king, having decided to besiege the castle, requisitioned men and weapons from many parts of the country – 25,000 arrows arrived from the royal arsenal at Corfe, carpenters trudged their way from Windsor, ropes and picks were brought over from Cambridge, and quarrymen were recruited from parts of Bedfordshire to manufacture stone balls for the siege-engines.

On 20 June, Henry began the siege. Although the defenders resisted vigorously, parts of the castle began to fall: first the barbican and then the walling of the outer bailey. The defenders withdrew into the inner bailey, then into the shell and some even into the great tower. The king had belfries moved against the inner bailey and barrages were fired into it. Simultaneously, sappers dug a tunnel underneath the shell wall and, when they had got in, troops followed them through the tunnel. Then another tunnel was dug under the cylindrical great tunnel itself, pit props were put up under the foundations

The castle was enlarged to a rectangular stone curtain enclosure with towers, the south wall of which bordered the river and contained a wall-tower acting as a water-gate. Recent excavations exposed several features. One was part of the moat along the inner bailey to the west of the motte. This moat was lined with stone. It is thought that the motte was surrounded by a stone-lined ditch. Other stretches of ditch along the sides of the outer bailey, at west and east, have also been revealed. To the west of the motte are the foundations of a Norman rectangular hall. The motte itself was lowered after the siege by digging out the top layers. The remainder of the castle was destroyed at the command of Henry III.

Matthew Paris described the siege, and

and were set alight. When these had burned through, a segment of tower wall collapsed and the besiegers started to move in. This was the signal for the defenders to surrender.

Henry had the ringleaders executed and ordered the castle to be slighted. When de Bréauté returned to the scene he saw his castle in ruins and his brother and others hanging on a line of poles. He fell into a swoon and begged the King's mercy – and was spared.

A thirteenth-century enclosure castle with many flanking towers, Beeston was built on a 152-metre (500-ft) crag overlooking the Vale of Chester.

another appears in the *Dunstable Chronicle*. Paris tells how the great tower was undermined by sappers and brought down. The great tower was cylindrical, as we have seen, and its collapse as a result of undermining, therefore, is a cogent argument against the received view that round towers are superior to rectangular towers when it comes to mining operations.

BEESTON CHESHIRE
(SJ 537593)

The sandstone crag at Beeston is about 152.4 metres (500 ft) above sea level at the top, and it commands one of the gaps in the hill range around Chester on the south and east. In the early 1200s the land belonged to the powerful Ranulf, Earl of Chester, who in about 1220

began to build Beeston Castle. He died in 1232 and his son died in 1237, whereupon the castle passed to the Crown, in the person of Henry III, who enlarged it. In the first years of the fourteenth century major new works were undertaken by Edward, Prince of Wales (later Edward II), including heightening three towers in the inner bailey, and inserting a drawbridge and an extensive wall before the bridge. The names of some of the masons and carpenters who worked there in the 1330s are documented: Master Robert, a carpenter, who also worked at Chester, Scarborough and Windsor in his time, received 6d a day.

The castle consisted of a strongly fortified upper enclosure with flanking D-ended towers and a substantial gatehouse, opening southwards into the lower bailey. The curtain round the tower bailey had seven towers, all of them cylindrical, and an easterly gatehouse. Tall, strong walls were not needed on the north or west sides of the crag. Beeston was maintained in good repair throughout the

fourteenth century and for part of the fifteenth, but in Henry VIII's reign Leland described it as ruinous.

It has many interesting features: one is that the well was cut into the sandstone crag to a depth of about 112.8 metres (370 ft), a prodigious feat (*see also* Bolingbroke Castle).

BELSAY NORTHUMBERLAND
(NZ 085786)

Built in the mid-fourteenth century, Belsay began as a substantial rectangular tower of about 21.3 metres (70 ft) in height to the top of the tallest bartizan, with three storeys, approximately 16.8 x 14.3 metres (55 x 47 ft), and with walls 2.7 metres (9 ft) thick. The tower has four bartizans in the top storey, each of them battlemented and machicolated, as is the rest of the parapet. On the top storey a brattice of stonework projects to cover the entrance door lower down, which is between two projecting wings. The roof of the spiral staircase is partly vaulted; the largest room at ground level has pointed tunnel vaulting and was used as a kitchen. A mansion was added to the castle in the seventeenth century. The tower may have been built by the same masons who built Chipchase and Cartington (qq.v.), as all three incorporate the same masons' marks.

BELVOIR LEICESTERSHIRE
(SK 820337)
Many centuries before the great stately home of the Earls and Dukes of Rutland was erected here, a motte castle was built on a natural mound by Robert de Todeni (or Todnei) some time before 1089. Whatever structures were raised afterwards – and these are thought to have included a shell enclosure – the castle was destroyed by King John. There was some rebuilding, but so much alteration was done by owners in medieval times, by the Earls of Rutland in the sixteenth and seventeenth centuries and by the Dukes of Rutland in the nineteenth, that it bears no resemblance to its original shape.

BENEFIELD NORTHAMPTONSHIRE
(SP 987884)
A rectangular, moated enclosure site, it once contained a castle in the twelfth century, which was confiscated by John c.1208.

BENINGTON HERTFORDSHIRE
(TL 296236)
Benington was raised as a motte castle early in the twelfth century. It is encircled by a wide and deep dry moat. Some time in the mid-twelfth century a small stone tower was erected on the motte, nearly square in plan, about 13.7 x 12.5 metres (45 x 41 ft), with walls 2.1–2.4 metres (7–8 ft) thick. In about 1176 Henry II ordered the tower to be demolished – the Pipe Rolls record payment for a hundred picks for the job – but Benington is mentioned in later years. One other interesting feature at Benington is that on one side there is a depression with two ponds and traces of a dam. This suggests that the depression could have been flooded for defence purposes, as at Saltwood in Kent (q.v.).

BERKELEY GLOUCESTERSHIRE
(ST 685989)
A motte castle was raised here on rising ground overlooking the plains between the Severn and the Cotswolds, probably by William FitzOsbern, one of the Conqueror's commanders at Hastings, who led the invasion of south Wales by the Normans. In the mid-twelfth century the castle became the property of Robert Fitzhardinge, a supporter of Henry II. He received permission to build a castle of stone. The motte was then sliced vertically and trimmed to make it more cylindrical, whereupon the sides were revetted in red sandstone with buttresses, and the stonework continued upwards above the top of the motte. This shell enclosure enclosing a motte is about 18.9 metres (62 ft) tall. It has three small semi-cylindrical turrets in the stonework. A forebuilding was constructed on the wall line between two of the turrets. One of the turrets contains a prison cell in which Edward II is said to have been confined before being murdered in another part of the castle.

The bailey in which this unusual shell enclosure stood was surrounded by a stonework curtain which makes the inner ward. There was a range of buildings inside, which have been replaced by later structures, many of them of fourteenth-century work.

The castle is still in the possession of direct descendants of the Fitzhardinges, the Berkeley family.

BERKHAMSTED HERTFORDSHIRE
(SP 996083)
One excellent way to see at a quick glance what a typical motte castle looked like (without its wooden tower and palisading) in the eleventh century is to visit Berkhamsted Castle. And there is a bonus because you can also see how some motte castles were converted to stone. Enough of the stone curtain round the bailey is standing and there are also traces of the shell enclosure on the motte summit that replaced the wooden palisade round the wooden tower (*see also* Pickering). A further bonus is provided in the restoration of the double moat around the whole castle.

Berkhamsted motte castle belonged to the Conqueror's half-brother Robert of Mortain. The motte was built to about 13.7 metres (45 ft) tall. The bailey, oblong and about 137 x 91.4 metres (450 x 300 ft), is joined to a segment of the motte base. Both motte and bailey were (and are) surrounded by a wet moat, giving the appearance of a castle standing in a lake. Outside the moat is a rampart, which in turn was almost completely encircled by another moat.

The castle received its first stonework in the twelfth century when it belonged to the Crown but was held by various lessees. One was Thomas Becket who held it from about 1155–65 and who spent money on 'the king's houses on the motte', which means buildings. It is thought that he raised the shell enclosure, some 18.3 metres (60 ft) in diameter, where the wooden palisade stood, and the curtain round the bailey, both of flint and rubble with ashlar dressings. Improvements were made to the castle by King John, including wing walls up the south slope of the motte from the bailey and round towers along the bailey curtain (*see plan, p. 19*).

In 1216 Berkhamsted was besieged by Prince Louis of France. The castle fell after a continuous barrage by day for about a fortnight. After John's death, his widow Isabella was allowed to live at the castle and some further works were done. Then in 1227 Henry III gave it to his brother Richard, Duke of Cornwall. He may have built a three-storeyed tower along the western part of the curtain: some foundations of a square tower have been identified. There is also thought to have been a tower inside the shell on the motte, mentioned in a survey of 1327.

In the fourteenth century the castle was given to Edward I's wife, who held it from c.1300 to 1317, and it was then occupied by Edward II's wife until 1326, and up to 1336 by her son John of Eltham. The Black Prince was the next holder. In 1360 Berkhamsted was used as a place of honourable confinement for King John of France who had been captured by the English at the Battle of Poitiers (1356).

BERRY POMEROY
NR TORQUAY, DEVON
(SX 839623)
Berry Pomeroy is on a wooded hill near the River Dart. It is a quadrangular fortified house with an unusual gatehouse whose towers are polygonal. Grooves for the portcullis can still be seen. Over the gateway there is a guardroom, with several loopholes, and this is divided by a wall supported by pillars and almost rounded arches. Berry Pomeroy was probably begun in the twelfth century and later enlarged. The castle became the property of Edward Seymour, Duke of Somerset, who was Lord Protector for part of the reign of the boy-king Edward VI (1547–53). He started to build inside the quadrangle a new Tudor

mansion which is totally out of keeping with the medieval ruins around it.

BERWICK-UPON-TWEED

NORTHUMBERLAND
(NT 994535)
Berwick Castle and Town Fortifications stand on rising ground between the east bank of the mouth of the Tweed and the North Sea. We are concerned only with the castle which was begun in the twelfth century.

It represented a very small part of the area of the fortified town, positioned in its north-west corner. The north-west to south-west wall still standing reaches the edge of the River Tweed. At that point there is the ruin of a cylindrical gun-tower of the fifteenth century. The last and steepest part of it is stepped like a roof step gable, and behind it is an incredibly steep and long flight of stairs known as Breakneck Stairs. At the top of the bluff are the remains of another cylindrical gun-tower.

BEWCASTLE CUMBRIA
(NY 566747)
This was an enclosure castle of uncertain origin. The remains include a small gate-tower on the west side.

BICKLEIGH NR TIVERTON, DEVON
(SS 937068)
A Norman motte castle of the late eleventh or early twelfth century was dismantled in the mid-twelfth. A small stone chapel was built inside the bailey and it is still standing. In the fifteenth century the Courtenay family raised a fortified quadrangular mansion on the site, incorporating some earlier buildings. An interesting gatehouse of the fourteenth century has earlier (Norman) bases to the imposts of the vaulted entry, two rooms on either side opening into the arch, a great hall stretching across the top of the arch at first-floor level, and at one time had a second storey, which was destroyed.

BIGGLESWADE BEDFORDSHIRE
(TK 184445)
A recent survey by aerial photography revealed at Biggleswade the remains of a motte castle with double ditch and a single one about the bailey. Both are curiously segmented with what appear to have been baulks across the ditching (*see Bedfordshire Archaeological Journal* Vol. III, pp. 15–18).

BISHOP'S CASTLE

NR CLUN, SHROPSHIRE
(SO 323891)
This was a motte castle, probably originating from the twelfth century. A shell enclosure was constructed at a later date, and the remaining fragments of stonework down the slope of the motte suggest that there was probably a wall connecting the shell to a curtain round the bailey. Fragments can be seen near the Castle Hotel.

BISHOP'S STORTFORD

HERTFORDSHIRE
(TK 490215)
Sometimes known as Waytemore Castle, Bishop's Stortford started out as a motte castle; remains stand beside Bridge Street. A rectangular tower was built on the motte top early in the twelfth century. The northern end of the tower was slightly curved outwards. In the north-east and south-east corners were sunken chambers. The castle was improved in King John's reign, and a licence to crenellate was granted some time in the mid-1300s, which seems oddly late in the day considering its history. Remains of the tower and the chambers can still be seen on the summit which is surrounded by flint rubble-walling.

BISHOP'S WALTHAM HAMPSHIRE
(SU 552173)
This was a fortified palace begun by Henry of Blois, brother to King Stephen, and Bishop of Winchester from 1129–47. The buildings were ranged round a quadrangle. One was a square tower of three storeys, another was a gatehouse. Possibly the earliest structure was the twelfth-century apsidal chapel which has a Romanesque crypt.

BITCHFIELD

NR BELSAY, NORTHUMBERLAND
(NZ 091771)
Like Belsay Castle, this tower has had a mansion built beside one of its walls. The tower itself, which is rectangular in plan, is three-storeyed and measures about 9.4 x 7 metres (31 x 23 ft). Each storey contained one main room, with a staircase leading to the next. On the first floor a garderobe was inserted in one corner. The tower walls are about 1.2 metres (4 ft) thick along three sides and over 1.8 metres (6 ft) along the north side on the ground floor. The tower has been restored.

BLENKINSOP

NR HALTWHISTLE, NORTHUMBERLAND
(NY 665645)
Blenkinsop is named after its builder, Thomas, who in 1349 was granted a licence to fortify a tower-house. It was square, with 2.1-metre (7-ft)-thick walls, a ditch on two sides and a stream along the third. The castle was later absorbed in rebuilding work of the 1880s.

BLETCHINGLEY SURREY
(TQ 323506)
An early enclosure of earthworks was fortified by the addition of a rectangular tower, with walls about 1.5 metres (5 ft) thick, later in the twelfth century. The castle was associated with Thomas Becket, and held for a time by the powerful de Clare family (*see* Caerphilly). It was besieged and taken by royal forces in the wars between Henry III and some of his barons in the 1260s: 1.5-metre (5-ft)-thick walls were not able to withstand much bombardment with stone shot from trebuchets or mangonels in the mid-thirteenth century.

BOARSTALL BUCKINGHAMSHIRE
(SO 624143)
A fortified manor-house of the late fourteenth century, remodelled much later. An interesting gatehouse remains from its medieval beginnings. Boarstall was licensed in 1312 and was a quadrangular-plan building. It was garrisoned during the Civil War by Parliament, captured by Royalists and retaken by Parliament.

BODIAM SUSSEX
(TQ 785256)
Bodiam Castle stands near the River Rother where it forms the boundary between Kent and Sussex. It was built by a veteran of Edward III's wars in France, a knight with the picturesque name of Sir Edward Dalyngrygge. In 1385 he was granted a licence to fortify his house against invasion from France, as the nearby Cinque Port of Rye had been sacked by the French only a few years earlier.

Dalyngrygge took his licence as one to start building afresh, and he put up his stone castle a little way from the site of his manor-house. He raised a symmetrical quadrangular castle and created an artificial lake round it by letting the river into a rectangle of marshy ground (*see* Chapter 5). The plan of the core, although originally believed square, has since been found to be slightly rhomboid (1990). The four corners of the quadrangle were fortified with substantial four-storeyed cylindrical towers, the east and west walls having square interval towers and the south wall a square postern. The north front has a formidable twin-rectilinear-towered gatehouse. These towers were later provided with gun-ports for covering fire all round the castle by adapting arrow-loops (the fortifications are elaborated on pp. 55–6 and 109–10).

Bodiam's defences were never severely tested: the castle was half-heartedly attacked in 1484; and in the Civil War a Parliamentary army threatened it with bombardment which produced an immediate surrender by the garrison. Thereafter, Bodiam deteriorated until in 1917 a new owner, the Earl Curzon (once Viceroy of India), rescued it and restored its outside elevations to their medieval appearance.

BOLINGBROKE LINCOLNSHIRE
(TF 349649)

Ranulf, Earl of Chester, built two major castles in the 1220s. One was Beeston in Cheshire (q.v.). The other was Bolingbroke, of which there are few remains. Recent excavations described in *Mediaeval Archaeology* have revealed some of its foundations. The layout appears to have been as follows: an irregular hexagonal curtained enclosure of stone with substantial and thick-walled semi-cylindrical towers on four angles; on the fifth the tower was semi-cylindrical but its base was semi-octagonal and there was a twin semi-cylindrical-towered gatehouse on the north-east angle.

Bolingbroke became the property of the Earl of Lancaster in 1311 and passed eventually to John of Gaunt, Duke of Lancaster, fourth son of Edward III, when he married Blanche of Lancaster in 1359. Henry Bolingbroke, later Henry IV (1399–1413), was born there. Works costing more than £1000 were carried out during the reigns of Henry IV and of his son, Henry V (1413–22), and also later in the sixteenth century.

The castle was held for the king in the Civil War, although by that time it had decayed considerably, and the only part of it capable of being defended was the gatehouse.

BOLSOVER DERBYSHIRE
(SK 471707)

An enclosure castle with an outer bailey, the original Bolsover was built in the twelfth century. It received a great tower of stone c.1173–4. More domestic buildings were added in the thirteenth century. Then it was allowed to deteriorate after Edward I and his successors leased the buildings to people not interested in fortification. In the seventeenth century it was ruinous.

It was obtained by Charles Cavendish, one of the ambitious sons of Bess of Hardwick, who began to build Chatsworth. Cavendish decided to rebuild Bolsover in medieval style, but with palatial accommodation, notably the 'Little Castle' which resembled a late medieval tower-house with battlements and corner turrets. The castle was taken by the Parliamentarians in the Civil War but it survived and was renovated.

BOLTON
NR LEYBURN, NORTH YORKSHIRE
(SE 034918)

High on the north slope of Wensleydale stands the considerable fortified manor-house of Bolton Castle. Granted a licence in 1379, Lord Scrope, Richard II's Chancellor, had already begun to build a formidable quadrangle with substantial rectangular corner towers. The builder was John Lewyn, a noted master-mason who also worked at Raby, Bywell and Dunstanburgh, and the building contract for the work has survived. It was constructed from local stone, with quoins and arches in freestone from Greets Quarry a little further away. The owner's quarters were separated from those of his retainers. All doorways into the inner buildings from the courtyard were filled with portcullises. The only entrance to the castle in Scrope's time was a gatehouse in the eastern wing, protected by the south-east tower which at ground level contained a guardhouse. The vaulted passage in the gatehouse was covered at each end by a portcullis. There were several later periods of building, one as late as the present century.

Bolton was held by one of the Scropes for the king in the Civil War, and it was besieged for over a year (1644–5) by Parliament before the garrison surrendered.

BOTHAL NORTHUMBERLAND
(NZ 240866)

Bothal Castle stands by the River Wansbeck, not far from Morpeth. It was a fourteenth-century manor-house which was fortified by its owner by licence in the 1340s. It consisted of a walled enclosure with towers and buildings. The main feature was, and still is, a splendid square gatehouse-tower with twin turrets with semi-octagonal front ends flanking the entrance, this being a vaulted passage in which are murder-holes and portcullis grooves. On the first floor is the great chamber, or hall, which was considerably embellished in later centuries. A survey of the 1570s recorded that Bothal was notable for 'fair gardens and orchards, wherein grow all kinds of herbs and flowers, and fine apples, plums of all kind, pears, nuttes, wardens, cherries…'.

0   8m

Bothal: plan of the ground floor of the gatehouse-tower with twin turrets.

BOURN CAMBRIDGESHIRE
(TL 322562)

Bourn was an earthwork enclosure with wooden buildings and was erected in the last years of the reign of the Conqueror. It was demolished in the time of Henry III, and

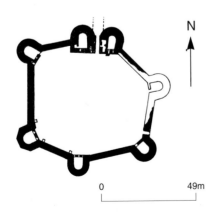

0   49m

Bolingbroke: plan.

Bourn Hall was built across part of the site. The original castle was held by the Picot family, one of whom was Sheriff of Cambridgeshire and as such is mentioned in Domesday.

BOURNE LINCOLNSHIRE
(TF 095199)
A motte castle of unusual plan was built here. The mound stood inside a bailey surrounded by a ditch and further encircled by another ditch, in concentric plan. It was raised in the later part of the twelfth century. Stonework was added in the thirteenth century, but there is no masonry to be seen.

BOWES DURHAM
(NY 992135)
This is one of Henry II's great tower castles. It was built in a corner of an old Roman fort overlooking the Yorkshire approach to the Stainforth Pass between the years 1170 and 1187. The recorded cost of about £600 may not represent the full expense, for the great tower, at 25 x 18.3 metres (82 x 60 ft) and probably reaching about 21.3 metres (70 ft) high, was a massive structure for its time, with pilaster buttresses at the corners and in the wall centres and with walls about 3.3 metres (11 ft) thick. It had mural chambers, vaulted passages in the walls, an off-centre cross-wall with the larger sector possibly divided by a second cross-wall, and a forebuilding on the east wall (now vanished).

Bowes' great tower is remarkable in that it appears to have been constructed on its own, with no buildings around it. It was built chiefly as a defence against Scottish raids. The tower is now in ruins.

BRAMBER NR STEYNING, SUSSEX
(TQ 185107)
This began as a 12.2-metre (40-ft) motte inside a D-shaped bailey beside the Adur, probably in the 1070s. The bailey is on a natural knoll which was flattened, and was surrounded at first with a wooden palisade. In the early twelfth century it was given a stone curtain. A square-plan gatehouse was inserted in the curtain, about 11.5 x 12.2 metres (38 x 40 ft), pierced by an entrance. Later in the century the entrance was blocked so the gatehouse could be given another storey and thus be converted to a gatehouse-tower. An alternative entrance to the castle was provided by a new gateway in the curtain nearby.

Recent excavations revealed the existence of buildings inside the curtain near the gateway, and that the curtain appears to have had more than one phase of construction. It was rebuilt in the fourteenth century using the early twelfth-century wall as the foundations. Bramber's chapel was not built inside the bailey but in a separate enclosure surrounded by ditching, just south of the gateway. Only fragments remain of the buildings.

BRAMPTON BRYAN
HEREFORD & WORCESTER
(SO 370726)
This fortress belonged to the Harley family. It has been considerably altered and extended, and the original form obscured. Brampton was a motte castle probably of the early twelfth century which, in the fourteenth century, received a curtain with towers and a square-plan gatehouse with a long barbican projecting outwards.

BRANCEPETH DURHAM
(NZ 223377)
Brancepeth Castle is largely a nineteenth-century restoration round the remains of a fourteenth-century castle that belonged to the Nevilles. The Neville castle followed an even earlier Norman building.

BRANDON
NR WOLSTON, WARWICKSHIRE
(SP 40875)
An earthwork enclosure of the early twelfth century whose ditches were provided with water from the River Avon by means of sluices. In the thirteenth century (c.1226) a great tower of unusual shape was added: it was rectangular with the centre of its two longer walls indented, providing a plan in the form of an 'H'. The indents were blank arches, each being 1.5 metres (5 ft) deep. The tower was held for Henry III during his war with Simon de Montfort and the barons, 1264–5. Some earthworks and some stone fragments remain.

BREDWARDINE
HEREFORD & WORCESTER
(SO 335444)
Traces of the stone walls of a rectangular great tower, about 23.8 x 13.7 metres (78 x 45 ft), are on a platform here beside the River Wye. This was probably of late twelfth-century construction. Beside it is an earlier mound which also had stonework.

BRIDGNORTH SHROPSHIRE
(SO 717927)
An enclosure castle on the narrow ridge of rock in Bridgnorth beside the River Severn, it was first mentioned in 1102. But its principal feature, a square great tower, was not built until the reign of Henry II who had taken the castle from the Mortimers (supporters of Stephen) in 1155. The great tower, of which only some ruined walls remain, is of cut and dressed sandstone, with pilaster buttresses. It leans about 10 degrees off the vertical. There was a forebuilding which has gone. The castle was severely damaged during the Civil War.

BRIDGWATER SOMERSET
(ST 302378)
William de Briwerre was licensed to build a castle at Bridgwater c.1200. It appears to have been a rectangular enclosure. There is part of a water-gate beside the River Parrett in the town. During the Civil War, Bridgwater Castle was fortified by the Royalists but nevertheless fell to the Parliamentarians.

BRIGHTWELL BERKSHIRE
(SI 578908)
The mound of an early twelfth-century motte castle can be seen near the village church.

BRIMPSFIELD GLOUCESTERSHIRE
(SC 941148)
There are some fragments on the site of a thirteenth-century castle here. The shape has not been determined.

BRINKLOW WARWICKSHIRE
(SP 438796)
A motte castle was raised at Brinklow in the early twelfth century. The motte was about 12.2 metres (40 ft) high. The bailey, surrounded by ditch and ramparts, was cut in two by another ditch with ramparts.

BRISTOL AVON
(ST 594732)
There is very little to see of the ancient castle of Bristol. A motte castle was raised on land between the Avon and the Frome, probably in the reign of the Conqueror. In King Stephen's reign, Bristol received a rectangular great tower said to have been about 27.4 x 22.9 metres (90 x 75 ft) and perhaps about 21.3 metres (70 ft) tall. This great tower was described in the thirteenth century (in Robert of Gloucester's *Chronicle*) as the flower of

English great towers. It had four corner turrets, one higher than the other three, and a forebuilding. Excavations of 1951 revealed traces of a substantial curtain wall, and work of the late 1960s produced evidence of a gateway and some tunnelling. Later still, a west tower in the curtain was found.

The castle was taken over by Henry II after the 1173–4 revolt led by his eldest son, and it remained in Crown hands up to the 1650s when, already in a state of deterioration, it was destroyed.

BROMWICH WEST MIDLANDS
(SP 158904)
A motte castle of unknown date was excavated here in 1968–9. Evidence of timber plank lining of the motte was uncovered.

BRONSIL HEREFORD & WORCESTER
(SO 749372)
A few remains of a fortified quadrangular manor-house, with corner and mid-wall towers, have been dated to the fifteenth century. The castle was surrounded by a moat.

BROUGH CUMBRIA
(NY 791141)
Brough stands in one corner of the remains of a rectangular Roman fort. The first work was a roughly triangular enclosure of stone begun late in the eleventh century, making Brough one of the earliest castles in Britain to have stonework. There are several building periods. Part of the original curtain on the north side has characteristic Norman herringbone masonry. The castle belonged to the de Morvilles until it was surrendered to Henry II in 1173, when soon afterwards it was attacked by William the Lion, King of Scotland, who captured it after a hard fight. But he was himself taken by the English under the walls of Alnwick Castle later in 1174, and Brough was returned to Henry II who granted it to Theobald de Valoires. He erected a rectangular great tower upon the remains of a previous tower in the west angle of the enclosure in the wall circumference, destroyed in William the Lion's siege.

The newer tower, about 16.8 x 12.2 metres (55 x 40 ft), was four-storeyed, built of sandstone-dressed rubble, with pilaster buttresses on the angles and centrally in the north and south walls. It was restored in the seventeenth century by Anne Clifford, Countess of Dorset, Pembroke and Montgomery (owner also of Brougham, q.v.). One of her works was the cylindrical tower in the south-east corner, called Clifford's Tower.

Brough: this twelfth-century castle was erected within the stone enclosure of a second-century Roman fort.

BROUGHAM NR PENRITH, CUMBRIA
(NY 537290)
A roughly quadrilateral enclosure on the south bank of the River Eamont, Brougham received stonework in the time of Henry II, probably about 1170. One of the first buildings was a substantial square great tower built of sandstone rubble, having ashlar dressings. The tower has pilaster angle buttresses on north, west and south walls, and on the east wall is a forebuilding. The tower appears to have been erected in two stages, the first three storeys followed by a top storey whose stonework is of better quality than the earlier work. Other buildings were added in later periods, the last being by the aged Anne Clifford, Countess of Dorset, Pembroke and Montgomery, who had enormous wealth and was owner also of Appleby and Brough castles. Anne Clifford restored all three castles to make them habitable. She died in Brougham Castle in 1678 at the (then) great age of almost 90.

BROUGHTON OXFORDSHIRE
(SP 418382)
Broughton is substantially a sixteenth-century house surrounded by a broad wet moat. It has some fourteenth-century military remains such as towers and battlements. The moat used to be crossed by a causeway into a barbican. During the early part of the Civil War, the castle was used for clandestine meetings of the opponents of Charles I. When the Royalists won the first major battle of the war at the nearby Edgehill, they then raced on to Broughton and captured it.

BRYN AMLWG SHROPSHIRE
(SO 167846)
Some remains of stone walling round an enclosure castle of the twelfth and thirteenth centuries, which had towers and a gatehouse, are to be found on this site, which is now privately owned.

BUCKDEN CAMBRIDGESHIRE
(TL 192677)
Buckden was for many years a residential palace, used by Bishops of Lincoln, including the famous Robert Grosseteste (1190–1252) who may have built a hall on the site. In the late fifteenth century, considerable building works were undertaken, including a brick gatehouse, a rebuilt hall and chapel, and a

great tower within the assemblage of other buildings, all surrounded by a moat and a stone curtain round the grounds, altering the palace into a castle by virtue of these fortifications.

BUCKINGHAM BUCKINGHAMSHIRE
(SP 695337)

There was a motte castle on the north side of the Ouse in Buckingham sited in a loop in the river which acted as the bailey. It may have been a castle held by the Giffard family. The site has been covered by a church, for which the motte would have had to have been levelled. Stone foundations were discovered in excavations on the motte site.

BUNGAY SUFFOLK
(TM 336896)

A motte castle erected in a loop of the Waveney at Bungay may date from the early twelfth century. The motte has been levelled. The castle was held by the Bigods who were powerful in East Anglia. In 1154 it was held by Hugh Bigod, but in 1157 Henry II confiscated it, restoring it to the earl c.1164.

Bigod then converted the castle to stone. The levelled motte received a substantial great tower, 21.3 metres (70 ft) square, rising, it is estimated, to about 27.4 metres (90 ft), with walls 5.5 metres (18 ft) thick. Only foundations up to the level of ground-floor loops remain. The great tower, which had a cross-wall, and a staircase in the north wall, was given a forebuilding over an entrance on the south wall. One dramatic discovery in the excavations of the early 1930s was an uncompleted mining gallery dug under the south-west corner of the great tower. This may have been dug when, after Bigod had joined Henry II's eldest son, Prince Henry, in his unsuccessful 1173–4 revolt, the king confiscated Bungay (among other estates) and began to demolish the great tower. The demolition was stayed on payment of a ransom, but the great tower decayed and was finally pulled down. It appears that it was later restored in some form.

In the 1290s, Roger Bigod, descendant of Earl Hugh, was granted permission to rebuild Bungay. He built a multangular curtain enclosure (somewhat similar in concept to

The twelfth-century great tower complex at Brougham, which was the first building in this quadrilateral enclosure.

Framlingham, which had been erected by Hugh Bigod's son), but without flanking towers. In the west of the curtain is a pair of twin cylindrical-towered ends flanking an entrance. These are the remains of a gatehouse, and there is argument as to whether this is the work of the 1290s or of a much earlier date. Parts of the curtain and the gatehouse remain.

BURGH SUFFOLK
(TG 475046)

This is the site of one of the famous Roman forts of the Saxon shore, built by the Roman occupying forces in Britain along the east coast in the third century AD. In early Norman times a small motte castle was raised in one corner of the fort quadrangle. The mound was levelled in 1839, but the ditch that separated the mound from the bailey has been identified by aerial photography.

BURLEY LEICESTERSHIRE
(SK 894119)
A motte castle of late eleventh-, early twelfth-century origin; it was excavated in the 1930s.

BURTON-IN-LONSDALE
NORTH YORKSHIRE
(SD 649721)
A motte castle with two baileys, probably of the early twelfth century. It is first mentioned in 1129, although the estate is noted in Domesday as belonging to the king. The motte was constructed of sand coated with clay. The bases of the ditches were paved with stone of varying sizes (cf. Bedford). The castle's history from the early twelfth century to the early fourteenth century is unknown, but in 1322 it was confiscated from the Mowbrays who held it in opposition to Edward II. The mound is visible.

BURWELL
NR CAMBRIDGE, CAMBRIDGESHIRE
(TL 587661)
A rectangular banked platform enclosed by a wide moat, this castle was excavated in the 1930s and found to have been raised on the site of a late Roman-British structure. The castle was built in the time of King Stephen (1135–54). The diggings revealed stonework remains of a curtain wall and a gatehouse of square plan with buttresses angled at 45 degrees on the two corners projecting into the ditch. It is clear the castle was not completed. There are some fragments near the church.

BUTTERCRAMBE
NR YORK, NORTH YORKSHIRE
(SE 533584)
William de Stuteville, who held Knaresborough Castle from about 1173 to 1203, was granted a licence to fortify a castle at Buttercrambe c.1200. The castle was probably a motte castle, although the remains have been greatly disfigured by later building work. If it was a motte castle, it was a late example. Motte castles were still 'thrown up' if a fortress was needed quickly for some purpose in the thirteenth century. With their wooden towers they made good watch-towers. The motte is still visible.

BYTHAM NR BOURNE, LINCOLNSHIRE
(SK 992186)
On a hill overlooking the village of Little Bytham stands the mound of the motte castle built possibly before 1086 and certainly by 1140. The earthworks contain traces of stonework, although not enough to say anything conclusive about the form which the castle originally took.

BYWELL NORTHUMBERLAND
(NZ 049618)
The main feature of Bywell was (and still is) its huge gatehouse-tower. Built in the 1430s by the Nevilles, Bywell backed on to the River Tyne. The gatehouse is a three-storeyed structure about 18.3 metres (60 ft) wide and 11.5 metres (38 ft) deep. A 3-metre (10-ft) arch and passage lead through the centre of the ground floor whose main rooms on either side are vaulted. It has machicolations on the battlements: there is a short stretch directly over the central arch, and on the tower corners are the remains of octagonal turrets

that are machicolated. The entrance was protected by a portcullis.

CAINHOE

Nr Clophill, Bedfordshire
(TL 097374)
An earthwork castle of the late eleventh or early twelfth century, with a motte and three baileys well protected by ditches. Stonework was added, but as yet the nature of the castle in its final form is not known. Some excavations were undertaken in 1972–3.

CAISTER Nr Yarmouth, Norfolk

(TG 504123)
Caister Castle was built between 1432 and 1446 by a self-made adventurer and knight, Sir John Fastolf, who acquired a fortune after many years of distinguished military service. The building work is particularly interesting because many details of the materials, labour and costs have survived. One of these was a note of an attempt by one mason, Henry Wood, to overcharge for his work.

Caister was built of locally made brick. The castle has a double enclosure in the form of two quadrangles surrounded entirely by water. The outer quadrangle was linked to the inner by a drawbridge, and was itself approached from outside by another drawbridge, on its north side. The inner quadrangle contained the main living quarters. The principal feature of the castle, however, was, and still is, the very tall, slim, cylindrical great tower, 27.4 metres (90 ft) with five storeys of residential accommodation, but equipped with machicolated parapet, gun-ports at several levels, and constructed of walls 1.2 metres (4 ft) thick. Adjacent to the cylindrical tower is a hexagonal turret running from ground level up to a little higher than the top of the tower. The top of the turret is pierced with gun-ports on each facet, for hand-guns. These were employed on at least two occasions, one of them in 1458 against the French.

Caister was occupied for a time by the well-known Norfolk family Paston, whose letters of the fifteenth century have survived to give a remarkable view of country life of the period.

(Left) Caister is a mid-fifteenth-century castle built largely of brick. Its cylindrical great tower is over 27 metres (90 ft) tall.

CAISTOR Lincolnshire

(TA 116012)
A mound near the church is possibly the remnant of a motte castle of the Anarchy (c.1140) – the prolonged civil war which followed Stephen usurping Matilda's throne.

CALLALY

Nr Whittingham, Northumberland
(NU 051099)
The present mansion at Callaly stands near the site of a motte castle raised in the twelfth century. A pele-tower was built in the fifteenth century and this forms part of the mansion which is seventeenth century with nineteenth-century improvements. The pele was 12.8 x 11.9 metres (42 x 39 ft) and rose to three storeys.

CAMBRIDGE Cambridgeshire

(TL 446592)
The mound in front of Shire Hall in Castle Street, Cambridge, is the sole remnant, except for earthworks, of a once important medieval castle. The motte was raised c.1068, and 27 houses were demolished to make room for it.

Some time, probably in the late twelfth century, the castle received its first stonework. There is a record of a charge of £41 for transporting stone, lime and sand for Cambridge Castle c.1190. Thereafter work on the castle was desultory.

Then in the years 1283–99 major works were undertaken by Edward I. They included a stone curtain, with gatehouse, barbican, cylindrical angle towers, a great tower on the motte, and a hall. These works amounted to the sum of £2630. Then the king appears to have lost interest.

In the fourteenth century the castle was 'raided' for stone to build colleges. By 1600 only a gatehouse was left complete. The castle was refortified during the Civil War, but slighted afterwards.

CANTERBURY Kent

(TR 145574)
An early motte castle raised before 1086, Canterbury was a royal castle for most of its history. It received a substantial great tower, on a sloping plinth, about 27.4 x 22.9 metres (90 x 75 ft), of which only the lower part survives. Various dates for the tower have been suggested: late eleventh century, *temp.* Henry I, and even early Henry II; but it remains unsettled. The great tower was of flint

A view of what remains of the massive twelfth-century rectangular great tower at Canterbury.

rubble with dressings of Caen stone and sandstone. It had pilaster buttresses on the angles and mid-wall, and had two cross-walls inside. It had two spiral staircases, one in the east corner and one on the south-west wall in the section of wall supported by the mid-wall pilaster buttress. Foundations of a forebuilding along the north-west wall were found recently, and excavations in 1975–6 revealed fragments of the great tower buried in the castle ditch which had been located for the first time.

The castle had gates, barbican, bridge, chapel and other buildings, chiefly of later

Canterbury: ground-floor plan of the great tower (after King's Works).

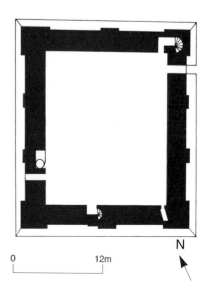

0   12m

N

twelfth- and thirteenth-century work. In 1380 a new gate with towers was built as part of a general move to improve the fortifications of many castles in the south-eastern counties.

CARISBROOKE Isle of Wight
(SZ 486877)

A very early Norman motte castle built c.1070. The motte rose to over 18.3 metres (60 ft). It was erected beside a bailey which was a raised platform of earth surrounded by ditching. By 1136, the motte had received an irregular polygonal shell enclosure built of squared rubble on the mound. A rectangular-plan stone curtain round the raised bailey has flanking square turrets on the south-west and south-east corners (converted in the 1580s into star-pointed gun-turrets for coastal defence). The shell enclosure has a buttress on the north side. It was once taller than it is at present, although the floor of the parapet walkway remains, and to the north is the well sunk to some 48.8 metres (160 ft). The north stretch of curtain wall ascends the motte to the shell and protects a flight of steps into the gateway on the west side of the shell. On the west side of the curtain is a twin cylindrical-turreted gatehouse with parapet machicolation over the central chevron-head arched entrance. The gatehouse is basically c.1335, with some later additions, and has grooves for three portcullises. The doors to the entrance are at least five centuries old.

The bailey inside the curtain has received a variety of buildings, erected against the inside wall and free-standing, sufficient for the castle to be a residence of some elaboration.

The castle was besieged in 1377 by a French commando force but the garrison held out. Carisbrooke is also famous for acting as the place of confinement for Charles I for a period after the First Civil War.

CARLISLE Cumbria
(NY 397563)

The earliest structure at Carlisle was a wooden, palisaded enclosure on the high bluff overlooking the River Eden. This was raised by William Rufus in 1092, in approximately triangular plan. Henry I is recorded as having ordered a 'castle and towers' to be raised to fortify the city in 1122, but what buildings followed this order is not clear, except for walling round the city, and those may well have been of wood. Carlisle was surrendered

to David I, King of Scotland, by Stephen in 1136. Some time between 1136 and 1174 the massive great tower was built, but whether by David I who held Carlisle until 1153, or his successor Malcolm IV, or Henry II of England who recovered it in 1157, we do not know. The dimensions were 20.4 x 18.3 metres (67 x 60 ft), and 20 metres (65 ft) high, approximately cuboid, like Dover although this is coincidental. It has been substantially altered over the years, but some features remain, such as the clasping pilaster buttresses on the corners. There was a forebuilding in Norman style, which contained a straight staircase to the first-floor entrance. The alterations have been considerable, and they are summarised in the Department of the Environment's booklet on Carlisle Castle.

Note the inner enclosure, whose north-east wall is deep-buttressed, with a fourteenth-century gatehouse at its south-eastern end. The inner enclosure occupies the north-eastern corner of the much larger outer enclosure whose curtain wall has several flanking towers.

CARLTON Nr Louth, Lincolnshire
(TF 395835)

A motte and some ditching survive from a (?) twelfth-century motte castle built here by the Bardolph family. The mound remains.

CARTINGTON
Nr Rothbury, Northumberland
(NU 039045)

Early in the fifteenth century a tall rectangular tower was built under the shadow of the Rothbury hills. It was about 12.5 x 9.4 metres (41 x 31 ft), with 1.8-metre (6-ft) thick walls. The tower was part of a quadrangle of buildings which were greatly altered in later years, with the result that the original ruins are partly obscured.

CARY Nr Wincanton, Somerset
(ST 641322)

There are remains of the foundations of a substantial great tower at Castle Cary, which had been built of rubble with ashlar facing. The tower, almost square in plan, was about 23.8 metres (78 ft) wide, and appears to have been enclosed within banks and moat, some of the banks being of later date. The great tower had a cross-wall. Dating is difficult, but there is mention of the castle in the time of Stephen. The tower is later twelfth century.

CASTLE ACRE
Nr Swaffham, Norfolk
(TF 819152)

Castle Acre has been the subject of some interesting excavations in recent years. It began as a Norman motte castle c.1080, or perhaps earlier, raised by the de Warennes, Earls of Surrey. The mound was low and it received its first stonework some time before the end of the eleventh century, when a hall-tower was built on it. It is unlikely that the hall was intended to be a fortified building. The lower courses of this have survived. Before the end of the century, the excavations suggest, a simple stonework gatehouse was erected in the perimeter of the wooden palisade round the motte.

The hall-tower was about 22 metres (72 ft) square, with a cross-wall, and a door in the south wall. Some time in the twelfth century, the castle was strengthened. The motte was enclosed by a polygonal-plan flint rubble curtain wall, raised upon heightened ramparts. Curtain walling was raised round the bailey, and the level of the bailey was raised in places. The hall-tower also received some attention. Interestingly, the tower walls were thickened inside: the evidence for this is instantly apparent. What was happening? The Ancient Monuments Inspectorate of the DoE considers that the hall-tower was being transformed into a fortified great tower. Then, probably about 1150, the work was halted and the southern half of the tower was pulled down, but work was continued on the north half. The curtain wall was also heightened in places, and the gatehouse was strengthened. The castle was being refortified. Excavations are continuing and more information will emerge.

CASTLE COMBE Wiltshire
(ST 837777)

There are some remains of a medieval castle behind the manor-house to the north of Castle Combe village. The castle began as a cluster of earthwork and timber enclosures with ditching, probably during the twelfth century. Some of the enclosure walling was converted to stone and some free-standing buildings were erected.

CASTLE RISING
Nr King's Lynn, Norfolk
(TF 666246)

Castle Rising stands in an enormous area of man-made ditches and banks (about 4.8

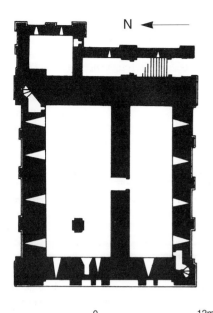

Castle Rising: plan of the ground floor of the great tower on this site.

hectares [12 acres]), which are in a fine state of preservation. The inner bailey, sandwiched between two smaller outer baileys, contains two buildings: the foundations of a Norman chapel of the eleventh century, raised before the great tower which is dated c.1138–40; and perched on the top of the inner bank of the inner bailey are the remains of the gatehouse, a rectangular tower pierced by an entrance passage with a room over, built at much the same time as the great tower.

The great tower is a squat, rectangular donjon whose horizontal dimensions, at 24 x 20.9 metres (78½ x 68½ ft), are greater than the height which reaches to 15.2 metres (50 ft) today, and was several feet higher when it had its parapet and tops to the corner turrets. The corner turrets are clasped by pilaster buttresses and there are three more shallow pilaster buttresses along each of three of the four sides. The fourth side has a forebuilding (with its own clasping corner pilaster buttresses) rising to the same height as the great tower. This is reached by a two-flight staircase behind a stout wall adjoining the forebuilding. The stairs begin to rise just behind a round Norman arch with corbelled frieze which is on the south front at the east end of the tower. Note the blind arch decoration of the higher level of the protecting wall. The great tower has an

off-centre cross-wall all the way up. Both side walls and the cross-wall have chambers and passages.

Built by William d'Albini, Earl of Sussex, Castle Rising was for some 30 years the home of Isabella, mother of Edward III. She was sent there by her son after he broke up the conspiracy between herself and her lover, Roger Mortimer.

CASTLETHORPE
HANSLOPE, BUCKINGHAMSHIRE
(SP 798446)

This was a motte castle with two baileys, and it was raised in the twelfth century. The castle was besieged and destroyed in 1215–16 by Faulkes de Bréauté who captured Bedford Castle in 1215. In 1292 William Beauchamp was granted a licence to crenellate a wall that he had built round a house and garden which appear to have stood on or near the motte castle site. Some traces still remain of the original earthworks.

CAUS SHROPSHIRE
(SJ 337078)

An eleventh-century motte castle covering an area of about 2.4 hectares (6 acres), Caus received a shell enclosure on the motte in the following century, as well as a rectangular curtain round the inner bailey. The curtain had cylindrical towers on each of the corners. The stonework was protected by extensive earthworks, which included double ditching. The castle was demolished during the Civil War and there are very few remains still visible today.

CAWOOD NORTH YORKSHIRE
(SE 573376)

An ecclesiastical fortified residence was built here in the fourteenth century. The gatehouse, a stone-clad brick structure, survives amid some farm buildings now occupying the site.

CHALGRAVE
NR TODDINGTON, BEDFORDSHIRE
(TK 009274)

Chalgrave was a motte castle of twelfth-century beginnings, whose motte once buttressed a square wooden building, which may have been a tower. The tower was dismantled and the motte was enlarged. Part of the bank surrounding the bailey was faced with stone.

CHARLTON
NR THE WREKIN, SHROPSHIRE
(SJ 597112)

There are fragments of earthworks of a thirteenth- and fourteenth-century castle here.

CHARTLEY STOWE, STAFFORDSHIRE
(SK 101285)

A motte castle with two baileys (created by a ditch that divided one bailey), which had a cylindrical tower on the summit. The tower had a small projecting lobe. Around the inner bailey was raised a rectangular-plan curtain along two adjacent sides, with semi-cylindrical turrets. The stonework is probably thirteenth century.

CHENEY LONGVILLE SHROPSHIRE
(SO 417847)

The remains of a moated castle of quadrangular plan round a courtyard, built c.1394 (when the licence was granted), are associated with a much later house on the site.

CHESTER CHESHIRE
(SJ 404657)

The Conqueror raised a motte castle here, with inner and outer bailey, just outside the site of the old Roman town, in 1069–70. For a time it was leased to the Earls of Chester but it is not possible to say much about its first 150 years. There are remains of what is considered a twelfth-century square tower on the motte. In 1237 the castle came into royal ownership, and an extensive improvement programme began soon afterwards. This was the start of the major stonework, which was partly new work and partly rebuilding of earlier work of

Chester in the eighteenth century. Ground plan dated 1769. C = Caesar's Tower. G = great hall. I = inner bailey.

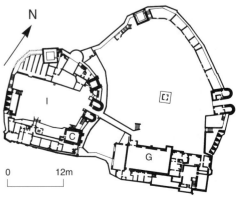

stone and wood. Henry III raised the outer bailey curtain with a tower and rebuilt the great hall. Edward I rebuilt the outer gatehouse and put up new domestic buildings. The inner gatehouse, leading into the inner bailey, is probably of the same period. Repairs and small improvements were carried out on a regular basis over the years up to the close of the fifteenth century. Chester was besieged in the Civil War.

CHICHESTER SUSSEX
(SU 863051)

A very early motte castle was built on the site of the north gate of Roman Chichester by Roger de Montgomery, one of the Conqueror's principal lords and commanders, c.1066–7. In time the castle passed to the Albini family (cf. Castle Rising); Philip d'Aubigny (Albini), one owner of the castle, was ordered to demolish it by King John, but he evidently ignored the command for he was told again to demolish it by John's son, Henry III, in 1217. The castle was destroyed a few years later and a Grey Friars priory built on the site of the bailey. There are earthwork remains on the site.

CHILHAM NR CANTERBURY, KENT
(TR 066533)

Chilham was a great tower castle inside a curtained enclosure surrounded by a ditch, a conventional plan for the twelfth century. The great tower was of polygonal shape

Chilham: ground floor of the great tower, with forebuilding c.1171–5.

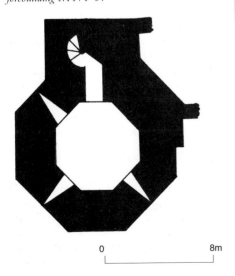

0   8m

(octagonal, with one side projecting into a turret to contain the spiral staircase). The tower was built of Kentish ragstone and dressed with ashlar quoins on the corners. The period of construction was between c.1171 and 1175, during which time over £400 was spent by Henry II who had taken it over as a royal fortress (cf. Tickhill, Odiham, Orford). The great tower has been partly restored but is not open to visitors. It can, however, be seen from the gardens.

CHILLINGHAM NORTHUMBERLAND
(NV 070249)

In 1344 a licence to fortify and crenellate his family mansion at Chillingham was granted to Thomas Heton. The structure seems to have been a quadrangle with corner towers. It has been extensively rebuilt.

CHIPCHASE
NR HAUGHTON, NORTHUMBERLAND
(NY 882757)

Chipchase Castle is today an imposing structure on the western bank of the North Tyne. The fortified part is principally the fourteenth-century rectangular tower, 15.5 x 10.3 metres (51 x 34 ft), which is at one end of the later Jacobean mansion. The tower is 15.2 metres (50 ft) tall and has machicolated cylindrical turrets on the angles reaching to another 3 metres (10 ft), with machicolation along the walls between. The entrance was guarded by an oak portcullis which is still *in situ*. The tower is four-storeyed and the parapet, battlement and turret area forms a fifth floor.

CHRISTCHURCH HAMPSHIRE
(SZ 160927)

A motte castle was raised here c.1100 by Richard de Redvers, cousin of Henry I. The motte received a rectangular great tower, about 15.2 x 13.7 metres (50 x 45 ft), with walls 2.7 metres (9 ft) thick. It was three storeys high, built of Freshwater limestone and local ironstone with ashlar dressings of Purbeck, Binstead and other stones. The great tower has not been dated beyond a presumption that it is c.1300. Beside a stream in the castle bailey there are the remains of a rectangular Norman hall of mid-twelfth-century construction. The south-east corner has a projection right into the stream and contains garderobes. The hall has angle and mid-wall buttresses. The ground floor was lit

by short arrow-loops in the stream-side wall and one other.

CHURCH STRETTON SHROPSHIRE
(SO 448926)

Also called Brockhurst Castle. A motte castle overlooking the terrain between Shrewsbury and Ludlow, protected by natural hills. Stonework curtain walling was found in recent excavations.

CLARE SUFFOLK
(TL 772452)

Clare Castle began as a motte of the late eleventh century. It had two baileys (in one of which the nineteenth-century railway station was erected). A polygonal shell enclosure was built round the motte top some time in the twelfth century, possibly by the de Clare family whose descendants became powerful in south Wales in the thirteenth century and built the castle at Caerphilly. Traces of a wall, which led down the motte slope from the shell to join up with the curtain around one bailey, have been found. Some remains are visible in Clare Park.

CLAVERING NR NEWPORT, ESSEX
(TL 471320)

Although it is now generally accepted that no castles, not even motte castles, were built in England before 1066, the enclosure at Clavering was for a long time considered to have been a structure raised by a Norman lord at the encouragement of Edward the Confessor. The moat round the enclosure was fed by the River Stort which may have driven a watermill nearby.

CLAXTON NR NORWICH, NORFOLK
(TG 335038)

This fourteenth-century enclosure castle, whose remains today consist of a long stretch of wall with six flanking towers, was licensed in 1333. On the north side of the south face are traces of a hall, with staircases and upper rooms. The ruins stand inside an area which is partly surrounded by a moat.

CLEOBURY
CLEOBURY MORTIMER, SHROPSHIRE
(SO 681761)

Earthworks beside the river here are possibly the remains of an early twelfth-century castle which is recorded as having been pulled down, perhaps by Henry II, in 1155.

CLIFFORD HEREFORD & WORCESTER
(SO 243457)

There are indications of three castles in this area. One was a simple motte castle near Old Castleton (SO 283457), probably the one mentioned in Domesday and thought to have been built c.1070. The second was another motte castle known locally as Newton Tump (SO 293441). The third, at grid reference SO 243457, near the church, was a motte castle on earthworks, about 1.4 hectares (3¹/₂ acres) in area. This was given a polygonal enclosure of local sandstone with five round towers, two of them flanking a gate, and a hall building, in the thirteenth century. The castle was held by the Clifford family and later passed to the Mortimers. Substantial remains have survived.

CLIFFORD'S TOWER YORK
(SE 605515)

A motte raised in 1069–70 on the north side of the Ouse – built of marl and clay in layers, with gravel and stones above and with layers of timber – supported a timber great tower. It was burnt down during the anti-Jewish riots in York c.1190, and rebuilt, which involved raising the height of the motte to the present height of 18.3 metres (60 ft). Then in 1228 the second tower was blown down in a severe gale. In 1245 Henry III ordered the rebuilding of the castle and over the next 25 years a curtain with several towers and two gateways was raised round the bailey, while on the motte was built an unusual great tower, now called Clifford's Tower. The plan of the tower is quatrefoil, in some respects similar to the great tower of Étampes, some 34.8 km (30 miles) south of Paris, which was built c.1140. A forebuilding was inserted at Clifford's between the in-turning arcs of two adjoining 'foils'. The timber joists of the ground/first floor were supported by corbels in the inner wall masonry (a few can still be seen). A portcullis was inserted in the inside archway to the exit.

CLITHEROE LANCASHIRE
(SD 742416)

A motte castle built on a natural rock outcrop was given a square great tower, about 10.7 metres (35 ft) wide, of limestone rubble dressed with ashlar. The tower corners have pilaster buttresses. The stonework is probably twelfth century, and the tower is among the smallest of the great towers. It has no garderobe and no fireplace, and the thick walls

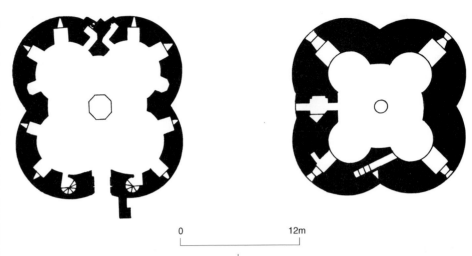

(Left) Clifford's Tower: quatrefoil in plan, this tower was built between 1245 and 1270, and has been compared with the great tower at Étampes (ground plan on right). Étampes was built between 1130 and 1150.

contain no useful chambers, leaving the core of the tower incapable of providing comfortable quarters. The castle belonged to the de Lacy family, but in 1399 it became Crown property. At some time the tower was surrounded by a curtain wall.

CLUN SHROPSHIRE
(SO 298809)

The castle at Clun began as a substantial motte castle with two baileys, close to the junction of the rivers Clun and Usk. The motte was joined to the baileys by causeways. In the twelfth century the top of the motte was surrounded with a stone curtain of irregular shape, with a twin-turreted gateway. Down the north slope of the motte a rectangular great tower, some 24.4 metres (80 ft) tall, was erected (c.1160), half on, half off, with its base at ground level. The great tower has buttressed corners and three storeys with a basement, the top three floors provided with windows (*see* Guildford). The tower, although derelict, is still upright.

COCKERMOUTH CUMBRIA
(NY 123309)

Cockermouth was built in the thirteenth century on a site by the junction of the rivers Cocker and Derwent, which gave it water defences for most of its flanks. It was an enclosure castle with curtains, towers and an

inner gatehouse. Considerable modifications, including an outer gatehouse and barbican, were made to it during the fourteenth century. Some of these were ordered by Edward III who held the castle for a period. Part of the earlier stonework is still present among the later buildings.

COCKLEPARK TOWER
NR MORPETH, NORTHUMBERLAND
(NZ 202910)

An interesting three-storeyed tower-house of the fifteenth century which has one end with corners embellished with machicolated bartizans at the wallhead, and machicolations between. The tower-house was later extended by a domestic building on one end. The castle was occupied and in use up to a few years ago, but it is now unsafe.

COCKLAW TOWER
NR HEXHAM, NORTHUMBERLAND
(NY 939712)

This rectangular tower is an interesting, large pele-tower, three storeys tall, each storey containing one main room. One wall was thick enough to accommodate several chambers and the spiral staircase. Cocklaw was built in the early fifteenth century. It has been well preserved.

COLCHESTER ESSEX
(TL 998254)

Colchester great tower was the first to be built in England (c.1075–80), after a serious raid on the town by the Danes, and it is by far the largest great tower in Great Britain. In plan the tower is much the same as that of the White Tower of London, notably with its apsidal extension on the east wall. Indeed, the similarities in the two plans have led some historians to think that both were designed and built under the direction of the same man, Bishop Gundulf of Rochester. The great tower was built partly over the remains of a *podium* of a Roman temple dedicated to the Emperor Claudius (41–54), for Colchester had been a Roman city.

The dimensions of Colchester were 46.2 metres (151¹/₂ ft) (north–south), 33.5 metres (110 ft) (east–west) and about 27.4 metres (90 ft) high, with the corner turrets rising to 32–33.5 metres (105–110 ft). The corner turrets project from the walls in a more pronounced manner than the White Tower, and they contain both staircases and chambers. The tower walls are about 3.8 metres (12½ ft)

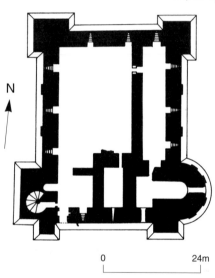

Colchester: ground plan of the great tower.

thick at the base (and so slightly thinner than London), leading down into a battered plinth where they widen out to 5.3 metres (17½ ft). The tower well in the south-west is 1.5 metres (5 ft) wide and over 12.2 metres (40 ft) deep, and is lined with septaria (clay nodules). The tower was built of Roman brick and dressed stone mostly quarried from the Roman ruins nearby, together with septaria lumps and Kentish ragstone. The dressed stone is said to have been Barnack or Reigate, with some ashlar from Caen. One interesting feature is the clear outline of battlements in the masonry at first-floor level, subsequently built on as the tower was continued upwards.

This is thought to have been because it was required to be defended at short notice, and the work level so far reached was hurriedly crenellated.

The tower was four-storeyed, but the top two storeys were pulled down in 1683 when the castle was sold to one John Wheeley for demolition. Evidently he abandoned the massive undertaking after reaching the bottom of the third floor. Today the great tower houses an excellent museum.

COMPTON Nr Paignton, Devon
(SX 865648)

A fourteenth-century fortified manor-house which belonged to the Gilbert family. It was fortified as a precaution against 'commando' raids which the French launched frequently upon the south Devon coast in the later years of the century. Towards the end of the sixteenth century Compton was owned by Sir Humphrey Gilbert, founder of the English colony in Newfoundland. It has been radically altered since, but still retains some of the original stonework.

CONISBROUGH

Nr Doncaster, South Yorkshire
(SK 515989)

Conisbrough stands on a natural mound which was given counterscarp banks to provide a wide and deep moat that almost surrounds the castle. The castle was built in the period c.1180–1200 by Hamelin Plantagenet, illegitimate half-brother of Henry II. It is a great tower castle enclosed in a curtain wall (which was 10.7 metres [35 ft] tall and 2.1 metres [7 ft] thick), with flanking solid half-cylindrical towers and a gatehouse with projecting barbican in front (of which there are a few remains). The barbican led out from the gatehouse, angled twice to the right, and then turned left downwards to the twin-towered gate half-way down the mound, the gate having a drawbridge across the moat.

The principal feature of the castle is the uniquely shaped great tower (unique, that is, in the UK, for there is a similar shaped tower in France). Built of limestone ashlar, the tower is basically cylindrical, but with six wedge-shaped buttresses placed equidistantly round the outer wall of the cylinder. Both cylinder and buttresses stand on a splayed plinth and rise to 29 metres (95 ft) tall, although the buttresses originally rose higher, to over 30.5 metres (100 ft). Only the south-east buttress

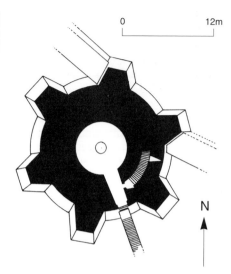

Conisbrough: ground-floor plan of the great tower. The outside staircase is not the original.

has accommodation of any size, a six-sided chapel. Two buttresses have water cisterns and two had space in the top where they emerged above the cylindrical wall for shelter leading to staircases. Otherwise, the stairs are in the wall thickness. There are fireplaces, hand basins and garderobes in the walls. The tower is notable for its scarcity of window openings and arrow-loops.

The great tower had the disadvantage affecting most cylindrical towers, namely, that the entrance was not protected by a forebuilding. Entry was gained via a flight of steps (not those at present in position) into a simple doorway.

The castle was not put to the test of siege.

COOLING Kent
(TR 755760)

A castle was built at Cooling in the 1380s to protect the approaches to the Thames from foreign raids. Sited near the Cliffe Marshes, Cooling was a double quadrangular castle with cylindrical corner turrets. Its building works were very well documented. Henry Yevele, the celebrated fourteenth-century architect/master-mason, worked there. The gatehouse, which survives today in remarkable condition, was built under the direction of William Sharnall. Cooling was attacked and taken by Sir Thomas Wyatt in 1554 during his rebellion against Mary I (Bloody Mary), which he led in protest against her plans to marry Philip II of Spain.

CORBRIDGE VICAR'S PELE

NORTHUMBERLAND .
(NY 987644)
The Vicar's Pele is one of the simpler Northumberland pele-towers and was built c.1300. It is called Vicar's Pele because it was the vicarage for the church next door. It is three storeys high, with one room to each storey, and is built largely of stone taken from the Roman fortress at Corstopitum nearby. The vicar's study/bedroom was on the top floor, reached by a staircase in the wall, and its windows were screened by battlemented parapets. The ground-floor entrance was through a thick, wooden door lined with an iron grating.

CORFE DORSET

(SY 958823)
Corfe Castle was King John's favourite fortress and he graced it with a remarkable 'gloriette', a block of apartments next to the great tower. These were the best appointed quarters in any castle in England at the time (c.1200–5).

Corfe began as a motte castle of the 1080s, erected on a steep hill. The outline of the castle precincts at this early period, viz. an ear-shaped plan, remained much the same for most of its history. The castle had received its first stonework by the end of the eleventh century: a small hall with some herringbone masonry on the south and pilaster buttresses on the west situated towards the western tip (now fragmented); and a rough-coursed rubble curtain wall round a high point on the north, roughly pear-shaped, that tapers to the west. This enclosure became and remained the inner bailey.

In the reign of Henry I a three-storeyed rectangular great tower was built along the south wall of the inner bailey. It had cross-walling, pilaster buttressing along its walls and blind arcading between some of the walls (reminiscent of Norwich great tower). This tower at Corfe is mentioned several times in medieval records, always as 'great tower'. The tower received a forebuilding in the mid-twelfth century, and much of this has survived to the present.

In the early thirteenth century King John lavished over £1400 on Corfe, including the gloriette, the curtain (with octagonal projecting tower on the extreme western tip) around the west bailey and the deep ditch and bank which divide the south-east outer bailey

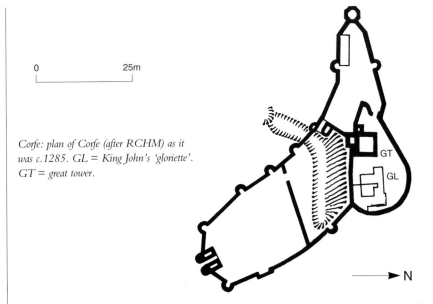

Corfe: plan of Corfe (after RCHM) as it was c.1285. GL = King John's 'gloriette'. GT = great tower.

from the rest of the castle. The outer bailey received some, if not all of the stone curtain and flanking towers. Henry III completed the curtain and inserted the south-east gatehouse, and also the inner gatehouse into the inner bailey. Corfe was used by Henry III and other kings as an arsenal as well as a fortress-residence. Edward I built an extra storey on the great tower. Thereafter, the castle was maintained rather than improved. It was used from time to time as a royal prison for top-rank captives.

The castle was besieged by parliamentary forces during the Civil War and it finally fell as a result of betrayal rather than enforced surrender. It was then ordered to be slighted, an order which was somewhat relished by the demolition gangs who virtually destroyed what must once have been one of the most fascinating castles ever to have been built in England.

COTHERSTONE DURHAM

(NZ 015200)
Cotherstone is a motte castle of the twelfth century which received stonework. Remains of the mound are situated to the north of the village itself.

COTTINGHAM

NR BEVERLEY, HUMBERSIDE
(TA 041330)
A motte castle whose motte was square at the top was built here in the twelfth century. In c.1200 King John granted William de

Stuteville, the holder (who also held Knaresborough and Buttercrambe castles), a licence to fortify the site. How this was carried out is not absolutely clear, but it may have been by means of constructing a tower on the motte. During the fourteenth century the site was completely transformed when a licence was granted to fortify a manor-house. The mound still survives.

COUPLAND

NR MILLFIELD, NORTHUMBERLAND
(NT 936312)
Coupland Castle, about 3.2 km (2 miles) from Millfield, is an L-plan tower of the late sixteenth century. The tower is three-storeyed, with the entrance staircase located in the 'L' extension which is actually taller than the main tower. It has been restored and extended.

COVENTRY WEST MIDLANDS

(SP 336788)
Coventry is a rectangular enclosure castle with surrounding ditchwork (part of which was excavated a few years ago). This was originally built as a priory, but it was taken by Robert Marmion during the Anarchy of King Stephen and converted into a fortress 'with pits and trenches'. Marmion is believed to have been killed when his horse stumbled and jerked him into one of his own trenches. The castle was dismantled by Stephen c.1147, but during Henry II's time it was repaired.

CRASTER
NR DUNSTANBURGH, NORTHUMBERLAND
(NU 256197)
Craster is a few kilometres south of Dunstanburgh. The pele-tower, probably built in the first years of the fifteenth century, is now part of a mansion. It has two storeys above the ground-floor part, which is vaulted. Craster Tower has been considerably altered, and has Gothic-style windows.

CRESSWELL
NR DRURIDGE BAY, NORTHUMBERLAND
(NZ 293933)
The tower at Cresswell is a fine rectangular building with one corner bearing a turret at the top. Cresswell was built in the thirteenth century and is still in good repair.

CREWKERNE SOMERSET
(ST 421107)
A mound at Crewkerne, known as Castle Hill, may have been a Norman motte castle. Excavations revealed some (?) twelfth-century pottery which has been taken to be housed at Taunton Museum.

CROFT LEOMINSTER
HEREFORD & WORCESTER
(SO 449655)
Croft is a fourteenth-century quadrangular-plan castle. The quadrangle has cylindrical towers on the corners and one rectangular flanking tower mid-wall on the north side. The north-west tower is in its original form, but the other towers have been altered. The old castle has been considerably modified to make it a more sumptuous residence, with a pair of semi-octagonal turrets flanking a one-storey gate turret of rectangular plan on the east wall. The gate leads into the hall, behind which lies the open courtyard.

The castle is named after the family that has owned it, with an interval of about 150 years, ever since its construction.

CUCKNEY NOTTINGHAMSHIRE
(SK 566714)
A motte castle probably raised in the time of the Anarchy (1135–54), it is also known as Castle Hill. The mound is near the church.

DACRE CUMBRIA
(NY 461266)
At Dacre there is a very fine pele-tower, which is still occupied. It was erected in the fourteenth century and given two wings, much in the Scottish tower-house manner. One of the wings has the staircase. Dacre was altered in the late seventeenth century.

DARTMOUTH DEVON
(SX 887503)
The earliest surviving English coastal castle specifically built to carry guns, Dartmouth was well sited on a rocky promontory on the west bank of the Dart estuary, about 1.6 km (1 mile) south-east of the town. Built by the corporation of the town in the period 1481–c.1495, it was tailored to fit the site, as can be seen in the plan. Basically, it is a square tower on the rock edge over the sea, buttressed on the northern side by a cylindrical tower, although internally the two towers are one structure. Both towers are battlemented, and all the walls are well provided with gun-ports, particularly at lower levels. There are well-crenellated gun platforms stretching out on both sides.

The corporation was granted an annual sum of £30 by Edward IV to 'repair and keep it garnished with guns…' and this was increased to £40 in 1486 by Henry VII. The masons building the castle in the 1480s were paid 7d a day, and labourers 5d. Some of the stone for the construction was brought from Charleton, near Kingsbridge.

Many additions and alterations were carried out in the sixteenth and seventeenth centuries. The castle was captured after a siege of one month by Prince Maurice on behalf of Charles I during the Civil War and held by a garrison of about 500 men for three years, until it was stormed by Sir Thomas Fairfax for Parliament in 1646.

DEDDINGTON OXFORDSHIRE
(SP 471316)
Deddington Castle began as an earthwork double enclosure of the twelfth century that accumulated stone buildings inside its structure over the years. There is very little to see today. Excavations revealed parts of a stone curtain and the base of a small rectangular tower, of the mid-twelfth century, erected on a mound, both within the inner enclosure. There are also remains of a hall of about 1160 and a chapel of the thirteenth century (some of the stained glass was found). Piers Gaveston, the favourite of Edward II, was held at Deddington before his execution in 1312.

DEVIZES WILTSHIRE
(SU 002613)
Devizes Castle began late in the eleventh century as an enclosure on a natural promontory, with two baileys. The 'Gesta Stephani' refers to its 'impregnable fortifications' but scarcely anything of these now remains. Suggestions have been made that it had an inner enclosure with a curtain wall and flanking towers, probably rectilinear, and including a great tower and an aisled hall. This enclosure was reached by a gatehouse from an outer bailey enclosed by a stone curtain with towers. Henry II acquired it in 1157 and used it as an official prison. Much work was done by Henry III who also used it as a prison for top-rank captives, including for a while his own justiciar Hubert de Burgh. The castle was demolished in the Civil War, although a few remains are detectable.

DONINGTON LEICESTERSHIRE
(SK 448276)
An earthwork enclosure of the early twelfth century, Donington probably had stonework by the time of King John. It was attacked during the Magna Carta war (1215–16). It passed in 1311 to Thomas, Earl of Lancaster, Edward II's cousin, and eventually became Crown property. The stone buildings probably included a rectangular hall (Leics. Arch. Soc. Trs. xxxii, p. 53).

DONNINGTON
NR NEWBURY, BERKSHIRE
(SU 464694)
This enclosure castle with added gatehouse-tower was built in the fourteenth century; its greatest days were during the Civil War when the garrison defending it on behalf of Charles I held out for nearly two years against Parliamentary forces (*see pp. 114–15*).

The castle stood on a high spur over the old London–Bath road. The enclosure was a rectangle with six flanking towers (four cylindrical and two square), inside which were ranges of buildings using the enclosure wall as outside walls. Along the eastern wall was the opening into the gatehouse inner part, protected by a portcullis, the grooves of which are still visible. The gatehouse was the principal and is now the sole feature of the original castle, for which a licence to crenellate was granted in 1386 to Richard de Abberbury, chamberlain to Richard II's Queen, Anne of Bohemia.

The rectangular-plan gatehouse-tower, with twin cylindrical towers flanking the entrance, is all that remains of Donnington.

The gatehouse is a rectangular-plan tower with twin cylindrical towers flanking the entrance, the whole tower on a splayed plinth. It is about 20 metres (65 ft) tall and resembles that at Saltwood in Kent, built at much the same time. It has three storeys, the two towers having four levels. The gatehouse is lit by slim loops in the towers and by windows over the entrance arch. A barbican projected in front of the entrance.

In the 1640s, the castle was surrounded by a remarkable five-pointed star defensive earthwork, which was reinforced with timber. Each of the five points was a bastion with a gun emplacement covering all flanks.

DORCHESTER DORSET
(SY 690908)
In medieval Dorchester there was a castle, probably of motte and bailey construction, in the north part where the later prison was built near Sheep Lane. There are no remains of the castle, although some pillar bases were said to have been found in the eighteenth century that suggest the one-time existence of a hall. The castle was fortified during the troubles of King Stephen's reign. For a time it was held by Henry II, and Exchequer records show several sums of money spent on it over about a century.

DORSTONE
HEREFORD & WORCESTER
(SO 312416)
A motte castle of the late eleventh/early twelfth century which survived into the thirteenth century without conversion to stone. The mound is over 6 metres (20 ft) in height.

DOVER KENT
(TR 326416)
Considering all its splendid features, its great military interest, its strategically important site and its long history of occupation and use, Dover has to be the greatest of all the thousands of castles in the British Isles, not excepting the Tower of London (picture on page 48).

Dover has everything. It is concentric, and began to be so nearly a century before any other British concentric fortress, new or

adapted. The great tower, an almost 30.5-metre (100-ft) cube, with walls from 5.2–6.4 metres (17–21 ft) thick all round and big enough to contain many sizeable chambers, is the most massive in Britain. The great tower's forebuilding, three-towered over three flights of stairs and wrapped round both edges of one corner, is more substantial than any other. The castle's inner curtain walls have 14 flanking towers (including gate-towers), while the outer curtain, which enwraps the inner at the north end and continues southwards right to the cliff's edge on the sea, creates an outer bailey of several hectares. The outer curtain has over 20 towers of varying shapes – square, D-ended, polygonal, rectangular, beaked – among which are gate-towers including the huge

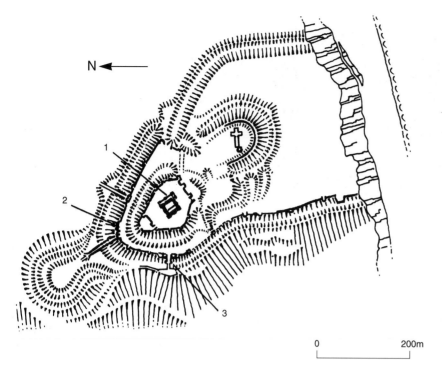

Dover: (after DoE). 1 = great tower. 2 = Norfolk Towers. 3 = Constable's Tower and Gate.

Constable's Gate which is perhaps the most elaborate gateway in any British castle.

This astonishing structure sprawls across the whole natural mound known as Castle Hill. In the middle of the outer bailey stand the ruins of a Roman pharos, or lighthouse, a clear sign of the strategic value of the site to the Roman forces of occupation. When the Conqueror defeated Harold II at Hastings, he headed not for London, principal town of his new kingdom, but for its 'gateway', Dover, where the Anglo-Saxons had already raised a *burh*. There, he improved the fortifications by erecting a motte castle, it is recorded, in only eight days.

But the incredible layout of stonework that is now Dover really began with Henry II, builder of many castles, who appointed as his master-mason Mauricius Ingeniator (Maurice the engineer) who had already built the great tower at Newcastle upon Tyne where he was known in the lower rank of Mauricius Caementarius (Maurice the builder). Between 1180 and 1189, Dover great tower, the whole inner curtain with its towers, and part of the outer curtain were all constructed. King John extended the latter, erecting several towers and the north gateway (incorporated in what

are now called the Norfolk Towers). Between them, Henry and John spent over £8000.

In 1216 there was a set-back. The King's agreement to Magna Carta had been followed by civil war in which the barons asked Louis, son of the French King, to come and take the English throne. He arrived in England and without wasting much time besieged Dover, which was held by John's staunch friend, Hubert de Burgh. Louis went straight for the King's newly completed north gateway and captured the barbican. Sappers, meanwhile, dug a tunnel under the gate and successfully brought part of its eastern tower crashing down. Hubert de Burgh and a handful of troops rushed to the gaping hole and plugged it with huge timber beams, wedging them down with other planks. They fought off the attackers who withdrew. Almost at once, news arrived that John had died at Newark and had been succeeded by his son, Henry. Louis thereupon called off the attack and the castle was saved.

Among the considerable building works done at Dover in Henry III's time was a quick but substantial repair to his father's gatehouse: the damaged eastern tower was rebuilt solid. The entrance was blocked by the insertion of a third (solid) beaked bastion. This is the cluster of three towers that make up the Norfolk Towers. A big round tower was raised in the ditch in front, and beyond that a

new outwork of earth. The outer curtain was finished, along with the rest of its towers, and the great Constable's Gate was constructed (*see* below), which became the residence of the castle's guardian. Dover was now complete, concentric and perhaps at last impregnable.

The great tower, 29 metres (95 ft) tall on a splayed plinth, and almost square – 29.9 x 29.3 metres (98 x 96 ft) – excluding the forebuilding, is built of Kentish ragstone, dressed with Caen stone, the two colours presenting a pleasing contrast. Each corner has a pronounced corner buttress turret, and there are equally pronounced pilaster buttresses mid-wall all round. The wall thickness of the tower diminishes from 6.4 metres (21 ft) at ground level to 5.2 metres (17 ft) at the top. There is a cross-wall nearly 2.1 metres (7 ft) thick all the way up. The tower has four storeys – a basement, first floor and second floor which is in fact two storeys tall with the upper level containing a mural gallery, like Hedingham (*inter alia*). The main entrance to the tower is at this second storey by means of the elaborate stairs, doors and landings in the wrap-around forebuilding of north–east to south–east. The forebuilding contains a chapel. The storeys in the great tower are connected by spiral staircases, in north and south corner turrets.

The well arrangements are interesting. There is a vaulted room on the second floor (in the wall thickness) which is a well chamber. The well-head comes up to this chamber and at one time provided direct water supply through pipes to the double storey and elsewhere. Remains of lead piping can be seen today near the well-head. The well itself is lined with Caen ashlar downwards for about 51.9 metres (170 ft) and continues thereafter for another 21.3 metres (70 ft) through natural chalk.

The Constable Gate is a remarkable structure. It was built into the outer curtain (at west) early in Henry III's time, and was a development upon a simpler tower at that point erected during John's reign. It consists of a cluster of different sized, rounded towers, the cluster curving outwards, set high above the ditch in front, dominating all angles of approach. The fronts of the rounded towers have spur bases dropping right down into the ditch. The central projection is a pair of cylindrical towers flanking the entrance passage, joined across the top. The rear parts of the cluster contain residential quarters for the castle's constable and his household, together with guard-rooms and fighting platforms. The central gatehouse was guarded by a drawbridge which bridged the ditch between the gate front and the barbican on the other side. The passage through the complex had a portcullis and doors. The Constable's Gate became the principal entrance after the siege of 1216, when the damaged gateway was repaired.

Much of this great medieval building work remains, but it has been altered over the centuries as the need to fortify Dover Harbour has from time to time become urgent. If it was 'the key to England' in the thirteenth century, it is hardly less so today.

DRIFFIELD HUMBERSIDE
(TA 035585)
A twelfth-century motte castle was built here at what came to be called Moot Hill. Excavations were undertaken in 1975.

DUDLEY WEST MIDLANDS
(SO 947907)
A motte castle mentioned in Domesday (1086) was strengthened with stonework in the 1130s. In the revolt by Prince Henry, eldest son of Henry II, against his father (1173–4), the castle was owned by Gervase de Paynel who supported the prince, and he paid for backing the wrong side by having his castle destroyed by the king in 1175. The site lay abandoned until the mid-thirteenth century when a descendant, Roger de Somery, began to rebuild. He died in 1272 before the works were anything like complete, and they were carried on by his son, John, said to have been one of the most hated feudal lords in the west Midlands.

John's works included a two-storeyed great tower of about 1300, rectangular in plan with cylindrical corner turrets, part of which remains, a square-plan gatehouse linked to the great tower by part of a new curtain wall round the whole castle. Other buildings were added in the fourteenth century including a barbican in front of the gatehouse, and in the 1980s evidence was found of a further curtain wall round the great tower (late fourteenth century) which provided concentric defence.

In the Civil War the castle was garrisoned by Royalists, but it was captured by Parliament in 1645 and the great tower was slighted two years later.

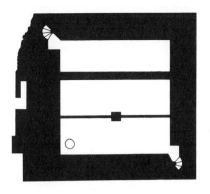

Duffield: (after D.F. Renn). This is a plan of the remaining foundations of the great tower.

DUFFIELD DERBYSHIRE
(SK 344441)
Duffield great tower was once one of the largest of the fortress-residences in England: today it is scarcely more than an outline of foundations on a site. The great tower was built in the 1160s–70s on the mound of an earlier motte castle by the de Ferrers family. It was 29 x 28.3 metres (95 x 93 ft), with walls about 4.6 metres (15 ft) thick, and it is estimated that it reached as high as 36.5 metres (120 ft). The tower was divided unequally by a thick cross-wall and the larger half by what may have been a pair of arcades. In the largest part was the castle well, sunk through shale to about 24.4 metres (80 ft). There had also been a forebuilding on the western end and spiral staircases in both east and west walls.

The remains of the tower show signs of having been subjected to great heat, suggesting that it may have been burned at some time in its history.

DUNHAM MASSEY CHESHIRE
(SJ 750878)
A motte stands in the grounds of Dunham New Park. It may be the castle of Hamo de Masci in the twelfth century.

DUNSTANBURGH
NR CRASTER, NORTHUMBERLAND
(NU 258220)
Dunstanburgh occupies about 3.6 hectares (9 acres) high on the cliffs above the sea. It was a stonework enclosure whose main feature was the huge gatehouse-tower at the extreme southern end. The enclosure had flanking towers and turrets of rectilinear shape. The first works were erected in the early fourteenth century and consisted of the entire enclosing wall, about 1.8–2.1 metres (6–7 ft) thick, but 3 metres (10 ft) thick for a stretch leading north-eastwards out of the gatehouse into the small Constable's Tower. They also included the massive gatehouse, now in ruins. This consisted of two D-ended towers flanking an arch-entranced passageway. In front of part of the gatehouse was a ditch cut into the rock, and a barbican projected towards it, although the ditch was not completed. The entrance was protected by a portcullis. The gatehouse was three storeys high but the cylindrical towers were two storeys taller. The gatehouse-tower had a

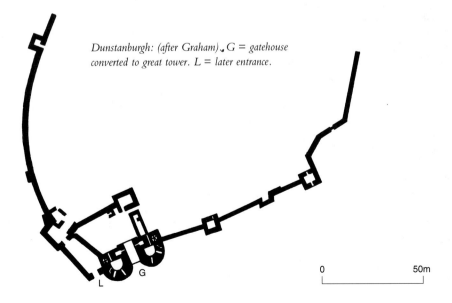

Dunstanburgh: (after Graham). G = gatehouse converted to great tower. L = later entrance.

0   50m

great hall on the second floor, with tall, mullioned and transomed windows positioned at each end.

All this work was carried out by Thomas, Earl of Lancaster, cousin of Edward II, whom he opposed because of the King's misgovernment and his infelicitous choice of friends. Lancaster was defeated at Boroughbridge in 1322 and executed at his castle at Pontefract. Dunstanburgh passed in due course to John of Gaunt, Duke of Lancaster, fourth son of Edward III. It was John who closed up the entrance to the gatehouse with a stone wall and a forebuilding in front (now disappeared) and turned it into a residential great tower, building an alternative gateway with barbican 30.5 metres (100 ft) or so along the curtain wall in a north-westerly direction. His works were carried out in the 1370s and 1380s.

Dunstanburgh was besieged during the Wars of the Roses when much damage was done to the fabric by the cannons, particularly those of Richard Neville, Earl of Warwick, the leading Yorkist general. It is now in ruins.

DUNSTER NR MINEHEAD, SOMERSET
(SS 991434)
The present imposing fortified manor-house known as Dunster Castle is a replacement of an earlier Norman earthwork castle which may be the same as that of Torre mentioned in Domesday. There are no remains of the earlier work except for a mound, scarped out of a natural hill, and we do not know if it ever received stonework. The castle of today began as a fortified manor-house in the fourteenth century. It came into the possession of the Luttrell family, who were famous for the *Luttrell Psalter* in the British Museum (so many revealing pictures of everyday life in fourteenth- and fifteenth-century England), and they have owned the castle ever since. It was besieged during the Civil War when its governor surrendered it to Parliament in 1646. It was restored by Salvin during the nineteenth century.

DURHAM DURHAM
(NZ 274423)
This began as a motte castle, raised against a cliff in a loop of the Wear c.1072, and granted to the Bishop of Durham. Its wooden tower rested on four posts, 'one post at each strong corner', according to a modern rendering of a twelfth-century description by Laurence, the Prior of Durham (cf. Abinger). In the early twelfth century a shell enclosure of sandstone in roughly octagonal plan was erected on the motte around the wooden tower which may have been retained for some time afterwards. The shell was destroyed in 1340 and rebuilt. In the banked and ditched bailey, partly curtained, domestic structures were raised over the years, one of the earliest being a chapel whose crypt – still in wonderful condition – has six pillars with carved capitals. The other buildings include a range to the north, a great hall (rebuilt), a gatehouse and a kitchen.

The castle was a bishops' palace rather than a fortress, although it was always kept in a state of defensibility. The walls were connected with the city's walls, and the whole peninsula was surrounded by the Wear, with the cathedral included. The castle is now part of Durham University. The Lower Hall is entered through an elaborate doorway of three orders, possibly the finest example of later Romanesque architecture in Britain.

DYMOCK GLOUCESTERSHIRE
(SO 711293)
Traces of a motte castle, probably of the twelfth century, have been found here in the village. It is known as Castle Tump.

EARDISLEY
HEREFORD & WORCESTER
(SO 311491)
This was a rectangular enclosure with a motte. The bailey was surrounded by a moat fed by a stream. It may have been built late in the eleventh century at the time of the Norman advance into Wales. The castle is mentioned in the reigns of Henry II and John, but there is little further information.

EATON SOCON CAMBRIDGESHIRE
(TL 173588)
Erected beside the Ouse, this Norman double enclosure for which Saxon houses were destroyed (according to excavations of 1962–3) was surrounded with moats filled with water from a diversion of the river, which also operated a watermill. There have been several investigations into its early history, but the origins are still uncertain. The Beauchamp family held the castle in 1156, but before that it was a fortress in the possession of the de Mandevilles. Some earthworks remain.

ECCLESHALL STAFFORDSHIRE
(SJ 827295)
Eccleshall began as an enclosure and was surrounded by a moat fed by the River Stow. Stonework was added, principally a curtain wall with polygonal flanking turrets, and there was also a stone bridge across one arm of the moat. In c.1200 Bishop Muschamp of Lichfield was granted a licence to fortify his house, and the stonework may be part of the works that were carried out. There are some remains of later stonework including a tower and some walling.

EDLINGHAM
NR ALNWICK, NORTHUMBERLAND
(NU 116092)
The ruins of Edlingham Castle show it to have been a triangular enclosure with a great tower outside the walls but connected to them. Recent excavations revealed several phases of construction, beginning in the late twelfth century. It began as a long rectangular hall-tower which later acquired some polygonal corner turrets. It was divided into several apartments. The hall-tower formed the south wall of the enclosure whose east and north walls later received ranges of buildings. One on the north wall and projecting outwards was a gate-tower of two or three storeys (of mid- to late-fourteenth-century construction) which in the fifteenth century was extended outwards still further, with a portcullis and pivoting bridge across the moat beyond.

To the south, the great tower, about 12.2 metres (40 ft) square with elongated corner buttresses, was linked to the hall-tower block by a small forebuilding (which has almost disappeared). The tower was three-storeyed, with vaulted first floor, and had a spiral stairway encased in a special projection on the east, next to the forebuilding.

EGREMONT CUMBRIA
(NY 010105)
A motte castle of the twelfth century created by scarping a natural mound, which is outside the present structure. This received stone walls and a gatehouse later in the same century, or perhaps early in the thirteenth. The gatehouse was faced with ashlar and was inserted in the curtain wall. Some of the curtain has herringbone masonry. There were other buildings in the enclosure. The mound and some stonework remain.

ELLESMERE SHROPSHIRE
(SJ 403347)

A motte castle of the late eleventh century, possibly built by Roger de Montgomery who led the Norman invasion into central Wales. The castle was given to the Peverels by Henry I but taken back by Henry II in 1154 who granted it to his brother-in-law David, son of Owain Gwynedd, Prince of Wales, in about 1177. The castle alternated between English and Welsh crowns up to the 1240s and then passed to the le Strange family.

ELMLEY HEREFORD & WORCESTER
(SO 979043)

There is very little left of this late eleventh-century earthwork castle which received stone additions in the twelfth and possibly the thirteenth centuries. The earthworks consist of ditching and banking of irregular plan. There are the remains of a stone rectangular structure with a projection that suggest a great tower with forebuilding. This may have been perhaps of the late twelfth century. There are also the remains of a curtain wall. The ruins are in Elmley Castle Park, near Pershore, whose bridge on the outskirts is thought to contain stone taken from the old castle. It was for more than two centuries the principal seat of the Earls of Beauchamp.

ELSDON NORTHUMBERLAND
(NY 939935)

An interesting and well preserved motte castle of the late eleventh century; the motte is separated from the bailey by a deep ditch. The motte is about 9.1 metres (30 ft) above the bailey, one side of which is itself some 18.3 metres (60 ft) above the water level of the burn at Elsdon. The other three sides of the bailey were protected by ditches. It is thought that Elsdon Castle was abandoned c.1156.

ELY CAMBRIDGESHIRE
(TL 541799)

Cherry Hill mound is probably the remnant of the very early motte castle raised by the Conqueror c.1070 during his campaign against Hereward the Wake. It may have been the same castle at Ely that was fortified by Bishop Nigel, during the reign of King Stephen, who also built a fort of lime and stone nearer to the site of the cathedral (Lib Eliensis). There is believed to have been a windmill sited on Cherry Hill in the thirteenth century.

EMBLETON TOWER
NORTHUMBERLAND
(NU 231224)

There is some uncertainty about the date of this tower-house – the building period is given as c.1330–40 and also as the end of the fourteenth century. The tower-house has two vaulted chambers in the basement. It was modified much later.

ETAL NR FORD, NORTHUMBERLAND
(NT 925394)

The castle at Etal was built on a roughly quadrangular plan, with a rectangular great tower (about 14 x 9.7 metres [46 x 32 ft]), half in and half out of the north-west corner of the enclosure (cf. West Tower at Dolbadarn in north Wales). The great tower was four-storeyed with one large room to each floor, and the ground-floor room was vaulted. The east wall had a projecting forebuilding with a portcullis. At the south-east corner of the enclosure was the castle's gatehouse, a large square-plan building, about 11 metres (36 ft) square, with projections on the east entrance on either side of the vaulted passage into the courtyard, protected by a portcullis and a gate. The enclosure wall was about 0.9 metres (3 ft) thick, running from the south-west of the gatehouse to another smaller rectangular tower in the south-west corner, but only stretches of it survive.

Etal was captured in 1513 by James IV of Scotland before the Battle of Flodden Field.

EWIAS HAROLD
NR PONTRILAS, HEREFORD
& WORCESTER
(SO 385287)

This is one of the castles claimed to have been built before the Conquest (*see* p. 16). It is referred to in the *Anglo-Saxon Chronicle* for 1052. In Domesday there is a reference to Castellum Ewias which William FitzOsbern *refirmaverat*, that is, had strengthened or reinforced. By 1086 Ewias had become a motte castle, and its motte was 15.2 metres (50 ft) tall. At one time the motte was believed to have received a shell enclosure of stone in the twelfth century. Today, only earthworks remain.

EXETER DEVON
(SX 921930)

Soon after the Conquest, William I went westwards towards Dorset, Devon and Cornwall. Arriving at Exeter in 1067, he was met by considerable opposition. The defenders assembled within the old Roman walls, which the Conqueror is supposed to have breached by means of undermining. In the northern corner of the walls, William raised a castle of earth and timber. The following year a simple single-tower stone gateway was built (which still stands as a good example of an early stone gate-tower).

Exeter Castle was in royal hands from Henry II's time to 1348. During that time many additions were made – towers, walls, extensive ditches (parts of which were discovered in recent excavations), hall and great chamber. Only the gateway remains, along with fragments of wall.

EYE SUFFOLK
(TM 148378)

Eye Castle was a motte castle built by William Malet in the Conqueror's reign. The mound is about 15.2 metres (50 ft) tall. There is flint rubble masonry on the motte slopes, which is medieval, and it is part of the walling that connected with a bailey curtain. There are several records of work done on repairs and strengthening, such as heightening the walls, in the Pipe Rolls of Henry II and Richard I. In the late 1980s remnants of a tower were uncovered on the north side of the motte.

EYNSFORD KENT
(TQ 542658)

One of the earliest examples of a stone enclosure castle in England, Eynsford's order of building periods was as follows: a platform of earth was raised beside the River Darent, a wooden tower about 11 metres (36 ft) square was erected upon it, and in about 1088 the platform was enclosed by a 1.8-metre (6-ft) thick curtain of coursed flint rubble up to about 6 metres (20 ft). This walling was carried on up to about 9.1 metres (30 ft) c.1100. The level of the platform was adjusted and associated earthworks were carried out.

The enclosure received stone buildings, mainly free-standing, in the twelfth century. The principal building was a rectangular hall with solar, and with undercroft below, erected across the site of the wooden tower. It had a forebuilding of some complexity. The hall is now only as high as its undercroft. A stone gate-tower was added at the same time, roughly c.1130, on the south side, and it led to a bridge across the moat. The bridge was

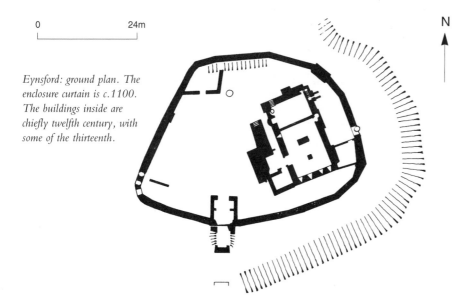

Eynsford: ground plan. The enclosure curtain is c.1100. The buildings inside are chiefly twelfth century, with some of the thirteenth.

timber-built, and its construction and operation (part of it appears to have been movable) have recently been the subject of considerable research.

FARINGDON OXFORDSHIRE
(SU 297957)
An earthwork enclosure castle was built here c.1144 by Robert, Earl of Gloucester, during the Anarchy of King Stephen's reign, and it was destroyed by the king a year or two later. There is a mound known locally as the 'Clump', which may be the original earthworks. Skeletons lying tangled and on top of each other were found in diggings in 1935, which suggest a siege. Stones found may have been reinforcements of the motte.

FARLEIGH HUNGERFORD
NR TROWBRIDGE, SOMERSET
(ST 801577)
This is a fourteenth-century double courtyard protected by a moat, walls and towers. Sir Thomas Hungerford, Speaker of the House of Commons, built it between c.1370–83. He appears to have been granted a pardon in 1383 for failing to obtain a licence to crenellate it. The site backs at the north on a deep dyke, with natural scarps to east and west. The castle began as a quadrangular enclosure with cylindrical towers on the corners and a substantial gateway of D-ended towers flanking an entrance. Inside, an extensive range of domestic buildings was erected. It is thought that these were grafted upon the remains of an earlier castle that had been

destroyed in the mid-fourteenth century.

Hungerford's son, Walter, enlarged the castle by building a polygonal enclosure curtain with a flanking cylindrical tower and two gateways (east and west). He surrounded the newer works with a moat extension along the southern end. He also constructed a masonry dam and sluice in the original western ditch to control the water flow from a large pond, thus creating a kind of 'water-castle' (*see* p. 52).

FARNHAM SURREY
(SU 839474)
Farnham is an interesting variant on the normal motte castle. Looking at the inner part, the shell enclosure as it is called, the visitor sees a mound enclosed within a many-sided shell of stonework, with a shallow

gatehouse and four rectangular-plan buttress turrets which originally rose higher and contained windows. On the summit of the mound (today almost the same height as the shell wall) is a large 15.5-metre (51-ft) square stone platform which is in fact a flange on top of an 11.3-metre (37-ft) square stone substructure extending down the middle of the mound to ground level. This contains a well shaft. The structure and its flange supported a square great tower (evidently of stone) about which little is known.

Whatever it was, and whether it had been finished, it was pulled down on Henry II's orders in 1155. The earth may have been heaped up round the substructure afterwards, to make a mound in much the same way as was done at Ascot d'Oilly, Wareham, Totnes and South Mymms, or the substructure may have been sunk into an already established motte, which was about 9.1 metres (30 ft) tall.

Farnham belonged to the Bishop of Winchester, Henry of Blois, brother of King Stephen, and when he left England to go to France after the death of his brother in 1154, the new king, Henry II, seized the castle and had it slighted. It was rebuilt, possibly by Henry of Blois, but in a different form. The mound was encircled closely by a substantial shell wall up to about 3 metres (10 ft) thick, rising considerably higher than the 9.1 metres (30 ft) of the mound, with the gatehouse and

Farnham: plan of the castle of several periods. Centre: late twelfth-century shell enclosure (K) revets the mound on which earlier (c.1138) the square great tower (T) was raised, with its basement within the earth of the mound.

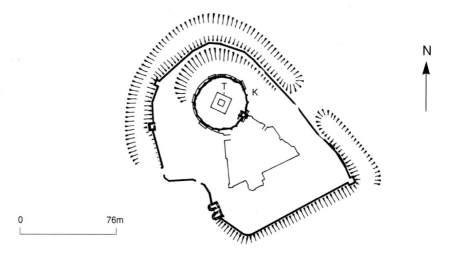

the buttress turrets built in. Garderobe chutes were inserted in the wall, and buildings were ranged round its inside. The space between the wall and the slopes of the mound were filled in later (thirteenth century). The whole structure was fortified by the erection of an outer curtain wall (much of which still remains), which had square-plan flanking turrets, and a twin semi-octagonal-towered gatehouse on the west side. The gatehouse is probably thirteenth century. The curtain has been extensively repaired, in many places using brick.

From about the 1280s right up to the seventeenth century, the castle was extended within the outer curtain, but these structures were of a domestic nature and the castle itself really ceased to have any defensive significance. Farnham was attacked during the Civil War and was then slighted by Parliament. It continued to be a residence of the Bishops of Winchester after an interval of about 20 years.

FEATHERSTONE
NR HALTWHISTLE, NORTHUMBERLAND
(NY 674610)
The present mansion at Featherstone, built in the seventeenth century, incorporates some much earlier stone building, including a very fine arch of the late twelfth century and a handsome square pele-tower which has an arm to make it L-plan. The pele-tower was erected in about 1330 by Thomas de Featherstonehaugh. It has the distinct feature of rising in three stages which are marked with sloping offsets. At the top the corners are crowned with bartizans.

FOLKESTONE KENT
(TR 214380)
This was an enclosure castle at the end of a natural mound protected on three sides by sheer cliff and on the fourth by a deep ditch and bank. There was an outer bailey, also with ditches. Inside the enclosure a well was sunk some 25.9 metres (85 ft) deep. Rubble masonry has been found which may have been part of a stone structure on the site, possibly of the early twelfth century. Traces remain on Castle Hill.

FORD NR ETAL, NORTHUMBERLAND
(NT 944375)
Ford Castle was built for defence against Scottish raids into Northumberland. A licence

to crenellate his home was granted in 1338 to William Heron, who built a quadrangle with towers on the four corners. The towers were different in size, and two of them were square, one nearly square and one rectangular. The strongest was the King James Tower on the north-west.

Ford was captured by the Scots in 1385 and dismantled by them. Evidently there was enough structure left to make it worthwhile restoring, for by the beginning of the sixteenth century it has been rebuilt and refortified. But in 1513 Ford was taken by James IV of Scotland a few days before the Battle of Flodden (*see* Etal Castle). The much later mansion grafted upon the old remains has largely obscured the original work.

FOTHERINGAY NORTHAMPTONSHIRE
(TL 061930)
Almost certainly, Fotheringay's greatest claim to fame is that it was the scene of the execution of Mary, Queen of Scots, in 1587. By that time it was more of a manor-house and was not fortified. Indeed, it was said that some of the walls were low enough to jump over. But it began as a Norman motte castle on the north side of the River Nene, with no ditch between motte and bailey. An investigation recorded in 1975 (RCHM)

---

*Framlingham: E = entrance through gate-tower.
GH = site of second great hall. FGH = position of
first great hall (c.1160).*

suggested that some masonry near the river may have come from the motte, which indicates a building or a wing wall. Mentioned early in the thirteenth century, the castle was held by William the Marshal, Earl of Pembroke, and also by Ranulf, Earl of Chester. Interestingly, the castle had been used for prisoners from Scotland several times.

FOULDRY
MORECAMBE BAY, LANCASHIRE
(SD 233636)
Known also as Piel Castle, Fouldry sits on an island in Morecambe Bay. In the 1320s a concentric castle was built here, consisting of a great tower inside an inner bailey, surrounded by an outer ward with broad ditches and thick stone walling. The great tower is square in plan, 18.3 metres (60 ft) wide, and rose to about 15.2 metres (50 ft), having pilaster buttresses on the corners. Much of the building was restored in the mid-nineteenth century.

FRAMLINGHAM SUFFOLK
(TM 287637)
Framlingham Castle was built between c.1189 and c.1200 by Roger Bigod, Earl of Norfolk, on the site of an earlier timberwork castle raised by his grandfather c.1102. This earlier castle had been destroyed on the orders of Henry II in 1175, but part of the hall survived and was built into the curtain wall enclosure which has 12 rectangular flanking towers and a gateway. The enclosure is a simple enough

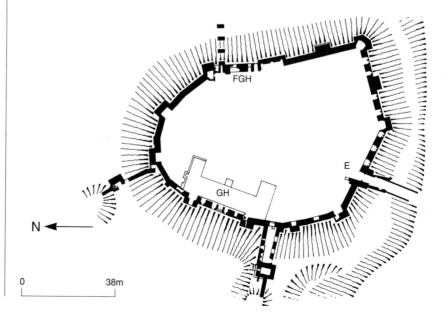

structure at first sight, and it is an excellent early example of this type of castle. But the walls are about 13.4 metres (44 ft) tall and 2.4 metres (8 ft) thick, and the flanking towers rise about another 6 metres (20 ft), which would have presented quite an obstacle to a besieging army. Added to that, the structure stands on a platform surrounded by extensive wide and deep ditching with higher counterscarp banking. A nearby stream was dammed to provide water for part of the ditching. The castle was besieged, however, in 1216 and taken on behalf of King John, but there is no evidence of major siege damage, which may suggest that the Bigod defenders gave in without much of a fight.

The enclosure was provided with additional buildings inside. Ten of the flanking towers were open-backed, which means they were of entirely military purpose: in time of war temporary backs of timber would be erected above the wall-walk level, making each tower-top a separate and integral fighting unit approachable only from the wall-walk. A great hall built by the Bigods on the west wall has disappeared into the masonry of a poorhouse which was built there in the seventeenth century.

FRAMPTON LINCOLNSHIRE
(TA 327391)
Remains of a rectangular moated enclosure here may be of that belonging to the castle mentioned c.1216.

FRODSHAM CHESHIRE
(SJ 514775)
In the eighteenth-century Castle Park House at Frodsham are traces of the earlier (Norman) castle, although it is not possible to suggest a clear plan. There are indications that a tower was built on the high ground.

GIDLEIGH NR CHAGFORD, DEVON
(SC 671884)
Remains of a possibly Norman tower, about 6.7 x 4 metres (22 x 13 ft), have been detected on this site.

GILLING
NR HELMSLEY, NORTH YORKSHIRE
(SE 611768)
The ground floor of a square tower-house built by the de Etton family in the mid-fourteenth century is incorporated in the later (sixteenth-century) tower block built by Sir William Fairfax. The block was remodelled in the eighteenth century. There is a possibility that the original tower was raised on an earthwork of eleventh-century origin. Gilling Manor belonged to Alan the Red who built Richmond Castle.

GLEASTON
NR FURNESS ABBEY, CUMBRIA
(SD 261715)
Gleaston was a simple quadrangle castle with corner turrets, built c.1330. The walls were 2.7 metres (9 ft) thick and built of crudely dressed limestone rubble blocks. There were some red sandstone dressings. There was a larger tower in the north-west corner, about 27.4 x 15.2 metres (90 x 50 ft), at the highest point of the castle site. The castle was dismantled in 1458. This may have been a by-product of the Wars of the Roses (1455–85), but under what or whose insistence we do not know.

GLOUCESTER GLOUCESTERSHIRE
(SO 828185)
Although there is nothing to see of Gloucester Castle, it is included because of some interesting aspects of its history that survive in medieval documents. One of these is a simple but revealing sketch of the great tower, drawn in the fourteenth century. Gloucester began as a motte castle of the Conqueror's reign (16 houses were demolished to make way for its site, according to Domesday). It was enlarged by William Rufus (eight more houses were taken down) and further extended by Henry I

Gloucester: fourteenth-century drawing of the great tower, from King's Works.

and Henry II. Henry I built the great tower c.1112, which may have looked like the drawing (below left). According to Leland, who saw it in the 1540s, the great tower was 'high'. Interestingly, it is one actually described in another medieval document as *magna turris* (in an Exchequer record dated 1328). Considerable repairs and some improvements were carried out by Henry III (including a bridge across the River Severn leading to a barbican in the outer wall). Gloucester was besieged twice in the war between Henry and Simon de Montfort in 1264–5. Further works were done in the reigns of Edwards I, II and III, and also in the fifteenth century.

GODARD'S NR THORNHAM, KENT
(TQ 808582)
A twelfth-century enclosure castle of flint masonry. Fragments of the gatehouse survive, together with portions of curtain wall.

GOODRICH
ROSS-ON-WYE, HEREFORD & WORCESTER
(SO 579199)
Goodrich Castle is sited on a high rocky spur over the right bank of the River Wye, commanding a crossing of the river. It is protected partly by a natural steep slope and valley, and partly by a moat cut out of the rock. The first stone building at Goodrich is mid-twelfth century, a square great tower built upon the site of an earlier undetermined castle which was probably wooden. The great tower is constructed of pink local sandstone ashlar, with clasping pilaster buttresses all the way up the corners and about two-thirds up the centre of the tower's walls. There is a doorway into the basement, with a chevron-headed arch, and above that another doorway into the first floor, with a round-headed arch, supported upon moulded side pillars. This has been partly blocked up and has a later window. The first-floor entrance was probably reached by an outside stair, for there is no evidence of a forebuilding. The tower has three storeys, reached by a spiral staircase in the north-west angle. It is over 18.3 metres (60 ft) tall today, and probably rose originally to nearer 21.3 metres (70 ft).

The tower stood on its own for a time. Then, in the late thirteenth century, when held by the de Valence family, the castle was substantially renovated. It was converted into a formidable quadrangle with massive cylindrical towers on three corners, and a vast

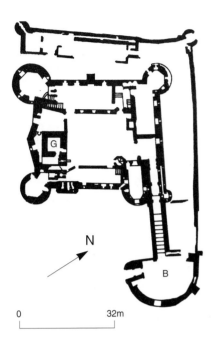

Goodrich: plan of the castle of several periods. G = great tower of the twelfth century, enclosed by late thirteenth/early fourteenth-century quadrangle with towers. B = barbican of fourteenth century (like the Lion Tower at the Tower of London, and Sandal in West Yorkshire [see pp. 178–80]).

gatehouse-tower on the fourth (north-east) corner. The cylindrical towers were raised on square bases with spurs that clamped the towers to the rock base upon which they stood. The south-west tower contains traces of foundations of an earlier tower of unknown date. Inside the quadrangle some elaborate apartments were built, including a great hall (20 x 8.2 metres [65 x 27 ft]), a solar abutting on to the north-west tower and kitchens. The north-east corner tower was erected as a gatehouse coupled with a chapel. This tower is not in good condition. The chapel has an apsidal east end.

Extending from the gatehouse is a sloping causeway and bridge which crosses over the moat, leading downwards for about 12.2 metres (40 ft) into a half-moon barbican whose exit is at right-angles, facing south. The outer wall of the barbican curves round into the outer enclosing wall of the castle which continues around the north and east sides. The barbican arrangement is similar to one built at the Tower of London, and also (earlier) at Sandal.

GRAFTON HEREFORD & WORCESTER
(SO 494369)

The remains of a motte castle lying inside an enclosure were detected on aerial photographs in 1990. At the time of writing, no reliable information about its origins has yet been established.

GREAT CANFIELD
NR DUNMOW, ESSEX
(TL 595179)

A substantial motte castle was raised here by the de Vere family which in the 1130s–1140s also built Hedingham great tower. The moats around the inner and outer baileys were fed from a diversion from the River Roding, which appears to have been regulated by a dam system.

GREYSTOKE CUMBRIA
(NY 435309)

The Greystoke family was granted a licence to crenellate their home, a pele-tower in Cumberland, in 1353. Little of this remains, for there have been many additions to the tower to make it into a mansion.

GROBY LEICESTERSHIRE
(SK 525076)

A motte castle, possibly of the eleventh century, was given stone buildings in the twelfth. The rubble from these was much later heaped over the remains of a tower which may have been a great tower. The castle was destroyed in the 1170s after the rebellion of Prince Henry against his father Henry II (1173–4). The site has disappeared under roadworks (Med. Arch. VIII, p. 235).

GUILDFORD SURREY
(SU 999495)

Guildford Castle has an almost square great tower, of Bargate rubble, flint and chalk courses. Note that some courses are set in herringbone. This was built in the mid-twelfth century upon the side of an earlier motte. The reason for setting the great tower to one side of the motte was in order to use part of the natural rock (from which the original motte was created) as foundation. There are also remains of a contemporary gateway and fragments of the curtain wall.

The castle was used as the county gaol for nearly 400 years (c.1200–1600). In 1381 it was a clearing house for prisoners taken during the disturbances caused by the Peasants' Revolt, but so many were brought to Guildford that half of them were transferred to Lewes and Arundel.

HADLEIGH NR LEIGH ON SEA, ESSEX
(TQ 810860)

This was a thirteenth-century creation, begun by Hubert de Burgh, the celebrated minister of John and the young Henry III. It was a polygonal curtain enclosure. Edward III took much interest in Hadleigh and lavished considerable sums on converting it to an extensive castle with several drum towers, and a large cylindrical tower that covered the north-west entrance to the enclosure. Domestic buildings included a great hall, a chapel, and suites for the king and queen. The majority of his works were done between 1361–70 and cost over £2300. The castle was intended to play both military and domestic roles: the substantial towers support the former. There are many references to domestic expenditure and to visits by the kings to Hadleigh in Exchequer records. The remains to be seen today are chiefly of the Edward III period.

HALLATON LEICESTERSHIRE
(SP 780967)

A very interesting motte castle, whose motte area occupied hardly less space (192 metres [630 ft] in circumference at the bottom) than its inner bailey. Excavations a century ago revealed some of the lumber assembled at the base of the motte, and this included tree trunks bearing axe marks, boulders and clay lumps (*Early Norman Castles*, p. 88).

HALTON NR FRODSHAM, CHESHIRE
(SJ 537820)

A timber and earth castle was built here in about 1071. Late in the twelfth century it was converted into a stone enclosure with flanking towers. During the fifteenth century a large, twin polygonal-towered gatehouse was also constructed, but little of it remains today.

HALTON
NR AYDON, NORTHUMBERLAND
(NY 997678)

The tower at Halton was erected in the fourteenth century. It adjoins a much later mansion. The castle is near the remains of a Roman fort whose stones were used in the tower's construction. The rectangular tower is about 9.4 x 7.3 metres (31 x 24 ft), and is four-storeyed, with cylindrical bartizans at the tops of the four corners, like the arrangement at Chipchase Castle.

HANLEY HEREFORD & WORCESTER
(SO 837415)

Hanley was built by King John between 1207–12, possibly on the site of an earlier rectangular-moated enclosure. From 1216, Hanley was held for about a century by the powerful de Clares (see Tonbridge and Caerphilly). A description of 1416 indicated the existence of several stone towers, a palisade (presumably wooden) and a chapel. Nash, the eighteenth-century historian of Worcestershire, stated that Hanley contained, *inter alia*, a great tower in the north-west corner. Nothing remains, however, except the moated site.

HARBOTTLE
NR ROTHBURY, NORTHUMBERLAND
(NT 932048)

Harbottle began as a motte castle on the north bank of the River Coquet, with the motte astride the southern curve of the bailey. It was raised in about 1157 by Robert de Umfraville, presumably to protect that part of Northumberland from the Scots. Part of the bailey wall was of stone, with a stone gateway and a turret towards the north. On the motte a rectangular tower was raised, although it is now much ruined. Gun-ports were added at a later date. In 1515, Margaret, widow of James IV of Scotland, was banished by the Regent, the Duke of Albany. She fled to Harbottle and towards the end of the year gave birth to a daughter there, who later became the mother of Lord Darnley, second husband of Mary, Queen of Scots.

HARTSHILL WARWICKSHIRE
(SP 325942)

A motte castle which later received a stone curtain round its bailey. There is a Tudor timber-framed house in the bailey.

HASTINGS SUSSEX
(TQ 822095)

Two castles were raised in England by the Conqueror after his landing on the south coast and before the great Battle of Hastings. They were at Pevensey (September 1066) and Hastings itself (October 1066, just before the battle). Hastings was a timber and earth castle raised just inland from the shore by his troops

and by local Anglo-Saxon labour pressed into service, and the scene is recorded on the Bayeux Tapestry which shows that the castle had a motte. It is possible that the wooden tower was assembled on the site from prefabricated parts shipped over from Normandy, and that the bolts and other iron parts were transported in casks.

The motte was almost certainly the mutilated mound remaining on Castle Hill which today has medieval stonework across it. The castle developed into one of stone with, among other things, a great tower and a gatehouse. Much of it has disappeared as a result of erosion from the sea which took place over the centuries and was commented upon in a fourteenth-century report, and such erosion would have led to neglect of the whole castle.

HAUGHLEY SUFFOLK
(TM 025624)

The motte at Haughley Castle is one of the largest surviving mottes in Britain. At 24.4 metres (80 ft) tall and about 24.4 metres in diameter at the top, it is the equal of Thetford. The inner bailey of the castle measured about 118.9 x 91.4 metres (390 x 300 ft), and the rampart round the encircling ditch is about 4.9 metres (16 ft) high in some places. Recent studies have suggested that the outer bailey enclosed Haughley church and much of the village. There are stonework remains on the motte that may be from a shell enclosure which was raised there. The castle was dismantled c.1173, during Henry II's war against his elder son.

HAUGHTON
NR HUMSHAUGH, NORTHUMBERLAND
(NY 918729)

Probably begun in the late fourteenth century, Haughton became a substantial castle based upon a narrow rectangular great tower with square corner turrets and an extra turret in the centre of the front wall at roof level. The tower was enclosed by a curtain, some of which remains.

HEDINGHAM ESSEX
(TL 787359)

This is one of the most famous Norman great towers in England. It is still privately owned but is open to visitors. The castle began in the late eleventh or early twelfth century as an earthwork and timber fortress held by the de

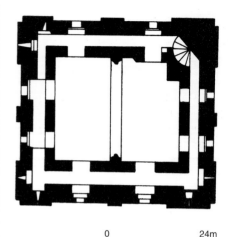

Hedingham: plan of the gallery level of the second floor. Note the overall gallery running round all four sides of the great tower.

Veres, one of whom became 1st Earl of Oxford in 1141. Some time late in the reign of Henry I or early in Stephen's time, the great tower was built on the flat, raised platform which had formerly held the wooden castle.

Built of Barnack oolite ashlar facing on rubble, the tower today stands to over 22.2 metres (73 ft) tall, with two corner turrets extending for another 6 metres (20 ft). It is rectangular in plan, 18.9 x 16.8 metres (62 x 55 ft), on a splayed plinth with flat pilaster buttresses on the angles and mid-wall. The tower has four storeys – or five, taking the second (great hall) storey as two. The entrance is at the first-storey level and its round-headed arch has chevron moulding. A forebuilding was added at a later date. This has disappeared, except for foundations, leaving only a flight of stairs, not all of which are original. The creasings where the forebuilding roof joined the west wall can be seen. The entrance had a portcullis.

The tower walls are between 3–3.6 metres (10–12 ft) thick. They are filled at every storey with chambers and passages. On the upper level of the great hall double storey, a wall passage runs right round through all the window bays, whose windows provided extra light into what was otherwise a dark hall. The windows at this level are paired. There is one staircase, a spiral, all the way up the north-west corner. The cross-walls, at first and second storey levels, take the form of flying arches, the arch on the double storey rising at its centre to over 6 metres (20 ft). The tower, which was well built and on the whole well appointed so far as accommodation is concerned, contained no chapel or kitchen. There is evidence of other buildings outside, including a hall and a chapel.

Hedingham Castle was on several occasions involved in warfare or drama. Robert de Vere, one of the barons who compelled King John to consent to Magna Carta, was besieged in his castle in the ensuing Magna Carta war and forced to surrender by the king. In 1918, the great tower was severely damaged by a fire which destroyed the interior woodwork and the present woodwork is a replacement.

The outer surface of the great tower contains several orderly rows of put-log holes, which have been used for the horizontal posts of the building scaffolding.

HELMSLEY North Yorkshire
(SE 611836)

The most striking things about this late twelfth-century stone enclosure castle with great tower are the huge earthwork ditch-and-bank defences. Simple enough as a quadrangle inside another quadrangle, the castle was in fact extremely well defended. The ditches are in the main over 9.1 metres (30 ft) deep. There may have been an earlier wooden castle on the site to which part, if not all, the earthworks relate. A thick curtain wall with D-end and round flanking towers was raised along the edge of the platform in the inner quadrangle. On the north-east of the wall was inserted c.1200 a D-ended rectangular great tower which originally rose three storeys (the gable line of its first height can be seen), but later (c.1300) two further storeys were added plus turrets on the square corners facing the inside of the quadrangle. It is possible that the rounded apsidal end which faces outwards over the scarping was added in stage two of the building of the tower. Several other buildings (some of them sixteenth century) were erected in the enclosure. A substantial western tower (rectangular) of c.1200 remains. The south-east inner gateway led out to a barbican and to a second gateway. The area between the two gateways was enclosed inside a smaller stone enclosure with turrets, built between the mid- and late thirteenth century.

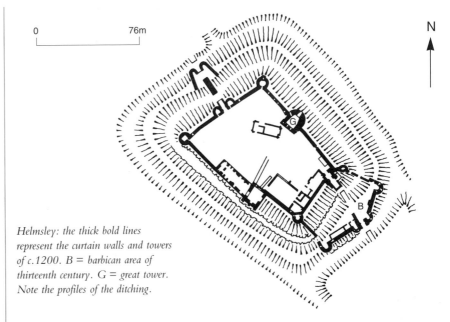

Helmsley: the thick bold lines represent the curtain walls and towers of c.1200. B = barbican area of thirteenth century. G = great tower. Note the profiles of the ditching.

The heightening of the great tower during the fourteenth century demonstrates the continuing value of great towers. Too much of it has been destroyed to work out its internal accommodation.

HEMYOCK Devon
(ST 135133)

This was a fourteenth-century enclosure castle with seven round flanking towers and a twin round-towered gatehouse in the east wall. Begun c.1380 (the date of a licence to crenellate it), it is now in ruins, but recent work has outlined its main features. The enclosure was five-sided with flanking towers on all corners. It was surrounded on the north, west and south sides by a moat fed by a stream that ran along the east. Other buildings were raised later, within and immediately outside the enclosure.

HEREFORD
Hereford & Worcester
(SO 509395)

Hereford is one of the castles once said to have been erected by Norman lords in the time of Edward the Confessor (cf. Ewias Harold and Clavering). But as it is now accepted that no castles were built before 1066, Hereford can probably be included among the first batch of motte castles erected by the Normans between 1066 and 1071. It was held by William FitzOsbern, one of the Conqueror's principal lords. It was a motte castle of which no trace remains, with a bailey, one side of which bordered the River Wye. Leland described the castle in the 1540s as having walls 'high and strong and full of great towers'. He also talks of one great tower encircled by ten semicircular towers. Recent excavations have revealed a confusion of stoneworks of medieval and much later origin. The documents certainly record considerable stoneworks of the thirteenth century, which include a great tower whose form we are not able to determine, but which was sited on the motte.

HERSTMONCEUX Sussex
(TW 646104)

Sir Roger Fiennes, a veteran of the wars in France, was granted a licence to build and crenellate Herstmonceux in 1441. It was constructed of brick, in basically quadrangular plan, with greensand stone dressings. It stands in a lake creating a wide moat round it. At each corner is a boldly projecting octagonal tower, and three semi-octagonal turrets project along its north, east and west fronts. On the south front are two turrets, in between which is a massive gatehouse, created by a further pair of semi-octagonal turrets flanking a handsome entrance arch, with machicolated battlements all round the top of the structure where the two turrets change from octagonal plan to cylindrical. Behind the parapet rising from the cylinders, as it were, are two inner cylinder towers, bringing the height of the gatehouse to about 25.9 metres (85 ft). The entrance arch is recessed and bears long slots for the drawbridge gaffs. Murder-holes are incorporated beneath the arch over the entrance. The gatehouse parapets have cross-arrow-loops which are also inserted in the flanking towers themselves. The middle tower on the north front has a postern gate, and is also recessed for a drawbridge and slotted for the bridge gaffs.

However, the castle was allowed to decline, although the outer masonry was carefully restored by two owners in the present century.

HERTFORD HERTFORDSHIRE
(TL 325125)

It is likely that Hertford began as a motte castle quite early in the Norman period, for a constable was appointed by the Conqueror. It was sited right by the River Lea which provided the water for its inner and outer moats. Renn thinks a small cylindrical tower about 9.1 metres (30 ft) across may have been built on the motte, which was low (about 6 metres [20 ft]). The earliest documentary evidence of work on Hertford is 1171–4. This may have included the approximately pentagonal stone curtain that surrounds the inner bailey and joins up with some stone walling up the motte sides. After this there was a lot of activity at Hertford over many years. The curtain acquired towers and an interesting three-storeyed gatehouse which is

probably fifteenth century. This gatehouse has been restored. Considerable excavation work has been done at Hertford in recent years, substantiating the motte-type origins of the castle (E. Herts. Arch. Soc. Trans.).

HEVER NR EDENBRIDGE, KENT
(TQ 477452)

Hever is basically a quadrangular, fortified manor-house, with great gatehouse, begun in the 1270s. It sits in a lake rather like Bodiam and Kirby Muxloe. A licence to refortify the manor-house was granted in 1340 to the owner, William de Hever. Yet another fortifying was carried out c.1380 by Sir John de Cobham.

Thereafter the castle changed hands several times, and c.1460 it became the property of Henry Boleyn (Lord Mayor of London) who was great-grandfather of Anne Boleyn (second wife of Henry VIII and mother of Elizabeth I). The castle was greatly modified by the Boleyns, and the artificial lake was probably the work of Henry Boleyn's son in about 1482. The three-storey gatehouse with square flanking turrets is probably of this date, although it has been altered and renovated.

Much restoration was done by William Waldorf Astor in 1903–7, who added a number of Tudor-style houses nearby to form a kind of village in which his guests could stay. William Waldorf Astor became 1st Viscount Astor of Hever. The castle is still owned by the Astors.

(Opposite) Hever is a late thirteenth-century castle with fourteenth- and fifteenth-century improvements. It is more usually regarded as a fortified manor-house.

HINTON WALDRIST BERKSHIRE
(SU 376991)

A motte castle was erected here late in the eleventh century.

HOLGATE
STANTON HOLGATE, SHROPSHIRE
(SO 562896)

Near the church are the remains of a motte castle mentioned in Domesday, thus dating it to at least 1085. The motte summit has traces of masonry in rectangular outline suggesting a tower or hall. There are remains of a round tower in the bailey, and of a thirteenth-century gatehouse. The tower is today part of a farmhouse.

HOME HEREFORD & WORCESTER
(SO 733618)

Remains of a twelfth-century motte castle can be seen by the stream.

HOPTON SHROPSHIRE
(SO 367779)

Hopton was a motte castle of the twelfth century which received a rectangular great tower on the motte some time in the (?) thirteenth century. The stonework was surrounded by wet moats. It was captured by Royalists in the Civil War. The great tower still stands.

HORNBY LANCASHIRE
(SD 587687)

A motte castle, with a low motte of about 6.7 metres (22 ft), held by Roger de Montbegon but seized by King John in 1205.

HORSFORD NR NORWICH, NORFOLK
(TG 205156)

A motte with some ditching is all that remains today of the Norman earthwork castle built here, possibly soon after the great motte castle was raised at Norwich c.1070.

HORSTON HORSLEY, DERBYSHIRE
(SK 375432)

Only fragments of this castle of early Norman times have survived. It is on a spur of rock. The principal feature was a rectangular (?) great tower with ashlar masonry dressings,

Hertford: (after King's Works). Plan of the castle as it is today. The bold line represents the remaining walls and towers. R = River Lea. M = mound of original motte castle. The internal buildings are omitted.

standing on a battered plinth and with pilaster buttress corner turrets. The great tower was battlemented c.1205. Further works were carried out in Henry III's time, and in 1264 Horston was captured by the de Ferrers family (of Duffield Castle fame) who began to dismantle it. Afterwards, Horston was held by others and repairs were carried out, but by the sixteenth century it was a ruin.

HUNTINGDON CAMBRIDGESHIRE
(TL 240714)
On his first expedition into the north of England in 1068–9, the Conqueror built several motte castles, some on the way up, others on the return journey. One of the latter was a two-bailey motte castle on the north bank of the Ouse at Huntingdon. The motte

is nearly 12.2 metres (40 ft) high. The second bailey may be of later date than 1068–9. A second mound was erected a few hundred yards from the first, in the twelfth century. Huntingdon Castle passed from the Conqueror's niece Judith to her daughter Matilda who married David I, King of Scotland, who was also Earl of Huntingdon. After the collapse of the revolt of Prince Henry, eldest son of Henry II, in 1174, Huntingdon Castle – which then belonged to William the Lion, King of Scotland, who had supported the prince – was besieged and captured and ordered to be demolished, for which iron hooks were employed to dismantle the woodwork palisade, suggesting that at least part of the castle was still wooden. Stone remains have been found.

HUNTINGTON
NR KINGTON, HEREFORD & WORCESTER
(SO 249539)
A motte castle with two baileys was raised on this site by the powerful de Bohun family. A stone tower was raised on the motte during the late twelfth century. Some fragments still remain. Henry Stafford, Duke of Buckingham, was captured here when he decided to betray his king, 1484.

HUTTONS AMBO YORK, YORKSHIRE
(SE 763674)
A rectangular enclosure raised on a spur above the River Derwent, with rampart and ditch. The earliest building was a timber hall, but this was replaced by a stone hall of sandstone rubble on the same site, in the thirteenth century.

HYLTON

Nr Sunderland, Tyne & Wear
(NZ 358588)

Hylton consists of the repaired ruin of a substantial gatehouse-tower built by Sir William Hylton (1395–1410). Apart from the ruins of St Catherine's chapel nearby, there are no remaining buildings, and it is hard to say what shape the original castle took.

The gatehouse-tower is interesting. It was a residential building – indeed, its internal appointments indicate that it was the Hylton family's main residence. The ground floor is pierced by an arched passage on the west front, which may at one time have passed through to the east side. This passage was once protected by a portcullis. The west front is broken by four square-plan buttress-turrets, capped with machicolated and battlemented octagonal tops. Between the two centre buttress-turrets the parapet is supported by a segmental arch. The carved figures on the battlements are not original. The façade of the west front has been altered, chiefly in the detail of the window and front arch arrangement. The north and south sides are relatively plain, but of fine-quality masonry. The east façade has a central projecting rectangular tower, also battlemented.

Inside, the gatehouse-tower, which is now a shell, once had a ground floor of guardrooms and chambers on both sides of the entrance passage, and the spiral staircase began its upward turn in the south corner of the east block. The staircase rose to the roof. Above the ground floor were three further main storeys. In the centre all the way up to the roof was a tall great hall. At each storey, at either end of the hall, chambers, kitchens (first and second storeys) and other rooms opened off.

INKBERROW

Hereford & Worcester
(SP 017572)

There was a castle here, erected between 1154 and 1216. Earthwork traces remain.

KENDAL Cumbria

(SD 522924)

Kendal was an enclosure with earth banking which in the twelfth or early thirteenth century received stone additions. There was a surrounding stone curtain with cylindrical corner towers, a hall and a square tower (which may be of the twelfth century). Recent excavations exposed a gatehouse-tower which has a cobbled road through the pierced arch, and traces of a bridge across the moat. It appears that there was also some form of motte castle on the site.

KENILWORTH Warwickshire

(SP 278723)

Kenilworth was granted c.1120 by Henry I to his chamberlain, William de Clinton. The first structure was a banked enclosure surrounded by a wide ditch, on which was raised a large mound with a tower. Later in the century, a substantial rectangular great tower was erected upon the motte, possibly after levelling the summit. A stonework curtain was raised along the line of the bank (also levelled). The great tower, on a splayed plinth, began as a three-storeyed building including basement, the basement being filled with the earth of the top of the motte. The two storeys above had one principal room each. Entrance to the tower was by means of a staircase protected by a huge forebuilding on the west, the door at second-storey level. Both great tower and forebuilding were altered in the 1570s.

In 1253 Henry III granted it to Simon de Montfort. King John had spent over £1000 on it, and this included part of the outer stone curtain, the gatehouse and some of the mural towers. Henry III had the royal apartments modernised. It may also have been he who ordered the construction of the formidable water defence system – a dam 'affording a broad causeway across the water to a large outer barbican, to pond back the currents of two streams, flowing respectively past the south and west sides of the raised platform on which the castle stands'. The lake thus formed was more than 40.5 hectares (100 acres) in area. When in 1266 Henry III came upon the castle to besiege it, held as it was by the son of Simon de Montfort who had rebelled in 1264, he was faced with assailing a castle completely surrounded by water, at almost every place too wide to allow a mine tunnel to be dug. The siege began in June and lasted for six months. During this time, the defenders as well as the attackers employed stone-throwing siege-engines. When the king brought up wooden belfries against the outer walls, young de Montfort smashed them down with stone shot from inside. The attackers replied with their artillery, and one account of the siege refers to stone balls colliding in mid-air and smashing to fragments. The garrison finally surrendered when food ran out. The castle had not been taken by siege: even a water-borne assault failed.

The castle became the property of John of Gaunt, Duke of Lancaster, in the 1370s and he remodelled it, raising large domestic ranges to the west and south of the great tower, including a fine great hall, kitchen with three fireplaces and great chamber. In the sixteenth century it was the property of Robert Dudley, Earl of Leicester, Queen Elizabeth I's early favourite, and he added an interesting range of buildings on the south-east corner of the inner curtain.

Kenilworth: ground floor of the great tower c.1160–80. The forebuilding at the left was converted in Tudor times into a courtyard.

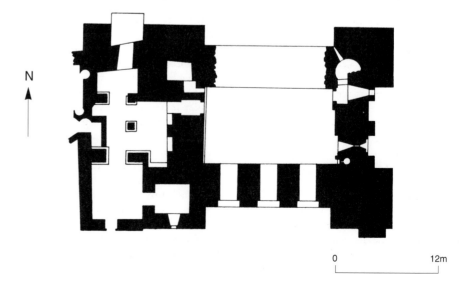

N

0   12m

KILPECK HEREFORD & WORCESTER
(SO 444305)
A castle of several building periods over the centuries, beginning as a motte castle in the late eleventh or early twelfth century. The mound received a shell enclosure in the later twelfth century. There are remains of later buildings, the exact nature of which have still to be determined.

KINGERBY LINCOLNSHIRE
(TF 056928)
This was a motte castle inside a rectangular-plan enclosure, itself surrounded by a ditch. The castle was burnt at the beginning of the thirteenth century. In later years a mansion was built next to the site.

KINGTON HEREFORD & WORCESTER
(SO 291569)
The remnants of an earthwork castle of mound and ditch, of possibly twelfth-century origin, are near the church at Kington. The castle was taken from its holder, Adam de Port, in 1172 by Henry II and remained in royal hands until about 1203 when John gave it to his friend William de Braose.

KINNARD'S FERRY LINCOLNSHIRE
(SE 806002)
Also known as Owston Ferry Castle, this is the site of a motte castle of the twelfth century built probably by the Mowbrays. It was dismantled on the orders of Henry II in 1175–6, perhaps following the rebellion of his son, Prince Henry, in 1173–4.

KIRBY MUXLOE
NR LEICESTER, LEICESTERSHIRE
(SK 524046)
Lord Hastings, who built the Hastings' great tower at Ashby de la Zouch, began to build this attractive fortified house in brickwork c.1480. The accounts for the building work have been preserved but the castle was never finished. Lord Hastings was executed during the works, and his widow could not afford to complete them.

The castle was a quadrangular structure with rectangular corner towers, tower projections mid-wall on three walls, and on the fourth a substantial gatehouse with semi-octagonal turrets flanking the entrance on the inner as well as the outer face. All that remains today are the gatehouse and one corner tower, still surrounded by a wet moat. It is evident

that much of the stonework on the edge of the bank and ditch is of an earlier date, probably fourteenth century, and so the structure initated by Lord Hastings was raised on the remnants of an earlier building. The surviving structures contain several gun-ports of ashlar strategically built into the brickwork and apparently covering every angle of possible attack. Parts of the wall of the surviving tower are over 3 metres (10 ft) thick. And the accounts indicate that the gatehouse was to have machicolation round the parapet. These are enough to establish it as a properly fortified residence.

The castle stood in an artificially constructed lake fed by a tributary of a local brook, which acted as a moat all round. Details of the work on the water arrangements have survived, and among them we read that men were paid to stay up all night to watch the level of the lake to see that it did not rise too high up the ramparts or up the sides of the castle. The water level was meant to be controlled by a system of dams, sluices and hollowed-out oak logs that could be plugged when required.

KIRKOSWALD CUMBRIA
(NY 560410)
A stone curtain enclosure with towers was built on this site in the thirteenth century, following the granting of a licence to fortify to Hugh de Morville c.1201. A tower still remains, along with some scattered masonry. The stone castle may have been erected on an earlier motte site.

KNARESBOROUGH
NORTH YORKSHIRE
(SE 348569)
Knaresborough Castle stands on a high rock overlooking the town and the Nidd valley. It began as an enclosure in the eleventh century. Some time in the twelfth century it received a roughly triangular stone curtain with flanking towers and other buildings inside. One was a tower which may have been a great tower. It was in royal hands on and off from the beginning, right through to the end of the fifteenth century, and most of the work done on it was carried out by the kings. The most extensive work was by Edward II and Edward III, between 1307–50, and the existing remains are chiefly of this period. Edward II had a tower (possibly the suggested great tower) demolished and a new rectangular

great tower built, about 19.5 x 15.8 metres (64 x 52 ft) with four storeys. The north wall protruding from the curtain is semi-hexagonal. The tower was built between 1307–12 at a cost of nearly £900. The staircase to the first floor was defended by three gates and three portcullises. The curtain wall is 12.2 metres (40 ft) high in places.

KNEPP SUSSEX
(TQ 163209)
A motte castle of the early twelfth century, which received a great tower of sandstone probably in the time of Henry II. The tower was raised on the mound. Some 9.1 metres (30 ft) or so of the structure remains in a ruinous state. The castle is believed to have belonged to the de Braose family.

KNOCKIN SHROPSHIRE
(SJ 334223)
A motte castle with a low motte, probably of the twelfth century, was reinforced with stone additions. There are traces of curtain wall round part of the bailey. There are no moats but the site lies between two streams that provided natural defences.

LANCASTER LANCASHIRE
(SD 473620)
Lancaster Castle stands on a knoll overlooking the River Lune, with steep west, north and east sides. It may have begun as a motte castle, but early in the twelfth century it received a great tower of stone, about 24.4 metres (80 ft) square, with 3-metre (10-ft) thick walls; this has been extensively restored. It had pilaster buttresses, a cross-wall and spiral staircases. It was surrounded by ditching, much of which has been filled in. Adjoining the great tower was a thirteenth-century rectangular hall along a curtain wall which ends in a cylindrical tower. At right-angles to the hall projects a further stretch of curtain, at the end of which is another tower, this time rectangular, also of the thirteenth century. When the castle came into the possession of Henry IV, by his right as Duke of Lancaster, in 1399, he began major new works. These probably included the handsome and formidable twin semi-octagonal-turreted gatehouse with boldly projecting machicolated and crenellated parapet round the top, and polygonal turrets emerging above the parapet. The gatehouse entrance arch is wide, and had a portcullis. The gatehouse is over 18.3 metres (60 ft) tall.

Some time in the mid-fourteenth century, Thomas de Lucy built the great tower at Langley, an H-plan structure which was four storeys high, with four substantial corner turrets reaching to about 20.1 metres (66 ft) on the arms of the 'H'. It was attacked and severely damaged by Henry IV during his

Lancaster: the splendid early fifteenth-century, twin polygonal-towered gatehouse is still in good condition.

campaign against the Percys and Archbishop Scrope in 1404–5. An early nineteenth-century description of Langley notes that the inside of the ruined tower was 'red with marks of fire'. The castle was eventually restored as a home in the 1890s.

LAUNCESTON CORNWALL
(SX 330846)
A motte castle was raised here early in the Conqueror's reign by his half-brother, Robert of Mortain. The motte received a shell enclosure of roughly cylindrical plan early in the thirteenth century, having walls about 3 metres (10 ft) thick. This has two stair flights in the masonry to higher levels. Later in the 1200s a cylindrical tower was built inside the shell. It has a pointed arch door on the west side. The stonework between the tower and the shell wall was at one time roofed, as it may also have been at Tretower and Sandal. The sides of the top of the motte were revetted with a stone wall for several feet, and this is sometimes referred to as a mantlet wall. The gateway at the south at bailey level leads to a flight of steps up the side of the motte.

The great seventeenth-century mapmaker Norden described the castle as 'this triple crowned mounde' and the visitor today can see exactly what he meant. Recent excavations exposed remnants of a large early thirteenth-century stone hall in the bailey. It measured about 18.3 x 5.5 metres (60 x 18 ft) internally, and is thought to have been used as a courthouse.

LAVENDON BUCKINGHAMSHIRE
(SP 917544)
A substantial motte castle was raised on the site at Lavendon, probably in the twelfth century. It had three baileys. The motte was demolished during the Second World War (Antiq. Jnl. xxxix).

LEEDS NR MAIDSTONE, KENT
(TQ 836533)
The two-island site in a lake is now occupied by a splendid group of buildings originating from Edward I's time and with later additions also having been made. The first castle was an earthwork enclosure whose wooden palisade was converted to stone and provided with two towers along the perimeter in the mid-twelfth century. This has now vanished. Traces of arches in a vault thought to be Norman were found at the beginning of this century. The castle came into the possession of Edward I c.1278 when the owner, William of Leybourne, handed it to him in part payment of some debts.

Edward I rebuilt much of the castle as it stood at the beginning of his reign, and enlarged it, providing an outer stone curtain

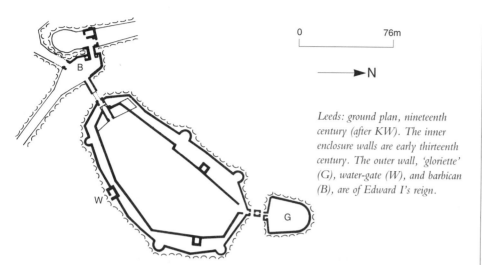

0   76m

→N

Leeds: ground plan, nineteenth century (after KW). The inner enclosure walls are early thirteenth century. The outer wall, 'gloriette' (G), water-gate (W), and barbican (B), are of Edward I's reign.

round the edge of the larger island, with cylindrical open-backed flanking towers and a square-plan water-gate on the south-east. The gatehouse at the south-west, a single tower pierced by an arched passage, was improved.

A medieval castle of several periods, beginning with an early thirteenth-century enclosure with towers, Leeds (Kent) was enlarged at the end of the thirteenth century by the addition of the outer wall, a barbican on the south-west and an isolated 'gloriette' on the north-east.

It led out via a drawbridge across to a smaller island on which was built the 'gloriette', a D-plan tower complex containing other buildings, extensively altered in Tudor and later times.

The castle was besieged by Edward II (1321) when Bartholemew of Badlesmere, holding it as a gift of the king, allowed his castellan to refuse entry to Edward's queen, Isabella. The king took the castle and hanged the castellan.

Much of what remains today is nineteenth-century reconstruction and addition.

LEICESTER LEICESTERSHIRE
(SK 585040)

Leicester Castle was a motte castle with inner and outer bailey, probably raised in 1068. Early in the twelfth century the castle received stone buildings, including a hall which has survived. It was probably built by the 2nd Earl of Leicester after he succeeded his father in 1118. The 2nd Earl's son joined Prince Henry's revolt against Henry II, 1173–4, and had Leicester Castle confiscated and severely damaged for his pains. But the family continued to reside there. It was held for a time by Simon de Montfort, Earl of Leicester, but when he was slain at the Battle of Evesham in 1265, it was taken over by Henry III who gave it to one of his sons, Edmund Crouchback, Earl of Lancaster. Eventually it became the property of John of Gaunt, Duke of Lancaster.

This was the most splendid period of Leicester Castle's history, by which time its military role had taken a marked second place to its residential role. It had become an enclosure with buildings round a square court, the most distinguished being the castle hall, oblong with sandstone walls over 1.2 metres (4 ft) thick.

Henry IV and V spent money on constructing new boundary walls, and a

gateway, the Turret Gateway, much of which still remains.

During the fifteenth century the castle deteriorated as the fortunes of the House of Lancaster declined. Richard III, the last Yorkist king, stayed there a few days before the Battle of Bosworth on 22 August 1485.

Leland described it in 1536 as 'of small estimation'. It has a later history which is not relevant here.

LEWES SUSSEX
(TQ 415101)

Lewes began as one of the few motte castles consisting of two mottes associated with one bailey. Both mottes stand astride the bailey limits. It was built by Gulielmus de Warenne, the Conqueror's chief justiciar, c.1069–70, and was provided with defensive earthworks and moat. The south motte was largely of compacted chalk blocks quarried locally. It carried a wooden tower and palisade which were later replaced by a flint rubble shell enclosure, some of it of knapped flint set in herringbone facework. The shell was built in the early twelfth century. In the thirteenth century this was given two semi-octagonal angle towers on splayed plinths along the wall. Other works included a new range of buildings against the inside of the shell wall, in particular a hall. This superseded an earlier free-standing hall of the early twelfth century that was demolished. A curtain wall was built along one side of the bank between the two mottes, but it is incomplete. A rectangular gate-tower was inserted at the south of this wall, and in the fourteenth century a

magnificent barbican was added to it. Restored, this barbican is one of the best in England – corbelled round towers on the corners, machicolated parapet over the centre pointed arch, the whole built of close-packed small-size knapped flints. The north motte, known as Brack Mount, contains traces of a flint shell wall.

LEYBOURNE KENT
(TQ 688589)

A circular enclosure with banked ditch and an additional banked area adjacent to it, with masonry remains, are the remnants of a castle here which has been incorporated in a much more modern structure.

LIDGATE NR NEWMARKET, SUFFOLK
(TL 722583)

This was a rectangular motte with one bailey, and a ditch and rampart on the south side. There were two other baileys, one encircled by a wet moat and the other by a dry moat. The motte castle appears to have been given its additional enclosures and buildings 'for manorial requirements'. There is some flint masonry which may be part of a gatehouse.

LINCOLN LINCOLNSHIRE
(SK 975718)

Lincoln is one of the handful of motte castles that had two mottes associated with one bailey (Lewes was another). It was started in 1068 on the Conqueror's orders and 166 houses were cleared to allow the castle with its earthworks

to be built. The site covered 2 hectares (5 acres). One of the mottes, raised astride the line of the enclosing bailey wall, was adorned, some time in the twelfth century, with an interesting shell enclosure, some 6 metres (20 ft) tall, 15-sided, bolstered by pilaster buttresses on the angles, with an entrance projecting out of one of the sides and having a fine rounded arch. This is reached by a steep flight of steps which may follow an original flight. There is another entrance at the south end of the shell. Inside the shell some of the stones on the angles are cut and set horizontally as wide-angled V-shapes, presumably to form a stronger join than several quoins cemented together. There was a barbican in front of the shell. In recent years the West Gate has been excavated: it was an early twelfth-century gate-tower, erected upon an earlier part-stone, part-timber gateway. It also had a barbican in front.

The shell enclosure, known as the Lucy Tower, has wing walls; one, in double thickness with parapet walk, leads in a curve down the motte slope and up the slope of the other motte right to the structure on the summit. This wing wall is stepped for some of its length. The other wing wall travels in the opposite direction from the Lucy Tower right round the castle, interspersed with gateways at

---

Lincoln: ground plan. Note the two mottes. The larger motte received the polygonal shell enclosure. Buildings within the enclosure have been omitted.

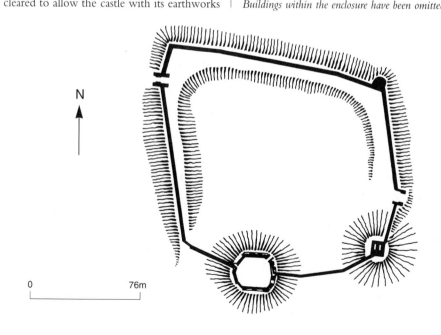

Lewes: (after R. Allen Brown). Ground plan. Note both mottes. The left-hand motte carried the oval shell with polygonal turrets. The dark lines indicate remaining medieval masonry. The barbican (B) is fourteenth century, with restoration of later years.

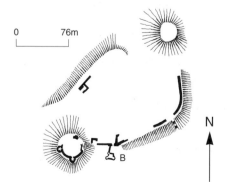

The Lucy Tower, a shell enclosure with wing walls, is one of the main surviving buildings of the important medieval castle at Lincoln.

west and east. The eastern gateway is a handsome structure, with pointed arch surmounted by two semi-cylindrical turret projections (containing spiral stairs) in between which is sandwiched a chevron-plan wall projection, whose apex is in line vertically with the keystone of the arch. This gateway is a reconstruction of the original and simpler gate, and is of thirteenth-century construction with some later work added.

The second motte carries a square-plan tower structure with a nineteenth-century Observatory Tower. The date of this motte is not known for certain. It has been suggested that Ranulf, Earl of Chester, who held the castle in the 1140s and who was granted leave to refortify it (with limitations) by King Stephen, raised it in the south-east corner in the line of the bailey wall and on it erected a wooden tower, which was later converted to

stone. But it has also been mooted that this was the original 1068 motte, and that the Lucy Tower stands on a much later one. The name Lucy stems from Ranulf's mother, Lucy, Countess of Chester, who died c.1136, passing the castle to him. This could date the motte and the shell enclosure to c.1130 or earlier. There is a reference to a stone curtain at Lincoln Castle in 1115. Perhaps this is the period of the building of the Lucy Tower and second motte.

Today the castle can be visited, and there is much to see.

LLANCILLO
HEREFORD & WORCESTER
(SO 367256)
Traces of stone walling can be seen at this motte castle site.

LONGTHORPE TOWER
NR PETERBOROUGH, CAMBRIDGESHIRE
(TL 163983)
This began as a square great tower c.1300, supported by angled buttresses at the lower

part of its height. It is three storeys tall, has walls 1.8–2.1 metres (6–7 ft) thick, and is built of small stone rubble with larger quoins. The ground floor is vaulted, but the room inside is not connected to the storeys above which are in fact reached by a passage at first floor level from the building next door (which is partly of a slightly earlier date). The first floor contains the great chamber, also vaulted, and this has recesses, including a possible garderobe, and a narrow staircase leading up to the top floor, above which was the roof with a parapet and wall-walk.

One particularly notable feature of Longthorpe is the series of medieval wall paintings in the great chamber. These had been whitewashed, possibly for centuries, but were revealed during cleaning soon after the Second World War.

LONGTOWN
HEREFORD & WORCESTER
(SO 321291)
A motte of some 10.7 metres (35 ft) in height at the corner of a rectangular double bailey,

probably constructed in the late eleventh century and later crowned with a cylindrical great tower of sandstone rubble on a battered plinth in the 1300s. Walling skirts down the motte slope towards a right-angle of curtain wall within the northern half of one bailey. The tower is interesting: its three lobes project slightly (at 120 degrees from each other) from the cylindrical plan, the lobes acting as buttresses. One has a staircase. Note the corbelled garderobe shoot halfway up the tower beside one of the lobe buttresses.

LOWER DOWN

LYDBURY, SHROPSHIRE

(SO 336846)

An early motte castle here is believed to have received a polygonal shell enclosure in the twelfth century. Only fragments remain.

LUDGERSHALL WILTSHIRE

(SU 264513)

An extensive earthwork enclosure beginning in the late eleventh century in which a motte castle was raised. The earthworks consisted of two adjacent double-ditched enclosures with double ramparts. Excavation has revealed a complex series of buildings of several periods:

1 Three phases of timber buildings, of late eleventh and early twelfth century, were found. There was some rough brickwork incorporated in the third phase.

2 An enclosed rectangle of stone and timber buildings of the same period, including a timber tower.

3 A phase in which some of these works were demolished and others preserved, and a great tower of stone was begun, in the mid-twelfth century, but evidently not finished. This was superseded by another larger great tower, with stone steps, which incorporated the smaller tower. This later tower was then pulled down and replaced by a tower set in a rampart with a timber rampart walk, c.1200. In the thirteenth century four more phases converted the castle to more of a residence, including a great hall (c.1244–5), and several ancillary buildings. There were three chapels, all of about the same period. By then the castle had become a hunting lodge for the king, Henry III.

LUDLOW SHROPSHIRE

(SO 508746)

This is a castle of considerable interest, much of it of great antiquity. The site stands upon

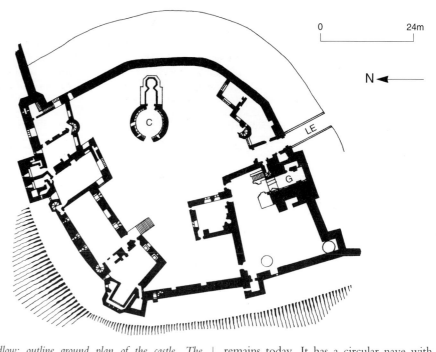

Ludlow: outline ground plan of the castle. The earliest buildings were the round chapel (C), the first gatehouse (G) and the enclosing curtain. The gatehouse was later altered to make a great tower. LE = later entrance.

the top of a rock promontory over 30.5 metres (100 ft) high overlooking the River Teme. Some time towards the end of the eleventh century, a stone curtain enclosure was raised in multangular plan, roughly an oval shape, whose north and west abut upon the steep and rocky south bank of the Teme, and whose east and south were protected by a rock-cut dry moat. The curtain, about 3 metres (10 ft) thick for most of its length, was provided with a simple stone gateway in the south (cf. Exeter). The curtain was also flanked with two square and two polygonal wall-towers along the north and west sides which indicate that the idea of a curtain wall with flanking towers as a form of defence was introduced much earlier into English castles than has previously been accepted (Allen Brown). This is lent weight by the existence of similarly dated walling having a flanking tower (incorporated in later work) at Rochester, and by flanking towers at Richmond, also of early date.

Ludlow had wooden buildings at first, but in the early twelfth century an unusual Norman chapel was built, much of which

remains today. It has a circular nave with a battlemented top and a billet-on-chevron moulded round-head arch at the entrance on the west. The chancel has disappeared. The chapel is among the earliest castle chapels to be built in Britain.

In the mid-twelfth century, the gateway was enlarged into a tower-cum-gateway. Afterwards, that gateway was blocked up (as happened much later to the gatehouse at Dunstanburgh) to make a great tower of nearly square plan. A fresh entrance was cut into the curtain beside the great tower (not unlike the arrangements at Roscrea, Co. Tipperary). In the later fifteenth century the great tower was substantially reduced in size: its northern and parts of its western and eastern walls were demolished and a new wall erected 3.6 metres (12 ft) or so further back.

The other buildings inside the enclosure, including great hall, great chamber, annexes, residential block and kitchen block, are mostly of fourteenth-century construction, altered and in some respects beautified in the Tudor period. The residential block was recently found to have wall passages and flights of steps from ground to first floor level.

LUMLEY

NR CHESTER-LE-STREET, DURHAM

(NZ 288511)

A quadrangular fortified manor-house erected in the 1390s following a licence to crenellate of 1389–90. The holder, Lord Lumley, was a supporter of Richard II who was deposed in 1399. The castle has a quadrangle about 24.4 metres (80 ft) square with substantial square towers at the corners. The towers were topped with octagonal turrets bearing machicolation. The east wing of the quadrangle has an interesting gatehouse.

LYDFORD DEVON
(SX 510848)

This is one of the castles whose great tower was raised before the motte which was subsequently piled up round the tower base (cf. Aldingbourne). The castle is very early: 40 houses were destroyed to make room for an enclosure soon after the Conquest. The square great tower (15.8 metres [52 ft]) is on a platform to the east of a sizeable banked bailey, and is of two periods: the lower part is of the twelfth century and the top is of the thirteenth. It was during the works of the thirteenth century that the motte was piled up round the bottom part, blocking up the windows. The tower has a cross-wall. In the east wall are two double-splayed windows.

The great tower decayed but in the eighteenth century it was used as a courthouse and prison for the Stannary Court.

LYDNEY GLOUCESTERSHIRE
(SO 617025)

In Little Camp, by Lydney Park, the remains of a Norman stone castle were excavated earlier this century. The plan was approximately pentagonal, with uneven sides, with a rectangular tower (15.2 x 17.4 metres [50 x 57 ft]) of local limestone rubble with squared sandstone facing in one of the corners. Next to the tower was a gateway, also rectilinear in plan. An iron mine was found in the courtyard. The dating is early twelfth century. The surrounding earthworks are all that remain.

LYMPNE NR HYTHE, KENT
(TR 117342)

A castle was built on the edge of a sheer cliff at Lympne in the 1080s. In the fourteenth century the remains of this early structure, whose form is not known, were replaced by a great hall with a tower at each end. The west tower is D-ended, the east tower is square. Lympne Castle was probably raised as a defence against raids from French naval forces coming across the Channel over which the

site commands a splendid view. It is also known as Stutfall Castle.

LYONSHALL
NR MADLEY, HEREFORD & WORCESTER
(SO 331563)

An earthwork enclosure with an additional bailey, the remains of which are near the church. A cylindrical tower was erected on a low platform in the enclosure, probably in the thirteenth century, and the enclosure was surrounded by a stone curtain.

MALMESBURY WILTSHIRE
(ST 935872)

There was a castle of some kind at Malmesbury, according to several records, but the design is not established. Probably raised during the Anarchy of Stephen's reign, Malmesbury Castle had stonework. It was pulled down in 1216 by monks from the abbey, with the king's consent. There are stretches of wall remaining which may be part of the old curtain.

MARISCO LUNDY ISLAND
(SS 141437)

A thirteenth-century rectangular tower inside a curtained enclosure was raised here, using local stone, but the lime and other materials were ferried over the sea from Devon. The name of the castle comes from a family of pirates who used the island as a haven. Some of the outer walls are still standing.

MARLBOROUGH WILTSHIRE
(SU 183686)

The earliest mention of Marlborough motte castle is 1110. The remains are in the grounds of the college. Henry II added stone buildings, using quarrels (squared stones). There are accounts for more than 176,000 shingles which suggest extensive roofing to buildings.

King John had new kitchens built, with ovens big enough to allow the roasting of two or three whole oxen at one time. He also built the circular shell enclosure with narrow pilaster buttresses on the motte summit, since vanished. Henry III spent over £2,000, including constructing a tower inside the shell, although it is now not possible to determine its plan. The castle was still garrisoned in the mid-fourteenth century. Today there is only the motte, over 15.2 metres (50 ft) tall, which stands in the grounds of Marlborough College.

MARSHWOOD DORSET
(SY 404977)

A motte castle of the twelfth century was later improved by the erection of a rectangular great tower on the mound. Some parts of the ground-storey masonry remain.

MAXSTOKE WARWICKSHIRE
(SP 224891)

A licence was granted c.1345 for this quadrangular fortified house with corner polygonal towers and a gatehouse. It was one of the earliest fortified houses of this kind to be built. It has been considerably modified since the fourteenth century. Maxstoke is surrounded by a wide and deep moat.

MEMBURY
NR RAMSBURY, WILTSHIRE
(SU 305745)

The site of an aerodrome during the Second World War, Membury was excavated under an emergency scheme in 1941. This revealed a rectangular earthwork inside which were building foundations. A twelfth-century tower was replaced by a thirteenth-century (or later) mansion.

MEPPERSHALL BEDFORDSHIRE
(TL 132358)

A motte castle with two baileys in front of it, in series, all ditched and banked, and these are inside a larger rectangular moated enclosure split into segments.

MERDON HURSLEY, HAMPSHIRE
(SU 421265)

A circular enclosure with ditch and bank, probably surrounded by a flint-built curtain and provided with a gate-tower having walls 2.1 metres (7 ft) thick. The castle was probably little more than a sparsely fortified manor-house of an early date, possibly c.1130–40. Fragments of stonework remain.

MIDDLEHAM
NR LEYBURN, NORTH YORKSHIRE
(SE 128875)

There was a motte castle some 396.2 metres (1300 ft) from the present ruins of the later stone castle at Middleham. This motte dates from c.1086. In c.1170, Robert Fitzrandolph, descendant of the original owner of Middleham, was granted leave to build a great tower, and a very substantial structure emerged: rectangular, 32.9 x 23.8 metres (108

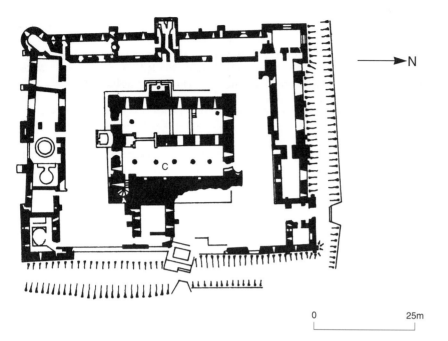

Middleham: ground plan. The great tower is in the centre. The great hall is over the cellars (C). The outer quadrangle is thirteenth and fourteenth century.

x 78 ft), two-storeyed, about 18.3 metres (60 ft) tall, the walls 3–3.6 metres (10–12 ft) thick, and with a cross-wall, two garderobe towers, clasping corner buttresses, one larger than the other three, splayed plinth on three sides, built of rubble inside and faced on the exterior with limestone ashlar. Entrance was (as usual with great towers) through a first-storey door, and in this case approached up a long flight of stairs on the east wall of the tower, once protected by a long forebuilding. All this is now in a very ruinous condition.

In the thirteenth century, the great tower was enclosed in a quadrangular curtain with buildings ranged along three sides, including corner towers and gatehouse. A tall chapel was built on to the east side of the great tower, abutting the forebuilding. Further buildings were added in the fourteenth and fifteenth centuries. It was also surrounded by a moat inside a further surrounding wall, with additional ditching and walling round what is presumed to have been a second courtyard sited to the east.

Middleham came into the possession of the Nevilles, passing to the great Richard, Earl of Warwick, the 'Kingmaker', and thence through his second daughter, Anne, to her husband, Richard, Duke of Gloucester, later

Richard III. He and Anne are thought to have loved the castle and enjoyed it as a residence. Its ruinous state today is a result of being severely slighted after the Civil War.

MIDDLETON STONEY
Nr Bicester, Oxfordshire
(SP 534233)
There was a motte castle at Middleton Stoney in the twelfth century, adduced from some pottery of that time discovered in excavations about 40 years ago. The earliest documentary mentions, however, are of later date, viz. 1215–16, and these include an order from John that the castle should be dismantled. By that time some stonework had been added. The levelling of some of the earthworks suggest that the order to dismantle was in part, if not totally, carried out. The motte has been dated c.1140.

MILEHAM Nr Litcham, Norfolk
(TF 916193)
A motte castle was raised here in the twelfth century. Later, the motte was given a square great tower of flint rubble, with splayed plinth. The mound remains, bearing some stone fragments.

MISERDEN Gloucestershire
(SO 945092)
A motte castle built in the twelfth century near the river was improved with added stonework. This consisted of a shell enclosure

of probably early thirteenth-century origin. But the castle was left to deteriorate, and by the fourteenth century it appears not to have been worth restoring.

MITFORD Northumberland
(NZ 170855)
Early motte castles were few and far between in Northumbria, but one was erected at Mitford in the 1100s. The later stonework additions are interesting; the motte top was surrounded with a D-shaped shell enclosure inside which was a great tower of five sides. The tower basement is vaulted, and the rooms are separated by a cross-wall. The structures stood on a natural mound of local sandstone. There are also some remains of a rough course rubble curtain round one bailey.

Mitford was confiscated by King John in 1215 from the holder for his part in the Magna Carta war. Two years later it was besieged by Alexander II, King of Scotland, but not captured.

MOCCAS Hereford & Worcester
(SO 348246)
A motte castle of the twelfth century was superseded by a late thirteenth-century fortified manor-house; there are no remains.

MONTACUTE Somerset
(ST 493169)
A very early castle built on a site obtained by the holder, Robert de Mortain, by exchanging land with Athelney Abbey in 1069–70. The castle was given to the priory of Cluniac monks nearby, c.1104, by Robert's son, and the stonework that had probably been added in the first years of the century was used for building works by the monks. Montacute was a motte castle whose motte was surrounded by a ditch; it stood inside a bailey that was also enriched by ditching.

MONTFICHET Addle Hill
City of London
A motte castle with a tower on a low motte was raised here in 1066–7 by the Conqueror soon after he had been crowned in Westminster Abbey. It was demolished in the thirteenth century.

MORETON CORBET Shropshire
(SJ 562232)
A sandstone and rubble great tower of diminutive size was built here c.1200, inside a

roughly triangular stone enclosure. Remains of this castle may be seen beside the ruins of the Elizabethan manor-house built for Robert Corbet c.1579. The castle was given a gatehouse, probably in the fourteenth century, and this has been restored.

MORPETH NORTHUMBERLAND
(NZ 200857)

A motte castle was built on Ha'Hill by the River Wansbeck in the reign of William Rufus. Stonework was added in the mid-twelfth century, but whatever type of castle emerged was destroyed by King John in 1215. Later in the thirteenth century a second castle was built nearby in part of the bailey of the original castle, and a gatehouse (of uncertain date) and some curtain wall remain. The gatehouse was given polygonal bartizans and a fine pointed arch to the entrance passage. In the Civil War, 500 Scots held out against a siege by Montrose for three weeks before finally surrendering.

MOUNTSORREL LEICESTERSHIRE
(SK 578148)

Mountsorrel began as a motte castle on a natural rock overlooking the town and the River Soar. It was held by the Earls of Leicester from c.1140 until taken by Henry II after the revolt of his son, Prince Henry, 1173–4. The castle was given stonework, including a tower, hall and also a chamber. Richard I spent money on Mountsorrel, and John ordered timber from Leicester (about 11.3 km [7 miles] away) to build hoarding (in 1215) along its walls. The castle was besieged in 1216–17 and finally dismantled.

MULGRAVE NORTH YORKSHIRE
(NZ 840117)

A polygonal-plan curtain enclosure, its gateway between two towers, encircled a great tower which had round angle-turrets and a forebuilding. The castle was begun c.1215, and the great tower was probably work of c.1300. Additions were made in later years. It is now in ruins.

MUNCASTER RAVENGLASS, CUMBRIA
(SD 103964)

A pele-tower of the late thirteenth century is incorporated in the south-west of the present castle at Muncaster. The castle guards an approach to Eskdale and overlooks the anchorage at Ravenglass which was once a busy harbour. The buildings were substantially reconstructed in the 1850s by Anthony Salvin, the well known Victorian architectural restorer. Muncaster is remarkable among castles for having been in the possession of the same family, the Penningtons, for more than seven centuries.

MYDDLE
NR SHREWSBURY, SHROPSHIRE
(SJ 469235)

A fourteenth-century small quadrangular castle with outer bailey was almost completely destroyed in the seventeenth century, reputedly as a result of earth tremors. There are remains of one turret.

NAFFERTON NORTHUMBERLAND
(NZ 072657)

Now known locally as Lonkins, the ruins of a castle also called Nafferton lie near a bridge across the Whittle Dean. The bridge itself is thought to have been built of stone blocks from the castle after it became ruinous.

NAWORTH CUMBRIA
(NY 560626)

This castle, built in the early fourteenth century, appears to have been a simple walled quadrilateral enclosure with a great tower in the wall at one end and a gateway at the other. A deep moat was cut on three of the four sides. It is possible that the great tower was the first building. A licence to crenellate was granted in 1335 to Ranulf de Dacre at a time of hostilities between England and Scotland. The tower has been alluded to as a pele, and it may have been just that. The considerable changes wrought in the buildings since the fourteenth century have obscured much of the castle's original plan. The present appearance is due largely to restoration by Anthony Salvin after a fire in the 1840s.

NEROCHE
NR BUCKLAND ST MARY, SOMERSET
(ST 272158)

This is an unusual structure. It began as an earthwork enclosure on a spur of the Blackdown Hills in the eleventh century, erected inside a larger and much earlier earthwork ring. Then in the 1100s the smaller enclosure was rendered into a motte castle by building a 7.6-metre (25-ft) tall motte across it. Later in the twelfth century part of the outer ditch was lined with stone, and a shell enclosure was also raised in one corner of the motte.

The eleventh-century castle was probably built by Robert of Mortain, William the Conqueror's half-brother.

NETHER STOWEY SOMERSET
(ST 187396)

An early motte castle with two baileys, Nether Stowey was given a substantial rectangular great tower, about 18.3–15.2 metres (60 x 50 ft), on the motte top which was itself several times larger in area. The great tower had a southern forebuilding and a cross-wall. The date of the tower is probably mid-twelfth century. There are a few ruins on Castle Hill.

NEWARK NOTTINGHAMSHIRE
(SK 796540)

Newark Castle stands on the west bank of the Trent, on a platform raised over an earlier inhabited settlement. It began as an earthwork enclosure raised in the 1130s by the Bishop of Lincoln, and it remained a church-owned castle throughout its active existence.

The first stonework was probably added in the reign of King Stephen. Major works were carried out in the time of John and Henry III. Approximately rectangular, the castle became a tall stonework quadrangle. The corner and mid-wall-towers were square and taller than the quadrangle. There is a remnant of a hexagonal tower of the thirteenth century on the south-west adjacent to an earlier postern. The gatehouse was a square-plan tower of three storeys pierced at ground level by a wide passage approached through a shallow round-headed arch. The present windows are replacements of later date than the original twelfth-century Norman ones. The gatehouse is 13.7 x 9.1 metres (45 x 30 ft) with walls 2.4–2.7 metres (8–9 ft) thick and buttresses on the corners. The front has sloping, offset buttresses supporting the lower part of the walls on either side of the entrance.

Newark was held for King John in the Magna Carta war, and he died there in 1216.

NEW BUCKENHAM NORFOLK
(TL 084904)

There are extensive earthworks at New Buckenham embracing part of the present village. The inner and smaller part is a figure-of-eight site divided by a ditch and with ditching all round. The ditch has been widened. Remains of a thirteenth-century gateway into one of the loops of the 'eight' are reached by a wooden bridge across the ditch, and some fragments are partly buried in a high rampart on one side. In the inner bailey – which is about 0.8 hectares (2 acres) in area and almost totally surrounded by the continuation of the high rampart, 6–9.1 metres (20–30 ft) tall – is the lower part of a flint rubble cylindrical great tower. This tower is of considerable interest and importance in the story of castles (*see* pp. 29–30).

The tower is about 20 metres (65 ft) in diameter. Its walls are 3.3–4 metres (11–13 ft) thick (4 metres at the base), and it has a cross-wall about 1.5 metres (5 ft) thick. In the basement there is an opening in the cross-wall with a rounded doorway with ashlar quoins at the base. There is a rough stonework entrance from which any dressings it may have had have been removed. It may not be the original entrance. The height of the tower is at present about 7.6 metres (25 ft) at the tallest point, and this appears to represent two storeys, judging from post-holes in the cross-wall that may be slots for floor crossbeams. Originally it was probably four storeys in all which, with parapet, could have taken it to about 20–21.3 metres (65–70 ft).

Its importance lies in its date, namely c.1140–50. This makes it probably the earliest cylindrical great tower in Britain, and helps to discredit the received idea that cylindrical great towers were an advance upon rectangular great towers. Clearly the two styles were being built concurrently.

NEWCASTLE TYNE & WEAR
(NZ 253639)

Sited by the Tyne, Newcastle began as a motte castle c.1080, with a bank and ditch. Part of the bank was clay-lined. In the late eleventh and early twelfth centuries the ownership of the northern counties of England was often disputed with Scotland and for a time Newcastle was held by Scottish kings, notably David I (1124–53). The motte was probably demolished to make way for the new stone castle begun by Henry II in 1168. Works continued for about ten years under Mauricius Caementarius (Maurice the builder), and included a substantial rectangular great tower, 18.9 x 17 metres (62 x 56 ft), enclosed within a curtain wall with flanking towers. This work cost over £1000 and may have included other buildings.

The great tower stands on a splayed plinth, has clasping angle buttresses (the north-west one is multangular), and buttresses in the centre of all four walls. The basement is vaulted. There are five storeys, one being the upper part of a double-height storey with chambers and passages in the walls at both levels. The walls are 4.6–5.5 metres (15–18 ft) thick. The top storey has a mural gallery all round. There is an extensive forebuilding along the east side which has been altered over the centuries. Originally, it had three towers, ascending from the entrance at ground level to a door into the great hall at third-storey level. The tallest tower contains a chapel, vaulted with a round-head arch with dog-tooth moulding.

The forebuilding stairs are in three flights with landings. The lowest tower has vanished. Inside the great tower, storeys are reached by spiral staircase in the south-east corner. The great hall was originally not accessible from the spiral stair but via an intermediate straight flight in the wall. The hall is 9.1 x 7.3 metres (30 x 24 ft) and is 12.2 metres (40 ft) tall with a brick vault roof, a nineteenth-century renovation of an originally lower ceiling. In the north-east corner is a vaulted chamber with access to the tower well, with basic recesses and pipe holes through which water was conveyed to other (lower) parts of the tower. The well is nearly 30.5 metres (100 ft) deep, and is ashlar-lined.

The curtain enclosure was many-sided, with postern gates and rectangular flanking towers, and had additional buildings raised against the inside in later years, notably the aisled great hall of c.1210, demolished in 1809. In 1247–50 the Black Gate, a rectangular tower, was built at the north-west, with a central passage piercing the ground floor, and with a drawbridge over a pit into a polygonal chamber, at the other end of which was an oval-plan gate-tower. This was pierced by a passage with gates, portcullis and drawbridge out front.

Newcastle was often attacked during hostilities with Scotland, and it was captured in the Civil War.

NEWCASTLE UNDER LYME
STAFFORDSHIRE
(SJ 845459)

The River Lyme was effectively dammed to produce a sizeable lake to protect the motte raised here probably in the twelfth century.

Remains have been found of a long and narrow building with pilaster buttresses, of the twelfth century. This was a tower that is said to have reached 21.3 metres (70 ft) tall. The mound is visible. Much work was carried out at the end of the twelfth century and over £200 spent on it by King John.

NORHAM
NR BERWICK, NORTHUMBERLAND
(NT 907476)

Norham stands on the south bank of the Tweed. Its site is protected on north and west by a steep cliff which forms part of the river bank. The east is protected by a ravine, and the south sides by an artificially deepened hollow which leads into the river at the south-west. In the north-east corner of this site is a roughly D-shaped inner bailey which is protected on its west and south by an inner ditch leading eastwards into the ravine, and its other two sides are actually along the ravine (east) and the steep part of the river bank (north). In the south-east corner of the inner bailey (which is enclosed by a thick stone curtain, now much ruined) is a massive rectangular great tower, also in ruins.

Other buildings in the inner bailey include a hall with kitchens (north) and, at south, a flanking tower with triangular front called Clapham's Tower, built in 1513 and equipped with gun-ports. The outer bailey is enclosed by a curtain wall, also much ruined, with several flanking towers and two gates, the West Gate and Sheep Gate (at the south), again, both buildings now ruinous. The West Gate leads out to a barbican, and the Sheep Gate once led out to a drawbridge across the outer moat, since replaced by a causeway.

Norham Castle belonged to the bishops of Durham. Founded by Bishop Flambard c.1120, it was destroyed by the Scots in the 1140s. It was rebuilt in stone in the 1160s at the demand of Henry II, and the bishop employed Richard de Wolviston as mason in charge (*see* p. 24). This was when the great tower was begun.

The castle was held by Henry II from 1173–89, and by King John from 1208–16. Norham stood in the front line for attack by the Scots and on numerous occasions it was besieged, and even captured. Each time damage was done, with the result that there is evidence of new work and repair work in nearly every generation between the twelfth and the sixteenth centuries. The DoE guide should be consulted in order to understand fully its history and its building story.

The great tower is 25.6 x 18.3 metres (84 x 60 ft), reaching 27.4 metres (90 ft) in some parts of the wall which remain standing. Rectangular in plan, it began as a three-storey building, two storeys above a vaulted basement. This work was done by the Bishop of Durham between 1158–74. The tower was heightened by two further storeys in the fifteenth century. A cross-wall was inserted above the vaulted basement for support of the new works. The new building was besieged in 1513 by James IV of Scotland who employed artillery, including the famous gun Mons Meg. The castle surrendered only a few days before the disastrous defeat of the Scots at Flodden Field, at which James was slain.

NORTHALLERTON
NORTH YORKSHIRE
(SE 365940)

An enclosure castle was built at Northallerton c.1068 but almost the whole site has been destroyed by nineteenth-century railway works. In c.1160, a motte castle was raised nearby by Bishop Pudsey, and this was employed on behalf of the rebel son of Henry II, Prince Henry, in 1173–4, whose revolt was crushed by the king. Bishop Pudsey's castle was levelled in about 1176. A later Bishop of Durham fortified a house on Pudsey's castle site and this saw military use during the revolt of the Mowbrays and Archbishop Scrope in the early years of Henry IV's reign. There are remains of the earthworks.

NORTHAMPTON
NORTHAMPTONSHIRE
(SP 748604)

There is practically nothing left of this once-important medieval castle. The first structure was a motte castle, built in the 1080s, on a site from which several Anglo-Saxon houses had been cleared. In c.1110 Henry I took over the castle and enlarged it. Works include a substantial ditch (over 27.4 metres [90 ft] wide and 9.1 metres [30 ft] deep) and a rampart (6 metres [20 ft] tall) round a large bailey. This was one of those occasions when the Crown paid compensation for encroaching upon another owner's land. By 1164 the castle had a great hall, a gateway, curtain walling and a chapel. Soon afterwards, a great tower was built although it is not possible to say what shape or size it achieved.

Northampton was besieged by the Magna Carta barons' forces using French-built siege artillery, but King John relieved the garrison and forced the attackers to withdraw. Major repairs were needed after this engagement but, despite continuing expenditure, the castle was not properly defensible by the time of the Barons' War against Henry III, led by Simon de Montfort who used the castle as a headquarters. There was more spent on it over the next century but it continued to deteriorate. The remnants were obscured by the erection of a railway over the site in the nineteenth century.

NORWICH NORFOLK
(TG 232085)

In 1067 the Conqueror ordered William FitzOsbern, one of his principal barons, to build a motte castle at Norwich, but it remained a royal castle. It was a huge mound, probably the largest ever built in England (although not as tall as Thetford), part of a natural protuberance and part-artificial. The artificial motte was over 12.2 metres (40 ft) tall, and big enough in area to carry a complete inner enclosure of palisade wall, great tower of timber and other buildings. One hundred and thirteen buildings were demolished to make room for it.

In 1075 the castle was besieged, and again in 1087–8, on the second occasion by Roger Bigod, a powerful Norman noble in revolt against William II. Some time in the reign of Henry I, probably between c.1125–35, the motte received a very substantial great tower. This was 29 x 27.4 metres (95 x 90 ft) and rose to 21.3 metres (70 ft) tall. It was built in somewhat similar style to the king's great tower at Falaise Castle in Normandy c.1120. The internal arrangements (which were destroyed in later centuries) included a large hall and chamber on the first floor, with garderobes, a chapel and a room for the castellan. The ground floor contained storage chambers and armour; the second floor, guardrooms and a gallery inside the walls all round. The tower also had a kitchen, one of the earliest built in a great tower in England.

The great tower was built of ashlar blocks of Caen stone facing a flintwork core. The walls had pilaster buttresses, interspersed with tiers of blind external arcading of varying size and punctuated with windows and loops (restored in the 1830s by Anthony Salvin). The present battlemented parapet (also of the 1830s) is probably a good reconstruction of the original. Evidently the great tower was built largely by masons released from working on Norwich Cathedral for a period, and presumably stone consigned for the cathedral was also diverted.

The castle was appropriated by Henry II in 1157 from the Count of Mortain, one of

Norwich: the great tower visible today was restored extensively in the early nineteenth century by Anthony Salvin, as closely as possible to its original twelfth-century form.

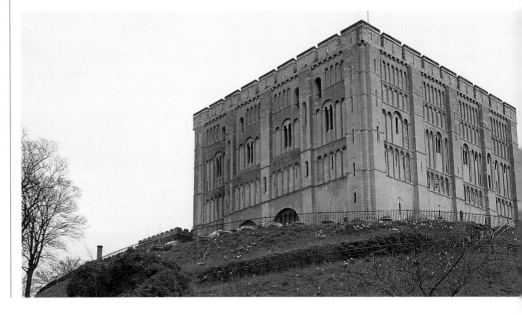

Stephen's sons. Work was carried out which included raising a palisade. During the 1173–4 revolt of Prince Henry against his father, Hugh Bigod, Earl of Norfolk, captured Norwich on behalf of the prince. When the revolt collapsed, Bigod lost nearly all his possessions and captures and Norwich reverted to the king, who spent money on further works. In 1268–70, the wooden wall around the castle was replaced by a stone curtain, at a cost of £500. Twenty years later Edward I spent a similar amount on rebuilding the hall in the great tower.

NOTTINGHAM NOTTINGHAMSHIRE
(SK 569394)

The present castle at Nottingham has little to do with the medieval castle that began as a motte castle c.1068. The motte was raised on what is now called Castle Rock. Henry II appropriated the castle in the 1150s and spent about £900 on it in the years 1170–5, which may have included a great tower. The castle remained in the Crown's hands for centuries, during which time it grew in magnificence until, in the mid-fifteenth century, it filled the land now occupied by the General Hospital and the Castle Rock. After the accession of Henry VII in 1485 it deteriorated, and it was almost completely destroyed in 1651 on the orders of Cromwell.

In 1617, John Smythson (designer of Bolsover Castle) drew a plan of Nottingham as it was then, although we do not gather from it the state of the buildings whose plans he includes. The plan is Pl. 48 of *The History of the King's Works, ii*. Some excavations of recent years have shown that the gatehouse in the outer bailey (which has been substantially restored) is of mid-thirteenth-century origin, and that the gatehouse into the middle bailey had a forebuilding and a barbican, and had been started in the time of Henry II and was completely rebuilt in Edward III's reign.

Of the many historical events associated with Nottingham Castle, one is of special interest. The castle was held by Queen Isabella (widow of Edward II whom she and her lover, Roger Mortimer, had put to death in 1327). She and her paramour attempted to hold out against the young Edward III (her son), but by tunnelling through the rock he entered the fortress and arrested the guilty pair. The actual tunnel is said to be that which is today called Mortimer's Hole and which can be inspected by visitors.

NUNNEY NR FROME, SOMERSET
(ST 737457)

The most dramatic feature of Nunney is the huge, gaping hole in the north wall of this high, compact, rectangular tower with huge corner cylindrical towers. The wall was smashed through by cannon of Oliver Cromwell at first-floor level above the entrance in 1645. The castle yielded two days afterwards and in due course some of the inside was stripped.

Nunney tower was described by the late S.E. Rigold (of DoE) as distinctly French, although there are similarities with the earlier Carlow, Co. Carlow, Terryglass, Co. Tipperary and Ferns, Co. Wexford. The towers were the same height as the two walls (north and south) – on the east and west side, the towers are coupled together – and the parapet at the top was machicolated all round. Each tower carried on top a small-diameter cylinder turret. The diameter of the towers was about 8.2 metres (27 ft), and the height from the straight plinth below to the parapet was 16.4 metres (54 ft). The tower walls are 1.5–1.8 metres (5–6 ft) thick. The lower part of each tower was lit by narrow loops only, as built in the 1370s (the licence to crenellate

Nunney: plan of the rectangular great tower with four cylindrical towers clamped on the corners. Built in the late fourteenth century, the style was very rare in Britain. In Ireland, however, several similar great towers were erected, although they are of early to mid-thirteenth century and were influenced by designs direct from north-west Europe (cf. Carlow, Ferns, Lea and Terryglass, qq.v.).

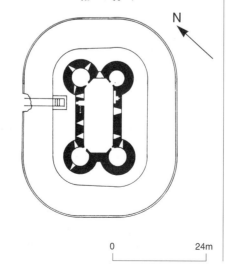

was granted to Sir John de la Mere in 1373), but some of these were enlarged in the sixteenth century to let in more light. The four-storey tower was entered through a very narrow door. The great hall was on the second floor.

OAKHAM LEICESTERSHIRE
(SK 861090)

The twelfth-century hall at Oakham is one of the best-preserved examples of a free-standing hall in a Norman castle. It is constructed of ironstone rubble with ashlar dressings and, although it has been repaired, it is a fine example of an early medieval hall. The castle began as a motte castle and acquired its first stoneworks in the twelfth century.

ODIHAM HAMPSHIRE
(SU 726519)

This was one of King John's favourite castles. Today, you can see the shell of the polygonal (octagonal) great tower built by him between 1207–12, at a cost of about £1000. The corners of the great tower had angle buttresses, but there was no forebuilding. Odiham was besieged in 1216, by which time it had part of its enclosure of curtain wall. In 1324–5, major repairs were carried out. After David II, King of Scotland, was captured at the Battle of Neville's Cross in 1346, he spent 11 years in exile in England. Some of this confinement was at Odiham.

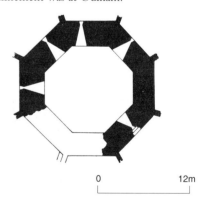

Odiham: (after D.F. Renn). Ground-floor level of polygonal great tower.

OKEHAMPTON DEVON
(SX 584942)

A motte castle of the Conqueror's reign (probably before 1070), set on the top of a naturally fortified ridge, was greatly extended for a long way down the ridge in the form of buildings round an elongated bailey, in the early fourteenth century. The castle has been compared with German hill-top castles such as Staufen and Rothenburg. There are in fact two distinct parts.

The motte first received a square great tower, built of shale rubble and granite with granite dressings, followed by a rectangular block joined to its south-west wall, with an entrance passage between the two in the wall. The tower was given garderobes with slate lining. The second part consisted of a number of buildings beginning below the bottom of a slope down from the tower, such as kitchen, lodgings, solar, hall, guardrooms and chapel, and then a gatehouse leading to a long barbican causeway which had its own outer two-storey gate block.

Excavation and analysis of results were carried out on the castle over the years 1972–90, and the interpretations are summarised in *Mediaeval Archaeology*, No. XXXVI, 1992, pp. 215–17. The ruins are extensive and worth a visit.

Sarum, and the earthworks became an enclosure for not only a new cathedral built before the end of the century but also a citadel. In the centre of the enclosure an inner ring of earthworks was raised. A circle of ditch banked round the outside surrounded a circular platform of earth, flattened down. Early in the twelfth century, inside the ring to the north, was built a quadrangle of apartments for the bishop, including a long hall, a chapel, a kitchen and a tower. Around the top of the platform a curtain wall of flint rubble was erected later, apparently upon the remains of an earlier wall. At the west was a postern tower-and-gate and at the east a main gatehouse was built.

The castle thus formed received several additional buildings in the thirteenth century, including a long rectangular hall, a bakehouse and some chambers which were added to the palace part at the north. In the early 1200s, the episcopal see at Old Sarum was moved to Salisbury where a new cathedral was begun in 1220, in which many of the stones of the earlier cathedral were used. It appears that

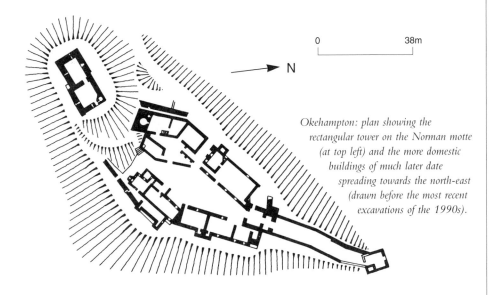

Okehampton: plan showing the rectangular tower on the Norman motte (at top left) and the more domestic buildings of much later date spreading towards the north-east (drawn before the most recent excavations of the 1990s).

OLD SARUM WILTSHIRE
(SU 138327)

The Anglo-Saxon *burh* at Old Sarum was converted by the Normans into a town. The greater part of the very extensive earthworks are of the late eleventh century, although some of them were modifications to much earlier work (possibly Roman or even Iron Age). In c.1078 the Conqueror transferred the Anglo-Saxon bishopric of Sherborne to Old

there was continual friction between the cathedral staff, clerical and lay, and the secular occupants of the castle. Old Sarum became an administrative centre and headquarters of the sheriff of Wiltshire.

Today, the visitor will see much of the earthworks, many foundations and fragments of buildings, including a fine stretch of splayed plinth of the postern tower. Many relics have been recovered and are in Salisbury Museum.

OLD WARDOUR
WARDOUR PARK, TISBURY, WILTSHIRE
(ST 939263)

Old Wardour was built by the 5th Lord Lovel, with a licence to crenellate of 1393. He raised a very unusual structure consisting of a hexagonal-plan range of apartments round a hexagonal courtyard. The range was not a perfect hexagon: the ends of the third and fifth arms joined into an elongated and widened sixth arm in which was recessed the entrance, making the two ends of the sixth arm look like towers. The inner hexagonal yard was perfect and had a central well. Much of this structure remains, although in poor condition.

During the Civil War, Old Wardour was besieged twice, the first time was by Parliamentarian forces in 1643 who captured it, and then again in 1644, this time by the original owner, Lord Arundell, who attempted to undermine the walls.

ONGAR ESSEX
(TL 554031)

A motte-and-bailey built in the early twelfth century by the de Lucy family, Ongar has a substantial motte, now 15.2 metres (50 ft) tall – it was probably taller in the early days of its existence. The motte is 61 metres (230 ft) in diameter at the base and was surrounded by a wet moat about 15.2 metres (50ft) wide. A tower of flint rubble was raised on the motte summit, probably in the 1150s, but was pulled down much later, for a structure of brick replaced it. That, too, was demolished. Ongar's motte-and-bailey plan is much like that of Pleshey.

ORFORD SUFFOLK
(TM 419499)

Orford stands on the Suffolk coast, at one time guarding the harbour which used to be a major port. Today, its only remaining structure is its unique great tower, which is in very fine condition. The castle was built by Henry II between 1165–73, cost £1413 (plus incidentals not listed in the records) and when finished consisted of an enclosure wall of stone with several rectangular flanking towers and a twin-towered gatehouse around the multangular great tower. Outside the enclosure was a very substantial ditch.

Orford was part of Henry II's programme of stone castle construction designed to show that he, not the barons, should govern the country. In East Anglia there were at the time no castles held by the Crown, but he rectified this by confiscating several, including fortresses belonging to Hugh Bigod, the most powerful magnate in the district. His own work at Orford was swift. The remarkable great tower was up and complete within two years (1165–7). The whole castle was ready by the time of the 1173–4 revolt led by his son, Prince Henry. The castle was garrisoned and supplies of all kinds were brought in – according to the records, bacons, cheeses, salt, iron, ropes, tallow and even hand-mills for grinding corn. But attack never came.

The design of the great tower is unlike anything else in Britain or Ireland, and it fits into no pattern. Basically, the tower is 21-sided on the exterior, and cylindrical inside. The 21 sides include three equidistantly placed rectangular-plan buttress-turrets, the south-east larger than the other two because it is a forebuilding-cum-turret (the turret has a spiral staircase all the way up). The tower is about 27.4 metres (90 ft) tall, has splayed plinths, rises five storeys (basement and two double storeys), plus a roof level (which had battlemented parapets between the three turrets projecting some 6 metres [20 ft] upwards). The buttress-turrets contain chambers all the way up: two kitchens, one chapel, a prison cell, closets. Each of the double storeys was a hall of two levels. On the western side, just north of the west turret in the outer wall face is a fine battery of four

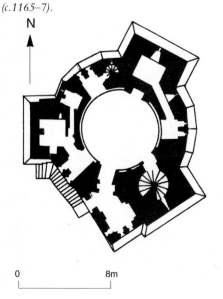

Orford: ground floor of the multangular great tower (c.1165–7).

N

0   8m

round-headed shoots from garderobes in the higher levels of the turret.

The great tower is built of local septaria with oolite dressings and some dressings of Caen stone.

Orford was captured in 1216 towards the end of the Magna Carta war, but not seriously harmed. Thereafter, its history is uneventful. The curtain, towers and gatehouse gradually decayed and collapsed through neglect. The last stretch of wall fell down in 1841.

OSWESTRY Shropshire
(SJ 290298)
A motte castle of the late eleventh century was erected by Rainald (or Reginald) de Bailleul (or Baliol), a Norman lord who was an ancestor of King John Baliol of Scotland (1292–6). Stonework was grafted on the motte in the form of a shell wall, some time in the twelfth century. Only fragments remain.

OXFORD Oxfordshire
(SP 510061)
Oxford was built c.1071 by Robert d'Oilly with the king's permission. Anglo-Saxon houses were cleared to provide the site for an enclosure to which an 18.3-metre (60-ft) motte was added later. When the motte was raised, clay was used to encase part of the sides to prevent the gravel slipping down into the ditch. Later, the motte was crowned with stone walling to produce a decagonal concentric shell wall, the inner wall 6.7 metres (22 ft) in diameter, the outer wall 17.7 metres (58 ft). Before this was built (mid-twelfth century), an earlier square tower had been raised and this is dated to before 1100. It is known today as St George's Tower, and is interesting because it is stepped inwards at several places up its height and has very few openings of any kind.

Money was spent on Oxford Castle by Henry II and John. In 1216 a church was dismantled to provide additional stone for fortifying the castle and to give it a barbican. But by the end of the thirteenth century the castle was in a poor state.

PEMBRIDGE
Hereford & Worcester
(SO 448193)
The castle occupies a roughly rectangular site and was partly surrounded by a wet moat. A cylindrical great tower was built, probably in the early thirteenth century, three storeys tall.

Other stone buildings included a two-storeyed gatehouse, a separate hall block also of two storeys, and a chapel block of three storeys. It was held for the king in the Civil War when it was besieged and most of its buildings ruined.

PENDRAGON
Mallerstang, Cumbria
(NY 782026)
A square great tower built of rubble, with intra-mural passages and angle buttressing, was raised inside an enclosure beside the River Eden at Mallerstang at the end of the twelfth century. Its position rendered it vulnerable to attack by raiding Scottish armies and it was burned in 1341. The dimensions, 19.5 metres (64 ft) square externally, 12.8 metres (42 ft) square inside (at second floor level), qualify it as a great tower, similar perhaps to Appleby. The remains stand on raised ground.

PENRITH Cumbria
(NY 513299)
The beginnings of Penrith Castle are obscure. Some time in the fourteenth century a tower was raised, and at the end of that century a quadrangular castle was built, in plan similar to Bolton, Yorkshire, but without the corner turrets. A licence to crenellate was granted in 1397–9 to William Strickland, later Bishop of Carlisle. Much of the interesting walling remains. The castle was intended to defend Penrith against Scottish raids. It is near the railway station.

PENWORTHAM Lancashire
(SD 524291)
A motte castle possibly built before 1086, in which the base of the wooden tower descended some 3.6 metres (12 ft) beneath the top of the motte, which was raised round it (cf. South Mymms, Totnes). The castle guarded the estuary of the River Ribble and a ford across it, which lay in the line of the road to the north. Only the mound remains.

PETERBOROUGH Cambridgeshire
(TL 195987)
In the deanery garden stand the remnants of a motte called Tout Hill, with a flat top about

---

(Opposite) At Peveril, the great tower of the early twelfth century rose to over 18.5 metres (60 ft). Peak District hills can be seen in the background.

12.8 metres (42 ft) across. It was probably erected in the last years of the eleventh century, before the foundation of the cathedral (cf. Ely).

PEVENSEY SUSSEX
(TQ 645048)
The Romans constructed one of their coastal forts of the Saxon shore at Pevensey in the third century AD. It was called Anderida. It was an elliptical enclosure with flanking D-ended bastions, unlike the other forts of the same time which were more generally rectilinear. Inside the remains of this fort, William of Normandy sheltered his forces once they had landed in Sussex at the end of September 1066. He cut a ditch in front of the remains of the Roman west gate in order to reinforce the ruins of the old fort which he considered usable.

Once William had won Hastings and made sure he had the south-east part of England under his control, he granted Pevensey to his half-brother, Robert of Mortain, who raised a castle in the east end of the fort in the shape of a roughly rectangular banked enclosure using a section of the original Roman curtain wall and two bastions on the south-eastern side. The remainder of the Roman enclosure became the outer bailey.

Soon afterwards, the first building work in stone began and this included the unusual great tower, started c.1100. It was a rectangular structure using the east wall as part of one wall and incorporating the Roman bastion. Three more projecting, round, solid bastions were added much later in the century. D.F. Renn suggests that they could have been used as siege-engine platforms for repelling assault: a number of rounded stones for use as shot were found in the castle grounds (and can be seen today).

The great tower may have been as tall as 24.4 metres (80 ft) and was 16.8 x 9.1 metres (55 x 30 ft) horizontally.

PEVERIL CASTLETON, DERBYSHIRE
(SK 150827)
Sometimes known as the Castle of the Peak, Peveril was a very early castle. Raised on a natural, easily defendable and almost inaccessible ridge with two precipitous sides, the first work was a stone curtain along the north side of a triangle, containing herringbone masonry; it was continued along other sides in the twelfth century. After the

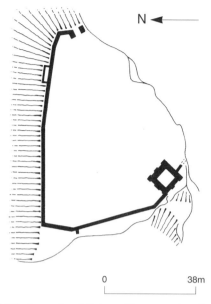

1173–4 revolt of Prince Henry against his father Henry II, the king fortified the castle by adding a 12.2-metre (40-ft) square great tower, 18.3 metres (60 ft) tall. This tower is a simple structure and was not really residential, although, of course, people did stay. It had no forebuilding – unusual for a square great tower. The tower was faced with ashlar and cost a little under £200.

(Left) Peveril: the north wall was raised before the end of the eleventh century, and the extension southwards in the early twelfth. The great tower is late twelfth century. Some later buildings are omitted.

Peveril is named after its original owners, the Peverel family. William Peverel forfeited it to Henry II in 1155 after he was disgraced, it is said, for having been involved in the murder of the Earl of Chester. The king took a fancy to the site, and the great tower was perhaps intended to be a kind of *pied-à-terre* for visits to Derbyshire and the Peak District.

PICKERING NORTH YORKSHIRE
(SE 800845)
This was a motte castle of the late eleventh or early twelfth century. The motte stood in its own surrounding ditch and two baileys surrounded that, in two curved halves, one half of later date than the rest, also ditched and banked. Some time in the mid-twelfth century a stone curtain was built along the northern bailey bank, ending on one side as a wing wall

Pickering: the motte in the foreground later supported a stone shell enclosure, which had two wing walls leading downwards to form two baileys.

up to the motte top. It appears that from c.1218–36 work was done on constructing a circular shell enclosure on the top. A long open stairway leading to a square entrance tower had been put up when the northern bailey wall was erected. Later still, c.1323–6, a second curtain was built, this time along the southern bailey bank, and this had three flanking rectangular towers. Various buildings were raised in the two baileys, including a King's Hall of c.1314, a chapel and constable's lodgings in the northern bailey.

The castle was besieged in the Magna Carta war of 1215–16. Edward II was fond of

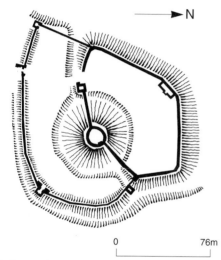

Pickering: the bold lines mark the principal stonework remains.

Pickering and lavished nearly £1000 on it in 1323–6 and this included the second (southern bailey) stone curtain and towers. The actual order for this work is preserved in the Public Record Office.

PLESHEY NR CHELMSFORD, ESSEX
(TL 666144)
Pleshey is a figure-of-eight motte castle with a very large outer bailey that now encloses the village of Pleshey. The motte, over 15.2 metres (50 ft) tall, is separated from the inner bailey by a deep ditch which surrounds the motte. There was a rectangular building on the summit, 20.4 x 17 metres (67 x 56 ft), with buttresses. It was built of flint and is thought to have been a great tower. Remnants of other stone buildings have been excavated on the castle site, including a chapel (thirteenth or fourteenth century) and round

towers. There is today a brick-built bridge from the inner bailey across the ditch to the motte and this is thought to be thirteenth century. An aerial view of Pleshey today gives a very good idea of what an early Norman motte castle looked like before its tower and wooden palisades were put up.

PLYMPTON
NR PLYMOUTH, DEVON
(SX 544557)
An interesting motte castle, whose motte is a local viewpoint, with a (now incomplete) cylindrical shell wall situated on the top, approximately 15.2 metres (50 ft) across. The stonework is mid-twelfth century at the very earliest.

PONTEFRACT WEST YORKSHIRE
(SE 460224)
Pontefract was for a long time the principal royal castle in northern England. Used as a residence, arsenal, court and prison, much money was spent on it but never enough to keep it in proper condition. Besieged three times during the Civil War and then slighted by Parliament, the great fortress almost disappeared under the weight of its ruins. Even now it is hard to reconstruct the castle's building history.

It had begun as a motte castle by 1086, on a natural rock mound inside an oval bailey whose site had considerable natural protection all round. Over the next two centuries it acquired two more baileys, and all three of these received buildings and walls, originally of timber which were later converted to stone, alongside other works built in stone from the beginning. One of the latter was a Norman chapel.

The castle was taken in hand c.1311 by Thomas Plantagenet, Earl of Lancaster (it is still technically owned by the Duchy of Lancaster) and from then on the major works began. These included a variety of flanking towers (chiefly and interestingly in rectangular plan), a gatehouse with two polygonal turrets, a barbican and, most important of all, a great tower situated on the mound. It is this great tower whose shape has stimulated so much dispute but which has now been more or less resolved.

Thomas of Lancaster started the work on it, but it was not finished until the castle came into the possession of John of Gaunt, Duke of Lancaster. Nowadays, it is a random and

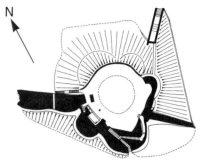

Pontefract: this is a modification of an early twentieth-century plan of the great tower. The thin line arcs inserted at the top indicate the approximate position of the two missing lobes, although the radii may well have been different from those suggested. The plan shows clearly that the tower was neither quatrefoil nor trefoil and that, whatever shape it was, there was no symmetry. All this is proved by aerial photograph.

incomplete cluster of stubs of towers a few feet tall. For long it was said to have been of quatrefoil, or trefoil, or even of sixfoil plan. Leland described it as 'cast into six roundelles'. The argument was not helped by well-known paintings of the castle as artists saw it at the time, which though dramatic were quite wrong about the great tower. Today it is possible to see four lobes, of different sizes and shapes, one of which is beaked (cf. Norfolk Towers at Dover), and a considerable arc where there are no lobes, indeed no stonework at all. An aerial photograph confirms this configuration, although still leaves the question of what fitted into the arc. In 1989 a document of 1643 was found in the Scottish Record Office relating to the castle, and it listed its apartments. In it the great tower is described as three-storeyed, with five rooms on each storey. It also says that there was a small courtyard inside the tower which suggests that the five rooms were set in a ring round an open centre area, at each level, an arrangement similar to that in the great tower at Flint (see pp. 309–10). What was in the empty arc? I think the answer is one large lobe, or two smaller and not necessarily equal lobes, making up a cluster not unknown in tower building in medieval castle architecture.

PORTCHESTER HAMPSHIRE
(SU 625046)
This is a really splendid fortress. It is a Norman castle built in the north-west corner

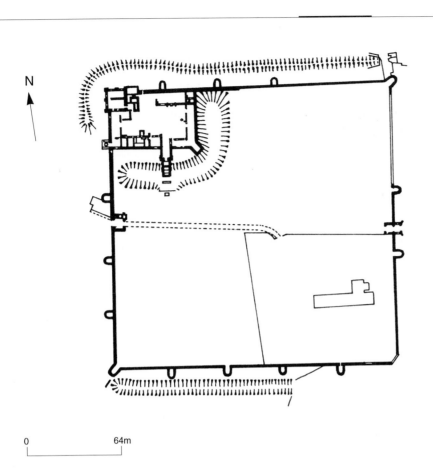

Portchester: ground plan. The Norman great tower (c.1120–30) is in the extreme top left corner. The enclosing walls are chiefly remnants of the Roman coastal fort of the late third century AD.

of an almost perfect Roman fort of the Saxon shore, the great majority of which is still standing. The Norman castle is a quadrangular enclosure with a great tower, the enclosure's north and west sides provided by the old Roman wall and the great tower built into the corner, but standing proud several feet north and west. A moat was cut round the east and south enclosure walls, while the north and west walls were protected by their own 'period' ditches and banks. The south-east walls of the inner enclosure had buildings ranged inside, and a tower and a gateway tower leading across the south moat. The square great tower itself is in very fine condition. It is faced in Caen ashlar and has pilaster buttresses mid-wall and on the corners. There is a forebuilding which appears to have been rebuilt more than once.

The tower is dated about 1120, but it went up two storeys only and was heightened later.

It had a cross-wall right up to the top. The dimensions are 17 metres (56 ft) square with walls 2.4 metres (8 ft) thick. The ashlar work seems of better quality in the lower part than higher up. The tower has few windows and these are small: there are also rows of very slim arrow-loops.

In 1133 an Augustinian priory was built in the south-east corner of the Roman fort, and the chapel of this remains there. The castle was probably appropriated by Henry II at the beginning of his reign, and it remained in royal hands thereafter. It was cared for by some of the kings. Edward I granted it to his mother and later on to his second wife. It was often garrisoned in the later fourteenth century as it was an embarkation point for English armies setting off to the wars in France, and also as a defence against invasion from the French.

POWERSTOCK

Nr Bridport, Dorset
(SY 522959)
A twelfth-century motte castle, possibly raised during the Anarchy of King Stephen's reign; it was taken by Henry Plantagenet, Count of

Anjou, who became Henry II in 1154. Some stone buildings were added later, the remains of which were still to be seen in the eighteenth century. They may have been put up by King John.

PRESTON Lancashire
(SD 512302)
This was an early motte castle, erected on the end of a projecting cliff. The castle is thought to have been abandoned as a fortress in the early 1100s, for the site was given to monks of the order of Savigny at Furness Abbey, a new monastic congregation, later amalgamated with the Cistercian order.

PRESTON CAPES
Northamptonshire
(SP 576549)
A motte castle formed from a natural sandstone mound, probably late in the eleventh century. The mound was surrounded on three sides by a ditch. The south side was possibly protected by a masonry wall.

PRUDHOE Northumberland
(NY 092634)
An extensive castle of Norman origins, it began as a motte castle of c.1080s. Then it developed into a roughly figure-of-eight plan enclosure, with the waist not much narrower than the two loops. This is about 1.2 hectares (3 acres) in area, on a natural spur on the south bank of the Tyne; it is well defended by a deep ravine on the south and east sides, with ditches to south and west. The second structure was an early twelfth-century earthwork. At some time, probably c.1175 or soon after, a great tower was raised in the western part of the enclosure, which by then may have been partly given a stone curtain.

The tower was almost square in plan, 13.4 x 12.5 metres (44 x 41 ft), three storeys tall with 3-metre (10-ft) thick walls, and with a forebuilding at the eastern end; it is one of the oldest in Northumberland. The gatehouse was also built in the twelfth century. The castle had been unsuccessfully besieged in 1173, and then again in 1174, by William the Lion, King of Scotland.

In the thirteenth century a barbican was added on the south side, 11 metres (36 ft) or so long, which led to a drawbridge across the moat, and a second barbican led from that to the gatehouse. The gatehouse was given a vaulted basement and a chapel on the first floor. This chapel is noted for its oriel window over the gateway, said to be the earliest oriel window in any castle in northern England, .

Prudhoe became a Percy possession in the year 1381.

PULFORD CHESHIRE
(SJ 375587)

A motte castle of probably mid-twelfth century is alluded to in a late twelfth-century record. It was sited near the River Alyn.

PULVERBATCH SHROPSHIRE
(SJ 423023)

There are two motte sites here, one at SJ 433016 and visible by Wilderby Hall, and the other, which has its bailey, at SJ 423023. The latter may be that mentioned in 1205. It is known locally as Castle Pulverbatch and the earthworks are visible.

QUATFORD SHROPSHIRE
(SO 738907)

On a cliff beside the Severn, Roger de Montgomery, one of the Conqueror's principal earls and commanders, built a motte castle some time between 1066–86. It is mentioned in Domesday. Some stonework was added, but in the early twelfth century the buildings were dismantled. There are traces of the original motte.

RABY NR STAINDROP, DURHAM
(NZ 129217)

Raby was aptly described by Britain's leading castellogist, Professor Allen Brown, as a 'rambling and ill-fortified castle'. It was built by the great Neville family in the late fourteenth century, as a quadrangular structure with high towers and a much lower surrounding curtain wall with crenellations. The licence was granted in 1378. One original building was the Neville Tower, the entrance gate-tower on the west. The castle evolved over the next few generations to become an extensive palatial residence of towers and ranges of apartments clustered round a small courtyard, with a series of stretches of inner curtain, and enclosed completely by an outer curtain with numerous open-backed rectangular flanking towers and a separate gatehouse to the north. The largest tower is Clifford's, which is about 24.7 metres (81 ft) tall, rectangular, with walls over 3 metres (10 ft) thick.

RAYLEIGH ESSEX
(TQ 805909)

A motte castle of the eleventh century whose motte slopes were revetted with ragstone and flint rubble, one of the very few to receive this treatment. The motte, 15.2 metres (50 ft) tall, was given a substantial wooden tower on its 21.3-metre (70-ft) diameter summit. Interestingly, the tower was never replaced with a stone tower, and indeed no stone buildings were ever erected at Rayleigh, although the castle was in use right into the middle of the thirteenth century. It was improved by several timber structures and some complex ditch and bank construction. The mound is situated just behind the main street of the town.

READING BERKSHIRE
(SU 718736)

Traces of a motte castle thought to have been built in the grounds of the abbey in the mid-twelfth century may be the remains of the Reading Castle that is recorded as having been destroyed by Henry II c.1154.

REDCASTLE SHROPSHIRE
(SJ 572296)

Two rock crests close together were the site of this thirteenth-century curtain wall castle with flanking square and cylindrical towers. There is little to see.

REIGATE SURREY
(TQ 252504)

Warenne, Earl of Surrey in William II's reign, built a castle at Reigate. It was an enclosure castle with a deep surrounding ditch.

Although there are no traces of later stonework, it must have been enlarged and improved with stone, since the castle was occupied by Royalists in 1648 during the Second Civil War. There is also a record of the castle having been captured in 1264 by Simon de Montfort during the Barons' War against Henry III, presumably around the time of his victory over the king at Lewes. It stood on the hill near the railway station, now the sight of a public park.

RESTORMEL
LOSTWITHIEL, CORNWALL
(SX 104614)

A very fine example of a shell enclosure castle raised on an earlier motte. The motte was raised in the twelfth century by Baldwin FitzTurstin. The shell enclosure, almost completely circular and 38.1 metres (125 ft) across, 2.4 metres (8 ft) thick, was erected c.1200. The top was crenellated. There was a ring of apartments of stone and wood raised around the inside of the shell, one-storeyed and two-storeyed, ranging over the later part of the thirteenth century. These included kitchen, great hall, solar and barrack room for retainers. The earliest stone structure was an early twelfth-century square-plan tower at the south-west, which was a gate-tower. It presumably sat in the circumference of an otherwise wooden palisade. Another square tower was inserted (c.1280) in the circumference once it had been converted to stone. This was in the east and it was two-storeyed, the top floor containing a chapel. A barbican was added to the south-west gate-tower in the thirteenth century. Holes for the

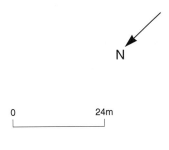

Restormel: plan of the shell enclosure. C = courtyard inside, surrounded by buildings ranged round the 'shell'. H = hall. G = gate-tower (the oldest stonework).

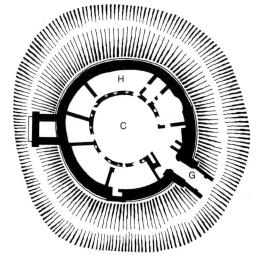

joists of hoarding are sited round the outer wall of the shell just below parapet level. The whole shell and mound were surrounded by a wet moat and high bank outside. Water was brought into the castle by lead pipes. A document of c.1337 mentions the conduits: recent archaeological excavations revealed lead piping. There was also a well dug to some 15.2 metres (50 ft).

Restormel was acquired by Richard, Earl of Cornwall, a son of Henry III, and it passed to Edmund, Earl of Cornwall. Both were responsible for the various stone-walled apartments inside the shell. The Black Prince held the castle from 1337–76.

RICHARDS CASTLE
HEREFORD & WORCESTER
(SO 484703)

Richards was a motte castle whose mound and inner bailey stand inside a larger outer bailey fortified by a ditch and rampart. Some time in the twelfth century (c.1175) a slightly asymmetrical octagonal great tower of sandstone ashlar was built on the 9.1-metre (30-ft) mound. The dimensions were 13.4 metres (44 ft) across, approximately 6 metres (20 ft) internally, and with walls up to 3.6 metres (12 ft) thick. Entrance was at first-floor level. Some form of apsidal extension was added to its eastern wall, although its purpose is not clear. A wing wall projected to the south but its purpose is not yet known.

The original inner bailey palisade was replaced by a stone curtain with turrets, some open-backed, and a gate-tower.

Richards, named after a Norman lord and friend of Edward the Confessor, was temporarily held by supporters of Simon de Montfort in his war with Henry III, 1264–5.

RICHMOND NORTH YORKSHIRE
(NZ 174006)

This is a very interesting castle of the earliest beginnings, of formidable aspect and dominating Swaledale from a great height, but which never saw military action. The first work at Richmond, on the edge of a very tall cliff over the River Swale, was a triangular curtain forming an enclosure, the south side being the cliff edge. The curtain has thick walling, nearly 3 metres (10 ft) in places. The site was granted to Alan the Red in the 1080s, and it was he who started the works. These also included one of the earliest stone halls in England, known as Scolland's Hall, although

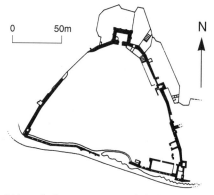

Richmond: the stone curtain and the hall at the bottom right are of late eleventh century. The great tower at the top is an early twelfth-century enlargement of a simpler gate-tower of the 1090s.

this may have been raised by his brother after Alan's death in 1089. The name comes from Scolland, steward to Alan the Red. The gate-tower was also begun in the eleventh century, in the north apex of the triangle. It was probably similar to that at Exeter.

Scolland's Hall may have been preceded only by the hall (which became a great tower later) at Chepstow, c.1067–71. It is two-storeyed and once had a cross-wall. At its east end is a gateway out of the triangle. Adjoining it on the extension of the curtain is the Gold Hole Tower, containing garderobes; the lower part is eleventh century, the remainder is fourteenth century. The curtain wall contains courses of herringbone masonry. There are square flanking towers on the east stretch of the curtain.

The great tower is the dominant structure at Richmond. It was built as an extension upwards of the original gate-tower and it is possible to see where the new work began. The tower was raised in the mid-twelfth century c.1150–70, and it reached 30.5 metres (100 ft) tall, retaining the fine archway of the eleventh-century gateway. This is at ground level. There is another, smaller entrance on the first floor, not protected by a forebuilding. Some think the original archway was blocked up when the tower was built, and if so it has been opened up again. The tower was built of squared ashlar, but much has been taken away and replaced with rubble masonry. Despite its height, the great tower is four-storeyed, the second floor (third level) opening to the roof. Each corner of the tower supports two-storeyed corner turrets. Along the wall-walk behind the battlements

you can see the pitch of the original roof of the tower, which has been replaced. The great tower has straight flights of stairs from floor to floor, like Bamburgh. There are also rooms and garderobes in the wall thickness of the tower, which is 3–3.6 metres (10–12 ft).

RIPLEY NORTH YORKSHIRE
(SE 283606)

Today, Ripley Castle is an eighteenth-century mansion incorporating some much earlier structures of a tower castle. The sole remaining part of military significance is the twin-turreted gatehouse, thought to have been built c.1418 by an ancestor of the present owners, the Ingilby family.

ROCHESTER KENT
(TQ 742686)

The motte castle at Rochester is mentioned in the *Anglo-Saxon Chronicle* entry for 1087–8 and is alluded to in Domesday (1086). It was held by the Conqueror's half-brother, Odo, Bishop of Bayeux, and was besieged by the Conqueror's son, William Rufus, and taken. This castle was probably on what is now Boley Hill, to the south of the stone buildings still standing.

A stone curtain was raised, probably in 1088, round a levelled platform north-east of

Rochester: ground floor of the great tower. The rounded corner of solid masonry on the south-east was the repair work done after the previous rectangular corner was undermined in the siege of 1215.

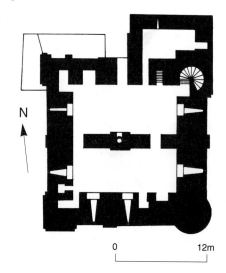

Boley Hill. The curtain was given one, possibly two, rectangular flanking towers on the south-east axis. These have disappeared (although the southern tower built by Edward III, which survives, may incorporate some of its stone). A gateway was inserted on the south side. Round three sides a ditch was cut, and the River Medway provided the defence for the fourth (west) side. This work was begun by Gundulf, Bishop of Rochester, who was also associated with the early stonework at the Tower of London, notably the White Tower, and at Colchester.

In c.1127 the great tower was begun and the work probably took 10 to 15 years. It is today more or less complete except for the roof (two gables), its floors and some of the forebuilding. It was built of Kentish ragstone with Caen ashlar dressing, it is 21.3 metres (70 ft) square, rises 34.4 metres (113 ft) to the battlemented parapet, and its four corner turrets rise 3.6 metres (12 ft) taller. The tower has pilaster buttresses mid-wall, north-west and south-east, and two buttresses along the north-east and one on the south-west (the second disappeared in 1215 when the corner tower collapsed after mining). It also has clasping pilaster buttresses on three corners, the west and east corners being larger than the north (and presumably the south, too, before the collapse during the siege).

The walls are 3.6 metres (12 ft) thick at lower level and 3 metres (10 ft) higher up. They stand on a straight plinth. The entrance is on the first floor. It is protected by a handsome three-storey (plus basement) forebuilding whose second floor is double, with a mural gallery at the higher level, and above this a chapel. The main tower has a cross-wall all the way up, centrally, and at the second storey (a double storey which has a higher gallery level with a mural passage all the way round through the window bays), the cross-wall pierced by arcading is of four round-headed arches with chevron moulding. Up through the centre of the cross-walls rises, from the basement, an ashlar-built well-shaft which served every floor.

In 1215 the castle was besieged and taken by King John. He undermined the south corner turret and it collapsed, allowing his troops to rush in. But even then, they had to fight almost inch by inch for the tower, since the defenders used the cross-wall to great effect to slow the besiegers down. Afterwards, probably about 10 years later, the corner

shattered in the siege was rebuilt in cylindrical shape, solid stone most of the way up, with a cylindrical turret at the top.

The castle was besieged again, this time in 1264, during the war between Henry III and Simon de Montfort, but the great tower was successfully defended by the king's men. It remained in royal hands until the seventeenth century, but despite repairs it has deteriorated, and only the great tower and some walling with two towers remain better than ruinous today – yet it should be visited.

ROCKINGHAM
NORTHAMPTONSHIRE
(SP 867913)

Rockingham is mentioned in Domesday. It was a motte castle built by the Conqueror on a steep hill overlooking the Welland valley, with two quadrilateral baileys. It seems probable that the early castle had a residential and recreational role rather than a military one. Archbishop Anselm had one of his periodic confrontations with William II here in 1095, which resulted in a trial before the king's court.

The castle was taken over by Henry II c.1156 and thereafter, over at least two centuries, many new works and repairs were recorded. Among the major features of this castle were its twin cylindrical-towered gatehouse, which is still impressive today and was built by Edward I (c.1280–90), and its *magna turris*, as recorded in Exchequer rolls, which is thought to have been more of a shell enclosure on the motte and which may have been built by King John.

RUFUS PORTLAND, DORSET
(SY 697711)

The present remains of a polygonal tower, built of Portland stone, stand upon the site of an earlier structure which may have been built as early as c.1100. A castle at Portland is mentioned by William of Malmesbury, the twelfth-century monk-historian. The tower is probably of the fifteenth century. The castle is also known as Bow and Arrow.

RUYTON-ELEVEN-TOWNS
SHROPSHIRE
(SJ 394222)

Fragments of a stone tower, about 13.7 metres (45 ft) square and with walls about 3 metres (10 ft) thick, remain on this thirteenth-century castle site on a ridge of ground.

SAFFRON WALDEN ESSEX
(TL 538385)

A late eleventh-century motte castle raised on a natural hill, Saffron Walden received, in the twelfth century, a substantial flintstone great tower of rectangular plan about 11.5 x 12.2 metres (38 x 40 ft). The tower is partly standing, although in ruins to two-thirds of its height. Remaining are two storeys, with substantial round arched recesses in the western and southern walls. There was a central pillar which may have supported a pair of arcades whose other ends rested perhaps on wall corbels. There was a forebuilding on the west wall of the great tower. The protruding wall-ends on the south-east angle are part of the buttressing. The corner contained a spiral staircase.

ST BRIAVELS GLOUCESTERSHIRE
(SS 559046)

An enclosure castle of the twelfth century, St Briavels received a square great tower probably in the time of Henry II, which is recorded as having finally collapsed in ruins in 1752. St Briavels still has its huge, twin cylindrical-towered gatehouse, built by Edward I, c.1292–3, at a cost of nearly £500. It can be seen from the road. The towers are supported at the bottom by spurs like those at Goodrich. St Briavels is situated within the Forest of Dean and in the thirteenth century it served as an arsenal for iron cross-bow bolts which were manufactured at the iron forges built in the forest.

ST MICHAEL'S MOUNT
OFF MARAZION, CORNWALL
(SW 515298)

There was a fort of some kind at St Michael's in the late twelfth century but no traces now exist. A Benedictine priory had already been established on the island in the previous century, c.1044. For a long time the island appeared to be a bone of contention between Normandy and England. Some time in the fifteenth century, when raids by French pirates against the island and against the nearby coast of Cornwall began to become too frequent for comfort, some military

(Overleaf) St Michael's Mount: a late medieval castle consisting of a cluster of towers, St Michael's Mount is built on a 61.5-metre (200-ft) rock on an island off Marazion.

defences were developed. A castle was built on the top of the rock, about 61 metres (200 ft) above sea level. It became a cluster of strong towers with battlemented parapets, including a platform for guns which were also housed in another gun battery part of the way down the path to the shore.

SALTWOOD Nr Hythe, Kent
(TR 161359)

At present this is the home of the Rt. Hon. Alan Clark, the eminent statesman and historian. It was a military enclosure surrounded by an oval curtain with open-backed square flanking turrets and square-plan interior towers, adjoined to the east by a triangular bailey surrounded by banking. The oval enclosure is thought to have been a motte, flattened possibly in the 1170s. It was surrounded by a moat. The inner enclosure was first raised by Henry of Essex in the 1150-60s. Further works were done in the fourteenth century. Buildings were raised in the oval enclosure, notably the Knight's Hall (c.1350), Thorpe's Tower, and the great tower started in 1170 was enlarged by Archbishop Courtenay of Canterbury (c.1381). The stone curtain was said to have been built round the triangular outer bailey by Henry Yevele, the celebrated designer of Queenborough and Cowling Castles, who also designed Saltwood's magnificent twin

cylindrical-towered gatehouse (c.1380).

Saltwood's moat was fed by a stream. This was dammed in order to keep the stream wide where it separated the oval enclosure from the rising ground nearby.

SANDAL
Nr Wakefield, West Yorkshire
(SE 337182)

One of the most dramatic castle excavations of the century has been uncovering the substantial remains of Sandal Castle. It began in 1963, took ten years, and was directed with great skill by Dr Philip Mayes. It revealed no less than the ruins of a complete medieval castle which had all but disappeared under 2.4 hectares (6 acres) of earth and scrub. The contrast between Sandal in 1963 and in 1973 is shown very clearly in the photographs on p. 179.

Sandal began as a motte castle c.1150, with a motte about 13.7 metres (45 ft) high. In c.1200, conversion to stone began and continued to about 1280. This is a summary of the excavations results:

1 The Public Record Office holds a drawing of Sandal c.1565 in the stylised manner of the time, a mix of accuracy with fantasy (*see* below). The accuracy was demonstrated when excavations uncovered features in the drawing. One was the remains of a polygonal tower added in 1484 by Richard III to the north-west corner of the great tower built earlier on the motte. It replaced a smaller half-round tower. In the drawing the polygonal tower can be seen beside the trees (at right). Another find caused great excitement. Towards the top left of the

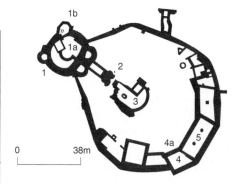

Sandal: ground plan of the castle after recent excavations. It follows the motte-and-bailey plan with later stone additions. 1 = great tower. 1a = inner curved wall (part of inner turret?). 1b = new polygonal tower (temp. Richard III). 2 = twin-cylinder tower structure. 3 = barbican (shape similar to Goodrich and Lion Tower, London). 4 = cellar with pantry over. 4a = base of pillar supporting staircase to great hall (see sixteenth-century picture of Sandal, below left). 5 = great hall.

drawing is a stairway to a balcony into the great hall, supported on a pillar with a conical dish. The base of a pillar matching the pictured pillar was uncovered beside the great hall, in the right position for it to have supported the stairway.

2 In the bailey, under several feet of earth, substantial traces of timber buildings of the motte castle were found, which included a hall 11.5 x 6.4 metres (38 x 21 ft), with narrow aisles about 1.2 metres (4 ft) wide.

3 The early thirteenth-century stone conversion had begun probably with the erection of the structure on the motte. This was a round tower 9.1 metres (30 ft) across, but it was not finished. Excavation revealed a half-cylinder with a turn-back flight of steps. It is a mystery why the tower was left when a larger, irregular cylindrical great tower was later built on the motte, with walls 3–3.6 metres (10–12 ft) thick. It had segmented chambers around its inside walls and two clasping round towers on the north and north-west sides, the north one rebuilt by Richard III.

4 One of the early stone buildings was the barbican, datable to c.1250, situated south-east of the gatehouse from which it is separated by part of the ditching that surrounds the barbican. It stands as it were on an island which at some time received very fine ashlar revetting at base level. It is basically D-shape, like barbicans at Goodrich and the

Sandal: as seen by a mid-sixteenth century artist. At top left is the pillar-supported balcony, whose pillar was discovered 400 years later in the 1963–73 excavations.

(Left) Sandal before
excavations began in
1963. (Above) The
castle exposed after
excavation
(1963–73). Note
the D-plan barbican
in the centre, similar
to that at Goodrich
and the Tower of
London.

now vanished Lion Tower at London, both of
which were later than Sandal's. The masonry
round the base of the barbican is of the highest
quality, cut and beautifully shaped.

5   The gatehouse block consisted of a pair
of wing walls running parallel and close down
the motte slope out of the south-east of the
great tower and into a twin round-towered
gateway flanking the end of the passage
between the walls. A drawbridge provided
access between gatehouse and barbican.

There were several other important stone
buildings within Sandal's stone curtain wall
whose ends 'fed' into the great tower at points
more than half-way up the motte. The

remains of these buildings form a semi-circular range including kitchen, larder, pantry, great hall and bailey gatehouse, all of the thirteenth century. The enclosure also had flanking rectilinear towers.

The history of Sandal from c.1200 to the 1640s was relatively uneventful. It was held by the Crown most of the time and after 1485 was neglected. In 1566 it was decided that it was 'especially to be meynteyned because it standith in a strong Contrie of men amongst whom (yf any rebellion shude happen, as God forbid) this castle must be the staie of it.' But little was actually done to preserve it in usable condition. By 1592 it was 'very ruynous and in great decay than th'other of our castles are'. It was garrisoned by Royalists in the Civil War, was twice besieged in 1645 and then slighted.

SAUVEY

WITHCOTE, LEICESTERSHIRE
(SK 787053)
A very late motte castle was built here by King John in the early thirteenth century. The site was put in the path of a stream which was dammed to provide water for a wet moat around it. The king appears to have liked the site, and there are records of money spent on fishponds at Sauvey in 1211. The castle remained in royal hands, although granted to the Count of Aumale for a few years. The castle had begun as a wooden one and what stone was added is impossible to determine. After about 1260 it was allowed to decay, and the site was 'quarried' for other castles, including Rockingham, which received supplies of lead, stone and timber. The earthwork remains can be seen.

SCALEBY NR CARLISLE, CUMBRIA
(NY 449624)
Scaleby began as a pele-tower built in the thirteenth century. This was enlarged to give it an extension on the eastern side consisting of a hall which is tunnel-vaulted at ground level. A licence to crenellate was granted to the castle's holder, Robert de Tilliol, and from this grew a fortified house with extra towers and a fourteenth-century gatehouse. Scaleby was garrisoned during the Bishops' War (1638–9) when an invasion from Scotland was feared. The castle has been restored and is occupied today. The original pele-tower is still standing but is in a deteriorating state.

SCARBOROUGH

NORTH YORKSHIRE
(TA 050893)
The castle on the edge of the cliff at Scarborough was begun in the 1130s by Count William of Aumale who started work on a stone curtain and probably built the first stage of the great tower. The curtain, with the steep, natural slopes of the cliffs, formed a roughly triangular site. There had been a Roman signal station on the headland within the site area. In the 1150s Henry II seized Scarborough and improved the fortifications. He raised the great tower on Aumale's first work. It is now ruinous, but was an approximately 16.8-metre (55-ft) square building and rose to over 30.5 metres (100 ft) tall. It had pilaster buttresses, except on the south face, walls between 3.3–3.6 metres (11–12 ft) thick, and 4.6 metres (15 ft) thick on the west side. The tower stood on a battered plinth. It had a forebuilding on the south, about 12.2 metres (40 ft) tall, 9.1 metres (30 ft) long and 6 metres (20 ft) wide, over a stone staircase some of whose steps remain (although the forebuilding has gone, like that at Hedingham). The tower was built of rough stone and mortar, faced with fine ashlar laid in beautiful courses. The windows were round-headed at the top, tall and slim, and in some places were in pairs. Lower down they were wider.

Scarborough is noted for its barbican. This emerges westwards from a narrowing of the inner bailey in front of the great tower, the narrowing carried as a stone bridge over a ditch. The barbican is triangular and has an entrance/exit in a large twin cylindrical-turreted gateway, and this was probably built in the 1240s.

SCOTNEY NR LAMBERHURST, KENT
(TQ 689353)
The very small, cylindrical turret at Scotney, with machicolation and a conical roof on its top, standing half-surrounded by water in a lake, is part of a fourteenth-century moated castle connected to a seventeenth-century manor-house which is in ruins. Both are in the grounds of a Georgian mansion.

SHERBORNE OLD CASTLE

DORSET
(ST 647167)
The Old Castle is a rectangular stone enclosure with canted corners raised inside a ditch that has a bank outside. Plain rectangular towers were inserted in the four canted corners and one in the north wall which was a gateway. The south-west corner tower was a gate-tower. This enclosure was probably the early twelfth-century part, put up some time between 1107–35. At some time in the mid-twelfth century, a small L-plan great tower was built into the south-west corner of the nearby palace quadrangle. But there is doubt as to whether the castle was ever seriously intended to be more than a large residence with some attempt at fortification. The castle came into royal possession c.1183, and King John later spent a little over £100 on it, presumably on fortification.

In the 1590s the castle became the property of Sir Walter Raleigh, who carried out several alterations.

SHERIFF HUTTON

NORTH YORKSHIRE
(SE 652661)
A very substantial, quadrangular fortified manor-house which had four large towers on the angles of four storeys (one had five), and an interesting gatehouse of later (fifteenth-century) date, some of which is standing. The castle was built of reddish rubble with ashlar dressing and quoins. It was built by the powerful Neville family c.1382, close to the site of a motte castle of the early twelfth century which was abandoned. The castle is now ruinous.

SHIRBURN

NR WATLINGTON, OXFORDSHIRE
(SU 697960)
This was a brick-built fortified manor-house, begun c.1380, with a section of dressed stone and chalk in the west front. It was quadrangular, with cylindrical towers on the corners and a gate-tower. Surrounded by a moat fed by local springs, the castle was greatly altered in the eighteenth and nineteenth centuries, incorporating much of the original brickwork.

SHOTWICK NR CHESTER, CHESHIRE
(SJ 350704)
A motte castle that was enlarged in the twelfth and thirteenth centuries into a roughly hexagonal enclosure of stone with a great tower inside. The curtain had four rounded flanking turrets. There was also a gate-tower. The great tower was rectangular, with pilaster

buttresses. The castle controlled a ford across the Dee. Little of this castle is left today, except for some earthworks.

SHRAWARDINE
NR SHREWSBURY, SHROPSHIRE
(SJ 400154)
Shrawardine was a motte castle beside the Severn. Begun in the twelfth century, it was held by the Crown. Fragments of a shell wall on the motte, of rubble but with some ashlar dressing, and other stonework, are probably of Henry II's time. Henry and his sons, Richard I and John, all spent money on repairs. The castle was attacked and severely damaged by the Welsh in 1215. The Welsh returned the castle to the English and it is believed to have been repaired c.1220. Shrawardine was razed to the ground in the Civil War.

SHREWSBURY SHROPSHIRE
(SJ 495128)
Fifty-one houses were destroyed in a loop of the River Severn at Shrewsbury some time in the years 1067–9 to make room for the motte castle built by Roger de Montgomery. Some of the woodwork was converted to stone in the twelfth century, and of this there are remains of the inner bailey wall and a gateway with a round-headed arch. Over the period c.1154–c.1350 several sums were spent on new works and repairs, although by no means all were specified. Some of this was spent on a stone curtain for the motte. A gatehouse was raised in the time of Henry III, possibly in the 1230s, and this may have been a twin cylindrical-towered type. A barbican was built in 1233–4. In c.1270 the tower on the motte collapsed, and it is thought that it was the original wooden great tower. There was a king's hall which received repairs c.1287–9. Works were also carried out intermittently on the palisades during the thirteenth century. By c.1350 the castle had become dilapidated.

SIZERGH
HELSINGTON, NR KENDAL, CUMBRIA
(SD 498878)
Sizergh is a roughly rectangular enclosure of three wings (there is no north-west wing) round a courtyard.

The south-east wing consists of an entrance hall in the centre (which was a great hall in the fifteenth century), the north-east of domestic apartments and the south-west the pele-tower. The pele-tower is mid-fourteenth century, about 18.3 x 11.9 metres (60 x 39 ft) and 18 metres (59 ft) tall. On the south side of the pele in the centre is a rectangular turret. This rises over 3 metres (10 ft) higher than the pele itself, and is called the Deincourt Tower. At ground-floor level this tower has walls 2.2 x 2.9 metres (7^1/$_2$–9^1/$_2$ ft) thick, and contained a dungeon, but it is less thick higher up. Both towers are battlemented. The other two wings were added much later, about the sixteenth century. Sizergh has belonged to the Strickland family since at least the fourteenth century.

SKIPSEA
NR BRIDLINGTON, HUMBERSIDE
(TA 163551)
This is one of the few motte castles where the motte is surrounded by its own ditch and rampart and also separated from its bailey, in this case by a marsh. There was a wooden causeway across the marsh. It was built c.1086 and its motte is about 13.7 metres (45 ft) tall with a flattened top which is nearly 0.1 hectares (^{1}/$_4$ acre) in area. The lake which surrounded much of the castle contained eels, then a staple fish diet, which produced revenue for the holders of the castle. The destruction of the castle was ordered by Henry III. However, earthworks can still be seen, and the remains of a harbour associated with the castle were recently discovered.

SKIPTON NORTH YORKSHIRE
(SD 995519)
This was initially an earthwork castle c.1080, which late in the twelfth century received the beginnings of stonework. The twin drum-towered gatehouse, now restored and dominant among the much later buildings of the castle, is thought to stem from the late twelfth century or early thirteenth century. The castle was given several more towers in the thirteen/fourteenth centuries, and the curtain walls were over 3.6 metres (12 ft) thick in places. It was surrounded by a moat. The castle was besieged and severely damaged in the Civil War, but it has been renovated and additions have been made.

SLEAFORD LINCOLNSHIRE
(TF 064455)
A rectangular enclosure was erected here probably early in the twelfth century, perhaps by the Bishop of Lincoln. It was surrounded on three sides by a moat and had an additional bailey. Fragments can be seen to the north-west of the station.

SNODHILL NR DORSTONE,
HEREFORD & WORCESTER
(SO 322404)
An early motte castle with an additional bailey. Fragments of an unusual elongated octagonal tower of sandstone rubble, dating from the thirteenth century, with a gateway flanked by solid drum towers, remain on the motte summit.

SOMERFORD WILTSHIRE
(ST 965831)
A twelfth-century motte castle with a low mound. The mound was excavated earlier this century and a stone wall fragment was found which contained a doorway. The wall was only about 0.6 metres (2 ft) thick, which raised the question of whether the wooden castle was replaced by a stone castle or a more residential and unfortified structure.

SOUTHAMPTON HAMPSHIRE
(SU 420110)
A motte castle was built at Southampton probably in the early twelfth century (certainly by 1153 when the castle is mentioned in a treaty). From the accession of Henry II, Southampton Castle, because of the extreme importance of its role *vis-à-vis* Southampton Water, is continually mentioned in Exchequer records up to the sixteenth century. Repairs and additions of many kinds are noted, including references to bridges, the king's house, castle quay and so forth. Some of the wall round the bailey survives today on Western Shore. The castle is recorded as being in a ruinous state in 1286, and although much money was spent by the kings and others over the next century, it seems to have remained in poor shape. The town, although partly walled, was attacked by the French several times.

Fresh refortification was carried out in the time of Richard II, and this included a cylindrical great tower raised on the motte which may have been reduced in height first. This would have entailed removing the earlier buildings. The tower was built by Henry Yevele at a cost of over £1700. A gatehouse, wall, barbican and other towers were added.

In the fifteenth and sixteenth centuries, decay set in again in some parts, although the great tower appears to have been kept in a condition fit enough for Elizabeth I to stay in it c.1569. Some of the castle walls are standing, as are remains of the water-gate, an eastern gate and other structures.

SOUTH MYMMS HERTFORDSHIRE
(TL 230026)

This was a motte castle built by Geoffrey de Mandeville c.1140–2. He may have had permission to do so from King Stephen (or from his rival, Matilda). It is an interesting site, and it was only recently investigated (1960–4 by Dr J.P.C. Kent). It stands on a low spur and consists of a bailey about 118.9 x 106.7 metres (390 x 350 ft). The bank around it is about 6 metres (20 ft) high. The motte in the north-west corner is about 8.2 metres (27 ft) tall and has its own ditch. The motte base was a ring of clay and flint, about 1.2 metres (4 ft) high, 6 metres (20 ft) wide, and 30.5 metres (100 ft) across. There was a break in the ring for the entrance. Inside the ring was a 10.7-metre (35-ft) square flint-based platform with slots for 22.9-cm (9-in) thick wooden beams laid round the square. Space was provided in the south of the square for an entrance. The superstructure erected on the base was battened inwards at a slope of about 80 degrees to give an inward-tapering tower of timber that may have been as high as about 18.3 metres (60 ft) or so. The spaces for the entrance were covered by a timber-lined passage. The lower part of the tower was covered with chalk rubble. Numerous objects found suggest that the tower was occupied in some comfort. The tower was one of those where the motte was thrown up round the base, as at Lydford, being raised as the tower itself went up. The outside of the motte was revetted with timber plans, set vertically. (Barnet Historical Society papers.)

SPOFFORTH
NR HARROGATE, NORTH YORKSHIRE
(SE 360511)

A rectangular hall-tower range of thirteenth-century beginnings with fourteenth- and fifteenth-century enlargements is what remains of Spofforth, which stands on a small plateau of rising ground. On the west side this ends in a rocky outcrop. The castle has been built against the rock. The present hall range may have been one wing of a larger structure round a courtyard.

The thirteenth-century part is the ground-floor undercroft to the later hall, whose eastern side is rock face, with a flight of stairs to it cut into the rock. A second stair flight is cut into rock further north, leading into the entrance passage and lobby. The fourteenth-century work is the two-storey chamber on the north side of the hall, which has a polygonal stair turret on the north-west corner. The fifteenth-century work included the upper storey of the hall part, namely the hall proper, which was a rebuilding job.

STAFFORD STAFFORDSHIRE
(SJ 902222)

Stafford Castle has been the subject of major excavation and rehabilitation in the past 20 years. The result has been an astonishing *tour de force* of reconstruction. Beginning as a motte castle of c.1070, this was destroyed by 1086, according to Domesday. By about 1102, however, it seems to have been restored in some form, for Henry I granted it to William Pantulf during a rebellion against the king led by Robert de Belleme. By the 1140s the castle was held by the Stafford barony, but there is no sound history for another two centuries. Then in 1348, Ralph, 1st Earl of Stafford, invited master-mason John of Burcestre to build a great tower on the old motte, and up went a rectangular core of three storeys, with octagonal corner turrets rising an extra storey above. The core was 36.5 x 15.2 metres (120 x 50 ft). The upper storey contained a Great Hall and a Great Chamber. Rooms for the owners, wardrobes, chapel and garderobes were all in the towers. A century later, Stafford enjoyed its heyday. By then it belonged to Humphrey Stafford who was married to the Buckingham family which backed the Lancastrians in the Wars of the Roses. By the 1460s, although the castle was intact, the settlement around it had been abandoned. When in 1521 the 3rd Duke of Buckingham, Edward Stafford, was put to death by Henry VIII, the king appropriated the castle. Thereafter it deteriorated: one owner referred to it in 1603 as 'my rotten castle of Stafford'.

In the nineteenth century it was partially restored by new owners who did not follow the plan entirely, but by the middle of this century it was ruinous again. Then in 1978 Stafford Borough Council initiated the imaginative project to rehabilitate the Great Tower and the grounds as a tourist attraction; they were opened by the present Lord Stafford in 1988.

STAMFORD LINCOLNSHIRE
(TF 027073)

Originally a motte castle of the late eleventh century, Stamford motte received a shell enclosure, about 18.3 metres (60 ft) across, before 1153, which may have been the tower surrendered to Henry of Anjou (who later became Henry II) in that year. The castle was considerably extended in several stages, and these included a hall with attached kitchens, cellars and chambers. Only fragments remain now, beside a car park.

STANSTED MOUNTFITCHET
ESSEX
(TL 516249)

An enclosure with bailey, surrounded with extensive ditching and ramparts. A small tower was raised in the enclosure, and other stone fragments suggest there were additional buildings, possibly including a gate-tower. Documentation for this castle is meagre. It is thought that the castle was dismantled in King John's reign.

STAPLETON
HEREFORD & WORCESTER
(SO 323656)

This is an example of a natural hillock adapted by scarping to form a motte castle. The castle is mentioned in 1207. The present ruins are those of a seventeenth-century house built on the site, for which the motte was levelled.

STOGURSEY
NR BRIDGWATER, SOMERSET
(ST 203426)

Stogursey was an enclosure with several baileys, raised at the end of the eleventh century. A stone curtain and mural towers were built in the twelfth century. The castle was besieged in the 1220s. Some stonework still remains.

STOKESAY SHROPSHIRE
(SO 436817)

This is one of the best-preserved medieval fortified manor-houses in England. The first structure was a simple two-storey twelfth-century tower of rubble masonry with ashlar quoins, roughly pentagonal in plan with a projecting square wall-turret on the north angle. Today, the top of the tower carries a seventeenth-century timber-framed gallery with gabled roofing, and this probably replaces a similar hoarding of the late Norman period,

to judge from the put-log holes. In the late thirteenth century, the owner, the rich wool merchant, Lawrence of Ludlow, built on to the tower's south wall a long hall with solar, 15.8 x 9.4 metres (52 x 31 ft) internally and without supporting aisles. At the south end of the hall was added, c.1290, a multangular tower of three storeys with battlemented parapet; these buildings formed one side of an enclosure of stone once surrounded by a moat. The stone curtain once reached to a height of about 9.1 metres (30 ft); in it is a timber gatehouse of the seventeenth century.

SULGRAVE NORTHAMPTONSHIRE
(SP 556452)
A fortified enclosure of triangular shape was created, probably soon after the Conquest, on the site of a pre-Norman residence that was not fortified. A tower of stone was discovered in the earthworks in recent years. This was probably early twelfth century.

SUTTON VALENCE
NR MAIDSTONE, KENT
(TQ 815491)
A great tower was built here in the mid- to late twelfth century; it was of limited size (11

metres [36 ft] square), like Clitheroe. It had angle buttresses on the corners. The walls were about 2.4 metres (8 ft) thick and contained small chambers and passages. Some time after it was erected a forebuilding was added, but there is evidence that this was demolished and replaced by a new staircase which was later encased by walls. The castle was abandoned in the 1200s. Fragments remain near the church (Arch. Cantiana, XXV, LXXI).

SWERFORD
NR CHIPPING NORTON, OXFORDSHIRE
(SP 373312)
Earthworks of a motte castle of the eleventh century can still be seen here. Excavations revealed pottery of the mid-twelfth century. The castle was raised by Robert d'Oilly who had been granted leave by William I. This is the same d'Oilly who built Ascot d'Oilly castle (*see* p. 121).

SWINESHEAD LINCOLNSHIRE
(TF 243410)
A motte castle of the twelfth century, mentioned in the Pipe Roll for 1185–6. Earthworks can be seen near the remains of the medieval abbey.

TAMWORTH STAFFORDSHIRE
(SK 206037)
There is still much to see of Tamworth. Most notable is its robust shell enclosure with a

square tower projection, wrapped round the original tall motte which was raised in the eleventh century. One wing wall remains in part on the motte slope, and some of its masonry is set in the familiar Norman herringbone pattern (*see* p. 38). The shell enclosure is an irregular polygon, and the shell wall is thick enough to contain two flights of straight stairs which presumably opened into a now-vanished shell enclosure gate-tower. Today the shell is interrupted by the presence of a residential building of Tudor origin slotted into the circumference.

TATTERSHALL LINCOLNSHIRE
(TF 210575)
The great tower at Tattershall Castle stands 30.5 metres (100 ft) high from the ground to the tops of the four battlemented turrets that clasp the corners. It is just about all that remains of a remarkable fifteenth-century castle, erected by Lord Cromwell, Treasurer of England from 1433 to 1443, but it dominates the countryside for miles around, and it is splendid proof of the fact that powerful lords had not given up building massive castles and that great towers were not out of date. Caister had just been completed and the Hastings Tower at Ashby de la Zouch was yet to come.

Tattershall was built from red brick made of local clay from nearby Edlington Moor, and dressed with freestone from Willesford and limestone from Ancaster. Accounts for the work survive and show that nearly one million bricks were made for the tower, other buildings, and the revetment round the 'platform' in the moat on which the castle stood. They also refer to the great tower as *Le Dongeon*, a corruption of donjon, the alternative medieval word for 'great tower'.

Lord Cromwell also intended that he should be able to enjoy living in the tower. Five storeys high (including the basement with its nearly 6-metre [20-ft] thick walls), it has large window openings and unguarded exterior doorways (at ground level) on the east wall fronting the inner enclosure ward. These appear vulnerable until one is close to the wall and looks upwards – to see at 24.4 metres (80 ft) or so a terrifying row of machicolations which were by no means merely decorative. The windows on the other three sides looked out on to the moat, defensive in itself.

The castle was an aggressive symbol of

Lord Cromwell's immense power, which was no less locally than it was throughout England. Once ready, he moved in and filled the tower and buildings with an army of servants and hangers-on, amounting to 100 people. Then he died without heir, and Tattershall passed to the Crown and thence to the Earls of Lincoln. Thereafter it fell into decay until rescued in 1910 by Lord Curzon (who also rescued Bodiam), who had intervened to save parts of the derelict structure from being shipped abroad. The attempts to take these out of the country aroused great public outcry and resulted in the passing of the Ancient Monuments Consolidation and Amendment Act by Parliament in 1913, an important landmark in the story of the State's involvement in helping to preserve ancient buildings.

TAUNTON Somerset
(ST 226247)

An early Norman earthwork enclosure castle, raised on the south side of the River Tone and surrounded by a moat, received a rectangular stone great hall building inside its north-west perimeter in the very early 1100s. Some time in the second quarter of the twelfth century, further stone buildings were raised, including a great tower, rectangular in plan, with corner turrets. Of this great tower only the foundations remain. The dimensions were 19.2 x 24.4 metres (63 x 80 ft) and the walls were from 3.6–4 metres (12–13 ft) thick.

Further improvements were undertaken in the early thirteenth century, including a constable's tower of about 15.2 x 10 metres (50 x 33 ft), which still has a vaulted undercroft, and a major reconstruction of the great hall which is well documented. There are details of accounts for building materials including 6,800 board nails, 16,000 tie nails and 32,000 lath nails. The hall has survived to a considerable extent, but with some modifications, and today houses the County Museum of Somerset. In 1662, the castle was slighted by government order and the great tower was demolished. The great hall was the scene of part of Judge Jeffreys' notorious Bloody Assize, held after the collapse of the Duke of Monmouth's rebellion of 1685.

THERFIELD Hertfordshire
(TL 335373)

A motte castle of the Anarchy of King Stephen's reign, Therfield was dismantled after the accession of Henry II. Excavations in 1958 showed that the rampart round the bailey had been lined with clay and then clad with wooden palisading.

THETFORD Norfolk
(TL 874828)

Thetford has one of the tallest mottes in Britain, about 24.4 metres (80 ft) high. The castle is mentioned in Chapter 3. The motte, of chalk rubble, was raised before 1086 on the site of an Iron Age fort. Thetford was an important castle, its site dominating the gently undulating area around it, overlooking the River Ouse, and yet it does not appear to have had any stonework additions. The surrounding double ditches and ramparts are impressive. The castle was owned for a time by the de Warenne family, but it was destroyed by Henry II in 1174. A second site at the other end of the town, TL 862830, known as Red Castle, was an earthwork enclosure inside which stood an eleventh-century church. Some of the earthwork still remains.

THIRLWALL Northumberland
(NY 660662)

This rectangular tower-house, which has turrets on three corners and a larger angle-tower on the eastern corner, is now ruinous. The walls are in places over 2.7 metres (9 ft) thick. The tower was built largely of stone quarried from a nearby section of Hadrian's Wall, near Greenhead. The tower-house has been dated at about 1360.

THIRSK North Yorkshire
(SE 428820)

Thisk is a motte castle, probably of twelfth-century construction, that was held by the Mowbrays. The castle was yielded to Henry II in 1174–5, following the collapse of the revolt of his son, Prince Henry, whom the Mowbrays supported, and it was then demolished. There are traces of the moat round part of the bailey site.

THORNBURY Nr Alveston, Avon
(ST 633907)

Said to be the last major fortified manor-house to be built in England, Thornbury was raised in the early 1500s by Edward Stafford, Duke of Buckingham. It was basically a small quadrangle with corner towers (polygonal on the south and west corners, square on the north and once also on the east). Attached to the south-west wall was a larger quadrangle consisting of two ranges of buildings, the fourth side open. These ranges were extensive, accommodating barracks for retainers (strictly forbidden by the Statute of Livery and Maintenance of 1504), and stables for horses for them and for the Buckingham family. The gatehouse in the western end of the smaller quadrangle is a twin semi-octagonal turret with a portcullis. Much of the walling is provided with gun-ports and loops. But it was never completed, for the duke was arrested in 1521 by Henry VIII on a manufactured treason charge, executed, and his estates attainted.

TICKHILL South Yorkshire
(SK 594928)

Tickhill was a motte castle, raised probably at the very end of the eleventh century by Robert de Belleme who was compelled to forfeit it to Henry I in 1102. The motte reached about 22.9 metres (75 ft) high and was about 24.4 metres (80 ft) in diameter on the top. The bailey was given a stone curtain early on, possibly c.1100, with an interesting gateway. On the motte was built an eleven-sided great tower, which had pilaster buttresses on all angles. This unusually shaped tower was erected c.1178–80 by Henry II at a cost of £120.

John inherited the castle when he succeeded to the throne in 1199 and he lavished over £300 on it. John had a penchant for polygonal great towers (see Odiham).

The great tower has now gone, but the

Tickhill: ground plan of the polygonal great tower, now only at foundation level.

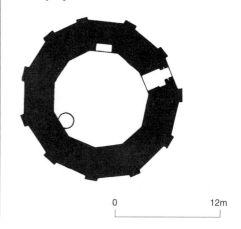

0   12m

motte remains. The foundations of the tower were excavated recently. The bailey wall survives for long stretches, and in its northern side can be seen (from the road) the square-plan gatehouse which has interesting features. Although part-ruined, it still has its walls, two shallow-rounded arches, a half-lozenge panel frieze across the front over the arch and, at second-storey height inside, on the west inner side, an early Tudor fireplace. This projects out of the wall but it has no hearth or floor. The second storey was rebuilt in the sixteenth century.

TINTAGEL CORNWALL
(SC 048891)
Tintagel Castle is not reliably documented before the twelfth century. That said, we are dealing with an interesting castle on a headland jutting into the sea. In the mid-twelfth century, the first structure, a narrow rectangular hall, was built on what was an isthmus between the headland and the mainland but which has been largely eroded by the sea, dividing the castle into two parts. It was raised by Reginald, Earl of Cornwall, who may also have built the twelfth-century chapel nearby. Little more than foundations survive of the hall. Evidence has recently been found of early timber structures situated on the mainland.

About a century later, Richard, Earl of Cornwall, raised two stone-walled enclosures on the mainland part, with a castle main gate and a curtain round part of the headland and enclosing the hall. Evidently, a bridge was constructed to connect the two parts. In the fourteenth century Tintagel belonged to the Black Prince as Duke of Cornwall, and he rebuilt the great hall. Apparently yet another hall was built over the remains of the previous two; this was in the late fourteenth/early fifteenth century.

TIVERTON DEVON
(SS 954131)
A quadrangular enclosure castle built by the Courtenay family, of pink sandstone, on the possible site of an earlier twelfth-century enclosure raised in the reign of Henry I. The quadrangle had towers on the corners (of which a cylindrical south-east and a square south-west remain) and it was surrounded by a double moat. The decayed gatehouse on the eastern side is also standing. It was built in the fourteenth century.

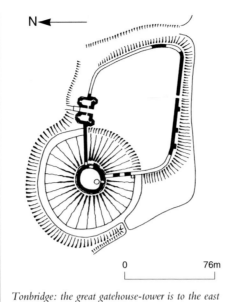

0   76m

Tonbridge: the great gatehouse-tower is to the east of the motte with its shell enclosure. It is similar in shape to the Great Gate at Caerphilly Castle.

TONBRIDGE KENT
(TQ 589466)
The *Anglo-Saxon Chronicle* in an entry for 1088 mentions the motte castle at Tonbridge on the River Medway whose bailey was surrounded partly by water meadows. In the twelfth century the motte received an oval shell enclosure of walls 1.5 metres (5 ft) thick, with buttressing on the south-east. Two wing walls ran down the motte sides. One eventually connected up with a massive gatehouse-tower; the other continued round a rough rectangle to form an enclosure.

The huge gatehouse-tower, the remains of which still stand, was raised by Gilbert de Clare, the castle's owner, who was also responsible for the construction of Caerphilly Castle. It is nearly 24.4 metres (80 ft) wide, oblong in plan with cylindrical turrets. The central passage had two arched openings, protected by stout doors and portcullis, and at the sides are guardrooms from which winding stairs led to the floors above. The tower contained sumptuous residential accommodation behind thick walls, and among these were the noble apartments to which I have referred in Chapter 5. Edward I was entertained in some state in this gatehouse-tower by the de Clares in 1275. He visited the castle again some years later on his way to Flanders when he handed the Great Seal of England to his son, Prince Edward, at the

castle. This event was commemorated in the coat of arms of Tonbridge UDC.

TONGE KENT
(TQ 933636)
An earthwork castle of Norman origin which, in the thirteenth century, received stonework. Some fragments were discovered in two excavations in the present century (1929–30 and 1964).

TOPCLIFFE WEST YORKSHIRE
(SE 410750)
A motte castle of the twelfth century raised by the River Swale. Its early history is unknown, but in 1174 Topcliffe was fortified by the bishop-elect of Lincoln, who was a son of Henry II and who backed his father in the serious rising of the king's eldest son, Prince Henry, in 1173–4. Topcliffe was for a time a possession of the Percy family. Part of the mound is visible.

TOTNES DEVON
(SX 800605)
One of the best-preserved shell enclosures in England, Totnes began as a motte castle sited on a natural rock jutting into the corner of the old Anglo-Saxon *burh* of Totnes. It is a large motte, and the top was a series of artificial layers of earth, rock and clay rammed down on the natural mound. About 3.3 metres (11 ft) down in the artificial motte was found a clay-packed rubble foundation, rectangular and about 4.9 x 4 metres (16 x 13 ft), of thin walls (0.8 metres [2 ft 6 in]). This is said by Allen Brown to have been the base for the wooden tower on the top, the artificial mound being finished round the foundations after they were laid. The foundations were to support the tower, as at Penwortham. Totnes stands in a valley configuration of the River Dart and is susceptible to 'funnelling' of high winds when the latter occur: a wooden tower would be helped by a stone 'anchor'. This early work is datable as very late eleventh century, or possibly c.1105.

The motte received a shell enclosure of limestone rubble, about 1.8 metres (6 ft) thick, in the thirteenth century. This was rebuilt in the early fourteenth century, with red sandstone dressings, following the original plan. The later shell enclosure was crenellated and the parapet is almost complete, with some repairs. The entrance is through the northern part of the shell. The inner bailey is a segment

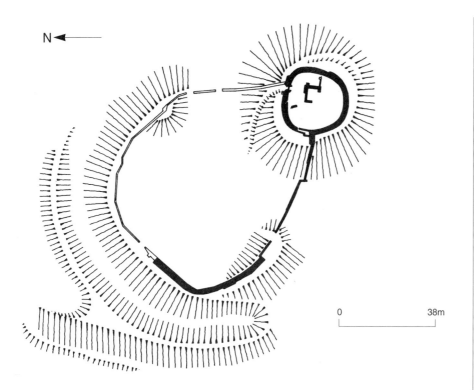

N◄

Totnes: the shell enclosure is on the motte at right. The site of the tower is inside the shell.

0   38m

turrets on the other three. This great structure was finished by his son Rufus, probably towards the end of the 1090s, and in 1100 it was to have its first prisoner, Ranulf Flambard, Bishop of Durham, who escaped a year later by having a coil of rope smuggled into him hidden in a jar of wine, and then letting himself down outside the window. Thereafter, for the next three centuries, the White Tower (first known as that in the reign of Henry III who used to have its walls whitewashed) accommodated a veritable galaxy of national and international celebrities as prisoners for one period or another – among these were David II of Scotland, John of France, Richard II who signed his abdication document there in 1399, and the Duke of Orleans, captured at Agincourt.

For most of the twelfth century the Tower had little done to it, apart from some fortification, but in the thirteenth century Henry III left his mark by a prodigious building programme, advancing a stage almost every year, and costing £10,000. He started the conversion of the castle into a great concentric fortress by erecting much of the inner curtain with nearly all of its eventual thirteen flanking towers. The construction of the outer curtain with six flanking towers along the south part of it was largely finished by his son, Edward I. In addition, Henry had built a variety of residential quarters and

of a circle to the north-west, surrounded by a stone curtain for most of its length.

TOTTERNHOE

NR DUNSTABLE, BEDFORDSHIRE
(SP 979221)
On the edge of a chalk down, 3.2 km (2 miles) from Dunstable, a motte castle was built using the promontory for part of the motte which was enclosed on three sides by a wide ditch. The south side was protected by the steep face of the promontory itself. Some stonework pieces were found in excavations. Was this local Totternhoe stone, from the same quarry that supplied stone for Windsor?

TOWER OF LONDON

What was to become one of the most famous castles in the world began as a simple earthwork enclosure erected in the first months of 1067. It was undoubtedly a personal enterprise of William the Conqueror who had to establish himself as undisputed ruler of England.

The works were begun in the south-east corner of what was left of the old Roman city.

In 1078 William started the White Tower, one of the first and largest great towers in Britain (see also Colchester), 32.6 x 36 metres (107 x 118 ft) and over 27.4 metres (90 ft) tall, not exactly rectangular, with an apsidal projection on its south-east corner and square

0   161m

Tower of London: simplified ground plan, to show the concentric scheme. In the centre is the first stone building, the White Tower, begun in 1078. At the extreme left are remains of the foundations of the Lion Tower, a barbican of the thirteenth century similar to those at Goodrich and Sandal.

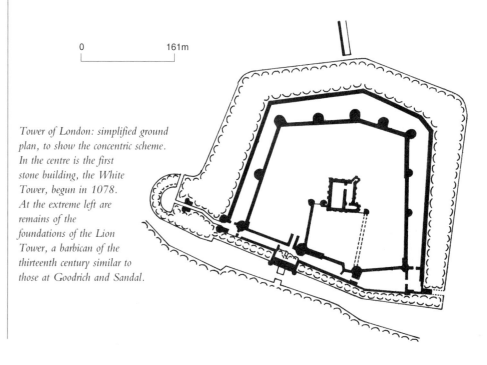

administrative buildings (most of which have vanished). The Tower had now become the greatest fortress in England, with the possible exception of Dover.

While most succeeding monarchs carried out works of one kind and another, none were on the scale of Henry III's or Edward I's. One work of Edward I's was the Lion Tower, which was a barbican, a D-shaped structure on the western extremity. This resembled the barbican at Goodrich (of slightly later date); and also the barbican recently excavated at Sandal, of earlier date.

Considering its history, the Tower is better documented than any other fortress. It played a dominant role in the affairs of the kings and their governments for centuries. Apart from its use as a palace, a castle and a prison, it has housed the Royal Mint, the Royal Menagerie, the public records and even for a time the Royal Observatory. It has been a major arsenal, it has held the Crown Jewels for centuries, and it has long had one of the finest collections of armour in the world. Just outside the outer curtain is Tower Hill, scene of the beheading of many great and famous people such as Thomas More, Thomas Cromwell, John Dudley (Duke of Northumberland), Thomas Wentworth (Earl of Strafford) and Archbishop Laud. Inside the south-west corner of the inner curtain is Tower Green. There, too, a sad roll of victims lost their heads, among them Anne Boleyn, second wife of Henry VIII, and Katherine Howard, his fifth wife; Margaret, Countess of Salisbury, last of the Plantagenets; and Lady Jane Grey.

The literature on the Tower of London is extensive, and in confining our discussion of the Tower to the briefest summary, I recommend the DoE's official guide (HMSO 1984) and the *Tower and its Institutions* (HMSO, 1978).

TREAGO HEREFORD & WORCESTER
(SO 490239)
A small, square, curtained enclosure with four angle-towers of different sizes, this castle is difficult to date, although it appears to be of the later Middle Ages, with alterations of the seventeenth century.

TREMATON SALTASH, CORNWALL
(SX 410580)
Trematon was an early motte castle, mentioned in Domesday. It received a stone

shell enclosure, probably in the twelfth century, and a stone curtain round the bailey that continued up the motte sides as two wing walls joining the shell. On the north-east side of the bailey is a gatehouse which began as a thirteenth-century gateway.

The castle came into royal possession in the 1270s when Richard, Earl of Cornwall, bought it. The shell walls are about 3 metres (10 ft) thick and they rise to about 9.1 metres (30 ft) for most of the circumference. There are indications of buildings ranged round the inside of the shell.

TROWBRIDGE WILTSHIRE
(ST 854579)
An earthwork enclosure of the early twelfth century was later given stonework of some kind. The suggestion is of a small tower, possibly raised in the time of King Stephen by Henry de Bohun. The moat of the castle is said to be partly defined in the curving main street (Fore Street) today.

TUTBURY STAFFORDSHIRE
(SK 209291)
The motte castle at Tutbury stood on a natural hill of rock, overlooking the Dove. It appears to have been dismantled by Henry II c.1175; after that it was neglected for more than a century. In the early 1300s, the site passed to Thomas, Earl of Lancaster, Edward II's cousin, whose rebellious activities over a period of years were to involve a number of castles in England. He may have rebuilt a wooden gateway in stone. The castle later passed to John of Gaunt, Duke of Lancaster, and from him to his son, Henry Bolingbroke, later Henry IV (1399–1413). Fifteenth-century improvements to the castle included a stone curtain with flanking towers and ranges of buildings within.

Tutbury was held for Charles I in the Civil War but was taken by Parliament and slighted. Today, it is largely in ruins.

TYNEMOUTH NR NEWCASTLE UPON
TYNE, TYNE & WEAR
(NZ 374695)
Tynemouth Castle was integrated with Tynemouth Priory, so much so that every time there was warfare between England and Scotland, in which the castle played a role as a border fortress, the monks of the priory had to contribute towards the costs of garrisoning and provisioning the castle.

The castle which began as an earthwork enclosure stood on a prominent headland with steep cliffs on three sides, on the north side of the mouth of the Tyne. Its late thirteenth-century curtain wall, with towers, surrounded the priory. There is a substantial gatehouse-tower with barbican built in the 1390s. The barbican was a tall passage protected at the entrance by two square turrets flanking the arch, and much of it remains today. The outer walls continue back to the rectangular-plan gatehouse-tower. There is a courtyard between the outer and inner gate. The gatehouse-tower has walls 1.5 metres (5 ft) thick and rises three storeys. The first floor was the great hall, the second a great chamber above it.

WAKEFIELD WEST YORKSHIRE
(SE 327198)
A motte castle with two baileys erected here may have remained an earthwork and timber castle for its entire existence. Excavations have revealed that nothing of stone work remains. The motte is about 9.1 metres (30 ft) tall, was surrounded by a moat, and the two baileys lay to the north-east, one behind the other. In the nineteenth century there were considerable intrusions upon the old site, which effectively spoiled much of it for excavating purposes. At the end of the century, Clarence Park, where the castle site lies, was opened as a public park. But some results have been obtained.

Pottery of the twelfth century was found on the north edge of the motte where it leads into the ditch, in the 1953 excavations. Similar pottery was found a little to the north-east of the first cutting. Digs in the baileys produced charcoal and more pottery. The castle has as a result been dated to c.1140–c.1150, a late date for a motte castle. Brian Hope Taylor thinks it may have been one of the adulterine castles so often mentioned (cf. *Anglo-Saxon Chronicle* entry in Chapter 2) and so rarely documented in any detail. The builder is also suggested – William, 3rd Earl de Warenne, or his successor William of Blois, second son of King Stephen.

WALLINGFORD OXFORDSHIRE
(SU 610897)
This appears to have been a very early motte castle, probably built c.1071. Eight buildings were knocked down to make space for the castle which eventually had three baileys. It guarded a useful ford across the Thames.

Wallingford was refortified during the Anarchy of King Stephen's reign, and was held for Matilda, surviving at least three sieges. Henry II, Richard I and John spent money on it; John made his formal submission to Pope Innocent III there in 1213. Exactly when the stonework buildings were begun we do not know, but it may have been in the mid-twelfth century. It was at some time given a great tower, although the size and shape are not known. In the period 1363–70, £500 was spent on general repairs to the castle, including the great tower.

It was a summer residence for Henry VI from c.1428, and was held by Francis, Viscount Lovell, friend of Richard III.

Wallingford was taken by Parliament in 1646. In 1652 it was demolished by order of the Commonwealth.

WALTON Nr Felixstowe, Suffolk
(TM 322358)

There was a castle here belonging to the Bigods, Earls of Norfolk, in the mid-twelfth century. The castle appears to have had a square tower, but this may have belonged to an earlier Roman fort on whose site the Norman castle was raised. Henry II appropriated the castle from the Bigods in 1157. It was demolished after the revolt of Prince Henry in 1173–4.

WAREHAM Dorset
(SY 920876)

There was a castle at Wareham in the time of Henry I. Some form of mound, probably the remains of a fort of earlier times, was discovered (in 1910) to contain the remnants of a substantial great tower, about 24.4 metres (80 ft) square, with pilaster buttresses. The bottom of the great tower was covered by gravel heaped up round the sides. The tower was built by Henry I. His elder brother, Robert, Duke of Normandy, who spent the first years of the reign, from 1100–06, attempting to seize Henry's throne, was finally defeated and imprisoned in one castle or another for 28 years. For part of that time he was held at Wareham, but we do not know if the great tower was ready for his reception in 1106, although it appears to have been completed by 1119. The castle was taken by Robert, Earl of Gloucester, c.1135, and, apart from a few intervals, remained in baronial possession until its destruction during the Civil War. The mound is still in existence.

WARK Northumberland
(NT 824387)

Wark started as a motte castle on the southern side of the Tweed. It was besieged and captured by David I, King of Scotland, and dismantled in 1138. Henry II recaptured it c.1158 and fortified it afresh at a cost of £380. This work probably included the polygonal great tower on the old motte, of which a few traces survive. From the early fourteenth century onwards, Wark Castle was allowed to deteriorate.

WARKWORTH Northumberland
(NU 248057)

A late motte castle of the mid-twelfth century, built on a large scale, Warkworth stands on rising ground in a loop of the River Coquet. It may have been built by Henry, Earl of Northumberland, a son of David I of Scotland, or strengthened by him with the conversion of the bailey's wooden palisade into a stone curtain, and given a hall alongside the west curtain wall which was later widened. There are some remains of this hall, which had a solar storey above. In 1173 the castle, which had reverted to the English Crown, was besieged and taken by William the Lion, King of Scotland, because it was 'feeble in wall and earthwork'.

Warkworth then passed into the holding of the Clavering family who built the first works of the great gateway at the south (later enlarged), and raised a massive ashlar-clad curtain with flanking towers round the bailey in place of the earlier wood palisade and incorporating the twelfth-century stretches of curtain. One tower raised in the fourteenth century was Grey Mare's Tail Tower, a polygonal wall tower which was equipped with 4.9-metre (16-ft) long fish-tailed cross-bow loops.

Before the end of the century the motte was part-flattened to receive a stone great tower, probably built by Henry Percy, Earl of Northumberland, who had been granted Warkworth by Edward II. This tower is multangular, on the following plan: a square core has rectilinear projections on four sides, the south one slightly off-centre; the corners of the core and of three projections (north, east, and west) are canted, and on the south the canting is sharper, producing a semi-octagonal shape. Within this plan (the nearest thing to it being Castle Rushen in the Isle of Man and Trim, Co. Meath, in Ireland) is a complete suite of apartments. Its southern wall joins the north-east and north-west lengths of the curtain round the bailey which are in fact wing walls. The great tower stands on a splayed plinth. It has been altered since construction and refaced but, withal, it seems a powerful building, despite the insertion of large windows in the upper storeys. The

Warkworth: the great tower is on the left. Some parts of the masonry of the east and west curtains of the outer bailey (OB) are probably of the twelfth century.

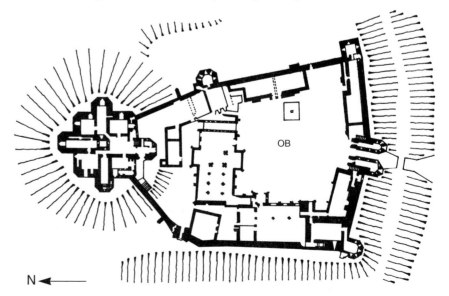

apartments inside are grouped round a square lantern turret which rises from ground level right to the top. The lantern collected rainwater and channelled it down to a tank in the basement where, by means of conduits, the water could be distributed to garderobes and basins. The tower has a square-plan watch turret which projects above the parapet line, in the centre.

These are the principal points of interest in Warkworth Castle. Its history is hardly less full. It was besieged in 1327 by the Scots, but not taken; it was attacked in the Percy rebellion against Henry IV (1403–5) and battered into surrender; and in 1644 it yielded to the armies of Scotland in the Civil War.

WARRINGTON LANCASHIRE
(SJ 609876)
An enclosure castle of earthworks beside marshes of the River Mersey. Excavations revealed artefacts of the late Norman period. Earthworks survive near the church.

WARWICK WARWICKSHIRE
(SP 284047)
Warwick Castle rises like a precipice above the River Avon. On this natural cliff William I founded a motte castle in 1068, on lands seized from a nearby Saxon convent. A wooden tower built on the motte was evidently still there in the reign of Henry II, by which time a polygonal shell enclosure had been raised round the motte top. Only fragments of the shell enclosure now remain, incorporated in the rebuilt shell, which is of much later date.

Late in the fourteenth century, by which time some additional buildings such as the great hall and residential blocks had been put up in the bailey, the castle passed to Earl Beauchamp who initiated a fresh programme of works. These were substantially what can be seen today. They included restructuring the great hall and a range of other buildings on the south-east, a water-gate, and on the west front a high and stout defensive curtain leading from a gatehouse to a very tall polygonal tower, known as Guy's Tower, which is 39.4 metres (128 ft) tall.

The gatehouse is a remarkable building: a pair of towers above the doorway passage, which had portcullises and murder-holes. Projecting from the east side of the gatehouse is a tall rectangular building leading to another tower. This latter tower is 45.2 metres (147

ft) tall, six storeys, trilobed (or six-lobed if the smaller bulges are counted) and capped by a two-fold system of battlements with machicolation all round below the battlements. It is called Caesar's Tower. The three main storeys in the tower are each vaulted, and have stone fireplaces.

The castle is completed by curtain walling and further, much smaller, flanking towers. The wall at the west leads up the motte to the restored shell enclosure and down again southwards to the south range. The whole is thus a powerfully defended enclosure.

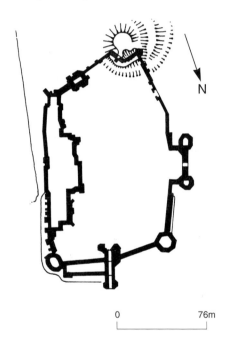

Warwick: the original motte is at the top. Caesar's Tower is at the bottom left, with Guy's Tower at the bottom right.

WATTLESBOROUGH SHROPSHIRE
(SJ 355126)
A castle whose three-storeyed stone great tower appears to have been enclosed by wooden palisading. The tower, about 9.7 metres (32 ft) square, with pilaster buttresses on the corners, is probably of late-twelfth-century origin. It has a spiral staircase in one corner turret. The top storeys were originally a kind of platform behind the parapet, the roof rising up to this level, but in the fourteenth century it is thought the roof was lifted to the top storey. The castle gradually lost its military role and became part of a manor-house.

WEETING NR BRANDON, NORFOLK
(TL 778891)
Weeting was a wet-moated enclosure castle, in which there was a two-storeyed hall-type structure, with a square tower adjoining one end, three storeys high. It was a strongly fortified manor-house. Some of the structures appear to be of late twelfth-century origin.

WELBOURNE LINCOLNSHIRE
(SK 968544)
Remains of an earthwork enclosure castle of the twelfth century can be seen.

WEOBLEY HEREFORD & WORCESTER
(SO 403153)
An enclosure of earthworks that was captured in 1138 and mentioned in the Pipe Rolls for 1186–7. The earthworks included double ditching. The later stonework is believed to have consisted of a quadrangle with corner and mid-wall towers, gateway and a great tower, but only the earthworks remain today (RCHM, Herefordshire, III).

WEST DERBY
NR LIVERPOOL, MERSEYSIDE
(SJ 397933)
A simple motte castle with enclosing ditch was built here probably before 1086 by Roger of Poitou. It was granted c.1115 to Stephen, Count of Blois. It is mentioned in Exchequer records for 1216, and was appropriated 15 years later by the de Ferrers family.

WEST MALLING KENT
(TQ 675570)
An early and interesting medium-sized great tower (known as St Leonard's Tower) 18.3 metres (60 ft) tall (but several metres taller originally). It was built of Kentish ragstone c.1100, a very early date for a great tower. It is attributed to Bishop Gundulf (cf., Rochester) although this has been questioned. The tower is four-storeyed, has corner pilaster buttresses (and one mid-wall) and a spiral staircase in the north-west corner. Remains of a curtain wall feed into the south-east corner.

WESTON TURVILLE
NR AYLESBURY, BUCKINGHAMSHIRE
(SP 859104)
Some remains of a motte castle built here probably in the twelfth century. They are in the grounds of Weston Turville Manor where, in the fourteenth century, a fortified

manor-house was erected by the de Moleyns family. That building was later dismantled.

WHITCHURCH BUCKINGHAMSHIRE
(SP 799207)

A twelfth-century motte castle here was given stonework later in the century. This may have been a stone great tower. In 1925, sites of drawbridges were discovered, which suggest a castle of some size. It is also called Bolebec Castle, and earthworks survive.

WHITCHURCH SHROPSHIRE
(SJ 543415)

A 4.6-metre (15-ft) tall motte surrounded by a wide ditch is the remnant of Whitchurch Castle today. There are ramparts, some as high as 3.3 metres (11 ft). The castle was sited near a lake, and this provided protection on the east side.

WHITTINGTON SHROPSHIRE
(SJ 325311)

Today the principal structure of Whittington which can be seen is the remnant of the twin cylindrical-towered gatehouse. The stonework was probably begun in the 1220s, for a licence to build upon the site of an earlier motte castle was granted by Henry III in 1220. This motte received a stone rectangular tower, of which today only the foundations remain. Then, the castle was surrounded by a stone curtain, and the resulting enclosure was divided unequally. The gatehouse was inserted in the outer enclosure, along with other towers. Outside the curtain was an extensive ditching system whose water levels from a nearby stream were controlled by means of drainage.

WHITWICK LEICESTERSHIRE
(SK 436172A)

An oval-plan motte surrounded on three sides by a stream, this was less than 3 metres (10 ft) high. The castle was held by the Earl of Leicester during the Anarchy of King Stephen's reign. The mound is on rising ground near the church.

WHORLTON NORTH YORKSHIRE
(NZ 481025)

Situated near the county boundary between Yorkshire and Durham, Whorlton was an earthwork enclosure on a spur of land. It received stonework later. Today, the fourteenth-century stone gatehouse remains.

WIGMORE NR MORTIMER'S CROSS, HEREFORD & WORCESTER
(SO 408693)

A motte castle was raised here c.1067 by William FitzOsbern, Earl of Hereford, and in 1086 it was held by Ralph de Mortimer. A sandstone rubble shell enclosure was built on the motte in the twelfth century, and a curtain wall with square and round towers was added, mostly, it appears, later. A square-plan gatehouse was also inserted in the curtain. There are traces of the shell enclosure to be seen today. Much reconstruction was done in the fourteenth century and also later, particularly when Edward IV and Richard III held the castle, between 1461–85, as they had been heirs to the Mortimer family.

WILTON
BRIDSTOW, HEREFORD & WORCESTER
(SO 590244)

A structure of Stephen's time, possibly a motte castle, sited near the Wye, but few remains of that period can be seen. The remains visible today are thirteenth and fourteenth century, and are of an irregular quadrilateral curtain wall, with towers at each angle and an additional one in the east wall which may be part of a gatehouse. The castle was surrounded by a wet moat but this has since been largely filled in. Further alterations were made in the sixteenth and seventeenth centuries.

WILTON NR SALISBURY, WILTSHIRE
(SU 100310)

A monastic structure at Wilton, probably of eleventh-century origin, was apparently altered to provide a fortified residence.

WINCHESTER HAMPSHIRE
(SU 472296)

In 1067 the Conqueror built a motte castle here 'hard (by) the south side of the west gate' of the Anglo-Saxon town, as Leland puts it. The castle was erected on rising ground. The motte was probably a low one: a platform over 6 metres (20 ft) high was found during recent excavations, and since then remains of timber structures have been detected beneath this, suggesting among other things that the motte had been revetted with timber planks. Some stonework was also found which replaced the timber revetting. The remains of a nave and apse of a chapel have also been found near the motte base, and the chapel has been dated to c.1070.

Winchester was the capital of England until the end of the twelfth century. The royal Exchequer was centred here, and Domesday was housed in the castle. The castle was the subject of an almost continuous programme of development from 1067 to at least the Tudor period. But nearly everything has aged into a fragmentary state, including a great tower, about 15.8 metres (52 ft) square, with walls about 4.3 metres (14 ft) thick, built in the time of Henry II or Richard I; a cylindrical tower said to have been raised on the motte in the reign of Henry III; and several other towers, curtain walling, apartments, etc. There is one exception, the splendid great hall built by Henry III between 1222–35.

Henry II favoured the castle and enjoyed it as a residence: records tell of a herb garden, of hedges round a new king's hall, and of a special aviary for royal falcons. King John spent a memorable Christmas there in 1206: 1500 chickens, 5000 eggs, 20 oxen, 100 sheep and 100 pigs were laid in for the festivities. The castle was captured by Louis of France in 1216 in the Magna Carta war. Henry III spent about £10,000 in restoring and improving it.

The great hall has been carefully tidied and restored in recent years, and can now be seen much as it must have been in the 1230s. Regarded by some specialists as second only to Westminster Hall, it has been in almost continuous use since its construction, and bears signs of only minor modification over the centuries.

WINDSOR BERKSHIRE
(SU 970770)

Windsor Castle's vast complex of palatial apartments, its huge and glorious chapel of St George, its towers, its enormous cylindrical shell enclosure, and its curtain wall with towers and gates, extending over half a mile in a rough figure-of-eight plan, is perhaps the nearest equivalent in Britain to the fairy-tale palace-castles depicted in *Les Très Riches Heures* of the Duc de Berry. Although much has been added and altered since the end of the Middle Ages, notably by Henry VIII, George III and George IV, it still resembles to a great extent the Windsor Castle seen by medieval visitors, official and private, travellers native and foreign. And by that time it had ceased to have any military significance, had already cost more than any other castle in the British Isles – over £50,000 was spent by Edward III alone, between c.1350 and c.1377

– and it had become the principal residence of the kings of England and Wales.

Windsor began very much more simply than that. It was a motte with two baileys (one on each side) – and an aerial view today instantly reveals this plan under all the succeeding stonework. It was raised by the Conqueror in 1067 by scarping a mound out of a chalk cliff beside the Thames.

It remained a wood and earth structure until Henry I began to convert the castle to stone by erecting a stone shell enclosure on the motte top (although there is a suggestion that this had already been done earlier).

Henry II raised the building in the upper bailey on a quadrangular plan like Old Sarum. Some of the stone was obtained from quarries at Totternhoe in Bedfordshire.

The shell was later refaced, probably in Henry II's time. Inside the shell, a large, slightly oval great tower was erected, with walls about 30.5 metres (100 ft) in diameter, 1.5 metres (5 ft) thick (later thickened), with pilaster buttresses some of the way up. The first height was about 10.7 metres (35 ft). The shell acted as a kind of surrounding base for the great tower. Inside the tower, timber buildings were put up against the walls, leaving a square courtyard in the centre. This was much as it is today and the two-storeyed, oak-framed buildings contain timberwork thought to have come from the Henry II structures. The tower has been much altered, and today stands nearly 20 metres (65 ft) above the height of the old shell enclosure.

Henry II favoured Windsor and treated it as a royal home, planting a herb garden and possibly a vineyard. Henry III also favoured Windsor and there is a record of an occasion when he gave the poor a meal on Good Friday. Edward III's extensive improvements included the first chapel of St George, and raising the height of the oval great tower. By the end of his reign, Windsor had become a palace and was no longer a real military structure.

Windsor was besieged in 1216, during the Magna Carta war.

WISBECH CAMBRIDGESHIRE
(TF 462097)
An earthwork castle was raised here early in the Conqueror's reign, possibly as part of William's campaign against Hereward the Wake (see also Ely) or perhaps just afterwards. Stonework was added much later. A few fragments are visible.

WOLVESEY
NR WINCHESTER, HAMPSHIRE
(SU 48429)
The ecclesiastical castle-palace at Wolvesey was begun c.1100, and major works were added by Henry of Blois, Bishop of Winchester, c.1129–c.1171. It became a quadrangular castle – very early for this plan type – which also contained a square great tower and a great hall. The site has recently been excavated with great thoroughness. The rectangular great hall was erected along the east wall of the quadrangle c.1130. This superseded an earlier hall of c.1110 on the western side, which thereafter was used as private apartments by the Bishops of Winchester. The great tower is thought to have been erected c.1138 as a defensive structure for the bishop during the Anarchy of King Stephen's reign, and is the next building to the great hall. Some of the decorative treatment of the great hall is similar to that at the monastery at Cluny where Henry of Blois had been a monk for a time. A square-plan gatehouse with central passage was inserted in the north wall of the quadrangle c.1160–1170. It is now in ruins.

WOODWALTON CAMBRIDGESHIRE
(TL 211827)
Although this castle is sometimes described as a motte castle, the raised ground was only a few feet above the earthworks surrounding it. The platform is about 41.1 metres (135 ft) in diameter. It falls more sensibly into the enclosure class of early earthwork castles. The earthworks are now known as Castle Hill.

WORCESTER
HEREFORD & WORCESTER
(SO 847550)
There is nothing left of the motte castle raised at Worcester c.1069, whose ditch encroached upon the cemetery of the cathedral priory. To begin with, the wooden castle was burned down in 1113. It was rebuilt, part in wood, part in stone, during the middle of the century, and a gateway of stone was added by King John in 1204. Interestingly, when King John was buried in 1216 in what became Worcester Cathedral, the monks asked the Great Council to return to them that part of the castle bailey which had once been church property, and this was granted. The castle lost its military importance. The motte was levelled in 1830.

WRESSLE HUMBERSIDE
(SE 707316)
The remains of this Percy family castle overlooking the River Derwent consist of two towers and part of a curtain of a quadrangular enclosure castle that had four towers at the corners, and a tower gatehouse. The castle was built c.1380 by Sir Thomas Percy, brother of Henry Percy, Earl of Northumberland, and it was surrounded by a moat. Wressle was damaged in a siege by Parliament during the Civil War.

WYCOMBE BUCKINGHAMSHIRE
(SU 868934) A
A Norman earthwork castle with a motte of about 9.1 metres (30 ft) in height. It was besieged during the Anarchy of King Stephen's time. The remains are at Castle Hill.

YANWATH CUMBRIA
(NY 508282)
A fourteenth-century pele-tower in good repair. Modifications were carried out in Tudor times.

YELDEN BEDFORDSHIRE
(TL 014669)
A motte castle was raised here, possibly in the mid-twelfth century, by Lord Traylly. The inner bailey was later enclosed by a stone wall with at least one flanking tower, traces of which were found in excavations.

YORK (BAILE HILL)
NORTH YORKSHIRE
(SE 603513)
The Conqueror built two motte castles in York in 1068–9. The first was on the west bank of the Ouse and the second on the east. In 1069, both were destroyed by the Vikings, and both were rebuilt. The second castle eventually became York Castle, and later still Clifford's Tower (q.v.). The first was described in the fourteenth century as *vetus ballium* (Old Baile), and the remains of the motte that lie near Skeldergate Bridge are still called the Old Baile. Excavations of 1968 revealed some steps cut in the slope. Traces of a square-plan building on the summit were also found.

Ireland

ADARE Co. Limerick
(R 4746)

The castle at Adare beside the River Maigue was among the biggest in Ireland. It was also an early structure, beginning as an earthwork enclosure with gateways, and outside it a ditch with additional banking. When this was built, and who built it is not clear. The

Adare, Co. Limerick: the thin-lined boxes denote areas of excavation in the 1970s (after Barry). The River Maigue runs along the south of the castle, past the edges of the two halls.

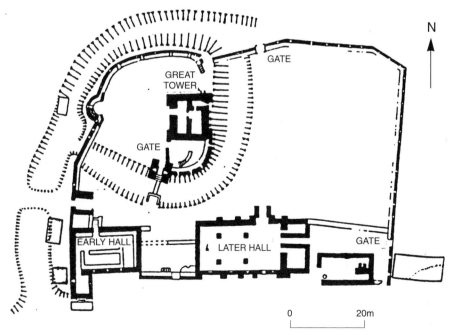

Anglo-Normans added a timber palisade to the enclosure then, soon after that, the first stone buildings. One was a rectangular two-storeyed hall on the edge of the river, outside the enclosure. The upper storey was the first great hall. This building has loops at ground level and, higher up, remains of fine Romanesque round-headed windows in pairs. Inside the enclosure, not long afterwards, a rectangular-plan great tower was raised, about 13.1 x 12.2 metres (43 x 40 ft), today largely demolished although one wall still stands to about full height. It had a north–south axis cross-wall, projecting pilasters at the end of

the east and west walls, and it was three storeys tall.

Some time in the mid-thirteenth century the palisade wall was replaced by a stone wall and a gateway put in on the south. And later in the century, a second and larger hall building was erected, about 22.5 x 10.7 metres (74 x 35 ft), also with its south wall along the river edge. In the fourteenth century, although there were additional buildings and more walling in stone on the east side of the site, the castle fell into decay and was never fully restored. The castle belonged to the Fitzgeralds for a long time. Restoration work is being done by the Office of Public Works.

ANTRIM Co. Antrim
(J 1586)

A motte survives from the early thirteenth-century motte-and-bailey castle. It is near the remnants of a much later stone castle which was burned in 1922.

ARDEE Co. Louth
(N 9690)

There are two tower-houses in the same street in Ardee; the larger is now used as a court-house. It began as an early thirteenth-century square tower with two projecting turrets at the front. Its present appearance is of a much later date. The tower is four-storeyed and has trefoil-point windows; some of the battlements are stepped. Nearby are remains of a late-twelfth-century motte. The other tower-house is known as Hatch's; it is also four-storeyed but is less tall than the first

The earlier hall and, next to it, the round arched west gate are in the left foreground of this view of Adare. Behind is the square great tower.

tower. The corners of the tower are rounded on the front face.

ARDFINNAN Co. TIPPERARY
(S 0818)

This is an example of the successful building of a stone great tower upon a motte summit. Here, a thirteenth-century cylindrical donjon of three storeys (including a vaulted basement) was raised on a motte of the 1180s. The donjon's staircase was located in a smaller cylindrical turret built into the donjon wall

and bulging as a semicircle outwards. Other surviving buildings are of much later date.

ARDGLASS Co. DOWN
(J 5637)

There were five separate fortified structures in Ardglass that can be classified as castles, and they were all tower-houses. The largest, known as Jordan's, has been restored and houses a museum. It is rectangular, with two projections along the north wall, one of which carried the spiral stair up to the roof, serving the four storeys. It has an extra small chamber on top of the stair turret. The tower's windows are narrow loops outside, although inside many have wide, splayed reveals. The two turrets are joined at roof

level by arched machicolation, and there is an additional machicolation at right-angles to the first, set higher, to cover the door into the staircase turret. The castle was built in the mid-sixteenth century and is probably the oldest of the five fortified buildings.

Among the others are King's Castle, a rectangular tower-house now only two storeys tall which has been converted into a nursing home, and Cowd Castle which is also two-storeyed.

ARDKEEN
STRANGFORD LOUGH, Co. DOWN
(J 5957)

Earthwork remains of a small motte-and-bailey of the 1190s.

A view of Askeaton, showing the fifteenth-century high tower.

ARDMAYLE Co. Tipperary
(S 0547)
Early thirteenth-century motte with D-shape bailey, and some remains of a much later square tower-house, sixteenth or seventeenth century.

ARDNAMULLIVANE Co. Galway
(R 4595)
A sixteenth-century tower-house with five storeys, the ground and third vaulted. The ground-floor ceiling shows the wickerwork on which the plaster was spread and held.

ARDMURCHER Co. Westmeath
(N 2638)
This began as a motte-and-bailey of the 1190s. Stonework was added, probably in the late thirteenth or early fourteenth century, to form a shell enclosure round a small tower erected on the motte summit.

ARDRAHAN Co. Galway
(M 4612)
This two-storey rectangular great tower of thirteenth-century origin, in hall style and

erected upon earlier earthworks, is now in a ruinous condition.

ARDREE Co. Kildare
(S 6698)
These earthworks are perhaps of the motte castle of about 1182 mentioned by Giraldus Cambrensis, opposite a similar site at Bigarz.

ARDTERMON Co. Sligo
(G 5844)
Ardtermon castle is a seventeenth-century rectangular tower-house of three storeys plus roof, which has been restored. The tower-house has round angle-towers and a D-plan turret with a staircase. It stands within a fortified enclosure.

ARKLOW Co. Wicklow
(T 2353)
Some fragments remain of a thirteenth-century structure of unknown size.

ASKEATON Co. Limerick
(R 3450)
Askeaton is basically an oval enclosure of stone inside a larger enclosure which skirts round a rock islet in the River Deel. The inner enclosure (much of whose walling has now disappeared) contains two rectangular buildings. One straddles the north arc of the enclosure. This began as a rectangular hall about 20.4 x 9.1 metres (67 x 30 ft), erected in the early thirteenth century by William de Burgo who started the castle a little earlier by creating a motte out of the rock top and putting up a wall round it. Very much later (fifteenth century), the hall was altered at its northern end and heightened to produce a tower-house, and later still a small tower was affixed on the west side, which contains chambers and garderobes. The enclosure's entrance was a gateway on the east just below the hall. At the south of the oval, a rectangular tower of the sixteenth century uses the enclosure wall as its fourth side. To the west, outside the inner enclosure, are the remains of a fifteenth-century banqueting hall which is rectangular with a small staircase turret on its west side. This was built by the Desmond family on the ruins of an earlier hall of similar plan, which had a vaulted basement.

The castle was held by the de Clares in the 1280s and was then granted to the de Welles family by Edward II (1307–27). The Fitzgeralds, Earls of Desmond, held Askeaton

from the late 1360s for about two centuries, after which there was a continuing succession of owners. In 1652 it was slighted by Parliamentary forces.

ASSAROE Co. Donegal
(G 8662)
A castle was built here in 1212 and it is recorded as having been destroyed during the following year.

ATHBOY Co. Meath
(N 7265)
Traces of an earth and timber castle of the early thirteenth century.

ATHENRY Co. Galway
(M 5028)
There was an Irish settlement at Athenry on the Clareen river probably as far back as the seventh or eighth century. In about 1235, Meiler de Bermingham founded a castle there, surrounded by a roughly D-plan stone enclosure with round towers on the corners. Inside the enclosure he raised a low-level, hall-type great tower, 16.4 x 10.3 metres (54 x 34 ft), of one storey at first-floor level set over a pronounced splayed plinth which surrounded a basement. Within a generation, Meiler's son Piers raised the height of the first floor, lifting its ceiling and walls, and embellishing its entrance with the fine arched door at the south-east end. This was reached from outside by a staircase from the ground, probably of timber (a reproduction stair exists there today), and it was protected by some sort of forebuilding. At the same time, he raised a banqueting hall along the east wall of the enclosure, which used the enclosure wall for its fourth side. Among the decorations Piers inserted were narrow windows with trefoil heads, which are some of the very few such castle windows anywhere in Ireland (Ferns, Wexford, and Lea, Laois, are two other examples).

In the fifteenth century, the tower was raised yet again to provide two more floors including an attic between two new gable ends. The basement, meanwhile, which had hitherto been accessible only by ladder through a trap in the first floor, now received its own entrance cut into the splayed plinth. The top of the tower was equipped with battlements whose rectangular merlons were more akin to Norman-style merlons such as were found in English great towers.

This interesting castle has been very carefully restored by the Office of Public Works. It was linked to the town that expanded beside it during the Middle Ages, which itself was enclosed by a comprehensive system of walls, towers and gates, much of which remains to be seen today. Among the buildings enclosed was a Dominican friary (now in ruins) which was founded soon after Meiler's first works.

ATHY Co. Kildare
(S 6894)
Known as White's Castle, this formidable-looking rectangular tower-house of either three or four storeys reaching to nearly 18.3 metres (60 ft), with battlementing, sits along the edge of the River Barrow in the town. Some of the present windows are replacements. There are also arrow-loops, notably in the rectangular corner turrets. The entrance on the east side is through a narrow, Gothic, arched door.

ATHLONE Co. Westmeath
(N 0341)
Athlone was one of the main fording points of the Shannon, an importance recognised by Toirrdelbach Ua Conchobair, King of Connacht and for a time *ard rí* (High King of Ireland). In about 1129 he raised a ring-fort here beside a new bridge he had built across

The thirteenth-century, three-storeyed tower-house at Athenry – one of the earliest in Ireland – has its entrance at first-floor level. The tower-house has recently been restored with great skill and care. Note the prominent sloping plinth.

the river. The fort was one of the seven pre-Norman 'castles' of the 1120s–1160s (*see* p. 87). Some time towards the end of the century, the Anglo-Norman Geoffrey de Costentin built a motte castle on the site, which was later burnt. Then in about 1210 King John ordered a stone castle to be built there, arranging at the same time for the wooden bridge across the river to be converted to a stone one. The old motte was encased in stonework, but it collapsed a year or two later, and a new ten-sided tower was built upon the ruins, which also encased the old motte. This structure, albeit altered and modified, can be seen today.

There has been considerable modification and addition to the castle in general, especially in the last two centuries, but some of the medieval curtain walling and relics of D-plan towers remain. Because of its strategic position, the castle has been described in some quarters as the gateway to the West. It figured in several sieges, such as in the Confederate War of the 1640s, in the fighting between

Athlone: in the centre, behind the enclosure walls with their D-plan towers, is the much-altered ten-sided great tower, begun in c.1210.

William III and ex-King James II in 1689–91 and even during Wolfe Tone's rebellion in 1798–99.

ATHLUMNEY Co. Meath
(N 8966)
This is a double structure overlooking the Boyne near Navan. It consists of a fifteenth-century tower-house, alternatively known as Dowdall Castle, and an end-of-sixteenth-century, semi-fortified stronghouse with gabled roofing and mullioned windows. The latter building is three-storeyed and about 30.5 metres (100 ft) long. Most of its gables are badly damaged. The tower-house projects eastwards from the stronghouse, is four-storeyed, with an attic whose gabling has partly survived, and it has rectangular corner turrets, each of different dimensions and which project from the main walls. The whole edifice was set on fire by its then owners, the Maguires, in 1649, when they were demoralised by the news of the siege of Drogheda not far away, and were determined not to let Cromwell take the castle.

AUDLEY'S Co. Down
(J 5851)
Inside a five-sided enclosure in the north corner is a fifteenth-century three-storeyed tower-house with projecting turrets on two corners which are bridged at the top by arched machicolation (cf., Ardglass [Jordan's], and Kilclief). The entrance is through a door in the south turret at ground level facing the other (east) turret. This is protected by a

drop-hole from the arched machicolation above. The spiral stair goes up the south turret to roof level. The east turret contains garderobes, shoots from which emerge at ground level outside along the north-east wall. The tower was raised in the fifteenth century by the Audley family, and in the seventeenth century it was sold to the Ward family of Castle Ward, situated nearby.

AUGHENTAINE Co. Tyrone
(H 4652)
This long, rectangular tower-house is early seventeenth century and had a squarish projection on the north wall. In the western corner thus formed was a cylindrical staircase turret leading up from the main hall to residential quarters above. The tower-house partly collapsed in the 1930s, and is today an almost total ruin.

AUGHER Co. Tyrone
(H 5654)
A restored square plantation tower-house of three storeys, about 9.1 metres (30 ft) square, whose four faces have a central triangular projection from ground to parapet, containing windows, and doors on one side. On the east wall is the entrance through a simple arched doorway covered by a box machicolation on the parapet above. The tower stood in a bawn of which only traces remain, including a small turret. A later, small mansion was built on to the west side.

AUGHINISH ISLAND Co. Limerick
(R 2853)
A late sixteenth-/early seventeenth-century tower-house within a circular enclosure whose walling is about 1.8 metres (6 ft) or so thick. There is an entrance on the south.

AUGHNANURE Co. Galway
(M 1544)
This is a interesting site on the edge of Lough Corrib. A substantial early sixteenth-century tower-house stands today six storeys high, reaching 17 metres (56 ft) to the parapet which has a square machicolation box centrally along each of the four parapets, including one over the entrance below. The tower-house is about 12.5 x 8.5 metres (41 x 28 ft) and it was built upon the remains of a much earlier castle of which little is known either about its shape or who held it and for how long.

The structure has square corner box machicolations, or bartizans, on the external corners at third-storey level. The tower stands on a sloping plinth, rises to stepped battlements, and inside there are various gun-ports, shot-holes and fireplaces. Two storeys are vaulted. At first-floor level there is a fireplace whose flue goes right to the top of the tower. Some of the ornamentation in the tower features such as the windows and doors is elaborate.

The tower-house has been carefully restored by the Office of Public Works. It stands in a large bawn that was once divided into two in the north-west by a short wall from the north down to a round watch-tower (also restored) and another wall due west meeting the west wall of the larger enclosure. These two walls have more or less vanished. Along the inside of the west wall of the larger enclosure are remains of a banqueting hall that used the wall as one of its sides.

BAGINBUN Co. Wexford
(S 5412)
This site was the earliest in Ireland on which the Anglo-Normans built a fortification, in the years before Henry II invaded Ireland (1171). It was an earth and timber enclosure and was put up by Raymond FitzGilbert le Gros. There are still some remains of the earthworks on the site.

BALIMORE EUSTACE Co. Kildare
(N 9311)
A motte castle was erected here in the early part of the thirteenth century for the Archbishop of Dublin.

BALLINAFAD Co. Sligo
(G 7808)
'The Castle of the Curlews', as it is called, was raised in about 1590. It has four cylindrical turrets with a square interior plan clasping a tower-house of rectangular plan, and rises to three storeys, although the turrets are higher. Although a late sixteenth-century tower, its plan is much like the thirteenth-century great towers at Carlow and Terryglass.

BALLINALACKAN Co. Clare
(M 1001)
A late sixteenth-century six-storey tower-house in good condition (although without its roof) stands in its bawn which has a round-headed entrance near the tower.

BALLINASLOE Co. Galway
(M 8531)
One of the first of the very few castles built by the Irish, half a century before the Anglo-Norman invasions. It was a timber and earth enclosure, of which some remains can be seen. Nearby is a nineteenth-century rebuild of a sixteenth-century tower-house.

BALLINCOLLIG Co. Cork
(W 5971)
This castle, with its walled enclosure, is recorded as having been built in the fourteenth century.

BALLINDONEY Co. Tipperary
(S 1122)
A four-storey (plus roof) tower-house of the fifteenth or early sixteenth century, with angle-loops, gun-ports, and standing on a sloping plinth.

BALLINDOOLY Co. Galway
(M 3229)
A fifteenth-century tower-house which is in good condition.

BALLINGARRY Co. Limerick
(R 2437)
A pre-Norman ring-fort platform was in later years heightened by the Anglo-Normans and topped with an L-plan three-storey 11.5 x 8.2 metres (38 x 27 ft) tower-house.

BALLINTOBER Co. Roscommon
(M 7274)
An early fourteenth-century stone enclosure, roughly square, with polygonal corner turrets, a twin drum-towered gatehouse on the east, this castle was attacked on many occasions almost from the start of its existence. In the seventeenth century the north-west and north-east corner turrets were enlarged and reinforced as tower-houses in their own right. Built probably by the Ua Conchobair family (which had once provided kings of Connacht) 16 km (10 miles) from Roscommon Castle (q.v.), it resembles the latter in plan. Was this perhaps deliberate?

BALLINTOTTY Co. Tipperary
(R 9178)
Here is an impressive ruin of a large, rectangular, four-storey tower-house, with rounded corners and arrow-loops in the angles as well as elsewhere.

BALLINTRA Co. Donegal
(G 9068)
A motte here was found to contain a square stone floor with walling, which may have been the core of a small tower-house.

BALLYCARBURY Co. Kerry
(V 4580)
A substantial fifteenth-century rectangular tower-house inside a rectangular enclosure, most of which is missing. It is 23 x 13.1 metres (75½ x 43 ft), with walls nearly 2.7 metres (9 ft) thick, and it rises three storeys plus attic level, although the top of the tower is very badly damaged. On the north-east corner is the remnant of a small square turret, with rooms at each level. Inside, the tower has been divided into three nearly equal accommodation areas separated by cross-walls, at ground- and first-floor levels, and the top storey below the attic is a hall which occupies two-thirds of the floor area. Large parts of this tower-house have collapsed, and now the remains are neglected. It belonged to the MacCarthaigh family.

BALLYCOWAN Co. Offaly
(N 2925)
Ruins of a substantial L-plan tower-house of nearly 18.3 metres (60 ft) in length and 10.7 metres (35 ft) in width, three storeys plus roof in height, built in the early seventeenth century, with the shorter arm of the 'L' slightly indented along the longer part. The ground floor has a cross-wall dividing the area into cellars and kitchen. This castle was begun in the early seventeenth century.

BALLYGALLY Co. Antrim
(D 3708)
A Scottish-style L-plan tower-house of about 1625, with conical topped bartizans on cone corbels, this is rectangular with a wing projecting north-eastwards at one end, which contains the entrance and spiral staircase.

BALLYGRENNAN Co. Limerick
(R 6475)
A sixteenth-century tower-house enclosed within a two-bailey system which has other towers of the seventeenth century.

BALLYHACK Co. Wexford
(S 7111)
Sited on a steep slope overlooking the Waterford estuary, this is a mid-fifteenth-century tower-house of five storeys, with box machicolations and gabled roof. The ground and second floors are vaulted, and there are interesting recesses on the third floor, including a chapel.

BALLYLOUGHAN Co. Carlow
(S 7458)
The great gatehouse of twin drum towers, three storeys tall, is the main remnant here of a once-substantial enclosure castle with corner towers. The south-west tower was almost square, with one wall nearly 3 metres (10 ft) thick to allow the insertion of flights of stairs. The castle is of late thirteenth-century origin, but Leask considers it was not well defended, apart from the gatehouse.

BALLYMALIS Co. Kerry
(V 8494)
This is an interesting example of a sixteenth-century, four-storey tower-house, having corner bartizans among its defences. There are two which clasp opposite corners of the tower at second-floor level. It is 14.9 x 9.7 metres (49 x 32 ft). The east wall is twice as thick as the others, and it contains a staircase and also chambers.

BALLYMOON Co. Carlow
(S 7362)
One of the major castles of the thirteenth to early fourteenth century, Ballymoon is an almost square enclosure. Surprisingly, there are no corner towers, but there are remains of rectangular projections on the east, south and north walls, all of which have garderobes. The enclosure wall is of granite, about 2.4 metres (8 ft) thick, and for much of its length about 6 metres (20 ft) tall. Along the walls are a variety of loops (especially cross-loops) and window openings, some spaced regularly to suggest they were part of domestic buildings built (or in some cases intended to be built) along the walls, of which some, if not all, may have been two-storeyed. On the west wall is a gateway with a portcullis groove, and outside are traces of what may have been a protecting barbican.

The history of the castle is barely known, and tradition maintains that it has never been inhabited. It may have been built by the Bigods, an East Anglian family of considerable power. Certainly, it does not seem to have been very defensible.

BALLYMOTE Co. Sligo
(G 6615)
An enclosure castle of the later thirteenth or very early fourteenth century, almost square in plan, it has massive round towers on the corners, a D-plan flanking tower along east and west walls, and a sally-port or postern tower on the south wall. But its main structure is a huge gatehouse of two half-round towers flanking the entrance on the north wall. This was 23.2 metres (76 ft) wide

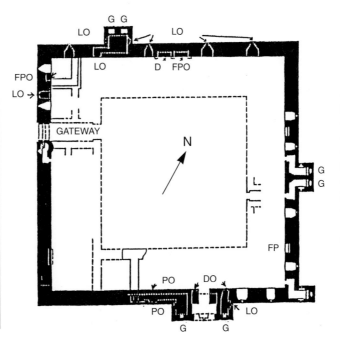

Ballymoon, Co. Carlow: the plan suggests that the structure was never completed. LO = loop over. D = door. FP = fireplace. G = garderobe. DO = door over. FPO = fireplace over. PO = passage over. There were two storeys of buildings all round the inside of the wall, with cellars underneath.

The south wall of the quadrangular enclosure at Ballymoon, with its rectangular mural tower.

(the size of an average class 1 great tower) and it was four-storeyed. Ballymote's enclosing walls are – where they survive intact – over 3 metres (10 ft) thick and they had a number of wall staircases leading to the wall parapets. At some stage, the gatehouse towers were strengthened by the addition of a protective skin of outer walling.

Ballymote was raised by the de Burgo family, but was besieged and taken by both the Ua Conchobair and MacDiarmaid families in the fourteenth century. Thereafter, there is a long history of further siege, capture, recapture and sale or lease. It also appears to have been left unoccupied for long periods.

BALLYNACARRIGA Co. Cork
(W 2951)
This sixteenth-century four-storey tower-house stands on a rock base beside its own lake. A date of 1585 is carved in a window on the top floor, but it is thought the tower may well be older. This top floor was for a time used as a chapel.

The remains of the north-west round corner tower of Ballymote and, to its left, part of the twin-towered gatehouse. The western D-plan mid-wall tower is on the right.

BALLYNAHOW Co. Tipperary
(S 0860)
One of only a few cylindrical great towers and tower-houses in Ireland (the finest of which is Nenagh, pp. 228–9), this 17.4-metre (57-ft) tall structure is of late sixteenth-century origin. It has five storeys, two of which are vaulted double storeys. The tower on a splayed base is 10.7 metres (35 ft) in diameter, and the wall thickness, of about 2.4–2.7 metres (8–9 ft) at ground floor, gets less thick in the higher storeys. The ground and first floor are cylindrical internally, but higher up, the apartment area forms a quadrilateral plan. Outside, the wall-walk and parapet are well preserved, and have four equidistantly placed box machicolations. The tower has some 28 gun-ports as well as several pairs of narrow arched windows, some rounded, some of ogee shape, and a murder hole covering the area inside the door.

BALLYNAKILL Co. Tipperary
(S 0985)
A three-storey rectangular tower-house, associated with later buildings.

BALLYNARRY Co. Down
(S 5644)
A motte castle, whose mound appears to have been heightened from time to time up to the thirteenth century, although it is not clear whether the last increase in height was Anglo-Norman or native Irish.

BALLYRAGGET Co. Kilkenny
(N 4472)
A fifteenth-/sixteenth-century tower-house of the Ormonde (Butler) family, Ballyragget still has its roof, and it stands inside a walled enclosure that has its original ditching most of the way round.

BALLYRONEY Co. Down
(J 2240)
A late twelfth-century motte castle, with a bailey on each side, which was excavated in the 1970s.

BALLYSONAN Co. Tipperary
(N 7804)
This is a curious castle, described by C.T. Cairns (from a sketch of 1648) as a large tower-house enclosed by a rectangular bawn, with two rectangular and one cylindrical corner turrets, further defended by star-plan fortifications and a wet moat. Outside the inner bawn, in a second bawn, was an Anglo-Norman motte still in use in the 1640s and being defended, although there is no sign of any building. A second, outer bawn protected two sides of the motte's bawn.

BARRY'S COURT Co. Cork
(W 8273)
A substantial castle of medieval origin which was rebuilt during the last quarter of the sixteenth century.

BEAL BORU Co. Clare
(R 6674)
This site probably began as an Irish ring-fort on the Shannon near Killaloe. Some time during the early thirteenth century, a motte was raised on the site, but this was apparently not completed.

BENBURB Co. Tyrone
(H 8152)
Site of a great victory by Owen Roe O'Neill commanding the Confederate army in 1646, Benburb had once been a seat of the O'Neills, leaders of opposition to English rule in Ulster. In about 1611, Sir Richard Wingfield built the castle there on a high cliff some 61 metres (200 ft) above the River Blackwater; this consisted of a triangular enclosure with walls about 4.9 metres (16 ft) tall. One of its sides is the cliff face, a sheer drop down to the river. On the north side are two three-storeyed rectangular towers, one at each end. At the south end of the north–south wall is a smaller round turret near the cliff edge, and this has a staircase. Nearby is a house of a much later period. The castle is today in the grounds of a Servite monastery.

BIGARZ Co. Kildare
(S 6698)
The low motte on this site, which is near Ardree (q.v.), may be that of Robert de Bigarz, erected in 1182, as recorded by Giraldus Cambrensis.

BIRR Co. Offaly
(N 0504)
The nineteenth-century 'reproduction' castle here began as a simple motte castle of c.1186, which the records say was destroyed in about 1207 and rebuilt five years later. It was for a time the property of the O'Carrolls. Its history and development thereafter are almost unknown until in the 1620s an imposing castellar-like house was erected on the site. This in turn was substantially modified in the early nineteenth century, eventually emerging as it appears now.

BLARNEY Co. Cork
(W 6174)
Blarney's tremendous rectangular great tower – one of the very biggest in Ireland – has an interesting building history. It was erected in two stages. First, in the early fifteenth century a small 6-metre (20-ft) square turret rising to four storeys and containing small rooms was built as part of some other building which has since been superseded. This original turret, not then machicolated, remained where it is when about 40 years later the castle owner, Cormac MacCarthaigh, decided to restructure whatever was there by imposing a huge rectangular great tower, 18.3 x 11.9 metres (60 x 39 ft), with five storeys, on the earlier building, but incorporating the small square turret at its north-west corner, making the whole an L-plan tower. The new rectangle has walls 3.6 metres (12 ft) or so thick at the lower levels, reducing a little on the way up towards the top. The second floor of the rectangle is vaulted, and the tower has its own staircase in the north wall. Meanwhile, the turret was refurbished by having its ground floor filled up with rubble, masonry, earth, etc., and its higher floors remained much the same but with a small spiral staircase up the north-east corner.

The most arresting feature of the newer tower, however, is the massive parapet with its machicolation all round the top of the fifth storey. This projects outwards over the top of the walling by a distance of more than 0.6 metres (2 ft) and is carried all round on a row of pyramidal corbels over 1.8 metres (6 ft) long. On the top of the parapet are stepped battlements. Received opinion is that the corbelling and machicolation are later than the MacCarthaigh tower, by perhaps as much as a century. In the eighteenth century the then owner added a Gothic-style extension at the south end; however, this was severely damaged by a fire in the nineteenth century and has remained derelict since. The castle is famous for the Blarney Stone, which is a stone set in the machicolation. By means of inverting oneself head downwards between two machicolations one can kiss the stone, an act that will, it is claimed, 'confer eloquence'.

BOURCHIER'S Co. Limerick
(R 6542)
A castle of unknown size and shape but noted as having been built during the thirteenth century lies under the later fifteenth-century tower-house known as Bourchier's. The latter is five-storeyed, about 16.8 x 11 metres (55 x 36 ft), with, among other features, a gun-port beside its entrance (cf., Claypotts, Scotland, p. 250). Excavations in the castle area revealed traces of two medieval houses which were part of a village which grew up around the original castle. It had been built by the Earls of Desmond.

BUNCRANA Inishowen, Co. Donegal
(C 3531)
This began as an almost square-plan tower-house of the early fourteenth century, and had its entrance at first-floor level. There were many passages, straight staircases and chambers in the wall thicknesses. The top of the tower is of much later construction, part of repairs by the O'Dochertys in c.1600. It was burned by the English in 1602 but repaired again later in the century.

BUNRATTY Co. Clare
(R 4561)
Begun by the Macconmaras and once the seat of the Thomond O'Briens, this is a vast great tower which is of mid-fifteenth-century construction. It has a rectangular central core with four massive square corner towers.

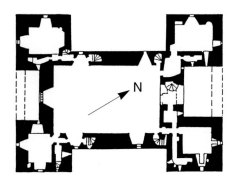

Bunratty, Co. Clare: plan of second (upper) hall. Note spiral staircases and passages in the wall thicknesses, many leading to individual rooms.

Originally, it stood inside an extensive enclosure with various buildings, but these have almost disappeared. The rectangular core of the great tower is 18.9 x 12.5 metres (62 x 41 ft) with walls over 2.1 metres (7 ft) thick. These walls contain a number of mural stairs, straight and spiral. The northern wall, 3 metres (10 ft) thick, contains the entrance, which leads straight into a great hall that is vaulted, as is the storage floor underneath. Above the great hall is a second hall which at one time was magnificently decorated with fine plasterwork in the seventeenth century, and which was restored not long ago. The core contains only the large rooms. It is the four huge corner towers, each over 7 metres (23 ft) square, which contain the many bedrooms, garderobes, a chapel, and a plethora of passages and stairways. There are five storeys in each tower. The two northern towers and the two southern towers are joined on the exterior at top-floor level by broad arches. The prominent parapets at the top of the core and at the top of the towers (different height) with their battlements are not original.

The great tower castle replaced an earlier, smaller stone castle of the late thirteenth century which had endured a number of sieges. That castle itself was the second on the site, which originally carried a motte castle of the mid-thirteenth century. The latest restorations were carried out in the late 1950s, and today the castle is open to visitors.

BURNCHURCH Co. KILKENNY
(S 4847)
Burnchurch is one of the fifteenth-century rectangular tower-houses which have the special feature of the two narrower sides being continued upwards for an extra storey higher than the wall-walk, in the manner of additional wide turrets. In these turrets there are passages or rooms, with their own wall-walk on the roof above. All the sides have (or had, as may be) battlemented parapets. Burnchurch, which although without its roof is in very good condition, slopes gently outwards on four sides from the second floor downwards, and is six-storeyed, with a vaulted ceiling on the fifth (hall) floor, where there is an interesting fireplace with joggle voussoir arch protruding from the wall.

BURNCOURT Co. TIPPERARY
(R 9518)
A many-windowed and gabled tower-house of the mid-seventeenth century, partly – although perhaps inadequately – defensible, this rectangular building with four huge square turrets on its corners (like Kanturk, q.v.,) is still more or less in the ruinous condition in which it was left after its owners set fire to it to prevent it being besieged and captured by the army of Cromwell, then under the command of General Ireton, in 1650. Between the top row of windows on the various wall faces, stone corbels were inserted

Burncourt, Co. Tipperary: plan.

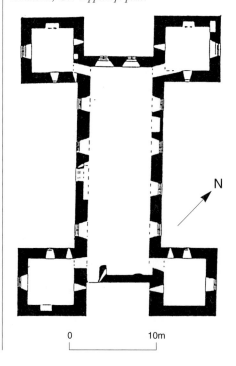

0   10m

during construction, probably to support protective hoarding, and more characteristic of medieval castle defensive mechanisms. Parts of its surrounding bawn have survived.

BURT Co. DONEGAL
(C 3119)
A late sixteenth-century, Z-plan tower-house, with two opposing cylindrical corner towers, much like the models found in Scotland (cf., Claypotts), Burt stands on a hill with fine views across the countryside all round. It is on the whole ruinous, but some parts are of interest, particularly its staircase-tower on the south-west corner. The core walls of the rectangle are over 1.8 metres (6 ft) thick on three sides. The tower stands to its full height of three storeys plus attic, and there are traces of machicolation on one corner. It was once enclosed inside a bawn, but not much of this remains. A drawing of the castle in 1601 survives in the Irish State papers.

CAHERCONLISH Co. LIMERICK
(R 6750)
Here, a motte castle of late twelfth- or early thirteenth-century construction was erected, and earthwork remains which are visible at the site may be of this structure.

CAHIR Co. TIPPERARY
(S 0525)
Cahir Castle was built on a rocky island in the River Suir, and it is among the biggest castles in Ireland. It was begun in the thirteenth century, had major additions in the fifteenth and lesser works in the sixteenth and seventeenth. Today, after some restoration work in the 1840s, which included renovating the great hall and the rectangular western tower, it still retains an almost unrivalled grandeur. From c.1375 the castle was for centuries the seat of the Ormonde Butlers, one of whom initiated the mid-nineteenth-century renovations.

The basic plan of Cahir consists of two large baileys and one small bailey placed in between. The north, inner bailey (or ward) is an original thirteenth-century work with two rectangular corner towers and one round corner tower, and a much larger rectangular tower block positioned on the fourth (west) corner. Much of this early bailey was built upon rock, and this can be seen 'splaying' out of the bottom of the walling. The principal building in the bailey, however, was a twin-

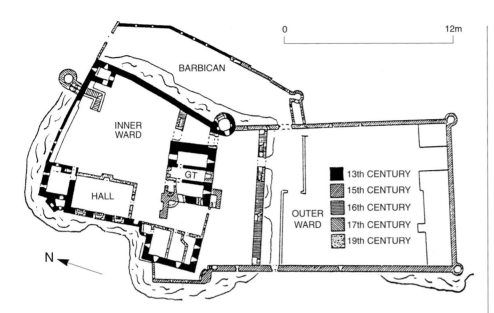

0   12m

Cahir, Co. Tipperary: GT = Great Tower.

13th CENTURY
15th CENTURY
16th CENTURY
17th CENTURY
19th CENTURY

rectangular-towered gatehouse which was built along the south wall.

The fifteenth-century work included converting this gatehouse into a great tower (similar changes of this kind were made at Roscrea, Co. Tipperary, and at several British castles, such as Dunstanburgh and Ludlow), and putting a new, smaller gateway nearby between it and the round tower on the east bailey wall. This gateway has a double-arch head and fronted a portcullis. The fifteenth-century work also included constructing a second (outer) bailey (or ward) to the south, roughly rectangular, with two southerly round corner towers, a new gateway at the east, and other walls and extensions. In the sixteenth century, the outer bailey was shortened at the north end by putting a wall across it from east to west, positioned not far from the great tower, to create the middle bailey (or ward).

These were the main developments. The fifteenth century also saw the enlargement of an already extensive eastern barbican with the east wall on the river edge.

Cahir was captured after a ten-day siege by the Earl of Essex, who was Elizabeth I's favourite, during his vainglorious Irish campaign which lasted from 1598–1600. It was captured again, this time without a fight, by Cromwell in 1650.

Today the castle is still preserved in remarkably good condition.

CAPPAGH Co. Limerick
(R 8948)

This late fifteenth-century great tower 21.3 metres (70 ft) tall is inside a walled enclosure that has turrets on the eastern corners.

CARBURY Co. Kildare
(N 6935)

A late sixteenth-century, irregularly shaped tower-house with additions of later date was raised on the site of a much earlier motte castle that had two baileys. The motte may have been of Henry II's time, although it has been cleared away. The tower-house appears to have begun as a large rectangular building with an off-centre cross-wall. On the west side a smaller turret probably contained the staircase. There were more extensions to the south. Most of the main walls were 1.8–2.1 metres (6–7 ft) thick. The remains include clustered chimneys and largish windows.

CARGIN (CARRAIGIN) Co. Galway
(M 2443)

A rectangular two-storeyed hall-house, possibly of the thirteenth century, with a vaulted lower storey, and a square-plan garderobe turret on the east corner. It has been much modified at various times, including within the last 30 years.

CARLINGFORD (KING JOHN'S)
Co. Louth
(J 1812)

One of the principal early castles of the Anglo-Normans, King John's at Carlingford

stands on a rock mound beside Lough Carlingford, overlooking the harbour. Possibly there was an earth and timber structure at the site put up during Prince John's lordship of Ireland in the 1180s. The stonework castle of basically D-plan was started towards the end of the century. How much was completed in the first stage of works is not certain, but probably it included the curve of the 'D', with a twin-rectangular-towered gateway at the west, linked southwards by a straight wall to a square tower with splayed plinth, and north and eastwards a curving wall (of short, straight lengths) on which there was another flanking tower facing north. This curving wall rests for much of its length on a bulging outcrop of rock (like, for example, part of the castle at Dunstaffnage, Scotland).

In the 1260s the gap between the ends of the north and south walls, however it had been filled in the early works, was now re-sealed with a large hall structure, a block of at least two storeys, and roofed, over a basement with cellars. This block contained a hall, smaller apartments and other chambers. Leask cites payments listed in the Irish Pipe Rolls for quarrying and transporting stone to Carlingford (and to Greencastle on the other side of the lough, *see* p. 219). In the fifteenth century, more apartments were added on the southern end of the 1260s work.

There are two other, much smaller, castles in Carlingford, of much later date. One is

Carlingford, Co. Louth: the black walling is the earliest work, of the late twelfth century. The hall is largely of the 1260s.

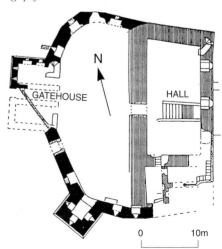

*Carlingford: the remains of the twelfth-century,
twin rectangular-towered gatehouse are seen on the
left, with part of the thirteenth-century hall block
on the right.*

called Taaffe's, a four-storeyed, rectangular
sixteenth-century tower-house which has a
projecting corner turret, and is joined to the
tower on the north wall by a two- or three-
storeyed hall-like building with large
windows. Another building nearby known as
the Mint is a rhomboid-plan tower-house in
good condition, also of the sixteenth century.

CARLOW Co. CARLOW
(S 7376 A)
Little remains of this once huge castle whose
central tower was a substantial rectangular
block of three storeys on a sloping plinth,
some 20.4 x 14 metres (67 x 46 ft), with
2.7-metre (9-ft) thick walls. Situated by the
River Barrow, it was built by William the
Marshal between 1207 and 1213. A century
later it was granted to Thomas Plantagenet de
Brotherton, Earl of Norfolk, and it remained
a Crown castle until 1537. In the Confederate
War it changed hands more than once.

The rectangular core was clasped on its
corners by circular towers, some 7.6 metres
(25 ft) in diameter and rising several feet

above the battlemented top of the core. All
that now remains is the west wall, damaged,
and with two clasping towers, and within its
thickness are straight flights of stairs. On what
remains of the north wall is the vestige of the
entrance on the first floor. There are few
loops in the west wall and they are narrow. At
second-storey level outside are two 'blisters'
which are garderobe shoots. The castle, which
contained other buildings and an enclosing
wall in addition to the great tower, was largely
demolished in the early nineteenth century to
make way for houses and for a lunatic asylum.

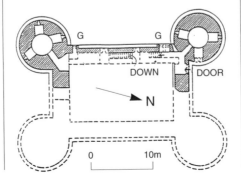

*Carlow, Co. Carlow: plan of remains of great
tower with clasping corner towers. The hatching
shows the areas of existing stonework above ground
(after Leask). G = garderobe.*

CARRICK Co. WEXFORD
(T 0023)
An oval enclosure of Henry II's reign, raised
after Strongbow's expedition and before the
king set out for Ireland (1171). Its ditch and
banking can still be seen. The nearby round
tower is not of the castle period.

CARRICKFERGUS Co. ANTRIM
(J 4187)
This is a large three-ward castle, the wards of
differing dates, situated on the northern shore
of Lough Belfast. It is often described as the
earliest stone castle in all Ireland and, short of
another candidate at the moment of writing,
we may accept that the first of its three phases
of building, carried out between 1178 and
1195, were at least started before any other
stonework. It was begun by John de Courcy,
the Anglo-Norman lord who conquered
much of Ulster and governed it for over a
quarter of a century (1177–1204). The early
phase included the polygonal enclosure that is
still there and is called the inner ward,
together with a great hall along its east wall,
now only in fragmentary condition. The
other work of this phase was starting the
nearly square great tower that still dominates
the castle and the adjoining town today. This
great tower, now 27.4 metres (90 ft) tall, and
measuring 17.7 x 17 metres (58 x 56 ft)
horizontally, rose to three storeys in de
Courcy's time. The lowest storey is barrel-
vaulted and divided by a cross-wall beside
which is the tower's well. In one corner is a
large spiral staircase that continues up the
height of the tower. Entry to the tower was
originally via an outside stairway up to the
first floor and through a round-headed
doorway. The stairs and the entrance were
once protected by a forebuilding (now
disappeared). The first floor and the next one
above also have cross-walls. The third floor,
which is the Great Hall, has a flying arch
across the centre, which supports the roof.
The roof may be part of the second phase of
building, c.1216–23. On the west side of the
second floor is a pair of garderobes whose
shoots emerge in a projection on the outside.
Nearby is another step-way to a separate
garderobe with its own outside shoot. This
may have been the private lavatory for the
castellan, or for the king himself when he was
in residence.

The castle was taken over by King John in
1210 and he made it an administrative centre

GATEHOUSE

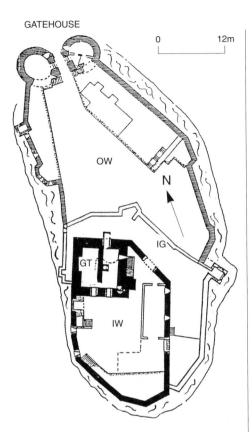

Carrickfergus, Co. Antrim: IW = Inner Ward. This, with part of the great tower (GT), was the first stage of the buildings. IG = inner gateway. The second stage included finishing the great tower and erecting the eastern wall along the edge of Belfast Lough, immediately south-east of the inner ward, and also the wall running east to west north of the inner ward, which formed a middle ward. The third stage included the outer ward (OW) and the great gatehouse at north, and other buildings, all shown by hatching.

for the English government, which it remained for over seven centuries. The second phase of building started after John's reign was over, in 1216, and included finishing the great tower and adding a middle ward by erecting a wall west to east ending in a square tower on the edge of the lough, and a further stretch of wall north to south feeding into the inner ward's walling to the south. The third phase, c.1226–42, consisted of an outer ward on the north which was given a twin cylindrical-towered gatehouse to the north, the towers being about 12.2 metres (40 ft) in diameter and flanking a passage protected by a portcullis. On the first floor of

the eastern of the two towers is a chapel which has a two-light ecclesiastical window in the east. The southern back of the chapel was cut off at some stage half-way across, creating a half-moon plan. This has led some to think that the gatehouse was not twin-cylindrical, but in fact it was, as may be swiftly deduced from looking at the surviving shape of the western of the two towers of the gatehouse.

Carrickfergus was besieged and damaged by Edward Bruce in 1315–16, and then again by the O'Neills in the 1380s. It was taken by one of William III's generals in the war between William and James II (then in exile) in 1689–91.

CARRICKKILDAVNET Co. Mayo
(L 7294)
A striking, narrow tower-house of four storeys plus attic, with box machicolations on each of the four parapets, it stands on an islet of the sea and was once enclosed by a bawn.

CARRICK ON SUIR Co. Tipperary
(S 4021)
This is an Elizabethan undefended house and courtyard built by the Earls of Ormonde, and bolted, as it were, on to a double-towered stone enclosure castle of the mid-fifteenth century. The fifteenth-century towers, of slightly differing dimensions but situated nearly parallel, were both five-storeyed, and one wall of each was continued southwards and parallel to a joining wall at right-angles, forming a courtyard. This latter wall vanished in the sixteenth century when new work was done, including extending the two parallel walls further southwards to meet a new end wall that bowed outwards in the middle. The Elizabethan house at the northern end is low, two-storeyed with a steep, gabled attic storey and impressive porch; it is much lower than the two earlier towers.

CARRIGAFOYLE Co. Kerry
(Q 9947)
A 24.4-metre (80-ft) tall rectangular tower-house standing centrally inside a high-walled bawn on the Shannon estuary, near Ballylongford, and belonging once to the Ua Conchobair family; it was built in the late fifteenth century. The enclosure reaches the water at one point and a dock for ships was built by the base of the tower. The tower is five-storeyed, with vaulted ceilings on the second and fourth floors. At one level it has an

arched recess between the spiral staircase inside and the main room, whose door opened inwards. The tower is badly damaged.

CARRIGAHOLT Co. Clare
(Q 8552)
This is a much-restored sixteenth-century tower-house. Tall, slender, with five storeys, it stands in the corner of a bawn. Its walls have gun-ports, the fourth floor is vaulted, and a fireplace on the fifth floor carries the date 1603, which may indicate the addition of that storey in that year. The castle was taken by Cromwell's forces in 1651 but it was restored to the O'Briens (its owners) by Charles II after the Restoration of 1660. In 1691, William III granted it to one of his army commanders.

CARRIGAPHOOCA Co. Cork
(W 2974 A)
A sixteenth-century rectangular tower-house of four storeys, the third storey double-vaulted; it stands on a rock base. It has two turrets remaining on opposite corners at the top. One wall contains straight staircases all the way up. The tower has no windows, only loops, nor does it have fireplaces or chimneys. There is only one room to each floor, with some mural recesses. It was built by the MacCarthaigh family, and it was sacked in 1601–2.

CARRIGOGUNNEL Co. Limerick
(R 5050)
This was an O'Brien possession on top of a rock over the Shannon. It is now ruinous, and the principal remains include a severely damaged tower-house, also a fragmentary enclosing wall, and a chapel. The first work here has been dated to the early thirteenth century when the rock top was converted into a motte. Probably the first stone building was the cylindrical tower some 10.7 metres (35 ft) across, now in remnants, sited on the edge of the rock, which replaced the motte castle. The main works were of the fourteenth and fifteenth centuries and included the hall block immediately south of the round tower, and an enclosing wall which swept south-eastwards, turned sharply north-eastwards, then north-westwards (at this point a gateway was inserted), then north-east again to swing north-west once more, and finally westwards back to the area of the round tower. There was more work in the sixteenth century, which included building an inner courtyard

beside the old round tower and an apartment block. The castle was slighted in the war between William III and the exiled James II, from 1689–91.

CASHEL Co. TIPPERARY
(S 0741)
Driving from Urlingford towards Cashel, you can see, miles before reaching the town, the High Rock of Cashel, 30.5 metres (100 ft) above the plain. This was where Cormac, a fourth-century king in Munster, built his capital. In the next century it became a Christian centre. In the 970s, Brian Boru, later to become *ard rí* (High King of Ireland) – and the greatest figure in all Irish history –

was crowned there as Munster's king. A century after his death in 1014 at Clontarf, his descendants gave the land to the Church and in 1127 Cormac MacCarthaigh started to build the small Romanesque church known later as Cormac's chapel. In 1169, a cathedral was started next door, where in 1172 the assembled Irish clergy did homage to Henry II. By the 1260s, the cathedral had gone but was to be replaced by another, whose ruins are still there. At the end of the nave of this later building, a tower-house was built in the early fifteenth century, 12.6 x 8.8 metres (41 x 28½ ft) and some 22.2 metres (73 ft) tall, with thick walls and lots of passages. It is now a ruin.

CASTLE ARCHDALE Co. FERMANAGH
(H 1859)
Overlooking Lower Lough Erne on its eastern side, this was a plantation castle of about 1615. It consisted of a T-plan stronghouse, not unlike Tully on the other side of the lough (q.v.), standing in a square bawn. The castle was ravaged by the Maguires during the Confederate War and was attacked again in the war between William III and the exiled James II, 1689–91. It is now quite ruinous.

CASTLE BALDWIN Co. SLIGO
(G 7614)
An early seventeenth-century rectangular L-plan tower-house whose shorter arm is a square tower. This carried the staircase – apparently of timber – to all three floors.

CASTLE BALFOUR Co. FERMANAGH
(H 3634)
An eccentrically shaped plantation castle was erected here at Lisnaskea in the early seventeenth century (c.1615–20) by the Balfours. It was a long, rectangular building of three storeys, on a north–south axis, having a square wing to the west, a later rectangular block put up on the northern end and, later still, more works at the south. It is located at the end of Lisnaskea's main street.

CASTLECARRA Co. MAYO
(G 1775)
Near Lough Carra, this is a thirteenth-century rectangular great tower of three storeys, about 15.2 x 10.7 metres (50 x 35 ft), with an east wall about 1.8 metres (6 ft) thick, the others slightly less, and with its entrance in the south. The tower was altered over the centuries and at one time given a cross-wall in the ground storey. An entrance tower was set on the south wall in the fourteenth century. The biggest development was the fifteenth-century five-sided enclosure about 1.8 metres (6 ft) wide around the great tower, which had a small circular flanking tower at the north-east angle.

CASTLE CALDWELL Co. FERMANAGH
(H 0261)
This very ruinous tower-house with rectangular projections on the west side is

The remains of the thirteenth-century great tower at Castlecarra.

three storeys tall. The west projections are linked to two further square two-storeyed turrets which have several gun-ports. Castle Caldwell was a plantation castle dating from about 1612.

CASTLE CAULFIELD Co. Tyrone
(H 7563)

A plantation castle of c.1611–19 erected by Sir Toby Caulfield (later Lord Charlemont) was burned down during the Confederate War in 1641. It had been built upon the site of an earlier native Irish enclosure, of which part of the twin-towered gateway remains to two-storey height. What emerged was a U-plan stronghouse, three storeys tall, with mullion windows. One of the wings is no longer standing. At the ground floor there are fireplaces low down in the wall indicating that the floor level is now much higher than originally. The earlier gateway has guardrooms on either side of the entrance passage, and one room contains a half-rounded turret in the corner for a spiral stairway up to the storey above which has traces of meutrières in the floor, over the entrance passage.

The castle is sited on the outskirts of the small town, and is now surrounded by a modern housing estate.

CASTLE COMER Co. Kilkenny
(S 5273)

A motte castle of the late twelfth century, which was attacked and burnt c.1200.

CASTLE CONNELL Co. Limerick
(R 6563)

Beside the village street at Castleconnell is a huge rock mass on which in the early thirteenth century a castle of unknown shape was raised. This was attacked by the Irish in about 1260 and wrecked, and the site was taken over by the de Clares who built an enclosure with cylindrical corner towers. There are some remains. The castle survived into the late seventeenth century but was blown up by the forces of William III in the war against the exiled James II.

CASTLEGRACE Co. Tipperary
(S 0415)

A thirteenth-century stonework enclosure of rectangular plan, with two round corner towers, and traces of rectangular towers on the other corners.

CASTLEGROVE Co. Galway
(M 3758)

Castlegrove is a fifteenth-century tower-house of four storeys and a roof storey above, of which the gable ends partly survive today. The parapet is rounded at the corners. There are plain and arched loops, and pairs of small windows.

CASTLE KIRK Co. Galway
(L 9980)

On an island in Lake Corrib are the remains of a substantial rectangular enclosure with square corner turrets, built in the early thirteenth century. A rectangular tower was raised against the south side of the enclosure at or soon after the first work.

CASTLEKNOCK Co. Dublin
(O 0836)

This twelfth-century castle of earth and timber origins today lies right next to St Vincent's College in north-west Dublin. It began as a motte castle of c.1180 (built by the Tyrell family), whose mound was situated on an already present natural hillock, creating a very tall mound. Within a few years, the mound top was encased in stonework and heightened to create a polygonal great tower of three storeys, of which a sketch was drawn by Francis Place in 1698.

Today there is still some of the stonework of the tower, notably around the entrance, and there are traces of other buildings. The mound top is now a cemetery. About 152.4 metres (500 ft) away is another mound which may have been an observation mound. It carries a very small round turret on the summit, although this structure is not of great antiquity. Castleknock was besieged and taken by Edward Bruce in 1316–17, and again by George Monck, later Duke of Albemarle, during the Confederate War.

CASTLEMARTYR Co. Cork
(W 9674)

An earth and timber castle was raised here, probably by the Anglo-Normans in the late 1170s. Nearly three centuries later, a quadrangular enclosure castle was built on the same site. This had a large square tower on the north corner, of which two storeys survive today, and positioned at the east, a five-storey tower-house.

CASTLEMORE BARRETT Co. Cork
(W 5792)

This is a site of some ruins. A rectangular hall-tower of the mid-thirteenth century was erected over an earlier enclosure castle. A wing was added to this tower at one end in the fifteenth century.

CASTLEROCHE Co. Louth
(H 9913)

Castleroche, close to the Ulster border, north-west of Dundalk, stands on a rocky cliff on guard, as it were, over a pass in the Armagh hills. It is mentioned in the Close Rolls for 1236 when a Lady de Verdon is recorded as building a fortified house against the Irish. This is probably the stone great tower whose ruins remain in the centre of the later high-walled and battlemented stone enclosure of the 1260s–70s. The latter, although now dilapidated through a mix of age and assault, is complete enough for us to see the arrangement of buildings in what was a major thirteenth-century castle. Triangular in plan, the enclosure's north wall, some 65.8 metres (216 ft) long and 1.8 metres (6 ft) thick, has at its east end the remains of a huge four-storeyed twin-cylindrical-towered gatehouse

Castleknock, Co. Dublin: from the view of the castle drawn in 1698 by Francis Place. There are still some remains of the polygonal great tower.

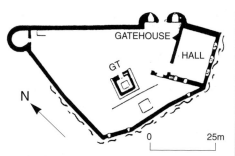

Castleroche, Co. Louth: GT = great tower, the earliest building in the castle.

with loops, and at the other end the lower levels of a cylindrical tower 8.2 metres (27 ft) in diameter. Immediately next to the gatehouse, and slanting some 10–15 degrees, is the shell of a substantial hall building, 17.7 x 14.5 metres (58 x 47½ ft), which points south. It is built on sloping rock and its south-facing wall has three large windows with seats. The hall occupied the higher levels, the lower part had rooms. The enclosure, hall, gatehouse and other works were built by Lady de Verdon's son John. The castle is well worth a visit.

CASTLE SKREEN Co. Down
(J 4740)

This is the site of an Irish ring-fort. The Anglo-Normans erected a fairly large motte here in the last years of the twelfth century.

CASTLETOBIN Co. Kilkenny
(S 4245)

An early Anglo-Norman enclosure castle here was excavated recently, and revealed to be about 51.9 metres (170 ft) across and partly surrounded by a ditch. One find was a stone gate-tower positioned across the ditch.

CASTLETOWN DELVIN
Co. Westmeath
(N 6062)

This began as a motte castle, built by Hugh de Lacy, mentioned in 1182 by Giraldus Cambrensis, and the motte is still visible today. Nearby, on the other side of the street, a century or so later, a long, rectangular stone tower-house with rounded corner turrets was built by the Nugent family. Originally it probably had four corner turrets, although today only two of these remain. The tower's main walls were nearly 2.4 metres (8 ft) thick.

CASTLETOWN GEOGHEGAN
Co. Westmeath
(N 3444)

A fine, prominent motte castle close to the road, it has most of its ditch surviving, and the lines of the bailey are clear. The motte is over 12.2 metres (40 ft) tall.

CASTLEVENTRY Co. Cork
(W 2942)

Excavation on this enclosure site revealed traces of a stone gate-tower similar to that found at Castletobin (q.v.).

CASTLE WARD Co. Down
(J 5750)

An early seventeenth-century tower-house in good external condition stands in the grounds of the eighteenth-century mansion which is now in the care of the National Trust. The tower is 8.5 x 7.9 metres (28 x 26 ft) and 14.9 metres (49 ft) to the stepped battlements.

CLARA Co. Kilkenny
(N 5747)

The five-storeyed (plus attic) fifteenth-century tower-house surrounded by its seventeenth-century bawn would be almost insignificant but for the relatively good condition of its outside and, more importantly, the survival of many of the original oak beams of the floor inside. Today you can look upwards from the ground through several horizontal 'trellises', as it were, to the vaulted fourth-storey ceiling. The storeys can still be reached by flights of winding stone stairs, lit by loops. A secret chamber on the third floor was reachable only via a lift-up seat in the floor above. Outside, it has nearly all its stepped battlements, angle-loops on corners, narrow loops along the wall faces, and pairs of round-headed windows.

CLAREGALWAY Co. Galway
(M 3833)

A fifteenth-century four-storeyed tower-house in good condition. It is nearly 18.3 metres (60 ft) tall, and has many original features such as gun-ports, angle-loops and even a meurtrière in the ceiling of the entry passage in the east wall.

CLOMANTAGH Co. Kilkenny
(S 3564)

A sixteenth-century tower-house which still has its roof.

CLONARD Co. Meath
(N 6644)

There are the remains of a de Lacy motte castle of c.1182 here, which was mentioned by Giraldus Cambrensis.

CLONCURRY Co. Kildare
(N 6544)

A motte from the twelfth or early thirteenth century has survived at this site.

CLONMACNOIS Co. Offaly
(N 0130)

Outside the famous monastic 'city' of St Ciaran, near the Shannon, is what is left of Clonmacnois Castle. This had begun as a motte castle, whose mound and bailey are still clearly visible, which had been built probably in the first years of the Anglo-Normans. Early in the next century, a substantial stone great tower was built on the motte, with encircling walls and a gatehouse in the bailey. The great tower was blown up in 1650 on English orders, and today huge chunks of mortared stone blocks straddling the mound top are all that remain.

CLONMINES Co. Wexford
(S 8413)

Clonmines, which became rich in the Middle Ages through the lead and silver mines nearby, has several buildings that appear to have been fortified in these times. There was the town hall (fifteenth century), the fifteenth-century church with its strong tower, and the Augustinian church of the late fourteenth century which may be associated with the wall fortifications nearby. Close by is a ruined fifteenth-century tower-house of four storeys, which has straight stairways.

CLONMORE Co. Carlow
(S 9676)

Now largely now in ruins, this castle was a late-thirteenth-/early fourteenth-century quadrilateral enclosure of stone with flanking towers along the walls and on the corners. Traces of buildings against the east wall inside remain, and in these there are interesting trefoil-pointed windows, and elsewhere some cross-loops.

CLONONY Co. Offaly
(N 0521)

A sixteenth-century tower-house with bawn, which has been neglected in recent years

resulting in deterioration of some structures. The castle is approached via an imposing round-headed gateway, lower down the slightly rising ground on which the tower-house stands. The tower is four-storeyed, has narrow loops and few of them, and it is surrounded by a bawn linked at various points to the tower. There are remains of much later additional buildings now in poor repair. Part of the parapet of the tower survives. The tower and its bawn stood in the north-eastern corner of a much larger outer enclosure, which appears to have had corner turrets.

CLOUGH Co. DOWN
(J 4140)

A motte castle of the late twelfth or early thirteenth century has been excavated here. Post-holes were found suggesting timber buildings, and artefacts such as axe heads, bowls, arrow-heads, buckles and coins of John's reign (1199–1216) were also found. Later, in the mid-thirteenth century, a hall was built in stone to the north-east of the motte summit and, towards the end of the

Clonony: in front of the tower-house are the remains of the later surrounding bawn, which include an entrance.

thirteenth century, a small rectangular tower was raised towards the south-west edge, to which in the fifteenth century an extension in a north-east alignment was added. Of these, the tower's walls survive to two storeys, and there are also remains of some of the fifteenth-century works. The castle has commanding views towards the Mourne Mountains.

CLOUGHEAST Co. WEXFORD
(T 1205)

A fifteenth-century tower-house whose battlements are stepped.

CLOUGHOUGHTER Co. CAVAN
(H 3405)

On an islet in Lough Oughter, a cylindrical great tower with a cross-wall, at least three storeys tall, was built in two stages in the thirteenth century. The first two storeys were followed after a long interval by one, possibly two, more. The original entrance was at first-floor level. There is now another entrance on the ground floor, of the sixteenth century. The tower is 10.7 metres (35 ft) in internal diameter, the inside walls 2.4 metres (8 ft)

Clough: the motte was raised in King John's reign (1199–1216). Later, two small structures were built on the summit, one a late thirteenth-century tower, the other a seventeenth-century extension to it.

thick. Its height is now over 18.3 metres (60 ft). Part of the tower has fallen away.

COLLOONEY Co. SLIGO
(N0521)

This was one of the few Irish pre-Norman 'castles' built in the 1120–60 period.

COOLHULL Co. WEXFORD
(S 8810)

The remains of a late sixteenth-century, long, rectangular tower-house of three storeys, rising to a fourth storey in a rectangular turret at one end for stairs, garderobes and the entrance. The tower top has stepped battlements all round, with a square bartizan on one corner. Inside the tower are interesting fireplaces, and the upper windows are round-headed.

COPPINGER'S COURT Co. CORK
(W 26636)

A substantial stronghouse – perhaps more accurately a tower block – of the early seventeenth century, this castle has an interesting plan. A long, rectangular main core on an east–west axis has two square projections, one at each end on the north side, while on the south there is a third central projection which has the staircases. The block is basically four-storeyed, with high gabled roofs and several chimneys. The north-facing wings are heavily machicolated round their parapets. Yet the whole block's walls are hardly more than a metre (yard) thick at any point. It was built by Sir Walter Coppinger in the years 1620–40.

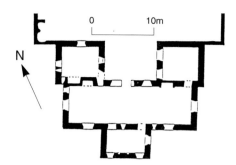

Coppinger's Court, Co. Cork.

CORK (SKIDDY'S) Co. Cork
(W 6771)
On North Island in Cork Harbour, a stone tower-house was erected in 1445 by John Skiddy on a timber raft tied to posts sunk into the peat-bog base.

CRATLOE Co. Clare
(R 5259)
A large rectangular tower-house of the end of the fifteenth century, Cratloe is 16.8 x 10 metres (55 x 33 ft), with thick walling on all sides, mostly over 2.1 metres (7 ft) thick. It has four storeys, the second and third vaulted, and has small rooms in one end wall. The staircases are straight, and they are set in the wall thicknesses.

CROM Co. Fermanagh
(H 3624)
By a lake here, the remains of a plantation castle of c.1611, which was gutted by fire in the eighteenth century, lie next to a nineteenth-century mansion. Surviving are parts of the outer enclosing walls and two small flanking turrets.

DALKEY'S Co. Dublin
(O 2827)
This is a sixteenth-century three-storeyed tower-house with machicolated parapet. It is also known as Archbold's Tower. It measures 10.3 x 6 metres (34 x 20 ft).

DANGANBRACK Co. Clare
(R 4375)
An early sixteenth-century tower-house, 14.3 x 9.1 metres (47 x 30 ft), with seventeenth-century modifications; the chief of these raised its height to five storeys and provided tall chimneys flush with the walls, and wall-walks which were confined to the corners, and were

The early seventeenth-century stronghouse at Coppinger's (see plan) had several stretches of large machicolations.

protected by box machicolations, two circular and two square.

DERRIHIVENNY Co. Galway
(M 8708)
A four-storeyed tower-house with an enclosing L-plan bawn with round towers on two opposite corners, and along one wall a hall-style building, makes up this interesting castle which can be dated to 1643 from an inscription in the north-east angle machicolation. It is in fair condition. Its parapet and wall-walk partly overhang the walls at the top.

DERRYPATRICK Co. Meath
(N 8272)
A castle of earth and timber on this site was given up as early as 1176.

The mid-seventeenth-century tower-house at Derryhivenny with its bawn, which has the remains of two round corner towers.

DESMOND Kinsale, Co. Cork
(W 6451)
Known as the French Prison, this fifteenth- or sixteenth-century tower-house of three storeys was from time to time used to contain foreign captives of many nationalities taken in war, including Spaniards, Dutch and even Americans. It has interesting windows and a fine doorway.

Doe: the tall, early sixteenth-century tower-house in the middle of the thick-walled enclosure was the earliest structure. The castle was enlarged in the late sixteenth and seventeenth centuries.

DOE Co. Donegal
(C 0832)

This is a much altered and improved castle centred on an original four-storeyed tower-house of the early sixteenth century, 9.1 x 7.6 metres (30 x 25 ft), with straight flights of stairs up to a plain parapet (which had once enclosed a gabled roof). The tower is 16.4 metres (54 ft) tall to the top of the parapet. It stood in a large, roughly square-plan bawn which had one round corner turret on the north-east corner. On the west wall is the gateway (a rebuild) from which projects a barbican and next to that a small square tower. The tower-house was later clasped on the east and south walls by a right-angled apartment block, and at the end of the south part of the block is a round tower, now battlemented. At

right-angles to the south wall of the block projects a 10 x 5.8 metres (33 x 19 ft) hall building, probably of the late sixteenth century. The moat on the landward side of the castle is cut into the rock on which it stands. Much of the castle to be seen now is

The original late fifteenth-century tower-house at Donegal. The upper storeys were remodelled in the 1620s, and the south-east end has been modified in recent years.

improvement work of the early nineteenth century, done after the original castle had been left derelict for over a century.

DONAGHMOYNE Co. Monaghan
(H 8506)
There are traces of a motte castle here, raised in about 1193.

DONEGAL Co. Donegal
(G 9377)
A great tower castle was begun here in the late fifteenth century by the O'Donnell family, lords of Tyrconnel. The first building was the great tower itself, rectangular, 16.8 x 10.7 metres (55 x 35 ft), with walls nearly 2.4 metres (8 ft) thick. Its five storeys began with a vaulted ground floor. It has been greatly altered, disguising its original form although not concealing its obvious defensiveness. The tower was set on fire by the family in about 1600 to prevent it being captured by the Earl of Essex's successor, Mountjoy. A few years later it came into the possession of the Brookes, a prominent Protestant family, who carried out major reconstructions, adding a substantial residential three-storey rectangular wing on the great tower's west side. The tower itself was restored, windows enlarged, and a huge bay window inserted just above the original entrance on the east side. The bartizans and other features on the top storey,

such as gabled parts, were all of this period. The work was surrounded by a five-sided walled enclosure with a south angle-tower. It is at present being restored yet again.

DONORE Co. Meath
(N 7149)
This is a good example of the 1429 and afterwards small tower-house type of castle known as the £10 castle. It has three storeys which are reached via a spiral staircase in a small round turret projecting on one corner. The corners of the tower are rounded. The ground storey is vaulted.

DOONMORE Co. Antrim
(D 1842)
On a rock outcrop here, excavation produced evidence of earth and timber works, including post-holes for (probably) a small watch-tower.

DOWNPATRICK Co. Down
(J 4844)
A motte castle of the early Anglo-Norman settlement, about 1177, occupied the whole summit of one of the low hills here. Its bailey rampart was probably part of a pre-Norman ring-fort. The motte was about 0.4 hectare (1 acre) in area, and it was raised by John de Courcy.

DROGHEDA Co. Louth
(N 0976)
Drogheda on the River Boyne has had a major harbour for centuries. The Anglo-Normans recognised its strategic value, and in their initial decades raised first a substantial motte castle on a prehistoric mound which is now known as Mill Mount (the structure on its summit is a nineteenth-century Martello-type tower). The motte may have been raised by de Lacy as early as the 1180s. A bailey wall of stone was erected afterwards, of which only parts survive. The motte is on the south side of the Boyne. On the other side of the river are the remains of a substantial four-storey twin drum-towered gateway with a round-headed entrance, known as St Laurence's Gate. It was built in the thirteenth century, along with other structures forming some sort of castle, but it is the only survivor of that work. The general view is that St Lawrence's is part of the castle barbican which protected the castle gatehouse. The tower's battlements survive, and it has long, narrow loops and a few windows at higher levels, some of them round-headed. You can still drive through the tower today, in much the same way as at Canterbury in Kent.

DROMANEEN Co. Cork
(W 5097)
An attractively sited, L-plan stronghouse of the sixteenth and seventeenth centuries on a rock base on the south bank of the Blackwater river, near the road into Mallow.

DROMORE Co. Antrim
(D 0413)
An Irish ring-fort on a gravel mound was taken over and possibly developed by the Anglo-Normans, although a case has been put for continued occupation by the Irish.

DROMORE Co. Down
(J 2053)
A motte castle, of Anglo-Norman origin, whose 12.2-metre (40-ft) motte appears to have been crowned with two circles of wooden posts. Traces of stone may relate to new work recorded as being carried out there in 1211–12.

DUBLIN Co. Dublin
(O 1534)
Possibly the castle least liked by the Irish because it was the headquarters of English government for so many centuries. Dublin Castle has also been through numerous changes, so that it is not possible today to get any real idea of what it looked like in the late Middle Ages. The first works were begun at the start of the thirteenth century (there is a royal writ for them dated 1205), and they were positioned on or near fortifications in Dublin that were almost certainly of mid-tenth-century Viking origin. Recent excavations revealed Viking battle buildings. According to a drawing surviving from the later seventeenth century, the castle was a five-sided enclosure, with no great tower, but with huge round corner towers on the angles. Parts of some of these have survived, incorporated in various later works. These include the base of the Bermingham Tower on the south-west end of the enclosure; parts of what is now the Record Tower on the south-east end, 17 metres (56 ft) in diameter, whose parapet and machicolation are of the nineteenth century; and stretches of the southern curtain. What was called the Storehouse Tower, on the north-east corner, may have been used as a residential tower in place of a great tower, but it was demolished in the eighteenth century. On the north-west corner was the Corke tower, a round tower that was rebuilt in the seventeenth century.

The castle is recorded in one source as being finished by about 1220 but in another as having only had its enclosing walls complete by 1228, with the rest of the works by the mid-thirteenth century. There have been several excavation programmes, one of which revealed part of the causeway from the city across a wide moat into the castle.

DULEEK Co. Meath
(O 0468)
This is a very early site. The first buildings, constructed of timber, are recorded by Giraldus Cambrensis as being restored in 1173–4. There used to be a motte but it has almost completely disappeared.

DUNAMARK Co. Cork
(V 9950)
An enclosure castle of the early period of Anglo-Norman occupation, described by the archaeologist D.C. Twohig as 'one of the best examples of a ring-work [enclosure] I have seen in either Britain or Ireland' (1978).

DUNAMASE Co. Laois
(S 5298)
Among the most impressive sites in Ireland, Dunamase was erected upon an early Christian site on the towering rock overlooking Portlaoise. For a time it was also the site of a fortress belonging to the kings of Leinster, which is how it came into the possession of Strongbow, who had married King Diarmait's daughter Aiofa. Strongbow seems to have been allowed to retain it but nothing is known of his works, and the first mention in Anglo-Norman history is in King John's reign, when the king granted it to William Marshal. Even his works are not fully known, and were either starting the great tower which is inside the inner enclosure, a roughly heart-shaped stone curtain enclosure on the rock top, or starting the enclosure itself. Only a part of the great tower remains and this is badly damaged. The enclosure had

(Opposite) Dunguaire: the sixteenth-century tower-house has machicolation boxes at parapet level in the centre of each of the four walls.

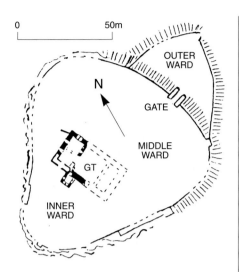

Dunamase, Co. Laois: GT = great tower.

walling over 1.8 metres (6 ft) thick on the east side, with flanking rectangular turrets, while the west wall was thinner. The great tower was rectangular, some 20.4 x 35.3 metres (67 x 116 ft), with two cross-walls. In the seventeenth century this was adapted to make the northern section into a tower-house of its own, presumably because the remainder of the great tower was ruinous. To the east of the great tower, sited in the east wall, are the remains of a twin round-ended towered gateway leading into a triangular outer ward, which is very much smaller than the enclosure on the rock top. The castle, although impressive and clearly having covered a lot of the rock, is in a very ruinous condition. It was taken and held by the O'Neills during the Confederate War, and then slighted by Cromwell's forces in 1650.

DUNBOY Co. Cork
(V 6644)
At Dunboy are remains of a tower-house castle of fifteenth-century origin, whose site and buildings were closely examined in 1967–73. The sequence was (1) a tower-house of sandstone erected on rock with a slightly sloping plinth, measuring 17 x 13.1 metres (56 x 43 ft), which is quite large. It is thought to have been about 20.4 metres (67 ft) tall, with three main storeys over the ground floor. The bawn wall had two turrets. At some time afterwards a square wing was added on one corner of the tower-house. (2) In about 1602, a second bawn wall was

added, in anticipation of attack which in fact did come soon afterwards, and the castle was taken and then slighted. Later on, in the mid-seventeenth century, the castle was replaced with a star-plan fort.

DUNDONALD Co. Down
(J 4274)
A motte was raised here in the late twelfth century, was captured in 1210 and then repaired in 1211–12. It is situated near the church. A fifteenth-century tower-house was built nearby.

DUNDRUM Co. Down
(J 4036)
Dundrum Castle was built on the site of an Irish ring-fort. It may have been converted into a timber-and-earth enclosure by John de Courcy, the conqueror of Ulster, but the earliest mention of Dundrum as a castle is not until 1205, by which time he had been

---

Dundrum, Co. Down (after Barry): UW = upper ward. OE = original entrance. G = garderobe(s). The cylindrical great tower at north-west and part of its curtain wall (in black) are the first works, late twelfth/early thirteenth centuries.

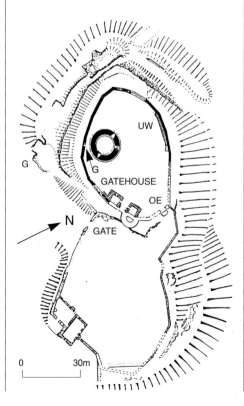

displaced as ruler in Ulster by Hugh de Lacy. The enclosure had been converted to stone probably before the end of the twelfth century, but the large 14.6-metre (48-ft) diameter cylindrical great tower may only have been started by then. The tower is mentioned in the 1211 Irish Pipe Roll as a *magna turris* (great tower), and by this date it was four storeys tall, standing on a sharp batter, with walls over 2.1 metres (7 ft) thick. Its original entrance was at first-floor level, leading straight into a two-storeyed hall with vaulted ceiling. The topmost storey contained a range of mural chambers and passages all the way round.

In the 1260s, the enclosure was given a square-plan twin-towered gatehouse on the south side, built on to the remains of an earlier cylindrical wall-tower. Two centuries later, a second enclosure of stone was erected as an outer (lower) ward on the south-west.

The castle was unsuccessfully besieged by de Courcy in 1205 in an attempt to recover it. In 1210, King John took possession of it and it remained a Crown possession until 1227 when it was granted to de Lacy, Earl of Ulster. The work of the mid-thirteenth century was carried out by the de Lacy family. By the mid-1330s it was apparently ruinous and was taken over by the Magenis family which held on to it for two centuries. Large and dominating as it is, its life as a feudal castle seems to have been short.

DUNGIVEN Co. Derry
(C 6908)
A castle was built by the O'Cahan family on the site of an Augustinian friary which was under their patronage. After the Dissolution of the Monasteries in the reign of Henry VIII (who made himself King, rather than Lord, of Ireland), the medieval castle was enlarged into a stronghouse surrounded by a huge bawn, 45.7 x 61 metres (150 x 200 ft), among the largest in Ireland. No remains of the original castle are visible.

DUNGUAIRE Kinvara, Co. Galway
(M 3811)
This is a sixteenth-century castle raised upon an old Irish ring-fort. It rises to four storeys and an attic, and the lower part of one of its walls makes up part of the wall of a six-sided surrounding bawn. It has a central machicolation box at parapet level on each of its four walls. The castle has been restored

with a great deal of care, and it is open to visitors during the day from April to September. During this season, medieval banquets are held in the tower-house.

DUNLUCE Co. Antrim
(C 9041)
One of the most dramatically sited castles in all Ireland, Dunluce stands on a rock surrounded by the sea, attached to the mainland by a wooden bridge, formerly joined by a drawbridge. The castle was originally a four-sided enclosure, approximately rectangular, with corner towers. Of this oldest work, only the south wall facing the land and the remains of two eastern towers, both about 9.1 metres (30 ft) in diameter, survive. This work is of the fourteenth century, possibly late thirteenth century. It had been erected upon the site of a prehistoric souterrain which had later been a Christian 'underground' harbour for ships. The Norman castle buildings were begun by Richard de Burgo, Earl of Ulster. The main

part of the castle, however, is of much later date, and includes a late sixteenth-century gatehouse capped on its outer angles by corbelled round turrets. At much the same time, the Great Hall was erected up against a somewhat earlier and rather unusual arcaded gallery, or loggia, some of whose pillars are still there. Other works included domestic buildings put up in two baileys.

The castle was held by the O'Donnells, taken from them in 1584, then restored at the end of the sixteenth century.

DUNMAHON Co. Louth
(J 0605)
A small, late fifteenth-century tower-house with turrets. It is four-storeyed, has a square-plan staircase turret and a second turret which

The ruins of Dunluce rise dramatically from the rock more than 30 metres (100 ft) above the sea. The round towers are the oldest parts.

has garderobes. Its height, however, is only about 12.2 metres (40 ft) to the wall-walk.

DUNMOE Co. Meath
(N 9070)
A large fourteenth-/fifteenth-century great tower overlooking the Boyne is now in much ruined condition. The tower originally had four turrets clasping the central rectangular core, and they are half round, half polygonal. One is fragmentary and the other has narrow loops and crude machicolation (which in fact may just be holes in the wall to drain water off the roof). The south walling between the towers – the only complete walling to survive – is four storeys tall. A quantity of stone rubble is heaped up behind it. On the east side of the great tower are remnants of a hall-type building, set back slightly from the remains of the south-east turret. This building has its own staircase approach at ground level on the south. There is much evidence of alterations of several periods.

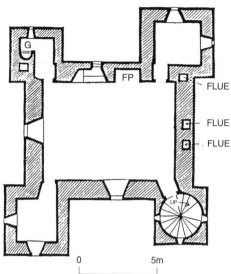

Dunsoghly, Co. Dublin: plan of the top floor of the Great Tower. FP = fireplace. G = garderobe.

Although built two centuries later, the long rectangular great tower at Dunmoe, with its rounded corner turrets (two are missing), closely resembles the thirteenth-century style of Carlow, Ferns, Lea and Terryglass. The rectangular extension on the right is of a later date.

DUNMORE Co. GALWAY
(M 5064)

A fourteenth-century rectangular great tower, later given an extra storey, or possibly two storeys, and a gabled attic on top, shows signs of repair work and modifications of more than one period. The castle measures 17 x 11.9 metres (56 x 39 ft) on a sloping plinth, and has walls about 2.1 metres (7 ft) thick. It was raised on the site of an earlier, thirteenth-century Bermingham castle built by the Irish.

DUNSEVERICK Co. ANTRIM
(C 9844)

Built on a rock promontory on the north coast, which was partly skirted by a bawn, this castle has a sixteenth-century tower-like building, now very ruinous, which may have been a gatehouse leading into the bawn.

DUNSILLY Co. ANTRIM
(J 1488)

A low-level motte, about 7.6 metres (25 ft) across on its summit, was raised on an earlier Irish ring-fort which had been built in three stages. The motte covered the remains of earlier residential buildings, and was itself built up in three stages. It appears that the motte was never used.

DUNSOGHLY Co. DUBLIN
(O 1143)

A few kilometres north of Dublin in a farmyard stands the very tall great tower of Dunsoghly, with some remains of other buildings and surrounding wall. The tower is remarkable in having its original timber roofing dating from the fifteenth century, which is not only an exceptional example of survival but also a valuable and authentic illustration of how roofs were built at that time. The great tower was erected by Sir Thomas Plunkett, a Chief Justice of the King's Bench, in the mid-fifteenth century. It is four-storeyed with four almost square corner turrets of differing dimensions, which taper inwards and upwards and project above the tower core. The tower's lowest storey is vaulted. One turret (north-east) contains the staircase. In the top of the south-west turret is the tower's 'prison', reachable only by means of a hole in the ceiling.

DURROW Co. OFFALY
(N 3131)

Near the monastery of St Columcille (Columba), where the famous Book of Durrow was compiled, are the remains of a motte castle. This was raised in the 1170s, probably by de Lacy, who is said to have pulled down a stone chapel nearby and used the stone from it for a building on the motte which he had raised within the chapel enclosure. This sacrilege is advanced as the reason for his murder in 1186 on or very near the site.

ENNISCORTHY Co. WEXFORD
(S 9739)

There was a major Norman castle here at Enniscorthy in the thirteenth century, but it has largely disappeared under a complete rebuild of the late sixteenth century and further modifications later still. The plan may have been the same as at present, that is a rectangular, four-storeyed tower (in this case with a cross-wall) on which four cylindrical towers were clamped on the corners. The two corner towers on the west wall also act as protector towers for the main tower entrance. The present 'reproduction' currently functions as a museum.

ENNISKILLEN Co. FERMANAGH
(H 2144)

This began as a fifteenth-century rectangular four-storey tower-house with prominent parapet and battlements round the top gabled attic storey, put up by the Maguires. A drawing of it was made in 1595 and this is reproduced in Salter's *Castles and Strongholds of*

Enniskillen: to the right along the huge enclosure wall of this fifteenth-century castle on the River Erne is the water-gate, which was added in the seventeenth century.

Ireland, 1993. The tower-house stood inside a bawn. It was destroyed in 1602, and a few years later a new Protestant English owner rebuilt it as a plantation castle. The lower part of the original tower was absorbed, and the water-gate was also added close to the river's edge, much of which can still be seen. This tower has two narrow and tall cylindrical turrets which begin not at ground level but resting on inverted cone corbels about one storey up, rising to more than one storey's height above the tower. There are newer buildings in the bawn, some of them at one time used for military purposes.

FANSTOWN Co. LIMERICK
(R 6428)
A sixteenth-century rectangular tower-house with bartizans.

FEARTAGAR Co. GALWAY
(M 3856)
This is a tower-house dating from the late sixteenth/early seventeenth century, known as Jennings Castle. It is four-storeyed and has staircases in the wall thicknesses. It was abandoned after the Cromwellian campaign in Ireland, 1649–51.

FENNOR Co. MEATH
(N 9674)
Sited just outside Slane, the seventeenth-century T-plan tower-house is three-storeyed plus attic. Its south wall has five window openings in line, giving it a mansion-like appearance. At the east and west ends of the main rectangular part are ruinous chimney projections. There are several surviving fireplaces but no floors. The tower-house overlooks the valley approach to Slane, yet does not seem to have been very defensive.

FERNS Co. WEXFORD
(T 0050)
This is one of the main early to mid-thirteenth-century large Anglo-Norman great tower castles (like Carlow, Terryglass and Lea), which consist of a central rectangular (or square) core with round towers clasping the corners. It is now not in very good condition, even though substantial parts remain. There were major excavations at Ferns in 1967–73.

Ferns began as an Irish 'castle' raised in the 1120s–1160s (*see* p. 87). There is also a record of Ferns in Giraldus Cambrensis for 1186. There was some structure there in the early thirteenth century when it was in the possession of William Marshal (d.1219), but

This view of Ferns shows one of the thirteenth-century great towers with corner turrets, a type peculiar to Ireland. This is the surviving south wall.

the great tower whose ruins we can see now is of a later date, probably 1230–50. It had a rectangular three-storey core of 27.4 x 23.2 metres (90 x 76 ft) which is huge, with walls about 2.4 metres (8 ft) thick, standing on a sloping plinth, but only half of it remains. Clamped on its corners were four four-storey cylindrical towers, only one of which is more or less whole, and contains on its third floor a fine circular vaulted chapel. Two towers have

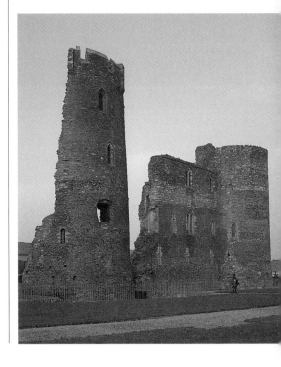

all but vanished, the third is a half-round. Traces of a drawbridge of the thirteenth century were found in the excavations. By the fourteenth century Ferns seems to have been run down and there is no evidence of major restoration at any time since. One sideline of the excavations is the discovery of what the thirteenth-century occupants ate as their main diet: bones of pigs, cattle, and sheep were found in the tower and just outside.

FERRYCARRIG Co. Wexford
(S 9727)
Ferrycarrig was said by Giraldus Cambrensis to have been one of the first Anglo-Norman castles in Ireland, which was given a ditch but not a motte. As it was raised on an outcrop of rock beside the River Slaney, it was presumably a fortified enclosure type.

FIDDAUN Co. Galway
(R 4196)
A tall, rectangular five-storeyed tower-house with attic, of the sixteenth century, with box machicolations on the outside walls at third-storey level, stands centrally inside a rectangular bawn whose gateway is on the north side, and on the west side of which is a sharp triangular projection like part of a star fortification. Fiddaun was held by the O'Shaughnessys up to the end of the seventeenth century. The bawn is one of the best preserved in Ireland.

GALTRIM Co. Meath
(N 7649)
An earth and timber castle, which may have had a motte, is recorded in *The Song of Dermot* as having been given up as early as 1176.

There is also a record of it being re-occupied by about 1211.

GARRAUNBOY Co. Limerick
(R 4345)
A fifteenth-century tower-house of five storeys, 14 x 9.1 metres (46 x 30 ft), with three walls about 2.1 metres (7 ft) wide and the fourth originally nearly twice as thick, with space for a spiral staircase. Part of this fourth wall has crumbled away. The tower stands surrounded on all sides by a rectangular enclosing wall, now fragmentary, which had cylindrical turrets, which are also fragmentary.

GARRYNAMONA Co. Clare
(R 3661)
This was an Irish ring-fort which continued to be occupied after the Anglo-Norman invasion had taken place, but by the Irish and not the Normans.

GEASHILL Co. Offaly
(N 4322)
Set back a little from the main village street, this castle is ruinous and covered with foliage. A low-level motte on rising ground, which falls sharply away to lower ground on north and west, is the first work of the beginning of the thirteenth century and it belonged to William Marshal. Some time later in the thirteenth century, or possibly the next, a stone great tower was built on the motte and surrounded by a stone wall, which is linked to the tower by tangential walling in at least two places. The tower is so ruined that it is impossible to identify its main features beyond noting that it was rectangular. There is a wall left with an exposed fireplace which has a square-section chimney going up at least three storeys. The remainder of the stonework is only a few feet high.

GLANWORTH Co. Cork
(R 7504)
This started off as a mid- to late thirteenth-century castle of the Roche family. Its first buildings included a rectangular great tower, 12.8 x 11 metres (42 x 36 ft), now only two storeys high, inside a trapezoid curtain with round turrets of later date, of which parts

The five-storey-plus-attic tower-house at Fiddaun. A square, corner machicolation box can be seen at third-storey level on the left corner of the tower.

Glanworth: the tall, narrow building is the garderobe tower added to the west side of the fifteenth-century tower-house.

remain. Some of the curtain is original. To the west of it were found remnants of a gatehouse built at much the same time as the great tower. The entrance through the gatehouse was blocked off in the fifteenth century to create a tower-house of five storeys with a garderobe turret which still stands. In the fifteenth century, a new curtain was built west of the first enclosure, in which a round tower was erected at the north-west and a square tower at the south-west.

GLENINAGH Co. Clare
(M 1910)
An L-plan tower-house of the sixteenth century, based largely on Scottish models of the same period, Gleninagh is four storeys tall above a basement, and it has an attic at roof level. The third storey is vaulted. Some window openings were later blocked up to allow for inserting fireplaces. The staircase is in the short arm of the 'L', where the tower is entered at ground floor. A box machicolation at top level covers the entrance. The three other corners of the tower-house have round bartizans at parapet level. The castle was occupied well into the nineteenth century.

The sixteenth-century L-plan tower-house at Gleninagh has its spiral staircase in the wing. The castle is on the shore overlooking Ballyvaghan Bay.

GLENOGRA Co. Limerick
(R 5942)
The early fifteenth-century castle here was an enclosure of six unequal sides. The north side was an 8.5-metre (28-ft) or so stretch of wall about 3 metres (10 ft) thick, at each end of which was an octagonal tower with similarly thick walls. One tower has survived, the other is residual. The survivor is about 12.2 metres (40 ft) across and still has its staircase.

GLENQUIN Co. Limerick
(R 2526)
A six-storey tower-house, of the mid-sixteenth century, which was rebuilt in the mid-nineteenth century.

GLINSK Co. Galway
(M 7266)
An imposing stronghouse with box machicolations on the outer front corners of its two projecting towers, this rectangular building is of the 1620s. There is a 3.3-metre (11-ft) square recess between the two towers where the entrance to the tower is at second-storey level. The tower is three storeys with tall chimneys and had a gabled attic storey above, of which not much remains. The interior of the tower is without its floors due to a serious fire early in its history. The exterior is well preserved, including many of its machicolations.

GORT Co. Galway
(M 4403)
A sixteenth-century four-storey tower-house at Ballylee, near Gort, was converted into a home for the great poet W.B. Yeats in the 1920s. After he left it in 1929 it fell into disrepair, but it has been restored as a national monument to Yeats. It contains a collection of first editions of his works.

Greencastle (Co. Donegal): the ruins of this once substantial enclosure castle, which features flanking towers and massive twin polygonal gatehouses at the south-west end, dominate the sea at the mouth of Lough Foyle.

GORTMAKELLIS Co. Tipperary
(S 0942)
A fifteenth-century or early sixteenth-century rectangular tower-house of four storeys, formerly with an attic on top which has now fallen away.

GRALLAGH Co. Tipperary
(S 1549)
This is a sixteenth-century four-storey tower-house inside a large bawn, much of whose walling remains.

GRANAGH Co. Kilkenny
(S 5815)
Granagh is known colloquially as Granny Castle. It was originally a rectangular- (almost square-) plan late thirteenth-century stone enclosure with, in the northern corner, a residential tower-house of the late fourteenth/early fifteenth century, of unknown height, which contained a long, rectangular hall block built on its west end,

This view of Granagh shows the fifteenth-century tower-house in the north-east of the enclosure. Next to it was the sixteenth-century hall, of which part of one wall remains on the left.

that was constructed during the sixteenth century. The south-east and south-west corners of the enclosure had cylindrical flanking turrets, the former of which is still lapped by the River Suir.

The tower-house is badly damaged but stands to its full height in parts, especially where there is a quaint seventeenth-century oriel window at the top.

GRANARD Co. Longford
(N 3382)
Here, a motte castle was raised upon a natural mound, heightening the castle to make it one of the tallest in Ireland. It has a clearly defined bailey, with ditching and an outer bank. It was built at the very end of the twelfth century. The foundations of a stone shell wall round the motte summit have been found, and also the remains of a cylindrical tower within. The stonework was probably early thirteenth century.

GREENCASTLE Co. Donegal
(M 6540)
Greencastle, Inishowen, was built by Richard de Burgo, who was Earl of Chester in 1305. It was a roughly rectangular stone enclosure of strong walling, with a projecting rectangular tower in the north wall which may be an earlier structure. The entrance to the enclosure was through a powerful gate-tower at the western end whose passage was protected by a pair of polygonal towers. The castle belonged for a time to Lionel, Duke of Clarence, Edward III's second son. It was attacked and taken by the Irish in the late fourteenth century and was finally demolished in the 1550s.

Greencastle (Co. Down) overlooks Lough Carlingford. The rectangular great tower, with square corner turrets, was built in the early thirteenth century and later modified internally.

GREENCASTLE Co. Down
(J 2411)

This was a royal castle begun in the mid-thirteenth century. Probably the first work was a stone enclosure, very little of which remains today. In about the 1230s, a substantial rectangular great tower of hall type, only two storeys tall, was erected inside the curtain. It had projecting corner buttresses. The tower was 21.3 x 12.2 metres (70 x 40 ft) and had a roof of steep pitch. It was intended as a guard to the ferry across Carlingford Lough to Carlingford Castle, being enlarged at much the same time.

The castle was sacked soon after the great tower was built, and it was besieged again by Edward Bruce in 1316. Then, in the mid-fifteenth century, major work was carried out on the great tower. Its walls were heightened to form a third storey. The ground floor, meanwhile, was divided into three long chambers by cross-walls, and all were given vaulted barrel ceilings. At the beginning of the sixteenth century, the castle was granted to Gearoid, Earl of Kildare, who may have been responsible for the enlargement of the upper windows. In the 1550s it reverted to the Crown, but during the seventeenth century it was abandoned.

Greencastle, Co. Down: the long, rectangular great tower is the earliest building, c. 1230. The partitioning of the lower part of the tower was carried out much later.

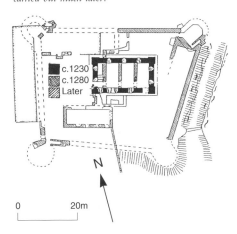

c.1230
c.1280
Later

N

0   20m

HARRY AVERY'S TOWER
Co. Tyrone
(H 3985)

A stone enclosure of the late fourteenth century built upon a hillock. What is visible today is the remnant of a rectangular tower having two half-circular projections of two storeys' height each, which were three-storeyed before assault by Viceroy Chichester in the first years of the seventeenth century. Originally the structure was a hall tower, having the two projections side by side guarding the entrance to the tower, the plan being B-shaped.

HOWTH Co. Dublin
(O 2839)

The present Howth Castle is largely an eighteenth-century modification of whatever the builders found there at the time. The main original structure of the fifteenth century is the slightly L-plan gate-tower with round-headed archway at left of the front face, leading through to the rear. There are two projecting pilasters on the front which slope into the wall half-way up, one of which contains a garderobe shoot. The tower has domestic-style windows. The parapet is battlemented, with stepped merlons.

IGHTERMURRAGH Co. Cork
(W 9973)

This interesting stronghouse of the early seventeenth century is of cruciform plan, with a long, rectangular block 22.2 x 9.7 metres (73 x 32 ft), with walls nearly 1.8 metres (6 ft) thick. Centrally across this block are a pair of opposite square towers projecting from the block, with somewhat narrower walls. All four arms of the 'cross' rise to four storeys plus the attic storey (18.3 metres [60 ft] to the top) behind a bold parapet with tall chimneys. Inside are several fireplaces, one of which has an inscription dated 1641.

The seventeenth-century, four-storeyed stronghouse of Ightermurragh was built on the cross plan. The projecting wing, seen in the centre, is repeated on the other side.

INCH Co. DONEGAL
(C 3222)

Remains of a three-storey rectangular tower-house inside an enclosure of the fifteenth century can be seen on the small peninsula of Inch Island in Lough Swilly. Access is possible but requires a lengthy tramp across farmland. It belonged for a time to the powerful Gaelic family of the O'Domhuaills who were, among other things, Lords of Tyrconnel and held sway in much of Donegal in the fifteenth and sixteenth centuries.

INCHIQUIN Co. CORK
(X 0176)

A substantial cylindrical great tower on a sloping plinth, beside the river, rises to two full storeys in its present ruined state, but was clearly three if not four storeys originally. The tower is nearly 9.1 metres (30 ft) in diameter internally, with walls about 4.1 metres (13½ ft) thick, making an overall width of about 17.7 metres (58 ft). The ground floor of the tower is vaulted.

INISCRONE Co. SLIGO
(F 2930)

A rectangular enclosure castle which once had cylindrical towers on the corners. Two survive in much reduced condition, the other two have vanished.

ISERT KELLY Co. GALWAY
(M 5212)

A mid-sixteenth-century tower-house with a vaulted first floor. It stands in the corner of a now fragmentary bawn.

KANTURK Co. CORK
(W 3801)

An early seventeenth-century castle having a four-storeyed rectangular core, on the four corners of which are sizeable five-storey square towers. The main entrance has pilasters and a round-headed doorway. Corbels for a wrap-round machicolated parapet were included although the parapet was not built. The windows are mullioned and take up much of the walls, curiously for a stronghouse originally intended to be defensible. It is said that the owner stopped work on the castle because neighbour lords complained to the English Privy Council about the size and fortifications. No stairways were built in stone, and probably not in timber, either.

KELLS Co. KILKENNY
(S 4943)

This is one of two castles of the same name (*see also* Kells, Co. Meath). It began as a motte castle of the late twelfth century, which had a later walled bailey. Nearby, the Augustinian priory, which was first fortified at the end of the twelfth century, was provided with several square towers positioned in the castle wall surrounding it, the remains of some of which can be seen.

KELLS Co. MEATH
(N 7475)

An Anglo-Norman castle was raised here in the first years of Anglo-Norman occupation, but it was abandoned by about 1176.

KILBARRON Co. DONEGAL
(G 8365)

Remains of a fifteenth-century enclosure spread across a cliff projection into Donegal Bay, at the east edge of which is a ruinous gate-tower, and fragments of other structures.

KILBEG Co. MEATH
(N 7780)

On the road between Nobber and Kells, and beside a graveyard, is a well preserved motte with much of its ditching clearly defined. The site is being excavated by the Office of Public Works.

KILBIXIE Co. WESTMEATH
(N 3162)

A motte castle without a proper bailey, but having a small terrace, was built in the early 1190s. Later on, a rectangular stone enclosure was built on the motte top.

KILBOLANE Co. CORK
(R 4221)

A late thirteenth-century square castle survives with two round turrets and two walls.

KILCASH Co. TIPPERARY
(S 3427)

This consists of a six-storey tower-house with bartizan and high chimney stacks, beside which is the remnant of a great hall block, two storeys high.

KILCLIEF Co. DOWN
(J 6046)

A fifteenth-century tower-house, roughly 1412–40, this has two turrets on its east wall, one for the entrance and staircase, one for garderobes. The turrets are linked higher up by arching, behind which are machicolations. Smaller turrets also project above the four-storey height.

KILDREENAN Co. Dublin
(O 2525)
Site of a castle near Killeney church, the structure was in existence by about 1200.

KILFEAKLE Co. Tipperary
(R 9938)
A motte castle of c.1193 which has some traces of stonework, including a smallish tower over part of the motte ditch.

KILKEA Co. Kildare
(S 7497)
This is a nineteenth-century rebuild in medieval style of a fifteenth- or sixteenth-century L-plan tower-house, with round and square turrets. Nowadays it is now a golf clubhouse. On the right-hand side of the road approaching the front of the tower-house, about 91.4 metres (100 yds) away from it, is the original motte of the motte castle mentioned by Giraldus Cambrensis in 1181, which is now covered with trees. It is about 12.2 metres (40 ft) tall, and part of its ditching survives.

KILKENNY Co. Kilkenny
(S 5155)
Beginning as a motte castle of c.1171, built by Strongbow and destroyed presumably by the native Irish in 1174, the castle at this important early Norman town was begun again by William Marshal during his years in Ireland (1207–12). He laid down a trapezoidal-plan enclosure of stone walling with massive round towers on the corners (three of which survive in differing conditions, and measure 11.3 x 8.2 metres [37 x 27 ft] and 7 metres [23 ft] in diameter). The original enclosure walling was over 1.8 metres (6 ft) thick, and some of it survives on the north side. If there were other buildings of this early period they have not yet been clearly identified, although there exists a description of the castle given in 1307, which summarises Kilkenny as it was in or about that date, namely, 'in which are a hall, four towers, a chapel, a mote, and divers other houses'. A century or so after this description, the castle came into the possession of the Butlers, Earls

Kilkenny is a very early thirteenth-century enclosure castle, begun by William Marshal and enlarged and improved over several centuries. The round tower in the centre is basically one of the original corner towers, with later modifications.

(and later, Dukes) of Ormonde who, over the centuries, especially in the reign of Charles II (1660–85) and again in the mid-eighteenth century and early nineteenth century, carried out extensive remodelling of the original works. Today, Kilkenny is an ancient monument and houses the National Furniture Collection of Ireland.

KILLARE Co. Westmeath
(N 2748)
A motte castle of c.1184 which was attacked and burned in 1187; this was recorded by Giraldus Cambrensis.

KILLARNEY (ROSS CASTLE)
Co. Kerry
(V 9589)
An impressive tower-house of the sixteenth century, with later additions and given a bawn with flanking round turrets, this is known as Ross Castle and it stands on an isthmus in Lough Leane which also laps the edge of Killarney town. The tower is five storeys to the parapet, has box machicolations on two opposing corners and is rectangular in plan,

with one shorter wall thicker than the other three, to accommodate small rooms at each level. It was captured by the English in 1652 as a result of a water-borne force attacking it from the lough.

KILLENURE Co. Tipperary
(S 0044)
A late sixteenth-century modified tower-house that had four cylindrical corner turrets, mostly now in a ruinous state. The ground floor had no living quarters and the windows were much smaller than those above. It was presumably made to be defensible. Cairns describes it as a tower-house that became more house than tower.

KILLESHIN Co. Laois
(S 6777)
A motte castle of 1181 mentioned by Giraldus Cambrensis and also in the *Song of Dermot*. It is near Leighlin. The mound is about 12.2 metres (40 ft) tall with steep sides. It has a commanding view over Carlow valley.

KILLYLEAGH Co. Down
(J 5253)
Close to Strangford Lough's western shore, this is a greatly modified castle. Beginning in the thirteenth century, the only original work now is part of the south-west substantial cylindrical tower clasping the central rectangular core. This tower was probably

built upon an even earlier motte. The tower has been materially altered to match its opposite and much newer tower on the south-east. The medieval work, in so far as we know it, was converted in the seventeenth century to a stronghouse by Sir John Hamilton, ancestor of the present owner, and that conversion was itself substantially altered in the nineteenth century to give it the present Continental château-esque look.

KILMESSAN Co. Meath
(N 8755)
A motte of the early thirteenth century here has disappeared in recent years.

KILMORE Co. Cavan
(H 3804)
A motte castle of the early thirteenth century which is mentioned in the Irish Pipe Rolls. It is near Lough Oughter.

KILSANTAN Co. Derry
See Mount Sandel, p. 228.

KILTARTAN Co. Galway
(M 4605)
A large thirteenth-century castle, now in ruins, which had a three-storey tower and a gateway flanked by powerful round towers set in an enclosing curtain.

KILTEEL Co. Kildare
(N 9821)
A five-storey tower-house of the late fifteenth century adjoining a gate-tower of the same period. This may have been part of a range of residential buildings belonging to the Knights Hospitallers (there are fragmentary remains a few hundred yards away from the tower). The tower-house has a cylindrical turret projecting on one corner, which has loops at each level. Part of the parapet and battlements remain.

KINNITTY Co. Offaly
(N 1508)
A motte and bailey of c.1213, about 1.6 km (1 mile) from the village. This is a low motte erected on rising ground. The ditching has become obscured now, probably through prolonged farming.

KINSALE Co. Cork
(W 6451)
South of this important and historic port town are the remains of a fifteenth-century fortified

area of headland known as the Old Head of Kinsale. Here, a long stone wall with flanking turrets was the front defence. Behind a gateway in the wall is the shell of a tall tower-house, which measures about 15.2 metres (50 ft) high, with five storeys now very badly damaged and incomplete. Two of these storeys were vaulted.

KIRKISTON Co. Down
(J 6458)
This tower-house and its enclosing bawn were built in the 1620s, and then restored a century or so later.

KNAPPOGUE Co. Clare
(R 4472)
A mid-sixteenth-century rectangular tower-house of five storeys and attic, with corner box machicolation, long, narrow loops, battlements, and two raised corner turrets with projecting machicolation, which has been restored and supplemented with newer buildings at the lower levels.

KNOCKGRAFFON Co. Tipperary
(S 0241)
This is probably the most famous motte castle in Ireland – it is certainly the most widely photographed. It was raised in about 1192. The site has commanding views over the Suir valley, and when the motte was first raised, with its wooden tower, it must have demonstrated great strategic control. The motte is about 16.8 metres (55 ft) tall and about 20 metres (65 ft) across its summit. It was built upon an earlier Irish hill site which may have been a seat for the Kings of Munster before they moved their residence to the site at Cashel, not far away (*see* p. 204). The motte has its ditch and counterscarp, and a prominent bailey. There are foundations of a stone structure on the summit, and also remains of another stone building in the bailey, which consist now of a segment of a corner where two walls join, one of which has a row of corbels at second-floor level and also an arrow-loop.

Below the mound is a churchyard with the ruins of a church and several rows of graves and tombstones. Beyond that, situated about 0.8 km (½ mile) from the mound, there is a sixteenth-century rectangular tower-house, built by the Cahir Butlers, which is 11.5 x 8.8 metres (38 x 29 ft) and which has round bartizans on two corners.

KNOCKKELLY Co. Tipperary
(S 2337)
A tall tower-house of the late sixteenth or early seventeenth century, with a large enclosing bawn having several strong turrets on the angles.

KNOCKTOPHER Co. Kilkenny
(S 7337)
A motte castle of the early 1180s, mentioned by Giraldus Cambrensis. It was later supplemented with buildings, possibly of stone as well as timber. The motte was levelled in 1973 and the bailey has left no trace of its existence.

LACKEEN Co. Tipperary
(M 9504)
A sixteenth-century rectangular four-storey tower-house on a sloping plinth, whose third storey is vaulted. The roof level has two opposite walls that are crow-stepped.

LAVAGH Co. Laois
(S 3283)
A motte castle, isolated from a ridge by a complex bank and ditch, is mentioned in 1207. It may have begun as an Irish ring-fort.

LEA Co. Laois
(N 5712)
This great structure must in its heyday have been one of the most imposing castles in all Ireland. It also had a stirring history, ending up with being slighted by the forces of Cromwell in 1650. Three and a half centuries afterwards, it is still a most dramatic and impressive aggregation of ruins.

It began as an oval motte with two baileys, constructed at the beginning of the thirteenth century by William Marshal (this was mentioned in a document of 1201). Half a century later it was owned by one of the Fitzgeralds, probably Maurice, 2nd Lord of Offaly, and it was then that the motte was used as a base for a major great tower, rectangular with four corner towers, like Carlow, Ferns and Terryglass (qq.v.); in this case the core was 21.3 x 15.2 metres (70 x 50 ft), with walls 3 metres (10 ft) thick, and the towers 8.8 metres (29 ft) across. It was four-storeyed including the basement, whose cross-wall is of later construction. The window openings were largely plain loops, as at Carlow (q.v.) and, like Carlow, the tower had a main staircase in straight flights in the core

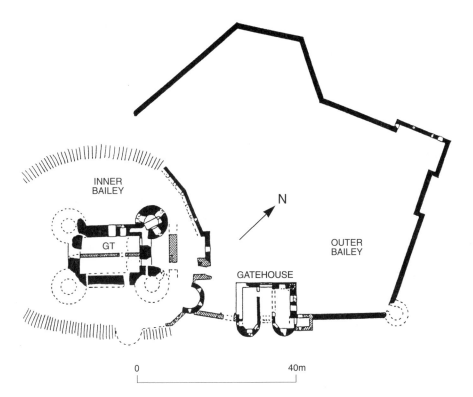

Lea, Co. Laois: note the similarity of plan of the great tower (GT) to those of Ferns, Carlow and Terryglass.

wall. The tower was surrounded by a stone enclosure, following the line of the old wooden palisade of one of the original baileys, of which some traces remain on the north-east side, and in which was inserted the original gateway, a simple rectangular gate-tower. There were also round flanking towers in this curtain wall, parts of two of which remain to a height of three storeys, although more or less ruinous. The gateway was at a later stage blocked by a structure which almost fills the space between it and the two round towers on the north and east corners of the tower core.

Outside the great tower's bailey, a second stone enclosure was raised, more or less on the site of the palisade of the second original bailey, extending north to the edge of the River Barrow. Most, if not all, of this work was done at much the same time as the great tower. At the end of the thirteenth century a twin-round-towered gatehouse with a 3-metre (10-ft) wide entrance passage was built in the outer enclosure, facing south-east. Although badly ruined, this still has grooving for two portcullises. In later years, possibly

before the end of the fifteenth century, the entrance to the great gatehouse was blocked up prior to converting it into a second great tower. Perhaps the original great tower was so badly damaged in some siege that it was easier and quicker to make the gatehouse conversion. There are accounts of several major assaults on the castle over the centuries.

LEAMANEH Co. Clare
(R 2494)
This tower-house castle belonged to the O'Brien family. It began as a tall, narrow, five-storey rectangular tower-house of about 1480, with loops and not windows. Three sides stand on a slightly sloping plinth. Inside, the main rooms are rectangular and take up about half of the tower, the other half containing the staircase. About 160 years later, a long rectangular stronghouse of four storeys was added on the west, the walls of which were much the same width as the original tower. In the newer work, the windows are large and mullioned, and at the second floor level on the west is a wall bartizan around its corner. Behind the west end is a square residential wing. The front entrance is a round-headed doorway. The castle ended up as an L-plan, about 20.4 x 10.7 metres (67 x 35 ft) with a 6-metre (20-ft) square wing.

LEIGHLIN Co. Carlow
(S 6465)
Also known as Leighlinbridge. A motte castle is mentioned in 1181 by Giraldus Cambrensis, built by Hugh de Lacy. A later work, namely a stone tower-house like Burnchurch (q.v.), was erected by the bridge in the sixteenth century; this is also known as the Black Castle. Only the western part remains.

LIMERICK (KING JOHN'S)
Co. Limerick
(R 5857)
Known as King John's Castle, this was begun about 1200 on the site of an Anglo-Norman earthwork enclosure dating to about 1175. It was developed over the thirteenth century into a stone castle of six sides. The longest side flanked the Shannon on the west. There is an entry in the Pipe Roll for 1212 about repairs, which must mean that much of the castle had been completed by then, and this may have included a large round tower at each end of the west wall, and a twin round-towered gatehouse in the northern wall, and slightly to the north-east another large flanking tower. The gatehouse was for a time the residence of the castle's constable. In Edward I's reign (1272–1307) more building was carried out, including the start of work on a substantial great hall along the Shannon wall (*see below*).

Limerick Castle was intended as an

King John's, Limerick: the western wall and two end towers skirt the edge of the River Shannon. On the right is the twin round-towered gatehouse. The location of the great hall (GH), the basement of which was recently excavated (1993–5), is marked as an addition to the plan, just below the riverside wall (see also Gazetteer entry, above).

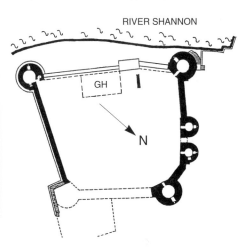

Limerick (King John's Castle) is one of Ireland's largest castles and was begun by King John as a stone enclosure with round corner towers and a twin cylindrical-towered gatehouse. Inside the wall by the river's edge are remains of the recently discovered great hall (see plan p. 223).

administrative centre to control not only the activities of the Irish north-west of the Shannon but also to check the expansionism of Norman lords. It has been altered over the centuries because of its key role. It was captured by Edward Bruce in 1316, and was taken over briefly in the mid-fourteenth century by the O'Briens; it declined in importance in the fifteenth and sixteenth centuries, and was then re-occupied in the seventeenth century. A British army barracks was built in the courtyard in c.1750.

Major excavations began at the castle in the early 1990s. The most interesting result has been the exposure of significant remains of the thirteenth-century great hall, rightly described by the leader of the archaeological team, Kenneth Wiggins, as 'some of the most spectacular structural remains ever unearthed in the excavation of an Irish castle'.

The great hall appears to have been built in two stages. The ground storey was raised in c.1280, with only four loops in a row along the western wall. This building stood on the floor of the courtyard, which was then 'several metres lower than the present-day ground level'. Some time around the turn of the fourteenth century a second storey was constructed on the original building, with its own entrance. At this time the level of the courtyard was raised to its present height, and the original ground storey became a large basement. The second storey was razed in the 1820s, and the original ground storey was filled with rubble. To quote from the excavation summary by Mr Wiggins:

'The excavated hall consists of a large room measuring over 19 metres (62 ft) in length (north-south), by over 8 metres (26 ft) in width (east-west), with a surviving height of around 4 metres (13 ft). The room was divided longitudinally in the centre by a spine wall which was inserted to support the roof when the second storey was added. As well as the four window loops in the western wall, the basement contains several other architectural features, such as archways and doorways, in varying degrees of preservation. In addition, the hall was skirted by a covered corridor, which allowed external access to the basement storey after the building of the upper storey. The corridor wall to the east of the hall was revealed by excavation in 1994.'

King John's Castle is managed by Shannon Development, and is open to visitors at regular hours throughout the year.

LISCANNOR Co. Clare
(R 0688)

A six-storey tower-house of the sixteenth century, Liscannor is now in ruins and has only its thick end-wall standing to the original full height.

LISCARROLL Co. Cork
(R 4512)

A large thirteenth-century castle consisting of a huge rectangular stonewall enclosure about 61.9 x 43.5 metres (203 x 143 ft) in size, with 8.2-metre (27-ft) diameter round corner towers; on the south wall is a substantial gatehouse measuring 12.2 x 7 metres (40 x 23 ft) with portcullis grooves, and on the opposite (north) wall a rectangular flanking tower. Later in the fifteenth century (or possibly early sixteenth) the gatehouse was altered to make a tower-house. Much of the castle walls and towers remain, even though they are badly damaged in places, but – curiously – there are few traces of any buildings inside, other than some structures on either side of the gatehouse, a situation roughly the same as that at Ballymoon (q.v.).

LISCARTAN Co. Meath
(N 8409)

This site has a pair of rectilinear tower-houses on the same axis, joined now only by a short wall. Their shapes are unequal: one is roughly T-plan with a small square corner turret at the bottom of the down-stroke of the 'T'; it is only two storeys high. The other is a nearly square tower-house with two projecting square turrets on one wall, one of them housing the staircase. Leask places the castle in the fifteenth century.

LISCLOGHER Co. Meath
(N 6862)

A residual example of a sixteenth- or seventeenth- century Z-plan tower-house with diagonally opposite round corner towers, one larger than the other and containing the staircase. It has a vaulted basement measuring 14.3 x 7.7 metres (46½ x 25 ft).

LISMAHON Co. Down
(J 4238)

A motte castle built by the Anglo-Normans c.1200 upon an earlier platform-type Irish rath. Some traces of buildings of timber were found; these included four post-holes probably for a small watch-tower or equivalent, and also a residential structure resting on courses of stone.

LISMORE Co. Galway
(N 9516)

A late sixteenth-century tower-house; three of its four walls are still standing, with a box machicolation on one corner. It was 12.5 x 9.2 metres (40½ x 30 ft), with the shorter end walls thicker than the long walls.

LISMORE Co. Waterford
(X 0498)

Near the River Blackwater a motte castle was erected c.1185, according to Giraldus. It is known locally as the Round Hill. The later castle in Lismore town is of the end of the thirteenth century, and this has a much later history; what is there is largely nineteenth-century re-modelling.

LISTOWEL Co. Kerry
(Q 9924)

An impressive ruin of a great tower that perhaps resembled Bunratty (q.v.). Listowel Tower was built in the fifteenth century. Only parts remain, chiefly a pair of square corner towers with a connecting wall, and fragments of other walling.

LOHORT Co. Cork
(R 4602)

A fifteenth-century tower-house, badly knocked about by Cromwell's forces in 1650, but restored in the eighteenth century and completely renovated in the 1870s. It had six storeys with rounded corners and a machicolated parapet most of the way round at the top. It has recently been allowed to decay and is now ruinous.

LORRHA Co. Tipperary
(M 9204)

A motte castle was erected here in about 1207, the mound created by in-filling with a circular ring bank with earth (*see* p. 90).

LOUGHLOHERY Co. Tipperary
(S 0284)

A rectangular tower-house of four storeys and attic which is enclosed by gables on all four sides. There are round bartizans on two of the corners.

LOUGH MASK Co. Mayo
(M 1560)

Lough Mask is a four-storey tower-house, 18.3 x 12.2 metres (60 x 40 ft), built in the

The west front of the stronghouse at Loughmoe. The original tower-house is on the right.

early seventeenth century. It is joined to part of the surviving bawn of an earlier castle building on the site, about which little is known. This later tower has substantial walls, in particular the east one which is nearly 6 metres (20 ft) thick, containing chambers and staircases.

LOUGHMOE Co. Tipperary
(S 1266)

This is a huge ruin of more than one period of construction. The first work was the fifteenth-century rectangular tower-house on the south end of the castle. It has four storeys, two of them vaulted, with rounded external corners,

Loughmoe, Co. Tipperary: the great tower with rounded corners, on the south end, is over a century older than the 26-metre (85-ft) long mansion added to the northern side.

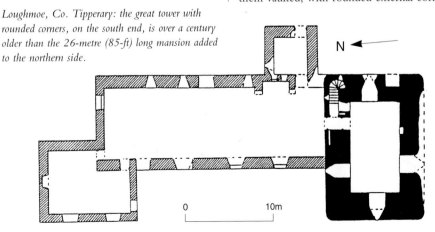

box machicolations at high level, and it measures 16.1 x 11.9 metres (53 x 39 ft). It is about 17.4 metres (57 ft) high to the wall walk. The two narrower walls extend a further storey upwards and contain mural passages and chambers. The tower's walls are nearly 2.7 metres (9 ft) thick on the two longer sides, and 3 metres (10 ft) thick on the shorter.

About two centuries later, a much less defensible long house was added on the north wall of the earlier tower, 26.2 metres (86 ft) long and only 10.3 metres (34 ft) wide, the rear wall continuing in the same line as the older tower's rear wall. The masonry of the new block was not keyed into the older tower. An arched entrance from the older tower into the new block was inserted at ground level. The new building was four-storeyed along its core, with mullioned windows at three levels. Projecting out of the rear wall where it joins the old tower is a small square porch tower facing east. Attached to the core and rising one storey higher is a rectangular wing, with some mullioned windows at four levels. This projects westwards and northwards out of the north-west corner of the core. The whole of this later structure was given parapets but not proper battlements.

LOUTH Co. LOUTH
(N 9800)
A motte, now known locally as Fairy Mount, with ditching all the way round and some counterscarp, it was attacked and burnt in 1196 but re-occupied in 1204. There are no signs of a bailey. The motte, raised on natural rising ground, is about 9.1 metres (30 ft) tall.

LURGANKEEL Co. LOUTH
J 0211
A motte castle here was excavated in the 1960s and remains found of a timber tower and some palisading. Not much of the motte now remains.

MALAHIDE Co. DUBLIN
(O 2446)
Although this much-modernised castle was the home of the Norman family of Talbot for several centuries, the remains of the original castle have been almost completely obscured. Nonetheless the present structure is handsome, and may even be described as formidable-looking; it is worth a visit, now

that it is in the care of Dublin County Council.

The castle's origins go back to about 1185 when Henry II granted the lands of the last Viking ruler of Dublin to Robert Talbot, one of his Norman knights who had come over to Ireland with him in the 1170s. There are some remains at ground and cellar levels, and the cylindrical tower on the eastern side is probably part of the first major re-building of the sixteenth century.

MALLOW Co. CORK
(W 5698)
This great stronghouse was built at the end of the sixteenth century. The front of its long, now badly damaged, rectangular core of three storeys and attic floor (whose gables have gone) is flanked by two hexagonal towers at the ends of the north wall and a pentagonal entrance tower in the centre of that wall. On the south wall of the core, in the middle, is another pentagonal tower which contained staircases and garderobes. This tower projects further than the entrance tower. There are no

---

This view of Mallow shows the long rectangular stronghouse, with two corner towers on the east long side and a projecting wing in the centre of the west long side (right of centre).

flanking towers on the rear wall. The core is 27.4 x 11 metres (90 x 36 ft), and it has a short kitchen block extension at the east. The castle was raised upon the remnants of a much earlier structure, probably dating from the thirteenth century.

MANORHAMILTON Co. LEITRIM
(G 8839)
This is a much-damaged stronghouse of the 1630s, which centred on a rectangular core 25 x 9.7 metres (82 x 32 ft) with two projecting wings, one at each end of the longer core wall at the north. The wings and the southern longer core wall had spur-shaped towers. The history of the castle is extremely short: it was destroyed in the aftermath of the Confederate War, barely fifteen years after being built.

MATRIX Co. LIMERICK
(R 3040)
A tall, 18.3-metre (60-ft) high rectangular tower-house, of seven storeys in the thick end wall and four storeys in the rest of the tower (an arrangement seen in the Scottish castle at Amisfield); it was built in the mid-fifteenth century and it has been renovated. Originally a Desmond castle, Matrix was a home for Edmund Spencer, the poet, during the 1580s.

MAYNOOTH Co. Kildare
(N 9337)

Maynooth has a substantial great tower, 22.2 metres (73 ft) (north–south) x 19.2 metres (63 ft) (east–west); it is inside an enclosure that is roughly rectangular. Very close to the great tower's south-east corner is a large, three-storeyed gatehouse, which has a round-headed entrance, and to the east of this is another rectangular tower, also three-storeyed, in line at the south with the gatehouse. Behind the tower are the remains of buildings extending north, which end in the remnant of an obliquely positioned smaller tower (at the north-east).

The great tower is an impressive ruin. It rises over 21.3 metres (70 ft). There are loops, larger windows, put-log holes and pilaster buttresses on three of the four walls. On the east side, which has no buttress, a timber staircase leads to where there was once a large fore-building. The actual entrance to the tower from the fore-building was a floor higher than the opening used now, and its arch is still there. The basement of the tower is divided by a cross-wall (a later work) and has rooms on both sides of it. The floor level of the basement is higher than it was originally, as is clear from the presence of two fireplace top arches very close to the floor. On the north side a spiral stair leads up to the first floor, which also has the remains of a cross-wall. There are chambers in the buttresses on the west and south sides. Around the inside of the tower, about half-way up, are beam-holes which were for a second floor. There is also evidence that the original roof gable began at about this level when the great tower was more of a hall-tower. Later, the walls were raised about two-thirds as high again and loops were inserted near the top at the level of the wall-walk. A damaged rectangular turret projects above the parapet on the north-east corner.

There is evidence of at least three stages of building of the great tower, from the first work of c.1200 up to the fifteenth century. It was probably begun by the Offaly Fitzgeralds. In the 1530s it belonged to 'Silken Thomas', Lord Offaly, son of Gearoid Og, Earl of Kildare, Lord Deputy, but in Thomas's rising of 1534–5 the castle was taken by the new Lord Deputy, William Skeffington. It was returned to the Fitzgeralds in 1552, and it was finally abandoned halfway through the seventeenth century.

MEELICK Co. Galway
(M 9314)

A small chapel here was filled with earth and gravel up to its gabled roof and then the whole was covered with more earth to create a mound, some time in 1203, according to documentation.

MILLTOWN Co. Louth
(J 0503)

A sixteenth-century tower-house which has one rounded corner turret for the stairs. A second, smaller turret for the garderobes is situated opposite.

MINARD Co. Kerry
(V 5598)

A large tower-house of uncertain age, but probably fifteenth century; it had four storeys, but is ruinous. The ground floor has thick walls, varying between 2.4 and 3 metres (8 and 10 ft). The first floor, equipped with chambers at one end, was reached presumably by step-ladder as there are no signs of staircasing. There are stairs up to the second floor above, which is vaulted. There was a top (hall) storey which is only a fragment now.

MONEA Co. Fermanagh
(H 1649)

Monea is an impressive ruin of a plantation castle of the early seventeenth century, built by Malcolm Hamilton, who imported some Scottish castle features in its design (such as the rectangular gabled tops of the circular towers flanking the entrance). Basically, it was a rectangular enclosure of stone with round towers on the north corners (these are now fragmentary), and an undetermined rectangular building at only foundation level in the south-west corner. The south-east of the enclosure contains a substantial rectangular

Monea, Co. Fermanagh: plan of the hall floor.

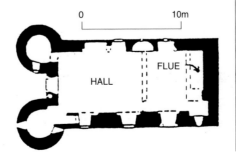

tower-house with two strong round towers at the western end flanking the entrance. This tower-house is 17.7 x 8.8 metres (58 x 29 ft) and was three-storeyed (four in the two entrance towers). The rectangular tops to the rounded entrance towers are supported by corbelled courses which 'serve to develop the round towers below into the square form above' (Leask).

These upper levels are crow-step gabled. Much of the interior of the tower-house is fragmentary: there is partitioning at ground level surviving from a kitchen and two cellars in line, plus a staircase into one of the entrance towers. There are also service stairs from the cellars to the first floor which once had a hall, and next to it a large chamber which was heated by a flue from the kitchen underneath. The third storey was originally divided into bedrooms.

The castle was badly damaged during the Confederate War, and was abandoned in the eighteenth century.

MONGAVELIN Co. Donegal
(C 3506)

A seventeenth-century, narrow, rectangular tower-house, 15.2 x 7.6 metres (50 x 25 ft), now ruinous, which had gabled roofing and round corner bartizans at roof level. The corbelling of some of them remains.

MONKSTOWN Co. Cork
(W 7666)

A seventeenth-century rectangular strong-house, of five storeys with gabled roofing, Monkstown is an interesting structure. It has two large projecting towers in front of its central core, and two similar towers projecting at the rear. The front towers have a corner box machicolation at parapet level on the outer side. Until recently, it was in good repair and in use as a golf clubhouse, but it has now fallen into serious decay. It must have been formidable in its time.

MONKSTOWN Co. Dublin
(O 2428)

A late fifteenth-century rectangular tower of four storeys, which was extended in later times. The main part of the tower has corner turrets which are now badly damaged. To the north of the tower is a gatehouse which has a Saracenic-style arch and a battlemented parapet. This structure is joined to the tower by a nineteenth-century wall.

MOORESTOWN Co. Tipperary
(S 1532)
A tower-house inside a bawn which has two round flanking towers and a gatehouse whose entrance is protected by a box machicolation at the top, but which has no portcullis.

MOUNT ASH Co. Louth
(H 9514)
A motte castle of the early Anglo-Norman period, it has traces of a polygonal tower on its summit.

MOUNTJOY Co. Tyrone
(H 9069)
A two-storey tower-house which was built for the Viceroy Mountjoy in 1601–02. Overlooking the south-west of Lough Neagh, it is constructed with a mixture of stonework and brickwork.

MOUNT LONG Co. Cork
(W 6573)
A seventeenth-century tower-house, not unlike Monkstown, Co. Cork, but which is in much more dilapidated condition. It has two projecting turrets on the front wall of the main rectangular core, and also two projecting turrets of similar shape and dimensions on the rear wall, although the latter are ruinous.

MOUNT SANDEL Co. Derry
(C 8530)
A motte castle near the River Bann. Three miles up-river at Mill Loughan is another motte. There is still doubt as to which of the two is mentioned in *The Annals of Ulster* as being erected in c.1197.

MOYCARKEY Co. Tipperary
(S 1554)
This sixteenth-century tower-house, now in ruins, was erected inside a large bawn. It measures 11.3 x 7.9 metres (37 x 26 ft) and has a thick end-wall for straight flights of stairs. There are no chambers in this wall below the fourth storey.

MOYGARA Co. Sligo
(G 6903)
A rectangular great tower, probably of the thirteenth century, was the first building here, and only fragments remain above ground. In the sixteenth century the tower was enclosed within a large square-plan enclosure, using the north wall of the old tower for part of its north side. At each corner of the enclosure is a square tower, well equipped with loops, one tower being taller than the other three.

MOYLOUGH Co. Galway
(M 6248)
A fourteenth-century three-storeyed tower-house built on an earlier motte of unknown date, measuring about 18 x 11.9 metres (59 x 39 ft), with 2.1–2.4-metre (7–8-ft) thick walls. It is now ruinous.

MOYNE Co. Mayo
(M 2549)
A late fifteenth-century rectangular tower-house, about 14 x 10 metres (46 x 33 ft) with walls over 2.1 metres (7 ft) thick; it had an east end-wall which was over 3 metres (10 ft) thick for chambers and stairs.

MOYRY Co. Armagh
(J 5715)
Lord Mountjoy, Viceroy in Ireland, built a small, towered castle here in the first years of the seventeenth century. It was a square-plan three-storey tower with rounded corners which was sited within a bawn. The tower walls and the bawn walls were equipped with numerous gun-loops.

NAAS Co. Kildare
(N8919)
A motte castle (now behind the post office) was raised here in the early years of the Anglo-Normans, and is mentioned by Giraldus Cambrensis for c.1180. It is about 10.7 metres (35 ft) tall, having been raised on rising ground, and is the highest point in Naas, with extensive views to north and west.

NARROW WATER Co. Down
(J 1319)
Sited at the northern edge of Carlingford Lough, in the Co. Down half, this three-storey plus attic tower-house of the mid-sixteenth century is 11.4 x 10 metres (37½ x 33 ft) and has 2.1-metre (7-ft) thick walling. It is protected by a quadrilateral enclosure, with a gateway on the north side and a corner turret on the lough edge. The tower-house has most of its battlements, and has been restored inside and out. It has interesting garderobes, splayed window reveals, straight flights of stairs in the wall thickness, and a Gothic arch entrance protected by a box machicolation on the third floor.

NAVAN Co. Meath
(N 8768)
A motte castle was raised here in the early years of the Anglo-Norman settlement.

NENAGH Co. Tipperary
(R 8679)
Nenagh Castle has as its main feature one of the finest cylindrical great towers in Ireland, and also one of the oldest. It is unusual in that, although round, it is placed in the perimeter of the whole castle, with the castle curtains coming out of it on opposite sides as they continue on to form the roughly horseshoe-shaped enclosure. The enclosure had two further cylindrical towers in its circuit and a twin-cylindrical-towered gatehouse as well. Taking the main tower first, it is now five-storeyed, built of coursed limestone rubble with some ashlar dressings, standing on a tall sloping plinth. Unusually for a cylindrical donjon in Britain and Ireland, it had a forebuilding, which has vanished. It had been formed between the east part of the curtain where that joined the donjon and a small projection further south, coming out of the tower. The spiral staircase, reached from the entrance, joined the floors above.

The donjon is some 16.8 metres (55 ft) in diameter at its base and reaches almost 30.5 metres (100 ft), including the battlemented parapet and also the arcade of openings

Nenagh, Co. Tipperary (after Leask): DO = door over. SP = sally port. W = walling. EO = entrance over. Between the walling on the south-east of the great tower and the projection a little further south there was once a forebuilding protecting the entrance.

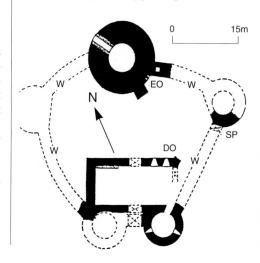

underneath, both of which features are of the mid-nineteenth century. The original tower was only about 22.9–23.5 metres (75–77 ft) tall and four-storeyed. The walls are about 4.9 metres (16 ft) thick at the bottom but less than 3.6 metres (12 ft) at the top level before the arcade, the whole tower tapering gently inwards. The entrance was on the first floor, like most early great towers.

Apart from the donjon, there are few remains; these include a short segment of the east round tower, one of the southern towers of the gatehouse, and behind that two storeys of a rectangular hall building whose southern wall was integral with both round towers. Most of this work, particularly the donjon (except for its nineteenth-century additions), is of the first years of the thirteenth century, carried out for Theobald Walter, the ancestor of the Ormonde Butlers, who held it for two centuries, lost it, recovered it in the 1530s and lost it again in 1548. In 1650 it was taken by Cromwell's forces after siege and again by forces of William III in 1689.

Considerable restoration work is at present being carried out by the Office of Public Works, notably on the great tower and on the rectangular hall, but the castle can be visited without difficulty.

NEWCASTLE Co. Wicklow
(O 2903)

A motte castle was raised here in about 1200 by building up on a natural ridge. The motte castle's history after that is vague, until in the sixteenth century a stone rectangular structure was built on the motte. This looks as if it was a gatehouse of three storeys, now in a very ruinous state.

NEWCASTLE LYONS Co. Dublin
(O 0234)

1 A low-level motte on flat ground, about 7.6 metres (25 ft) tall; this lies in a field next to the main street.
2 A small, L-plan tower-house on the side of the road about 0.4 km (¼ mile) from the motte (above); it is two-storeyed now, but may have been taller. It is about 4 metres (13 ft) square and has a projection 1.2–1.5 metres (4–5 ft) square, which has loops.

NEWTOWN Co. Clare
(M 2206)

Not far from Ballyvaghan Bay at the top of Co. Clare is the recently restored round tower-house at Newtown. This belonged first to the O'Briens and then to the O'Loghlens who for a time called themselves Kings of the Burren, an extraordinary group of mountains almost completely covered with smooth rock.

The tower-house was begun in the fifteenth century. It is a cylindrical tower standing on a four-spur base (q.v., Goodrich, England). The approach to the tower is covered on all angles by pairs of gun-loops all round at the first floor, and just above each spur is a loop with double gun-ports. Ingeniously placed to provide extra protection, especially on the entrance side, is a shot-hole concealed under a flat-pointed arch between each spur. The tower is over 15.2 metres (50 ft) tall, has four storeys below the roof level, and measures about 9.1 metres (30 ft) in diameter.

The restoration in the early 1990s has been done very well, with much thought for the tower's history and the original building skills employed. This work included a new conical roof-truss of timber encased in slates, a restored parapet with new and repaired stepped battlements made from local stone, and refurbishment of the storeys inside. The spiral staircases are in good condition, there have been tasteful renovations to fireplaces, windows and window reveals, and wickerwork-plastered ceilings in the vaulted storeys have been tidied up.

NEWTOWN STEWART Co. Tyrone
(H 4086)

Slight remains of a plantation castle of c.1618, which was burned down in 1690.

NOBBER Co. Meath
(N 8286)

A small motte with bailey, recorded in existence in 1186. Built by de Lacy, the motte's present height is a little over 7.6 metres (25 ft).

OLD CONNELL Co. Kildare
(N 8016)

A motte castle was erected here in the early Anglo-Norman period.

OLD ROSS Co. Wexford
(S 7927)

The motte castle was built at the end of the twelfth century by Isabel de Clare, daughter of Richard de Clare (Strongbow), leader of the Anglo-Norman invaders of the 1160s.

OMAGH Co. Tyrone
(H 4472)

The castle here was besieged in 1471 by the O'Brien family who had once owned it. It was besieged again in 1602 and taken by English forces.

ORANMORE Co. Galway
(M 3825)

Right down on the water's edge in Galway Bay, just east of the city of Galway, this sixteenth-century rectangular tower-house has two projecting turrets on the north-east wall, between which is the arched entrance at ground-floor level. The tower has few windows in any of its four sides, and openings are otherwise arrow-loops at all levels. One window frame has a sculptured gargoyle-type face on one of its exterior pillars. There are traces of a machicolation box at parapet level over the entrance. The parapet itself, however, is missing.

OUGHTERARD Co. Kildare
(N 9526)

A small rectangular tower-house with rounded corners, 7 x 5.5 metres (23 x 18 ft), four storeys tall but in dilapidated condition. The first floor is vaulted. Its second floor has its own entrance.

PALLAS Co. Galway
(M 7608)

An impressive and well preserved tower-house of the sixteenth century inside an equally well preserved bawn with a two-storey gatehouse and corner towers, Pallas is five-storeyed, rectangular in plan, with one wall more than twice the thickness of the other three, to take in staircases, garderobes and chambers. The exterior has a number of narrow loops but few windows. The parapet is machicolated over the entrance side, and the tower still has its roof.

PARKE'S Co. Leitrim
(G 7835)

An early seventeenth-century plantation castle, in the form of a tower-house with extensions, of formidable appearance; it has recently been restored. Parke's began as a sixteenth-century rectangular tower-house, about 12.2 x 9.1 metres (40 x 30 ft), with both east and west walls much thicker than the other two. Around it was a five-sided bawn with round flanking towers on two corners

Parke's (Co. Leitrim): this view shows the sixteenth- and seventeenth-century pentagonal enclosure with two round corner towers, and residential block and gatehouse.

(north and north-east) of differing sizes. Part of the bawn skirts the edge of Lough Gill. The date of the bawn is not known precisely but seems much later than the original tower-house. There are traces of other buildings along the inside walls.

After the defeat of the Spanish Armada (1588), the tower-house was destroyed by the English allegedly because its owner had given sanctuary to a Spanish sea captain, Francisco de Cuellar, who described his stay. The stone from the tower was used in the 1620s by Robert Parke to build a plantation castle inside the bawn, using the east bawn wall as one of the sides and rebuilding the round flanking tower as part of his new tower-house. On the other end the original gateway was enlarged to provide a well defended entrance passage. The remains of the old tower, such as they were above the ground, were levelled and the whole area was covered over with a cobbled yard.

PIPER'S FARRANFAD, CO. DOWN
(J 4343)
This is a site still argued about as to whether it was an Irish ring-fort or an early Anglo-Norman motte castle that was never completed. The finds in excavation work served rather to confuse than clarify: souterrain-ware pottery, cobbled flooring and post-holes for timber building. There is more to be done before the mystery is solved.

POLLARDSTOWN CO. KILDARE
(N 7715)
Excavation here uncovered what seemed like an Irish ring-fort, yet the artefacts were almost all representative of an Anglo-Norman settlement, many with military connotations such as iron arrow-heads, metal stirrups, metal buckles and so forth.

PORTAFERRY CO. DOWN
(J 5950)
This early sixteenth-century L-plan tower-house of three storeys, with the shorter arm being a staircase wing on the south side, was raised to command the narrow passage between Strangford Lough and the sea. The entrance was placed in the re-entrant angle between the tower and the wing. The wing carries the stair to the first floor. Thereafter, access to the levels above are by stairways in the wall thickness of the tower's west wall.

PORTNASCULLY CO. TIPPERARY
(S 5113)
There are the remains of a motte castle here.

PORTUMNA CO. GALWAY
(M 8502)
Walking up the refurbished drive in front of this substantial stronghouse-type mansion of the period c.1610–18, one might easily be lulled into thinking the castle was not properly defended. One would be wrong.

Approaching the front door, the unwanted visitor of the seventeenth century would be confronted by a number of guns poking through shot-holes in the door jambs. Above the door an extra threat came from a box machicolation at parapet level. Meanwhile, the four corner towers clamped onto the central rectangular core represented a formidable all-round defence by means of battlements and more gun-ports.

Portumna's interior is at present being restored by the Office of Public Works. Basically, the core, some 30.5 x 21.3 metres (100 x 70 ft), has two cross-walls running parallel east to west and rising to three storeys, between which was the staircase, or possibly two staircases, upwards to corridors on each floor in which doors opened into rooms along both sides. Most rooms were of massive proportions, and some surviving fireplaces are huge.

The castle, built by Richard Burke (de Burgos), 4th Earl of Clanricarde, Lord President of Connacht, who is believed never to have seen his palace completed, was gutted by fire in the 1820s. In the basement there is an unusual well-head, elliptical in plan (well-heads are usually round or square).

The fortress-residence stands in its own bawn which has strong round turrets at the east and west ends of the northern wall, with gun-ports along the east and west bawn walls.

QUIN Co. Clare
(R 4274)
An enclosure castle of stone, of symmetrical plan, was built here by the de Clares in 1278–80, but it did not last long. It was destroyed by the Irish Macnamara family before the fourteenth century. In the fifteenth century, descendants of the family used the ruins as a framework for a Franciscan friary, within the enclosure of 3.3-metre (11-ft) thick walling of the de Clares. It is possible by looking down from the friary church tower to see the original castle plan in outline, namely, a square enclosure with large round corner towers. Parts of three towers remain.

QUOILE Co. Down
(J 4947)
Part of this sixteenth-century tower-house has been repaired and is incorporated into a country amenity centre beside the Downpatrick to Belfast road. The lowest storey has a cross-wall dividing it into two vaulted rooms which are equipped with several gun-ports.

RAHEENE Co. Limerick
(R 5949)
An Irish ring-fort in which a later Anglo-Norman castle was erected.

RAHINNANE Co. Kerry
(Q 3601)
A large, circular ring-fort of Irish origin situated here was in Anglo-Norman times given a stone two-storeyed tower-house of roughly L-plan. This probably took place in the sixteenth century.

RAPHOE Co. Donegal
(C 2603)
A seventeenth-century rectangular three-storeyed stronghouse, reinforced with four-storeyed corner towers which are square-plan on the two inner sides and slightly extended to arrow-shapes on the outer two. There are remains of a cross-wall on the ground floor on the side facing downhill, which is somewhat thickened by having a fireplace in it, while the continuation of the cross-wall is much thinner. This is in part missing in the centre of the ground floor. All the walls have large window openings, many of which were added in the eighteenth century. Raphoe Palace, as it is sometimes called, was built in the 1630s by Bishop Leslie, but it was besieged in 1641 in the Confederate War and captured by Cromwellian forces in 1650. It was restored in parts after Cromwell's time, but was sacked by forces loyal to the exiled James II in 1689.

RATHCONRATH Co. Westmeath
(N 2953)
A motte castle was built in 1191 near the church (*Song of Dermot*).

RATHFARNHAM Co. Dublin
(O 1529)
This building today is in good condition, due largely to major renovation carried out in the eighteenth century by the then owners, the Loftus family. It is now a national monument and is in the care of the Office of Public Works. It began as a substantial rectangular-plan stronghouse built in the 1580s for Adam Loftus, Archbishop of Armagh. It had four corner towers affixed to a central core, whose outer angles are pointed, like those at Raphoe (q.v.). The castle suffered greatly in the seventeenth century but this enabled it to be renovated later.

RATHMACKNEE Co. Wexford
(T 0414)
A smallish, five-storey nearly square tower-house, about 12.8 metres (42 ft) tall, whose walls have very little illumination; it stands in the corner of an irregular pentagonal enclosure of thick walling, which is 5.5 metres (18 ft) tall. Next to the tower is a gateway with an outside pointed arch, protected by a machicolation box above. The wall is partly battlemented. The tower has square turrets on top, and all have stepped battlements. Rathmacknee was built in the late fifteenth century and early sixteenth century and is in good condition today. It has a rounded box machicolation on one corner of the bawn.

Rathmacknee, now a national monument, is a very good example of a fifteenth-century tower-house with connecting bawn.

RATHMORE Co. Meath
(N 7566)
A four-storeyed L-plan tower-house; the 'L' is formed by a rectangular projection out of one corner, which contains the staircase.

RATHMULLEN Co. Down
(J 4737)
A motte castle here was raised on the top of an Irish ring-fort which itself was built on a natural hillock, at the beginning of the thirteenth century.

RATHURLES Co. Tipperary
(R 9280)
The remains of a cylindrical tower-house of the sixteenth century which was about 12.2 metres (40 ft) in diameter.

RATHWIRE Co. Meath
(N 5343)
A motte castle of the early Anglo-Norman period, built by Hugh de Lacy. Stonework foundations of a later castle structure have been found in the bailey.

RATOATH Co. Meath
(O 0351)
On the edge of the village, at the end of a track towards a stream, is a motte of the early thirteenth century.

REBAN Co. Laois
(S 5898)
A motte castle here is mentioned in a charter of c.1200.

The five-storeyed tower-house on one corner of the bawn at Rathmacknee. Note the gateway in the walling next to the tower-house, which has a machicolation box above.

ROCKFLEET Co. Mayo
(L 9395)

A small, sixteenth-century tower-house on the shore by Clew Bay. It is a simple tower-house of four storeys with box machicolations at the top on two opposing corners of the parapet. There are very few windows but a number of narrow loops. It belonged for a time to Grace O'Malley during the reign of Elizabeth I. Grace beat off an attack from the water by an English force, and later was received by the queen.

ROODSTOWN Co. Louth
(N 9993)

Probably one of the £10 castles of the 1430–40s (*see* p. 100), Roodstown is a rectangular tower-house in good external condition, with two polygonal turrets at the top on the summit of two diagonally opposite projecting square turrets emerging from the tower, in the form of a prolongation of the wall. It is four-storeyed, five if you take the turrets as an extra level. No battlements remain. The ground floor is vaulted. Round the top is a crude form of machicolation which may be little more than a series of holes to drain off the water from the gabled roofing. One of the turrets has a staircase running all the way up to the top. The other has chambers, of which two were garderobes. There are good views over the surrounding flat countryside from north to east, and towards hills to the south. There is a meurtrière above the entrance door.

ROOSCA Co. Tipperary
(S 0619)

A stronghouse on a sloping plinth in a corner of its enclosing bawn, which has a flanking turret in another corner. The whole castle is ruinous. The tower was only three storeys high, including the attic, some of whose gabling remains.

ROSSCLOGHER Co. Leitrim
(G 8455)

The remains of a fifteenth-century cylindrical tower situated on an island on the southern edge of Lough Melvin.

RINNDOUN Co. Roscommon
(N 0054)

The original castle here, on a small peninsula on the west side of Lough Ree, was built in about 1227 by the Justiciar Geoffrey de Marisco. It was besieged by the Irish soon afterwards, and then rebuilt by Henry III or his son Edward in the 1270s, who erected a rectangular great tower. This had three principal storeys, was 19.2 x 13.7 metres (63 x 45 ft), and contained a substantial hall and a vaulted ground floor. It was incorporated into the enclosure wall on one side, as at Carrickfergus and others.

The castle was (and is) on the southern side of the peninsula, and north of that was a small town, possibly of earlier beginnings, which was protected on its north side by a stone wall right across the peninsula neck. In 1315, during Edward Bruce's invasion of Ireland, Rinndoun town was sacked and the castle was damaged. It was deserted altogether in the middle of the century. Since then it has slipped slowly into continuing neglect, and the ruins are overgrown. The great tower still has its north wall up to about 10.7 metres (35 ft) high, but not much else remains.

ROSCOMMON Co. ROSCOMMON
(M 8764)

This is one of a number of castles in Ireland raised in the second half of the thirteenth century, more or less according to the same basic plan, namely, a rectangular or square enclosure of strong, high walls clasped at the corners by massive towers, taller than the walls, with a powerful gatehouse in the curtain wall on one side of the enclosure. At Roscommon, the enclosure is 49.4 x 39.6 metres (162 x 130 ft), the corner towers are circular, three-storeyed and with narrow straight staircases in the walling, and the gatehouse is on the east curtain; this has two massive D-ended towers, also three-storeyed and which project outwards, and the backs of the towers stick out deep into the enclosure. The passage between the gate-towers was in fact only 3 metres (10 ft). Leask reckoned Roscommon's gatehouse to be the finest in Ireland. There is also a small, rectangular postern gate on the west curtain wall, whose entrance passage is vaulted, and there are traces of a drawbridge mechanism.

Roscommon was begun by Robert de Ufford, Lord Justice of Ireland, on ecclesiastical land, like several Irish castles (such as Swords). It was intended to discourage the O'Conchobair family of Connacht who were descendants of the old Irish Connacht kings, but in the 1270s, the then Ua Conchobair chief, Aedh, attacked

Roscommon, Co. Roscommon: (after Leask). This plan may be compared with that of Harlech, Wales (p. 311). The Roscommon design precedes that of Harlech. GH = gatehouse. G = garderobe(s). DB = drawbridge. WG = water-gate. The dotted lines indicate remains of ranges of buildings.

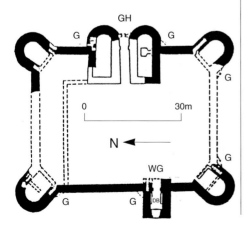

and destroyed the new buildings, such as they were. Soon after, about 1280, the ruins were re-taken and a new castle built along the above-described lines, similar to Harlech (q.v.) but *before* that castle was built. The curtain walls between towers, gatehouse and postern gate were about 2.7 metres (9 ft) thick, tall and battlemented. The castle was maintained by a royal garrison into the first years of the fourteenth century. Then over the years it changed hands several times, including being taken over by the O'Conchobair family again in 1341 and held by them for many years. There were several changes of ownership in the sixteenth century. In the 1580s a range of domestic buildings forming a kind of mansion was erected inside along the north wall and round to the west wall of the great gatehouse, but these have all disappeared. At this time, the north-east circular tower was changed inside, as was the gatehouse.

ROSCREA Co. TIPPERARY
(S 1389)

The first evidence of building here is documentary. King John had a motte castle erected in 1213, but nothing remains. Much later, about 1280, a stone castle was raised beside the earthwork. It was a rambling shaped enclosure, vaguely polygonal, in whose northernmost wall was inserted a substantial rectangular gatehouse, some 16.4 x 10.3 metres (54 x 34 ft), which rose to three storeys (higher still in the seventeenth-century work). At much the same time, a round tower was inserted at each end of the south part of the enclosure, which was in chevron-plan. Although there is little evidence of other buildings of the period inside, it is clear from the openings in the curtain wall that something was intended. Later, in the fifteenth century, the gatehouse had its entrance passage closed up to make a tower-house, while entry into the castle was provided through a new gateway in the wall next to the converted building. Later still, this access was given a rounded arch.

The castle was held from the early fourteenth century for more than three centuries by the Earls, and later Dukes, of Ormonde (the Butler family). Inside the enclosure there is a Queen Anne mansion built in the early eighteenth century, called Damer House.

This interesting castle, which fronts onto

the town's main street, has recently been consolidated by the Office of Public Works as part of the new Roscrea Heritage Town project. They have done splendid work which has included opening up the centuries-old blocked entrance to the original gatehouse (later, the residential tower), making it a gatehouse again, and re-creating the drawbridge and portcullis mechanisms just as they were in the castle's earliest days.

ROSSLARA Co. CLARE
(R 5382)

Rosclara is a fifteenth-century tower-house which has vaulting.

ROUGHAN Co. TYRONE
(H 8268)

A seventeenth-century plantation castle consisting of a rectangular core tower of three storeys with cylindrical turrets on all corners, with a high-level arch across the space between two turrets on the south side. It is now ruinous. The entrance is through a doorway in one of the westerly turrets which contains the staircase.

SEAFIN Co. DOWN
(J 2238)

A polygonal stone enclosure was put up here in about 1252 by the Justiciar; it was nearly 30.5 metres (100 ft) across. It made use of banks of an earlier Irish hilltop rath. Within the enclosure was built a rectangular great tower of the same period, little of which now remains.

SEEFIN Co. GALWAY
(M 5116)

Part of a five-storey tower-house is standing. It is the section that houses the staircase.

SHANID Co. LIMERICK
(R 2445)

This began as a 10.7-metre (35-ft) tall motte castle of the end of the twelfth century. It still has an impressive ditch. Soon afterwards, the motte was adorned with an oval shell enclosure of stone on its summit which itself surrounded a similarly dated multangular tower, half of which has disappeared. Like some polygonal towers elsewhere in the British Isles, such as Orford and Conisbrough, the interior was cylindrical, and was 6.7 metres (22 ft) in internal diameter. The surviving half of the tower is about 10.7 metres (35 ft) tall and its remaining wall is 4

The tower-house at Roscrea, showing the re-opened gateway through its north wall (at right).

metres (13 ft) thick (as it had been all round). The present ruin still has a row of narrow loops around what is left of the top. Below the tower and the motte on which is stands, the bailey is oval in shape and has its own ditch. The castle belonged for a time to the Fitzgerald Earls of Desmond.

SHIPPOOL Co. Cork
(W 5755)
Remains of a fifteenth-century rectangular tower-house with a cylindrical turret which projects out of the north-east corner. The staircase was in the east wall, however, and not in the turret. The latter has gun-ports on each of its floors.

SHRULE Co. Mayo
(M 2753)
A sixteenth-century tower-house consisting of four storeys, with polygonal-plan corner machicolations at the top. The tower's four walls splay outwards sharply from the top of the first storey downwards.

SKETRICK Co. Down
(J 5363)
A fifteenth-century tower-house, now badly damaged and with much of it missing, Sketrick was once a four-storey rectangular building which was enclosed by a bawn. There are some remains.

SKREEN Co. Meath
(N 9458)
A motte only about 4.1 metres (13½ ft) tall, which clearly has been reduced, together with traces of a bailey; they are situated in the garden of a modern property here. This could be the motte castle mentioned in 1181 by Giraldus Cambrensis.

SLADE Co. Wexford
(X 7597)
A fifteenth-century L-plan tower-house of different phases but having most of its battlementing. The first part was a narrow tower which is still 17 metres (56 ft) tall. Then next to it was erected a two-storey rectangular wing (sixteenth century). The entrance to the first tower is protected by a machicolation box at top level.

SLANE Co. Meath
(N 7657)

The Gothic Revival castle of Slane is not part of the current survey. On the Hill of Slane, on the north edge of the town, is a motte and its bailey, originally erected in the mid-1170s, destroyed by the Irish soon afterwards and then rebuilt, probably by about 1180. Later, stonework was added, of which only traces remain and are incorporated in the much later house, but it is not clear what shape the medieval stonework took.

STRANGFORD Co. Down
(J 5950)

A late sixteenth-century tower-house, only about 7.6 metres (25 ft) square, which guarded the entrance to Strangford Lough. It is three-storeyed and has some of its battlements. There are no signs of staircasing, and access will have been by ladder, as in the case of a number of Border castles in Northumberland and also elsewhere.

SWORDS Co. Dublin
(O 1847)

Swords Castle, in the northern half of the present town of Swords and cared for by Fingal County Council, was a bishop's castle and was started in about 1200. Although its five-sided enclosure of stone remains standing and in reasonably good condition, even with plenty of battlements (mostly stepped), and although there are considerable remains of what seems at first sight a formidable gatehouse and also corner towers, the castle does not really convey much sense of strength, and indeed may never have been meant to be more than a relatively safe place for a bishop or archbishop to have as a home. The enclosure has towers on the east and west corners, both square, and on the north side was a three-storey rectangular tower-house, of somewhat later date, in which the castle's constable or castellan lived. The two largest buildings, both somewhat damaged and both later than the early thirteenth-century work, are the four-storeyed gatehouse on the south (which has twin rectangular towers protecting the entrance passage) and, adjoining it on the east, a large chapel, probably fourteenth century. The staircase to the gatehouse on the

The gatehouse (centre) at Swords, flanked by buildings.

first floor is in a turret on the north-east corner. The western tower of the gatehouse has a rectangular extension projecting into the enclosure. The chapel, now without first or second floors, roofing or interior fittings, is the equivalent of three storeys, and the ground storey was probably a crypt. There are the remains of a tiled floor.

Inside the enclosure, not quite central, is a large earth mound which is the motte erected in the early thirteenth century. Along the inside of the curtain are various features of interest, mostly relics of buildings no longer there, such as the ruins of a three-storey tower along the east wall, whose lowest storey was vaulted, a fireplace in the enclosure wall, a recessed doorway and a garderobe.

SYNONE Co. Tipperary
(S 0847)

Synone is a sixteenth-century cylindrical tower-house, which has dome vaulting at the top of two double storeys inside, and some machicolation round the parapet. The stairs were built in the thicker parts of the tower wall.

TERMON Co. Donegal
(G 1066)

An early seventeenth-century rectangular tower-house, 11.9 x 9.4 metres (39 x 31 ft), whose walls taper outwards in the lower levels (cf., Shrule, Co. Mayo), and which has a large

cylindrical turret on the north-east corner containing a staircase to three storeys above the ground floor. The turret base on the ground floor is solid masonry. Entrance to the first floor was by step-ladder from the ground level. This ground floor was clearly intended as a military defensive area, and there are gun-ports at chest level along the walls. At the top, there is machicolation remaining along two sides. The tower-house stands inside a large bawn, backing onto the south wall.

TERMONFECKIN Co. Louth
(O 1480)

This three-storey tower-house of the fifteenth or sixteen century had vaulting made by overlapping stone slabs positioned in a similar manner to corbels.

TERRYGLASS Co. Tipperary
(M 8600)

A number of castles based on this plan were built in the thirteenth century in Ireland, although each was quite individual in many of its features. Here, a thirteenth-century rectangular great tower with four cylindrical towers on the corners was built near Lough Derg. At present the building is only two storeys high. Its corner towers, of different diameters (two are nearly 9.1 metres [30 ft] across), are lower than the core now. The smallest tower, about 6 metres (20 ft) across, contains the staircase. The core itself stands on

a sloping plinth and has the residue of a cross-wall at ground-storey level, but this is thought to be a later work.

THADY'S FORT Co. Clare
(R 3762)
This was an Irish ring-fort, and possibly constructed soon after the Anglo-Norman invasion and settlement.

THREE CASTLES Co. Wicklow
(O 0105)
The title relates to the one-time existence of three separate tower-houses here. Now there is but one damaged tower left, and this is less than its original height.

THURLES Co. Tipperary
(S 1258)
A motte castle of c.1189 belonging to Theobald Walter. A century and a half later, a great tower was built in the bailey, of which there are some remains.

TIBRAGHNY Co. Kilkenny
(S 5715)
A motte castle of c.1185 mentioned by Giraldus Cambrensis. It is near a later church.

TIMAHOE Co. Laois
(S 5390)
Just outside the present village is a motte of c.1182, listed by Giraldus Cambrensis. In the village, close to a tall, 29-metre (95-ft) monastic round tower of uncertain period, is a one-time fifteenth-century chapel of stone on which was grafted a stone tower-house, which entailed destroying most of the chapel.

TOOME Co. Antrim
(H 9990)
The remains of a plantation castle were found here by accident a few years ago. They include about 7.6 metres (25 ft) of 2.1-metre (7-ft) thick walling, together with traces of a turret on the north-west corner. The turret was five-sided.

TRIM Co. Meath
(N 8056)
Trim is among the greatest of the Norman castles in Ireland. Built beside the River Boyne, it occupies 1.2 hectares (3 acres) in slightly triangular plan. One side is a bank sloping down to flat ground leading to the river. At the north-east end of the bank is a square-plan tower (described as a sally-port by Leask). At the other end is a small round tower. In between is a fragment of another square tower and a stretch of wall from the north-east tower, but otherwise no walling remains. The second side is a straight line of walling from the north-east tower leading south-west to a small round tower. Half-way along is a rectangular gate-tower. The third side is a curve of walling from the south-west tower which joins up with the south-east of the first side. Along the curve are three equidistantly placed round towers, then a longer stretch of wall, and then, due south, a larger round gate-tower. This consists of two semicircles with guardrooms flanking a narrow entrance passage which leads out into a barbican that spans the moat. The curving wall continues out of the east of the gate-tower to meet the most easterly tower.

The castle may have begun as a moated enclosure of timber and earth, erected not long after the arrival of the Anglo-Normans. The stonework probably began towards the end of the twelfth century. At one time it was thought the castle contained a motte (on which the later great tower was built) but excavations in the 1970s showed that the mound was in fact earth covering the splayed plinth of the great tower.

The great tower itself is of considerable interest: it is a square core of some 20 metres (65 ft) all round, with four square turrets, centrally placed on the four walls. The turrets are 6.7 metres (22 ft) square. The height of the great tower is almost 23.2 metres (76 ft). This type of plan is similar to that of Castle Rushen in the Isle of Man, and also Warkworth in Northumberland. The core walls are 3.3 metres (11 ft) or more thick, although the turrets are about half this. The turret on the north wall is missing today although fragments of where it was keyed into the core can be seen. It is believed the tower was erected in two stages, the first, from c.1200–10, which took it up to two full storeys, and the second, c.1220s. There are signs of the first roof. The windows of the first stage are rounded, whilst those of the later stage are squared. The lower half had the entrance at first-floor level, using a staircase in the east turret which acted as a forebuilding and which has a chapel over the entrance into the core. The first floor of the first work was divided in two by a cross-wall,

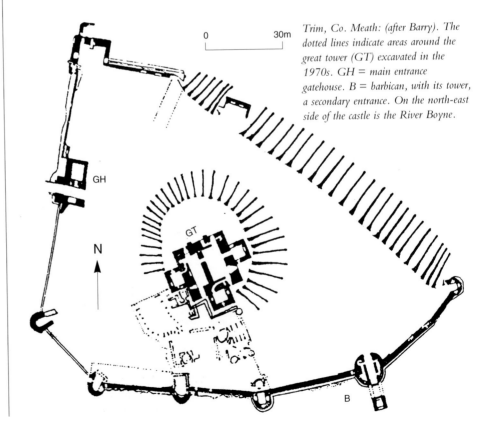

Trim, Co. Meath: (after Barry). The dotted lines indicate areas around the great tower (GT) excavated in the 1970s. GH = main entrance gatehouse. B = barbican, with its tower, a secondary entrance. On the north-east side of the castle is the River Boyne.

providing a great hall and a lord's bedroom or chamber. When the core was heightened, the extra storey contained a variety of rooms.

The castle appears to have been begun by the de Lacys. Some time in the thirteenth century it passed to the Mortimers. It was neglected in the second half of the fourteenth century until, in 1399, Richard II of England, on his famous visit to Ireland, arranged for two of his Crown wards to live there. They were Henry of Monmouth (later Henry V) and Humphrey, his brother, both sons of Henry Bolingbroke (Richard's first cousin). Little is known of the great structure in the fifteenth century or the sixteenth century until during Silken Thomas's rebellion in the 1530s there are records of repairs being made to the buildings. It was ruinous again by the end of the sixteenth century, and after the Confederate War it was finally yielded to the Cromwellians in 1650.

TUAM Co. Galway
(M 4352)

This is the site of one of the seven pre-Norman Irish 'castles' of the 1120s-60s (*see* p. 87). The fort has disappeared.

TULLABARRY Co. Kilkenny
(S 4572)

A motte castle north of Ballyragget (q.v.) was built at the start of the thirteenth century.

TULLIRA Co. Galway
(M 4795)

A seventeenth-century tower-house, much added to at the end of the nineteenth century.

TULLOW Co. Carlow
(S 8574)

A motte castle, on whose motte a chapel was later built. The castle itself was begun c.1181 (Giraldus Cambrensis).

TULLOW Co. Tipperary
(S 1972)

A basically rectangular tower-house with one corner clasped by a round turret of about 6 metres (20 ft) in diameter, immediately adjacent to which is the staircase to the tower's higher levels.

TULLY Co. Fermanagh
(H 1357)

A plantation castle of about 1610, beside Lower Lough Erne, Tully is a T-plan tower-house inside a roughly square enclosure (whose foundations were recently tidied up). The ground-floor main room is vaulted. At one end is a rounded arch fireplace at low level (lower than the original). On the south side is an entrance turret with splayed gun-ports on three sides. The first floor of the main block has large windows. Beam-holes of the second floor can be seen. The main staircase went up in the entrance to the first floor, then continued upwards as a spiral in a rounded turret pushed out on the right. The enclosure had rectangular and square turrets on the four corners, whose remains can still be seen. It was attacked by the Maguires in 1641 in the Confederate War and burned down, and was apparently never occupied again.

TURBET Co. Cavan
(H 3617)

This is a motte castle on Turbet Island in the River Erne, which is recorded as being strengthened, 1211–12.

URLANMORE Co. Clare
(R 3766)

There is a three-storey tower at one end of this building and an adjoining extension, with remains of a large first-storey hall. In the tower part is a small room which has wall paintings of animals. The castle has been partly destroyed.

WATERFORD Co. Waterford
(S 6012)

This important town on the Suir was in Norman times surrounded by a fortification of walls and tall towers. The walls were linked to earlier Viking walls. The principal interest to the castle enthusiast is Reginald's Tower, at the extreme east end of the fortifications, on the edge of the river. This is still about 15.2 metres (50 ft) tall and 13.1 metres (43 ft) in diameter, four-storeyed with only a few windows, an unbattlemented parapet, and presenting a formidable defence. Its origins are certainly Anglo-Norman, probably about 1200, but it is situated on the site of an earlier structure erected by the Viking ruler Reginald in about 1000.

WEXFORD Co. Wexford
(T 0522)

A motte castle was erected here in 1173, mentioned by Giraldus Cambrensis, which has largely been built over. It was captured in 1176. In the thirteenth century a stone castle was built in Wexford, which some authorities think may have been on the same basic plan as Carlow or Terryglass (qq.v.); but whatever was constructed has disappeared.

WICKLOW Co. Wicklow
(T 3194)

A castle with stonework was noted by Giraldus Cambrensis at Wicklow as early as 1173. It may have been on the headland, a triangular apex with a rock-cut ditch, later occupied by what came to be known as Black Castle. The original castle was given by Henry II to Strongbow in 1173. The plan of Black Castle is shaped like a motte-and-bailey, although without the mound, and only a raised platform.

Scotland

ABERCORN LOTHIAN
(NT 082792)
Once thought to have begun as a motte castle in the twelfth century, it is now believed that Abercorn rose from scratch in stonework, although its shape has not been determined. It belonged to the mighty Douglas family and featured in the power struggle between them and the king, James II, in the 1450s. It was besieged in 1455 by James, using cannon, mentioned specifically in Scottish Treasury accounts. It was probably destroyed, for a mansion was later raised on the site, using masonry from the older fortress.

ABERDOUR FIFE
(NT 193854)
Aberdour is a rambling assemblage of ruins of several periods. It was begun in the thirteenth century, some time after the site had been granted by Robert Bruce to his great friend and nephew Thomas Randolph, Earl of Moray. After centuries of improvements and also changes of family ownership, it was burnt some time towards the end of the seventeenth century and thereafter allowed to deteriorate, although an ornamental garden was erected in the courtyard to the south.

The castle started as a rhomboidal great tower, of which not much remains today beyond some walling. The tower is 15.8 x 11 metres (52 x 36 ft) with angle-buttresses on two corners. The walls are almost 1.8 metres (6 ft) thick. Unlike most great towers, the entrance was at ground- (and not first-) floor level. It has a spiral staircase in the wall thickness on the east corner. The tower was

modified in the fifteenth century to enlarge the accommodation, and this entailed rebuilding the top part. It also included erecting a new square-plan staircase tower on the south-west corner adjacent to the part of the wall containing the original spiral staircase.

In the sixteenth century a fresh range of buildings was raised on the south-east, abutting at the top on the staircase tower. This range extends in a north-easterly direction and was added to in the seventeenth century, the principal building being a long rectangular structure with a square-plan tower on its extreme east corner.

Aberdour passed on to the famous Douglas family in the mid-fourteenth century. It belonged to the Regent Morton from about 1548 to his execution in 1581. It has been the subject of recent excavations.

ABERUCHIL TAYSIDE
(NH 745212)
A seventeenth-century L-plan tower-house in poor condition.

ABOYNE GRAMPIAN
(NO 523995)
Aboyne was a motte castle raised in the thirteenth century which received stone additions, probably by the time of the War of Independence (c.1296–c.1307). The motte received a stone great tower. In the seventeenth century the great tower was drastically altered to a tower-house, and altered again in the nineteenth century into a mansion which, after a period of decay, was restored in the 1970s.

ACHADUN STRATHCLYDE
(NM 804392)
This was an irregular quadrilateral stone enclosure, the great part of which has collapsed and is ruined. Part of the north-west wall stands to a maximum height of about 6.7 metres (22 ft) and 1.5–2.4 metres (5–8 ft) thick. It dates from the early thirteenth century. The castle has a small rectangular turret projection in one corner, and a garderobe built into the curtain wall itself.

ACKERGILL WICK, HIGHLAND
(ND 352547)
A rectangular great tower of the end of the fifteenth century, approximately 14.6 x 10.3 metres (48 x 34 ft), and which has received later additions and restorations. Its history is not known.

AFFLECK MONIKIE, TAYSIDE
(NO 495388)
This is a well-known L-plan tower-house of the late fifteenth century which is still in very good condition. It is built of local reddish sandstone rubble, with fine-quality dressings on the angles, around windows, arrow-loops and so on. It is four storeys to the parapet which has two square corner turrets and two small corner roundels. Although sparsely provided with windows, which at upper levels have iron grilles, and more liberally supplied with arrow-loops, Affleck tower-house has elaborate internal appointments, including a chapel at the top storey (over the top of the wheel stair in the staircase tower), and a well-designed solar, also on the top floor, which

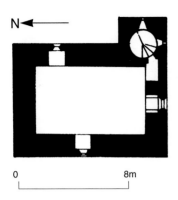

Affleck: plan of the first floor of the tower-house. The main room was the Common Hall.

has a remarkable fireplace, a garderobe and several wall chambers which were probably bedrooms. The wing at Affleck contains five storeys including three flights of spiral stairs, up from ground level, which then stop. The next floor is a mezzanine chamber, and above that is an oratory, or private chapel, which is vaulted. The solar in the main block is reached by another spiral stairway from the hall in a different corner, making the oratory accessible only from the solar. The mezzanine chamber, meanwhile, is attainable only by a mural flight of stairs from the hall, and a garderobe leads off the chamber.

Affleck was – and still is – a fine residence. It was also a well-fortified one: the walls are 1.8–2.1 metres (6–7 ft) thick, there are inverted keyhole gun-ports at lower levels, and there are battlemented cap-houses acting as watch-turrets at the top on two corners.

AIKET STRATHCLYDE
(NS 388488)
This began as a rectangular tower-house of the late fifteenth century.

AIRLIE KIRRIEMUIR, TAYSIDE
(NO 293522)
On a promontory over the junction of the Isla and Melgund rivers stands the greatly renovated castle of Airlie, belonging as it has for centuries to the Ogilvy family. The first work began c.1432 and was probably a large enclosure castle. There is a stretch of wall of this surviving, about 36.5 metres (120 ft) long, 3 metres (10 ft) thick and 10.7 metres (35 ft) tall in places. In the wall is a gateway with a portcullis. The remainder of the original is no

longer detectable, and a more modern mansion occupies part of the north area of the enclosure. The original ditch to the south of the long wall is still there. The old castle was burnt by the Duke of Argyll in 1640.

AIRTH CENTRAL
(NS 900868)
Airth Castle is basically fifteenth century, raised on an earlier castle site. The tower is 10 x 8.5 metres (33 x 28 ft). In the sixteenth century a wing was added on the east wall of the tower, and a further north wing was joined to that at a point where a small rectangular stair turret abuts on the end of the east wing.

ALDIE TAYSIDE
(NT 050977)
Aldie has been well restored, both in the seventeenth century and in recent years, and is no longer known as a castle. But its original purpose was as a fortified home, built in the late fifteenth century. The tower is four-storeyed with garret. The top part has been rebuilt, and the original wing containing the staircase was removed and replaced by a lower structure. The tower has bartizans corbelled out at the corners, although these were added after the need for fortification and so are decorative rather than military. Other additions made in the seventeenth century, and also later, converted the castle into a courtyard mansion.

ALDOURIE HIGHLAND
(NH 601372)
An early seventeenth-century tower-house which has been absorbed in later buildings.

ALLARDYCE ARBUTHNOTT, GRAMPIAN
(NO 817739) C
A late sixteenth-century rectangular tower-house which has been considerably altered and expanded, Allardyce now has a cluster of turrets and label-moulding in the corbelling of the turrets and parapet. There is also an interesting old archway into the courtyard.

ALLOA CENTRAL
(NS 888925)
Once a massively tall tower of the fourteenth century, it was greatly altered in the seventeenth century. New features included bigger windows and a Renaissance-style entrance.

ALMOND TAYSIDE
(NS 968722)
Almond Castle was probably begun in the fifteenth century as an L-plan tower of four storeys plus a garret in the roof. Later additions were built on the north-east and south-east. The castle was once surrounded by a ditch fed by a nearby stream which has dried up. It is a ruin today.

AMISFIELD DUMFRIES AND GALLOWAY
(NX 992837)
Amisfield Tower is a very tall tower-house of about 1600. In its way it embodies the Scottish anxiety to build tall and strong. Amisfield incorporates a variety of features that might almost be described as having been thrown together, its lower-storey walls built of random rubble, its higher levels of better ashlar work. It is five-storeyed to the main garret level, but one end rises for two further storeys as a narrow double cap-house. Scattered – for that is the appropriate word – around the top are bartizans and rectangular projections. Lower down on one corner is a roundel that stops about 3 metres (10 ft) from the ground. Its top end supports a square-plan chamber of two storeys with its own attic inside a gable roof. The basic dimensions of the tower are 9.1 metres (30 ft) square and over 21.3 metres (70 ft) tall.

The weird appearance of Amisfield's design is heightened by the different shades of colour of the stone used.

ARDBLAIR CENTRAL
(NO 163445)
An L-plan tower-house with courtyard, probably built in the sixteenth century, which has been little altered and is a substantial ruin.

ARDROSSAN STRATHCLYDE
(NS 232422)
This is a courtyard castle sited on part of a rock detached from a large promontory. Parts of a large gatehouse on the north-east side still survive. There are also remains of another tower at the south-west. The lower level of the gatehouse is the earliest work of the castle, probably late thirteenth century. There was reconstruction in the fourteenth century when the gatehouse was rebuilt from the first floor upwards. In the fifteenth century the gatehouse was converted into a gatehouse-tower and heightened, and fortified with gun-ports in the sixteenth century.

The seven-storeyed tower-house at Amisfield is over 21 metres (70 ft) tall.

ARDTORNISH MORVERN, HIGHLAND
(NM 692426)

This castle was built in the thirteenth century. It was a rectangular great tower, of which only the walling of the ground floor now remains, this being some 2.7–3 metres (9–10 ft) thick and several metres high. Ardtornish belonged to the Macdonalds, who were Lords of the Isles.

ARDVRECK ASSYNT, HIGHLAND
(NC 239236)

Perched on a rocky promontory jutting into the north side of Loch Assynt, Ardvreck is now a ruin. It was raised in the late sixteenth century as a simple, rectangular tower with a cylindrical staircase turret at the south-east corner, corbelled out on the upper storeys. The three chambers on the ground floor were vaulted. The tower had three storeys, and the windows in the top storey were served by a gable passage. After his defeat at Invercharron in 1650 Montrose took refuge at Ardvreck, but was betrayed and handed over to Parliament, which hanged him in Edinburgh.

ARNAGE ELLON, GRAMPIAN
(NJ 935370)

A late sixteenth-century Z-plan tower with two square wings, still in sound condition, and which has been renovated. It was enlarged in the nineteenth century by the addition of a wing which obscured some of the original work.

ASLOUN GRAMPIAN
(NJ 543149)

Ruins of a late sixteenth-century Z-plan tower-house include one round tower and some walling.

ASSYNT HIGHLAND
(NC 195250)

Vestiges of dry stone-walling on this castle site, reaching to 1.5 metres (5 ft) in various places, are almost the only remains of a fortress of uncertain shape which was recorded as having been given to Torquil McLoyd of Lewis c.1343. There still remains some of the retaining wall to be seen round the edge of the island.

AUCHEN Dumfries and Galloway
(NT 063035)
This interesting castle was begun in the thirteenth century. It was partly demolished in the Wars of Independence, possibly in furtherance of Robert Bruce's policy of 'slighting' castles. It was rebuilt in the fourteenth century as an irregularly shaped, thick-walled quadrangle castle with cylindrical corner turrets, whose lower levels are solid masonry. The quadrangle was surrounded by a deep and wide ditch, providing a formidable defence, although not really a concentric defence as has been suggested. The east wall of the quadrangle has a mural passage with a corbelled roof. There was a drain running from the castle into the moat. It is now in ruinous condition.

AUCHENHARVIE Strathclyde
(NS 363443)
A late fifteenth-century great tower in ruins.

AUCHINDOUN Montlach, Grampian
(NJ 349374)
A late fifteenth-century L-plan tower-house inside the limits of a prehistoric hill-fort, Auchindoun has ribbed vaulting in the remains of the great hall. It was designed by Robert Cochrane, who was the court mason and favourite of James III (1460–88), responsible (among other works) for the great hall at Stirling Castle. The castle has been in ruinous condition for some time, but restoration is in progress by the Scottish Development Department.

AUCHNESS Kirkmaiden, Dumfries and Galloway
(NX 107446)
A small, rectangular tower-house of the sixteenth century, which rose to three storeys and a garret, Auchness has been absorbed into a farmhouse, with many alterations. Turrets have been added for decoration.

AUCHTERARDER Tayside
(NN 943133)
A very early rectangular tower, possibly twelfth century, enclosed by a moat. Some fragments of the tower walls remain, to a height of about 4.9 metres (16 ft). The castle is reputed to have been associated with Malcolm III (1057–93) but if this is so, then it will only have been an earth and wood castle at the time. Nothing is known about its later structural history.

AULDEARN Highland
(NH 917556)
A castle of the time of William the Lion (1165–1214) is mentioned in an early charter (1187–8). Remains consist of a raised area enclosed by a rampart.

AULDTON Dumfries and Galloway
(NT 094058)
This is a twelfth-century motte in good preservation. It has the remains of a ditch around the base. Unfortunately, nothing is known of its history.

AYR Strathclyde
(NS 335222)
Traces have been found of the late twelfth-century castle built here probably by William the Lion, King of Scotland. It began as an earthwork enclosure and received stone additions. It was besieged in 1298 by the English, using siege-engines sent to the site from Carlisle by sea (S.H. Cruden).

BALBEGNO Grampian
NO 639729
Balbegno was built in the late 1560s on a roughly L-shape plan, and has considerable

The oldest part of Balgonie is the four-storeyed rectangular tower-house, which was built with ashlar facing in c.1450.

additions of the seventeenth, eighteenth and nineteenth centuries. The upper hall in the earlier tower part is particularly notable for its ribbed vaulting.

BALBITHAN Grampian
(NJ 812189)
Now called Balbithan House, this began as a sixteenth-century L-plan tower, the projecting arm of which is extended much more than normal in towers of this design. It is occupied and open seasonally.

BALFLUIG Alford, Grampian
(NJ 596150)
An L-plan tower-house of the mid-sixteenth century which was ruinous for a long period. It has recently been restored and is occasionally open.

BALFOUR Tayside
(NO 337546)
A sixteenth-century round tower (a shape rare in Scottish castles) was built here.

BALGONIE Markinch, Fife
(NO 313007)
A substantial castle of fifteenth-century beginnings standing on the south bank of the Leven, Balgonie is a gaunt, dilapidated structure as seen from a distance, but restoration work has been in progress for some while. The main rectangular great tower of four storeys plus garret was built of ashlar blocks and is complete to the roof. This was renovated very recently. Additional buildings were raised in the sixteenth and seventeenth centuries, the latter by the 1st Earl of Leven, and remains of these are still standing.

BALLINSHOE Tayside
(NO 417532)
A sixteenth-century tower-house, of which little original work remains.

BALLINDALLOCH Grampian
(NJ 179365)
A Z-plan tower-house of the late sixteenth and early seventeenth centuries, considerably enlarged and modified since.

BALLONE Highland
(NH 929837)
A late sixteenth-century Z-plan castle, which was already in ruins by the mid-eighteenth century. The main central rectangular tower, lying north–south, rose three storeys with a garret above, and of the diagonally opposing towers one was cylindrical, the other square. In each angle a narrow staircase turret was inserted. The remaining two corners of the main block still have corner turrets. The present ruins are three storeys high. Gun-ports were placed all round the tower-house at ground-floor level.

BALNAGOWN Highland
(NH 763752)
This is a great tower castle of the thirteenth/fourteenth century that has been considerably modified.

BALQUHAIN Inverurie, Grampian
(NJ 731236)
A large quadrilateral great tower was built here in the fourteenth century. The walls were thick, with deep recesses and narrow window loops. It was destroyed in 1526 and rebuilt soon afterwards to smaller dimensions. A curtain wall enclosed the tower and also some outbuilding. Mary, Queen of Scots, is thought to have taken refuge here before the Battle of Corrichie in 1562. The castle was finally destroyed by the Duke of Cumberland in 1746.

BALTHAYOCK Tayside
(NO 174230)
A simple but impressive ruin of a fifteenth-century rectangular great tower; it is approximately 15.8 x 11.3 metres (52 x 37 ft), with thick walls.

BALVAIRD Tayside
(NO 169115)
A fifteenth-century L-plan tower-house with a separate square-plan staircase tower in the angle. The tower-house is its full height, and several other features are visible, such as battlemented parapets, a rectangular cap-house on the wing tower with its own parapet and bartizan corners, and part of the barmkin which was added somewhat later than the tower's construction period. Balvaird has the remains of an interesting plumbing arrangement: latrines were flushed out by means of a chute in the wall thickness, with an outlet at the bottom covered by a stone 'plug', called a 'grund-wa'-stane' (ground wall stone, cf., Corgarff).

BALVENIE Dufftown, Grampian
(NJ 326408)
This is an interesting castle of late thirteenth-century origin, which began as a substantial stone quadrilateral enclosure with walls basically 2.1 metres (7 ft) thick, and probably up to 10.7 metres (35 ft) high. There are remnants of a small latrine turret on the north corner, and of a larger square-plan tower on the west corner, and other buildings were raised inside. In the mid-sixteenth century, the eastern part was completely remodelled by the then owner, John Stewart, 4th Earl of Atholl, who constructed a range consisting of three storeys facing south-eastwards, with a cylindrical tower on the east corner, about 8.5 metres (28 ft) in diameter, three storeys tall and which once had a 'pepper-pot' roof. The tower has wide-mouthed gun-ports, as has the lower storey of the range.

The castle was an extensive building in the sixteenth century, about 45.7 x 39.6 metres (150 x 130 ft) in area, with buildings round three inside walls, and it is today an equally extensive ruin. It stands on a platform surrounded on three sides by a 12.2-metre (40-ft) wide moat, the fourth side falling away

Balvenie: this view shows the sixteenth-century, three-storeyed round tower on the south-east corner of this large enclosure castle.

as a steep cliff. The moat has stone facing. Balvenie once belonged to the Douglases. When the mighty family was brought low by James II in the 1450s, Balvenie became Crown property, but the king gave it to John Stewart, 1st Earl of Atholl. It was occupied until the eighteenth century.

BALWEARIE Kirkcaldy, Fife
(NT 251904)
Only ruins remain of this fifteenth-century tower-house inside an enclosing curtain wall. The tower was 13.1 metres (43 ft) by about 8.5 metres (28 ft), with 1.8-metre (6-ft) thick walling. The masonry was ashlar, set in courses of 25–30 cm (10–12 in).

BANFF Grampian
(NJ 689641)
There is very little to see here of the original stone enclosure castle that was raised in the thirteenth century, apart from a stretch of wall about 42.7 metres (140 ft) long, up to about 5.5 metres (18 ft) high and up to 1.9 metres (6½ ft) thick.

BARCALDINE Strathclyde
NM 908406
Sited about 24.1 km (15 miles) north of Oban with a fine view of Loch Creran towards Glencoe, Barcaldine was built to L-plan in 1601–9. The main tower block was 13.1 x 8.2 metres (43 x 27 ft), with the walls varying between 1.2–1.8 metres (4–6 ft) thick. The south-west wing was 7 x 6.7 metres (23 x 22 ft). The tower-house rose three storeys plus attic (which has been rebuilt). It was allowed to decay, but in the final years of the last century it was restored and is occupied.

BARDOWIE Strathclyde
(NS 578737)
This sixteenth-century tower-house has later additions, which are not castellar. The tower is four-storeyed, with walls 1.9–2.4 metres (6½–8 ft) thick, and is built of rubble.

BARHOLM Kirkmabreck, Dumfries and Galloway
(NX 521529)
Situated high above the sea, Barholm is now a ruinous L-plan tower-house of three storeys plus garret with parapet, to which has been added a wing of greater height, containing the staircase. The tower wing is topped with a cap-house. Around the tower was built a curtain wall, about 3 metres (10 ft) tall and about 0.9 metres (3 ft) thick. Barholm was built during the late sixteenth and early seventeenth centuries.

BARJARG Dumfries and Galloway
(NX 878901)
A late sixteenth-century L-plan tower-house forms the eastern wing of a mansion built here in the early nineteenth century. It was built of red rubble and rises to four storeys plus attic, and has corbelled angle-turrets on the corners of the parapet (which were probably built in a later period).

BARR TOWER Strathclyde
(NS 502364)
A plain tower castle of the sixteenth century that has received modifications.

BARRA Bourtie, Grampian
(NJ 793258)
This is a fortified stone rectangular building of the seventeenth century with a wing which joins the main block towards the south so that there are two angles. In the eighteenth century a second wing was added projecting eastwards from the north, and the three sides of a rectangle thus formed were completed by the building of a curtain wall across. The castle is occupied.

BASS OF INVERURIE Grampian
(NJ 781206)
A natural mound some 15.2 metres (50 ft) tall was altered into a motte by scarping the sides and excavating a ditch round it. The work was probably done c.1180 by David, Earl of Huntingdon, brother of William the Lion, King of Scotland. The remains of an oak gangway up the south face of the motte were found in recent excavations. The motte is thought to have been given a shell enclosure of stone at a later date, but this has not yet been finally determined.

BAVELAW Penicuik, Lothian
(NT 167627)
This possibly seventeenth-century L-plan tower-house built around an earlier structure, three storeys high with an attic, is equipped with gun-ports. A cylindrical turret projects from the north-east angle of the main tower block, and a rectilinear turret abuts on the southern edge. The earlier work may be part of a hunting lodge used by Mary, Queen of Scots.

BEDRULE Borders
(NT 598180)
Bedrule began as an oval, stone-wall enclosure on the bluff jutting westwards from the rising ground on the right bank of Rule Water. A gatehouse was inserted on the north-west and a cylindrical flanking tower on the south-east, with two further round towers at the west and south-west. The structure was built in the late thirteenth century and was put up by the Comyns during the John Balliol-Edward I contention. Robert Bruce captured it during the War of Independence and gave it to his friend and counsellor, Sir James Douglas. It is a complete ruin.

BELDORNEY Grampian
(NJ 423369)
An altered Z-plan tower of the sixteenth century, with one round and one square (staircase) turret. It has a courtyard.

BEMERSYDE Mertoun, Borders
(NT 592333)
A modernised mansion which incorporates a sixteenth-century tower-house whose original height was five storeys. The walls of the tower are 3 metres (10 ft) thick. Bemersyde has been held by the Haig family for centuries. By far its most celebrated occupant was Field Marshal Sir Douglas Haig, 1st Earl Haig of Bemersyde, Commander-in-Chief of the British army in France, 1915–18.

BENHOLM Grampian
(NO 804704)
This uncomplicated tower-house of the fifteenth century is in a ruinous state.

BLACKNESS Nr Linlithgow, Lothian
(NT 055802)
Once a very important Scottish fortress by virtue of its position by the waters of the Firth of Forth, Blackness is a castle of the fifteenth/sixteenth century whose overall plan is very much like a ship. It is sited on a rocky outcrop at the sea end of a promontory. I say fifteenth/sixteenth century to cover its two distinct phases. The fifteenth century saw the erection of the rectangular great tower, which was given, probably in the seventeenth century, a cylindrical staircase corner turret on the north-east angle. The tower stands inside the 'ship-shape' courtyard of mainly sixteenth-century construction, which has another tower at one end, and a triangular

tower-like bastion at the 'bow' end of the courtyard. Blackness was used as a prison for Covenanters in the 1660s.

BLAIR TAYSIDE
(NN 866662)
This is the palatial home of the Dukes of Atholl; it is largely a late eighteenth-century reconstruction grafted upon the remains of an earlier and complex tower-house castle. The first building, of which some lower portions of wall survive, was the Comyn Tower, built c.1270 of square plan. It is now called the Cummings Tower. It was subsequently enclosed in a barmkin along with further buildings including a lord's hall. The medieval castle was for a time the seat of the first Earls of Atholl, who were royal Stewarts. It was occupied for a few weeks by Bonnie Prince Charlie, the Young Pretender, during the Second Jacobite Rising, 1745–6. After the flight of the prince, Blair was taken over by the Hanoverian government. The Duke of Atholl attempted to recover it by siege but was fought off. This was probably the last siege of any castle in Britain.

BLERVIE GRAMPIAN
(NJ 071572)
A well-preserved, Z-plan tower-house of the seventeenth century, which still has a five-storey tower.

BOGHALL NR BIGGAR, STRATHCLYDE
(NT 041369)
A sixteenth-century T-plan tower-house, three small round towers and a gate-tower in an enclosure wall; these are all now ruined.

BONSHAW TOWER
ANNAN, DUMFRIES AND GALLOWAY
(NY 243721)
An unadorned late fifteenth-century small rectangular tower, 10.3 x 7.6 metres (34 x 25 ft), three-storeyed to the wall-head and with a roofed attic. The basement is vaulted.

BORTHWICK LOTHIAN
(NT 369597)
Borthwick is one of the greatest tower-houses in all Britain, certainly the most imposing in Scotland. It has been in almost continuous occupation since it was constructed in 1430–2, and is today preserved and lovingly cared for by its present owner in a way that the first Lord Borthwick, who was granted a

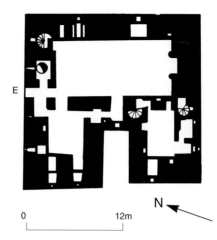

Borthwick: first-floor plan of the tower. Note the massive wall thickness. E = entrance.

licence to build it by James I in 1430, would have appreciated.

It is built of large ashlar blocks. It is a rectangular tower with two wings projecting from the ends of one longer (west) side. The longer sides of the rectangular part are 21.7 metres (71 ft) long, the shorter sides 13.7 metres (45 ft). The wings are slightly dissimilar in dimension: the more northerly wing measures 9.7 x 7 metres (32 x 23 ft), the southerly wing 8.5 x 6 metres (28 x 20 ft). The walls of the tower-house are 3–4.3 metres (10–14 ft) thick in most places, particularly impressive when one looks at some of the window sills. The great hall takes up the whole first floor of the rectangular part, and has a tall, barrel-vaulted roof. At south is a magnificent canopied fireplace, 6 metres (20 ft) high, flanked on either side by a deep window with stepped sills. From the hall, four spiral staircases wind their separate ways up to chambers and thence to the roof, and downwards to dungeons and cellars. A large kitchen opens off the hall into the northerly wing, while the southerly wing contains a solar on the same floor. Next to the solar is a garderobe, whose chute discharged into a system of movable containers for subsequent opening. The tower-house is 30.5 metres (100 ft) tall and has machicolated parapets.

Borthwick Tower was later enclosed by a curtain wall with one large cylindrical corner tower flanking a gateway in the wall, positioned just to the south-west of the southerly wing of the tower.

The great tower-house was bombarded by

Cromwell in the war between England and Scotland in 1650. The 9th Lord Borthwick, a staunch Royalist, refused to yield to Cromwell after the great man's victory over the Scots at Dunbar. Cromwell formally demanded surrender in a letter which included the threat: '... if you necessitate me to bend my cannon against you, you may expect what I doubt you will not be pleased with...' Borthwick refused, whereupon Cromwell's guns opened fire and fragmented the battlements and some wall stonework on the top part of the east main wall. Then Borthwick surrendered, and the tower-house was spared. The results of the bombardment can still be seen today. They mar the otherwise noble and tidy appearance of the castle's masonry.

BOTHWELL
UDDINGSTON, STRATHCLYDE
(NS 688593)
We have encountered this important thirteenth-century Scottish castle (with later additions) in Chapter 9. Its great tower was the first structure, raised in the 1270s at the latest, by the Moravia family (later Moray) who also owned Duffus.

The castle was built on rock upon the south bank of the Clyde. The masonry is red sandstone quarried nearby, finely cut and dressed. The great tower, or donjon, was over 20 metres (65 ft) in diameter, rose to at least 24.4 metres (80 ft) and had walls about 4.6 metres (15 ft) thick. It had four storeys, a spiral stair in the wall thickness on the north-east side, and a mural passage at first-floor level leading out of the south-east side into a wing wall jutting out south-eastwards. This wall led to a cylindrical turret. This was just about all of the stonework completed by c.1290, although foundations have been discovered of parts of a planned curtain wall, a twin-towered gatehouse and other towers laid out to form a quadrilateral enclosure. These northerly structures were never completed, and indeed some may never have risen higher than a few feet above ground. We may assume that it was intended to continue this building plan, and even that the curtain line was temporarily followed by wooden palisading. The positioning of wide ditches to north-east and east suggests that an area of some size was to be fortified. A ditch was also cut into the rock in front of the donjon, between the two wing walls.

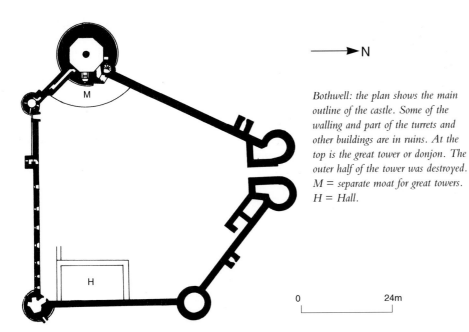

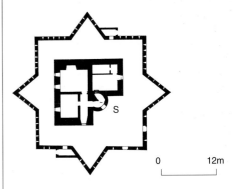

N

Bothwell: the plan shows the main outline of the castle. Some of the walling and part of the turrets and other buildings are in ruins. At the top is the great tower or donjon. The outer half of the tower was destroyed. M = separate moat for great towers. H = Hall.

0   24m

In the 1290s, the castle fell into English hands after the deposition of John Balliol (1296). In 1297, the Scots attacked Bothwell and captured it after a 14-month siege. In 1301 Edward I recaptured it. To do so he employed a variety of artifices including a huge belfry of prefabricated parts made in Glasgow and moved 12.9 km (8 miles) in two days to Bothwell by thirty wagons. But after Bruce's great victory at Bannockburn (1314), the castle reverted to Scotland, and it may have been dismantled under Bruce's policy of slighting castles likely to be useful to the English again.

In c.1331, during renewed hostilities between Scotland and England, Bothwell was captured by Edward III who used it as a headquarters. Much restoration work was done to the great tower, and a hall was built on the eastern side of the quadrilateral, but possibly not completed. In 1337, Sir Andrew de Moravia recovered the castle once more from the English and dismantled it. The donjon was partially thrown down, so that only half of it remained standing to almost its full height.

In the 1360s, the castle came into the possession of the Black Douglas family who rebuilt the hall, a chapel and some walling, and erected a new wall from east to west. Further work was done in the fifteenth and sixteenth centuries, but its history from the end of the fourteenth century is not our concern here.

BOYNE BOYNDIE, GRAMPIAN
(NJ 611656)
The ruins of a courtyard castle of the late sixteenth century, Boyne was protected on three sides by Boyne Water and a dry ditch on the fourth. At each corner of the courtyard was a cylindrical tower, about 6.7 metres (22 ft) in diameter. The connecting curtain wall was on average 1.5 metres (5 ft) thick. Inside the courtyard, ranges of domestic buildings were put up on three sides. The entrance consisted of a walled walkway covered by a pair of cylindrical towers.

BRAAL HIGHLAND
(ND 139601)
This is a rectangular tower-house dating from the fourteenth century, about 10.7 x 11.3 metres (35 x 37 ft) and rising today to the second storey only. The walls are 2.4–3 metres (8–10 ft) thick. It is a simple structure with no vaulting. The entrance is at first-floor level at the south-west. The tower was surrounded by a wet ditch.

BRACO ARDOCH, TAYSIDE
(NN 823113)
A tall, square tower-house with projecting staircase tower, of the sixteenth century. This was given an extension on the south side absorbing the stair tower (seventeenth century) and a further extension of L-plan (eighteenth century), rendering the castle three sides of a square round a courtyard.

BRAEMAR GRAMPIAN
(NO 156924)
Not far from Balmoral (the Scottish home of the royal family), lies the castle of Braemar. It is basically an L-plan tower-house with some interesting additions. Begun c.1628, it was burned in 1689 and restored in 1748 to be used as a military base for the Hanoverian army after the Second Jacobite Rising of 1745–6. The corners of both wing-ends were provided with cylindrical turrets corbelled out from second-storey level upwards, and these turrets were battlemented at the top. A large cylindrical staircase tower was inserted in the angle and around the tower was raised a star-shaped barmkin, or stone curtain, battlemented and supplied with gun-ports all round (see also Corgarff). Later, its bartizans were heightened.

0   12m

Braemar: ground plan (after Fenwick). Star-shaped enclosing wall is the mid-eighteenth-century addition to the original L-plan tower-house. S = stair twist in re-entrant.

BRAIKIE KINNELL, TAYSIDE
(NO 628508)
An L-plan tower-house built by the Fraser family in 1581 (according to a date stone). It has been altered but little in the four centuries, and has the usual features of sixteenth- and seventeenth-century smaller Scottish tower-houses, such as crow-stepped gables, corbelled embrasures and an iron yett at the entrance. It is now derelict.

BREACACHADH STRATHCLYDE
(NM 160539)
This is a medieval great tower castle with curtain wall and other buildings, mainly of the fifteenth century, which has been partly restored.

BRECHIN TAYSIDE
(NO 598599)
A late thirteenth-century structure of uncertain shape, which has been incorporated in later buildings.

BRODICK ISLE OF ARRAN, STRATHCLYDE
(NS 007379)
Now built of red sandstone, Brodick began as a Viking fort, probably of the twelfth century. In the fourteenth century it was converted to an early stone L-plan tower-house. The north wing is all that remains of the original building. The remainder of the structure is chiefly nineteenth-century work, and was designed by Gillespie Graham for the owner, the Duke of Hamilton.

BRODIE FORRES, GRAMPIAN
(NH 979578)
Brodie Castle belongs to the Brodie family: the land on which it stands has done so since the twelfth century. The present structure is basically of the sixteenth and seventeenth centuries but was raised on an earlier castle site. It is a Z-plan formed from a strong, centre rectangular tower with two projections. The tower is four-storeyed to the parapet which rests on highly decorated corbelling, and there is a garret above, with crow-stepped gable. It is equipped with loops and gun-ports, and is part of a nineteenth-century mansion.

BROUGHTY BROUGHTY FERRY, TAYSIDE
(NO 465304)
About 3.2 km (2 miles) from Dundee, Broughty has been extensively altered. It started as a tower-house of the last years of the fifteenth century. It appears to have been allowed to decay, probably as a result of damage by the English in 1547, and more damage when it was retaken in 1550. In c.1603, Broughty was restored, but again damaged, this time in 1650. The actual shape of the castle in its earlier state is difficult to determine but its main tower block foundations are still visible. In 1855 the castle was purchased by the War Department and modified as a coastal fort. Parts of the east block are the only upright remains of the fifteenth-century castle.

BRUCE'S ST NINIANS, CENTRAL
(NS 857878)
Not connected with the illustrious King of Scotland, this castle stood on a rocky spur. It was built of sandstone rubble and was of rectangular plan with walls which were nearly 3 metres (10 ft) thick. It was begun in the fifteenth century. Only the ground floor and parts of the first storey remain.

BRUNSTANE LOTHIAN
(NT 201582)
Brunstane is a sixteenth-century courtyard-plan castle, with a medium-sized tower-house of earlier date on the south-east side, of two storeys and a garret. The castle was burnt down in 1547 and rebuilt in the 1560s, at which time it received the main part of the courtyard buildings.

BUITTLE DUMFRIES AND GALLOWAY
(NX 819616)
This is a thirteenth-century enclosure castle with cylindrical towers on the angles, now in ruins. There is an entrance at the north-west which appears to have led out through a twin-towered gateway to a drawbridge. Nearby is a seventeenth-century L-plan tower-house.

BURGIE GRAMPIAN
(NJ 094593)
A seventeenth-century Z-plan tower-house. One interesting feature is its groups, or batteries, of gun-ports which are set in groups of three in the walls. It is largely in ruins, after part-demolition.

BURLEIGH MILNATHORT, TAYSIDE
(NO 129046)
Close to the north edge of Loch Leven, the early sixteenth-century tower of Burleigh stands without roof and in ruins, being about 9.7 x 8.2 metres (32 x 27 ft) in its horizontal dimensions. A stretch of enclosure wall joins on to a round tower which has several interesting features, including gun-ports and shot-holes, in a few of which the wooden sills still remain in place.

BUSBIE STRATHCLYDE
(NS 397390)
Ruins of a seventeenth-century tower-house.

CADZOW HAMILTON, STRATHCLYDE
(NS 734536)
There is thought to have been an early castle here in the twelfth century, used by David I and succeeding kings. It stood on a natural hill overlooking the Avon, and was later surrounded by a formidable curtain and a wide ditch. Two round towers project into the ditch, one at each end of a stretch of the curtain that is less well protected. One tower has wide-mouth gun-ports, inserted in the sixteenth century, which cover the ditch, since the tower is hardly higher than the ditch. The other, now only fragmentary, presumably had gun-ports as well. The artillery-type fortifications (c.1542–4) are the work of the 2nd Earl of Arran.

CAERLAVEROCK
DUMFRIES AND GALLOWAY
(NY 026656)
'Caerlaverock was so strong a castle that it feared no siege … it had but three sides round it, with a tower at each corner but one of them was a double one, so high, so long and so wide, that the gate was underneath it, well made and strong, with a drawbridge and a sufficiency of other defences … and it had good walls, and good ditches filled right up to the brim with water …'. This comes from a translation of a contemporary French rhyming account of the siege of the castle in 1300 by Edward I, *Le Siège de Karlaverock* and it is an apt summary of the castle's defensive features which are hardly less imposing to look at today. It was probably built c.1280–90, although it may have been raised c.1290–1300 by the English during the struggle between Edward I and the Scots.

It was besieged c.1300 by Edward I, and it

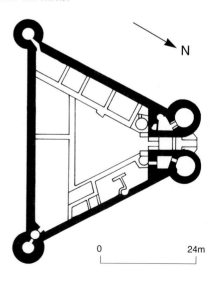

Caerlaverock: the only triangular-plan castle in the UK. The bold lines represent the earlier fortified walls and towers.

N

0   24m

surrendered. The English held it for 12 years. The constable then changed sides and declared for Robert Bruce, dismantling the castle in accord with the Scottish King's policy of slighting castles. Caerlaverock deteriorated but it was rebuilt in the fifteenth century, carefully following the original design. The massive gatehouse was strengthened and altered internally to make it residential, and the quarters were protected from dangers at ground level. Gun-ports were inserted into the stonework for cannons and other small guns some time near the end of the sixteenth century, and this may have helped the garrison defending it for the king against the Covenanters in 1640.

Caerlaverock's triangular plan is unusual but simple; an enclosure of three massive curtains covered by angle-towers on two corners and the huge gatehouse on the third. It was made concentric by surrounding it with an inner moat, then ramparts of earth which in their earlier years were topped with palisading, then another moat and finally a higher ring of earthworks. Attackers had to cross two separate bridges before even reaching the daunting gatehouse, rendered more forbidding still (in the fifteenth century) by the addition of machicolated parapets and toughened stonework over and round the gateway.

It was besieged several times, large parts of it demolished and then rebuilt, abandoned and then reoccupied and garrisoned for war. In the 1630s, its owner, Lord Nithsdale, built a three-storeyed residential block against the inner face of the eastern wall, in Classical Renaissance style and quite out of character. Nonetheless, much remains of its formidable defensive building work.

CAIRNBULG RATHEN, GRAMPIAN
(NK 017639)

Cairnbulg is situated on the right-hand bank of Philorth Water near Fraserburgh. It used to be called Philorth. It was raised in the mid-thirteenth century by the Comyn family and was a rectangular tower, some 21.3 metres (70 ft) tall, which had a smaller tower as a wing. Additions were made in later years, and it was converted largely to a mansion at the end of the last century. The old parts can be seen.

CAIRNS MIDCALDER, LOTHIAN
(NT 090605)

Cairns is in ruinous condition. It was a roughly L-plan tower-house of the fifteenth century. The main tower was 8.2 x 7.1 metres (27 x 23½ ft), with walls from 1.4–1.8 metres (4½–6 ft) thick, and it was three-storeyed to the parapet. The extension making it L-shaped was a wing about 5.5 metres (18 ft) square. The staircase is in a rounded extension on the outer angle between the two towers.

CAISTEAL DUBH PITLOCHRY, TAYSIDE
(NN 947589)

Caisteal Dubh means Black Castle. It is a ruin of a thirteenth-century rectangular stone enclosure which had cylindrical corner towers. The enclosure was about 33.5 x 25.9 metres (110 x 85 ft). Some walling remains to a height of about 3 metres (10 ft). The castle is also known as Moulin Castle.

CAKEMUIR NR CRICHTON, LOTHIAN
(NT 412590)

Cakemuir belonged to the Wauchope family. Built in the sixteenth century as a rectangular tower-house, 9.1 x 7.5 metres (30 x 24½ ft), four storeys tall with gun-loops along the top-storey wall level, it has been added to since then, notably in the nineteenth century. The castle is in good condition.

CAPRINGTON STRATHCLYDE
NS 408362

A fifteenth-century castle of towers and curtain walling that has been absorbed in much later buildings.

CARBERRY INVERESK, LOTHIAN
(NT 363696)

A small but massive tower of early sixteenth-century construction, possibly on an earlier building's remains. The tower is at the north-west end of a later building which incorporates it. It is 9.1 x 10.3 metres (30 x 34 ft), with walls over 2.1 metres (7 ft) thick in most places. There are four storeys to the heavy rounded parapets, which have wide-mouthed gun-ports. Note that the parapet is supported in places with corbels bearing carved faces of angels.

CARDONESS NR GATEHOUSE OF FLEET, DUMFRIES AND GALLOWAY
(NX 590553)

Cardoness is much ruined. It stands on a rock platform overlooking the Water of Fleet. Its principal feature is a fifteenth-century great tower, about 16.1 metres (53 ft) to a roofless top, 13.1 x 9.7 metres (43 x 32 ft), with walls over 2.4 metres (8 ft) thick. This tower is in better preservation than the rest of the buildings. The basement storey is vaulted. One interesting feature is that two rooms which are positioned end to end on one storey are served by a corridor in the wall thickness. The tower has both wide-mouthed and keyhole gun-ports. Inside, the now floorless great hall has a fine fireplace with clustered pillars on moulded bases.

CARNASSERIE
NR KILMARTIN, STRATHCLYDE
(NM 838009)

Carnasserie was once the home of John Carsewell, Bishop of the Isles (after the Reformation), who translated John Knox's *Liturgy* into Gaelic. Built in the second part of the sixteenth century, it is based on a tower-house and is square-plan, with parapet and rounded turrets projecting over the corners. Gun-ports were inserted in the walls for hand-guns. The tower has many interesting architectural details, and the quality of the masonry is high. It was built of a local stone called schist. There is well-cut heraldic carving in the stonework, particularly round the entrance. There are remains of walling that once formed a courtyard to the south and west. The castle was captured during the rebellion of the Duke of Argyll in 1685 and was blown up, although enough remains to see something of what it would once have been like.

CARNOUSIE FORGLEN, GRAMPIAN
(NJ 672504)

The remains of this derelict castle reveal an original Z-plan tower-house that had one square tower and one round tower diagonally opposed. Built in the 1570s, the tower-house was modified in the seventeenth and eighteenth centuries to include a rectangular building attachment. It has been restored in recent years.

CARRICK STRATHCLYDE
(NS 193945)

The remains of an early fifteenth-century rectangular tower-house, four storeys high, stand on a rock projecting into Loch Goil. It was once a hunting lodge which was used by the Stewart kings. Note the interesting garderobes, the exits of which are in ashlar in otherwise rubble walling.

CARSCREUGH
OLD LUCE, DUMFRIES AND GALLOWAY
(NX 223599)

A sixteenth-century tower-house consisting of a main block of four storeys plus garret, two square towers, one at the north-west and one at the south-west end, and a cylindrical staircase tower. The stair tower and the south-west tower remain standing, but the castle is pretty ruinous.

CARSEWALL
KIRKCOLM, DUMFRIES AND GALLOWAY
(NW 991714)

A fifteenth-century rectangular great tower, 12.8 x 10 metres (42 x 33 ft), with walls about 2.4 metres (8 ft) thick, Carsewall was raised on a mound. Today, there is little to see above the vaulted ground floor.

CARSLUITH
NR CREETOWN, DUMFRIES AND GALLOWAY
(NX 495542)

A basically L-plan tower-house castle of the sixteenth century standing on a promontory overlooking Wigtown Bay. The main block is rectangular, 9.7 x 7.3 metres (32 x 24 ft), with

The fifteenth-century, four-storeyed tower-house is on the right in this view of Castle Campbell.

the wing tower containing the spiral staircase. The staircase leads to the second floor, but after that the top levels are reached by another staircase in the wall thickness. It is thought that the staircase tower was added later.

CARY NR FALKIRK, CENTRAL
(NS 786775)

A late fifteenth-century tower-house built by the Livingstones, which has seventeenth- and eighteenth-century additions. It is L-shaped, the main wing being 10 x 6.7 metres (33 x 22 ft). The tower incorporates some stone from a Roman fort which had been built on the Antonine Wall nearby. There is not much left of the remainder of the castle, due to railway works carried out in the late nineteenth century.

CASKIEBEN GRAMPIAN
(NH 788213)

This is a sixteenth-century Z-plan tower-house whose remains are absorbed by a later baronial mansion.

CASSILIS KILMICHAEL, STRATHCLYDE
(NS 340128)

Cassilis House is a reconstruction of an older, massive rectangular tower of the fourteenth century. To this tower was added a square-plan staircase tower at the south-east in the

seventeenth century. The original tower had walls over 4.6 metres (15 ft) thick at the base, and it rose to four storeys. In the thickness of the northern wall was a pit prison.

CASTLE CAMPBELL DOLLAR, CENTRAL
(NS 961993)

A complex of buildings round a tall, rectangular tower sited on a rocky mound in Dollar Glen, Castle Campbell is a castle of three building periods. The rectangular tower was the earliest stone building, raised in the late fifteenth century on what may have been a much earlier motte castle site. This tower is in a very good state of preservation. It has four storeys, three of which are vaulted. The dimensions are about 13.4 x 8.8 metres (44 x 29 ft), rising to about 18.3 metres (60 ft) to the parapet. It has two entrances, one on the west on the ground floor, and another on the first floor on the south. Interestingly, the north wall has no openings at all in the first two storeys. Originally, floors were reached by straight-flight mural stairways, but in the sixteenth century a square-plan stair tower with spiral staircase was built against the south wall, providing access to all floors. The tower contains a pit prison. The top-floor ceiling was vaulted at a later date, probably the late sixteenth century, and it bears masks painted on the stonework. The present roof is a much later replacement, which has helped to keep the tower in such good condition.

The second building period was some time in the sixteenth century, probably the earlier half, and the main work was a southern range outside the original barmkin of the fifteenth-century tower (since disappeared). And in the late sixteenth century (possibly stretching over into the seventeenth century), a shorter range was added at the east, joining the original tower to the south range. A curtain at the west and at the north-west (with a gateway) completed a quadrangle.

CASTLE DONNAN KINTAIL, HIGHLAND
(NG 881258)

Also known as Eilean Donan, this much-photographed castle is a major twentieth-century reconstruction of a strong, early thirteenth-century fortress probably built by Alexander II (1214–49) during his campaigns against the Vikings, determined to hold the Western Isles and parts of the western mainland. The thirteenth-century castle, a stone curtain enclosure (which was given a

rectangular great tower measuring 17.4 x 13.1 metres [57 x 43 ft] with 3-metre [10-ft] thick walls in the fourteenth century) evidently replaced an original Iron Age vitrified fort. The castle stands on an islet and is joined to the mainland by a causeway.

CASTLE FRASER
MONYMUSK, GRAMPIAN
(NJ 722125)

A National Trust for Scotland castle that has been restored and maintained, Castle Fraser was a rectangular tower castle originally built in the fifteenth century. In the late sixteenth century it was converted to Z-plan. In the early seventeenth century, the main core was enlarged under the supervision of John Bell, a noted mason in his time, who left his mark on a plate on the north face. The diagonally opposing towers are cylindrical (south-east) and rectangular (north-west). They are four-storeyed, with an attic above, and are equipped with ornamented shot-holes. The corbelling at the wall-head of the rectangular central block consists of a band of false gun-barrel gargoyles. It is also provided with a 'luggie' between the vaulting of the hall and the chamber above, formed in the thickness of the wall which was attained from behind a window shutter. The 'spy' or 'eavesdropper' could slip into a cubicle by lifting a stone slab, replace it and listen quietly to goings-on in the hall.

CASTLE GRANT HIGHLAND
(NJ 041302)

An L-plan tower-house of the sixteenth century, built probably in two stages, was absorbed by a new mansion of the 1740–70 period. It has been neglected for a long time.

CASTLE KENNEDY
STRANRAER, DUMFRIES AND GALLOWAY
(NX 111605)

Kennedy was built probably in the early seventeenth century. It was a rectangular tower block with a square wing at one end, well built with dressed quoins. The tower was burned in 1716, but the shell stands today.

At Castle Fraser, the basic rectangular tower-house of the fifteenth century was converted to a Z-plan in the late sixteenth century, with one round tower and one square tower diagonally opposite. There is a further extension on the left.

Then it was home to the 2nd Earl of Stair, subsequently a Field Marshal in the British army.

CASTLE LACHLAN STRATHCLYDE
(NS 005592)

This is an interesting ruin. From the outside it appears to be a large, rectangular tower-house. Its external dimensions are 21.3 x 16.4 metres (70 x 54 ft) and today it reaches over 12.2 metres (40 ft) high. But inside it is in fact in two parts round an open inner courtyard. It belonged to the Maclachlans, but during the Second Jacobite Rising (1745–6) it was fired on by government warships. Apparently, the Maclachlans abandoned the castle and it has not been occupied since.

CASTLE LEOD
STRATHPEFFER, HIGHLAND
(NH 486593)

Leod was a late sixteenth-century L-plan tower-house with bartizans at the angles and an open parapet. It has been modified, and it is in excellent condition. It can be visited on application.

CASTLE OF PARK
OLD LUCE, DUMFRIES AND GALLOWAY
(NX 188571)

Castle of Park stands over the shore of Luce Bay. It was built c.1590 as a four-storey plus

attic tower-house. It received two wings, one a two-storeyed block at the south-east and the other a single-storey building at the north-east, both in the eighteenth century, but these have since disappeared. The remaining tower building has been restored and can be seen from the outside.

CASTLE ROY HIGHLAND
(NJ 007219)

A very early stone castle, beginning in the thirteenth century as a quadrilateral stone enclosure surrounded by a ditch beside the River Spey. There is a square tower on the north-west of the quadrilateral and a small garderobe tower along the west wall, worked into the wall. Timber buildings were erected against the inside of the enclosure wall, as is shown by grooves in the stonework. The wall is about 2.1 metres (7 ft) thick, and is now from 3–4.6 metres (10–15 ft) high. The entrance was through a doorway in the north.

CASTLE STALKER
CREAGAN, STRATHCLYDE
(NM 921473)

You can see this relic on a small island in Loch Laich from the road driving from Ballachulish down towards Oban. Access to Stalker has apparently always been by boat. The building was a rectangular tower-house,

about 13.7 x 11 metres (45 x 36 ft), and with walls about 2.7 metres (9 ft) thick. The ground storey contained a pit prison. The entrance was at first-floor level, originally reached by a wooden ladder or stairway, later converted to a stone stepway. Stalker was built in the mid-sixteenth century, fell into disrepair after the Second Jacobite Rising (1745–6) and was restored in the present century.

CASTLE STEWART
DUMFRIES AND GALLOWAY
(NX 379690)
A seventeenth-century courtyard castle which has a square great tower with rounded angles.

CASTLEMILK GLASGOW, STRATHCLYDE
(NS 609593)
There was a tower-house of the fifteenth century here, used by the Stewarts, but it has been absorbed by the present children's home, formerly a Stewart mansion.

CAWDOR HIGHLAND
(NH 847499)
This palatial range of buildings belongs to the Earl of Cawdor, whose family has owned the castle since the sixteenth century. Before that it was the seat of the Calders, who were also Thanes of Cawdor. There was an earlier stone building, a tower-house of the fourteenth century, on the site. This was absorbed by a later rectangular great tower built in 1454 following a licence to fortify his home granted to John Calder, Thane of Cawdor, by James II of Scotland. This licence allowed him to erect his castle '… with walls and ditches and [to] equip the summit with turrets and means of defence', but on the understanding that it was always to be open to the king and his successors. The tower which resulted was substantial, and the lower parts of it survive today, heightened by one of the Cawdors in the sixteenth century. The walls are between 2.7–3.3 metres (9–11 ft) thick, and the basement is vaulted. In the fifteenth century it was enclosed by a deep ditch with drawbridge across. The entrance had an iron yett and was at first-floor level (which today has a large window in the space).

The later extensions and improvements were residential and are not relevant to this gazetteer, but the castle is most certainly worth a visit not merely for the great tower, but also to see how a simple structure can

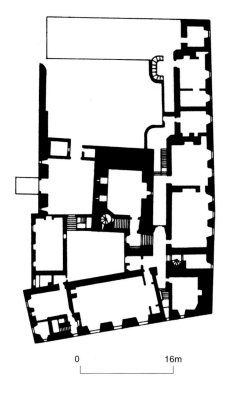

Cawdor: ground plan. Note the original rectangular tower-house in the centre, with thick walls and very limited window allowance.

have 'an expansive establishment built round it' (S.H. Cruden).

CESSFORD ECKFORD, BORDERS
(NT 738238)
Once regarded as one of the strongest castles in Scotland, Cessford was a massive L-plan great tower of the early fifteenth century, with very thick walls and vaulted basement, and possibly vaulted all the way up in the smaller arm of the 'L'. The stone is local red freestone. The tower was dismantled in the mid-sixteenth century, later restored, and then damaged once again.

CLACKMANNAN CENTRAL
(NS 906919)
A substantial L-plan tower-house, with additional buildings, stands on the summit of King's Seat Hill by Clackmannan. The oldest part is the north end of the L-plan, an oblong tower of the late fourteenth century. The 'L' wing was added in the fifteenth century and is five storeys tall, thus one storey higher than the original tower. The castle was once

surrounded by a moat with a drawbridge across it. Note the machicolations and battlements round the parapets. The castle has a fine commanding view of the land beyond the town towards the Firth of Forth.

CLAYPOTTS NR DUNDEE, TAYSIDE
(NO 453318)
Claypotts is a Z-plan castle, and it was built in the 1570s by John Strachan, lord of Claypotts. It began as a rectangular, gabled four-storeyed great tower-house of hard local stone. Cylindrical towers were grafted diagonally on to the north-east and south-west corners, which rose to the same height as the bottom of the central tower's gable, thus forming a Z-plan (see plan). The towers were topped with overhanging square cap-houses (inside which are garrets) and the towers were large enough to contain rooms all the way up. Each of the towers covers two surfaces of the centre building which in turn covers both towers. In theory it was impossible to approach the castle from any angle without being in the direct line of fire at ground level through a series of wide-mouthed gun-ports a few feet up the

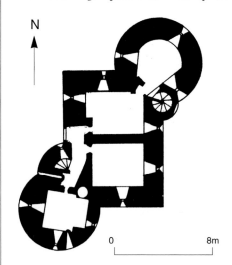

Claypotts: ground-floor plan.

walls on every face. One shot-hole was put in the back of the kitchen fireplace, on the eastern side of the south-west tower. Another was put just outside the entrance door, at right-angles and about 1.2 metres (4 ft) up.

Claypotts is one of several dozen Z-plan castles built in Scotland in the sixteenth and seventeenth centuries (cf., Noltland, Kilcoy), and is in an excellent state of preservation.

There were other buildings round it but these have vanished. The all-round defensiveness of Claypotts was never put to the test. In the 1620s Claypotts was sold to Sir William Graham of Claverhouse, and it was his great-grandson, John Graham, who was to become famous through Scotland as Bonnie Dundee: he became 1st Viscount Dundee, and raised an army to help the cause of James II (and VII), driven off the English throne late in 1688 by English supporters of William of Orange. When James II was deposed, Claypotts was forfeited to William III who gave it to the Marquis of Douglas, and it has descended through the family to the late Lord Home who put it under the guardianship of the Scottish Development Department.

CLEISH TAYSIDE
(NT 082979)
Restored in the 1840s, Cleish Castle is L-plan and was built of ashlar masonry in the sixteenth century. The main rectangular block of the tower-house is 12.2 x 8.8 metres (40 x 29 ft) and rose to five storeys. The two bottom levels are thought to have been built earlier than the upper three, which may have been as late as the early seventeenth century. The outer angles are rounded.

CLONBEITH STRATHCLYDE
(NS 338456)
A tower-house of plain rectangular plan, of the late sixteenth century, of which only the basement survives.

CLUNY CRICHTON
NR BANCHORY, GRAMPIAN
(NO 685997)
This L-plan tower-house was built in the 1660s. It had a rectangular staircase tower set in the angle. The tower-house was three-storeyed with a garret. The entrance was protected by gun-ports.

COLLAIRNIE DUNBOY, FIFE
(NO 306171)
A fortified building which had ornamented shot-holes, Collairnie was once of L-plan within a stone barmkin. It was built in the sixteenth century. A tall wing was added in the 1580s with four storeys plus garret. The castle has been substantially mutilated, probably by time and exposure, and the main tower is now only one storey tall. It is used as a farm building, and thus may be missed when driving by. The wing contains painted ceilings, which bear the arms of several families associated with the castle and with Fife generally.

COLLISTON ARBROATH, TAYSIDE
(NO 613464)
A Z-plan castle of conventional shape, built in 1553, Colliston's main block is 13.7 x 7.3 metres (45 x 24 ft), and has two diagonally opposite cylindrical towers. The castle's original entrance was guarded by two shot-holes, but a seventeenth-century modification moved the entrance into the middle of the main block (this is dated 1621). Further modifications were carried out in the eighteenth and nineteenth centuries which altered the castle into a residence without a military role.

COMLONGON
DUMFRIES AND GALLOWAY
(NY 079689)
This is a really splendid Scottish tower-house of c.1435, which dominates the north shores of the Solway Firth. It is one of three great fifteenth-century castles (the others are Borthwick, and Elphinstone before it was partly demolished) in which the great tower predominates and which are perhaps the nearest equivalent in Scotland of the English (and Welsh) great towers. Comlongon is a seat of the Earls of Mansfield (Murrays) and is in fine condition. It is occupied but not open.

The great tower is a massive structure of four storeys, the basement vaulted and the others having timber floors. At the top of the tower is an over-sailing parapet upon multiple corbelling, the parapet battlemented on three sides and provided with cap-houses on two corners. The fourth side has a later roofed gallery. Inside, each floor consists of one main large room, with chambers, closets and stairs opening off into the tower's wall thicknesses. The first floor has the great hall. This has two fireplaces, one at each end. One is in an arched recess which was once a kitchen, and which is reached directly from the spiral staircase passing up and down the corner of the tower. The recess is now separated from the hall, but at one time probably had a screen with serving hatches.

The tower's storeys are reached by means of an unbroken spiral staircase from beside the entrance passage in the basement right to the parapet where it emerges into a turret. Like Borthwick, Comlongon's great tower was not provided with gun-ports or arrow-loops.

COMRIE TAYSIDE
(NN 787486)
An L-plan castle of the Menzies clan, built in the sixteenth century, Comrie is now ruined.

CONZIE GRAMPIAN
(NJ 095450)
A seventeenth-century castle, with little original work remaining.

CORGARFF COCK BRIDGE, GRAMPIAN
(NJ 255087)
A well-restored, plain, rectangular tower-house of the sixteenth century, about 10.7 x 7.3 metres (35 x 24 ft), Corgarff was modified after the Second Jacobite Rising by the Hanoverian government: a single-storeyed building was added to each short end, and the whole tower was enclosed inside a star-shaped barmkin with narrow vertical loops for guns. This provided a useful fortress for guarding crossings of the rivers Dee, Don and Avon by Cock Bridge. A peace-keeping garrison was maintained at Corgarff for many years, right into the 1830s.

Corgarff was the scene of an appalling crime in 1571. During a quarrel between the Forbes family, holding the castle, and the Gordons of Auchindoun, the 'ground wall stone' of the garderobe chute was removed by one of the Gordons and fire was inserted up the flue which set the castle alight (cf., Balvaird). Margaret Forbes and her family and servants were burned to death. Corgarff was burned again in 1689.

CORSBIE LEGERWOOD, BORDERS
(NT 607438)
A rectangular-plan fortress with walls about 1.8 metres (6 ft) thick was raised on rising ground. The tower was about 12.2 x 8.2 metres (40 x 27 ft), but it is now in a state of considerable decay.

CORSE GRAMPIAN
(NJ 549074)
This is a sixteenth-century L-plan tower-house which was built by the Forbes family. Patrick Forbes is quoted as saying, 'I will build me such a house as thieves will need to knock at ere they enter' (S.H. Cruden). This was after the previous building there had been destroyed in a raid.

A sixteenth-century tower-house stands inside Corgarff's eighteenth-century star-plan barmkin, which is equipped with prominent vertical loops.

CORSINDAE GRAMPIAN
(NJ 685088)
Now called Corsindae House, the castle was a sixteenth-century L-plan tower. It has been absorbed in the present building.

CORTACHY TAYSIDE
(NO 398595)
This enclosure castle of the fifteenth century was considerably altered in the nineteenth century to include towers and turrets which were purely decorative. Originally more simple, the castle had four cylindrical flanking towers, and of this structure some of the curtain and three towers remain, absorbed in the newer work. The castle belonged to the Ogilvys, as it still does today.

COULL GRAMPIAN
(NJ 512022)
Coull Castle was built in the mid-thirteenth century. Its plan seems to have been roughly a pentagonal courtyard walled in stone. The remains of three flanking towers were discovered in excavations earlier this century, but the castle is in such a poor state that it is not very easy to determine its true shape. It was dismantled c.1307 by Robert Bruce, following his policy of slighting castles.

COULTHALLEY
CARNWARTH, STRATHCLYDE
(NS 971481)
This castle is mentioned in a late twelfth-century document, although we do not know its form. It was rebuilt c.1375, altered c.1415 and again c.1520. It emerged as an enclosure with three towers, one of them as part of the curtain wall. The castle was besieged in 1557 and rebuilt. Part of the rebuilding was an L-plan tower, but not much of the castle is left.

COVINGTON STRATHCLYDE
(NS 975399)
Covington was an earthwork castle of the late twelfth or the early thirteenth century, surrounded by a ditch. In the fifteenth century a rectangular four-storeyed tower-house was built on the site, with walls 3 metres (10 ft) thick, some of which now reach as high as 13.7 metres (45 ft). The tower was built with some skill. The four corners have ashlar quoins, and the arrow-loops are dressed with ashlar at all levels. A garderobe was discovered in 1982.

COXTON TOWER
Nr Elgin, Highland
(NJ 262607)

Coxton Tower was built in 1644. It has four storeys, measures 7 metres (23 ft) square, with walls 1.4 metres (4½ ft) thick, and the principal entrance is on the south wall, 2.7 metres (9 ft) above the ground. It has corbelled bartizans on two opposing corners and rectangular crenellated bartizans on the other two. The four storeys are all vaulted. The roof is unsound.

CRAIG Highland
(NH 632638)

Craig is an L-plan tower built in the sixteenth century, situated on the Black Isle. The tower is now in ruins.

CRAIG Auchindoir, Grampian
(NJ 470248)

Built in the mid-sixteenth century as an L-plan, three-storeyed (plus garret) castle with battlements, which was given ribbed vaulting and provided with wide-mouthed gun-ports at lower levels, Craig has been extensively altered and enlarged to include, among other features, a small courtyard of the eighteenth century. S.H. Cruden states that there was originally an oratory over the entrance to the great hall (as at Towie Barclay). The castle was built by the Gordon family.

CRAIGCAFFIE
Inch, Dumfries and Galloway
(NX 088641)

A very small castle consisting of a rectangular tower with vaulted ground floor and rising to three storeys plus attic. It is about 9.1 x 5.8 metres (30 x 19 ft) and hardly big enough for a comfortable residence, one might suppose. There are fragments of some kind of courtyard. The tower-house well rises in the ground floor. The parapet is crenellated, with rounded corner half-turrets. The tower-house was built in the 1570s.

CRAIGCROOK
Nr Edinburgh, Lothian
(NT 210742)

A sixteenth-century tower-house: the three-storeyed main block, 18.3 x 6 metres (60 x 20 ft) with wing towers (one cylindrical and one square staircase tower),is incorporated in later renovations and additions.

Craigie began as an early thirteenth-century hall-tower castle, and was enlarged in the fifteenth and sixteenth centuries.

CRAIGIE Strathclyde
(NS 409317)

Most Scottish tower-houses were vertical rather than horizontal buildings, but there were some, generally of the earlier centuries, which were long, rectangular hall-towers constructed in the manner of Chepstow in Wales or Christchurch in Hampshire. One was Craigie (but see also Skipness and Kindrochit). Craigie probably dates from the early 1200s, and the original long hall structure was incorporated in a later fifteenth-century tower-house. The earlier hall had a flush battlemented parapet round its wall-tops. The embrasures were subsequently filled in and the walls built up and widened outwards to form a new hall-tower, which had rib-vaulting at the top. The ribs sprang from sculptured corbels set in the wall-walk of the first hall-tower. The original entrance was a round-headed arch at ground-floor level on the northern long side.

The hall-tower stood on a mound which was enclosed by a moat. There was a shot-hole near the entrance, inserted probably in the sixteenth century. It is largely ruined.

CRAIGIEVAR Alford, Grampian
(NJ 566095)

This stepped L-plan castle is tall, substantial and formidable to look at. Built c.1620–6, it has been described as being in the front rank of European architecture. Internally, it is luxuriously appointed, with a vaulted roof to the great hall bearing much decoration, including a moulded plaster ceiling of which there are more in other main rooms, straight flights of stairs with landings, as well as spirals. And it has been changed but little since the

Craigievar: first-floor plan (after S.H. Cruden).

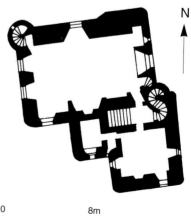

0   8m
N

1620s. Moreover, it has been continuously occupied since its foundation.

Craigievar has seven storeys, and is topped with finely corbelled, well-proportioned cylindrical turrets with conical roofs. The re-entrant tower is surmounted by a pillar balustrade. The top half of the tower is well provided with windows but lower storeys have few, and these are mostly small. Palatial rather than military, it was fortified with ramparts, and a courtyard wall with towers and an outer gateway. There was only one way in – through a massive iron-studded door, past a yett and through a pair of equally stout doors.

The castle is in excellent condition and, high in the hill, has a fairy-tale appearance.

CRAIGMADDIE STRATHCLYDE
(NS 575765)

A sixteenth-century tower-house, of which only one storey remains. The dimensions are 8.5 x 7.3 metres (28 x 24 ft) and the walls are 1.5 metres (5 ft) thick, presumably all the way to the parapet.

CRAIGMILLAR

LIBERTON, EDINBURGH, LOTHIAN
(NT 285710)

This castle is famous chiefly because it was the place where the murder of Darnley, husband of Mary, Queen of Scots, was planned while the queen was actually staying there in 1566–7. It is also interesting by virtue of its plan, which is the result of four main periods of building.

The castle began in the late fourteenth century as a large L-plan tower-house, 16.1 x 14.9 metres (53 x 49 ft). It has walls over 2.7 metres (9 ft) thick, and is built with close-texture rubble of red-grey sandstone, with long, dressed quoins. The entrance to the castle is positioned in the small extending wing from the south side of the tower, which also contains a spiral staircase.

The great tower-house was fortified in the 1420s by a massive quadrangular enclosure wall on both sides of the south of the tower where a cliff forms a natural defence, and extending wide on the other three sides to form a courtyard, with rounded towers on the corners which were machicolated. The enclosure wall is 1.5 metres (5 ft) thick and about 8.5 metres (28 ft) tall. Ranges of buildings were erected along the inside of three sectors of the enclosure. The entrance is in the north wall.

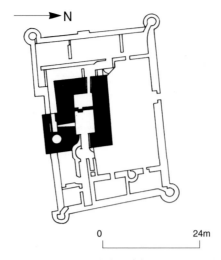

Craigmillar: the ground plan of the inner courtyard. The L-plan tower is from the late fourteenth/early fifteenth century, and the remainder is largely fifteenth century.

Gun-ports were built in the north-east and the south-east corner towers. There are also gun-ports of later insertion in three of the four towers.

Extensions were added to the quadrangle in the sixteenth and seventeenth centuries and, to its north, a large outer courtyard enclosed in a curtain wall was created in the late sixteenth or early seventeenth century. On the east corner of this outer enclosure is a dovecot with gun-ports.

Craigmillar was attacked and burned by the Earl of Hertford (later the Duke of Somerset) on behalf of Henry VIII in 1544. But it was restored in time for Mary, Queen of Scots to reside there from 1566–7, after the murder of her Italian secretary, David Rizzio, by her husband Darnley. During her stay, a band of conspirators, Argyll, Huntly, Bothwell, 'Mr Secretary' Maitland and Gilbert Balfour, met and plotted to ensure that 'sic ane young fool and proud tirrane suld not reign nor bear reull over thame: and that … he sould be put off, by ane way or uther …' that is, Darnley was to be dispatched.

CRAIGNETHAN

NR LANARK, STRATHCLYDE
(NS 815463)

Craignethan stands on a rocky promontory overlooking the Clyde. Although in ruinous condition, it possesses numerous features of interest. A great deal of careful restoration work has been carried out by the Scottish Development Department.

Craignethan was built to incorporate artillery defences. It consists of a western outer

In the foreground of this view of Craignethan is the fourteenth-century L-plan tower-house, and to its right part of the later quadrangular enclosure with ranges of buildings.

courtyard, dating from c.mid-sixteenth century, rectangular in plan with two square-plan corner towers, and surrounded on three sides by a curtain wall. On the east side the yard is protected by a ditch. In the west wall is a fine battlemented gateway, defended at low level by businesslike gun-ports. In the south-west corner was built a private house, a century after the courtyard. This house is still standing. To the east of this courtyard is the older part of the castle, built mostly between 1525 and 1545. This consists of a second courtyard surrounded by a thick barmkin with two rectangular towers on the east, at the north-east and south-east corners, a median tower on the north and a turret projection containing a wheel staircase on the south. On the west was built a huge stone structure, running from north to south across the ends of the barmkin, three storeys equivalent in height, with walls over 4.9 metres (16 ft) thick, with its ends turning at right-angles inwards to meet the barmkin. This was equipped with gun-ports and battlements. This structure has now disappeared down to ground-level. It edged the ditch separating the inner courtyard from the outer courtyard.

The principal feature of the inner courtyard was the substantial rectangular tower-house, much of which still stands. It is about 10.7 metres (35 ft) tall, three-storeyed to the parapet, and built of rubble masonry. It is about 15.8 x 20 metres (52 x 65 ft). Its west wall is about 3.6–4 metres (12–13 ft) thick. The roof is missing but there is a wide parapet wall-walk. The tower has no gun-ports but they were plentiful in the flanking towers along the barmkin. The south-east tower today shows gun-ports near the top which covered the slopes of the promontory at this particular point.

Craignethan was built by Sir James Hamilton, bastard son of the 1st Earl of Arran, but because the Hamiltons had backed Mary, Queen of Scots against the forces of the Regent, the castle was slighted by order of the government in 1579.

CRAIGSTON GRAMPIAN
(NJ 762550)

Built in 1604–7 (according to an inscription on a wall), Craigston belonged to John Urquhart, who was the grandfather of Sir Thomas Urquhart, the translator of François Rabelais' *Gargantua*. Craigston is a massive structure, with two wings at the front which

are linked by an *arc de triomphe* over the entrance (*see* Fyvie). The castle contains a fine great hall, 9.1 metres (30 ft) and nearly 6.4 metres (21 ft) high.

CRAIL FIFE
(NO 614075)

Crail is on the north coast of the Forth Estuary. The site is practically bare, but there is a stretch of mortared wall about 4.9 metres (16 ft) long, 1.2 metres (4 ft) wide and 1.2 metres high which may be the remains of a hall-tower. It is thought to date from perhaps the twelfth century.

CRATHES BANCHORY, GRAMPIAN
(NO 735968)

This is an impressive tower-house castle, considerably restored and in fine condition; Crathes is well known for some interesting painted ceilings, notably in the Chamber of the Nine Muses. One end has had a modern extension added.

Crathes began as an L-plan tower-house in 1553. A date panel of 1596 suggests the completion of improvements rather than the end of the original building work, for a period of 43 years is long for a simple tower-house. Many of the alterations and improvements were done by masons from the Bell family. There have also been further alterations, including a three-storeyed east wing, another later wing, and some ornamental corbelled turrets. The original tower was equipped with a 'luggie', an iron yett by the door and a re-entrant tower for a staircase.

CRAWFORD STRATHCLYDE
(NS 954214)

Crawford is mentioned in documents of c.1175–8. It was a motte castle which by that time had probably received a stone curtain of rectilinear plan round the summit. Traces of a hall were found. But the remains there today are chiefly of a much later seventeenth-century structure which is not easy to define.

CRICHTON NR PATHHEAD, LOTHIAN
(NT 380611)

Crichton Castle is a formidable structure of several periods, whose buildings are ranged round a square courtyard; from the top of the old tower-house it is possible to see Borthwick Castle, 8 km (5 miles) away. It is now in ruins and has little more than its walls, yet it is possible to trace the various building

periods. The first structure was a rectangular tower-house of coursed rubble, which originally rose three storeys (now only two storeys tall), measuring 14.6 x 10.7 metres (48 x 35 ft), with walls about 2.4 metres (8 ft) thick. This was built probably by John de Crichton towards the end of the fourteenth century. The basement is vaulted, and has a prison cell and a kitchen. The tower-house was originally surrounded by a barmkin, later demolished and built over.

In the second phase the once massive gatehouse-tower at south-west was built a few feet away from the tower-house. This was erected probably in the 1440s by John de Crichton's son, William, who became Lord Chancellor, and who virtually managed Scotland during some of the minority years of James II. The gatehouse-tower was a powerful structure. Entrance was through a passage in the centre of the ground floor, but this was blocked up in a later building period. The storey above the ground floor was principally taken up by a long hall right across. The walls of this gatehouse are 1.8 metres (6 ft) thick, and the rectangular dimensions of the block are 21 x 11.5 metres (69 x 38 ft). The top storey of the building, which contained a second hall, carried a machicolated parapet outside.

The third phase, later in the fifteenth century, was a range of buildings on the north-west, at right-angles to the original tower-house and projecting out beyond its north-west wall. The fourth phase, built perhaps only a short while after the third, was a western range, three storeys high except for

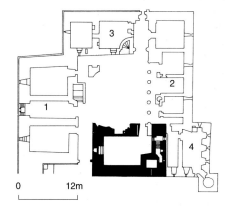

Crichton: (after S.H. Cruden). The bold lines indicate the original rectangular tower of the late fourteenth century. The other ranges were added later, in order of numbers.

the south-west end which actually rises to six storeys. This range contained a variety of living rooms, cellars, offices and so on, and a postern gate on the north-west corner. The castle was besieged and captured in 1559 in the struggle between Protestant and Catholic parties during the Scottish Reformation.

The last major phase, c.1580–90, was not of military significance but is interesting, nonetheless. The north range was heightened and developed and given an arcade at ground-level facing into the courtyard. Above this, the wall of the whole range was dressed with a spectacular diamonded facade in the Italianate manner, like the Palazzo dei Diamanti at Ferrara. This was the work of Francis, Earl of Bothwell, a cousin of Mary, Queen of Scots' Bothwell, who had spent some time adventuring in Spain and Italy and who held the castle.

CROMARTY HIGHLAND
(NH 792671)
A motte castle of the twelfth century which received a stone tower in c.1470. The remainder of the structure was added in the seventeenth century, rendering the castle L-shaped (*see* Dunskeath).

CROOKSTON GLASGOW, STRATHCLYDE
(NS 525627)
This was a substantial rectangular tower-house castle whose origins go back to the late twelfth century. The tower-house is fifteenth-century. Its plan was a rectangular tower with four rectangular corner towers (not unlike Hermitage, but much less pronounced). The walls were in part 3.6 x 4.6 metres (12–15 ft) thick, and contained numerous passages and stair flights, garderobes and chambers. There is a noticeable shortage of defensive arrow-loops

This view of Crichton shows the west range (left) with its six-storeyed tower, and to the right the mid-fifteenth-century large gatehouse-tower, the gateway of which was later blocked up.

or gun-ports, which has prompted the idea that Crookston was not a real fortress, despite its thick walls.

CRUGGLETON
DUMFRIES AND GALLOWAY
(NX 484428)
Only fragments remain of this once-important castle sited on a promontory, which began as a motte-and-bailey in the twelfth century. Traces of part of its original moat survive on the west, about 10.7 metres (35 ft) wide. In the mid-thirteenth century, stonework was added, principally a walled enclosure, which

appears to have been reinforced with some towers, and what seems to have been a great tower. Cruggleton belonged to the lords of Galloway, who ruled south-west Scotland as semi-independent princes during the Middle Ages. Excavations in the early 1980s uncovered more of the enclosure wall, a latrine tower, a kitchen and some wooden buildings.

CRUIVIE Nr Logie, Fife
(NO 419229)
A late fifteenth-century L-plan tower-house with what may have been an encircling ditch, Cruivie has some walls today rising to over 6 metres (20 ft).

CUBBIE ROO'S Isle of Wyre, Orkney
(HY 442264) SDD
One of the earliest stone castles built in Scotland, Cubbie Roo's is a slightly rhomboid great tower constructed in the mid-twelfth century. The walls are about 1.5 metres (5 ft) thick and the dimensions are about 7.6 metres (25 ft) square.

Today it rises to about 1.8 metres (6 ft) in height. At a later date, a projection was added to the north-east corner, of which only traces now remain. The tower is enclosed in an oval-shaped earthwork with ditching.

Cubbie Roo's was probably the castle (*steinkastala*) built c.1145 by Kolbein Hruga, a Viking chief, which is mentioned as the 'fine stone castle ... a safe strong-hold' in the *Orkneyinga Saga* (translated). The origin of the castle's name is explained if it was built by Kolbein Hruga.

CULCREUCH Fintry, Central
(NS 620876)
A rubble-built sixteenth-century tower-house is now part of a larger building. The tower is in a good state of repair.

DAIRSIE Fife
(NO 414160)
Two castles were built on this site. The first was probably a simple rectangular great tower constructed in the fourteenth century. In the sixteenth century it was enlarged and converted to what appears to have been a Z-plan tower-house: the main tower has three storeys with cylindrical towers at diagonally opposite corners. The castle is in poor condition, and little more than a shell of the tower remains.

DALCROSS Highland
(NH 779483)
A seventeenth-century L-plan tower-house in fine condition. It is occupied.

DALHOUSIE Nr Cockpen, Lothian
(NT 323635)
Dalhousie began as a fifteenth-century great tower-house in a courtyard enclosed by a tall, thick curtain wall. The tower is four-storeyed and L-shaped, and a staircase turret was added in the seventeenth century. Considerable alterations have been done since then. One of the entrances was protected by a drawbridge, whose lifting slots can still be seen clearly in the walling above. Dalhousie was occupied by Cromwell during his campaign in Scotland.

DALKEITH Lothian
(NT 333678)
Dalkeith House is a palatial residence of about 1700. It incorporates part of the much earlier (fifteenth-century) L-plan tower-house which was later encircled by a curtain wall. The castle belonged to the Douglases of Dalkeith, notably James Douglas, 4th Earl of Morton, Regent of Scotland, 1572–8.

DARNAWAY Nr Forres, Grampian
(NH 994550)
One of the homes of the Earls of Moray from the fourteenth century, Darnaway Castle has few remains left of its original work. But one interesting survival is the great hall, about 27.4 x 10.7 metres (90 x 35 ft), which had, and still has, an open oak roof. In the early years of the nineteenth century a substantial mansion was erected in front of the great hall.

DARNICK Nr Melrose, Borders
(NT 532343)
Sir Walter Scott was so attached to Darnick when a boy that he was called 'Duke of Darnick'. Still in remarkably good condition, it is basically a T-shaped sixteenth-century tower-house built on an earlier site. The main rectangular tower has three storeys. The south wall has a square projecting turret with a cap-house, inside which is a staircase. Entrance to the castle was through the stair turret.

Darnick is built of rubble with freestone dressings. The larger windows are of much later date. The walls of the tower are up to 2.4 metres (8 ft) or so thick, and the parapet is battlemented. There are later buildings attached to the tower.

DEAN Kilmarnock, Strathclyde
(NS 437394)
A straightforward fourteenth-century high, rectangular tower-house which has had many additional buildings erected next to it, some of them in the fifteenth century, some of much later date, and all of them now restored. The tower is almost square, rises four storeys with a battlemented parapet, and a gabled garret above, bearing in one corner a small square turret. Although part of the present palatial structure, the tower has no communication with the rest of it. Beside the stonework is the remnant of a low motte. Dean belonged to the Boyds of Kilmarnock, the *parvenu* but ambitious family which dominated the young King James III during some of his minority years in the late 1460s.

DELGATIE Turriff, Grampian
(NJ 754505)
Built c.1570–80 on the site of an earlier castle possibly of the thirteenth century, whose main feature had been a four-storeyed rectangular great tower, Delgatie was L-plan, incorporating some of the original structure. The features of this late sixteenth-century structure, notably rib-vaulted rooms, resemble contemporary work at Towie Barclay, and the question arises, were the same builders at work on the two? The castle has survived remarkably well. A mansion was added to the tower in the seventeenth century.

DIRLETON Lothian
(NT 516839)
Dirleton began as an earth and timber castle built by the de Vaux, a Norman family encouraged to settle in Scotland by David I in the twelfth century. Some time in the early thirteenth century (possibly c.1225 if the 'castellum de Dyrlton' mentioned for that date in *Liber St Marie de Dryburgh* is the stone castle of Dirleton), a cluster of towers was erected upon the earlier site. The chief structure was the substantial cylindrical great tower, facing south, about 11.3 metres (37 ft) in diameter and on a splayed plinth; it rose three storeys, two of them vaulted, and was polygonal in plan inside with a spiral staircase at the north-west corner. This is not a complete cylinder: its north-west face was chamfered off. To the west, as a projection from it, is a square-plan tower. Emerging from the north-west of this is a walled passage into a second cylindrical tower of smaller size than the great tower.

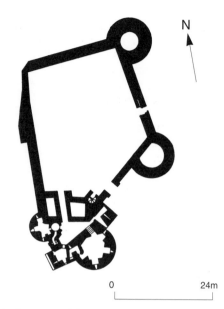

Dirleton: ground-floor plan (after S.H. Cruden). Outline of the castle as it was in the mid- to late thirteenth century. The original two round towers at right are only at foundation stage.

The cluster was joined to a curtain which travelled north-east into another cylindrical tower (only the base of which remains below later work) of smaller size than the donjon, and on the north side of that tower the curtain continued at a changed angle – northwards – to a second cylindrical tower, also reduced to traces at foundation level and now bearing later work on top. This first stage is complex, and the arrangements inside are best understood by reference to the official guide book.

In the fourteenth and fifteenth centuries, alterations and extensions were made, converting the castle into a more elaborate enclosure with ranges of buildings along the east, a more powerful gatehouse (remains of which can be seen) on the south-east, and a block on the north-east.

The cluster at the south still presents a formidable front mass. Some of its lower rooms and prison pits are hewn out of the rock on which the castle stands. It was almost surrounded by ditching, most of this cut into the rock, some of which has since been filled in. Dirleton was besieged in 1298 by Edward I's orders and the garrison was compelled to surrender. Later it was retaken by Robert Bruce who may have ordered it to be slighted. Dirleton was besieged in 1650 by General Lambert on behalf of Cromwell, since Royalists were using the castle as a refuge.

DOUNE CENTRAL
(NN 728011)

The name 'Doune' is derived from *dun*, the ancient word for a fortified town, and there are traces of prehistoric earthworks around this splendid stone enclosure castle. It was built towards the end of the fourteenth century for Robert Stewart, Duke of Albany, Regent of Scotland from c.1396–1420. Much of it has been restored in the last and the present centuries.

Doune Castle is basically an irregular pentagonal stone enclosure with a powerful frontal range on the north side, and on the west a rectangular building which breaks the obtuse angle between two of the sides. The frontal mass of the castle consists of a thick-walled (2.4–3-metre [8–10-ft]), roughly rectangular block which is made up as follows: the eastern end is a substantial gatehouse-tower, nearly 29 metres (95 ft) tall now and probably taller still in its heyday, shaped in plan like a rectangle with the two shorter sides tapering outwards; a bulging semi-cylindrical turret, five storeys tall, at the north-east; and adjacent to that a flat, rectangular projection, similarly tall,

Doune: an aerial view of the frontal mass, including the gatehouse-tower.

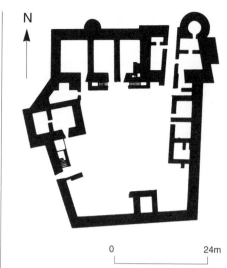

Doune: (after W. Simpson). Ground floor. The great gatehouse-tower is in the north-east corner.

solid and acting as a buttress. The entrance passes through the rectangle at a slant centrally at basement level into the open courtyard, and is protected by arrow-loops in the passage walls. The gatehouse-tower, which had a portcullis, is the strongest point of the castle. Above the entrance passage is the lord's hall, which has no way of access from the basement, but which is reached by a protected staircase to be found inside the courtyard.

In the same frontal mass, west of the

gatehouse-tower, is the retainers' hall block with tall roof (restored) and parapet. Midway along the north wall is a projecting semi-cylindrical turret with an open battlemented parapet of its own, providing a platform for covering fire against attack.

Behind the frontal mass, the castle tails off, as it were, into a quadrangle, whose curtain wall is about 12.2 metres (40 ft) high and 2.1 metres (7 ft) thick. The western rectangular building astride the join of two sides of the curtain is itself a substantial tower structure. This contains the remnants of the massive kitchen on the first floor, which is vaulted and has a remarkable fireplace about 5.5 metres (18 ft) across, spanned by a segmental arch. So substantial a kitchen is understandable for the scale of hospitality that the Regent Albany would feel obliged to extend.

Albany died in 1420. His son, Murdoch, inherited the castle, but he was put to death by James I in 1425 and Doune was taken over by the Crown. It was held for more than a century by royalty and then passed to the Earls of Moray, relatives of the King, James VI, whose descendants still hold it.

DOUNE OF INVERNOCHTY
STRATHDON, GRAMPIAN
(NJ 351129)

A very fine Norman-style motte castle was raised here with moat and encircling rampart. The summit of the mound, which is nearly 18.3 metres (60 ft) tall, is surrounded by a low mortared stone wall, about 1.8 metres (6 ft) thick, which was once much taller. The entrance is at the south end, with a square-plan tower nearby, inside the curtain. The shell of a rectangular building lies in the north segment. The rampart at the north extends as a dam, and by means of sluices controlled water from the River Don to fill the moat.

DROCHIL NEWLANDS, PEEBLES, BORDERS
(NT 162434)

Drochil is a version of a Z-plan castle. It is a four-storeyed rectangular block of two rows of apartments separated by a corridor on each floor. On the north-east and the south-west are cylindrical towers about 7.9 metres (26 ft) in diameter. The main block is 25.6 x 21 metres (84 x 69 ft). The walls are 1.8–2.1 metres (6–7 ft) thick. The towers are provided with wide-mouth gun-ports which cover the walls of the central block, but the block has no corresponding covering gun-ports. The

doorway is largely unprotected. The castle is in poor condition. It was built during the 1570s by the Regent Morton who was executed in 1581.

DRONGAN STRATHCLYDE
(NS 450178)

There are fragments of a fifteenth-century great tower castle.

DRUM NR ABERDEEN, GRAMPIAN
(NJ 796005)

The castle at Drum is a fine surviving example of a late thirteenth-century great tower. It has rounded corners, its walls are about 3.6 metres (12 ft) thick, and its original entrance was at first-floor level, as with many English great towers. It adjoins a mansion built c.1620. William Irvine, armour-bearer to Robert Bruce, was given the castle in the 1320s. His descendants held it until 1976 when it passed to the National Trust. The tower is over 21.3 metres (70 ft) tall, it has very few window openings anywhere, and contains a spiral staircase from the first floor up to the battlemented parapet and wall-walk. S.H. Cruden states that the narrow way round the wall-walk was made easier to negotiate by the insertion of special footholds and that this is not repeated in any Scottish castle.

DRUMCOLTRAN
KIRKGUNZEON, DUMFRIES AND GALLOWAY
(NX 869683)

A rectangular L-plan tower-house of the mid-sixteenth century, 10.3 x 8 metres (34 x 26½ ft), three storeys tall, with gabled roof and a staircase wing. There is an overhanging parapet supported on corbels, and a narrow wall-walk behind. The tower stands amid farm buildings and can be seen at any time.

DRUMMINOR NR RHYNIE, GRAMPIAN
(NJ 513264)

Now only a fragment of its original size, this was begun between about 1440 and 1456 by the head of the Forbes family (who still own it). Curiously, the licence to fortify was granted *after* the structure was raised. The Forbes family were continually under attack by a rival family, the Gordons, and clearly needed a stronghold. But it was ultimately to no avail, for in 1571 it was sacked. It was a tower-palace connected with buildings round a courtyard, and it has been restored with great care to attain something of its original

shape and atmosphere. The staircase positioned behind the entrance is said to be one of the widest in Aberdeenshire. The yett at the entrance was apparently stolen from the Gordons. The tower was four-storeyed, including the basement.

DRUMMOND TAYSIDE
(NN 844180)

The present mansion to be found at Drummond incorporates the lower part of a fifteenth-century tower-house in its entrance gate. The original castle was badly damaged by Cromwell in 1650.

DUART ISLE OF MULL, STRATHCLYDE
(NM 748354)

Duart Castle has been extensively rebuilt. It stands high upon a rocky mound over the entrance to the Sound of Mull and it belongs, as it did from the thirteenth to the eighteenth centuries, to the Clan Maclean. It began as an enclosure castle of late Norman construction, and its first stonework was a quadrilateral of walling, probably about 3 metres (10 ft) thick all round. This has been greatly built upon and today much of the enclosing wall is 9.1 metres (30 ft) tall. Adjacent to the enclosure was built a rectangular tower, about 19.2 x 14 metres (63 x 46 ft), also of the fourteenth century, which has been considerably restored and modified.

DUCHRAY CENTRAL
(NS 480999)

A rectangular tower, about 10.7 x 6.4 metres (35 x 21 ft), with a cylindrical tower containing the staircase on the south-east corner. It was three-storeyed, the ground floor having a barrel-vault roof. Erected in the late sixteenth century, it is in good repair.

DUDHOPE DUNDEE, TAYSIDE
(NO 395307)

Predominantly an L-plan tower-house of the very early seventeenth century, Dudhope belonged to the Grahams of Claverhouse. The tower formed part of a courtyard castle, the remaining sides of which were high stone walls which have since disappeared. The tower began with three storeys and a fourth was added later. The entrance was in the centre of the east front between a pair of squat cylindrical turrets.

Dudhope was owned by the celebrated Graham of Claverhouse, otherwise known as

Bonny Dundee, who commanded the Jacobite forces at Killiecrankie in 1689 but was killed at the moment of victory. The castle was used as army barracks for much of the last century.

DUFFUS ELGIN, GRAMPIAN
(NJ 175687)

Duffus is one of the oldest motte castles in Scotland to be later converted to stone. Founded by Freskin de Moravia, a Norman-Scottish baron in the reign of David I (1124–53), it began as a tall motte surrounded by a ditch and associated with a ditch-

Duffus: the late thirteenth-century great tower at bottom left split and its north-west corner fell away. The range leading east is mainly fifteenth century.

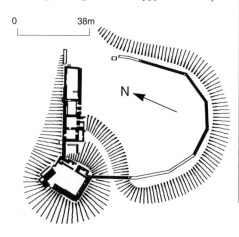

encircled bailey. The wooden tower and walling were completed probably by the mid-twelfth century, for David I stayed there in 1151. Duffus remained in the Moravia, later Moray, family's hands for some time.

Duffus was held by a supporter of Edward I of England in his vain-glorious campaign to establish himself as a King of Scotland, and it was burnt by Scottish patriots. It was rebuilt c.1300, and it is thought this was the time when the motte was given a new stone great tower and the timber palisade round the bailey was replaced by a stone curtain. The stone great tower is rectangular, rising from a splayed plinth of ashlar. The stonework was of good quality but the foundations were unstable. There are three storeys, these are about 20.4 x 15.2 metres (67 x 50 ft) in exterior dimensions, with walls about 2.4 metres (8 ft) thick. The staircase is a straight-flight type in a projection to the south-east which is a thickening of the tower wall. Some time later, the north-west corner of the great tower broke away from the rest of it and slid down the motte. (The breakaway corner can still be seen today.) This was due to the faulty foundations and the unstable condition of the motte soil (see Chapter 2).

In the fifteenth century further works were added, including a range of buildings along the north side of the bailey whose curtain wall joins into the great tower after crossing the ditch which was filled in. These are now in ruins.

DUMBARTON STRATHCLYDE
(NS 400745)

Dumbarton Castle is built upon Dumbarton Rock, a volcanic neck of basalt jutting out into the Clyde, on which a fortified structure was raised during the last years of Roman occupation of Britain in the fifth century AD.

The medieval history of Dumbarton is one of continual change of holder: sometimes it was in firm control under the kings who appreciated its strategic value, or in the hands of the allies of the Crown; sometimes it was in the charge of the Lennox family, some of whose members held it against the kings. It was besieged several times, which must have been a difficult and hazardous operation in view of its geography.

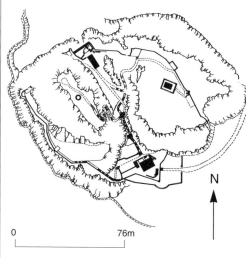

Dumbarton: the walls are delineated in bold lines.

The plan of the rock and the structures upon it (see plan) do not reveal the full extent of whatever medieval castle buildings were erected there, for the remains are too fragmentary. Certainly, dating is quite unreliable. Buildings were raised upon the flat ground between the two rock mounts and on the incline to the river. Some wall lengths remain. The western mound contains on its summit the foundations of a cylindrical tower. The site of the governor's house at the south end of the rock contains traces of the wall of a medieval hall. From the seventeenth century, Dumbarton castle was refortified with assorted walling, batteries and gates, but these are beyond the scope of this book.

DUMFRIES DUMFRIES AND GALLOWAY
(NX 973765)
There are some remains of a motte castle at the site of Dumfries Castle (D.F. Renn holds that these are the remains of two castles). The existing earthworks indicate a raised earth structure with associated ditching and a second mound 15.2 or 18.3 metres (50 or 60 ft) from the first. A castle existed in the 1180s and was strengthened in 1263. The structure was refortified by the English-employed carpenter, Adam de Glasson, 1299–1302, which suggests it was taken from the Scots by the English.

DUNBAR LOTHIAN
(NT 678793)
Scene of several key struggles in Scottish history (notably the siege by England in 1339 which was relieved when supplies reached the Scottish defenders by sea, and the famous battle nearby in 1650 when Cromwell routed the Scots), Dunbar was dismantled in 1568 by the Regent Moray. Built of red freestone, it is now a jumble of ruins scattered over its high position 24.4 metres (80 ft) above the sea. The castle plan was a stone enclosure with gatehouse, although the gatehouse was erected later than the walls, suggesting an earlier and simpler gate-tower. In the sixteenth century the masonry was given gun-ports. The castle may have been raised in the very late thirteenth century.

DUNBEATH HIGHLAND
(ND 158282)
Sited on a cliff, this elaborate building has absorbed the original fifteenth-century four-storeyed tower, which had walls about 1.5 metres (5 ft) thick. The first additions were in the seventeenth century when three corners were adorned with angle turrets two storeys high. The castle was successfully besieged by Montrose in the Civil War.

DUNDARG GRAMPIAN
(NJ 895648)
Dundarg ruins stand inside the site of an Iron Age fort on a promontory in Aberdour Bay. In the thirteenth century a castle of local red stone

was raised here by the Comyn family, who were lords of Buchan. It was probably a simple enclosure castle with a great tower inside. In 1308 Dundarg was besieged by Robert Bruce during his consolidation of power as King of Scotland. In 1334 it was rebuilt, but almost immediately it was attacked again, siege-engines being used, as is recorded in a verse from Andrew Wyntoun's *Chronicle*:
> The wardane gert his wrichtis syne.
> Set up richt stoutly ane ingyne.

Dundarg was rebuilt yet again. Among the features of which traces remain are an inner gatehouse and a tower at the western end.

DUNDERAVE INVERARAY, STRATHCLYDE
(NN 143097)
Although this castle was built as the seat of Iain, chief of the MacNaughtons, c.1590, there are charters relating to Dunderave going back to the fifteenth century. MacNaughton's castle was L-plan with a substantial cylindrical tower on one corner, something like Killochan. It was substantially restored by Sir Robert Lorimer (1864–1929).

DUNDEUGH DUMFRIES AND GALLOWAY
(NX 601880)
Little is known of this castle, and only a few fragments remain, enough to indicate that it had been a small L-plan tower-house, with walls only 0.9 metres (3 ft) or so thick. The date is conjectured as sixteenth century.

Much of the extensive walling of Dumbarton is clearly visible on the rock.

DUNDONALD STRATHCLYDE
(NS 363345)
Dundonald is particularly interesting. A twin-D-end-towered gatehouse was built for residential as well as military purposes by Walter Stewart, ancestor of Robert II of Scotland, some time in the early thirteenth century. It stood on a hill at Dundonald and was part of a stone, curtained enclosure. Robert II inherited the castle in 1371, appreciated its defensive position, and converted the original work which had been slighted in Robert Bruce's time into a bigger, rectangular tower block, using its stone. This entailed blocking the passage through the gatehouse and altering the entrance arrangements, in effect turning the accommodation the other way round to face inwards. The king used the castle as a residence and died there in 1390. Much of the tower still stands but is ruinous. The walls are over 2.1 metres (7 ft) thick.

Recent excavations have revealed stretches of a later barmkin (fifteenth-century), and of extensions to a much earlier rectangular building, which was possibly an early hall. There were three main phases of building at Dundonald: c.1250–1370; c.1370–c.1450; and finally c.1450–1550.

DUNGLASS CENTRAL
(NS 435736)

A fifteenth-century L-plan tower-house now in ruined condition.

DUNIVEG ISLAY, STRATHCLYDE
(NR 406455)

Sited on a rock jutting into the sea, Duniveg (or Dunyvaig) now shows only foundations and fragments of wall somewhat buried by grass and heather. It was probably an enclosure of stone with an outer bailey. There are remains of a stone cylindrical tower and foundations of a rectangular building. Duniveg is possibly a Viking fortress but the dating is extremely uncertain. There are some remaining fragments that have been ascribed to the 1500s.

DUNNIDEER GRAMPIAN
(NJ 612281)

There was a first-century BC vitrified fort within earlier earth outworks on Dunnideer Hill. In the early thirteenth century, a simple great tower was built using much of the ancient fort materials found in the vicinity. Little remains of this castle, one of the earliest towers in Scotland. The basement had arrow-loops. The castle was mentioned in the Lindores Abbey Charters for c.1260; it belonged to the Balliol family.

DUNNOTTAR GRAMPIAN
(NO 881838)

Dunnottar is a rambling collection of ruins that were never an integrated castle. Some of the ruins have been restored. The site, on a promontory jutting into the North Sea, is surrounded by the sea except for a small low-level isthmus connecting it to the mainland. The first structure was an earthwork and clay castle of the twelfth century (of which there is practically nothing left). Towards the end of the fourteenth century, William Keith, hereditary Great Marischal of Scotland, erected an early L-plan tower-house on the headland near the isthmus. This still stands to its full height but is roofless.

In the late sixteenth and early seventeenth centuries, the castle was converted to become a more palatial and residential structure. A quadrangular courtyard with ranges all round emerged. But one wall nearest the mainland was equipped with gun-ports, suggesting that the Keiths had not entirely neglected to defend the castle. It was as well, because Dunnottar was besieged by Montrose in 1645, and again in 1651, on the later occasion by the forces of Cromwell. It was slighted by the government after the collapse of the First Jacobite Rising. Considerable excavations and restoration work have been undertaken in the present century, notably by Viscountess Cowdray in the 1920s to help alleviate local unemployment. Several rooms in the quadrangle are now open.

The part-restored remains of Dunnottar, a castle of several periods, occupy a dramatic position on the rock high above the sea (see also Dunluce, Co. Antrim).

DUNOLLIE STRATHCLYDE
(NM 852315)

Dunollie is partly ruinous. It was the site of a fortress owned by the great Somerled, Lord of Argyll, who died in 1164 and was father of the founder of the MacDougall clan which still owns the castle. The principal structure is the four-storeyed rectangular tower-house (of the fifteenth century), which has a barrel-vaulted basement. Associated with the tower are the remains of a later curtained enclosure which had buildings along the inner walls. Only remnants of this work survive. There was also a second enclosure, of which only traces remain. A postern gateway in the first enclosure has a dog-tooth ornamented arch which suggests a much earlier period than the fifteenth century, probably late Norman or the twelfth/thirteenth centuries.

DUNOON STRATHCLYDE
(NS 175763)

The earliest castle here was raised on an artificial mound in the late twelfth/early thirteenth centuries. It was a royal residence. Later, it was enlarged to consist of three cylindrical towers arranged in a triangular plan. Today it is in ruins.

DUNROBIN GOLSPIE, HIGHLAND
(NC 850008)

This palace is largely the creation of the eighteenth and nineteenth centuries; it is a superstructure built upon an early fifteenth-century great tower, and has a vaulted ceiling on each floor. The tower originally belonged to the Earls of Sutherland (then Morays), and is still in the family. The first major enlargements to it were carried out in the seventeenth century at which time it was converted to a courtyard-plan castle-mansion.

DUNSCAITH MIGG, HIGHLAND
(NH 807689)

Also spelled as Dunscath, this began as a low motte castle built c.1179 by William the Lion (1165–1214). The surviving remains are two concentric semicircular ditches with ramparts.

DUNSKEY
PORT PATRICK, DUMFRIES AND GALLOWAY
(NX 004534)

Dunskey is on a promontory jutting into the sea. It is protected by a ditch separating it from the landward side. The tower-house is L-plan, with walls about 1.5 metres (5 ft) thick, but it is roofless. Outside the tower are remains of enclosure walls built across the rocky site. The castle was erected in the sixteenth century, on the site of an earlier building which is said to have been burned down.

DUNSTAFFNAGE
NR OBAN, STRATHCLYDE
(NM 883344)

This is a well preserved, basically thirteenth-century fortress on a rock on the south edge of Loch Etive which it commands. It is a quadrangular enclosure castle of stone with cylindrical projections on the corners which are embryo towers. The walls are about 3 metres (10 ft) thick and, very interestingly,

Dunstaffnage: this interesting thirteenth-century enclosure castle with towers rests upon rock, notably along one side, where the rock face actually makes up part of the castle wall itself (see also Cahir, Co. Tipperary).

they can be seen to follow the contours of the rock on which they stand (see also Cahir in Ireland). The base of the south wall, for example, starts low down at the east and rises at an incline, so that the base at the west end is about 9.1 metres (30 ft) above the ground outside. The walls are 18.3 metres (60 ft) tall overall. The entrance is in the east corner about 6 metres (20 ft) up, through a tall, arched doorway, which is protected by a simple forework. Positioned over the entrance passage is a tower which was added in the seventeenth century.

In the highest part of the castle, the north-west corner, there is another tower, larger than the seventeenth-century example, whose outer wall is curved, as it forms a corner tower to the enclosure. This projects square with one rounded corner into the courtyard, and is reached by a staircase outside into its ground floor several feet higher than the courtyard. The top storey is reached by a wall-walk

behind the battlemented parapet. There are tower-like projections in the other two corners. Dunstaffnage was very well provided with long, fishtail arrow slits, many of which were later modified to act as shot-holes. Its postern, however, was a natural one of great defensive capability.

It features in several important periods of Scottish history. Alexander II and Alexander III used it during their campaigns against the Vikings in the Western Isles. Edward I of England also recognised its importance as a checkpoint to the approach to Glen Mor. It was captured by Robert Bruce from the MacDougalls (owners also of Dunollie, q.v.), who sided with Edward I. It is also traditionally on the site of an earlier building of the ancient Kings of Dalriada, where the Stone of Destiny was kept until it was removed to Scone (whence it was stolen by Edward I of England and taken away to Westminster in London).

DUNTREATH CENTRAL
(NS 536810)

A quadrangular castle whose principal structure is a fifteenth-century rectangular tower-house, 14.3 x 7.9 metres (47 x 26 ft), with walls about 1.2 metres (4 ft) thick.

DUNTROON Kilmartin, Strathclyde
(NR 793955)
This late thirteenth-century small enclosure castle was raised on a promontory jutting into the northern side of Loch Crinan. The curtain wall is 7.3–8.5 metres (24–28 ft) high and about 1.8 metres (6 ft) thick, and the inner area is about 1067 metres (3500 ft) square. In the seventeenth century an L-plan tower-house was erected in the southern angle of the courtyard, possibly over the site of an earlier (demolished) tower. The castle was owned by the Campbells of Duntroon.

DUNTULM Kilmuir, Skye, Highland
(NG 409743)
A rectangular structure of the sixteenth century, some 25 x 9.1 metres (82 x 30 ft), was raised on a site above the sea at the extreme north end of the island. In the seventeenth century a smaller tower was added. The castle is in poor condition.

DUNURE Strathclyde
(NS 252158)
Dunure occupied a promontory overlooking the sea. It was a great tower castle of the thirteenth century, whose great tower was of irregular shape, possibly similar to Castle Sween. The basement was vaulted. A range of buildings was added in the sixteenth century. Only fragments remain of the castle today. Dunure was the scene of a frightful act: in the 1550s the Earl of Cassilis seized the abbot of Crossraguel Abbey and roasted him alive in order to get him to sign over the Crossraguel lands to him. The abbot survived to sue his tormentor and recover damages.

DUNVEGAN Skye, Highland
(NG 247481)
This romantic fortress is still occupied by the Macleod family whose ancestors erected it in the Middle Ages. The present structure is a nineteenth-century transformation of a castle that was begun in the thirteenth century.

Dunvegan stands on the top of a rock projecting into the sea. The first detectable building is the substantial great tower, 14.6 x 10.7 metres (48 x 35 ft), which stands in the north-east and which has been embellished. The tower has 3-metre (10-ft) thick walls, and it is used today, among other things, to display many historic Scottish relics. One early feature of the castle still visible is the remnant of a sea gate which enabled the castle to

receive supplies if the landward side was blockaded by enemies.

EARLSHALL Leuchars, Fife
(NO 465211)
Earlshall has been much restored. In its original shape of 1546 it was nearly Z-plan, but not quite. A rectangular tower block with thin walls had a cylindrical tower on the north-east corner (with its own spiral stair). Projecting southwards from the main block, and at the western end, was raised a square-plan tower whose southernmost walls at first and second storeys are considerably thicker (2.4 metres [8 ft] and 2.1 metres [7 ft] respectively). In the angle between this tower and the main block was built a rounded-cornered staircase turret. The castle was later extended at the south to contain a courtyard, at the other end of which was built, in the seventeenth century, a rectangular range, forming the third side of an enclosure. All this work became ruinous, and was not restored until the present century.

EDEN Grampian
(NJ 698588)
Ruins of a sixteenth-century L-plan tower-house, changed into a Z-plan in the seventeenth century.

EDINAMPLE Central
(NN 625235)
A Z-plan castle of the early seventeenth century, erected by the Campbells of Glenorchy, Edinample; it contains an example of a bottle dungeon.

EDINBURGH Lothian
(NT 252736)
Edinburgh is probably the most famous of all Scottish castles. The most prominent in a city of conspicuous buildings, its history is largely bound up with the story of Scotland. Its periods of construction span many centuries, beginning at least from the eleventh when Malcolm III erected a wooden fortress upon the huge rock mass that towers some 82.3 metres (270 ft) above the valley that is now occupied by Waverley Station and Princes Street Gardens. The castle has been a palace, a treasury, the home of Scotland's records, a refuge for several Scottish kings during their minority years, and a prison.

The top of the rock is girt with a wall erected in several stages, and inside that is the

citadel which contains several buildings. The castle that can be seen today, however, bears small resemblance to the medieval castle, and only a few buildings that date from earlier than the seventeenth century remain. Notable among these is the small chapel of St Margaret on the highest part of the castle. This is a fine Norman building of the early twelfth century, and is named after the wife of Malcolm III, Queen Margaret, who was canonised. It has been considerably altered and repaired over the centuries, but still retains some original features. Another early structure of which there are remnants is a tower that was L-shaped and which rose to about 18.3 metres (60 ft). It had a drawbridge. This is known as David's Tower, named after David II (1329–71) who built it probably between 1368 and 1371.

Today, the ruins that include a vaulted chamber are submerged in the great Half-Moon Battery (or Great Half Bastion Round). This was built in the late sixteenth century by the Regent Morton, and later heightened. David's Tower had been largely destroyed in a siege of 1583.

Edinburgh Castle was besieged many times in the Middle Ages: for example, it was attacked and taken by Edward I of England in 1296, and recaptured by Robert Bruce's valiant nephew Thomas Randolph, Earl of Moray, in 1313. Moray destroyed the castle, but not the St Margaret Chapel.

EDZELL Nr Brechin, Tayside
(NO 585691)
Edzell began as a substantial rectangular L-plan tower-house of the early sixteenth century, with a square-plan projection out of the north-west corner to contain the stairs. Later in the century a quadrangle of buildings was raised beside it, anchored on the tower's north-west wall, and connected to it by an entrance hall.

Finally, in the very first years of the 1600s, a spacious pleasaunce was added to the eastern side of the courtyard. This was a huge walled garden, with a square-plan bath-house tower on the south-east and a summer-house on the north-east corner. The garden is one of the most notable in any British castle. As a fortress, Edzell had a peaceful history. Although fortified, it never sustained siege, but it was garrisoned for a while by troops of Cromwell in 1651–2. It was abandoned in the mid-eighteenth century.

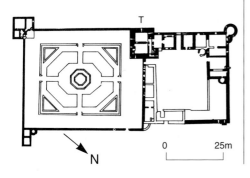

Edzell: this tower-house castle is well known for its formal garden, which was first laid out in the early seventeenth century.

(Below) Edzell: ground plan. T = tower-house. At left is the famous Edzell garden.

T

0   25m

N

ELCHO Nr Perth, Tayside
(NO 164211)

A massive five-storeyed, rectangular tower-house of the sixteenth century which is today in splendid condition after restoration. The castle is particularly fascinating for its tower attachments. A substantial square-plan tower projects from the south-west corner of the block. It has walls 1.8–2.4 metres (6–8 ft) thick. On the north long wall of the block are three more tower projections, west to east, one square and slightly tilted to north-east, one semi-cylindrical and one cylindrical (on the north-east corner). The castle windows are protected by iron grilles and the walls are

(Right) Elcho: first-floor plan. Note the very wide ceremonial-style staircase on the south-west corner (top left).

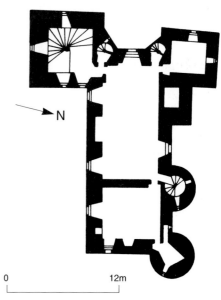

N

0   12m

equipped with gun-ports, most of them wide-mouthed. There is evidence that the tower-house was at one time enclosed inside a barmkin with a ditch outside.

ELGIN GRAMPIAN
(NJ 212628)
Mentioned as early as the 1220s, Elgin Castle was a simple stone enclosure with a great tower. Very little remains of the building which is thought to have been derelict since the fifteenth century. The enclosure that can be detected was about 19.2 x 9.7 metres (63 x 32 ft) with rubble-built walls about 2.4 metres (8 ft) thick.

ELLON GRAMPIAN
(NJ 960307)
A four-storeyed sixteenth-century tower-house that was extended and then largely demolished to make room for a mansion.

ELPHINSTONE LOTHIAN
(NT 390698)
Elphinstone was one of three massive, rectangular tower-houses of the early fifteenth century (Borthwick and Comlongon are the other two) which are regarded as the finest of their kind anywhere in Scotland.

Elphinstone was built c.1440. The plan is rectangular, 15.2 x 10.7 metres (50 x 35 ft), with walls up to 2.7 metres (9 ft) thick, the tower once rising five storeys to the parapet, some 17.4 metres (57 ft) from the ground, plus an attic storey above. Each storey had a substantial main room. The lower two storeys were split by a wooden floor, but the upper ceiling was barrel-vaulted. Above that was the great hall, vaulted but not split in two storeys. And above that were two more storeys, plus the attic. In the wall thickness was a virtual honeycomb of chambers, passages, staircases and cubicles. From the mezzanine storey to the lower half of the hall storey there were three separate wheel stairs, and a straight flight up to the upper half and its many passages and chambers off.

The flue of the fireplace in the great hall contained a chamber with a window looking over the hall. The chamber opened off a secret set of rooms in the north-west corner of the tower, which had an exclusive wheel stair leading from the hall. The tower was equipped with 'luggies'. The whole tower was amazingly short of window space, and had no gun-ports or shot-holes, and yet was

Elphinstone: elevation of tower-house before it was demolished to the lowest floor level in the 1950s.

strongly defensive. Sadly, it was recently demolished down to the lowest storey because of subsidence.

ELSIESHIELS
LOCHMABEN, DUMFRIES AND GALLOWAY
(NY 069850)
A much modernised L-plan tower-house of the sixteenth century, three-storeyed with attic, with a square stair-tower extension on the north wall of the tower. The stair-tower is five-storeyed. The modern additions include bartizans on the south-east and south-west corners of the main block.

ERCHLESS KILTARLITY, HIGHLAND
(NH 410408)
This castle has been renovated and modernised but it was originally an L-plan tower-house of the period c.1590–c.1625.

ESSLEMONT ELLON, GRAMPIAN
(NJ 932297)
Two castles have occupied this site. The first, built in the fourteenth century, was destroyed by fire in the 1490s: marks of burning have been found. A licence to start again was granted c.1500, and an L-plan tower was raised. This was replaced in probably 1570–90. The later structure was a three-storeyed L-plan tower with a square-plan staircase turret in the angle. A cylindrical

tower at the east corner projects into the ditch. Some of the tower masonry appears to be of earlier date, presumably remains of the destroyed fourteenth-century building. The main tower block measures 16.8 x 12.8 metres (55 x 42 ft), and the walls are 1.8–2.1 metres (6–7 ft) thick.

ETHIE INVERKEILOR, TAYSIDE
(NO 687468)
Basically an E-plan tower-house built in the fifteenth century, which has received considerable alterations that obscure the original shape. By the mid-sixteenth century, Ethie had grown into a courtyard castle with the main building on the south and a second yard on the northern end. It was enclosed by a moat which is now covered. The castle is well maintained and occupied.

EVELAW WESTRUTHER, BORDERS
(NT 661526)
A partly ruinous sixteenth-century tower-house, three-storeyed, and still whole to its parapet. The tower-house is L-plan, with rounded corners, corbelled out to square at the level of the eaves. Evelaw has wide-mouth splayed gun-ports in the south and east walls. Another building has been raised against the tower-house, and this also has gun-ports.

EVELICK KILSPINDIE, TAYSIDE
(NO 204257)
A four-storeyed L-plan tower-house of the early sixteenth century. Evelick is now derelict. There is a later building adjoining it, and this contains masonry that is thought to have come from another building of the original construction.

FAIRBURN TOWER
URRAY, HIGHLAND
(NH 469523)
This is a ruined tower-house dating from the late sixteenth/early seventeenth century, the earlier part being the square great tower with angle-turrets. It was equipped with gun-ports in each wall. The Fairburn Tower was a Mackenzie stronghold.

FAIRLIE LARGS, STRATHCLYDE
(NS 213549)
This castle is in ruinous condition. It was a late fifteenth-century rectangular tower, about 13.7 x 8.8 metres (45 x 29 ft), with a great hall on the first floor served by a kitchen separated

by screens, similar to Skelmorlie and Law in the neighbourhood. The first floor at Fairlie was reached by a spiral staircase at the ground floor next to the entrance. Fairlie was given a rounded angle-turret at each corner.

FALKLAND Fife
(NO 254076)
The present magnificent palace at Falkland was begun by James II (1437–60) in about 1458, and work was continued by his successors, notably James V (1513–42). It was raised upon the remains of an earlier castle whose origins can be dated to the thirteenth century, but of which only a few fragments remain; these include the bases of two round towers. Falkland is not within the scope of this work, but the palace is well worth a visit. Note some keyhole and wide-mouth gun-ports, inserted in the sixteenth century.

FALSIDE Tranent, Lothian
(NT 377709)
Falside began in the fifteenth century as a rectangular tower, 9.1 x 11.9 metres (30 x 39 ft), with four storeys, the top storey of which was vaulted. This tower was badly damaged by the English after the Battle of Pinkie (1547). In the seventeenth century Falside was enlarged by adding an L-plan tower-house to the south wall of the original tower, constructed to the same height. It has been restored.

FARNELL Tayside
(NO 624555)
This is today a tidy, modern, three-storeyed building, with a semi-cylindrical projecting turret containing the entrance door and a staircase. It is a rebuild of a late thirteenth-century castle. The first renovation was begun in the 1570s and it was restored in the 1960s. Farnell has absorbed features of the thirteenth-century castle which had been a palace-fortress of the Bishops of Brechin.

FAST Borders
(NT 595182)
A motte castle of the twelfth century, sometimes known as Castle Knowe. It was erected on the left bank of Rule Water only 0.8 km (½ mile) from Bedrule Castle. The mound was about 13.7 metres (45 ft) tall in natural height, and about 3 metres (10 ft) of extra height was added to it before erecting the wooden great tower on the summit.

FATLIPS Minto, Borders
(NT 581208)
This is one of two castles of this name in Scotland, and it stands in a commanding position. The basic structure is sixteenth-century. Some restoration has been done. The original rectangular tower was 8.2 x 9.7 metres (27 x 32 ft), and rose to four storeys with an additional garret. It was built of local whinstone with freestone dressings. The castle contains a museum of interesting relics including a breech-loading gun, a muzzle gun of the seventeenth century and, outside, a cannon of c.1637.

FATLIPS Symington, Strathclyde
(NS 968340)
There is very little to see of this sixteenth-century rectangular great tower built of coursed rubble. It was about 13.4 x 8.5 metres (44 x 28 ft), with 1.5-metre (5-ft) thick walls, and the south-west corner was rounded. The tower contained a cross-wall, like English great towers. At present, some of the walling stands, but not higher than about 1.5 metres.

FEDDERATE Grampian
(NJ 897498)
Said to have been built in the sixteenth century, only some stone fragments remain.

FENTONS TOWER
North Berwick, Lothian
(NT 543820)
A sixteenth-century rectangular L-plan tower-house with small area wing attached. The walls are about 1.2 metres (4 ft) thick, hardly adequate as fortification.

FERNIE Monimail, Fife
(NO 316147)
A tall, L-plan castle of the sixteenth century with many additions of the seventeenth century and later. It is in good condition and is used as a hotel.

FERNIEHURST Jedburgh, Borders
(NT 632179)
This castle is largely a sixteenth-century reconstruction of an earlier building. It consists of a long, rectangular block of three storeys, at one end of which are two wings, making the plan approximately T-shaped. One of the wings contains the principal staircase. The wings are provided with corner turrets corbelled out on the corners with

conical roof tops. The earlier building, whose remains are incorporated in the present structure, was seized by forces of Henry III during the 1547 war between Scotland and England, but they were driven out.

FETTERESSO Grampian
(NO 842855)
A rectangular block of the fifteenth century with a courtyard which had a second block added in the seventeenth century to make two sides of a quadrangle. Montrose burnt the eastern block in 1645 and it was rebuilt later in the century. The castle was further renovated in the nineteenth century, but is for the most part derelict today. The Old Pretender, James Edward, was proclaimed King James VIII of Scotland here in 1715.

FIDDES Grampian
(NO 804812)
A roughly L-plan castle of unusual shape, built at the end of the sixteenth century. It has a cylindrical staircase tower on the top edge of the lower arm of the 'L', and a second cylindrical tower on the bottom edge. Yet a third cylindrical tower is corbelled out on the first floor and rises to the second floor, containing another staircase. This is in the middle of the other arm of the 'L'. It has several gun-ports. Fiddes is much restored.

FINAVON Tayside
(NO 497565)
A late sixteenth-century square tower-house which has interesting double shot-holes.

FINDLATER Fordyce, Grampian
(NJ 542672)
Now in ruins, this was a substantial castle on a high rock almost entirely encircled by the sea and reached across an isthmus. A ditch on the mainland gave extra protection. The castle appears to have had several towers and some curtain walling. Remains are scanty.

FINDOCHTY Grampian
(NJ 456674)
A sixteenth-century L-plan tower-house whose original work is ruined.

FINGASK Kilspindie, Tayside
(NO 228274)
The more modern structure here contains remains of a late sixteenth-century tower-house which was besieged during the Civil

War (1642–6), and is recorded as having been dismantled in 1746 at the end of the Second Jacobite Rising.

FINLARIG KILLIN, CENTRAL
(NN 575338)

A panel over the entrance dates this Z-plan tower-house to 1609. It was raised on a mound of earth which indicates that an earlier castle had once been on the site, and this is lent support by traces of a moat. The tower-house, which reaches about 9.1 metres (30 ft) high, is dilapidated. There are gun-ports in the walls. It had square towers at diagonally opposite corners.

FORDELL DALGETY, FIFE
(NT 147853)

Fordell was a Z-plan castle built in about 1580 on the site of an earlier fortified building. The plan is a main rectangular block (running east to west) with two wings containing staircases, one on the north-west edge and the other on the south-east. The wings were square-towered, with a cylindrical turret corbelled out of the north-west wing. There were cylindrical turrets on the north-east and south-west corners as well. Although it is a small structure, its 1.5-metre (5-ft) thick walls indicate that it was a fortified residence. It has been modernised in recent years.

FORDYCE GRAMPIAN
(NJ 555638)

A three-storeyed tower-house of L-plan of the late sixteenth century, Fordyce has a tall semicircular projection which is corbelled out from the first-floor level upwards to the roof of the main rectangular block. The turrets and walls have shot-holes. A second tower extension was added later against one wall of the main block.

FORFAR TAYSIDE
(NO 456508)

There is nothing to see now of an early castle built here, probably in the twelfth century when it is first mentioned. It may have been a stone enclosure built upon an even earlier earthwork. There is evidence that remains were visible in the seventeenth century.

FORRES GRAMPIAN
(NJ 034587)

There is nothing now to see of what appears to have been a thirteenth-century castle here.

The suggestion from excavation is that it was a rectangular enclosure castle of stone, with towers on the western side. Forres was destroyed and rebuilt more than once.

FOWLIS TAYSIDE
(NO 321333)

Remains of a seventeenth-century four-storeyed tower block which has been enlarged by a more modern wing.

FRAOCH EILEAN STRATHCLYDE
(NN 108252)

This began as a rectangular hall-tower of the thirteenth century. The north wall was built thicker than the other three and it contains a straight staircase. Wooden buildings were raised at the same time, or even earlier. They were then all enclosed by a stone curtain with a gateway at the south, traces of which remain. In the 1600s, the hall-tower, which had been abandoned, was taken over and adapted to contain a house which was enlarged before the end of the century. The house was later abandoned. Today the hall-tower remains rise about 4 metres (13 ft).

A view of the south and west façades of the great fortress-palace of Fyvie.

FRENDRAUGHT FORGUE, GRAMPIAN
(NJ 621419)

The present mansion contains fragments of a rectangular tower of the (?) fifteenth century.

FYVIE GRAMPIAN
(NJ 764323)

This is a magnificent castle to look at today, one of Scotland's great fortress-palaces. Its long, rectangular block has a four-storeyed rectangular tower with garret and cylindrical corner bartizans on each end. In the centre is a massive gatehouse-like projection of twin semi-cylindrical towers, flanking a recess containing a doorway at ground level. This whole south front is about 45.7 metres (150 ft) long and has a formidable appearance, but in fact it is not properly fortified. The work is a series of impositions on an earlier castle which may go back to the fourteenth century. The first mention of stonework at Fyvie is c.1390. The south-east tower (the Preston Tower) was raised c.1390–1430; the south-west (the Meldrum) tower, some time between c.1433 and c.1590.

The gatehouse is from the very late sixteenth century. Later still, additions were made, right up to the 1890s. One interesting feature is the wheel staircase which has wide sweep steps and a solid newel.

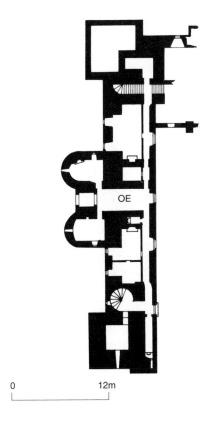

Fyvie: plan of the south facade at ground floor. OE = old entrance.

GALDENOCH
DUMFRIES AND GALLOWAY
(NW 973632)
This is now a ruin. It was an L-plan tower-house built between 1547 and 1570. It may have been three storeys tall, but the present height is about 6 metres (20 ft) maximum.

GARDYNE KIRKDEN, TAYSIDE
(NO 574488)
Gardyne has been well maintained, and is still occupied. It began in 1568 as an L-plan tower-house with a rounded staircase turret bearing a rectangular cap-house (like Claypotts). The eastern end has a cylindrical turret on each corner. Later additions include a block on the north-west.

GARTH COSHIEVILLE, TAYSIDE
(NW 764503)
Garth has been very well restored after a long period of decay. It is a square-plan tower-house about 18.3 metres (60 ft) tall to the parapet, with walls 1.8 metres (6 ft) thick and built of rough boulders. The tower was raised in the fourteenth century for Alexander Stewart, the 'Wolf of Badenoch', brother of Robert II of Scotland, who is thought to have died at Garth in 1396.

GIGHT METHLICK, GRAMPIAN
(NJ 826392)
Built in the third quarter of the sixteenth century, Gight is a ruin. It was an L-plan tower-house which had ribbed vaulting (some remains today). The gun-loops are interesting: a crosslet (arrow slit in the shape of a cross) at the top of a slit and an oillet at the base, like Tillycairn and Towie Barclay and others.

The castle was built by the Gordon family which, in the sixteenth and seventeenth centuries, had a reputation for violence. The burning of Corgarff Castle in 1571 is a terrible example (*see* Corgarff).

GLAMIS TAYSIDE
(NO 386480)
This magnificent mansion of the Earls of Strathmore and Kinghorne, one of the finest in Scotland, conceals a number of castle structures reaching back to the early fourteenth century. In 1376 Robert II granted the site, which probably contained a fortress of some kind, to John Lyon who constructed an L-plan tower-house. This had outer defences of barmkin wall and flanking towers, and the structures were surrounded by a moat which was later filled in. Remains of this castle are incorporated in the much later conversion to a baronial mansion.

GLASCLUNE TAYSIDE
(NO 154470)
A sixteenth-century Z-plan tower-house.

GLENBUCHAT GRAMPIAN
(NJ 398149)
A late sixteenth-century castle on the Z-plan, with square towers. There is a staircase from the first floor upwards in a half-cylindrical projection in the re-entrant between the north-east tower and the main block (1), and another on the exterior between the south-west tower and the main block (2). Both of these staircases are supported by squinch-arches and not corbelling.

The entrance to the castle building is in the east wall of the south-west tower, and it had an outer door and an inner yett. The door could not be opened until the yett behind had opened. A staircase led up from opposite this entrance to the first floor where, at right-angles, access was available to the spiral staircase in the cylindrical projection (2). The tower walls were equipped with gun-loops all round. The castle is standing with most of its walling, but no roof.

Glenbuchat belonged to the Gordon family who were extremely powerful in Aberdeenshire. It was built c.1590. One owner was John Gordon, a hero of both Jacobite Risings. Known as Old Glenbuchat, his devotion to the Pretenders' causes was such that George II was haunted by him in his dreams and would wake up screaming 'De gread Glenbogged is goming', in his thick German accent.

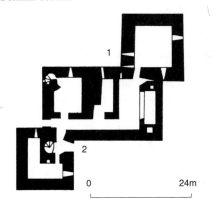

Glenbuchat: ground-floor plan of the c.1590 Z-plan tower-house.

GLENDEVON CENTRAL
(NN 976055)
Glendevon is a seventeenth-century Z-plan tower-house developed from an earlier, possibly fifteenth-century, rectangular tower. It has been considerably modified since, and is today a hotel.

GLENGARNOCK
KILBIRNIE, STRATHCLYDE
(NS 310573)
This castle was based upon a square great tower integrated in a roughly polygonal stone-curtained courtyard, which had other buildings against the inside of the curtain. It was begun in the fifteenth century. The tower was 13.7 x 10.7 metres (45 x 35 ft) with vaulted ground and first floors. Its condition today is so bad that it is not possible to say what height the tower reached.

GRANDTULLY Nr Aberfeldy, Tayside
(NN 891515)
Principally a late sixteenth-century Z-plan tower-house of three storeys, which has had a large modern house of the same building style erected on its north and east sides. The corner turrets are rectangular. This Z-plan is thought to have been raised upon the remains of a c.1400 square-plan tower-house, which itself was enlarged to L-plan in the early sixteenth century. There is a gatehouse containing oval gun-loops. Another noteworthy feature of seventeenth-century origin is the tall, cylindrical stair turret sited not on a corner, nor in an angle, but projecting out of one long side; it is six-storeyed with an ogee roof.

GREENAN Strathclyde
(NS 312193)
A rectangular tower-house of the sixteenth century, with seventeenth-century additions.

GREENKNOWE TOWER
Gordon, Borders
(NT 639428)
An interesting tower-house of L-plan, built c.1581 (this date is etched on the doorway lintel), by the Seton of Touch family. It stands on rising ground once enclosed by marshy ground. The tower is 11 x 6.7 metres (36 x 22 ft), with walls 1.5–2.1 metres (5–7 ft) thick. The shorter wing is about 5.2 x 3.3 metres (17 x 11 ft) and contains the spiral staircase. The entrance is in the angle, and is still guarded by its iron yett. On the first floor there is a second staircase in a turret staircase corbelled out over the angle. This leads to the three higher floors.

GUTHRIE Tayside
(NO 562505)
A modern mansion has been added to the older square-plan tower at Guthrie. The old tower is 12.2 x 9.4 metres (40 x 31 ft), and the walls vary between 1.5–2.4 metres (5–8 ft). It was raised in the fifteenth century, and has had various additions.

HAILES Nr East Linton, Lothian
(NT 575758)
An early castle with a dramatic history, Hailes is today a ruin on the south bank of the Tyne. It is one of the few Scottish castles which still displays masonry of the thirteenth century. This is to be found in the lower part of the tower in the north range of buildings

overlooking the river, which has a pit prison. In the fourteenth century, the castle was granted to the wild and dangerous Hepburns (who later became Earls of Bothwell) who raised the height of this north tower and built additional structures, including a substantial square-plan tower at the west, and some lofty curtain walls, much of which can be seen though in a dilapidated state. The west tower also contains a pit prison, this one in the thickness of the wall. Later work included a chapel in the sixteenth century.

Hailes was besieged but not taken c.1400 by the Percys from Northumberland in the Border hostilities with England. It was attacked in 1544 during the 'Rough Wooing', and in 1650 by Cromwell, whose cannon reduced it.

HALLFOREST Kintore, Grampian
(NJ 777154)
A ruined rectangular tower, still over 18.3 metres (60 ft) tall, with 2.1-metre (7-ft) thick walls, Hallforest was built in the late thirteenth/early fourteenth century. It had six storeys (including an attic) and measures 14.6 x 9.1 metres (48 x 30 ft). Little remains of the tower which is said to have been built at the encouragement of Robert Bruce and granted in 1309 to Sir Robert Keith, Great Marischal of Scotland, who commanded a major wing at Bannockburn (1314). No staircase of stone appears to have been provided, which means that access to floors was by wooden ladder.

HARTHILL Oyne, Grampian
(NJ 686252)
Harthill is now a roofless ruin of a Z-plan tower-house, with barmkin and gatehouse, built by the Keiths c.1600. There is a stone slab with the date 1601, but doubt has been raised as to whether this relates to the original building work or was inserted at a later date of building. The plan was a rectangular tower with one square corner tower diagonally opposite a cylindrical corner tower. The masonry was provided with a limited number of gun-ports and the tower does not appear to have been designed for defence against anything except a frontal assault. No gun-ports were put in the barmkin.

HATTON Newtyle, Tayside
(NO 302411)
Lord Oliphant built a three-storeyed Z-plan tower-house with gable top here in the 1570s.

The main tower is rectangular and has square towers on the north-east and south-west angles. The building was equipped with gun-ports all round at ground-floor level providing defensive fire over every direction of assault.

HAWICK Borders
(NT 499140)
Hawick motte is an artificial mound of the twelfth century, now measuring about 7.6 metres (25 ft) tall, but which may have been reduced in height by several feet. A coin of Henry II was found in the earth round the motte, which confirmed the date for its erection. Today, it has a flight of stone steps to the top which vividly re-creates the appearance it probably had 800 years ago, when the steps would have been timber. It was probably a watch tower.

HAWTHORNDEN Lothian
(NT 286636)
Sited on a triangular promontory at the eastern end of a ravine above the North Esk, not far from Edinburgh, Hawthornden has a ruined fifteenth-century tower at the north which adjoins a seventeenth-century L-plan house. The tower was originally three-storeyed. Its owner, William Drummond, helped to organise the celebrations of the coronation of Charles I.

HELMSDALE Highland
(ND 027151)
Fragments remain here of a medieval castle of uncertain date, which was altered in the (?) fifteenth century into an L-plan tower-house.

HERMITAGE Borders
(NY 497961)
This is a massive tower-house castle of several periods of building. It has figured in many episodes of Scottish history and for a time was held by the wild and dangerous James Hepburn, Earl of Bothwell, whose liaison with Mary, Queen of Scots was the scandal of the sixteenth century in Scotland.

The original structure was a small rectangular enclosure of stone of the late thirteenth/early fourteenth century, with walls about 1.5 metres (5 ft) thick on three sides, and about 3 metres (10 ft) thick on the north side where the spiral staircase was enclosed. This was more of a domestic structure. In 1338 it was captured by the Knight of Liddesdale, Sir William Douglas,

from the English baron, Ralph Neville, who held it by gift of Edward III. Later in the century it was granted to William, 1st Earl of Douglas, nephew of Sir James Douglas (one of Robert Bruce's three trusted advisers). Hermitage was thereafter held by the Douglases to the end of the fifteenth century, and during that time developed from the simple stone enclosure into the huge structure it is today.

Hermitage: the bold area is the original tower-house of the fourteenth century. The rectangle immediately enclosing the original tower represents the first additional work, of the late fourteenth century.

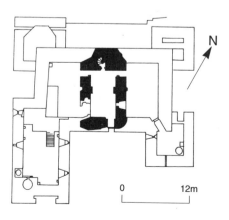

The west front of Hermitage. The entrance to the original great tower (later enclosed by the rest of the castle) is between the two projections on the right.

First of all it was wrapped round by a much larger rectangular enclosure whose north and south (longer) walls are about 2.4 metres (8 ft) thick and extend to about 22.9 metres (75 ft). In the south-west corner, the wall projected westwards into a wing in which the entrance was placed several feet above the ground. At the very end of the fourteenth century, projecting square towers of great strength were added to the corners of the rectangular mass. These towers are close together (they encased the corners of the mass), and on the east and west sides they are linked at the top by a continuous storey presenting the appearance of a huge stone wall with a great central pointed arch reaching to the top storey from the ground. There have been subsequent alterations, notably the provision of wide-mouth gun-ports in the 1540s.

HODDOM DUMFRIES AND GALLOWAY
(NY 156729)

An interesting variant on the L-plan, Hoddom's tower-house has cylindrical turrets on the corners. The walls of the main tower are up to 3 metres (10 ft) thick, and rise to four storeys plus a garret. The building is on a strong site surrounded by a moat. It was built in the sixteenth century, incorporating some stonework of an earlier building.

HOLLOWS TOWER
CANONBIE, DUMFRIES AND GALLOWAY
(NY 382786)

This is also known as Gilknockie. A rectangular tower-house of the sixteenth century, 7 x 4.6 metres (23 x 15 ft), with walls 1.8 metres (6 ft) thick, it rose to four storeys plus an attic, with a bold parapet. The tower was equipped with gun-ports on all sides, some of which are still in sound condition. The tower belonged to the wild, aggressive and lawless Armstrongs, who terrorised much of the Border district in the sixteenth century and some of whom were caught and hanged. It has been restored.

HUME BORDERS
(NT 704414)

This began as a high-walled enclosure castle of the thirteenth century. Hume was extensively altered and enlarged in later centuries, and little remains today of the early buildings.

HUNTERSTON
WEST KILBRIDE, STRATHCLYDE
(NS 193515)

Basically a long, rectangular block tower of two main periods. The first structure was a rectangular tower four storeys high. This was raised in the fifteenth century, and is about 7.3 x 6.7 metres (24 x 22 ft) with walls 1.2–1.5

The fifteenth-century tower-house castle situated at Hunterston was raised on the site of a much earlier earthwork castle.

metres (4–5 ft) thick. The small square stair turret at the south-west corner was added in the seventeenth century, at the same time as the extension to the tower, slightly longer but of equal width. This new block contained the great banqueting hall. The tower (the first building) is battlemented, although the crenellations may have been altered. The castle itself was surrounded by a moat.

Hunterston was probably built on the site of a much earlier castle, an earthwork enclosure, which had been raised by the Hunter family (of Norman origin) in the twelfth century.

HUNTINGTOWER Nr Perth, Tayside
(NO 0842252)
This tower-house is made up from tower blocks of two periods. It began as a rectangular tower of the early fifteenth century which was renovated at the end of the century. It had an entrance in the south wall beside the east wall, which has since been

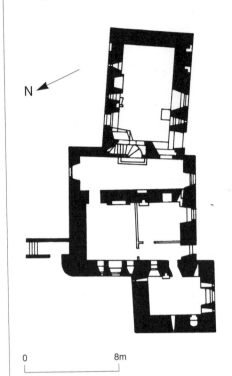

Huntingtower: plan of ground floor (after SDD).

0   8m

A view of the south front of Huntingtower. The fifteenth-century masonry is in the lower courses of the east tower-house.

filled in. This entrance led right through to an inner yard, and there was a door leading off to the west into the tower which rose to three storeys. The top of this tower can still be seen, for the extra floors erected above at a later date are of different masonry work. This tower contained the great hall. The walls were plastered, and the ceilings were decorated with painted designs between and on the wooden ceiling joists.

In the late fifteenth and early sixteenth centuries, a second tower was constructed, rectangular, three-storeyed plus garret, with a square jamb, or out-tower, on the south-west corner one storey taller. The first floor of the western tower was given over to a great hall, reached by a spiral staircase inside on the north-west corner, and outside by a flight of steps in through a door in the north wall. In the seventeenth century the space between the two towers was completed by adding walling up to three storeys plus garret.

Huntingtower is perhaps most famous as the scene of the Ruthven raid of 1582, when William Ruthven, Earl of Gowrie, and the Earl of Mar, friends of the boy-king James VI, kidnapped him to get him away from the influence of their rivals, the Duke of Lennox and the Earl of Arran.

HUNTLY Grampian
(NJ 532407)
Described as one of the noblest baronial ruins in Scotland, this remarkable structure, a mixture of building periods, was the fortified residence of one of the most powerful families in Scotland, the Earls (and later Marquises) of Huntly. Originally there had been a twelfth-century motte castle on the site. The mound and some ditching are still there. The first stonework was undertaken perhaps at the end of the fourteenth century. It was a very substantial L-plan tower with walls over 2.4 metres (8 ft) thick, although this has now vanished except for foundations. It had been placed to the east of the motte.

In the mid-fifteenth century, the 1st Earl of Huntly, who owned the castle, began to put up what was called the 'new werk' to the south of the 'auld werk' (the great tower). This is now in ruins but its shape is easy to determine – a rectangular block about 21 x 10 metres (69 x 33 ft), four storeys tall, with walls about 2.4 metres (8 ft) thick.

On the south-west corner is a boldly projecting cylindrical tower of five storeys

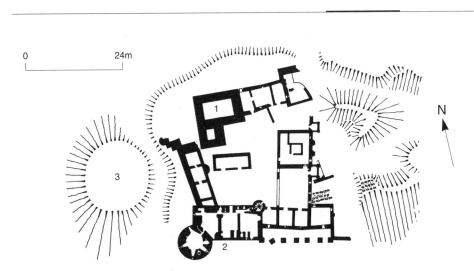

Huntly: (after SDD). 1 The 'Auld Werk' (fifteenth century). 2 'New Werk'. 3 Site of Norman motte.

equipped with gun-ports, and on the north-east corner is a smaller cylindrical tower.

The whole block is fascinating. The top storey has oriel windows. The façade above and below the oriel window line has an inscription bearing the name of the 1st Marquis of Huntly and his wife. It may seem as if the block was not a defensive building, but its thick walls, particularly so at basement- and ground-floor level, its gun-ports, vaulted ground floor and iron yett in front of the door all belie this.

The structure is not all of one period, however. The basement is largely fifteenth-century, but the storeys above date from the sixteenth century, and there was also rebuilding of those upper levels in the seventeenth century. The work was extensive and spread over many years. It was seriously interrupted in 1594 when the 5th Earl of Huntly foolishly joined a revolt against James VI. The revolt however collapsed and Huntly paid for his folly by having his fine home blown up. But later he made his peace and was advanced by James to become the 1st Marquis of Huntly. He celebrated this by rebuilding the castle, particularly the 'new werk' which had been severely damaged by the explosion. It was at this time that the inscriptions over the oriel range were put in, namely c.1606.

Huntly: the 'New Werk' of the late sixteenth and early seventeenth centuries.

INCHDREWER GRAMPIAN
(NJ 656607)
Inchdrewer castle was constructed in the sixteenth-century. It is an L-plan tower-house which was destroyed by fire in 1713, following the murder of the owner, Lord Banff, an unpopular local laird.

When the castle was restored later in the eighteenth century, the L-plan was enlarged and given a cylindrical staircase tower at the south end and ranges of buildings to form a courtyard castle.

Gun-ports were inserted. This castle was recently restored even more magnificently by the present owner.

INCHMURRIN STRATHCLYDE
(NS 373863)
This is an early tower-house castle which was built round a courtyard. The tower was probably raised in the fourteenth century. The remains of its wall are mainly 0.6 metres (2 ft) or so thick.

INNERPEFFREY TAYSIDE
(NN 905179)
Remains of an L-plan towered castle of the seventeenth century.

INNISCHONNEL STRATHCLYDE
(NM 977119)
Also spelled Inchconnell, this began as a rectangular stone enclosure of the early thirteenth century, which had pilaster buttresses like those at Sween. The castle was greatly altered in the fifteenth century, but it retained the older work, much of which can be seen. Additional buildings included a tower on the south-east and a range of buildings adjoining, including a four-storey block. The castle was for a time the chief stronghold of the Campbells.

INVERGARRY HIGHLAND
(NM 315006)
An L-plan tower-house built during the seventeenth century.

(Opposite) Two towers in the enclosure of thirteenth-century Innischonnel, which was added to in the fifteenth century.

INVERLOCHY

NR FORT WILLIAM, HIGHLAND
(NN 120754)

Old Inverlochy Castle was built c.1270–80 as a quadrilateral stone enclosure with four corner cylindrical towers. The north-west tower is larger than the other three and is a donjon. The enclosure has an entrance at north and south, both of which have plain arches. Foundations of later barbicans in front of both gates have been found. There was a moat round three sides of the enclosure with a rampart behind that, and the fourth side was defended by the River Lochy, attainable by means of a water-gate, whose waters fed the moat. Although the castle is dilapidated, it has survived well. The cylindrical towers and the curtain stand 9.1 metres (30 ft) high. Its walls are nearly 3 metres (10 ft) thick.

INVERMARK LOCHLEE, TAYSIDE

(NO 442804)

A tower-house of two major building periods, Invermark rose to four storeys plus a garret. The lower storeys were raised in the sixteenth century, and it is possible that the gun-ports in the basement level were inserted at this stage. Then in the seventeenth century the upper parts were completed. One of these was a

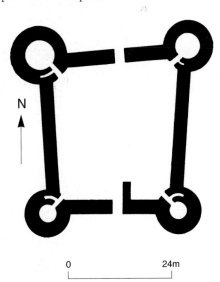

Inverlochy: a plan of the thirteenth-century enclosure with towers.

cylindrical turret which has pistol-holes below a loop. The entrance to the castle is at first-floor level and is still guarded by an iron yett. Foundations of other buildings have been found to the south and east.

INVERNESS HIGHLAND

(NH 666451)

The first castle at Inverness was built in the twelfth century, possibly by David I. It guarded the routes to and from the Highlands. It was an earthwork structure which later received stonework, whose shape we are not able to determine. It had also had a hall built of timber boards, a *domus Scoticana*, for Alexander III. Its earthen outworks were also reinforced in 1263. The castle was captured by the Lord of the Isles in 1491 but retaken by James IV soon afterwards. It was severely damaged in Mary, Queen of Scots' reign, damaged again during the Civil War, and finally all but razed by the Young Pretender, Bonnie Prince Charlie, in 1746. The only remains are parts of the ancient curtain wall and some earthworks. It has been transformed by a variety of works dating from the eighteenth and nineteenth centuries and is used as a courthouse.

INVERQUHARITY

KIRRIEMUIR, TAYSIDE
(NO 411579)

A smaller tower-house of the fifteenth century, which began as an L-plan, although the smaller wing has gone. Inverquharity was built by the Ogilvy family. The main block is 13.7 x 10.7 metres (45 x 35 ft) with walls about 2.4 metres (8 ft) thick, and it rises four storeys to the parapet, behind which is a wall-walk and an attic storey. The disappeared east wing has been replaced by a later building. The castle remained empty for a long time but restoration work has been carried out recently. The second storey of the main block has the great hall of which the timber roofing is the original fifteenth-century work (cf. Dunsoghly in Ireland).

JEDBURGH BORDERS

(NT 647202)

A motte castle was built on a site at Castle Hill, probably by David I. The castle is mentioned in a mid-twelfth-century charter. It was appropriated by Edward I in 1296, taken back by Wallace in 1297 and recaptured by Edward I in 1298. It was finally destroyed

c.1410 by the Regent Albany. In the 1820s, a building was erected over the site. This was originally designed as a prison and used as such for many years.

KAMES BUTE, STRATHCLYDE

(NS 063075)

Originally a five-storeyed tower-house of the late sixteenth century, Kames was rectangular in plan, about 11 x 7.6 metres (36 x 25 ft), with walls over 1.5 metres (5 ft) thick.

KEIRS STRATHCLYDE

(NS 430080)

Fragments remain here of a stone enclosure castle of the thirteenth century. The castle was attacked by Wallace in 1297–8.

KEISS HIGHLAND

(ND 357616)

A Z-plan tower-house of the late sixteenth century, with two round turrets, now in ruins.

KELBURN LARGS, STRATHCLYDE

(NS 217567)

This interesting castle is really in two parts. One is a four-storeyed, late sixteenth-century rectangular tower-house of Z-plan with cylindrical flanking towers on the south-west and north-east corners. In the early eighteenth century this was enlarged by the erection of a mansion house by the owner, David Boyle, 1st Earl of Glasgow. The site is said to have belonged to the Boyle family since the thirteenth century.

KELLIE NR ARBROATH, TAYSIDE

(NO 608402)

Kellie was raised on rock overlooking Elliot Water. It is a substantial L-plan tower of the sixteenth century, raised upon the site of a late twelfth-century castle built by the Mowbrays. The tower-house has associated buildings around it.

KELLIE PITTENWEEM, FIFE

(NO 520052)

Owned by the Oliphants, and later the Lorimer family, Kellie is huge. Three towers are joined to a main block, the plan roughly in the shape of a 'T'. The north tower was built in the fifteenth century, the east tower was added in the sixteenth and the two were joined by the substantial main block in the seventeenth, with a south tower. There is evidence of the north tower having been raised over earlier remains and it is conjectured that the first 3 metres (10 ft) or so of wall above the ground is of fourteenth-century origin.

KENMURE DUMFRIES AND GALLOWAY
(NX 635764)

Kenmure was an L-plan tower-house of the sixteenth century which was burnt down at the end of the century. In the seventeenth century it was rebuilt and extended into a courtyard castle of two adjacent ranges (south and west), reaching to three storeys plus attic. It fell into decay again, and was abandoned until the nineteenth century when some remodelling altered its character. Then it was left once again.

KIESSIMUL

ISLE OF BARRA, WESTERN ISLES
(NL 665979)

Kiessimul is an enclosure castle of the late twelfth/early thirteenth century. Of irregular shape, its walls are 1.5–2 metres (5–7 ft) thick, and follow the contour of the rock on which it stands, with a square-plan tower in the south-to-south-west wall. It is the westernmost castle in Scotland, stands on a splayed plinth and was probably used as a stronghold in the national struggle against the Vikings in the first half of the thirteenth century. Eventually, the castle came into the ownership of the MacNeils, descendants of whom still hold it today, and who have restored it.

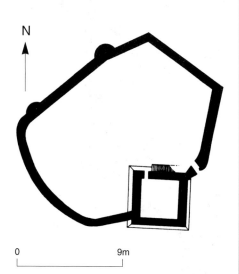

Kiessimul: ground plan.

Kilchurn: the first building – a large fifteenth-century, five-storeyed square tower-house – is on the right. The castle stands on a peninsula jutting into Loch Awe.

KILBIRNIE NR LARGS, STRATHCLYDE
(NS 304541)

Now known as Kilbirnie House, this began as a fifteenth-century castle of towers and curtain wall; however, it has received considerable modifications over the centuries.

KILCHURN STRATHCLYDE
(NN 133276)

Sited on a peninsula in Loch Awe, Kilchurn Castle stands, a splendid ruin, among reeds and marshes. It began as a five-storey, square tower at the east, built in the mid-fifteenth century by Colin Campbell of Glenorchy, 1st Earl of Breadalbane. Additions were made during the sixteenth century, and by the end of the seventeenth the buildings were grouped round a courtyard. It then seems to have been abandoned in the mid-eighteenth century, and is a gaunt shadow of its obvious former splendour. Work has been done to secure some of its dangerous remains and the ruins may be seen from the grounds.

KILCONQUHAR FIFE
(NO 493027)

Kilconquhar is a much altered L-plan tower-house built during the sixteenth century which now forms part of a nineteenth-century mansion.

KILCOY KILLEARNAN, HIGHLAND
(NH 576512)

An interesting Z-plan castle of seventeenth-century construction, which has been restored. Its extension towers (built at the north-west and south-east) are cylindrical, the latter being smaller than the former. Unlike Claypotts, which it resembles in plan, the ground floor here has apartments separated from one main wall by a corridor. Kilcoy incorporates vertical and horizontal gun-loops. The castle belonged to the Mackenzies of Kintail.

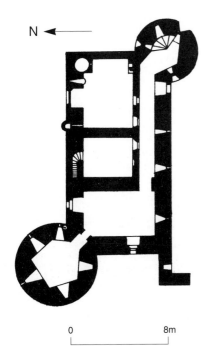

Kilcoy: ground-floor plan of early seventeenth-century Z-plan tower-house.

KILDRUMMY Nr Alford, Grampian
(NJ 455164)

A remarkable early thirteenth-century castle, Kildrummy superseded a twelfth-century motte castle and was put up in the reign of Alexander II (1214–49).

Built of red sandstone, Kildrummy was a substantial enclosure castle, roughly seven-sided – one of the longer sides of a rectangle being pushed out to form a multangular curtain with a large twin-cylindrical-towered gatehouse at the apex (south-east). Each of the four corners of the rectangle had towers: D-shaped at south and east; cylindrical at north; and a much larger cylindrical great tower to the west. A range of buildings was erected along the inner face of the north-west curtain, and the whole structure was surrounded by banks and ditches.

This interesting structure is now ruinous, although there is something left of the towers, the range and the gatehouse. The chapel straddled the east wall of the enclosure at an oblique angle; the twin-towered gatehouse is considered to have been of later construction,

Kildrummy: bold lines indicate the main works of the thirteenth century.

probably the close of the thirteenth century. The great tower is now only visible above ground for a few feet, but it apparently rose five storeys, each of them vaulted. The first floor had a gallery in the wall thickness with arrow-loops all round the outside. The gatehouse, recently excavated and carefully examined, was guarded by a barbican, probably of the fifteenth century. This has a deep pit which was traversed by a drawbridge. The gatehouse appears to have been burned at some time.

Kildrummy was besieged by the English under the Earl of Gloucester in 1306. The castle was besieged again in 1335 and again in 1361, on the second occasion by David II who kept it for several years.

KILHENZIE Strathclyde
(NS 308082)

This rectangular tower-house of the sixteenth century has been much restored. Part of a much larger mansion, it is open seasonally.

KILLOCHAN Strathclyde
(NS 227003)

Said to be one of the finest fortified houses in southern Scotland and today in very good repair, Killochan is a late sixteenth-century, roughly L-plan tower-house, whose main block is five storeys tall. Straight flights of

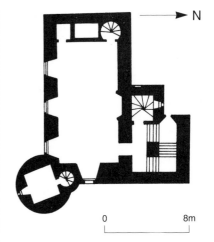

Killochan: first-floor plan (after Renwick) of late sixteenth century stepped L-plan tower-house with straight flights of stairs.

stairs with landings were constructed in the stair tower in the re-entrant angle.

KILMARONOCK Strathclyde
(NS 455877)

Kilmaronock is today derelict. It was a rectangular great tower measuring 13.7 x 12.2 metres (45 x 40 ft) and reaching five storeys tall. Dating from the late fifteenth century, it has ashlar dressings.

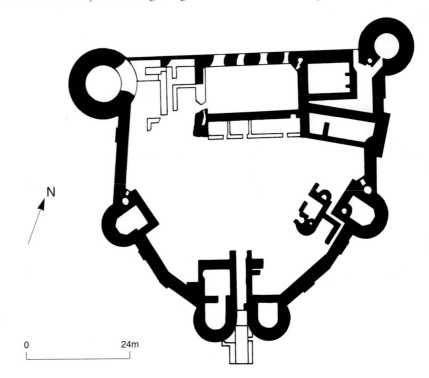

KILRAVOCK CROY, HIGHLAND
(NM 814494)

A small rectangular great tower, 11.9 x 9.4 metres (39 x 31 ft), was built here c.1460. In the seventeenth century it received a square-plan stair tower on the south-west corner and a rectangular structure extended from that to make half a quadrangle. It has been added to in later times. The original works can be seen.

KINCARDINE GRAMPIAN
(NO 671751)

Kincardine is a very early Scottish castle of thirteenth-century origin. It was a simple enclosure castle of curtain wall on a natural hill which was surrounded by marsh land. There were rectangular gate-towers on the south wall. There was also an outer wall with battered plinth.

Kincardine was a royal castle for a time. John Balliol (1292–6) is thought to have drafted his abdication document there. Only fragments remain.

KINCLAVEN TAYSIDE
(NO 158377)

A ruined rectangular enclosure of stone, with projecting square corner towers; it had a curtain which was 2.1 metres (7 ft) thick, overlooking the junction of the Tay and Isla rivers. The stonework is probably twelfth century, although it has been attributed to Malcolm III (1057–93). Only fragments remain. Kinclaven was a royal castle in the reign of Alexander II (1214–49). The design resembles that of Ballymoon, Co. Carlow, Eire (*see* p. 197), and may have been modified early in the thirteenth century.

KINDROCHIT NR BRAEMAR, GRAMPIAN
(NO 151913)

An impressive ruin, this fourteenth-century castle began as a royal hunting lodge in the reign of Robert II (1371–90). The king then granted the site to his friend, Malcolm Drummond, who in the 1390s erected a substantial hall-tower of horizontal rather than vertical shape, about 30.5 x 9.1 metres (100 x 30 ft). Evidently, as shown from excavations in the present century, the hall-tower was erected across the remains of the hunting lodge which had had a basement storey. The earlier building appeared also to have had rectangular turrets on the corners. The Drummond hall-tower was among the largest of this type of tower built in Scotland.

KINGENCLEUCH STRATHCLYDE
(NS 503256)

A borderline castle, that is, a house built as a castle but not well fortified. It was a four-storeyed L-plan tower-house with ashlar dressings. The walls were less than 1 yd thick. The north-west wall stands to about 7 metres (23 ft) with a crow-step gable above. The ground-floor chamber was vaulted.

KINKELL HIGHLAND
(NH 554543)

A tower-house of the sixteenth/seventeenth century built on the 'E' plan. It has been greatly restored.

KINNAIRD FRASERBURGH, GRAMPIAN
(NJ 999675)

An interesting sixteenth-century tall, rectangular tower-house, with cylindrical bartizans at the angles and square bartizans in the straight sides. The tower is 18.3 metres (60 ft) tall, measures 11.9 x 8.2 metres (39 x 27 ft), and was raised in the 1570s. In the 1780s, it was converted for use as a lighthouse which it is today.

KINNAIRD NR BRECHIN, TAYSIDE
(NO 624571)

Kinnaird's first buildings were destroyed by fire in 1452. By the end of the fifteenth century the castle had been rebuilt, with a substantial rectangular tower as the core. Considerable improvements were made in the sixteenth and seventeenth centuries, and more changes later still, but parts of the walls of the earlier building have been incorporated. The castle has been owned by the Carnegie family since the seventeenth century.

KINNAIRD PERTH, TAYSIDE
(NO 241289)

A late fifteenth-century, rectangular tower-house, five storeys tall, which later received a two-storey extension. The tower-house was enclosed inside a curtain wall. The castle is in good repair and is occupied.

KINNAIRDY MARNOCK, GRAMPIAN
(NJ 609498)

This is a structure of several periods and features. It began as a twelfth-century motte castle, possibly contemporary with Duffus. A stone tower was raised on the motte which was partly encased within the stonework. Something of this can be seen today. A curtain wall was built with a tall arched entrance at the north-west. At a later date, possibly 1480, a six-storey tower with a crenellated parapet round its roof was built in the north corner of the enclosure. In the eighteenth century the two highest storeys of the tall tower were pulled down and a gabled attic substituted. By that time Kinnairdy had become a mansion.

KIRKCUDBRIGHT
DUMFRIES AND GALLOWAY
(NX 677509)

Only some earthworks and stone foundations remain of this thirteenth-century castle. It appears to have been a rectangular stone enclosure, comprehensively protected by ditching and banks. The curtain walls were between 2.1–2.7 metres (7–9 ft) thick. There were cylindrical towers on the corners, measuring about 11 metres (36 ft) in diameter. The entrance was guarded by two flanking cylindrical towers.

KNOCKHALL FOVERAN, GRAMPIAN
(NJ 994265)

A three-storeyed L-plan tower-house of the mid-sixteenth century, Knockhall was rebuilt in the seventeenth century and severely damaged by fire in 1734 (recorded as accidental). A cylindrical tower built on the south-east of the tower-house has collapsed. The castle is a ruin.

LAURISTON NR EDINBURGH, LOTHIAN
(NT 203760)

A nineteenth-century mansion has been grafted round the late sixteenth-century tower-house built here, near the southern side of the Firth of Forth. The original tower-house was a rectangular structure, 12.2 x 7.3 metres (40 x 24 ft) with a central projecting tower on the north side which contained the staircase. The castle was the birthplace of John Law, the financier who established the National Bank of France in the eighteenth century. This collapsed, bringing ruin to the economy of France. Recent excavation located a well, 14.9 metres (49 ft) deep, whose water level was about 7.6 metres (25 ft) down.

LAW WEST KILBRIDE, STRATHCLYDE
(NS 211484)

This rectangular tower of c.1460, now roofless, but whose walls are intact, has four storeys and a garret. Restoration work has now begun.

LENNOXLOVE LOTHIAN
(NT 514720)
This used to be known as Lethington Castle because it belonged to the famous Maitlands of Lethington (William Maitland was 'Mr Secretary' Maitland, the Protestant statesman in the time of Mary, Queen of Scots). It began as an L-plan tower in the early fifteenth century, built of rubble, the main block 16.8 x 11.5 metres (55 x 38 ft) and the wing 7 x 9.4 metres (23 x 31 ft). The walls were 2.4–3 metres (8–10 ft) thick. The parapet was altered in the sixteenth century. There were more alterations in the seventeenth century and in more modern times. The tower survives in good condition, and among the original features of interest are dungeons and two iron yetts.

LESLIE GRAMPIAN
(NJ 599248)
Built in 1661, Leslie Castle is often said to be the last fortified tower-house built in Scotland. This claim can, however, be countered by later dates for others, such as Lethendy in Tayside (1678) and Cluny Crichton (1667). Leslie Castle was owned by the Forbes family. It was a stepped L-plan tower-house with a square stair tower in the angle. The staircase was given straight flights. It had vaulted cellars and bartizans. Gun-ports were inserted, one of which covered the entrance to the tower. The castle was built upon the site of a previous structure and the traces of moat round part of it belong to that earlier building. Restoration work is being carried out.

LETHENDRY CROMDALE, HIGHLAND
(NJ 084274)
A sixteenth-century L-plan tower-house, now in poor state, that had at least three storeys. The castle was taken over by the supporters of James VII (James II of England, 1685–8) during the campaign between James and his son-in-law, William of Orange (William III).

LETHENDY TAYSIDE
(NO 140417)
Lethendy Tower is thought to be one of the very last tower-houses to be built in Scotland (c.1678), although for an earlier building date has been argued, perhaps very late sixteenth century. It was a three-storey, L-plan tower-house with attic. Despite extensive alterations, the original form can be seen.

LIBERTON NR EDINBURGH, LOTHIAN
NT 265696
The rectangular tower-house, 10.7 x 7.9 metres (35 x 26 ft), with four storeys beneath its parapet and a garret in the roof, was raised here in the fifteenth century. The parapet encloses an interesting wall-walk. There are few windows or loops in the tower walls.

LICKLYHEAD INSCH, GRAMPIAN
(NJ 627236)
An L-plan tower-house possibly of the late sixteenth century, it has been much altered. A tall roundel staircase turret rises in one corner, corbelled out only a few feet above the ground. The tower is three storeys to the wall-head, with a garret above.

LINLITHGOW LOTHIAN
(NT 003744)
Sited on a mound overlooking Linlithgow Loch, Linlithgow is today a ruin of a great palace-cum-castle. It is roofless but has most of its walling, giving the visitor a good idea of its impressive size and architecture. The fabric is of several building periods, from the 1400s to the 1600s. Its defensive features hinge chiefly upon thick outer walls and tall corner towers which are almost great towers.

Linlithgow may have begun as a royal manor-house for Scottish kings, first of all for David I (1124–53). The site fell into English hands c.1300, and in 1302–3 an enclosure with turrets made of 'great logs not split too small' was erected on the mound by the English King Edward I's order, under the supervision of Master James of St George. These works cost over £1,400 and they are notable also for the workmen failing to be paid their money properly. The works were among one of the last projects supervised by Chester James.

The new enclosure was besieged in 1303 but was not taken. Ten years later, however, it was captured by the Scots and then it began to deteriorate. In 1425, James I of Scotland decided to build a fortified palace on the site at Linlithgow, and during the next decade over £4,500 was spent. The structure that arose was a fine mix of the best contemporary residential appointments, with up-to-date fortifications. The palace was based upon a square courtyard-plan with buildings on all four sides. The extensive works were spread over many years.

Linlithgow: ground-floor plan. E = Old Entrie. The great hall is over the east range which contains the old entrance. The extension at the extreme north-east is the outer great bulwark (Utter Gret Bulwerke, a forebuilding which is now ruinous).

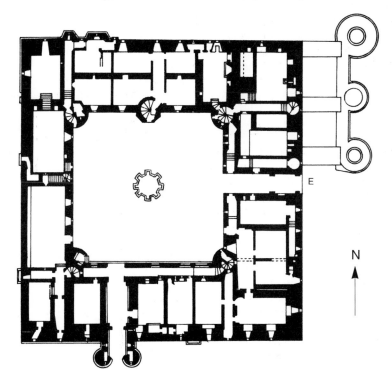

The eastern side of the palace contains, on the first floor, the Lyon Chalmer (or Great Hall). This remarkable structure runs the entire length of the side from the north-east to the south-east corner towers. It had a hammer-beam roof over the main floor space, and a stone barrel-vault over the fireplace at the south. The hall was lit by high clerestory windows. At the north end was a massive stone screen with serving hatches opening into the kitchens in the north-east corner tower. Entrance was via a wheel stair leading up from the courtyard below, but there had also been a stairway. The fireplace is in three sections and, with its many embellishments, is considered to be the finest surviving in the whole of Scotland.

This great hall was built c.1430. The northern side was reconstructed in the 1620s and the resulting range, known as the New Wark, is an interesting building of five storeys with the wheel stair tower on the west, and a polygonal wheel stair tower in the mid-wall position.

Other notable features include the Old Entrie, a round-head arch into the passage through the east side range beneath the great hall, with guardroom and prison flanking one side of the passage. This passage had portcullises. The outside of the entrance passage also has a rounded arch with a carved heraldic panel of the royal arms mounted on the wall face above. There was once a drawbridge, massive oak doors and also an iron yett.

Mary, Queen of Scots was born in the palace on 8 December 1542, scarcely a week before her father, James V, died, broken by the news of the defeat of the Scottish army at Solway Moss.

LITTLE CUMBRAE Bute, Strathclyde
(NS 152513)

There was a fortress on this site dating back to the fourteenth century, which was probably owned by the Crown (Robert II). This was considerably enlarged so that by the sixteenth century it had a rectangular great tower measuring 12.5 x 8.8 metres (41 x 29 ft), and rising to about 14 metres (46 ft) to the parapet. The walls measure 1.8–2.1 metres (6–7 ft) thick, and in the north-west corner a kitchen was arranged partly in the wall thickness of the first floor. Wide-mouthed gun-ports were inserted low in the front façade of the castle.

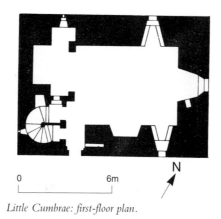

0   6m

Little Cumbrae: first-floor plan.

LOCH DOON Strathclyde
(NX 484950)

If you can build a castle in stone, you can also take it down and re-erect it elsewhere. This was done with Loch Doon, a late thirteenth-century enclosure castle of stone, erected originally upon an island in Loch Doon. The plan of the castle is polygonal with the longest side about 18.3 metres (60 ft) long. The walling is up to 8.5 metres (28 ft) tall, averages 2.4 metres (8 ft) thick and is splayed outwards at the base all round, except for the entrance which is about 2.7 metres (9 ft) wide and has a pointed arch, with two gates. The entrance is not complete.

This was the stonework that was moved piece by piece from the island to the west shore of the loch in 1934–5, a situation brought about when the water level in the loch was raised to service a hydro-electric scheme. The castle was shifted with the greatest skill and care by the Ministry of

Loch Doon: this is the late thirteenth-/early fourteenth-century simple enclosure castle that was moved from its original site, stone by stone, to a new site in the present century. The buildings in outline were later than the enclosure.

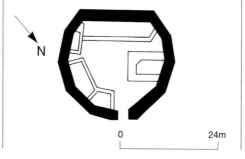

0   24m

Works (now the Scottish Development Department); indeed, every one of the stones was numbered in advance.

The original castle received buildings inside the enclosure at the time of constructions and further buildings later, notably a sixteenth-century range. This later work was not moved in the 1930s.

LOCHINDORB Grampian
(NH 974353)

A very interesting early thirteenth-century stone quadrilateral enclosure castle raised on an island on the Moray-Nairn border, with slightly projecting small cylindrical towers on the angles. Lochindorb resembles Inverlochy in plan. There are substantial remains to be seen. The southern end has an extra courtyard inside an outer wall which has its own gateway with portcullis, but curiously no access to the main enclosure. Presumably the outer yard was a later work. The main enclosure walls are noticeably thin.

Lochindorb was Scottish-built, probably by the Comyn family, but it seems to have been held for a time by Edward I of England in the first years of the fourteenth century. One point of interest is the masonry – large blocks of hard stone brought to a level course every 1.8 metres (6 ft) or so by flat pinnings.

LOCH LEVEN Tayside
(NO 138018)

One of the earliest tower-houses in Scotland, Loch Leven Castle stands inside an enclosure on an island in the loch and was begun in the

Loch Leven: the fourteenth-century tower-house (bold lines) along the north curtain of the later, mainly sixteenth-century enclosure.

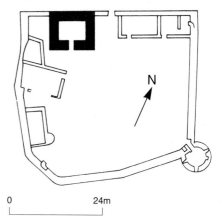

0   24m

fourteenth century. The tower-house is a simple building, an almost square-plan tower some 11 x 9.4 metres (36 x 31 ft), rising to five storeys, the lowest two of which are vaulted, with walls about 2.4 metres (8 ft) thick. The bulging parapet has corbelled roundels on three corners. The principal entrance to the tower was at the second floor on the east wall, leading into the great hall, and a spiral staircase in the wall thickness goes down to the first floor which was also accessible from the basement by a similar stair. Today, the entrance to the castle is in the basement, through a converted window opening. Loch Leven is famous for having been the place where Mary, Queen of Scots was imprisoned from June 1567 to May 1568, when she escaped.

LOCHMABEN

NR DUMFRIES, DUMFRIES AND GALLOWAY
(NY 088811)

Lochmaben began in the late twelfth century and appears to have been an earthwork enclosure with a motte and some extensive ditch and rampart defences. Some time in the 1290s it was given a wooden tower and this may have been the tower upon which the head of Robert Cunynghame, castellan of Caerlaverock, was impaled in 1299 by the English. It is attributed as being a stronghold of the Bruce family, and Robert Bruce's father had for a while been on Edward I's side in his conflict with the Scots, probably because he wanted the Scottish throne which John Balliol had abdicated and which Edward had then assumed.

Some time in the early fourteenth century, Lochmaben received the first stonework, an enclosure curtain, rectangular in plan. Supports for the bridge from the enclosure across the inner moat have survived. The enclosure walls are not in good condition, although parts are still standing high.

LOCH MABERRY

KIRKCOWAN, DUMFRIES AND GALLOWAY
(NX 285751)

This is an island site that has the remains of a substantial dry stone wall, between 1.8–2.1 metres (6–7 ft) thick, and as tall as 2.1 metres in some places, surrounding it. Traces of buildings inside the enclosure remain, and there are entrances on the east and west sides. A great deal of doubt surrounds the origin of this structure, and its history is unknown.

LOCHNAW DUMFRIES AND GALLOWAY
(NW 993632)

Fragments of a rectangular tower-house of large dimensions, about 36.5 x 17 metres (120 x 56 ft), are all that can be seen of the castle built here in the mid-fourteenth century.

LOCHRANZA

ISLE OF ARRAN, BUTE, STRATHCLYDE
(NR 933507)

There are substantial remains of this castle which stands on the edge of a promontory jutting into Lochranza, at the north end of the Isle of Arran. These are of two main periods and it is difficult to separate the two completely because the later period, the sixteenth century, saw a reconstruction of the earlier work (of the late thirteenth/early fourteenth century), using the older masonry and, to some extent, the older layout. In the first period, Lochranza was given a rectangular hall tower of two storeys, the greater part of which remains, with a small square-plan tower (having small rooms and long arrow-loops in the wall face) projecting from one corner. The reconstruction work done in the seventeenth-century included heightening the tower and rearranging the interior.

LOCHWOOD

JOHNSTONE, DUMFRIES AND GALLOWAY
(NY 084968)

There was a motte castle here, thought to be of the twelfth century, with some evidence of a terraced bailey edged with palisades. In the fifteenth century the Johnstone clan erected near the motte 'a fair, large tower' (as a description of 1547 gave it). The tower was rectangular with a stretch of wall extending beyond the north end against which other buildings were raised. The north wall of the tower was about 2.7 metres (9 ft) thick but the other three were only 1.8 metres (6 ft). The tower contained a pit prison. Little remains of this fortress today.

LUFFNESS ABERLADY, LOTHIAN
(NT 475804)

The roughly T-plan, three-storey house at Luffness which overlooks Aberlady Bay was raised in the sixteenth century on the site of a much earlier structure. The castle was positioned inside a strong arrangement of fortifications, built by the French in 1549, which were de-militerised in 1560 by agreement with France.

MACDUFF'S WEMYSS, FIFE
(NT 344971)

Not very much remains of this castle which was originally a late fourteenth-century rectangular tower-house whose entrance was in the west wall. Much later, in the sixteenth century, a range of buildings was built on to the south wall of the tower, and at the end of the range was another rectangular tower, with a rounded projecting turret on the north-east corner, containing the staircase. Some outer walling was looped for guns. The original entrance in the older rectangular tower was blocked up, probably in the sixteenth century.

MACLELLAN'S KIRKCUDBRIGHT,
DUMFRIES AND GALLOWAY
(NX 682510)

MacLellan's Castle is another 'borderline' castle. Basically L-plan, built in 1582, it has an extra, small square tower at one corner. The tower-house is four-storeyed with a double-height garret. It was built from the stones of an older convent of the Greyfriars that stood on the site, and which had become derelict as a result of the Reformation. Features that put MacLellan's into the defendable castle category include minimum window space in the lower storeys, no direct access between the basement and the hall, staircase access upstairs independent of lower storeys, and a spy-hole (which doubtless could be used as a shot-hole) in the back of an inglenook in the great hall.

MAINS EAST KILBRIDE, STRATHCLYDE
(NS 627560)

Mains is now in good repair. This tower-house of the late fifteenth/early sixteenth century, about 11.5 x 8.2 metres (38 x 27 ft), is surrounded by ditching. It stands to the side of an earlier motte castle. There were probably several other buildings ranged around it.

MAUCHLINE STRATHCLYDE
(NS 498273)

A fifteenth-century tower-house, which has ribbed vaulting.

MAYBOLE STRATHCLYDE
(NS 301100)

This was a property of the notorious Cassilis family (*see* Dunure) and it was built in the

early seventeenth century. It was an L-plan tower-house of four storeys plus garret. The tower was given corbelled circular turrets on the angles. The castle has been greatly restored and altered.

MEARNS STRATHCLYDE
(NS 552553)

Mearns Tower was built in the mid-fifteenth century. A licence to 'surround and fortify it [the castle] with wall and ditches, to strengthen by iron gates and to erect on the top of it all warlike apparatus necessary for its defence' was granted to Lord Maxwell in 1449. The result was a rectangular great tower, four storeys tall, 12.2 x 9.1 metres (40 x 30 ft), with walls 3 metres (10 ft) thick, built of rubble masonry. The entrance was inserted at first-floor level, with a spiral staircase to the top. The tower has been restored and converted into a church hall. There are also remains of an enclosing barmkin.

MEGGERNIE TAYSIDE
(NN 554460)

A sixteenth-century, simple, square tower with rectangular corner turrets, each five storeys tall, attached to a later hunting lodge. It was owned in the eighteenth century by James Menzies who introduced the larch tree into Scotland from Austria.

Menzies: this recently restored, large Z-plan castle has two massive, diagonally opposite corner towers.

MEGGINCH INCHTURE, TAYSIDE
(NO 242246)

A late fifteenth-century L-plan tower-house with gun-ports, Megginch became part of a larger and less fortified structure in the seventeenth century. It has been restored and the gardens are open.

MELGUND NR ABERLEMNO, TAYSIDE
(NO 546563)

A ruined castle of the mid-sixteenth century, it began as a rectangular tower-house more typical of the great Scottish fifteenth-century tower-houses. The tower is four-storeyed plus attic, with gun-ports at lower-storey levels. A tall staircase tower was built on the west end, rising higher than the main tower.

MENSTRIE CENTRAL
(NS 849967)

The birthplace of Sir William Alexander, founder of Nova Scotia, Menstrie is a late sixteenth-century L-plan tower-house that was enlarged by adding a second wing and joining with a curtain wall the two wings to form a quadrangle. The castle deteriorated and, by the 1950s, only the two wings

survived in any reasonable state. It was proposed to demolish the castle altogether but, after a considerable and sustained public protest, the local authority stepped in and rescued it.

MENZIES WEEM, TAYSIDE
(NN 837496)

Also called Castle Menzies, this seat of the Clan Menzies is Z-plan and dates from the second half of the sixteenth century (1571–7). The diagonally opposite corner towers of Menzies are massive constructions, described by S.H. Cruden as 'no less commodious than many an isolated tower-house of the same period'. The castle is indeed a substantial fortified residence of formidable appearance. The central block is three-storeyed, with a substantial attic as a fourth, and with a wide, squat bartizan on the two free corners. The diagonally opposed towers which are four-storeyed, plus attic, also have these squat bartizans. There are gun-ports by the entrance. The masonry is in excellent condition. In recent years there has been much restoration.

MERCHISTON EDINBURGH, LOTHIAN
(NT 242718)

Still in fine condition, Merchiston tower-house, built in the fifteenth century, rises five storeys and has walls 1.8 metres (6 ft) thick. Its entrance is on the second floor. The castle received alterations in later years including several sash windows which gave the tower much more interior light. Merchiston was originally enclosed by a curtain wall. It was attacked in 1572 by troops loyal to Mary, Queen of Scots, by then a prisoner of Elizabeth I of England. It was also the family home of the Napiers, notably John Napier, Lord of Merchiston (1550–1617), the inventor of logarithms, who was born there.

METHVEN TAYSIDE
(NO 042260)

A considerably modified rectangular tower-house castle of the seventeenth century, with five storeys.

MEY NR JOHN O'GROATS, HIGHLAND
(ND 290739)

Originally a Z-plan castle of the late sixteenth century with later alterations. It has now been completely restored and is the home of Her Majesty Queen Elizabeth the Queen Mother.

MIDHOPE LOTHIAN
(NT 072786)

The remains of this late sixteenth-century rectangular tower-house, five storeys tall with an attic, are situated in the grounds of Hopetoun House. In the seventeenth century two extensions, one storey lower, were added to the east end, as well as a gateway of ashlar, standing at right-angles to the castle.

MIDMAR GRAMPIAN
(NJ 704052)

This is one of the Z-plan castles which was given diagonally opposite smaller towers of different shapes; the north-west tower is square-plan, the south-east is cylindrical. The main block has a passageway along east and north on the ground floor. There is a half-cylindrical staircase turret in the southern re-entrant between the main block and the cylindrical tower. The north-west tower has straight flights of stairs inside and is adorned with capped roundels on the corners. No gun-ports were fitted.

Midmar was built by the Bell family of masons (who also worked at Crathes) between c.1570 and 1575. The original structure was badly damaged in the 1590s and was reconstructed. The castle belonged to the Gordon family who were powerful in north-east Scotland.

MIGVIE GRAMPIAN
(NJ 436066)

The remains of a thirteenth-century enclosure castle, probably destroyed in the time of King Robert Bruce (1306–29).

MINGARY ARDNAMURCHAN, HIGHLAND
(NM 503631)

Mingary is an irregular hexagonal enclosure castle with rounded angles, which was begun in the thirteenth century. It has walls 1.8 metres (6 ft) thick and between 9.1–12.2 metres (30–40 ft) tall.

It received additions and alterations in later centuries, including buildings erected inside the enclosure, even a barrack block of the eighteenth century. Mingary is thought to have been used as a prison for Covenanters in the seventeenth century. The section of wall that strengthens the north-west corner of the enclosure is thickened on both sides of the entrance at that point, to incorporate a stairway rising over the entrance and leading to a wall-walk.

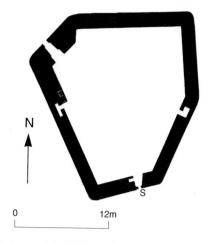

Mingary: (after S.H. Cruden). S = sea gate.

MONIACK HIGHLAND
(NH 552436)

Originally an L-plan tower-house of the mid-seventeenth century, Moniack (or Moniac) has been modernised.

MONTQUHANIE FIFE
(NO 348212)

The remains are left of a sixteenth-century rectangular tower house, with courtyard.

MORTON DUMFRIES AND GALLOWAY
(NX 891992)

An interesting rectangular hall-tower, with a cylindrical turret projecting from one corner, Morton is similar to Rait. It is almost complete to the parapet but has no roof or floors. The principal entrance was through an arch at first-floor level at one end into the main hall. The ground floor is an undercroft. There were other buildings in the castle complex, including a twin-towered gatehouse set in an enclosing curtain. The castle stands high on a promontory overlooking Morton Loch. It was begun in the fourteenth century but is now roofless.

MOTE OF ANNAN DUMFRIES AND GALLOWAY
(NY 192668)

A motte castle of the early twelfth century on the east side of the River Annan, which is mentioned in a document of 1124. The motte was raised to about 15.2 metres (50 ft) tall, and a ditch was cut to separate it from its bailey. The site has been altered. The castle was built by the Brus (Bruce) family.

MOTE OF URR DUMFRIES AND GALLOWAY
(NX 815649)

Excavated in the early 1950s by Dr Brian Hope Taylor (*see* Abinger Motte, Surrey), the Mote of Urr is a motte castle of the mid-twelfth century, perhaps c.1130–50, which was surfaced with clay. The castle was destroyed in 1174 and later rebuilt, with an additional few feet of earth and rubble upon the summit and a new timber tower. The wooden palisade which encircled the motte summit is thought to have had turrets projecting inwards.

MOY STRATHCLYDE
(NM 617247)

This is a ruined tower-house raised in the fifteenth century.

MUCHALLS GRAMPIAN
(NO 892918)

Built in the 1620s round a courtyard, Muchalls has two sides and part of the third as a tall range of apartments, the square closed by a high wall for the rest of the third and the whole of the fourth side. There is a vault with barrel roof in a tower structure on the south side and this may be the remains of what is thought to have been a thirteenth- or fourteenth-century castle on the site. Muchalls was burned by the Duke of Cumberland in 1746, during the Second Jacobite Rising, but was later rebuilt.

MUGDOCK CENTRAL
(NS 550772)

Fragments of a fourteenth-century courtyard-plan castle are still to be seen on this site. It has later additions. The walls are massive and part of the gatehouse is standing.

MUNESS UNST, SHETLAND
(HP 629013)

A late sixteenth-century, Z-plan tower-house with cylindrical corner towers, Muness is built of local rubble. It was very well provided with shot-holes of dumb-bell and quatrefoil design. The rectangular tower block has a straight flight of stairs in the wall's thickness. Some of the shot-holes in the external wall were served by a protected passage in the wall. The tower-house was four-storeyed, although the top-most storey has all but disappeared. This is the most northerly castle in the UK.

MURTHLY Nr Stanley, Tayside
(NO 072399)
Sited on the south side of the Tay, and today enveloped in woodland, Murthly was begun probably in the late fifteenth century, and the earliest building may have been the surviving tall, slim, 4.3-metre (14-ft) square tower, with slightly projecting stair turret at the south-east. The tower was at the south-west angle of a later courtyard with western range, built in the late sixteenth century, and this acquired subsequent additions during the next 200 years. In the nineteenth century a substantial mansion was built adjacent to this earlier part.

MYRES Auchtermuchty, Fife
(NO 242109)
The greater part of this castle is of modern building upon a small sixteenth-century three-storeyed house (plus attic), consisting of a central rectangular block 9.7 x 7.3 metres (32 x 24 ft), with two towers projecting from opposing corners, with a most interesting corbelled-out square-plan turret at the top levels of the north-east angle.

NEIDPATH Nr Peebles, Borders
(NT 236404)
This massive L-plan tower-house, built at the end of the fourteenth century on a rocky slope leading down to the Tweed, is in remarkably good exterior condition. Its plan is interesting: both arms of the 'L' are parallelograms, not rectangles; the corners are rounded, not squared. The top two storeys of the four have been remodelled. There are

Neidpath: basement plan. The basement is vaulted.

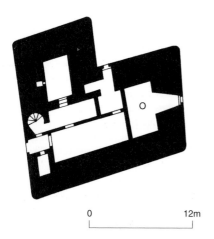

0   12m

other buildings of later date, chiefly of the sixteenth century, including an interesting gateway with a round-headed arch in the east wall of a range of building. The walls of the tower-house are 3 metres (10 ft) thick in some places.

Although the castle has a formidable appearance, its only siege experience appears to have been in the time of Cromwell.

NEWARK Borders
(NT 421293)
Newark tower-house was a Douglas-held castle built on a mound c.1423–4. It was a rectangular tower-house with end gables, surrounded by a barmkin. Keyhole gun-ports were added in the tower walls in the later part of the fifteenth century. After the Battle of Philiphaugh in 1645, at which Montrose was defeated by the Covenanters but escaped, many of his followers were taken and put to death in the courtyard of the castle. Newark is a ruin today, but well preserved.

NEWARK Strathclyde
(NS 322173)
A sixteenth-century tower-house, 9.7 x 8.2 metres (32 x 27 ft), on rising ground once surrounded by a moat (now filled), Newark rises to four storeys with a battlemented parapet enclosing a garret. Additions in the seventeenth century included another tower built on to the western wall, which has five storeys. In the nineteenth century the castle was further renovated.

NEWTON Tayside
(NO 172452)
A seventeenth-century Z-plan castle built upon the ruins of a sixteenth-century mansion that was later destroyed by fire. Masonry from the first building appears to have been used for the foundations and lower walls for the second.

NEWTON Strathclyde
(NS 339223)
Only ruins remain of the fifteenth-century castle of towers and curtain walling.

NIDDRY Kirkliston, Lothian
(NT 095743)
Niddry, a tall, massive tower of L-plan shape, was built in the early sixteenth century on a rocky mound near Kirkliston. It was given a curtain wall, of which traces can still be seen

on the western side. The tower is four storeys high to the parapet, although the top storey was added in the seventeenth century. The tower walls are 2.1–2.4 metres (7–8 ft) thick. In recent years much excavation has been carried out, and finds include a rectangular building, 14 x 6.7 metres (46 x 22 ft), a smithy and other outbuildings.

Mary, Queen of Scots was brought to Niddry by Lord Seton on the evening of her escape from Loch Leven in 1568.

NOLTLAND Isle of Westray, Orkney
(HY 429488)
Founded in the 1560s by Gilbert Balfour (who was party to the murder of Cardinal Beaton in 1546), Noltland is one of the earliest of the Z-plan castles. Noltland has square-plan towers on diagonally opposite corners of a long, rectangular main tower block. The tower-house was extremely well fortified. Both main block and corner towers are fitted with tiers of gun-ports, wide-mouthed and both square- and round-cornered, enough to give covering fire in all directions – some 70 gun-ports in all. The south-west angle-tower was not completed. In almost every respect the castle's military features overwhelmed the domestic: even the great hall on the first floor had windows on only one side. And the solar was effectively separated from the hall by a thick wall with a stout door. The walls of the tower-house are basically 1.8–2.1 metres (6–7 ft) thick.

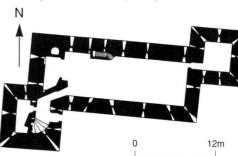

N

0   12m

Noltland: ground floor of the sixteenth-century, powerfully fortified, Z-plan castle. Note the proliferation of gun-ports on this floor.

Gilbert Balfour was also involved in the murder of the Earl of Darnley, second husband of Mary, Queen of Scots, in 1567, and the castle at Noltland was a hideout for him and his followers.

OLD DUNDAS DALMENY, LOTHIAN
(NT 117767)
Old Dundas has the distinction of being the earliest Scottish castle for which a proper licence to crenellate was issued, in 1424: 'to build a tower … of Dundas in the manner of a castle with the kernels, etc., usual in a fortalice of this sort according to the manner of the Kingdom of Scotland …' And to bear this out, it has to this day an impressive crenellated parapet round the top of its L-plan and its second wing on the north-west angle. The crenellation is thought to be of the sixteenth century but this may be too late an estimate. Its entrance is protected by a yett, and its walls are in places 3 metres (10 ft) thick. Old Dundas has experienced certain internal alterations: it was once used as a distillery. It is now empty.

OLD SLAINS GRAMPIAN
(NK 053300)
The sole remains of the castle of Old Slains are the ruins of a fourteenth-century tower-house and some vestiges of barmkin to the south. The castle was built by the Hay family, the chief of which became Hereditary High Constable of Scotland.

OLD WICK HIGHLAND
(ND 369488)
Old Wick stands on a promontory of rock, three of the four sides protected by cliffs and the fourth defended by a ditch. The castle began as a rectangular great tower of the thirteenth century, with four storeys, walls up to 2.1 metres (7 ft) thick, and measuring about 9.7 x 7 metres (32 x 23 ft). The walls still stand to a maximum height of 12.2 metres (40 ft). There was no entrance on the ground floor and that storey is lit only by a few loops. The entrance was in the first storey and was reached by an outside staircase which was probably made of wood, since no traces of a stone flight of steps have been detected.

Old Wick is thought by some authorities to have been of Viking origin. Today, the castle is a ruin.

OLIVER'S TWEEDSMUIR, BORDERS
(NT 099250)
Considerable doubts surround this castle site. Some fragments of a fortress on a low hill have been found. The site was protected on one side by a long slope falling 61 metres (200 ft) to the Tweed valley. On its other sides it appears to have been protected by two lines of ditch and scarp. A castle at Oliver is mentioned in a document of c.1200. Is this ruin of the same castle?

ORCHARDTON NR CASTLE DOUGLAS, DUMFRIES AND GALLOWAY
(NX 817551)
This is one of the very few cylindrical tower-houses built in Scotland. It was raised in the mid-fifteenth century by John Caryns (or Cairns), Provost of Lincluden. The internal arrangements of the tower are much the same as those of a rectangular tower-house of the same period: in Orchardton's case the basement is vaulted; entrance to the tower is at first-floor level by means of a stairway outside; the internal plan of the basement is rectangular but the plans of the first, second and top storeys are circular. There is no access from the ground floor to the higher floors. The tower walls are basically 1.8 metres (6 ft) thick, and the tower's spiral staircase is in the wall thickness. The top of the tower had a gabled cap-house resting on a corbelled parapet. It is 10 metres (33 ft) tall from the ground to the parapet. Nothing is known of the history of the tower.

PEEL OF LUMPHANAN GRAMPIAN
(NJ 576037)
Lumphanan was the site of the battle where the great Scottish king, Macbeth (1040–57), was killed, having lost to Malcolm Ceanmor who became Malcolm III (1057–93). A motte castle was built here in the twelfth century. The mound is over 9.1 metres (30 ft) tall, and was surrounded by a ditch about 15.2 metres (50 ft) wide, banked and enclosed by another ditch. In the late twelfth or early thirteenth century a shell enclosure was raised on the motte, whose wall was about 0.9 metres (1 yd) thick. Against the curtain of the shell was built a hall, about 15.2 x 3.6 metres (50 x 12 ft), possibly after the raising of the curtain. The castle is now ruinous. There has been further excavation in recent years, and it was established that the original height of the mound had been artificially raised in the thirteenth century, presumably to support the shell enclosure.

PENKHILL GIRVAN, STRATHCLYDE
(NX 232985)
A sixteenth-century tower-house which has been modernised.

PITCAPLE GRAMPIAN
(NJ 727260)
A Z-plan castle of c.1570, renovated in the 1830s, Pitcaple's main building is four storeys tall with two round towers on diagonally opposite corners. The tower on the west corner contains the staircase and is smaller than the east tower. High walling was added to form a sort of courtyard, and the whole was provided with ditching although there are no signs of it now. There are grounds for believing that the central block is earlier than 1570, possibly by a century or more. In the nineteenth century an extra block was added.

PITCRUVIE FIFE
(NO 414046)
Little remains of the original sixteenth-century tower-house beside a farm here.

PITCULLO LEUCHARS, FIFE
(NO 413193)
A small, late sixteenth-century three-storey tower-house, basically L-plan, with a cylindrical staircase tower centrally placed along the northern long wall. A second staircase was provided in the south-west corner of the wing. There is a surviving undercroft at the east end, vaulted, and now used as a dining room. Another tower, of rectangular plan, was added later and juts out of the south and east corners. The castle was restored after the Second World War.

PITFICHIE MONYMUSK, GRAMPIAN
(NJ 677166)
A half Z-plan rectangular tower of the late sixteenth/early seventeenth century with one cylindrical corner turret. It has been restored in recent years.

PITHLEAVIS TAYSIDE
(NO 103228)
An early sixteenth-century rectangular tower with a square projecting tower at the south-west and two corner turrets. The tower is provided with gun-ports.

PITSLIGO GRAMPIAN
(NJ 937670)
Pitsligo Castle is largely in ruins. There is an outer shell of a tower of the early fifteenth century, about 15.8 x 11.3 metres (52 x 37 ft), with 3-metre (10-ft) thick walls rising to the second storey. The third storey was demolished c.1700. In the sixteenth century

the tower was absorbed into a quadrangular-plan mansion. The castle was surrounded by a ditch. The tower appears to have had one large room on each floor, the normal arrangement found in many earlier and smaller English and Welsh great towers, viz. basement kitchen, ground-floor dining hall (with screened-off solar for the owner and his wife) and room for family guests on top.

PITTEADIE
KINGHORN, KIRKCALDY, FIFE
(NT 257891)
This ruinous castle stands about 2.4 km (1½ miles) north of Kinghorn. It began as a rectangular tower-house of the late fifteenth century, about 10 x 8.2 metres (33 x 27 ft), with four storeys and a cap-house on top of one corner. There are signs of alterations of later date, but the whole is in a poor state.

PITTULIE PITSLIGO, GRAMPIAN
(NJ 945670)
The ruins of a seventeenth-century rectangular tower-block about 21.3 x 7.3 metres (70 x 24 ft); it has walls which are 0.9 metres (3 ft) thick. The block had a square tower in the north-west corner, which still stands to roof height.

PLEAN TOWER ST NINIANS, CENTRAL
(NS 849869)
A rectangular tower-house built in the fifteenth century, it had a courtyard partly bounded by a range of buildings, of later date. Although restored at the beginning of the present century it is now in ruins.

PLUNTON DUMFRIES AND GALLOWAY
(NX 605507)
An L-plan tower-house, of only 6.4 x 4.6 metres (21 x 15 ft), with a staircase turret at the west angle, Plunton was three-storeyed with an attic; however, it is now roofless and decaying.

PORTENCROSS
WEST KILBRIDE, STRATHCLYDE
(NS 175489)
This ruinous castle on the coast of the Clyde began as a rectangular tower of three storeys and a garret. The walls were massively built and most of them remain today. A wing tower of one storey extra in height, with a vaulted ground floor, was added to one long side. The vaulted storey incorporated a

kitchen and a second kitchen was provided at first-floor level. The tower had two entrances and two stairs, the staircase beginning from the ground floor being straight, the first-floor ascending as a spiral. From ground level it was possible to climb to the battlements without disturbing the occupants of the hall in the main tower block. The castle, which was begun in the fourteenth century, was given by Robert Bruce to the Boyd family of Kilmarnock. It guarded a crossing to Bute.

POWRIE TAYSIDE
(NO 421346)
A large, fifteenth-century Z-plan castle with barmkin wall and other buildings, of which little remains.

PRONCY DORNOCH, HIGHLAND
(NH 771925)
A small rectangular tower, about 6 x 3.6 metres (20 x 12 ft), with walls about 1.5 metres (5 ft) thick, was built on a motte here probably in the fourteenth century. There are few remains to be seen.

RAIT NAIRN, HIGHLAND
(NM 894525)
Rait Castle is complete to its wall-tops. It was an unusual rectangular hall-tower of the early fourteenth century whose larger horizontal dimension was greater than the height: 16.4 x 6.7 x 11 metres (54 x 22 x 36 ft) tall to the

Rait: first-floor plan.

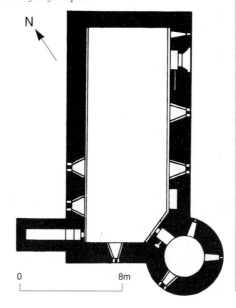

wall-top. Entrance to the tower was at the end of the first-floor level, protected by a portcullis, and at the south corner of the other end was built a cylindrical tower. On the west corner is an 2.4-metre (8-ft) wide garderobe tower, about 3.6 metres (12 ft) long. The walls of the hall and the cylinder tower are about 1.8 metres (6 ft) thick, except the north-east end which is about 0.4 metres (1½ ft) thinner.

RAVENSCRAIG KIRKCALDY, FIFE
(NT 290924)
Ravenscraig was the first castle in Britain to be designed specifically for defence by guns. It was intended by James II of Scotland, who initiated the work in the year of his death, 1460, to be a coastal fortress to guard against any attack from the waters of the Firth of Forth. The building work accounts for the years 1460–3 and have largely survived. It was equipped to store gunpowder and armaments in spacious and well protected cellars, in addition to its remarkable offensive gunfire capability.

The castle is positioned on a prominent and exposed rocky site jutting into Kirkcaldy Bay. The rock rises as sheer cliff on the west side to about 21.3 metres (70 ft) above the beach and falls away to the east in steep terraces. A wide, natural gully divides the site from the mainland, and this was artificially extended. The front of the castle facing the northern landward end of the promontory consists of a range of buildings with a well-fortified entrance passage in the middle, on the ground floor. At each end of the range was a huge D-plan tower with walls 3–4.3 metres (10–14 ft) thick, both projecting into the ditch. The west tower is still four storeys tall plus garret but without its roof, and has a vaulted basement which was at the same level as the ground floor of the centre range whose chambers and passages are also vaulted. The towers were given keyhole gun-ports, some of them designed to accommodate falconets (very small cannons). The central range has a second-storey artillery platform with a parapet in front, and this parapet contained wide-mouth openings for small guns. The eastern tower, three-storeyed and with a round front projecting into the ditch, has its basement storey and half the first storey below the level of the ground floor of the central range, the top of the top storey being in line with the central range's ceiling. Each tower had a well.

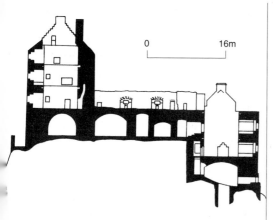

Ravenscraig (Fife): elevation facing inland.

The outer wall of the western tower stands sheer on a slope down to the beach.

The western tower is in reality a great tower, fortified and residential. Each storey had mural chambers as well as main centre rooms, with garderobes. There were kitchens and other offices in a detached range behind the tower towards the end of the promontory. The whole front of the castle presented a most formidable array of gun-ports through which, if provoked, the garrison could have discharged the most murderous fire. Its position on the shore meant that, if it was besieged, a garrison could hold out for a very long time because it could be supplied from the sea (cf. Tantallon).

RAVENSCRAIG GRAMPIAN
(NK 095488)
A fifteenth-century L-plan tower-house which has interesting gun-loops. They are positioned at ground level and are for the most part long slits with shorter crosslets near the top and circular openings at the bottom. The castle was licensed c.1490.

RED CASTLE (OF LUNAN)
INVERKEILOR, TAYSIDE
(NO 687510)
There was a fortified house raised on a promontory and partly surrounded by ditches in the twelfth century. It was used by William the Lion (1165–1214) as a hunting lodge. Fragments of a thirteenth-century high curtain wall (1.8 metres [6 ft] thick) and of a fifteenth-century rectangular tower still remain. The castle was besieged in 1579 and has remained in a ruinous state ever since.

RENFREW STRATHCLYDE
(NS 513674)
A fortification is mentioned in a mid-twelfth-century manuscript (c.1163–5). Its shape is unknown. It was replaced by a stone castle in the thirteenth century, which in turn was demolished c.1777 and replaced by a mansion, also demolished (1924) according to the Ordnance Survey at Edinburgh.

REPENTANCE
ANNANDALE, DUMFRIES AND GALLOWAY
(NY 155722)
Repentance Tower was constructed by John Maxwell, Lord Herries, in the mid-sixteenth century. It was on a square plan, with three main storeys to the parapet, and built of coursed rubble. It was equipped with more gun-ports and shot-holes than windows. It has been repaired and is in fine condition.

ROSSEND BURNTISLAND, FIFE
(NT 228858)
An ecclesiastical castle at first, built by the abbots of Dunfermline in the thirteenth century. In the sixteenth century Rossend was converted to a T-plan tower-house which incorporated some of the original stonework at lower levels. It has been restored and so its original shape is not definable.

ROSSLYN LASSWADE, LOTHIAN
(NT 275627)
Rosslyn Castle, also spelt Roslin, stands on a strong position on a peninsula created by the River Esk, which provides protection on three sides. Owned by the St Clair family, Princes (and later Earls) of Orkney, the 2nd Earl erected a tower-house on the site in the 1390s. It was added to in later generations but is now derelict, due chiefly to the artillery, first, of the Earl of Hertford in the 1540s and, second, that of Cromwell in the late 1640s. Extensions were also added to it in the late seventeenth century.

ROSYTH NR DUNFERMLINE, FIFE
(NT 108821)
The castle lies in the Royal Naval Dockyard at Rosyth. It consists of a rectangular enclosure of the sixteenth/seventeenth century, inside which at the north-east angle is an earlier (fifteenth-century) tower-house. The tower-house, which was free-standing, is about 12.5 x 14.6 metres (41 x 48 ft), three storeys tall, with walls about 3 metres (10 ft) thick. It was built with ashlar facing, and the ground and first floors were vaulted. There is a small wing at the south-east with the staircase.

ROTHESAY BUTE, STRATHCLYDE
(NS 088646)
The castle probably began as a low-level earth platform surrounded by a broad wet ditch, erected in the twelfth century. Then, some time in the thirteenth century, the motte was crowned with a huge and tall circular stone curtain of sandstone some 45.7 metres (150 ft) in diameter, making it an enormous shell enclosure. It is one of the few shell enclosures in Scotland. It was battlemented right round the top but, when part of the curtain was later heightened, the battlements were sealed up and used as the base for the extra wall height which was raised on top of them.

Early in the thirteenth century, four stout cylindrical towers were added to the outside of the shell, placed equidistantly round the circumference, and between the west and east towers a simple but tall square-plan gateway was inserted which was considerably altered and enlarged by James IV in the early 1500s. There were other later buildings situated inside the enclosure.

In 1230 Rothesay was besieged by Vikings from the Western Isles and Scandinavia under a chief called Uspak, whose men succeeded in breaking through the wall under the protection of a penthouse by hacking away at the stonework with axes, for the stone and the mortar were soft. The castle fell again to the Vikings, this time under their king, Haakon of Norway, in 1263, but a few weeks later Haakon and his forces were decisively defeated by Alexander III at the great Battle of Largs.

Rothesay: one of the few shell enclosures in Scotland. The shell wall was built in the late twelfth century and the round turrets added in the thirteenth century.

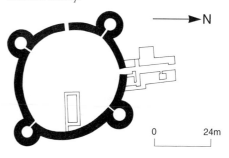

When the Stewarts became Kings of Scotland in the fourteenth century, Rothesay passed into royal hands.

ROWALLAN STRATHCLYDE
(NS 435424)

A mansion from the sixteenth/seventeenth century of thin walls that was built as a castle. The plan was approximately L-shaped, with two ranges of buildings at right-angles, the 'square' being completed by curtain walling and a further tower. In the south front there is a twin-cylindrical-towered gatehouse approached up a flight of stairs. The gatehouse has a passage nearly 6 metres (20 ft) long leading into the courtyard formed by the 'square'. The two ranges have their own spiral staircases. The gatehouse has a very formidable look, but is in fact a showpiece: the walls are less than 0.9 metres (1 yd) thick. The whole structure, the west range of which is equipped with dumb-bell gun-ports at ground level, was built upon the remains of an earlier mid-thirteenth-century rectangular great tower castle. The original great tower was 10.7 x 8.5 metres (35 x 28 ft) and probably rose to three storeys.

ROXBURGH BORDERS
(NT 713337)

Roxburgh was once a major Border fortress. It began as a motte castle raised on the north side of the Teviot early in the twelfth century (mentioned in a charter of c.1128). Whether the motte castle was built by a Scot or a Norman is not known, but from 1175 to 1189 it was held by Henry II of England. Roxburgh was garrisoned during Edward I's campaigns in southern Scotland at the end of the thirteenth century, but in 1314 it was captured by the Scots after an attack by night and, according to the Lanercost chronicler, was pulled down. In 1335–7, it was taken and rebuilt by Edward III; this work included a small pele-tower of wood, the prefabricated parts for which were transported by sea from Newcastle to Berwick and then by river (or land) to Roxburgh. The castle was retaken in 1342 by David II but lost again after the Battle of Neville's Cross in 1346. In Richard II's reign, a gatehouse was built and other fortifications were undertaken; this included heightening the existing towers, and a great wall 9.1 metres (30 ft) tall, with towers. The works cost about £2000.

In 1436, James I of Scotland besieged Roxburgh but failed to capture it. His son, James II, also besieged the castle in July 1460. This was when he was killed by one of his cannons that exploded beside him. But a few days later the castle fell and once more the Scots destroyed it.

In the 1540s, Roxburgh fell into English hands again and it was partially rebuilt. But by the 1550s it was once more in ruins, as it is today. Fragments remain of some of the towers, of the Richard II gatehouse and stretches of the curtain wall as high 4 metres (13 ft) in places.

RUSKO (RUSCO)
DUMFRIES AND GALLOWAY
(NX 584604)

A sixteenth-century rectangular tower-house, still three storeys plus attic in height. The tower is about 11.5 x 8.8 metres (38 x 29 ft), and the walls 1.8–2.4 metres (6–8 ft) thick. Its parapet is battlemented. A two-storey wing on the north, added in the seventeenth century, is ruinous but the castle has been restored.

RUTHERGLEN STRATHCLYDE
(NS 614617)

The site of this once-important castle in the Glasgow area has been built over. It was taken by the English during the War of Scottish Independence, besieged by Robert Bruce but did not fall until his brother, Edward Bruce, attacked and took it c.1313.

The castle was besieged again, in the war between Mary, Queen of Scots and the Regent, James, Earl of Moray, to whom it fell in 1568.

SADDELL
MULL OF KINTYRE, STRATHCLYDE
(NR 789315)

An interesting tower-house built between 1508 and 1512; it stands among some later buildings that are not of concern to us here. The tower has four storeys plus garret, a battlemented parapet with open angle-turrets, with a cap-house on one side. The entrance is on the ground floor. The tower-house was enclosed by a barmkin over 1.2 metres (4 ft) thick and about 3.6 metres (12 ft) tall, some of which remains today. For a time the castle belonged to the Bishops of Argyll and it later became a Campbell possession. After years of neglect, it has been restored and is now used as a guest house.

ST ANDREWS FIFE
(NO 513169)

This interesting fortress stands on a rock promontory to the north-east of the ancient city. The first stonework was erected in the late twelfth century and was the inner part of the Fore-Tower on the south (inland) side of the promontory. The Fore-Tower cannot have stood alone because it was too small to serve any purpose other than as a gateway, and it may be presumed that the tower was flanked on either side by wooden palisading that might have followed the lines of the present ruins of the late stonework enclosure. Timber buildings were doubtless raised inside. The castle was protected by a deep ditch on the south side.

In c.1336, the Fore-Tower was enlarged, but was demolished a year later when Andrew Moray slighted the castle. Towards the end of the fourteenth century, a major building programme was started; this included erecting a substantial curtain round the whole enclosure with two new towers (the Sea Tower at north-west and the Kitchen Tower at north-east), and re-building the Fore-Tower. Much of the west and south-west curtain is still standing. The castle later became a favourite residence of the Crown: James III was probably born there in 1451.

The next building phase was in the first half of the sixteenth century, when the south-east and south-west corners were given cylindrical towers; these were destroyed in the 1546–7 siege. This siege resulted when Cardinal Beaton, Archbishop of St Andrews, was murdered in the castle by Protestant infiltrators during the religious strife of the mid-sixteenth century in Scotland. The Protestants captured the castle and held it for a year against Catholic forces under Mary of Guise, mother of Mary, Queen of Scots. The Catholic siege was fierce and sustained, and extensive damage was done to the stonework. It was during this siege that the attackers sank a mine through the rock on which the castle stood, tunnelling towards the Fore-Tower. The defenders got to know of the attempt, calculated the direction the tunnel was taking, and sank a counter-mine, just outside the Fore-Tower, hoping to join up with the besiegers' tunnel and fight them off. The mine and the counter-mine, cut in the living rock, have survived to this day. The former is about 2.1 metres (7 ft) high and about 1.8 metres (6 ft) wide and slants downwards to pass under

This view of St Andrews shows the Fore-Tower on the left and, behind to the right, the courtyard, with the remains of the Sea Tower (left) and the kitchen tower (right). At ground level and just to the right of the Fore-Tower is the entrance to the counter-mine.

the ditch. The counter-mine is much the same size, and it reached the head of the besiegers' mine nearly 12.2 metres (40 ft) out from the Fore-Tower. Today, visitors can walk (or crawl) through the tunnels which are lit and are provided with railings.

The castle fell after nearly a year, and among the Protestant prisoners taken was John Knox, later to become the champion of the Scottish Reformation. He was sent to serve as a galley slave in the French fleet and spent two years chained to an oar.

SALTCOATS LOTHIAN
(NT 486818)
A late sixteenth-century courtyard castle, as it were, whose principal structure was a 22 x 7 metres (72 x 23 ft) building with two projecting angle-towers at the western end. The castle is partly ruinous and much of the walling is missing. It had been pulled down two centuries ago to provide materials for another entrance.

SANQUHAR DUMFRIES AND GALLOWAY
(NS 785092)
Sanquhar is now in ruins. Begun by the Crichton family in the fourteenth century, it was a rectangular courtyard castle with a substantial front mass (like Doune), with a tall tower at the south corner, which has been restored. The site was protected naturally on the north-west, south and east sides by a cut-ditch of which little remains, and which is flanked by a rampart. The quadrangle had a range of buildings on each inner side, of varying periods, beginning in the fifteenth century. There are remains of associated buildings in front of the rectangular enclosure, dating chiefly from the seventeenth century.

SAUCHIE ALLOA, CENTRAL
(NS 896597)
A square-plan tower of the fifteenth century is the principal feature of this courtyard castle. The tower was built of ashlar, and parts are still in good condition. There are three storeys to the parapet which has a bartizan on one edge. Buildings were added later.

SCALLOWAY NR LERWICK, SHETLAND
(HU 405393)
Scalloway is a four-storeyed tower-house of the end of the sixteenth century. Today its garret and roof are missing. Its plan is rectangular, with the north-east corner bulging into a cylindrical stair turret from the first storey upwards, and its south-west provided with a large square-plan tower containing straight flights of stairs to the top. There is also a secondary spiral staircase in a curved projection in the angle between the main block and the south-west tower, on the north side, also from the first floor upwards. Fortification was provided by the insertion of shot-holes in window breasts (many have since been blocked), and by gun-ports, especially in the south-west tower. The ground floor of the stair tower has a vaulted chamber under the stairs; this was a guard-room, with platforms and gun-ports.

Scalloway was built by Patrick Stewart, Earl of Orkney, a man of violent and cruel disposition believed to have mixed the blood of his victims with the mortar for his castle – almost certainly a myth. Animal blood, however, may have been used. The castle was allowed to deteriorate for a long time, but some restoration has been carried out by SDD.

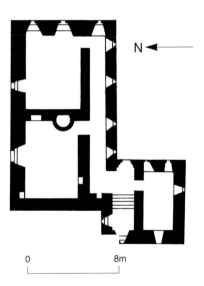

N ◄—

0   8m

Scalloway: ground-floor plan. This is an early example of a Scottish tower-house having straight flights of stairs.

SCHIVAS TARVES, GRAMPIAN
(NJ 897368)
A sixteenth-century L-plan tower-house incorporated now in a more modern mansion. It is notable for its ornamental shot-holes designed mainly for pistols.

Scotstarvit: the six-storeyed tower-house has an impressive machicolated parapet all round.

SCOTSTARVIT TOWER

NR CUPAR, FIFE
(NO 370113)
A fine tower-house of L-plan design, built between 1550 and 1579. It was the home at one time of Sir John Scot, brother-in-law of the poet William Drummond, who wrote a book called *Scot of Scotstarvit's Staggering State of Scots Statesmen* (later described by Carlyle as a 'homily on life's nothingness enforced by examples'). The tower is six-storeyed, including mezzanine (between ground and first floors) and attic (surrounded by parapet). The very small wing of the 'L' contains the spiral stair all the way up, and the wing was topped with a cap-house of stone. The six storeys contained six rooms of equal floor area, one above the other. The tower is notable for the scarcity of windows.

SELKIRK BORDERS

(NT 470281)
A large, natural mound north of Loch Haining formed the basis of an early twelfth-century motte castle which was later given stone buildings, probably by Edward I, in the very late thirteenth century. The mound received a pele-tower. The surrounding ditch was about 12.2 metres (40 ft) wide on average. The castle was taken by the Scots in 1301–2.

SKELBO DORNOCH, HIGHLAND

(NH 792592)
Now a ruin, Skelbo appears to have begun as a rectangular great tower in the fourteenth century, enclosed inside a barmkin. Some of the barmkin has been rebuilt in later style. The tower is 13.1 x 8.8 metres (43 x 29 ft),

with walls about 1.5 metres (5 ft) thick, and much of this is still stands. It is clear that the tower was repaired for use in much later times. There are remains of other buildings within the barmkin.

SKELMORLIE LARGS, STRATHCLYDE

(NS 195658)
A rectangular tower-house of c.1500 with additions of the 1630s which included a smaller tower in the barmkin. It was renovated in the nineteenth century and converted into a mansion. In the original tower part, the kitchen was divided from the dining hall by a screened passage.

SKIPNESS KINTYRE, STRATHCLYDE

(NR 907577)
Skipness is an enclosure castle of thirteenth-century origin, which has been greatly modified over the centuries. Today, it is a ruin in fair condition, basically a stone quadrangle with a tower-house of L-plan in one corner. The masonry of the earliest work is good quality.

The first structure was a rectangular stone hall-house. This was enclosed by a timber palisade upon an encircling rampart. Nearby, and at more or less the same time, a chapel was built, and it was dedicated to St Columba. Towards the end of the thirteenth century, the hall-house was reduced and absorbed in some new building work and the palisade was converted to stone. These buildings included a larger hall and some towers, one of which, in the north-east corner, used part of the original hall-house's east wall. This tower was later developed into an L-plan tower-house, whose remaining shell rises four storeys to the parapet. The stonework enclosure received an arched entrance gate on the south wall, equipped with a portcullis, which faces the sea. A second arch was inserted in the north wall later. Note the quality of the early masonry, the ashlar cross-loops in the west curtain, and the interesting siting near the sea.

SMAILHOLM BORDERS

(NT 637346)
This four-storey rectangular tower-house stands on a spur which was enclosed by a ditch and by stone walling. Three sides of the spur are rock cliff. The tower walls are nearly 3 metres (10 ft) thick and the tower reaches nearly 18.3 metres (60 ft). The building is chiefly seventeenth-century work. Smailholm was a favourite castle of Sir Walter Scott. It is now a ruin.

SORBIE TOWER

DUMFRIES AND GALLOWAY
(NX 451470)
This L-plan tower-house of the sixteenth century was abandoned after the Second Jacobite Rising (1745–6). The main block is 12.2 x 7.3 metres (40 x 24 ft), and probably rose to four storeys.

SORN STRATHCLYDE

(NS 548269)
A sixteenth-century great tower and curtain wall castle of rectangular plan, which was later restored and modified.

SPEDLIN'S TOWER

LOCHMABEN, DUMFRIES AND GALLOWAY
(NT 097875)
This is an interesting ruin of a once-splendid rectangular tower-house. It began as a three-storeyed tower (including basement) with a pit prison of dimensions of only 2.2 x 0.8 metres (7½ ft x 2½ ft). In the seventeenth century, the tower was considerably modified by adding two further storeys, the top of which was surrounded by a parapet, at each end of which was inserted a round corbelled turret with 'pepper-pot' roof. The roof of Spedlin's was unusual: it was a double one with two gables in between which ran a horizontal stretch. The horizontal stretch roofed a central corridor in the storey below, which had rooms off both sides. The tower is now without its roofs, but the stonework is in good condition considering its age.

STANE STRATHCLYDE

(NS 338399)
A sixteenth-century tower-house, which is now in ruins.

STAPLETON TOWER

DORNOCK, DUMFRIES AND GALLOWAY
(NY 235689)
This is a rectangular tower, about 13.1 x 8.2 metres (43 x 27 ft) and over 12.2 metres (40 ft) tall to the parapet. It was built in the sixteenth century but is now a shell. It abuts upon a much more modern house.

STIRLING CENTRAL

(NS 790941)
Perhaps more than any other castle, Stirling represented Scotland's military resistance to English aggression in the Middle Ages. In the War of Independence it was constantly being

attacked, its buildings destroyed and then rebuilt. In 1296, it was seized by Edward I of England. A year later, Wallace recovered it but lost it again in 1298. In 1299, the Scots took it again and held it until 1304, the year of the great siege by Edward I which was planned with some care. For three months the garrison resisted everything the old warrior could hurl against it, including a battery of siege-engines weighted down with lead stripped from neighbouring church roofs, under the general control of Master James of St George. These engines hurled Greek fire, stone balls and possibly even some sort of gunpowder mixture (see Chapter 5). At the end of July the garrison surrendered. The English held the castle for ten years, but in 1314 it was yielded to the Scots after their great victory nearby at Bannockburn, and it was then dismantled.

The structure that endured so much battering had begun as a timber and earthwork castle tailored to the great basalt rock some 76 metres (250 ft) high at Stirling, which commanded the main route into the Highlands. Alexander I (1107–24) built a chapel, and died there. David I stayed there on many occasions and his grandson, William the Lion, died there in 1214. But of the buildings of these years nothing remains. The complex of stone structures and walls that graces the huge rock today stem from the fifteenth century and later.

Stirling became a more permanent Crown residence under the Stewarts. The oldest surviving stone buildings, although doubtless not the first to be erected, are the gatehouse with its square centre block containing the entrance passage, and two narrower side entrances. The block is flanked by the great hall and also by substantial cylindrical towers which once had roof caps but which were replaced in the eighteenth century by crenellations.

The great hall was designed and built by Robert Cochrane, favourite of James III (1460–88), and it was one of the first and certainly the finest of the fifteenth-century Renaissance buildings erected anywhere in the British Isles. James IV began the great Palace Block with its rich carving on the north and south faces, and this was continued by his son, James V. In c.1594, James VI rebuilt a much earlier chapel, probably of c.1470–80.

James, the infant son of Mary, Queen of Scots, was baptised in Stirling in 1566, and a few months later he was crowned there as James VI, aged only 13 months, when his mother was forced to abdicate. Stirling's last military experience was an attack by Bonnie Prince Charlie in 1745.

STRANRAER DUMFRIES AND GALLOWAY
(NX 061608)
Stranraer Castle has recently been restored. It is in the middle of the town and was used as the town gaol from the seventeenth to the nineteenth century. It began as an L-plan tower-house of the sixteenth century whose main block is 10.7 x 8.5 metres (35 x 28 ft). It was heightened in the seventeenth century and given a cap-house with a wall-walk.

STRATHHAVEN STRATHCLYDE
(NS 702444)
A substantial rectangular tower, 21.3 x 11.5 metres (70 x 38 ft), with a four-storeyed round tower extension. There is little left of this fortress standing. It was originally a castle of the great Douglas family.

STRATHENDRY LESLIE, FIFE
(NO 225019)
Now incorporated in a modern mansion, the military part of Strathendry was a sixteenth-century tower-house, about 11.9 x 7.9 metres (39 x 26 ft). The tower-house, now restored, has a staircase turret projecting outwards from the north wall.

STROME LOCH CARRON, HIGHLAND
(NG 862354)
A rectangular hall-tower, about 30.5 x 9.1 metres (100 x 30 ft), now in ruins. It has a cross-wall. The highest part of the tower is about 6 metres (20 ft) tall, but much of the tower has crumbled away. Strome was a fortress of the Lords of the Isles. It was begun in the fifteenth century.

STRUTHERS FIFE
(NO 377097)
A sixteenth-century L-plan tower-house incorporates some earlier work. Major alterations were carried out during the eighteenth century. The castle is now in a ruinous condition.

SUNDRUM COLYTON, STRATHCLYDE
(NS 411212)
The original part of what is now a hotel is an early rectangular tower of fourteenth-century construction which has walls about 3 metres (10 ft) thick.

SWEEN KNAPDALE, STRATHCLYDE
(NR 713789)
Castle Sween stands on the rocky coast of Knapdale, half-way down on the western side. It is a quadrilateral stone enclosure, the two shorter sides parallel, the longer two not so. The walls are about 2.1 metres (7 ft) thick and as tall as 12.2 metres (40 ft) for much of the perimeter. The south wall has a small entrance with rounded arch. The walls have pilaster buttresses mid-wall and clasping the corners, and no windows. There is a sea-gate on the west wall. Inside the enclosure is an open straight flight of stairs against the wall just east of the entrance. This rose to the wall-walk behind the parapet, and in doing so traversed over the entrance passage. Against the north wall were built two small towers, one square and one round, at later dates. There are the remains of apartments ranged against the enclosure wall inside, and some of these have been investigated in recent excavations. The date of the castle cannot be given precisely but is reckoned to be from the late eleventh or early twelfth century, which suggests a structure begun at least under Norman influence. This is supported by the Norman-type wall pilaster buttresses.

It was started by the McSwine family (the name possibly coming from the Viking 'Sweyn') who were the owners until the mid-

Sween: plan of the earliest wall. S = sea gate.

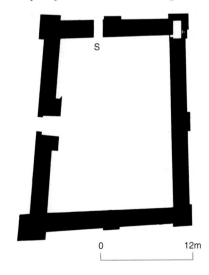

thirteenth century. It was for a time owned by the Stewart Earls of Menteith, who re-modelled some of the structure and built additions outside. Towards the end of the fourteenth century it was held for the Lords of the Isles when more works were carried out, including a number of buildings along the east wall inside.

Regarded as the first stone castle to be built in Scotland, Sween is a remarkably well-preserved ruin.

TANTALLON

NORTH BERWICK, LOTHIAN
(NT 596850)

This is a fascinating castle that makes the most of its coastal site on the Firth of Forth. A promontory with north-west, north-east and south-east sides juts into the Firth and consists of sheer rock cliffs about 30.5 metres (100 ft) tall falling straight down to the sea. On the fourth (south-western) side, a ditch, about 6 metres (20 ft) wide cut into the rock in the shape of an arc, straddles the promontory, effectively sealing off the rough rectangular site from the mainland. Inside the ditch, set back (south-eastwards) about 9.1 metres (30 ft) or so, is a massive battlemented curtain wall of dressed red freestone, some 15.2 metres (50 ft) tall, and 3.6 metres (12 ft) or so thick. In the curtain is a central mid-tower containing the entrance, and remains of end towers at the north-west and south-east

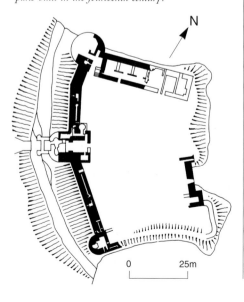

Tantallon: ground plan. The bold lines are the parts built in the fourteenth century.

N

0   25m

extremities. The ruins of all three towers rise to nearly 24.4 metres (80 ft).

The north-west (Douglas) tower had six storeys above the basement. It was cylindrical, but today only a short segment remains. The south-east tower (known as the East Tower) rose to five storeys, originally with wooden floors but later given stone vaulting. A cylindrical section of the height remains to the second storey, but above that only parts of two sides survive to the top. The gatehouse-tower is 12.8 metres (42 ft) square; it had four storeys of residential accommodation above

Tantallon: this once-powerful enclosure castle dominates both land and sea.

the room which contained the portcullis mechanism, and consisted at the front of a pair of square-plan wings up to the second storey, flanking the entrance, which then changed to cylindrical turrets on corbelling. The tower contained a drawbridge mechanism, and this was protected by a barbican projecting into the ditch.

This structure, together with a two-hall

(one above the other) block at the north attached to the Douglas Tower and a sea-gate protecting the castle interior on the north-east side, was erected in the fourteenth century. Additions and alterations followed in the fifteenth and sixteenth centuries.

Tantallon belonged to the Earls of Fife in the fourteenth century but probably the great stonework frontal wall with towers had not been built when it passed c.1360 to William, 1st Earl of Douglas, of the Black Douglas family. It later passed to the Red Douglas family (cousins of the former). One of its holders was Archibald Douglas, 5th Earl of Angus. He was besieged in Tantallon by James IV in 1491 who used both cross-bows and culverins (small cannons). In 1526, Tantallon, held by Archibald's grandson, was besieged by James V whose troops marched to the siege chanting the refrain 'Ding, Doon, Tantalloun! Ding Doon, Tantalloun!' The king failed to take the castle, despite the employment of 'two great cannones … two double falkons and four quarter falkons', but in 1529 it was surrendered to him, and it stayed in Crown hands until 1543. Its history thereafter was a somewhat chequered one, and it is mentioned in numerous documents.

In 1651, Tantallon was attacked by General Monck on behalf of Cromwell, and it was surrendered after twelve days of bombardment. Afterwards it fell into decay.

TARBERT
KILCALMONELL, STRATHCLYDE
(NR 868690)

An interesting agglomeration of ruins beside the sea, about which little is known. Even the dating is open to much question. The castle appears to have been begun in the thirteenth century, when a plain rectangular tower was built on one side of an irregularly shaped curtain. A further tower was raised in the fifteenth century in the wall of an earlier second outer enclosure, which may be of the fourteenth century. There are traces of projecting turrets in the enclosure walls. Tarbert was equipped with inverted keyhole gun-ports which were probably inserted in the sixteenth century.

TARINGZEAN STRATHCLYDE
(NS 556205)

A much restored and altered tower-house which was begun in the fifteenth century beside a thirteenth-century hall-house.

TERPERSIE ALFORD, GRAMPIAN
(NJ 546202)

This was one of the earliest Z-plan castles in Scotland. It was raised in 1561 and was smaller than the majority of those that followed. Terpersie was a rectangular tower block, 8.5 x 5.5 metres (28 x 18 ft), with small cylindrical towers on diagonally opposite corners, 5.2 metres (17 ft) in diameter. The cylindrical towers were equipped with gun-ports and pistol-holes. Today the castle is ruinous.

THIRLESTANE ETTRICK BORDERS
(NT 280154)

Thirlestane is an L-plan tower of the late sixteenth century, now in ruins.

THIRLESTANE LAUDER, BORDERS
(NT 533479)

This is a splendid building of interesting design. It began as a fourteenth-century structure, sometimes known as the Old Fort of Lauder, which was extended in the sixteenth century by the then owners, the celebrated Maitlands (see Lennoxlove). The major work, however, was done by John Maitland, Duke of Lauderdale (the last of the five men who ruled Britain under Charles II from 1666–73, whose initials formed the word CABAL – Clifford, Arlington, Buckingham, Ashley, Lauderdale). He employed the well known architect, William Bruce, who took the original shell of the tower-house (about 32.9 x 6.7 metres [108 x 22 ft] contained by massive cylindrical towers with curved lobes extended at the corners, the longer sides of the tower divided by semi-cylindrical towers, three on each wall), and crowned the whole building with a tower bearing an ogee roof. Parapets, cap-houses, conical turrets and fine windows were all added to make it even more sumptuous. By this time, however, it was no longer a fortress.

THREAVE NR CASTLE DOUGLAS,
DUMFRIES AND GALLOWAY
(NV 739623)

Threave stands on an islet in the Dee, and even as a ruin it is a mighty and forbidding structure. It is a massive great tower partly enclosed by a powerful 'artillery' wall which today has the remains of three cylindrical corner turrets. The castle has been the subject of major investigation in the 1970s and the results are interesting.

The first building was the great tower:

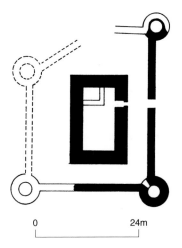

Threave: the 'artillery' wall runs from north to south between the cylindrical turrets and then at right angles from south to west. The space in the east wall indicates the position of the gatehouse. The great tower is in the centre.

today, 18.6 x 12.2 metres (61 x 40 ft), four-storeyed and rising to over 21.3 metres (70 ft) to the remnants of the battlements, with walls nearly 3 metres (10 ft) thick. It was built by Archibald 'the Grim', 3rd Earl of Douglas, Lord of Galloway, in about 1370, and it was a defensive structure as well as a building intended to impress.

During the reign of James II (1437–60), the Earls of Douglas were locked in a deadly quarrel with the king who was determined to break their power once and for all. In 1454, perhaps a year or two earlier, Threave great tower was reinforced an 'artillery' wall along the east and south sides which faced the mainland. The wall was 5.5 metres (18 ft) tall (the remains are less high today), and it was provided with vertical loops with embrasures for hand-guns and for cross-bows (both types of weapons were often used together in the fifteenth century).Its towers were equipped with two types of gun-port, inverted keyholes and dumb-bells. There was a gatehouse in the middle of the eastern wall. The wall used to be dated c.1514, but recent work puts it squarely in the mid-fifteenth century and makes it the earliest 'artillery' wall in Britain.

Additionally, the excavations revealed the existence of buildings and facilities of the mid-fifteenth century (such as a blacksmith's shop, carpenter's workshop and lead-smelting hearth) that suggest the castle's community in its isolated site was self-supporting. Threave was besieged in 1455 by James II using the latest cannons and bombards, including Mons Meg (*see* p. 57), and was eventually taken.

TIBBERS DUMFRIES AND GALLOWAY
(NX 863982)
Not much of this castle remains. It was one of the castles built by the English towards the end of the thirteenth century, during Edward I's attempts to take over Scotland after the deposition of King John Balliol. It was a simple, quadrangular curtain enclosure of stone with a cylindrical tower on each corner, of which one was a flanking tower for an entrance in the walling. There was a second flanking tower on the other side of the entrance. In front of this side of the enclosure are the rock-cut ditch and bank. The enclosure walls were between 2.1–2.7 metres (7–9 ft) thick. Enough stretches of this masonry remain to indicate the plan, which resembles that of Inverlochy.

TILLYCAIRN GRAMPIAN
(NJ 665114)
A mid-sixteenth-century L-plan castle. The main tower was 12.5 x 11.3 metres (41 x 37 ft), and probably rose to four storeys. The staircase wing, circular in plan, was one storey taller. Tillycairn has some interesting gunports; crosslet top and oillet bottom loops, one of which covered the door in the re-entrance; wide-mouth ports all round; and pistol shotholes in the roundels. It has been restored.

TILQUHILLY NR BANCHORY, GRAMPIAN
(NO 721941)
Tilquhilly is a Z-plan castle and was built c.1576, almost contemporary with Claypotts (q.v.). One end-tower was square-plan, the other rectangular. The towers had been well provided with gun-loops.

TIMPENDEAN TOWER BORDERS
(NT 635226)
The remains of this rectangular tower-house of the late sixteenth century consist of walls, two opposites reaching to gable height. The tower is 8.8 x 7.3 metres (29 x 24 ft). It was equipped with wide-mouth gun-ports.

TIORAM MOIDART, HIGHLAND
(NM 662724)
Tioram stands on an island in Loch Moidart, high on a rock which makes the castle stand well clear of the water. It is a stone enclosure,

Tioram: an early thirteenth-century stone enclosure castle in Loch Moidart. The corbelled turrets are a later addition.

approximately five-sided, whose angles (like Mingary's) are rounded. It occupies the whole summit of the rock on which it stands. Buildings including a great tower were erected inside, and are now ruined. The enclosure walls reached about 9.1 metres (30 ft) and are about 2.4 metres (8 ft) thick.

TOLQUHON TARVES, GRAMPIAN
(NJ 874286)
Tolquhon belonged to the Forbes family. It is a castle which derives from two main building

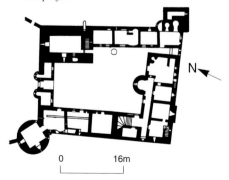

Tolquhon: ground floor plan. The 'Auld Tour' is at the top left.

0   16m

periods, the late fifteenth-century and between 1584–9. The first period saw the construction of the 'auld tour' (old tower). This tower is now ruined: only the vaulted basement and parts of the first floor remain. The walls are 2.1–2.7 metres (7–9 ft) thick and contained mural staircases.

In 1584, William Forbes enlarged the castle by building round the 'auld tour' a substantial irregular quadrangular enclosure with ranges of buildings along the inside of three of its walls. On the north-west corner of the enclosure he erected a cylindrical tower measuring some 7.9 metres (26 ft) in diameter, and on the south-east corner he built a tower about 6 metres (20 ft) square. The ranges contain well-appointed apartments on two levels, including a great dining hall, a long gallery and a laird's private room. On the inward face of the south range is a semi-cylindrical tower containing a spiral staircase in the upper half.

Tolquhon was equipped with wide-mouth gun-ports, notably in the masonry of the two semi-cylindrical towers on the north face which flank the entrance (which has a small round-headed arch). Behind the two semi-cylinders are guardrooms (at ground-floor level). Both the corner towers were equipped with gun-ports, each to cover two sides of the quadrangle. Some of the gun-ports are ornamented. The parapet of the 'auld tour' had been machicolated.

TORTHORWALD
DUMFRIES AND GALLOWAY
(NY 033782)
Torthorwald is nowadays a shell of a tower-house which was once part of a stone curtain enclosure. The ruin, which used to have two vaulted storeys, rises to about 18.3 metres (60 ft) tall and is partly shored up by more modern building works. The castle is of mid-fourteenth-century construction but was raised upon the site of an earlier earthwork castle. The site has the remains of considerable ramparts and ditches.

TORWOOD DUNPACE, CENTRAL
(NS 835843)
An L-plan tower-house whose main block is now roofless. It was built in the 1560s (a date panel of 1566 has been found), and the ground floor was vaulted. The tower is three-storeyed, with a wing tower containing the staircase. In front of the angle is a courtyard with other domestic buildings.

TOWARD STRATHCLYDE
(NS 118678)
A recently restored fifteenth-century tower of four storeys and a later courtyard. The castle was besieged and taken by the Argyll Campbells in 1646.

TOWIE BARCLAY
TURRIFF, GRAMPIAN
(NJ 744439)
A late sixteenth-century L-plan tower-house which has the unusual feature of a rib-vaulted great hall, reached by a spiral staircase within the tower wall thickness. Above the entrance to the hall is a small oratory reached by another mural staircase that rises unseen over the doorway. In the late eighteenth century, Towie Barclay was altered, the most substantial change being the removal of two storeys of the tower. It has been further restored and is now open.

TROCHRIE TAYSIDE
(NN 978402)
An early fourteenth-century hall-house with a remarkable undercroft, rib-vaulted from central piers. The hall received additions, including a strong curtain wall round most of the central structure. Tullialan is built on a natural rock outcrop, and was partly protected by a deep ditch. Note an interesting hooded fireplace with sconces.

TULLIBOLE TAYSIDE
(NO 053005)
Finely restored after the Second World War, Tullibole was begun in the first years of the seventeenth century, on the site of an earlier building which is mentioned in fourteenth-century documents. This was probably an unfortified structure. The newer castle was fortified with turrets and gun-ports. Two interesting features are a 'luggie', a seventeenth-century form of room 'bugging', and a shot-hole positioned beside the main entrance door.

TURNBERRY STRATHCLYDE
(NS 196072)
Raised on a promontory to the south of Maiden's Bay, Turnberry began as a cylindrical great tower castle of the thirteenth century. It is thought to have been the childhood home of Robert Bruce, for the castle belonged to his father. The great tower was probably surrounded by a stone curtain which in turn was enclosed by a moat.

UDNY GRAMPIAN
(NJ 882268)
This five-storeyed rectangular tower, with rounded corners like Drum Castle, was built in the fifteenth and sixteenth centuries. It is thought that originally the tower rose only to

Urquhart: plan of the buildings, as they probably were in the late seventeenth century. The great tower of the sixteenth century is on the extreme right.

three storeys, and that the extra two floors were added in the sixteenth century. Two of the original storeys have vaulted ceilings and very thick walls. In the nineteenth century a new mansion was built on to the tower, but this has since been demolished, leaving the ancient tower much as it was, with restorations of the last decade or so.

URQUHART
DRUMNADROCHIT, LOCH NESS, HIGHLAND
(NH 5331286)
Urquhart stands on a sandstone promontory jutting into Loch Ness from the north-west, overlooking Urquhart Bay. The site was defended from attack from the landward side by a ditch up to about 30.5 metres (100 ft) wide and 4.6–5.2 metres (15–17 ft) deep, and this was crossed by a bridge with high walls on either side of the path, broken in the middle by a drawbridge. This bridge led out from a massive twin-cylindrical-towered gatehouse in the length of the high stone curtain wall that skirted the west side of the castle. The curtain followed the contour of the irregular rocky ground of the promontory, and it survives in part, although not to its full height. At the north-east end of the curtain is the ruined shell of the great tower which has its south wall missing, and which is built of rubble with freestone dressings. Its walls are 3–3.6 metres (10–12 ft) thick and it rises to four storeys.

The period of the tower seems to have been three-fold: the basement is fourteenth century; the next storeys are sixteenth century

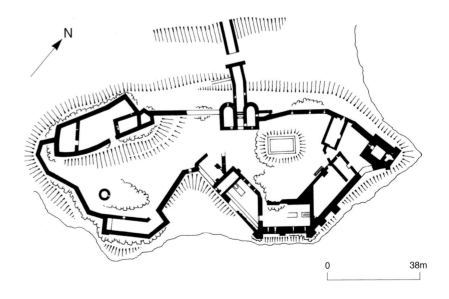

Perched on rock on the edge of Loch Ness, Urquhart's building history spans several centuries, beginning with a motte in c.1150. The great tower is on the extreme left.

(probably rebuilding of older work destroyed); and the top is seventeenth-century. Gun-ports were inserted in the sixteenth century.

To the south of the great tower is a semi-hexagonal-plan range of buildings skirting the top of the promontory containing the great chamber, hall and kitchen, now all ruined. The southern end of this range forms one side of an inverted V-shaped inlet for the loch water, and a landing place. At the apex of the 'V' is a water-gate, built in a length of curtain that continues along the promontory and round to join up with an irregularly shaped, polygonal, thick stone-walled enclosure which skirts the top of a natural mound. This mound was once a Norman-style motte, which centuries earlier had been the base for an Iron Age vitrified fort. The curtain continues north-eastwards out of the polygonal enclosure to join up with the western gatehouse, thus completing the circuit of a substantial enclosure castle with buildings whose ground-plan is roughly in the shape of a figure-of-eight, like Prudhoe. The motte enclosure remains to about 5.5 metres (18 ft) tall, and contained buildings inside, of which traces can be seen.

The beginnings of Urquhart as a motte castle were probably mid-twelfth-century. It passed to the powerful Durward family, and thence to the Comyn family. Edward I of England put it under English control, but it was retaken by the Scots in 1303, changed hands twice more, and in 1313 became the property of Randolph, Earl of Moray, one of Bruce's three greatest friends and counsellors. Thereafter it had a turbulent history in the struggle between the kings and the Lords of the Isles.

VAYNE TAYSIDE
(NO 494599)
Vayne is an interesting Z-plan castle of the sixteenth century, now in ruins. One diagonally placed tower is square-plan, the other is round.

WALLACE'S GAMRIE, GRAMPIAN
(NJ 773605)
There are fragments of walling on Ha'Hill in Glen Minonie which are of thirteenth-century date. They are thought to be the remnants of a simple tower or enclosure which may have been used by William Wallace during his war against Edward I, c.1297–1305. Wallace was helped by Anthony de Moravia who was operating in and around Morayshire.

WAUGHTON PRESTONKIRK, LOTHIAN
(NT 567808)
A terrace of rock supported an L-plan tower-house here, of which a wing remains.

WEMYSS FIFE
(NT 329951)
A fifteenth-century tower-house built on the 'E' plan. This has been considerably altered, enlarged, altered again and reduced in size during its history, and now looks magnificent in its palatial glory.

WESTER KAMES STRATHCLYDE
(NS 062681)
A much-restored rectangular tower-house of the sixteenth century.

WESTHALL OYNE, GRAMPIAN
(NJ 673266)
A much-modified seventeenth-century L-plan tower-house with a cylindrical staircase tower projecting in the angle. A second cylindrical tower containing another staircase was added later, and there were further alterations in the nineteenth century.

WHITTINGHAME LOTHIAN
(NT 602732)
An L-plan tower of possibly fourteenth-, or more probably fifteenth-century beginnings, which was added to in the seventeenth century. The castle has been restored.

WIGTOWN DUMFRIES AND GALLOWAY
(NX 437550)
Fragmentary remains of an early thirteenth-century enclosure castle of stone, circular in plan and about 0.2 hectares ($^{1}/_{2}$ acre) in area. The enclosure is partly surrounded by a ditch and partly by the sea, as it stands on the shore.

YESTER LOTHIAN
(NT 556667)
Yester Castle is one of the oldest fortresses of Scotland, whose remains now stand in the grounds of Yester House, on a peninsula into Hopes Water, 3.2 km (2 miles) from Gifford. The first work was a motte castle, perhaps of the twelfth century. In the middle of the thirteenth century, a rectangular great tower was erected partly on the side of the motte. This had an undercroft, some 11.3 x 4 metres (37 x 13 ft), with a high pointed barrel-vaulted ceiling. The great tower was later reduced in height when alterations were made in the layout, probably in the fifteenth century, to include an enclosure curtain between 1.8–2.4 metres (6–8 ft) thick. Part of the curtain survives, one length being nearly 21.3 metres (70 ft).

Wales

ABER BANGOR, GWYNEDD
(SH 656727)
Only a motte remains of the castle built here by Hugh d'Avranches, Earl of Chester, in the last decade of the eleventh century. It overlooked the narrowest part of the Menai Strait to the Isle of Anglesey. It is sometimes known as Bangor Castle.

ABER AFAN WEST GLAMORGAN
(SS 762901)
There was a motte castle here which was attacked in 1153 at the end of the Anarchy in England. Possibly the attack was carried out by the Welsh.

ABERCOWYN ST CLEARS, DYFED
(SN 297136)
Alternatively known as Castell Aber Taf or Castell Aber Carwy, this was a motte castle with an oval bailey, the motte astride the bailey. The motte is 7.6 metres (25 ft) high, although much of it has been ploughed up. The bailey was near the river. It is said to have been destroyed by the Welsh c.1116.

ABEREDW NR BUILTH WELLS, POWYS
(SO 076474)
Aberedw was an enclosure castle with small towers. It was a royal castle of Llywelyn the Last, Prince of all Wales (c.1246–82). After being defeated in north Wales by Edward I of England in 1282, Llywelyn escaped into mid-Wales and headed for Aberedw. However, near Builth Wells he was ambushed and killed. The site was built over for railway construction in the nineteenth century.

ABEREINION DYFED
(SN 687968)
Abereinion was a fortified mound enclosed by a ditch, built by Rhys ap Gruffydd in the mid-twelfth century.

ABERGAVENNY GWENT
(SO 299139)
The ruins of Abergavenny Castle stand on a spur of land at the southern end of the town, overlooking the junction of the rivers Usk and Gwenny. It was first a motte castle and then received stone additions. A square great tower was let into the mound on one side and traces of this survive, together with the remains of a curtain wall and two towers along it. The gatehouse and barbican are probably thirteenth-century structures. The castle was captured by the Welsh in c.1172, but it was soon recovered by its Norman owner.

ABERLLEINIOG
NR LLANGOED, ANGLESEY, GWYNEDD
(SH 617793)
Hugh d'Avranches, Earl of Chester, built the motte castle here, probably just after the end of the Conqueror's reign. It was attacked and burned by the Welsh under Gruffydd ap Cynan, Prince of Wales, c.1095. The stonework was not added to the earthworks until the seventeenth century.

ABERLLYNFI POWYS
(SO 171380)
An earthwork castle was built here in the twelfth century. It was captured in 1233, probably by the Welsh.

ABERRHEIDOL
NR ABERYSTWYTH DYFED
(SN 585790)
An earthwork enclosure situated 1.6 km (1 mile) to the south of Aberystwyth, where some of the timberwork has been deduced from post-holes and other imprints discovered in recent excavations. There is evidence of a motte formed out of the top of a spur emerging from the greater area of rising ground on which the castle stood. The castle was raised by the Norman lord, Gilbert FitzRichard, c.1110. It was attacked by the Welsh in 1116, and again in 1136 when it was burned down. It figures in the *Brut y Tywysogyon* (*The Chronicle of the Princes* [*of Wales*]), as having been burned (again) some time between 1162 and 1164.

ABERYSTWYTH DYFED
(SN 579815)
When Edward I put in train the first phase of his great castle-building programme in Wales in 1277, work was begun on Flint, Rhuddlan, Builth and Aberystwyth. At Aberystwyth his brother, Edmund, arranged the construction of a substantial lozenge-plan concentric castle of two curtain enclosures of stone (one inside the other), each being on raised ground and supplied with flanking round towers on the angles, and each with a twin-towered gatehouse. The outer and smaller gatehouse led to a barbican; the inner was a substantial fortified residential gatehouse with D-ends to the east. A hall, 18.3 x 12.8 metres (60 x 42 ft), was built between this gatehouse and the south tower of the inner curtain. There

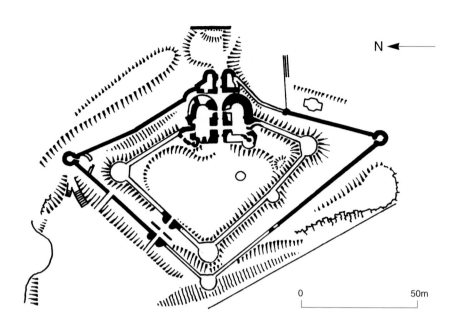

Aberystwyth: the bold lines indicate the masonry still visible (after C.J. Spurgeon).

were additional gates at the north-west in both curtains. Today much of the castle is in ruins, but there are stretches of curtain, some height in a few towers, and substantial remains of the great gate. There is thought to have been a third bailey to the north-west beyond the outer curtain, which has since been eroded by the sea.

For construction work, 120 masons and 120 carpenters were recruited from the West Country of England, transported by sea from Bristol to Carmarthen. Their journey probably finished by land in 1277, where they were joined by additional workers.

The building work started badly. Some years of what was probably 'jerry-building' were followed in 1282 by a sudden attack by Welsh patriots who destroyed the castle. Master James of St George, who was working at Rhuddlan Castle at the time, was asked to go to Aberystwyth to rebuild it. He put the work in the hands of his colleague, Master Giles of St George, and this went on for some years, ending, after interruptions, c.1290, having cost nearly £4500.

Aberystwyth was taken by Owain Glyndwr in 1403 and he held it for five years. During that time he made a treaty with Charles VI of France and the document was said to have been sealed in the captured fortress. In 1409 Henry of Monmouth, eldest son of Henry IV, recaptured it and thereafter it gradually decayed. In the Civil War Parliamentary forces besieged and took it, and in 1649 it was blown up.

AMROTH EARWERE, DYFED
(SN 170073)
Amroth began as a motte castle built by Norman invaders early in the twelfth century. At some point, probably in the fourteenth century, a stone enclosure with an interesting gateway was erected a few hundred yards away towards the sea, presumably within the original bailey.

BALA GWYNEDD
(SH 928361)
A low-level motte castle here was captured in 1202. It was near Lake Bala.

BASINGWERK NR HOLYWELL, CLWYD
(SJ 220734)
A motte castle of the twelfth century. It was taken by Owain Gwynedd, Prince of all Wales, c.1166.

BEAUMARIS ANGLESEY, GWYNEDD
(SH 607763)
Beaumaris is the last of the castles built by Edward I during and after his conquest of Wales. Its design, by Master James of St George, is almost perfectly concentric. It cost nearly £15,000; it took over 35 years to build, and even then was not completed. At one time over 3500 people were working on it, which is thought to be about 1 in 1000 of the total population of England and Wales at the time (1295). It was considered impregnable, but this was never put to the test. No shot appears to have been fired at Beaumaris in anger. And within 20 years of the last, but unfinished, building operations (c.1330), the castle was reported to be deteriorating: most of the timberwork was in decay and some stonework was dilapidated.

Beaumaris is situated strategically in flat, marshy land on the south edge of the Isle of Anglesey. The castle is basically two concentric wings of walling with flanking towers and gatehouses. The inner ring, square in plan, with walls about 4.9 metres (16 ft) thick and nearly 13.1 metres (43 ft) high, has cylindrical towers on the four corners, D-end towers mid-wall on the west and east and, on the north and south, a substantial twin-cylindrical-towered gatehouse mid-wall, the northern one completed, the southern one lacking its rear portions. None of the towers or gatehouses was completed to its full height. Both gatehouses were fitted with two suites of apartments, making them residential. Indeed, the gatehouses were the strongest parts of the castle, acting as great towers.

The outer ring, whose wall is 8.2 metres (27 ft) tall and about half as thick as the inner walling, is octagonal in plan and has cylindrical flanking turrets all round from the extreme south-west to the extreme south-east – there are twelve in all. On the north-east side is an outer gateway, and on the south-west is the sea gate, which abuts on to a dock provided for supply vessels to moor close to the castle. The whole castle is surrounded by a broad wet moat supplied by the waters of the Menai Straits.

The castle was built of grit and limestone rubble from a nearby quarry at Penmon. Both rings of wall and also the towers and gatehouses were equipped with arrow slits all round, providing the maximum covering fire from all angles against attack from any direction. The southern gatehouse was further protected by a barbican.

BENTON DYFED
(SN 005069)
A small enclosure castle, with a cylindrical tower and a smaller cylindrical turret on one side, built in the thirteenth century. It has

been merged in with later buildings. The cylindrical tower is still standing and is part-residential.

BLAENLLYNFI CATHEDINE, POWYS
(SO 145229)

A stone castle built on a knoll below Llangorse Mountain, probably of the twelfth century. The knoll was surrounded by a ditch fed by local streams, and continued by an earthwork dam. The stonework is now fragmentary but indicates a curtain-walled enclosure with towers and with a gateway in the east. The castle was destroyed in the 1230s by Llywelyn the Great, Prince of all Wales.

BLAENPORTH ABERPORTH, DYFED
(SN 266488)

Otherwise called Castell Gwythian, it was a motte castle which today shows good traces of a stone shell enclosure on top. The motte may have been raised by the de Clares, c.1110. It was destroyed c.1153.

BLEDDFA POWYS
(SO 209682)

A motte castle, altered at some period, with fragments of a square tower. A mural staircase, erected on the mound in the late twelfth century, was discovered in recent excavations.

BOUGHROOD POWYS
(SO 132391)

A recently excavated motte castle site on the side of the west road leading into the village. Masonry was found in the mound earth. This could mean either a stone tower which collapsed into the earth through insufficient foundations, or a tower built first and the earth heaped up round the basement level afterwards, as at Aldingbourne and Lydford. The castle was mentioned in 1206.

BRECON POWYS
(SO 043288)

The remains of Brecon Castle stand in the grounds of the Castle Hotel in Brecon. It began as a motte castle erected at the end of the eleventh century. In the twelfth century a polygonal shell enclosure was built on the motte, and later on further buildings including a hall and towers were added. Some of the stone for the shell enclosure and the other stone buildings was probably taken from the old Roman fort of Brecon Gaer nearby.

The castle was held alternately by Welsh and English. In c.1380 it became the property of Henry of Bolingbroke (later Henry IV) through marriage. Owain Glyndwr tried to take it by storm c.1404 but failed, and the constable was rewarded with an annuity for his stout defence of it.

BRONLLYS NR TALGARTH, POWYS
(SO 149346)

A twelfth-century motte castle with two baileys was given a cylindrical great tower c.1176. This is thought to have been after a fire in the 1170s, mentioned by Giraldus Cambrensis. The cylindrical tower is three storeys tall, the lower stage sloping slightly outwards. This was encircled by a curtain, and in the fourteenth century domestic buildings were added. Bronllys was captured in 1233 by the Welsh.

BUILTH POWYS
(SO 044510)

Builth was one of Edward I's ten new castles erected in Wales in the 1270s–80s as part of his scheme of conquest and government. There had already been a small castle on the site, a motte castle with a double bailey and deep wet ditch of the end of the eleventh century, which received a polygonal stone shell enclosure in the mid-twelfth century, and was further fortified by King John, c.1208. In 1260 Builth was taken by Llywelyn the Last, Prince of all Wales, and destroyed. Edward was thus able to rebuild from scratch, and over five years, 1277–82, he spent some £1666. John FitzAdam of Radnor was *custos operacionum*.

The principal works were a great hall, a kitchen block, a wet moat and a great tower. In 1278, the works are thought to have come under the general control of Master James of St George, and by 1280 the great tower (which may have been more like a shell enclosure since it had 'houses' within it), a stone curtain with six flanking turrets for the inner part of the castle, and a gate-tower had been proceeded with, if not finished. Works ended in 1282, and the records seem to suggest that they had petered out uncompleted, probably due to a shortage of money. In 1278, the master-mason received 7½d a day and ordinary masons 2s a week, and about 140 men were on the payroll. Most of the stone was quarried locally, but freestone was waggoned over from Cusop and Clifford on Wye, while stone for burning for lime came from Llyswen (near Bronllys, another castle site).

Builth Castle was famous as the place near which Llywelyn the Last was ambushed and slain in 1282. It was severely damaged by Owain Glyndwr in his campaigns of the early fifteenth century. Today, there is nothing to be seen except earthworks and a few foundations.

BWLCH Y DINAS POWYS
(SO 179301)

A small enclosure castle with rectangular turrets raised in the twelfth century inside the remains of a hill-fort of (?) Iron Age times. The castle was given a rectangular great tower but its dimensions are not clearly known. Today, it is ruinous.

CAEREINION POWYS
(SJ 163055)

Otherwise known as Twmpatch Garmon, Caereinion was a motte castle of Henry II's time, but built by a Welsh lord. The castle was attacked in 1167 and burned.

CAERGWRLE NR MOLD, CLWYD
(SJ 307572)

This ruined castle stands inside earthworks, probably of Iron Age origin. The stonework consisted of an enclosure with flanking towers. Recent excavations disclosed free-standing buildings in the enclosure, including what appears to have been a blacksmith's workshop. One report says the enclosure had the feel of a builder's yard. Caergwrle's existence was short, from construction in the later thirteenth century to abandonment in the 1330s.

CAERLEON GWENT
(ST 342905)

A motte castle of steep sides erected c.1086 on the outskirts of the site of the Roman fortress there. Giraldus Cambrensis mentions a vast tower on the motte, and remains of a tower foundation about 6 x 9.1 metres (20 x 30 ft), and several metres thick, were found in excavations. The tower may have been built between 1158 and 1173. There was also a twin-towered barbican at the motte base, leading to the bailey, and the bailey wall had flanking towers, of which one has survived; these may be of thirteenth-century origin.

Caerleon castle was attacked several times by the Welsh.

CAERNARFON Gwynedd
(SH 477626)

Caernarfon Castle was intended by Edward I to be symbolic of his conquest and new government of Wales. There had once been a Norman motte castle on the northern edge of the Seiont River where it flows into the Menai Strait, and this had been captured and held by the Welsh for over a century. Edward constructed his new hourglass-plan castle, with high curtain walls, polygonal flanking towers and great twin-towered gatehouses right round that castle.

His symbol had to be novel, vast, majestic and derived in some way from Imperial Rome because he had visited Constantinople when commanding an army on the Eighth Crusade (1270–72) and seen the great wall outside. Even the masonry was made to look like the wall, by dint of using limestone from the Penmon quarries in Anglesey, whose tiers of courses were interleaved every so often with darker brown sandstone courses, from quarries in Menai. But the whole project must have been a great disappointment to him. Begun in 1283, it was never finished. Severe and extensive damage was done in an attack by Madog ap Llywelyn in 1294–5. Edward had had to use press-gang methods to get English craftsmen and workers to come to the wilds of north-west Wales to build it, as he could not trust the native Welsh. By 1304 barely half the work had been done.

Despite this, the castle became the grandest of all his structures in Wales, and the sophistication of its defences still amazes.

Caernarfon: ground plan. The southern part from the Eagle Tower on the left along to the north-east tower on the right was built in the first stage, c.1283–93.

Below the battlemented parapet along the south side, upper and lower shooting galleries were constructed, with access to arrow slits in the curtain, which meant that a rain of missiles could be discharged against attackers from three levels and at several angles at once. To enter the lower courtyard by means of the King's Gate, a vast twin-towered fortress in itself, it would have been necessary to go across a drawbridge, through five doors and under six portcullises, turn right, and then across a second drawbridge. This progress would be subject to continual attack from defenders using arrow slits and spy-holes flanking all approaches at various levels, and in the gatehouse vaulting a collection of murder-holes presented yet another obstacle.

Although Caernarfon is one of the most sophisticated castles in all Britain, it is nonetheless a simple enclosure with curtain walls, towers and gatehouses. Its site on tidal waters meant it could be supplied by sea, like Harlech. There is a water-gate access to the huge polygonal Eagle Tower (at the west) with its three projecting turrets above the crenellations. The access led to a basement above which are three storeys of a residential kind. The masonry of the whole enclosure was tailored to fit the rock on which the castle was built, which explains its figure-of-eight plan. In the eastern half, a little higher than the west, was the original Norman motte, and this mound explains why the entrance through the Queen's Gate (a twin-polygonal-towered gatehouse) is so high up, at first-storey level, reached by a ramp up to a drawbridge leading to it. The gatehouse sits across the slope of the motte, and sloping stonework continues to the left and right of it.

The arrangement of the polygonal towers and gatehouses in the curtain, each one well equipped with loops at several levels, ensured maximum covering fire on every part of the castle, not only upon attackers outside trying to get in, but also upon them once they had entered the upper or lower bailey.

The building work fell into two main periods: the west, south and east curtain lengths with their towers and the Queen's Gate were raised mainly between 1283 and 1292, with top work to the Eagle Tower added afterwards; and the north side with the great King's Gate was built, although never completed, between 1296 and 1323.

Caernarfon Castle was part of a larger defensive arrangement incorporating the town which was enclosed inside a fortified wall with towers all round.

CAERPHILLY Mid-Glamorgan
(ST 155870)

Caerphilly was the first concentric castle to be built from scratch in Britain. Its combination of land and water defences represented a very high level of military architectural sophistication. Despite several sieges, long periods of neglect and, after the Civil War, serious attempts to demolish it, the great bulk of the castle has survived. Much has now been restored with detailed care, and it is now one of the most spectacular military ruins in Europe, if not the world.

Some time during the early Norman occupation of south Wales, a castle of earth and timber was raised at Caerphilly, but it is not clear whether this was a Norman or a Welsh work, for the hilly district around was in Welsh hands right into the 1260s. In 1266 or 1267, after the war between Henry III of England and Simon de Montfort, Gilbert de Clare, Earl of Gloucester and Hertford and one of the richest barons of England who owned large tracts of Glamorgan, moved into the Caerphilly district. With Henry III's leave he began to construct a stone castle, to counter the activities of Llywelyn, Prince of Wales, who had been in alliance with Simon de Montfort and who, after the latter's defeat at Evesham, had come to an agreement with Henry III by which the Prince was recognised as Prince of Wales. The English king realised, however, that Llywelyn constituted a danger to English holdings in South Wales, for it was the latter's policy to recover the whole of Wales and govern it as an autonomous kingdom – a perfectly legitimate aspiration.

In the autumn of 1270, Llywelyn descended upon the embryo fortress and

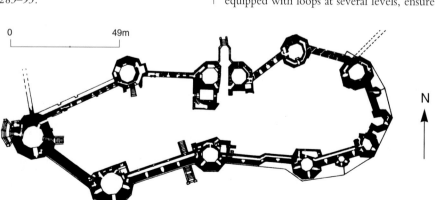

0   49m

N

burnt it. By this time, considerable progress had been made on the inner part, much more than has been previously supposed because the date of Llywelyn's first raid used to be taken as 1269. Probably the entire inner quadrangle of walls with corner cylindrical towers and twin-cylindrical-towered gatehouse in the east and west walls had been largely completed, and a start had also been made on the outer wall with its two gatehouses (also east and west). Work had also begun on the south defensive platform outside the outer wall. How much damage was done by Llywelyn is not absolutely clear, but if the account that Llywelyn burnt the castle is taken literally, that probably applies to the wooden and not the stone parts.

De Clare pressed on with the work, however, and by autumn 1271 the castle was almost completely concentric. Llywelyn attacked it again but this time was defeated, and he called off the siege.

The third building stage began in about 1277, when the two outer gatehouses were finished and other buildings added. Thereafter, work seems to have been done at a desultory rate, and masons and carpenters were still busy in 1326. By that time the artificial lake surrounding the castle, the western hornwork which barred the approach to the west side, and the unique screen of curtain walls and platforms, fortified by projecting turrets and buttresses, running from south to north on the eastern front, were complete. So was the second lake separated from the inner one on the north side by a mole. The first lake may have been controllable by means of dam and sluice-gates by the time the third work stage began.

These drawn-out later building works were not uninterrupted. In 1316 Caerphilly was besieged by Llywelyn Bren in a revolt against English rule, and a drawbridge was burnt. In 1326, when Edward II was on the run from his estranged wife Isabella and her paramour Roger Mortimer (*see* Nottingham Castle), he took refuge at Caerphilly. The queen caught up with his supporters there and besieged the castle for several weeks (although Edward had already fled). The garrison surrendered in 1327, and the besiegers discovered that Edward had left half his treasure and clothes behind.

For a time Caerphilly remained in Despenser hands (although Hugh had been executed in 1326). It was threatened by Owain Glyndwr in the early 1400s and was probably yielded to him. Thereafter it was allowed to deteriorate. During the Civil War it played some part, although one difficult to determine. Cromwell wanted it dismantled, and there are telling signs today of the effects of Parliamentary slighting, in particular the 'leaning' south-east tower of the inner ward.

Caerphilly has received considerable restoration to its fabric, and its lakes have been re-flooded. The great hall was re-roofed, and its floors and windows were restored.

CAERWENT Nr Chepstow, Gwent
(ST 475917)

Caerwent was once a Roman town inside a stonewall enclosure with bastions, banks and ditches. In the extreme south-east corner of the rectangle, in a space left when a section of the Roman wall was cleared away, a Norman motte was raised, probably between 1067 and 1070. Its summit is now about 2.1 metres (7 ft) above the Roman bank. It was provided with extra ditching which, together with the Roman ditching already there, surrounded the motte. Nothing is known about its

Caldicot: the substantial fourteenth-century gatehouse, built of fine ashlar blocks, has a garderobe tower at each end.

history, although it might be the same as Castell Gwent mentioned in about 1150.

CALDICOT Gwent
(ST 487885)

Beginning as a motte castle with two baileys, built beside a stream, probably in the early twelfth century, Caldicot developed in the late twelfth and early thirteenth centuries into a large stirrup-shaped stone enclosure castle of high walls, flanking towers, unusual gatehouse and a great tower erected on the motte in one corner. The great tower is cylindrical and made of local gritstone. It stands on a splayed plinth and has a mural staircase to the basement and spiral stairs upwards to the second floor, whence another mural stair continues to the top. The parapet was battlemented and the holes remain for the hoarding beams. The cylindrical plan is augmented with a bulging half-round turret which is solid except for the basement.

Caldicot's fourteenth-century gatehouse is rectangular with square garderobe turrets at each end. The longer sides of the rectangle are positioned lengthways in the curtain. The entrance passage has two portcullises and two pairs of folding doors. The gatehouse has handsome accommodation above the passage and was built as a residential structure. There were more additions in the fourteenth century.

CAMLAIS POWYS
(SN 956260)

Also known as Cwm Camlais, this was a motte castle built on a natural rocky mound very high, over 305 metres (1000 ft) above sea level, on the edge of Mynyold Illtyd. The motte was given a cylindrical tower, of which the base remains.

CAMMAIS DYFED
(SN 082401)

Alternatively called Nevern or Nanhyfer, Cammais was a motte castle which received a stone square-plan tower, among other buildings, in the late twelfth century.

CANDLESTON
NR BRIDGEND, MID-GLAMORGAN
(SS 871772)

This castle dates from the fourteenth century. It had a polygonal courtyard enclosing a square tower, and more domestic buildings were added later. The castle was held for a time by the Cantelupes, a powerful Norman family. It is now in a ruinous state.

CARDIFF SOUTH GLAMORGAN
(ST 180767)

When looking at the interesting castle at Cardiff, it is helpful to forget about the eighteenth- and nineteenth-century additions to this very old fortress. Basically, Cardiff began as a motte castle, raised by about 1080. The motte is over 12.2 metres (40 ft) tall, sitting in a surrounding moat. On the summit was erected a 12-sided shell enclosure, with one side having a tower-like projection. This was built in the twelfth century. Robert, Duke of Normandy, eldest son of William the Conqueror, was imprisoned here (c.1110–34) by his youngest brother, Henry I of England. Among the medieval additions were the Black Tower (1200s), below the motte and connected to the motte by a wing wall, an octagonal tower (c.1420s) on the south side of the shell enclosure and standing taller, and a substantial gatehouse linked to the Black Tower by a massive wall across the bailey.

The castle stands on the site of a Roman fort, with a stone curtain with flanking turrets. Later in the castle's history, apartments were raised in the bailey including a range against the western wall, substantially remodelled in the eighteenth and nineteenth centuries. The octagonal turret on the shell enclosure is one of these additions.

Cardiff is a very good example in Wales of how an earth-and-timber motte castle was converted to a stone fortress (like Berkhamsted and Pickering). The castle was attacked several times by the Welsh.

CARDIGAN DYFED
(SN 177459 and SN 164464)

There is confusion over two castle sites here. The first was a Norman enclosure of c.1093 (at SN 164464) which was converted to stone by the Welsh who probably captured it, c.1170, and then sold it to King John in 1199. John and Henry III both spent money on it. Then in 1231 it was taken by Llywelyn the Great and destroyed. Cardigan town was recovered by the English c.1240 and a castle was built near the older structure. This may have included the curtain wall and flanking towers, and the cylindrical great tower. In 1254 the castle was in the custody of Edward, eldest son of Henry III and later Edward I. Repairs were carried out in later reigns, including work on the roof of the 'great round tower' in the mid-fifteenth century.

CAREW DYFED
(SN 045037)

Carew stands on a rock above the shore where the Cleddau enters the sea. It began as an earthwork castle in the early twelfth century. This may have been the time when the rectangular gatehouse of rubble masonry was put up. Later in the century the gatehouse was altered to make a tower, when the vaulted passage was blocked and, later still, a square-plan curtain wall was built round the tower, with a double line of defence on one side. The curtain had four large flanking towers of various shapes, two of which were cylindrical on spur bases (cf. Goodrich). This was in the late thirteenth century when an outer ward with its own gatehouse into the main enclosure was added. The outer ward received buildings, but much later conversion of the ward into a walled garden has obscured the details. Meanwhile, the main enclosure was considerably altered in the fourteenth and fifteenth centuries, rendered more into a mansion, with a great hall and imposing porch. There were further changes in the sixteenth century in Tudor style. Carew was besieged and badly damaged in the Civil War. Some of the medieval buildings were changed, notably the windows, which were replaced by rows of wide, mullioned ones in the north front.

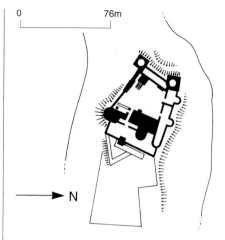

0   76m

Carew: ground plan. The two spur-based cylindrical towers, on the west, are among the oldest buildings and they confirm the military aspects of the castle.

CARMARTHEN DYFED
(SN 413420)

Carmarthen began as a motte castle of the very early twelfth century (possibly even before). The motte was revetted for part of its height. It was Norman-built, attacked several times by the Welsh during the century and was strengthened in 1181–3 for £170. In 1215 it fell to Llywelyn the Great who probably damaged it beyond repair, for in the following decade it received stonework. By 1275 it had an inner bailey with five towers, a great tower (actually described as *magna turris*), a hall, chapel, gate and curtain wall. Edward I made Carmarthen the centre for his administration of south-west Wales, and over the fourteenth and fifteenth centuries the castle was maintained in reasonable condition. Owain Glyndwr captured it c.1403 and held it for six years. Henry IV spent about £100 on the gate, converting it to the gateway which can be seen today. Recent excavations revealed more buildings, including a gatehouse, which is one of the few remaining features that can be seen today.

CASTELL CARNDOCHAN
GWYNEDD
(SH 846306)

A small Welsh-built castle of the mid-thirteenth century that commands the valley of Afon Lliw. It is a curtained enclosure with an integrated apsidal tower at the south-west end and a round turret on the north-east side. In the enclosure is a square-plan building.

CARREG CENNEN

Nr Llandeilo, Dyfed
(SN 668191)

This powerful courtyard castle, clasped on the north-east and east sides by two outer stone-walled baileys with flanking solid turrets and a gateway, stands on a 91.4-metre (300-ft) high limestone crag overlooking the Towy valley. The stonework was begun in the late thirteenth century and the first work was the inner enclosure with a long range occupying the whole east wall and containing a hall, the northern twin-semi-octagonal-towered gatehouse (of three storeys) and the cylindrical tower on the north-west corner. The east range was three-storeyed for most of its length and contained hall, solar, kitchen on the middle (first) floor and a chapel on the top in what is called the chapel tower. The range was flanked by a square-plan, north-east corner tower with canted edges, three storeys tall. The gatehouse served in a defensive role as a great tower in as much as it was the last refuge in the event of assault. The passage

Carreg Cennen: this great castle stands on a 92 metre (300 ft) crag overlooking the Towy valley. It was damaged in Owain Glyndwr's campaign to win independence in the early fifteenth century.

through the ground floor had a portcullis at each end. In between was a gate, and there were several arrow slits along the walls of the passage between gate and portcullis. You could walk from the gatehouse at first-floor level to the north-west and north-east towers through mural galleries, and at second-floor level above these galleries a wall-walk behind parapetting led round the whole enclosure.

The remains of the barbican show it to have been formidable. Projecting northwards from the gatehouse is the ruined Prison Tower, which was three-storeyed with thick walls. At right-angles leading eastwards is an opening into a long, narrow, walled passage, extending beyond the easternmost part of the main castle block. This passage slopes on its easterly path downwards and the floor is a stepped ramp. Along its course are deep pits which were crossed by movable bridges. It was thus difficult to get up to the Prison Tower entrance. At the east end the passage turns sharp right, emerging at a south access. The ground in front of the north wall falls sharply away down the rock slope.

Carreg Cennen is much ruined, but its general layout and sophisticated defences are clear. (Note the castle cave, reached by a door in the south-east corner of the inner enclosure.) Very considerable damage was done to it by Owain Glyndwr, who destroyed most of the defences. It was finally rendered useless as a castle by the Yorkists in the Wars of the Roses.

CARREGHOFA Powys
(SJ 255222)

An earthwork enclosure built c.1100 was captured in 1163 by the Welsh. It was retaken at the end of the century and repaired.

CASTELL-Y-BERE

Abergynolwyn, Gwynedd
(SH 667086)

This was a native Welsh castle raised on a spur of land in the shadow of Cadair Idris. It resembles the medieval German hill castles such as Staufen. It was begun probably in 1221 by Llywelyn the Great, Prince of all Wales (c.1196–1240), and consisted of an irregular curtained enclosure with flanking towers, one of them in the manner of a great tower, and a triangular barbican. It was not equipped with a drawbridge over the moat cut out of the rock, but had a fixed timber pontoon. It was formidable, nonetheless, because of its position. In April 1283, Bere was besieged and captured by Edward I's forces. After the ending of hostilities between England and Wales, Bere was restored to use by Edward who spent over £260 on works over the years 1286–90. This was mainly devoted to building a considerable stretch of tall curtain wall round the outside of the original castle. The castle appears to have been abandoned after c.1295. All the buildings are now ruined to their foundations.

CEFNLLYS Powys
(SO 089614)

There was once a substantial castle here, inside a hill-fort. Fragments of a great tower were found in the north corner of the fort, and of a round tower in the south.

CHEPSTOW Gwent
(ST 533941)

Begun c.1067 as one of the very first stone castles in Britain, Chepstow's building periods cover several centuries. Standing on a natural limestone ridge whose north face falls in a steep vertical cliff into the River Wye, it was started by William FitzOsbern, whom the Conqueror had recently made Earl of Hertford, and his first work became the first stone great tower in Britain. It was a

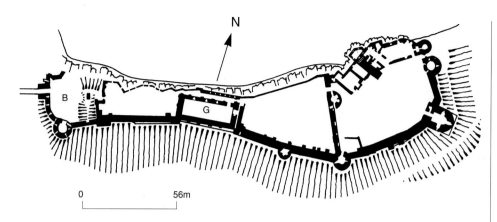

Chepstow: a castle of several periods, beginning with a great tower (G) c.1067–71; the barbican (B) was built c.1225–45.

substantial quadrilateral two-storey building, about 30.5 x 12.2 metres (100 x 40 ft), standing on a splayed plinth, with the ground scarped away from its south side. In the mid-thirteenth century, the upper storey had an extra storey added at the west end which, towards the end of that century, was extended for the rest of the tower's length, to give a three-storeyed great tower, with a cellar of unequal dimensions. Interestingly, different types of stone were used in the construction of the tower, notably old red sandstone, yellow sandstone and great oolite rock.

The next stage was a thick curtain wall on the east side of the ridge, with cylindrical towers and a gate. This work was carried out by William Marshal, Earl of Pembroke, c.1190–1220. It divided the central bailey from the lower bailey. Almost immediately after that, c.1225–50, the great tower was heightened, the upper (western) bailey was constructed, and next to it the interesting barbican with cylindrical tower at the south; the central bailey southern wall was raised, and also the lower (eastern) bailey received its easterly curtain and a twin-cylindrical-towered great gatehouse, three storeys high; this had a prison in the northern tower, which contained only an airshaft. From c.1270–c.1300, the western gatehouse was built at the extreme west end of the barbican and various domestic buildings were erected in the lower bailey. At the south-east corner of the lower bailey, a huge D-end tower was built (later called Martens Tower after Henry Marten, the regicide, imprisoned there after

the Restoration of Charles II). It was 19.2 metres (63 ft) tall, with pyramidal spur bases, and later was given gun-ports, in the seventeenth century.

These are the principal features still to be seen. The visitor is particularly recommended to explore this castle in some detail.

Chepstow overlooked a harbour on the Wye by means of which the castle could be provisioned by ships coming from Bristol. The castle was held for a few short periods by the Crown. It was never attacked in the Middle Ages, but it was besieged twice in the Civil War while being held for the king. Much renovation was done in the seventeenth century to fit the castle out for guns and musketry, although more probably after the Civil War than before it, which suggests it may have been intended that Chepstow should be a prison for political offenders, such as Henry Marten.

CHIRK CLWYD
(SJ 268380)

There was a motte castle here, of the mid-twelfth century. Nearby, in the 1280s, the Mortimers started to build a lordship castle (*see* Chapter 7), with a view across Cheshire to the Pennines. The fortress became a quadrangle with squat but substantial cylindrical corner towers and half-round towers on the mid-walls, which remain in the present, more modern, mansion. It is thought that the work went on into the 1320s, and was stopped when Roger Mortimer was disgraced and put to death. In 1595 the castle was sold to Thomas Myddleton, later Lord Mayor of London, and his descendants still own it. It was besieged in the Civil War. Myddleton's son surrendered it rather than have it blown up by Parliamentary cannons.

CILGERRAN DYFED
(SN 195431)

Built on a rocky promontory of great natural strength overlooking the Teifi River, with rock-cut ditches at the south end, Cilgerran began as a Norman enclosure castle with outer bailey in the early twelfth century. About a century later, a powerful stone castle was raised, using the Norman enclosure as an inner enclosure and giving it a stone wall, and raising another curtain round the old outer bailey. Cylindrical towers were built into the inner curtain c.1233 and a strong gate inserted. The outer enclosure was also strengthened but there is little to see of any of this work. By the 1320s the castle was ruinous. Repairs were ordered in 1377, one of Edward III's last acts, and probably enough was done to help it hold out against Owain Glyndwr in the early fifteenth century.

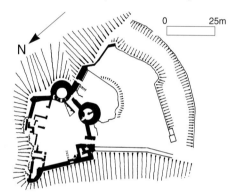

Cilgerran: plan of the enclosure castle. The two cylindrical mural towers at the south are early thirteenth century. Note how they are sited bulging out of the curtain and that the walls outside are much thicker than inside.

CLYRO POWYS
(SO 214436)

Only fragments remain of this castle on a hillock which was surrounded by good ditching. It is not clear when the castle was first raised.

COITY NR BRIDGEND, MID-GLAMORGAN
(SS 923816)

'Marry my daughter and you can have the castle of Coity without having to fight for it.' This, in so many words, is what the Welsh Lord Morgan said to a Norman knight, Payn de Turbeville, who had threatened to storm Coity some time during the last years of the

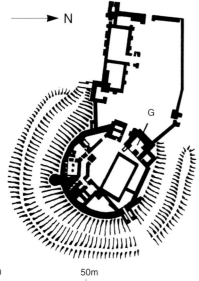

G

0   50m

Coity: the wall in the lower half of the enclosure at left and the great tower at G are the oldest parts (late twelfth century) of this castle of several periods.

eleventh century, according to an old legend. At that time, however, Coity was simply a circular earthwork enclosure, with a variety of good banks and ditches. A century elapsed before stonework was added to the site, and this comprised a curtain round the greater part of the inner bailey (surrounded for three-quarters of the circle by a moat). On the arc of the remaining part of the circle was built a rectangular great tower, some 12.2 x 10.7 metres (40 x 35 ft), at the north-west. The ribbed vaults and other features to be found internally are of a much later (fourteenth-century) date. There were some more additions and alterations made during Tudor times, including an abutting square turret, four storeys tall, on the north-east side of the great tower.

(Right) Coity: the remains of the late twelfth-century great tower, seen from the outer ward (left), are on the north-west of the inner ward beyond.

A view of the two large round towers in the south enclosure of Cilgerran.

COLWYN LLANSANTFFRAID, POWYS
(SO 108540)
An enclosure castle with marked bank, possibly of early twelfth-century beginnings, and said to have been rebuilt c.1144. The earthworks stand in farm premises.

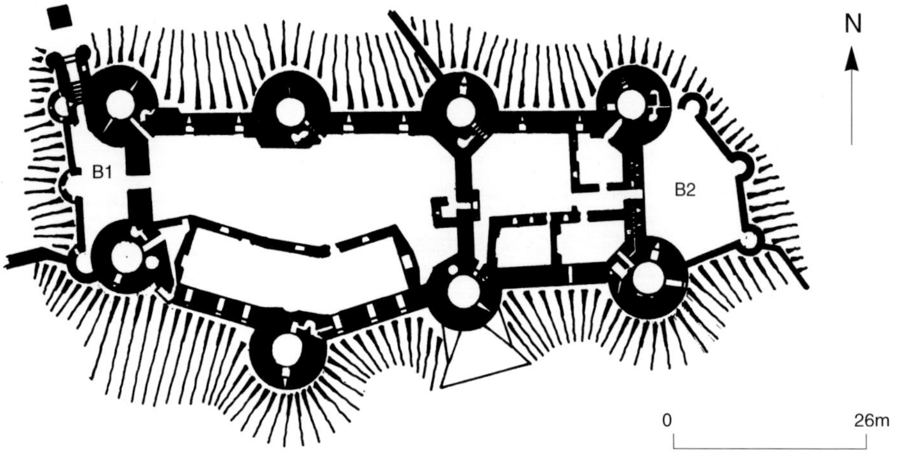

Conwy: ground plan. Despite the concentration of towers, the castle is basically a simple enclosure. B1 and B2 are barbicans.

CONWY GWYNEDD
(SH 781777)

One of Edward I's second tranche of castles in Wales (*see* pp. 62–5), Conwy was designed by Master James of St George and completed very quickly – 1283–7. Over 1500 men of one skill and another worked on the huge structure during the summer of 1285, and the workforce could hardly have been much less for the remaining building time. The bill came to nearly £20,000, which was the biggest sum spent on any castle in Wales between 1277 and 1304. And at the end of it, Edward I was presented with an almost perfect structure of a high, thick curtain wall with eight huge cylindrical flanking towers, the most compact agglomerate of turretry in the British Isles.

Tailored to fit the rock site chosen for guarding the entrance to the River Conwy, the castle was a vast enclosure divided into an inner and an outer ward, separated by a thick wall at each end of which was one of the eight flanking towers. The towers themselves are massive, well over 9.1 metres (30 ft) in diameter with walls up to 4.6 metres (15 ft) thick. Reaching to over 21.3 metres (70 ft) tall, they are like great towers, with several storeys equipped with rooms and staircases. This massive construction represented all that Edward I stood for – strength, terror, dominion, permanence – and it was hated by the Welsh for just those things. Yet it was not besieged until the Civil War, perhaps because it really did seem too big to challenge, and within a generation the mighty fortress began to show signs of decay. Timber in the tower roofs was rotting away and stonework was crumbling here and there.

In 1294, Prince Madog ap Llywelyn, a cousin of Llywelyn the Last, organised a rising against English rule in north Wales and, descending upon some of the Edwardian castles, wreaked a great deal of damage, particularly at Caernarfon (q.v.). The king marched rapidly to Wales, assembled a small force and set out to establish a base for operations in Conwy, leaving his commanders to marshal the main army for dealing with the revolt. He was no sooner inside the great castle than the waters of the river rose, effectively trapping him within and cutting off supplies. The king spent anxious days waiting for the waters to subside, his temper not at all improved by the deteriorating diet on which he and his men were compelled to subsist – salted meat, suspect water and coarse bread. Then at last the river went down and Edward emerged to deal with the revolt.

Conwy Castle was part of a walled town to which it was joined. The castle was used sporadically during the fourteenth century and then gradually began to decay over the years. In 1609 it was described in an official report as 'utterly decayed'. It was subsequently sold – for £100!

CRICCIETH GWYNEDD
(SH 500377)

Originally raised by the Welsh during the reign of Llywelyn the Great (c.1196–1240), Criccieth began as a roughly triangular curtain enclosure of grey stone upon a high peninsula. Nearly half its perimeter was protected by the steep slope of the cliff leading to the sea shore. Ditches and banks were cut and raised on the remaining sides which also had scarps. The enclosure was covered by a rectangular great tower at the south-west corner, let into the curtain, and by a second rectangular tower at the north corner, called the Engine Tower, also let into the curtain. Both towers commanded the slopes. The Engine Tower is so-named because it was equipped to mount a siege-engine on the top behind the protection of a parapet. The great tower, which has been compared with the great tower at Dolwyddelan, was about 20.7 x 12.2 metres (68 x 40 ft), and rose three storeys with a battlemented parapet above. There was a simple gateway at the south corner. The great part of this work was done in the first half of the thirteenth century.

In the years following the conquest of Wales by Edward I, an inner enclosure of reddish stone was erected inside the older work. This was given a rectangular tower on the south-east called the Leyburn Tower, named after the castle's constable in that period, possibly on the site of an earlier Welsh-built tower. The enclosure was also fortified by the insertion of a powerful twin-half-cylindrical-towered gatehouse.

Considerable repairs were carried out in Edward II's reign. Over £500 was spent on

Criccieth: the outer walling and two rectangular towers at right are the first (Welsh) parts, of early to mid-thirteenth century. The inner ward (I) with north-east gatehouse is Edwardian.

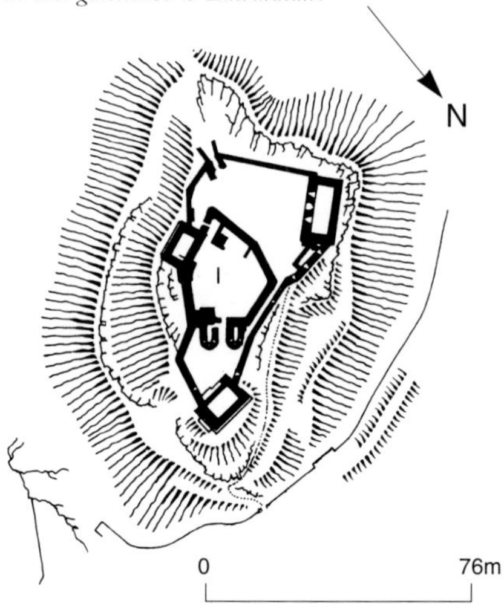

the castle between 1285 and 1326. It was captured by Owain Glyndwr in 1404, and soon afterwards appears to have been badly damaged by fire, to judge from charred timber discovered in excavations of the building ruins in the 1930s.

CRICKHOWELL POWYS
(SO 217182)
A motte castle of late date, probably the early thirteenth century, which was given a stone shell enclosure on the summit, with possibly a gate at bailey level. A pair of conjoined towers (cylindrical and rectangular) in fragmentary state are close to the motte. The pair are like those at Brecon and Abergavenny.

CASTELL CRUGERYDD
LLANFIHANGEL-NANT-MELAN, POWYS
(SO 158593)
Otherwise known as Crug Eryr, this was a motte castle on the side of a high hill. It was mentioned by Giraldus Cambrensis towards the end of the twelfth century.

CYMARON POWYS
(SO 152703)
A motte castle of the early twelfth century which was rebuilt c.1144 and appears to have been rebuilt again in 1195.

CYMMER GWYNEDD
(SH 732195)
A castle was built here in 1116. It appears to have been destroyed in the same year.

DEGANNWY GWYNEDD
(SH 781794)
A Welsh castle that began as a double motte castle of c.1090 (mentioned by Ordericus Vitalis). Two hillocks side by side were made into a double motte castle and linked by ramparts and ditching. This was taken by the Welsh in the twelfth century and was in the hands of Llywelyn the Great c.1200. It was taken again by the English c.1210, refortified with timber by the Earl of Chester, but retaken by Llywelyn c.1213. It was attacked in 1241 by Henry III of England and taken. In 1257, Llywelyn the Last recaptured it and then destroyed it.

This chequered history has obscured the building details. It was the site itself that was of value to both sides. Certain buildings were raised, of which traces remain or evidence is available regarding their existence. These

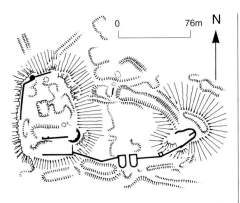

Degannwy: fragments remain of this once-formidable castle of the thirteenth century, built by Henry III and destroyed by Llywelyn the Last. There were powerful towers on the two hills (bottom left and right). Note also the remains of the twin-towered gateway. Degannwy combined geographical features with stonework in a cohesive plan.

included a great tower on one of the hillocks, an enclosure with three towers on the other, and a twin-D-ended-towered gateway of the thirteenth century in between the two, on the saddle, so to speak.

The Exchequer records indicate that Henry III took much personal interest in the building work in the 1240s. In 1245 he camped nearby for two months to supervise operations. The great tower was probably started in 1247. The *History of the King's Works* reckons that about £10,000 must have been spent in all, which is a very substantial sum. Henry gave the castle to his son Edward in 1254. Within 20 years it had been utterly destroyed by Llywelyn the Last, and only traces of the work can be seen today.

DENBIGH CLWYD
(SJ 051657)
There was a motte castle here of unknown date, but mentioned in the Pipe Rolls at the end of the twelfth century. During Edward I's campaigns in Wales he encouraged some of his barons to build castles for themselves. Henry de Lacy, Earl of Lincoln, an enormously rich and powerful magnate, erected Denbigh Castle over the years 1282–1311, in two main periods: in 1282–6 the west and south curtain walls of an enclosure, with round flanking towers, were built, and 1286 onwards saw the completion of the enclosure with polygonal flanking towers and the insertion, in the north face, of

a remarkable triangular complex of three polygonal towers to make a gatehouse. The question has been asked: did Master James of St George, then working at Caernarfon Castle (q.v.), advise de Lacy to complete his castle in this fashion? Inside the enclosure, domestic apartments were raised, including a great hall with a dais, and a barbican was added to the south postern tower, access being provided through an entrance in the curtain wall.

The great gatehouse has been described in Chapter 5. It was by far the most imposing feature of the whole castle, and still dominates the ruins today, notwithstanding the disappearance of much of it.

Denbigh: the great gatehouse. B = octagonal hall with stone vaulting.

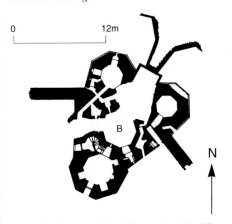

Denbigh was, like Flint and Rhuddlan, associated with an adjoining town which was fortified with a thick wall, towers and gates. The castle was besieged during the Civil War, in an assault lasting nearly six months, from April to October 1646. The Royalist garrison finally surrendered and the castle was used by Parliament as a prison for captured Royalists.

CASTELL DINAS BRAN
LLANGOLLEN, CLWYD
(SJ 223430)
An early castle of Welsh construction, probably twelfth century, Dinas Bran was a stone-walled enclosure, roughly rectangular, containing a square great tower. The curtain was flanked by a large D-ended tower, inserted in the thirteenth century. There was also a twin-towered gatehouse, likewise probably thirteenth century. The castle was taken from the Welsh some time in the Edwardian wars, between 1277 and 1282.

CASTELL DINAS EMRYS
NR BEDDGELERT, GWYNEDD
(SH 606492)
A Welsh-built castle consisting of the remains of a rectangular tower, erected on an earlier (?) Roman site. Dinas Emrys is in a district once rich in copper deposits, and the castle was raised by Llywelyn the Great in the early thirteenth century to protect them.

CASTELL DINAS POWYS
ST ANDREWS MAJOR, SOUTH GLAMORGAN
(ST 152716)
Two structures are at this site. The first was an earthwork enclosure surrounded by a rubble-reinforced bank on which a wooden palisade was set (whose post-holes have been found), with a ditch cut in rock. This is at ST 148722. There were additional banks and ditches outside associated with the enclosure. Nearby, the second castle (ST 152716) contained a square tower of late twelfth-century date beside a later rectangular enclosure of stone, with no towers but with a gateway. The curtain is of rubble, 6 x 9.1 metres (20–30 ft) tall and 1.8 metres (6 ft) thick. This contained buildings, including a hall and (?) a chapel on the south of the curtain near the west end.

DINEFWR DYFED
(SN 611217)
A polygonal inner stone enclosure was raised on an earlier earthwork castle on the top of a

Dinefwr: plan of great tower castle, mainly of thirteenth-century construction, with more domestic buildings added later.

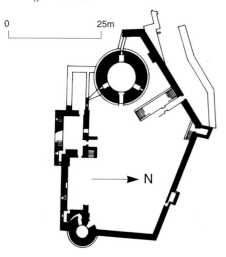

cliff here in the late twelfth century or early thirteenth century. The curtain has been repaired at later dates. Inside the enclosure, a cylindrical great tower was built at the east, between 1150 and 1250. The north side had a defensive moat cut out of the solid rock. There was also an outer enclosure. Domestic buildings were added in later periods, after the conquest of Wales by Edward I. Dinefwr was besieged c.1402 by Owain Glyndwr but not taken. Today, the remains stand in Dinefwr (Dynevor) Park. The 'summer house' cap on the great tower is a folly added in the eighteenth century.

DINGESTOW GWENT
(SO 455104)
A motte castle by the River Trothiu, probably built c.1180.

DINHAM GWENT
(ST 480923)
Parts of a small rectangular tower of possibly the thirteenth century, and traces of other stonework.

DINIERTH
LLANBADARN TREFELGWYS, DYFED
(SN 945624)
A motte castle of c.1110 was badly damaged by Gryffyd ap Rhys c.1116, and again in 1136. The castle was destroyed c.1208. There is some masonry rubble on the motte surface but it is thought that the rubble is part of the motte's own construction material and not of any building thereon.

DOLBADARN NR LLANBERIS, GWYNEDD
(SH 586598)
From its boomerang-shaped, rock-based platform between the Peris and Padarn lakes, Dolbadarn Castle commanded the entrance to the Llanberis Pass. The east side of the platform slopes down to the Padarn. The west side is protected by a sheer rock cliff down to a marsh. The castle site is peppered with rock crops where the platform was not flattened. The principal structure is a cylindrical great tower of mortared local slate and grit rubble, with splayed plinth and a curving outside stairway on the west arc, which may replace an earlier small forebuilding. The walls are 2.1 x 2.4 metres (7–8 ft) thick and contain a spiral staircase within the north-west facing segment, the overall diameter is over 12.2 metres (40 ft), and the height at present is

some 12.2 metres with three storeys, but once reached nearly 15.2 metres (50 ft). The tower forms part of the curtain round the site, which is interspersed with other buildings such as a south tower, a thick-walled west tower of which only the base remains and a rectangular hall at the north-west.

The whole castle was probably erected as one operation over several years by Llywelyn the Great in the early thirteenth century, although it has been argued that the great tower and west tower were raised shortly after the other works.

In the campaign against Wales, 1281–3, Dolbadarn was abandoned after Llywelyn the Last's death and Edward I declined to rebuild it. Instead, it was used as a quarry for materials for other buildings, including Caernarfon.

DOLFORWYN
BETTWS CEDEWAIN, POWYS
(SO 152950)
A Welsh-built castle on a ridge, with a stone curtain enclosure of rectangular plan, with various towers. The castle, which has been the subject of very recent excavations, dates roughly from the mid- to late thirteenth century and was probably raised by Llywelyn the Last, Prince of all Wales. The excavations revealed the details of, among other features, a square great tower 14.3 x 7.3 metres (47 x 24 ft) (internally) and a round tower about 7 metres (23 ft) in inside diameter, which is thought to have been an armoury in the fourteenth century. The castle was taken by Edward I in 1278 and was used by the English for some time.

DOLWYDDELAN GWYNEDD
(SH 722523)
Built upon a rock ridge towering from the slopes of Moel Siabod, Dolwyddelan was built by Iorwerth Trwyndwn (the Flat-nosed) in the 1170s. Here, c.1173, was born Llywelyn ap Iorwerth, who was to become Llywelyn the Great, Prince of all Wales, from c.1196–1240. The castle is surrounded by rock-cut ditches and is protected on all sides by its fine position. The first building was a rectangular great tower, Welsh-built on Norman lines about 13.4 x 9.4 metres (44 x 31 ft), with its entrance at the first floor, and the approach to it covered by a forebuilding which had a drawbridge over a pit inside to deflect direct assault on the tower door. At first the tower was two-storeyed, and its third

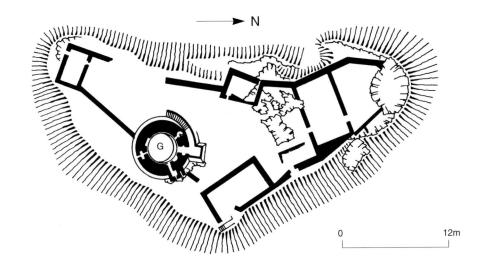

storey, battlements and new roofline are later works. The castle rock was skirted by a stone curtain whose two arms projected from either end of the great tower (north-east and south-west) along to two ends of a second rectangular tower. This was of later date, c.1270, was also two-storeyed, and about 15.2 x 9.1 metres (50 x 30 ft), using part of the north and west curtain as two of its four walls.

Dolwyddelan was captured by the English in January 1282, and it was maintained.

Dolwyddelan: the great tower at right was raised in the twelfth century. The remainder of the enclosure is thirteenth century.

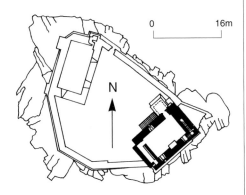

DRYSLWYN Dyfed
(SN 554203)
Dryslwyn was a Welsh-built castle of twelfth-century origin upon the possible site of an early Celtic hill-fort. It consisted of a large earthwork enclosure containing three stonework enclosures in line. The inner ward

Dolbadarn: ground plan of castle. G = great tower.

---

contained a large rectangular building discovered in 1980, measuring 16.1 x 17.7 metres (53 x 58 ft), with a cellar reached by a flight of steps. This was a great hall, begun in the twelfth century and which was altered over the next two centuries.

The castle figured in an interesting siege in 1287. The holder, Rhys ap Maredudd, rose against the new English dominion in Carmarthenshire. Edward I responded by besieging the castle. One detachment led by Lord Stafford dug a tunnel in the hope of coming up under one of the towers, but the earth collapsed. Most of the detachment, including Lord Stafford, were asphyxiated. Some of those behind, however, dug through the fallen earth and eventually gained access to the chapel.

DYSERTH Clwyd
(SJ 060799)
A castle was built near the present structure (which is not part of this gazetteer) c.1241–2 by the English. It had two baileys, the outer one with masonry for part of its circumference, the inner one completely enclosed in stone, set well back from its moat. A twin-towered gatehouse and two further polygonal towers were inserted. The site was on rock near the church. It commanded an approach to the Vale of Clwyd. It was besieged by David ap Llywelyn, Prince of all Wales (1240–6), in 1245, and was captured in 1263 by David's nephew, Llywelyn the Last, Prince of all Wales (c.1246–82), who

---

demolished it so thoroughly that 'not one stone was left upon another' (*Annales Cambriae*). The ruins have been used as a quarry, and practically nothing remains.

EWLOE Nr Hawarden, Clwyd
(SJ 288675)
A possible motte castle raised by Owain Gwynedd, Prince of all Wales (1137–70), c.1150, which was converted to a stone castle in the very early 1200s by Llywelyn the Great. The earliest building was probably the substantial two-storeyed, D-shaped great tower, known as the Welsh Tower. This stands in the eastern (upper level) bailey of a two-bailey enclosure surrounded by extensive earthworks. The tower had a forebuilding along its south wall. The inner bailey was partly enclosed by a stone curtain. The outer (lower) bailey, polygonal in plan with a stone curtain, had a cylindrical two-storeyed West Tower at the extreme west end on a boss of rock. This outer work was probably by Llywelyn the Last, in the late 1250s. The castle is set upon a slope.

Ewloe: plan of the castle as it was c.1260. G = great tower, of c.1210. The enclosure and the cylindrical tower at left were built in the 1250s.

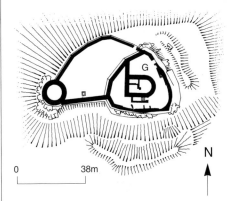

FLINT Clwyd
(SJ 247733)
Flint was the first of the Edwardian castles to be built in Wales during the king's campaign there of 1277. It was planned, like Rhuddlan of the same time, to be associated with a fortified town nearby and, like Rhuddlan, it was given direct access to tidal waters, in this case the estuary of the Dee. It was not concentric – it really had no need to be: the basic part of it, a roughly rectangular stone enclosure with three substantial cylindrical

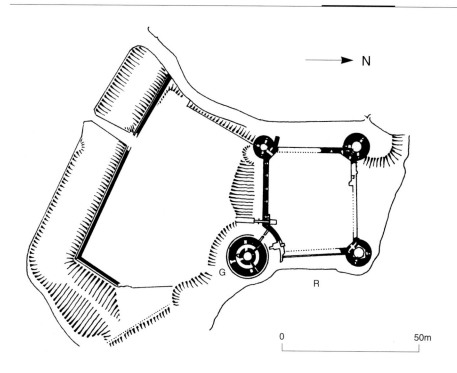

N

0   50m

corner towers, and on the fourth corner (separated by its own moat) a huge cylindrical great tower, was protected by the waters of the Dee. The south wall of the enclosure was also protected by a moat, in front of which was fa walled outer bailey and beyond that a second and very large moat fed from the Dee.

The inner enclosure's three towers were placed on the corners, built into them and, where the segments of the cylinders 'fed' into the walls, the walls were mitred off for additional strength. The dominating feature of the castle, however, was the great tower. Cylindrical in plan, its basement was a centre room around which was walling. On the other side of the wall was a circular wall gallery inside an outer wall, that is, the tower was concentric. Above the basement for two more storeys, the gallery space was partitioned off and provided with mural chambers and apartments. The centre core, however, remained hollow and changed from cylindrical to polygonal, was open to the sky and thus provided light for the rooms through indoor openings. There is doubt as to whether the space in the central core was used for rooms. Certainly, the mural chambers included a chapel, kitchen, garderobes and residential rooms. This arrangement would in fact have made the tower somewhat cramped for prolonged residence, and it has been suggested that the tower was used for short

Flint: R = line of River Dee. G = great tower, with its own moat.

stays, possibly as judge's lodgings.

The work on Flint Castle was spread mainly over the nine years 1277–86, and cost a little over £6000. In the Civil War the castle changed hands several times, surrendering finally to Parliament in 1646. It was slighted

so thoroughly that, as an eye-witness stated six years afterwards, it was 'almost buried in its own ruins'. But there is enough left to see the general plan of the castle, and notably of the cylindrical great tower.

FONMON
PENMARK, SOUTH GLAMORGAN
(ST 047681)
Founded c.1200, this was a stonework structure with two round towers and one square tower (presumably) flanking a stone curtain. The buildings were subsequently absorbed into a later seventeenth-century mansion. It was further modified in the eighteenth century. The square tower may have been a residential great tower.

GARN FADRYN GWYNEDD
(SH 278352)
A small fort inside an Iron Age fort, probably built c.1190.

GROSMONT GWENT
(SO 405244)
This is a very interestingly planned castle on the border between Wales and England. It is a compact enclosure of stone surrounded by a moat. It contained a rectangular hall tower, with a gatehouse building at the south-east corner and a rectangular building with D-ended tower at its west end at the north-west corner. A stone curtain with two semi-cylindrical flanking towers formed an arc to

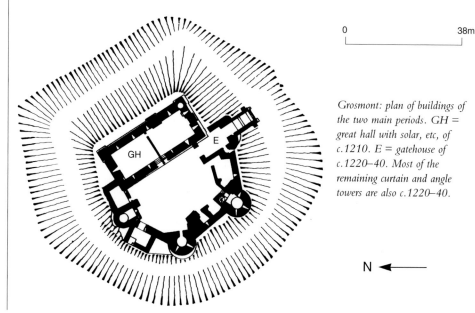

0   38m

Grosmont: plan of buildings of the two main periods. GH = great hall with solar, etc, of c.1210. E = gatehouse of c.1220–40. Most of the remaining curtain and angle towers are also c.1220–40.

N

Grosmont: the western side of the compact stone enclosure castle built on an earlier twelfth-century motte (see plan opposite).

complete the enclosure. The earliest structure was the hall tower, built c.1210, on the site of an earlier earthwork castle, probably of the late eleventh century. The hall is 29.3 x 9.7 metres (96 x 32 ft), and has pilaster buttresses on the corners and on three walls. It is likely that the great hall on the first floor was one long room, although there could have been a solar partition at one end. The gatehouse and the four-storeyed cylindrical towers are of c.1220–40, and were partly the work of Hubert de Burgh who held Grosmont. The gatehouse was three-storeyed with a large passage about 4.9 metres (16 ft) wide and 12.8 metres (42 ft) long, and it had a drawbridge out front. The northern building between the hall tower and the D-ended tower was raised in the fourteenth century.

Grosmont was attacked by the Welsh in a night raid in 1233, and it was besieged by Owain Glyndwr in 1405.

HARLECH GWYNEDD
(SH 581312)

The second phase of Edward I's fortress construction programme in Wales in the 1280s embraced four of the biggest castles in all Britain – Beaumaris, Caernarfon, Conwy and Harlech. Two of these, Beaumaris and Harlech, are concentric. While the former took over 35 years to build and was never finished, Harlech was completed inside 7 years, 1283–90.

Costing about £9000, Harlech was designed and personally supervised by Master James of St George. It was one of his most splendid creations, and from 1290–93 he was its constable, a well-paid job that gave him status as well as the time to superintend the other castles being built to his overall design, notably Beaumaris and Caernarfon. Harlech's design was simple yet immensely formidable: an inner trapezium of high curtain, with huge cylindrical towers on the corners and buildings ranged round the inside including a great hall, is surrounded by an outer and much lower wall enclosing a fighting platform. The south and east sides of the castle are further protected by a deep moat cut into the rock on which the castle stands, while the west side is sheer rock cliff sloping to the sea of Tremadoc Bay (now marsh and dune, for the sea has receded) and the north is protected by a mass of rock obstacles. At the extreme north end of the west side are the remains of the sea gate. Along the stretch of rock in front of the outer west wall are traces of specially cut artificial platforms for siege-engines. On the eastern side there is an outer gateway (now incomplete) which let out over a bridge (now a causeway) across the moat.

The dominant structure in the castle is the gatehouse, set in the east inner wall. This is a massive, oblong structure like a great tower, 24.4 x 16.4 metres (80 x 54 ft), three-storeyed, with twin cylindrical towers out front that flank the entrance passage which was once further guarded by three portcullises and three sets of doors. The structure also projects inwards into the inner bailey, with two more cylindrical towers, one placed at each end of the west wall, both containing spiral staircases leading to the fine residential apartment suites above. The gatehouse walls were 2.7–3.6 metres (9–12 ft) thick, equipped with arrow-loops, and the passage has murder-holes in the ceiling. Harlech's seeming impregnability was tested in 1294, when it was attacked by Welsh patriots led by Prince Madog ap Llywelyn, whose forces had wreaked great destruction at Caernarfon (q.v.). Thirty-seven men successfully beat off the assault then, unaccountably, this magnificent fortress was allowed to decay to an alarming extent. There were some repairs, but in the mid-fourteenth century phrases like 'weak and ruinous' were already being used.

In c.1404 Owain Glyndwr surrounded the castle and settled down to besiege it. The structure proved too strong to take by storm so he decided to starve the garrison. For months his forces controlled every road to the castle and watched every entrance. Inside, provisions began to run out. There was no chance of revictualling by sea, one of the main reasons for the castle having been sited on the

Harlech: plan of concentric castle built 1283–90.

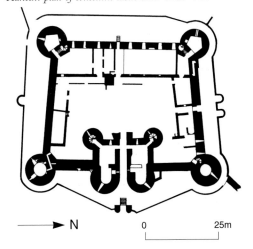

coast in the first place. Then disease broke out and some defenders tried to escape but were caught and put to death. Finally, Owain demanded surrender and the garrison filed out.

Owain moved in with his family and set up his headquarters. He may have held a second Parliament of Welshmen (the first had been at Machynlleth), and for four years he managed his remarkable campaign to free Wales from English rule. Then, in 1409, the English king, Henry IV, sent a strong force under Gilbert Talbot against Harlech and after a short siege the Welsh yielded. Owain's wife and four children were taken but the great Welshman had already slipped away. The fall of Harlech marked the end of his career.

HAVERFORDWEST DYFED
(SM 953157)
Strategically placed upon a ridge about 24.4 metres (80 ft) above the River Cleddau in the town of Haverfordwest, this castle has two enclosures. The inner enclosure contains two towers, one of which is a great tower. This has an unusual plan. The stonework is local gritstone called Boulston, and some Nolton sandstone was also used, for dressings.

The castle may have begun as a stone structure, for no earthworks are in evidence. The dating is possibly early twelfth-century for the beginnings. The curtain wall, of probably the late twelfth or early thirteenth century, was 3.6 metres (12 ft) wide, which is extraordinarily thick. The castle was attacked by Owain Glyndwr, whose army was assisted by a force of some 3000 Frenchmen, but the garrison held out.

HAWARDEN CLWYD
(SJ 319653)
Hawarden was one of the four lordship castles (see Chapter 7) in north Wales built or fortified at the instigation of Edward I (but at the lord's expense!) in the years leading up to the conquest of north Wales (c.1277–82). It had begun as a motte castle with two ditches, which received stonework in the early thirteenth century, including a cylindrical great tower on the motte, a hall and a simple curtain round the bailey. A small round tower was added as part of the Edwardian improvement, and a complex barbican in the fourteenth century.

Hawarden was besieged and taken in 1282 by Dafydd, brother of Llywelyn the Last, but when Dafydd was captured and executed, the castle was returned. In the Civil War, Hawarden was held for Charles I, fell to Parliament, was retaken by Royalists and taken again by Parliament. It was slighted by Cromwell in 1647–8.

HAY-ON-WYE POWYS
(SO 229423)
There are two earthwork sites close to one another at Hay. One was a motte castle and one an enclosure castle. The motte, at SO 226422, was built in the early 1100s and was destroyed in 1216 by King John. The other site, SO 229423, now having stonework remains which are incorporated in an Elizabethan period mansion, was an enclosure of timber and earth converted to stone in the twelfth and thirteenth centuries, including a curtain wall and a square gate-tower.

HEN DOMEN POWYS
(SO 214980)
Sometimes called Old Montgomery Castle, Hen Domen has been the subject of much excavation in recent years. First of all it was a motte castle of c.1071, built by Roger de Montgomeri, one of the Conqueror's principal generals who received large tracts of land in the border district between England and Wales and who led the invasion of central Wales. It is a motte astride the line of the oval bailey. There was a timber palisade round the base of the motte as well as a ditch. The whole castle was given a double ditch, like Berkhamsted. Access from the bailey to the motte top was by timber bridge stepped at intervals, at the foot of which was a forebuilding. A number of timber buildings of varying periods has been revealed, including a chapel and a hall, as well as towers along the wooden palisade round the castle. It declined after about 1223 when Henry III started to build the nearby Montgomery Castle (q.v.).

HOLT CLWYD
(SJ 412537)
There is little to see of this Edwardian-period lordship castle built on the bank of the River Dee soon after 1282 by John de Warenne, Earl of Surrey, on land granted to him by Edward I. It was a single enclosure castle, roughly pentagonal in shape, with flanking round towers and with buildings against the sides of the curtain. It is probable that Warenne had the services of Master James of St George as building consultant. The castle was demolished in the late seventeenth century and the stonework was used in the construction of Eaton Hall in Cheshire.

HOLYWELL CLWYD
(SJ 186762)
A small motte castle was raised here in the early thirteenth century. It is known more locally as Castle Hill.

HUMPHREY'S NR LLANDYSSUL, DYFED
(SN 440477)
A motte castle of c.1110 founded by one Humphrey, a follower of Gilbert de Clare. It was raised on a spur of land in the Teifi Valley. The castle was destroyed by the Welsh c.1137 and rebuilt in 1151.

KENFIG
NR PORT TALBOT, MID-GLAMORGAN
(SS 801827)
Kenfig is an example in Wales of the variation on a motte castle found at Aldingbourne and Lydford in England, where the earth is heaped up round the basement storey of a great tower. This castle is at low level by the river. The great tower was built of local rubble with Sutton ashlar quoins, its basement having a vaulted ceiling, the basic dimensions of the tower being 14 x 13.4 metres (46 x 44 ft) with walls about 3.3 metres (11 ft) thick. The tower stood on a splayed plinth under the earth mound. The date is uncertain but was probably the late twelfth century. The tower was enclosed by a narrow curtain wall. There was also an outer enclosure (or bailey), likewise walled with a gatehouse, and this may have been of the thirteenth century.

Kenfig was attacked in 1232 and it was burned, possibly as the result of hostilities, in 1295. It is now in ruins.

KIDWELLY DYFED
(SN 409070)
This well-preserved, almost concentric castle stands on a bluff beside the estuary of the Gwendraeth Fach river. Kidwelly began as an extensive Norman earthwork castle of c.1106, which consisted of a banked, roughly oblong site surrounded by ditching, with an oval site in the centre (which may have contained a motte) along the edge of the scarp facing the river. There is a record that the castle was captured and burnt by the Welsh in 1215. It was attacked again in 1257 but it was not taken.

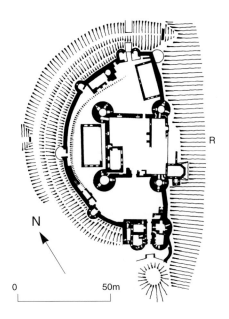

Kidwelly: the inner quadrangle is c.1275. The outer curtain, towers and gatehouses are predominantly early fourteenth century. R = Gwendraeth Fach River.

The first stonework is of the 1270s and consisted of an enclosure of a square curtain with cylindrical towers on the four corners. The towers had very thick walls. The south tower has five storeys. Adjoining this is a slightly later semi-octagonal chapel supported on a spur base, which is built into the slope of the bluff. The north tower flanked a postern which had gate and portcullis. The enclosure was surrounded on three sides by a second stone enclosure curtain with flanking half-cylindrical towers, and at each end (north-east and south-west) is a gatehouse. This work, making the castle concentric on three sides, was carried out in the fourteenth century. The south-west gatehouse is substantial, of three storeys, with semi-cylindrical towers flanking the entrance. Its south-east wall bulges outwards to cover attack from the river and up the scarp. The gatehouse had spacious accommodation on the first floor.

Kidwelly was attacked by Owain Glyndwr in the period 1403–7, when one of the gatehouses was burned.

KNIGHTON POWYS
(SO 284722)
There are two early motte castle sites at Knighton, one in the town near the church,

the other 0.4 km (¼ mile) or so away near the river (SO 290722). The first-named is thought to have lasted until the 1260s when it was captured, probably by the Welsh.

KNUCKLAS BEGUILDY, POWYS
(SO 250746)
This is a castle on a hill-site that was probably a hill-fort in much earlier times (perhaps Iron Age); the principal medieval remains are a small square stone block with what appear to be round corner turrets, dating from about the thirteenth century.

LAMPETER DYFED
(SN 579482)
Otherwise known as Llan Ystyffan, a motte castle was raised in what are now the grounds of St David's College, Lampeter. It was a Norman castle and was destroyed in 1136.

LAUGHARNE DYFED
(SN 302107)
A castle of unknown shape was built here in the twelfth century. Subsequently, rebuilding took place, probably in the thirteenth century, and this included a cylindrical great tower, another tower and a gatehouse which may have been fourteenth century. There were two baileys, and the inner bailey was converted into a mansion in the sixteenth century by Sir John Perrott. The remaining medieval gatehouse is an interesting structure, four storeys tall, containing an entrance arch of Perpendicular style which was probably added in the sixteenth century. The cylindrical tower has its battlements.

LLANBLETHIAN SOUTH GLAMORGAN
(SS 989742)
Otherwise called St Quentin's Castle, this was a late thirteenth- or early fourteenth-century stone enclosure with flanking towers, one square, two cylindrical and a fine twin-towered gatehouse (now the principal feature of the remains of the castle). There appears to have been a great tower in the centre of the enclosure of early fourteenth-century or possibly late thirteenth-century date.

LLANDAFF SOUTH GLAMORGAN
(ST 156780)
This is a small, irregular, quadrilateral-plan castle, consisting of stone curtain with flanking towers and possessing a good gatehouse. Two towers (one square, the other

cylindrical) remain today. Llandaff was a bishopric castle, and it is believed to have been destroyed by Owain Glyndwr c.1402. It was modified in later centuries – for example, mullioned and transomed windows were inserted at first-floor level in the western tower of the gatehouse during the late sixteenth century.

LLANDEILO TALYBONT
WEST GLAMORGAN
(SN 587027)
A motte castle was raised here in the twelfth century near the river.

LLANDOVERY DYFED
(SN 767342)
In the grounds of the Castle Hotel stand the remains of the castle founded by the Norman lord, Richard Fitzpons, in the early twelfth century. It was taken by the Welsh in 1116 and recovered by the family c.1158, when it was strengthened. It changed hands several times up to the reign of Edward I of England. Llandovery began as a motte castle. Stonework was added in the twelfth century, including a D-end tower of some strength and a gatehouse.

LLANELLI DYFED
(SN 501004)
Alternatively known as Carnwillion Castle, this motte castle has been almost submerged in the reservoir at Llanelli.

LLANFAIR DISCOED
CAERWENT, GWENT
(ST 445924)
Llanfair Discoed is a small, square-plan enclosure with curtain, two cylindrical turrets and part of a square-plan gatehouse built in the mid-thirteenth century. The castle has been added to in later years which has obscured much of the original work. No recorded history has yet been found but research is still continuing today.

LLANGADOG DYFED
(SN 709276)
A motte castle, 9.1 metres (30 ft) tall with a narrow ditch, was raised on this site in the twelfth century. The bailey is horseshoe-shaped, and was at one time bordered on one side by the River Sawdde. The castle was taken by the Welsh c.1209, but its later history is unknown.

LLANGIBBY LLANGYBI FAWR, GWENT
(ST 364974)

Also known as Tregrug Castle, Llangibby stands on a high site and was one single huge enclosure with a large gatehouse and a rectangular great tower. There were also four turrets on the walls, and a second (smaller) gateway. It was built in the fourteenth century. There are also references to an earlier earthwork structure at ST 369973 nearby.

LLANGWYNYD MID-GLAMORGAN
(SS 852887)

A small castle probably of the thirteenth century that may have been Welsh-built. Traces of a twin-towered gatehouse have been found.

LLANQUIAN SOUTH GLAMORGAN
(ST 019744)

There was once a stone revetted mound here. Its history is unknown.

LLANSTEPHAN DYFED
(SN 352102)

Llanstephan Castle was a double enclosure, the inner being in the north-east corner of the outer. The inner enclosure, or ward, was the first structure, a simple irregular polygon of stone with a gate-tower at the south-west, the

whole standing on a ridge with all but one of its sides protected by natural scarping. The remaining side was given a ditch for protection. This early work dates chiefly from the twelfth century, with early and mid-thirteenth-century completion. The outer enclosure was protected by a double ditch which is earlier than the stonework. The enclosure was fortified with a stone curtain in the thirteenth century with flanking towers and a bastion at the eastern corner.

Some time in the late thirteenth century, the great gatehouse was erected in the southern side of the enclosure wall. It is a typical gatehouse of the later thirteenth century, not unlike Tonbridge, and much of it stands today. The gatehouse was later blocked at its entrance (in the last years of the fifteenth century) to convert the building into a residence.

Llanstephan was captured by Owain Glyndwr in the early fifteenth century.

LLANTRISANT GWENT
(ST 047834)

The origins of this castle appear to go back to the early thirteenth century, when it was constructed with two baileys, the inner one smaller than the outer. The inner bailey contains fragments of wall and of a large cylindrical great tower thought to be of mid-thirteenth-century construction. The fragments of the cylindrical flanking tower on the curtain wall suggest that the curtain was a tall one.

Llanstephan has been consolidated in recent years. This view shows the gate-tower of the upper bailey of this double enclosure castle.

LLAWHADEN NR NARBERTH, DYFED
(SN 073174)

Llawhaden was a fortified palace built by the bishops of St Davids. It was originally an earthwork enclosure of the twelfth century, about 45.7 metres (150 ft) in diameter and surrounded by a dry moat, 21.3 metres (70 ft) wide, and a bank. The palace was destroyed c.1192 by Lord Rhys, satrap ruler of south-west Wales, and demolished. Soon afterwards, stonework was raised. This included a small cylindrical tower, 8.5 metres (28 ft) in diameter, and a curtained wall, of irregular shape but following the line of the earlier earthwork. This may have been done by the bishop of St Davids of the time.

In the 1280s, Bishop Thomas Bek converted the castle into a palace, obliterating much of the earlier work in the process, although there are still remains of the cylindrical tower and traces of the curtain. The new construction work produced a courtyard surrounded by ranges of buildings with two polygonal towers on two angles, and a gatehouse was erected during the late fourteenth century, the façade of which still stands to its full height today.

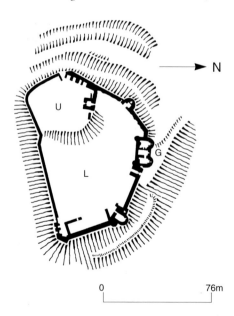

Llanstephan: the curtain of the upper bailey (U) is end of the twelfth century. The curtain of the lower bailey (L) with its towers is mainly thirteenth century. The gatehouse (G) is c.1280 and is similar to Tonbridge, Harlech, St Briavels, inter alia.

LOUGHOR West Glamorgan
(SS 564980)

Loughor consists today of a tower projecting from a curtain wall on a natural mound. The stonework is from the thirteenth/fourteenth century, raised on the twelfth-century motte castle site originated by the Normans and demolished c.1150 by the Welsh. The castle was repaired and demolished again in 1215. It is sited over the remains of a Roman fort.

LYCHEWEIN Dyfed
(SN 578148)

A castle at Lychewein was destroyed in 1206.

MACHEN Gwent
(ST 226887)

A Welsh castle built in the thirteenth century on a rocky ridge, of which little remains. It had a cylindrical tower. The site is in the neighbourhood of ancient lead mines used by the Romans.

MANORBIER Nr Tenby, Dyfed
(SS 064978)

This was the birthplace in 1146 of Giraldus Cambrensis (Gerald of Wales), the celebrated Welsh scholar who served Henry II, Richard I and John. The castle began as an earthwork of the late eleventh century, and in the twelfth century it received a square great tower of three storeys, with the entrance on the first floor. Other stone buildings were added, including a hall block, and by the thirteenth century it consisted of two high stone curtain enclosures in line, with flanking towers (cylindrical in the case of the outer enclosure), and with a strong square gatehouse which may not have been completed until well into the thirteenth century. The castle well was sunk to 9.1 metres (30 ft). Giraldus described the castle as 'excellently well defended by turrets and bulwarks'. Manorbier's residential features were pronounced, notably the state apartments in the inner enclosure, the fish-pond and the park.

The castle is superbly sited on the coast and is in a remarkable state of preservation. Its plan is not unlike that of Framlingham Castle in England (qv.).

MEURIG Gwnnws Issa, Dyfed
(SN 702675)

Also known as Castell Ystrad-Meurig, this is one of the few Cardigan castles to have been refortified with stone buildings and defences. The principal structure was a substantial rectangular great tower, possibly 18.3 metres (60 ft) square, date unknown but possibly late twelfth-century. There is a record of the castle being destroyed c.1208 but, as there are two castle sites in the neighbourhood, it is not clear if the 1208 date refers to this great tower. Only fragments remain.

MOLD Clwyd
(SJ 235644)

A late motte castle which retained its earthwork and timber structures right into the thirteenth century. It is mentioned in the 1160s and again later.

MONMOUTH Gwent
(SO 507129)

An earthwork enclosure castle was built here in the period 1067–71, probably by William FitzOsbern. It stands on a bluff overlooking the Wye and Monnow rivers. In c.1120–30, a rectangular two-storey hall tower like that at Chepstow was raised on the motte, with a west wall over 3 metres (10 ft) thick, and it was built of sandstone rubble with ashlar dressings. The tower has pilaster buttresses and stands on a splayed plinth. A length of curtain wall projected south-eastwards from the south wall and this later became part of a rectangular great hall, built c.1270.

The castle came into royal possession in 1399 when its owner, Henry Bolingbroke, became Henry IV. Twelve years earlier his son, Henry of Monmouth (later Henry V who was to win glory at Agincourt in the early fifteenth century) had been born in the castle gatehouse. The castle was slighted at the end of the Civil War when the Round Tower, which is said to have stood on the motte, was demolished.

MONTGOMERY POWYS
(SO 221968)

There was a stone double enclosure castle begun in the 1220s. It superseded Old Montgomery Castle (Hen Domen, q.v.), an eleventh-century motte castle. It has been extensively excavated.

Montgomery was built upon a promontory of greenstone (limestone) running roughly north to south, the northern end protected by sheer rock cliffs. The first work in stone was the inner ward at the north end, raised between 1224 and 1235, and it featured a D-ended flanking tower at north, and at south a twin-cylindrical-towered gatehouse whose lower parts were solid. A large D-ended tower projecting out of the western wall, in which the castle well was situated, was added in the mid-thirteenth century. Various buildings were put up within this enclosure in the fourteenth century.

At about the same time as the inner enclosure was begun, a second enclosure, this time of wood, was built adjoining the southern side. This was the middle ward, and it was separated by a ditch cut from west to east which was crossed by a bridge from the south gatehouse of the inner ward. This second ward was converted to stone in the mid-thirteenth century, for there was added to it a twin-towered gatehouse of stone at the southern extremity which is dated c.1250. The curtain walls were thick and were flanked by rounded turrets. Outside the south gatehouse was a rock-cut ditch which was crossed by a timber causeway.

MORGRAIG SOUTH GLAMORGAN
(ST 160843)

An irregular hexagonal curtain with horseshoe-shaped towers on four corners, nothing on the fifth, and one side of a large rectangular tower making up the bulk of the sixth side, built of local sandstone and limestone rubble, with limestone dressings. Built on an east–west ridge that was artificially enlarged to accommodate it, Morgraig was never completed and was probably allowed to decay as early as the mid-thirteenth century. It was a Welsh-built castle.

MORLAIS
MERTHYR TYDFIL, MID-GLAMORGAN
(SO 048097)

This was a thirteenth-century castle raised probably in the time of Edward I after his final conquest of Wales (1282–3). It appears to have been the cause of friction between two lords because it lay on a common boundary between their lands. Morlais contained a cylindrical great tower, a curtain enclosure with probably four flanking turrets, and extensive ditching. The ruins overlook the Taff Gorge. It is thought to have been begun by Gilbert de Clare, constructor of Caerphilly (among other castles).

NANTCRIBBA POWYS
(SJ 237014)

Traces of a stone curtain and towers, surrounded by a moat.

NARBERTH DYFED
(SN 110144)

This castle was a stone enclosure on a ridge at the south end of the town of Narberth. It contained a cylindrical great tower, and the ruins of four out of five original round flanking towers can still be seen. The stone castle was built during the thirteenth century, near the site of a Norman motte castle constructed c.1100, which had been destroyed by the Welsh in 1116.

NEATH WEST GLAMORGAN
(SS 753977)

There was a motte castle here, of which no trace remains, founded by the Norman knight, Richard de Granville, c.1130. Nearby, in the 1180s, another motte castle was raised in a bend of the river which supplied the ditch with water, and which could isolate the motte from attackers. In the thirteenth century the motte was revetted with stonework and two towers were built on the north side towards the river. The existing wall round Neath town was brought within the castle grounds by enclosing it with a curtain. Between the western tower and the town wall a strong outer gatehouse was constructed, and about 3.6 metres (4 yds) of its staircase can be seen.

Neath was attacked in 1231 and 1258, and captured in 1321 and the buildings levelled. The whole castle was then remodelled and new buildings erected on a level about 0.6 metres (2 ft) higher than earlier main ground level. The original round towers were modified to D-end towers.

NEWCASTLE
BRIDGEND, MID-GLAMORGAN
(SS 902801)

A stone enclosure of the mid- to late twelfth century raised against a steep spur overlooking the Ogmore river, probably upon the site of an earlier earthwork castle of c.1106. The plan is polygonal of nine unequal sides, with two almost square-plan towers in the curtain, one at the west angle, one at the south. The second tower is nearly 9.1 metres (30 ft) square and could be called a great tower, for it was residential (fireplaces, windows, staircases) and rose to three storeys. But there were also other buildings in the enclosure which were used for residential purposes. The entrance to the enclosure was adjacent to the south tower, through an elaborately decorated round-headed arch. The angles of the sides in the curtain have ashlar quoins.

NEWCASTLE EMLYN DYFED
(SN 311407)

Situated on a fine site overlooking the Teifi river in this picturesque town, Newcastle Emlyn was raised as a quadrangle in the 1240s by the Welsh. The twin-polygonal-towered gatehouse ruin is Welsh, but the second polygonal tower is thought to have been English-built. The castle changed hands several times in the 1281–3 war between England and Wales. It was also held for Charles I in the Civil War but was captured and blown up.

NEWPORT DYFED
(SN 057389)

A castle built in the early thirteenth century, on a natural mound with a moat cut round it, Newport now has only ruins. A few traces of

Newport (Gwent): plan of the 'harbour' level of the central water-gate tower at Newport. The double gates could be closed at low tide and thus keep out the rising river level.

the curtain may be seen and the remains of three towers and a twin-towered gatehouse (of later date). The present mansion, of nineteenth-century origin, absorbed these medieval remains. There is a surviving dungeon of the thirteenth century.

NEWPORT Gwent
(ST 312884)

A castle here is referred to as the 'new castle on the Usk' by the chronicler of the *Brut y Tywysogyon* for the year 1172. What is left at Newport today, however, is part of a later castle consisting of a long curtain wall facing the Usk, with three towers, the curtain once having been part of a quadrangle. The centre tower is a square gate-tower with an arched entrance. The river came up to this gate giving access to the castle: in other words, we have a specially designed water-gate that allowed the river to come into the ground floor of the tower at high tide, making a pool in which boats could draw up alongside a quay at the rear of the tower. The arch to the gateway had two strong portcullises. There was a chapel in the top of the gateway. Presumably the portcullises lifted up into the chapel (*see* Tonbridge).

Flanking this gateway on either side are two polygonal towers in the curtain, supported on spur bases. There was a hall in the range between the gateway and the north polygonal tower. There are remains of other parts, including some walling of the remainder of the quadrangle. Most of the building work is of the fifteenth century, much of it remodelling of the earlier stonework which was probably mid-thirteenth-century.

Newport (Gwent): the centre tower in the frontage on to the River Usk contains a hall above the water gate. Small ships could dock in the lower part at high tide.

OGMORE

NR BRIDGEND, MID-GLAMORGAN
(SS 882769)

Ogmore Castle is a stone-walled enclosure on an earlier earthwork site of c.1110, on the edge of the Ewenny river. It is entirely surrounded by a moat except for the north side which is bounded by the river, and it guards an important ford in which a unique row of stepping stones leads from the outer bailey across the river. The earliest stone building was the rectangular great tower of the late twelfth century, which was constructed of boulders in brown mortar with roughly hewn quoins at the lower end, and better ashlar higher up. It was three storeys tall, with 1.8-metre (6-ft) thick walls and measuring about 13.4 x 9.7 metres (44 x 32 ft), and was reached by an exposed staircase on the east side leading to the first floor. A gateway was built next to the great tower during the thirteenth century.

Opposite the great tower was built, also in the twelfth century, a rectangular building with one storey which was a kind of cellar, but its use is not absolutely clear. In the thirteenth century, the old earthwork rampart line was roughly followed by the erection of a stone curtain to form a polygonal enclosure. At the north end of this was built a long, rectangular two-storeyed hall with a solar. There were other buildings in the enclosure, and some in the outer bailey, including a court house dating from the fourteenth century. It was once used as a prison.

OLD BEAUPRE

NR COWBRIDGE, SOUTH GLAMORGAN
(ST 009721)

This castle is an Elizabethan quadrangular mansion (with extension at the south-east), which incorporates stonework remains of an earlier structure of the late thirteenth/early fourteenth century. The principal medieval remains include a gatehouse, incorporated in the south wing of the quadrangle and which may have led to other buildings now vanished, other segments of the same wing which are now part of the Elizabethan structure, and a block adjacent to and projecting north along the east wing. The differences in the periods of masonry can best be seen in the medieval gatehouse and the inner porch beside it to the west which is c.1600, where the porch joins the north wall of the south wing.

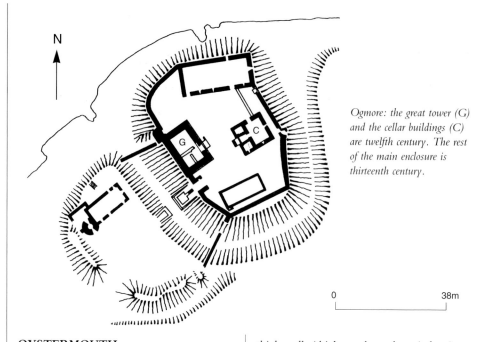

N

Ogmore: the great tower (G) and the cellar buildings (C) are twelfth century. The rest of the main enclosure is thirteenth century.

0   38m

OYSTERMOUTH

NR SWANSEA, WEST GLAMORGAN
(SS 613883)

A castle of c.1099 on a natural rock hill-site with bailey beside, overlooking Swansea Bay, was abandoned for a masonry enclosure of later date. The enclosure contained a rectangular tower of the late thirteenth century, and it received a twin-towered gatehouse at the other end. Today the tower remains with decorated windows, added in the fourteenth century, adjoining a second rectangular building and an attached gateway, which are in ruins.

PAINSCASTLE POWYS

(SO 167461)

A substantial motte castle, raised in the 1130s by Sir Payn FitzJohn. Fragments of walling on the motte suggest a cylindrical tower, and there are remains of another stone tower in the bailey, work of the rebuilding c.1230–1. It is recorded as having been captured in 1215.

PEMBROKE DYFED

(SM 982016)

This was one of the grandest of the earlier castles built in Wales. Its dominating feature was, and still is, its cylindrical great tower (built c.1200–10), massive, four-storeyed, over 16.1 metres (53 ft) in diameter, rising from a splayed plinth to almost 24.4 metres (80 ft) tall, with 4.6–5.1-metre (15–16½-ft)

thick walls (thickest where the spiral staircase ascends), and capped by a remarkable stone dome, over 1.2 metres (4 ft) thick at the top.

Pembroke began as an oval earthwork enclosure erected by Arnulf de Montgomery in the 1090s. The enclosure was divided into two, an inner smaller bailey of triangular plan, two sides of which were cliffs overlooking the Pembroke river. This bailey was given a stone hall of trapezoid shape in the twelfth century and surrounded with stone walls. The third side of the triangle was a substantial curtain wall with flanking towers. The larger outer bailey was enclosed with a stone curtain and several cylindrical corner towers on the angles, plus a substantial twin-rectangular-towered gatehouse and a powerful postern tower. Part of the southern curtain wall along the outer bailey was of double thickness for extra defence.

The great tower contained no mural chambers. All the storeys were cylindrical inside. The parapet at the top of the fourth storey protected a wall-walk, on the inside of which was a second wall with a parapet top; at one time this protected the dome and provided a second fighting platform. This parapet was severely damaged during the Civil War when the castle endured a prolonged siege by Cromwell.

Pembroke was held by William Marshall who was Earl of Pembroke and one of King John's staunchest allies. It was at Pembroke also that Henry Tudor, later to become King Henry VII, was born in 1456.

PENCADER
LLANFIHANGEL-AR-ARTH, DYFED
(SN 445362)
A motte castle of the mid-twelfth century. The motte was 7.6 metres (25 ft) tall.

PENCELLI POWYS
(SO 095249)
A motte castle, of which not much is left following the raising of modern farm buildings. The motte was surrounded by a ditch. There are fragments of a tower which appears to have been about 15.2 metres (50 ft) square. In the thirteenth century it was given a twin-towered gatehouse. It was captured in 1215 and 1234, possibly by Llywelyn the Great, Prince of all Wales.

PENCOED NR NEWPORT, GWENT
(ST 406894)
The remains of a thirteenth-century tower and curtain are situated beside a sixteenth-century mansion.

PENHOW NR NEWPORT, GWENT
(ST 423908)
Penhow is a small enclosure castle of irregular polygonal plan, with buildings round a tiny courtyard. The principal feature is a rectangular-plan tower, battlemented, three

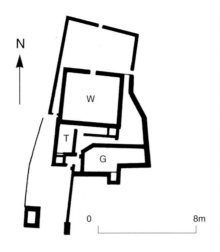

Penhow: late nineteenth-century plan of the castle. G = great hall. T = great tower (twelfth century). W = sixteenth-century wing added.

storeys tall, with walls 1.8 metres (6 ft) thick. Its entrance used to be at first-floor level, but a doorway was inserted later in the ground floor. The tower has a mural staircase and two garderobes, one of which was later altered to lead into the great hall. The castle was probably begun in the early thirteenth century by the then holder of the land, Sir William St Maur, a name later adapted to Seymour. He was an ancestor of Edward Seymour, brother-in-law of Henry VIII and Protector during

the reign of Henry's son, Edward VI. Alterations were carried out in the fifteenth and sixteenth centuries.

PENLLINE SOUTH GLAMORGAN
(SS 979761)
Also spelled Penllyn. So little of the twelfth- and thirteenth-century buildings remain that it is difficult to determine its original shape, which is also obscured by a later mansion.

PENMAEN WEST GLAMORGAN
(SS 534880)
Known also as Penmaen Burrows Motte, this was an earthwork enclosure castle which had stone rubble as part of its structure. Traces of a timber gateway have been found, approximately 6 metres (20 ft) square. This was burned down and later replaced by an entrance formed by drystone walls. There was also a timber watch-tower, about 5.2 x 3.6 metres (17 x 12 ft), and again replaced by a drystone structure of larger dimensions.

PENMARK
NR FONMON, SOUTH GLAMORGAN
(ST 059689)
A possibly thirteenth-century stone enclosure with cylindrical turrets and an outer bailey. There are a few fragments of wall and towers.

PENNARD WEST GLAMORGAN
(SS 544885)
An enclosure of earth and timber on rock was erected here probably in the early twelfth century. Later in the century a stone rectangular hall was raised. The castle was further expanded into an enclosure with towers and gatehouse (probably of the late thirteenth century), the buildings being mainly of light construction. It is thought that the stone hall replaced an earlier timber one.

PENRICE WEST GLAMORGAN
(SS 497885)
An enclosure castle of c.1100 where remains of some wooden parts were found in excavations of about half a century ago. This is sometimes called Old Penrice Castle, and the site is at SS 492879. A second (stone) castle was raised nearby in the mid-thirteenth century at SS 497885, and there are remains of a hall block and enclosure walls with small solid turrets, and a gatehouse of three towers, bunched like those at Denbigh Castle. Later, a residential complex was built beside an

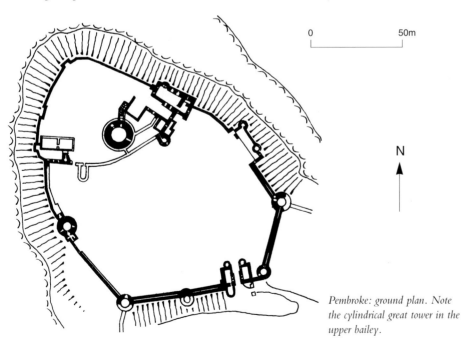

Pembroke: ground plan. Note the cylindrical great tower in the upper bailey.

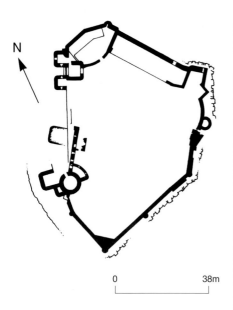

Penrice: plan of the enclosure castle of several periods. The cylindrical great tower at the south-west is of the later thirteenth century.

earlier tower, and stood as a separate fortified structure on higher ground within the enclosure.

PENTREFOELAS Clwyd
(SH 870522)

A motte, with some traces of stone wall.

CASTELL PEN-YR-ALLT Dyfed
(SN 158420)

A small earthwork enclosure, with ditching and some stone fragments.

PETERSTON South Glamorgan
(ST 084764)

There are traces of a square-plan tower.

PICTON Dyfed
(SN 011135)

A motte castle built in the time of William II (1087–1100) at the top of a stretch of rising ground, with a (?) bailey to the north. This was not converted to stone. About 150 years later, c. mid-thirteenth century, a second castle was built near the original site, which presumably had decayed. The new castle was a quadrangular enclosure with strong corner towers and mid-wall towers, one of which guarded the entrance in the east curtain. The castle is still occupied, but has been drastically altered over the centuries.

POWIS Nr Welshpool, Powys
(SJ 216064)

Powis Castle, today a graceful residence of towers and battlements, mullioned windows and turrets, compressed together and standing by the site of a thirteenth-century castle, belies the original. The latter was destroyed by Llywelyn the Last in the 1270s because its owner had taken sides with the English. It had two baileys, with a twin-towered gatehouse which was considerably modified.

PRESTATYN Clwyd
(SJ 073833)

A low-level motte castle with a half-moon bailey inside a larger rectangular enclosure, Prestatyn received stonework in the twelfth century. It was destroyed in 1167.

PRYSOR Gwynedd
(SH 758369)

A motte castle, the motte partly revetted, with some stone fragments. No date.

RADNOR Powys
(SO 212610)

There appear to have been three castles of some kind at various times in this area. The reference SI 212610 is of New Radnor, of which some evidence exists of strong earthworks of the late twelfth century. There may have been some stonework.

RAGLAN Gwent
(SO 415083)

Raglan Castle stands on the site of a Norman motte castle of c.1070. That earlier castle

survived in some form up to the early 1400s and included a lord's hall. In 1432, it became the property of Sir William ap Thomas, a Welsh knight who had fought at Agincourt (1415). It was he who started to build the structure whose magnificent ruins still dominate the landscape.

The first building was an unusual hexagonal-plan great tower, whose foundations and lowest courses of walling encase the old Norman motte. Known as the Yellow Tower of Gwent, it has three storeys above the basement (and had one more before it was slighted after the Civil War, in 1646). It was built over the years c.1430–45, given combined arrow-slit and gun-port openings at ground-floor level, and was equipped with a boldly projecting machicolated parapet all round the top. The tower tapered outwards slightly from the top downwards on all six sides and, at ground level, the walls were nearly 3 metres (10 ft) thick. Each storey consisted of one main room, with chambers off where needed, served by a spiral stair positioned in the walling.

Around the outside of the basement is the remnant of a low curtain wall, added in c.1450–60, also hexagonal with rounded projecting corners which were turrets with battlements, whose tops were approximately as tall as the gun-port/arrow-slit openings, enabling defenders inside the tower to give protected covering fire to other, more exposed defenders behind the battlements. This tower stood completely surrounded by its own wide and deep ditch, at first crossed by means of two drawbridges with elaborate

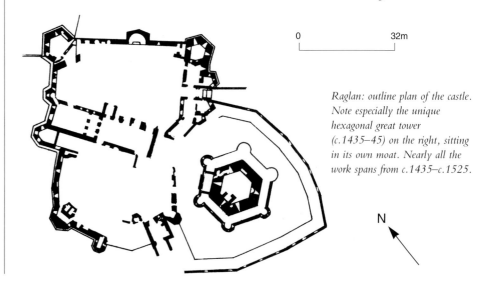

Raglan: outline plan of the castle. Note especially the unique hexagonal great tower (c.1435–45) on the right, sitting in its own moat. Nearly all the work spans from c.1435–c.1525.

mechanisms on the north-west face. When the castle was enlarged in a second building period, c.1450–69, a great gate was built, approached from outside the castle, and the drawbridges were abandoned. A new approach from the great tower into the newer parts was constructed in the form of a three-storey forebuilding which led to a bridge across the moat, and which joined with the parlour/dining room block on the north-east side of the new works.

The new works were ranges of buildings round two courtyards, the Pitched Court and the Fountain Court. The principal buildings in both were of polygonal (chiefly hexagonal) plan. In the Pitched Court (north-east) the gatehouse and its adjoining huge Closet Tower (three storeys plus basement) were equipped with gun-ports and with extensive machicolation at parapet level. There are several more domestic structures including the office wing, kitchen tower, pantry, buttery, great hall and the chapel lying alongside the hall. This side of the Pitched Court was also the north-east side of the Fountain Court, so-called from a marble fountain that once graced its courtyard. The court had apartment blocks on three sides and included the South Gate which is almost square, not polygonal. The base of this tower may well be a relic of the earlier castle.

Raglan Castle was held by the Somerset family who, in the sixteenth century, were Earls of Worcester. The 5th Earl, who became 1st Marquess, sided with Charles I in the Civil War, and Raglan was besieged in June 1646 by Parliament, sustaining a devastating bombardment for several weeks and surrendering in August.

RHAYADER POWYS
(SN 968680)

A motte castle built by the Welsh, known as Tower Mount, which confirms the motte-and-bailey character. It is dated late twelfth-century and was destroyed soon afterwards.

RHUDDLAN CLWYD
(SJ 024779)

A motte castle was raised here c.1070 which is mentioned in Domesday. It appears to have changed hands several times between the Welsh and the Normans. The mound can still be seen south of the later Edwardian concentric castle built by Master James of St George in 1277–82, and associated with the

fortified town. This later castle is a roughly lozenge-shaped inner stone enclosure with cylindrical towers at the north and south corners, and substantial twin-cylindrical-towered gatehouses at the east and west corners. This was surrounded by a larger polygonal stone curtain with flanking rectilinear turrets on every angle and occasionally mid-wall, some of them solid bastions. Three-quarters of the outer curtain was surrounded by a wide moat, the fourth quarter at the west by the River Clwyd. To provide a 3.2-km (2-mile) long, deep-water channel wide enough to accommodate supply ships from the sea, the river was diverted, an operation which took three years and employed about seventy men working six days a week. The cost of the castle, which included the walls of the town, did not fall far short of £10,000. The water channel rendered the construction works easier since building materials such as stone, timber and lead (for roofing) could be brought from many sources by ship, such as timber from Delamere Forest.

Rhuddlan's building works were interrupted when the castle was attacked by Llywelyn the Last's forces, probably under the command of his brother Dafydd, and materials taken for the Welsh prince's own uses. The castle otherwise survived throughout the Middle Ages and served as a centre for civil administration in north Wales. In the Civil War, Rhuddlan was held for the king but surrendered to Parliament in 1646. Two years later, it was slighted.

Four kinds of stone were used in the

construction of Rhuddlan Castle: dark, purple sandstone from a quarry near St Asaph; a lighter, red stone from Cheshire, chiefly for windows; a yellow sandstone from the neighbourhood of Flint; and a grey limestone, also quarried locally.

RHYMNEY GWENT
(ST 210789)

Otherwise known as Rumney Castle, this timber and earth enclosure castle was first mentioned in Exchequer Records in 1184 but was probably founded at the end of the eleventh century. It was developed over the first half of the twelfth century by the addition of more timber buildings and then a stone donjon and gate-tower later in the century. After about 1270, it was given up as a castle and converted into a manor-house. The site was recently excavated extensively.

ROCH DYFED
(SM 880212)

Built on a 'horn of a double upburst of igneous rock' and consisting of a D-end tower with lengthened sides, of the late thirteenth century, surrounded by earthworks and a double ditch, Roch has been considerably altered in later centuries. The basic tower was residential and still is. The castle's moments of glory were during the Civil War, when it changed hands several times.

RUTHIN CLWYD
(SJ 124579)

Now part of the Castle Hotel, Ruthin was one of the new lordship castles ordered by

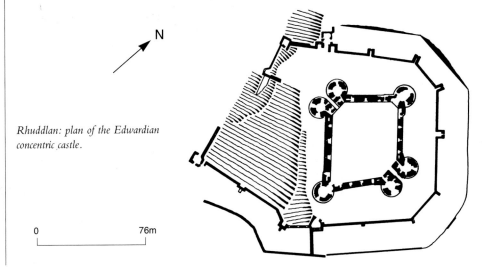

Rhuddlan: plan of the Edwardian concentric castle.

N

0   76m

Edward I to be built between 1277 and the 1280s as part of his scheme of the conquest and annexation of Wales. This castle was in its time formidable but the bulk of its structure has either disappeared or been absorbed, and it is difficult to define its shape. Its basic plan appears to have been two stone enclosures, each with a twin-towered gatehouse and flanking cylindrical towers, three of which have survived in some form. The castle stood on a red sandstone ridge gently rising above the Clwyd.

The building work began in the summer of 1277. Then it seems the castle and the lands about were granted to Dafydd, brother of Llywelyn the Last, and records are not clear as to what was done over the next years or by whom. In 1283, by which time Llywelyn had been slain and Dafydd taken and executed, Ruthin reverted to Edward, and it is possible that work was continued. Master James of St George is mentioned as being involved, though in some undisclosed capacity. The reconstruction work is considered tasteful and elegant but it is nonetheless unhelpful in assessing the original form.

ST CLEARS DYFED
(SN 280154)

A motte castle near the river, of unknown date but perhaps the mid-twelfth century, changed hands between the Welsh and English on at least three occasions between c.1153 and 1215, when it was destroyed.

ST DONATS

NR LLANTWIT, SOUTH GLAMORGAN
(SS 934681)

Now Atlantic College, an adult education centre, St Donats was a formidable double-enclosure castle of the late thirteenth century on a striking foreland site. The inner enclosure was flanked with towers, but the outer polygonal curtained enclosure was unflanked. Considerable alterations have been made in subsequent centuries.

ST FAGANS SOUTH GLAMORGAN
(ST 120771)

A small castle of two enclosures, one round and one rectangular. Little remains of the original works, as they have been obscured by the sixteenth-century mansion built on the site. Received opinion is that there was a great tower of the thirteenth century where the remains of the mansion now stand.

Skenfrith: the early thirteenth-century cylindrical great tower within the quadrilateral stone enclosure. The tower was erected on an earlier motte.

ST MELLONS SOUTH GLAMORGAN
(ST 227803)

Also referred to as Cae Castell, St Mellons is an earthwork enclosure castle which may date from the twelfth century.

SENNYBRIDGE POWYS
(SN 919283)

Probably a Welsh-built castle of the late twelfth/early thirteenth centuries, this consisted of a residential block of unclear shape and a tower. The works appear not to have been finished.

SKENFRITH GWENT
(SO 457202)

A small but compact quadrilateral enclosure with corner cylindrical towers of great strength, surrounding a cylindrical great tower that has a semi-cylindrical buttress on its western side. The tower, of thirteenth-century construction, stands on an earlier low-level motte of the late eleventh century, which was raised with gravel from the moat, and it has a slightly splayed plinth. The tower is about 10.7 metres (35 ft) in diameter and rose certainly to three storeys including the ground floor. There was no connection between the ground and first floor, except by trap-door. The entrance to the first floor was by timber staircase to an arched door. Access to the second storey was by spiral stair in the semi-cylindrical buttress.

The quadrilateral has a strong curtain wall with a fifth cylinder tower of later date on the south face, and outside was a moat with its sides revetted in stone. The River Monnow completed the water defences on the east side.

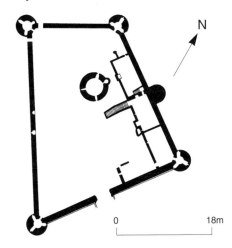

Skenfrith: ground plan. The cylindrical great tower and the enclosure curtain are of c.1220–40.

SWANSEA West Glamorgan
(SS 657931)

There was a motte castle here, built by Henry Beaumont, Lord of Gower. It was attacked and burned in 1115–16. It was probably not rebuilt as a motte castle. Later, an enclosure castle with towers was built near the site. This appears also to have declined and parts of it are incorporated in a third structure raised there, in the late thirteenth/early fourteenth centuries; for example, the outer walls of the south block are most probably the curtain of the previous bailey. To this was added in the fourteenth century the interesting arcaded parapet and a rounded-end tower bearing a corbelled offset (which can be seen today) with the wall as part of a new set of buildings unconnected with the castle. The castle itself was severely damaged during Owain Glyndwr's struggle for independence.

SYCHARTH
Nr Llangedwyn, Clwyd
(SJ 205259)

A very interesting site. Today, a mound sits surrounded by a dished moat, the two being on rising ground. Excavations of 1962–3 revealed stone fragments and traces of burnt timber. There were foundations of what appears to have been a rectangular hall and beside it, on the edge of the summit, another rectilinear building which the archaeologists think was a latrine block. The charred timber suggests a stone and timber structure that was burned down. The date of the building may have been twelfth century. It appears that the site was occupied by Owain Glyndwr in the very early fifteenth century and, if so, the hall may have been part of a residence. Was the structure attacked and burned down by the English? There is a record that it was destroyed in 1403.

TENBY Dyfed
(SN 138005)

Now in ruins, this interesting castle is sited on a headland overlooking what is now Tenby harbour. It began as a late Norman tower-gate complex, a square tower with D-ended barbican. This was probably built after an earlier earthwork had been captured in 1153, as is recorded in the *Brut y Tywysogyon*. Later, further buildings were added, but the town nearby was likewise fortified with wall and flanking towers, one of which is a large cylindrical battlemented tower with five arched entrances in its walling, and in time the town was much better defended than the structures on the headland.

CASTELL TINBOETH Powys
(SO 090755)

Some stone foundations of an enclosure and of a gateway of the (?) twelfth century.

TOMEN-Y-MUR
Maentwrog, Gwynedd
(SH 705386)

A motte castle, some 9.1 metres (30 ft) tall and about 91.4 metres (300 ft) round the base, sited inside the remains of a Roman earthwork fort. Remnants of masonry, including ashlar blocks, have been found on the motte site. William Rufus is thought to have built it c.1090. Supposedly he encamped there on one of his expeditions against Wales.

TRETOWER
Nr Crickhowell, Powys
(SO 184212)

Here is a Norman motte castle of about 1100, which was converted to stonework in the twelfth century, with additional work in the thirteenth century. The motte was revetted with stone because the water supply to the original moat was undermining it. Some time in the twelfth century the motte summit was surrounded by a thick stone curtain within which buildings were ranged round the walls in the manner of a shell enclosure, and a strong square-plan gate-tower inserted in the wall at the east. Then in the thirteenth century, probably 1220–30, the buildings were pulled down and in their place a cylindrical great tower was erected, with three storeys plus basement, and walls 2.7 metres (9 ft) thick on a splayed plinth. The entrance was at first-floor level. On the first storey, now floorless, is a fireplace with sloping hood of ashlar on corbels supported by pillars. there are two mural staircases.

The castle is associated with a mansion of the late Middle Ages, which is not pertinent to this gazetteer. It seems possible that the castle was taken by Llywelyn the Last in the 1260s and held for a while.

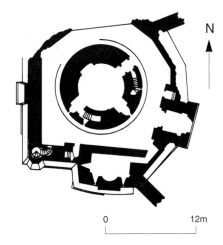

Tretower: ground plan. The great tower is the centre ring (first half of the thirteenth century). The outer range and curtain are largely earlier (mid-twelfth century).

UPTON Dyfed
(SN 020047)

Once a thirteenth-century small enclosure castle, with hall, towers and gate, it has been absorbed by later works.

USK GWENT
(SO 377010)

An earthwork castle of c.1138 built by de Clare, which had a second structure of stone raised in its bailey during the reign of Henry II. A small square tower of rubble and ashlar quoins projects from a curtain of later date. Considerable improvements were made in the thirteenth and fourteenth centuries, but it was besieged and severely damaged by Owain Glyndwr c.1403–4. Repaired, it was held for Charles I in the Civil War but slighted by Parliament after the war. The well-preserved three-storeyed gatehouse, which is probably of fourteenth-century origin, is incorporated in Castle House at Usk.

WELSHPOOL POWYS
(SJ 230074)

Considerable confusion exists about the castle at Welshpool. Recent investigation has revealed that there was a motte castle here, and that it was captured by mining some time in the twelfth century.

WEOBLEY WEST GLAMORGAN
(SS 478927)

A small, compact enclosure castle consisting of an irregular square of buildings joined together, principally of thirteenth- to fourteenth-century construction. It is more in the manner of a fortified manor-house and is set on high ground over the estuary of the River Loughor. Work was started towards the end of the thirteenth century, when a rectangular, almost square, tower – probably a great tower of three storeys – was raised in the south-west corner. This had a splayed plinth, walls 2.1 metres (7 ft) thick and was entered at first-floor level (as is normal with early great towers). On the north side of the earthwork enclosure, an interesting hall and kitchen block was erected at the same time.

The square consists of a variety of towers or tower-like buildings of square, cylindrical, or polygonal shape, which for the most part are still in remarkably good condition, although much of this is due to fifteenth- and sixteenth-century rebuildings. Note the polygonal garderobe tower on the north-east corner of the great tower, which had three storeys of latrines and also an interesting quatrefoil loop which provided light for the middle-storey garderobe. Weobley was damaged in an assault by forces of Owain Glyndwr c.1403–4.

WHITCHURCH SOUTH GLAMORGAN
(ST 156804)

Sometimes known as Treoda, a motte castle was built here probably in the early twelfth century. No stonework has been found.

WHITE CASTLE
NR ABERGAVENNY, GWENT
(SI 380168)

White Castle appears to have been predominantly a military structure and little attempt was made to render it comfortable as a residence. It consisted of a central pear-shaped enclosure, flanked on the north-west and south-east by two outer enclosures, all three moated, the south and the central surrounded by one moat which also separated the two. The north enclosure has a curtain wall with flanking cylindrical towers and an outer gateway. This curtain is thirteenth-century. The central enclosure also has a stone curtain with cylindrical flanking towers, and a twin-cylindrical towered gatehouse at the north-west end. The towers and gatehouse are late thirteenth-century but the curtain is earlier, c.1184–6, and cost £128.

At about the same time as the curtain was raised, there had been a square great tower built on the south-east arc of the original earthwork enclosure, whose foundations survive. At a later date, the tower was partly demolished to extend the curtain and join up the original two arcs. This was done when the flanking towers were inserted. Within the enclosure after the great tower was abandoned, various buildings were erected against the inside wall, including a hall, a solar and a kitchen and oven block.

The curtain walls of both the outer and central enclosures and their towers were formidable, and the whole defence system was of considerable sophistication. White Castle is so-named because it was once coated with white plaster on the masonry, traces of which may still be seen.

WISTON DYFED
(SN 022181)

A motte castle, whose mound was 12.2 metres (40 ft) tall and about 167.6 metres (550 ft) round the base. It is possible that the mound was increased in height to take the polygonal shell enclosure with sloping plinth that was erected in the early twelfth century, and of which only a few feet in height remain. The mound was surrounded by a 3-metre (10-ft)

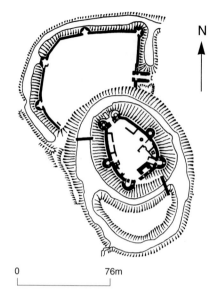

White Castle: the inner enclosure in the centre is largely twelfth century but the gatehouse is thirteenth century, as are the round D-end towers.

deep ditch, and the bailey attached was rectangular. Remains of a doorway into the shell enclosure can be seen. The castle was destroyed by Llywelyn the Great, Prince of all Wales (c.1196–1240).

WREXHAM CLWYD
(SJ 327487)

A motte castle, also referred to as Erddig Castle, lying against Offa's Dyke on raised ground by the Clywedog river, was mentioned in the Pipe Rolls in 1161. Remains of masonry were reported in 1912.

YSTRADFELLTE POWYS
(SN 936145)

The date for this is uncertain, and only traces of stone fragments survive.

County Listing

ENGLISH CASTLES

AVON
Bristol
Thornbury

BEDFORDSHIRE
Bedford
Biggleswade
Cainhoe
Chalgrave
Meppershall
Totternhoe
Yelden

BERKSHIRE
Brightwell
Donnington
Hinton Waldrist
Reading
Windsor

BUCKINGHAMSHIRE
Boarstall
Buckingham
Castlethorpe
Lavendon
Weston Turville
Whitchurch
Wycombe

CAMBRIDGESHIRE
Bourn
Buckton
Burwell
Cambridge
Eaton Socon
Ely
Huntingdon
Longthorpe
Peterborough
Wisbech
Woodwalton

CHESHIRE
Aldford
Beeston
Chester
Dunham Massey
Frodsham
Pulford
Shotwick

CORNWALL
Launceston
Restormel
St Michael's Mount
Tintagel
Trematon

CUMBRIA
Appleby
Armathwaite
Bewcastle
Brough
Brougham
Carlisle
Cockermouth
Dacre
Egremont
Gleaston
Greystoke
Kendal
Kirkoswald
Muncaster
Naworth
Pendragon
Penrith
Scaleby
Sizergh
Yanwath

DERBYSHIRE
Bakewell
Bolsover
Duffield
Horston
Peveril

DEVON
Bampton
Barnstaple
Berry Pomeroy
Bickleigh
Compton
Dartmouth
Exeter
Gidleigh
Hemyock
Lydford
Okehampton
Plympton
Tiverton
Totnes

DORSET
Corfe
Dorchester
Powerstock
Rufus
Sherborne
Wareham

DURHAM
Barnard
Bowes
Brancepeth
Cotherstone
Durham
Lumley
Raby

ESSEX
Clavering
Colchester
Great Canfield
Hedingham
Ongar

Pleshey
Rayleigh
Saffron Walden
Stansted Mountfitchet

GLOUCESTERSHIRE
Berkeley
Brimpsfield
Dymock
Gloucester
Lydney
Miserden
St Briavels

HAMPSHIRE
Ashley
Basing
Bishop's Waltham
Christchurch
Merdon
Odiham
Portchester
Southampton
Winchester
Wolvesey

HEREFORD & WORCESTER
Brampton Bryan
Bredwardine
Bronsil
Clifford
Croft
Dorstone
Eardisley
Elmley
Ewias Harold
Grafton
Hanley
Hereford
Home
Huntington
Inkberrow
Kilpeck
Kington
Llancillo
Longtown
Lyonshall
Moccas
Pembridge
Richard's
Snodhill
Stapleton
Treago
Weobley
Wigmore
Wilton
Worcester

HERTFORDSHIRE
Anstey
Benington
Berkhamsted
Bishop's Stortford

Hertford
South Mymms
Therfield

HUMBERSIDE
Cottingham
Driffield
Skipsea
Wressle

ISLE OF WIGHT
Carisbrooke

KENT
Allington
Canterbury
Chilham
Cooling
Dover
Eynsford
Folkestone
Godard's
Hever
Leeds
Leybourne
Lympne
Rochester
Saltwood
Scotney
Sutton Valence
Tonbridge
Tonge
West Malling

LANCASHIRE
Aldingham
Clitheroe
Fouldry
Hornby
Lancaster
Penwortham
Preston
Warrington

LEICESTERSHIRE
Ashby de la Zouch
Belvoir
Burley
Donington
Groby
Kirby Muxloe
Leicester
Mountsorrel
Oakham
Sauvey
Whitwick

LINCOLNSHIRE
Bolingbroke
Bourne
Bytham
Caistor
Carlton
Frampton

Kingerby
Kinnard's Ferry
Lincoln
Sleaford
Stamford
Swineshead
Tattershall
Welbourne

LONDON
Montfitchet
Tower of London

LUNDY ISLE
Marisco

MERSEYSIDE
West Derby

NORFOLK
Baconsthorpe
Caister
Castle Acre
Castle Rising
Claxton
Horsford
Mileham
New Buckenham
Norwich
Thetford
Weeting

NORTHAMPTONSHIRE
Barnwell
Benefield
Fotheringay
Northampton
Preston Capes
Rockington
Sulgrave

NORTHUMBERLAND
Alnwick
Ancroft
Aydon
Bamburgh
Belsay
Berwick
Bitchfield
Blenkinsop
Bothal
Bywell
Callaly
Cartington
Chillingham
Chipchase
Cocklaw Tower
Cocklepark Tower
Corbridge Vicar's Pele
Coupland
Craster
Cresswell
Dunstanburgh
Edlingham

Elsdon
Embleton Tower
Etal
Featherstone
Ford
Harbottle
Haughton
Langley
Mitford
Morpeth
Nafferton
Norham
Prudhoe
Thirlwall
Wark
Warkworth

NORTH YORKSHIRE
Bolton
Burton-in-Lonsdale
Buttercrambe
Cawood
Clifford's Tower (York)
Gilling
Helmsley
Huttons Ambo
Knaresborough
Middleham
Mulgrave
Northallerton
Pickering
Richmond
Ripley
Scarborough
Sheriff Hutton
Skipton
Spofforth
Thirsk
Whorlton
York (Baile Hill)

NOTTINGHAMSHIRE
Aslockton
Cuckney
Newark
Nottingham

OXFORDSHIRE
Ardley
Ascot d'Oilly
Bampton
Banbury
Broughton
Deddington
Faringdon
Middleton Stoney
Oxford
Shirburn
Swerford
Wallingford

SHROPSHIRE
Acton Burnell
Alberbury
Bishop's Castle
Bridgnorth
Bryn Amlwg

Caus
Charlton
Cheney Longville
Church Stretton
Cleobury
Clun
Ellesmere
Holgate
Hopton
Knockin
Lower Down
Ludlow
Moreton Corbet
Myddle
Oswestry
Pulverbatch
Quatford
Redcastle
Ruyton-Eleven-Towns
Shrawardine
Shrewsbury
Stokesay
Wattlesborough
Whitchurch
Whittington

SOMERSET
Bridgwater
Cary
Crewkerne
Dunster
Farleigh Hungerford
Montacute
Neroche
Nether Stowey
Nunney
Stogursey
Taunton

SOUTH YORKSHIRE
Conisbrough
Tickhill

STAFFORDSHIRE
Alton
Chartley
Eccleshall
Newcastle-under-Lyme
Stafford
Tamworth
Tutbury

SUFFOLK
Bungay
Burgh
Clare
Eye
Framlingham
Haughley
Lidgate
Orford
Walton

SURREY
Abinger
Bletchingley
Farnham

Guildford
Reigate

SUSSEX
Aldingbourne
Amberley
Arundel
Bodiam
Bramber
Chichester
Hastings
Herstmonceux
Knepp
Lewes
Pevensey

TYNE & WEAR
Hylton
Newcastle
Tynemouth

WARWICKSHIRE
Beaudesert
Brandon
Brinklow
Hartshill
Kenilworth
Maxstoke
Warwick

WEST MIDLANDS
Bromwich
Coventry
Dudley

WEST YORKSHIRE
Almondbury
Barwick
Pontefract
Sandal
Topcliffe
Wakefield

WILTSHIRE
Ashton Keynes
Castle Combe
Devizes
Ludgershall
Malmesbury
Marlborough
Membury
Old Sarum
Old Wardour
Somerford
Trowbridge
Wilton

IRISH CASTLES

ANTRIM
Antrim
Ballygally
Carrickfergus
Doonmore
Dromore
Dunluce
Dunseverick

Dunsilly
Toome

ARMAGH
Moyry

CARLOW
Ballyloughan
Ballymoon
Carlow
Clonmore
Leighlin
Tullow

CAVAN
Cloughoughter
Kilmore
Turbet

CLARE
Ballinalackan
Beal Boru
Bunratty
Carrigaholt
Cratloe
Danganbrack
Garrynamona
Gleninagh
Knappogue
Leamaneh
Liscannor
Newtown
Quin
Rosslara
Thady's Fort
Urlanmore

CORK
Ballincollig
Barry's Court
Blarney
Carrigaphooca
Castle Martyr
Castlemore Barrett
Castleventry
Coppinger's Court
Cork (Skiddy's)
Desmond (Kinsale)
Dromaneen
Dunamark
Dunboy
Glanworth
Ightermurragh
Inchiquin
Kanturk
Kilbolane
Kinsale
Liscarroll
Lohort
Mallow
Monkstown
Mount Long
Shippool

DONEGAL
Assaroe
Ballintra

Buncrana
Burt
Doe
Donegal
Greencastle
Inch
Kilbarron
Mongavelin
Raphoe
Termon

DOWN
Ardglass
Ardkeen
Ballynarry
Ballyroney
Castle Screen
Castle Ward
Clough
Downpatrick
Dromore
Dundonald
Dundrum
Greencastle
Kilclief
Killyleagh
Kirkiston
Lismahon
Narrow Water
Piper's
Portaferry
Quoile
Rathmullen
Seafin
Sketrick
Strangford

DUBLIN
Castleknock
Dalkey's
Dublin
Dunsoghly
Howth
Kildrennan
Malahide
Monkstown
Newcastle Lyons
Rathfarnham
Swords

FERMANAGH
Castle Archdale
Castle Balfour
Castle Caldwell
Crom
Enniskillen
Monea
Tully

GALWAY
Ardnamullivane
Ardrahan
Athenry
Aughnanure
Ballinasloe
Ballindooley
Carraigin

Castlegrove
Castle Kirk
Claregalway
Derryhivenny
Dunguaire
Dunmore
Feartagar
Fiddaun
Glinsk
Gort
Isert Kelly
Kiltartan
Lismore
Meelick
Moylough
Oranmore
Pallas
Portumna
Seefin
Tuam
Tullira

KERRY
Ballycarbury
Ballymalis
Carrigafoyle
Killarney
Listowel
Minard
Rahinnane

KILDARE
Ardree
Athy
Balimore Eustace
Bigarz
Carbury
Cloncurry
Kilkea
Kilteel
Maynooth
Naas
Old Connell
Oughterard
Pollardstown

KILKENNY
Ballyragget
Burnchurch
Castle Comer
Castletobin
Clara
Clomantagh
Granagh
Kells
Kilkenny
Knocktopher
Tibraghny
Tullabarry

LAOIS
Dunamase
Killeshin
Lavagh
Lea
Reban
Timahoe

LEITRIM
Manorhamilton
Parke's
Rossclogher

LIMERICK
Adare
Askeaton
Aughinish
Ballingarry
Ballygrennan
Bourchiers
Caherconlish
Cappagh
Carrigogunnel
Castleconnell
Castlematrix
Fanstown
Garraunboy
Glenogra
Glenquin
Limerick
Raheene
Shanid

LONDONDERRY
(DERRY)
Dungiven
Kilsantan (Mount Sandel)

LONGFORD
Granard

LOUTH
Ardee
Carlingford
Castleroche
Drogheda
Louth
Lurgankeel
Milltown
Mount Ash
Roodstown
Termonfeckin

MAYO
Carrickkildavnet
Castlecarra
Lough Mask
Rockfleet
Shrule

MEATH
Athboy
Athlumney
Clonard
Derrypatrick
Donore
Duleek
Dunmoe
Fenner
Galtrim
Kells
Kilbeg
Kilmessan
Liscartan
Lisclogher

Navan
Nobber
Rathmore
Rathwire
Ratoath
Skreen
Slane
Trim

MONAGHAN
Donaghmoyne

OFFALY
Ballycowan
Birr
Clonmacnois
Clonony
Geashill
Kinnitty

ROSCOMMON
Ballintober
Rinndoun
Roscommon

SLIGO
Ardtermon
Ballinafad
Ballymote
Castle Baldwin
Collooney
Iniscrone
Moygara

TIPPERARY
Ardfinnan
Ardmayle
Ballindoney
Ballintotty
Ballinahow
Ballynakill
Ballysonan
Burncourt
Cahir
Carrick-on-Suir
Cashel
Castlegrace
Gortmakellis
Grallagh
Kilcash
Killenure
Knockgraffon
Knockkelly
Lackeen
Lorrha
Loughlohery
Loughmoe
Moorestown
Moycarkey
Nenagh
Portnascully
Rathurles
Roosca
Roscrea
Synone
Terryglass
Thurles

Tullow

TYRONE
Aughentaine
Augher
Benburb
Castle Caulfield
Harry Avery's
Mountjoy
Newton Stewart
Omagh
Roughan

WATERFORD
Lismore
Waterford

WESTMEATH
Ardnurcher
Athlone
Castletown Delvin
Castletown Geoghegan
Kilbixie
Killare
Rathconrath

WEXFORD
Baginbun
Ballyhack
Carrick
Clonmines
Clougheast
Coolhull
Enniscorthy
Ferns
Ferrycarrig
Old Ross
Rathmacknee
Slade
Wexford

WICKLOW
Arklow
Newcastle
Threecastles
Wicklow

SCOTTISH CASTLES

BORDERS
Bedrule
Bemersyde
Cessford
Darnick
Drochil
Evelaw
Fast
Fatlips
Ferniehurst
Greenknowe Tower
Hawick
Hermitage
Hume
Jedburgh
Neidpath
Newark
Oliver's

Roxburgh
Selkirk
Smailholm
Thirlestane
Thirlestane Lauder
Timpendean

CENTRAL
Airth
Alloa
Ardblair
Bruce's
Cary
Castle Campbell
Clackmannan
Culcreuch
Doune
Duchray
Dunglass
Duntreath
Edinample
Finlarig
Glendevon
Menstruie
Mugdock
Plean Tower
Sauchie
Stirling
Torwood

DUMFRIES & GALLOWAY
Amisfield
Auchen
Auchness
Auldton
Barholm
Barjarg
Bonshaw Tower
Buittle
Caerlaverock
Cardoness
Carscreugh
Carsewall
Carsluith
Castle Kennedy
Castle of Park
Castle Stewart
Castlemilk
Comlongon
Craigcaffie
Cruggleton
Drumcoltran
Dumfries
Dundeugh
Dunskey
Elsieshields
Galdenoch
Hoddom
Hollows Tower
Kenmure
Kirkcudbright
Lochmaben
Loch Maberry
Lochnaw
Lochwood
Maclellan's
Morton

Mote of Annan
Mote of Urr
Orchardton
Plunton
Repentance
Rusco
Sanquhar
Sorbie Tower
Spedlin's Tower
Stapleton Tower
Stranraer
Threave
Tibbers
Torthorwald
Wigtown

FIFE
Aberdour
Balgonie
Balwearie
Collairnie
Crail
Cruivie
Dairsie
Earlshall
Falkland
Fernie
Fordell
Kellie
Kilconquhar
Macduff's
Montquhanie
Myres
Pitcruvie
Pitcullo
Pitteadie
Ravenscraig
Rossend
Rosyth
St Andrews
Scotstarvit
Strathendry
Struthers
Tullialan
Wemyss

GRAMPIAN
Aboyne
Allardice
Arnage
Asloun
Auchindoun
Balbegno
Balbithan
Balfluig
Ballindalloch
Balquhain
Balvenie
Banff
Barra
Bass of Inverurie
Beldorney
Benholm
Blervie
Boyne
Brodie
Burgie

Cairnbulg
Carnousie
Caskieben
Castle Fraser
Cluny Crichton
Conzie
Corgarff
Corse
Corsindae
Coull
Craig
Craigievar
Craigston
Crathes
Darnaway
Delgatie
Doune of Invernochty
Drum
Drumminor
Duffus
Dunnideer
Dundarg
Dunnottar
Eden
Elgin
Ellon
Esslemont
Fedderate
Fiddes
Findlater
Findochty
Fordyce
Forres
Frendraught
Fyvie
Gight
Glenbuchat
Hallforest
Harthill
Huntly
Inchdrewer
Kildrummy
Kincardine
Kindrochit
Kinnaird
Kinnairdy
Knockhall
Leslie
Licklyhead
Lochindorb
Midmar
Migvie
Muchalls
Old Slains
Peel of Lumphanan
Pitcastle
Pitfichie
Pitsligo
Pittulie
Ravenscraig
Schivas
Terpersie
Tillycairn
Tilquhilly
Tolquhon
Towie Barclay
Udny

Wallace's
Westhall

HIGHLAND
Ackergill
Aldourie
Ardtornish
Ardvreck
Assynt
Auldearn
Ballone
Balnagown
Castle Donan
Castle Grant
Castle Leod
Castle Roy
Cawdor
Coxton Tower
Craig
Cromarty
Dalcross
Dunbeath
Dunrobin
Dunskeath
Duntulm
Dunvegan
Erchless
Fairburn Tower
Helmsdale
Invergarry
Inverlochy
Inverness
Keiss
Kilcoy
Kilravock
Kinkell
Lethendy
Mey
Mingary
Moniack
Old Wick
Proncy
Rait
Skelbo
Strome
Tioram
Urquhart

LOTHIAN
Abercorn
Bavelaw
Blackness
Borthwick
Brunstane
Cairns
Cakemuir
Carberry
Craigcrook
Craigmillar
Crichton
Dalhousie
Dalkeith
Dirleton
Dunbar
Edinburgh
Elphinstone
Falside

Fenton's Tower
Hailes
Hawthornden
Lauriston
Lennoxlove
Liberton
Linlithglow
Luffness
Merchiston
Midhope
Niddry
Old Dundas
Rosslyn
Saltcoats
Tantallon
Waughton
Whittinghame
Yester

ORKNEY
Cubbie Roo's
Noltland

SHETLAND
Muness
Scalloway

STRATHCLYDE
Achadun
Aiket
Ardrossan
Auchenharvie
Ayr
Barcaldine
Bardowie
Barr Tower
Boghall
Bothwell
Breacachadh
Brodick
Busbie
Cadzow
Caprington
Carnasserie
Carrick
Cassilis
Castle Lachlan
Castle Stalker
Clonbeith
Coulthalley
Covington
Craigie
Craigmaddie
Craignethan
Crawford
Crookston
Dean
Drongan
Duart
Dumbarton
Dunderave
Dundonald
Duniveg
Dunollie
Dunoon
Dunstaffnage
Duntroon

Dunure
Fairlie
Fatlips
Fraoch Eilean
Glengarnock
Greenan
Hunterston
Inchmurrin
Innischonnel
Kames
Keirs
Kelburn
Kilchurn
Kilhenzie
Killochan
Kilmaronock
Kingencleuch
Law
Little Cumbrae
Loch Doon
Lochranza
Mains
Mauchline
Mearns
Moy
Newark
Newton
Penkhill
Portencross
Renfrew
Rothesay
Rowallan
Rutherglen
Saddell
Skelmorlie
Skipness
Sorn
Stane
Strathaven
Sundrum
Sween
Tarbert
Taringzean
Toward
Turnberry
Wester Kames

TAYSIDE
Aberuchil
Allfeck
Airlie
Aldie
Almond
Auchterarder
Balfour
Ballinshoe
Balthayock
Balvaird
Blair
Braco
Braikie
Brechin
Broughty
Burleigh
Caisteal Dubh
Claypotts
Cleish

Clunie
Colliston
Comrie
Cortachy
Drummond
Dudhope
Edzell
Elcho
Ethie
Evelick
Farnell
Finavon
Fingask
Forfar
Fowlis
Gardyne
Garth
Glamis
Glasclune
Grandtully
Guthrie
Hatton
Huntingtower
Innerpeffry
Invermark
Inverquharity
Kellie
Kinclaven
Kinnaird
Kinnaird (Perth)
Lethendy
Loch Leven
Meggernie
Megginch
Melgund
Menzies
Methven
Murthly
Newton
Pitheavlis
Powrie
Red Castle
Trochrie
Tullibole
Vayne

WESTERN ISLES
Kiessimul

WELSH CASTLES

CLWYD
Basingwerk
Caergwrle
Chirk
Denbigh
Castell Dinas Bran
Dyserth
Ewloe
Flint
Hawarden
Holt
Holywell
Mold
Pentrefoelas
Prestatyn
Rhuddlan
Ruthin
Sycharth
Wrexham

DYFED
Abercowyn
Abereinion
Aberrheidol
Aberystwyth
Amroth
Benton
Blaenporth
Cammais
Cardigan
Carew
Carmarthen
Carreg Cennen
Cilgerran
Dinefwr
Dinierth
Dryslwyn
Haverfordwest
Humphrey's
Kidwelly
Lampeter
Laugharne
Llandovery
Llanelli
Llangadog
Llanstephan

Llawhaden
Lychewein
Manorbier
Meurig
Narberth
Newcastle Emlyn
Newport
Pembroke
Pencader
Pen-yr-Allt
Picton
Roch
St Clears
Tenby
Upton
Wiston

GWENT
Abergavenny
Caerleon
Caerwent
Caldicot
Chepstow
Dingestow
Dinham
Grosmont
Llanfair Discoed
Llangibby
Llantrisant
Machen
Monmouth
Newport
Pencoed
Penhow
Raglan
Rhymney
Skenfrith
Usk
White

GWYNEDD
Aber
Aberllleiniog
Bala
Beaumaris
Caernarfon
Castell Carndochan
Castell-y-Bere

Conwy
Criccieth
Degannwy
Castell Dinas Emrys
Dolbadarn
Dolwyddelan
Garn Fadryn
Harlech
Prysor
Tomen-y-Mur

MID-GLAMORGAN
Caerphilly
Candleston
Coity
Kenfig
Llangwynyd
Morlais
Newcastle Bridgend
Ogmore

POWYS
Aberedw
Aberllynfi
Blaenllynfi
Bleddfa
Boughrood
Brecon
Bronllys
Builth
Bwlch y Dinas
Caereinion
Camlais
Carreghofa
Cefnllys
Clyro
Colwyn
Crickhowell
Castell Crugerydd
Cymaron
Dolforwyn
Hay-on-Wye
Hen Domen
Knighton
Knucklas
Montgomery
Nantcribba
Painscastle

Pencelli
Powis
Radnor
Rhayader
Sennybridge
Castell Tinboeth
Tretower
Welshpool
Ystradfellte

SOUTH GLAMORGAN
Cardiff
Castell Dinas Powys
Fonmon
Llanblethian
Llanquian
Llandaff
Morgraig
Old Beaupre
Penmark
Peterston
St Donats
St Fagans
St Mellons

WEST GLAMORGAN
Aber Afan
Llandeilo Talybont
Loughor
Neath
Oxwich
Oystermouth
Penmaen
Pennard
Penrice
Swansea
Weobley
Whitchurch

Glossary

apse circular or polygonal end of tower or chapel

arcading rows of arches supported on columns, free-standing or attached to a wall (blind arcade)

arrow-loop or slit long, narrow and usually vertical opening in a wall or merlon, through which arrows were shot. Round or triangular ends were for cross-bows, as were horizontal cross-slits, sometimes called 'crosslets'. These gave greater side-to-side range

ashlar blocks of smooth, squared stone of any kind

bailey or ward courtyard within the walls of a castle

ballista siege-engine in the form of a large bow for shooting missiles, usually iron bolts

barbican outward continuation of a gateway or entrance, erected to defend it.

barmkin outer defensive walling (generally Scottish)

barrel vault semicircular roof of stone or timber

bartizan small turret projecting from the corner or flank of a tower or wall, usually at the top

bastion tower or turret projecting from a wall length or at the junction of two walls

batter sloping or splayed part of a wall at ground level, particularly of a great tower

battlements (or crenellation) the parapet of a tower or wall with indentations or openings (embrasures or crenelles) alternating with solid projections (merlons)

bawn outer defensive walling (generally Irish)

belfry tall, movable wooden tower on wheels, used in sieges

berm horizontal space between a curtain or tower and its moat

billet one of a row of rectangular blocks raised as an ornament in Norman architecture

brattice see hoarding

buttress projecting pillar added to a wall to strengthen it

cap-house small chamber at the top of a spiral staircase in a tower or turret, leading to the open wall-walk on the roof

chevron moulding moulding in the form of an inverted 'V', a Norman feature

clunch hard chalk used as a building material. Often plastered with limewash for durability

corbel stone bracket projecting from a wall or corner, to support a beam

counterscarp outer slope or wall of a ditch. *See* scarp

crenellation *see* battlements

cross-wall internal dividing wall in a great tower

crow-steps step-gabled end to a roof. Also called corbie steps

curtain general term for castle walling, inner or outer, enclosing a courtyard. Sited between towers or a tower and a gatehouse, giving the appearance of being hung between, from which 'curtain' was derived

dog-legged with right-angled bends (passages, etc)

donjon alternative word for great tower

drawbridge wooden bridge which could be raised and lowered, sited in front of a tower or gatehouse, across a ditch

dressing carved or smoothed stonework around openings and along edges

embrasure *see* battlements

forebuilding structure on the outside wall of a great tower protecting the entrance and all, or part, of the approaching staircase(s). Some forebuildings contained chambers and chapel(s) over the stairs

freestone soft, easily worked stone

gallery long, narrow passage or room

garderobe latrine

groin junction of two curved surfaces in a vault

gun-loop or gun-port opening in a wall for a gun

hoarding covered wooden gallery affixed to the top of the outside of a tower or curtain to defend the castle. It was supported on wooden beams inserted into put-log holes. The floor was slatted to allow defenders to drop missiles or liquids on to besiegers below

jamb straight side of a doorway, archway or window

light window pane or window division

lintel horizontal beam of stone or wood positioned across an opening at its top

machicolation projecting part of a stone or brick parapet with holes in the floor, as in hoarding

mangonel stone-throwing machine worked by torsion

mantlet mobile wooden protective shield on wheels

merlon *see* battlements

meurtrière alternative word for murder-hole

mullion vertical member dividing the lights of a window

murder-holes openings in the roof of a gateway or part of a gatehouse over an entrance passage, popularly thought to be used for dropping missiles or shooting weapons at besiegers, but more probably for rapid water discharge over wooden parts, such as gates, set on fire by besiegers

newel centre support for a spiral stair

offset ledge in a wall followed by reduced thickness of the wall

oriel window projecting curved or polygonal window

oubliette dungeon or pit under the floor, reached by a trap-door, used for incarcerating prisoners (in Scotland, usually a pit prison)

pilaster buttress buttress with a projection, positioned on a corner or mid-wall

portcullis wood and iron grille-pattern gate which was raised and lowered in grooves by ropes or chains in, in front of or behind an entrance

postern small gateway, usually in the side or rear flanks of a castle, used as a get-away

put-log beam inserted into a special hole in a great tower, gatehouse or curtain to support hoarding, or as scaffolding for building or repairs

quatrefoil four-lobed

quoin dressed corner stone at an angle of a building

re-entrant angle that points inwards (opposite of salient)

relieving arch arch built in a wall to relieve the thrust on another opening

revet face with a layer of stone, stone slabs etc, for more strength. Some earth mottes were revetted with stone

rib vaulting arched roof with ribs of raised moulding at the groins
rubble uncut or only roughly shaped stone, for walling
salient angle that points outwards (opposite of re-entrant)
sally-port side gate for defenders to go out on an attack
scarp inner wall or slope of a ditch or moat (*see* counterscarp)
segmental less than a semicircle (for example, segmental arch)
shot-hole hole for firearms, generally smaller than a gun-port
six-foil six-lobed
slight to damage or destroy a castle to render it unfit for use or occupation as a fortress
solar lord's parlour or private quarters, sometimes adjacent to a great hall, and sometimes over it
squinch arch arched support for an angle turret that does not reach the ground
stepped recessed in a series of ledges
stronghouse a mansion capable of being defended
trebuchet stone-throwing engine worked by a counterweight
trefoil three-lobed
voussoir wedge-shaped stone forming part of an arch
wall-walk path along the top of a wall, protected by a parapet
ward *see* bailey
wing-wall wall descending the slope of a motte

Bibliography

An enormous amount of literature and reference material was studied in preparing this work; first, for its original edition of 1980, again for the reprints, and once more for this enlarged version. It has been all along a uniquely rich and rewarding experience. The study included practically every county archaeological and historical journal in Britain and Ireland, and almost every other learned journal in which castles are discussed in any detail. It was my aim to examine as many volumes as possible that carried references to castles individually or in general, in many cases going back to publications of the last century. The study also took in every worthwhile book on British and Irish castles in the English language, written between about 1880 and 1995. A considerable number of more general works was also consulted, embracing the political, military and social history of England, Scotland, Wales and Ireland in the periods concerned. The majority of these are listed. Many works on the medieval history of other European countries were consulted. Numerous medieval works, documents and records were read, mostly in translation, and these, too, are listed.

Extensive work was done in the record departments of the Department of the Environment; the Welsh Office; the Scottish Development Department; the Department of the Environment, Northern Ireland, and the Office of Public Works (Ireland); the Ordnance Surveys of the four countries; the Royal Commission on Historic Monuments; the Royal Commission on Ancient and Historical Monuments in Wales; likewise of Scotland; the Public Record Office, London; the Scottish Record Office; the Public Record Office, Ireland; and in numerous city and university libraries in all four countries. To everyone associated with these august institutions who helped – and there were many – my very deep gratitude.

Numerous local authorities, public bodies and private individuals and organisations have produced valuable booklets and I have read as many of these as have been available. They include of course the unique series of DoE, Welsh Office and Scottish Development Department official handbooks, wherever possible in their most recent editions. These last-named are a gold-mine of information for anyone seriously interested in castles.

Medieval sources (translations or later editions)
Anglo-Saxon Chronicle (tr. Garmonsway, Everyman, 1954)
Annales Cambriae (c.444–1288, Rolls series, 1860)
Annales Monastici (AD 1–1432, ed. Luard, Rolls series, 1864–9)
Annals of Connacht (ed. Freeman, A.M., Dublin, 1944)
Annals of Inisfallen (ed. MacAirt, S., Dublin, 1951)
Annals of the Kingdom of Ireland by the Four Masters (ed. O'Donovan, J., Dublin, 1848–51)
Annals of Loch Cé (ed. Hennessy, W.M., Dublin, 1871)
Annals of Ulster (ed. Hennessy, W.M. and MacCarthy, B., Dublin, 1887–1901)
Brut y Tywysogyon: Red Book of Hergest version (ed. Jones, T., Cardiff, 1973)
Chartularies of St Mary's Abbey, Dublin and Annals of Ireland (1162–1370), (ed. Gilbert J.T., 1884–6)
Chartulary of Lindores (c.1195–1479), (ed. Dowden, Edinburgh, 1903)
Chronica: Roger of Hovedon (c.732–1201), (ed. Stubbs, W., Rolls series, 1868–71)
Chronica Gentis Scotorum: John Fordun (to 1383), (ed. Skene, W., Edinburgh 1871–2)
Chronica Majora: Matthew Paris (to 1259), (ed. Luard, Rolls series, 1872–83)
Chronicle of Lanercost (1272–1346), (trans. 1913)
Chronicle of Melrose (tr. Stevenson, London, 1856)
Chronicles of reigns of Stephen, Henry II and Richard I (ed. Howlett, Rolls series, 1884–9)
Chronicon Anglicanum: Ralph de Coggeshall (1066–1223), (ed. Stevenson, Rolls series, 1875)
Chronicon ex Chronicis: Florence of Worcester (c.450–1117), (ed. Thorpe, 1849)
Chronicon Richardi Divisiensis de tempore regis Richardi primi: Richard of Devizes (ed. Appleby, 1963)
Domesday Book (Public Record Office, London)
Expugnatio Hibernica: the Conquest of Ireland, Giraldus Cambrensis (ed. Scott, A.B., and Martin, F.X., Dublin, 1978)
Flores Historiarum: Roger of Wendover (to 1235), (ed. Cox, 1841)
Ecclesiastical History of Ordericus Vitalis (c. AD 1–1141), (ed. Chibnall, M.,1969)
Gesta Normannorum Ducum: William of Jumièges (c.1028–70), (ed. Stubbs, Rolls series, 1887–9)
Gesta Regis Henrici Secundi (1169–92), (ed. Stubbs, Rolls series, 1867)
Gesta Regum Anglorum: William of Malmesbury (c.449–1127), (ed. Stubbs, Rolls series, 1887–9)
Gesta Stephani (tr. Potter, K., London, 1955)
Histoire de Guillaume le Conquérant: William of Poitiers (ed. Foreville, Paris, 1962)
Historia Anglorum: Henry of Huntingdon (55 BC–AD 1154), (ed. Arnold, Rolls series, 1879)
Historia Novella: William of Malmesbury (1125–42), (tr. Potter, K., London, 1955)
Historia Rerum Anglicanum: William of Newburgh (ed. Howlett, Rolls series, 1884–9)

Historical Collections of Walter of Coventry (to 1225), (ed. Stubbs, Rolls series, 1872–3)

Historical Works of Gervase of Canterbury (to c.1210), (ed. Stubbs, Rolls series, 1879–80)

Historical Works of Symeon of Durham (tr. Stevenson, London, 1853–8)

Historie and Chronicles of Scotland: Robert Lindsay of Pitscottie (1437–1575), (ed. Mackay, 1899–1911)

Itinerary: John Leland (ed. Toulmin Smith, 1904)

Itinerary in Wales: John Leland (ed. Toulmin Smith, 1906)

Liber Eliensis (Ely: ed. for Royal Historical Society, 1962)

Liber Landavensis (Llandaff: ed. Evans & Rhys, Oxford, 1893)

Liber St Marie de Dryburgh (ed. 1874)

Metrical Chronicle of Robert of Gloucester (to 1270), (ed. Wright, Rolls series, 1887)

Monasticon Anglicanum: William Dugdale (Caley's edition, 1846)

Opera Historica: Ralph de Diceto (ed. Stubbs, Rolls series, 1876)

Original Chronicle of Andrew de Wyntoun (ed. Amours, Edinburgh, 1902–14)

The Red Book of the Earls of Kildare (ed. MacNiocaill, G., Dublin, 1964)

The Red Book of Ormond (ed. White, N.B., Dublin, 1932)

The Song of Dermot and the Earl (tr. Orpen, G.H., Oxford, 1892)

Textus Roffensis (Rochester; to c.1150), (ed. Hearne, 1720)

Topographia Hibernica: the History and Topography of Ireland, Giraldus Cambrensis (ed. O'Meara, J.J., 1982)

See also records such as:

Exchequer records, including Pipe Rolls: Issue Rolls; Memoranda Rolls; Calendar of Ancient Correspondence Concerning Wales (Board of Celtic Studies, 1955); Calendar of Patent Rolls (1232–1509) (Public Record Office); Calendar of Liberate Rolls (John and Henry III) (HMSO); Calendar of Close Rolls (1272–1485) (HMSO); Register of Great Seal of Scotland (1306–1668); Register of Privy Seal of Scotland (from 1488); Scottish Rolls (1296–1516); Exchequer Rolls of Scotland (1264–1600) (ed. 1878–1908); Acts of the Parliament of Scotland (1124–1707); Calendar of Documents relating to Scotland (1108–1509) (ed. 1881–8); Ancient Records of Dublin (1889–1994); Irish Close Rolls; Irish Pipe Rolls; Documents relating to Ireland (1171–1307); Calendar of Ormond Deeds (1172–1603); Calendar of Patent Rolls (1892–1971); Historic and Municipal Documents of Ireland (1172–1320) (ed. Gilbert, J., London, 1870).

More recent books

Anderson, William *Castles of Europe* (Elek 1970)

Armitage, Ella S. *Early Norman Castles of the British Isles* (1912)

Ashdown Charles *British Castles* (A & C Black, 1911)

Ashurst, J., and Dimes, F. *Stone in Building* (Architectural Press, 1978)

Barrow, G.W.S. *Feudal Britain* (Edward Arnold, 1956)

Barry, T.B. *The Archaeology of Medieval Ireland* (Routledge, 1987)

Braun, Hugh *The English Castle* (Batsford, 1947)

Brown, Prof. Allen *English Castles* (Batsford, 1976)

Brown, Prof. Allen *The Normans and the Norman Conquest* (Constable, 1969)

Cairns, C.T. *Tower-houses of Co. Tipperary* (TCD thesis)

Caulfield, D.A. *Mottes of Kilkenny* (TCD thesis)

Clark, G.T. *Medieval Military Architecture in England* (London, 1884, 2 vols)

Cosgrove, A. *Late Medieval Ireland (1370–1541)* (Dublin, 1981)

Cosgrove, A. *Medieval Ireland, 1169–1534* (vol. 2 of *New History of Ireland*, Oxford, 1987)

Cruden, S.H. *The Scottish Castle* (Nelson, 1960)

Davin, A.K. *Tower-houses of the Pale* (TCD thesis)

Dickinson, W.C. *Source Book of Scottish History* (Edinburgh, 1952–4)

Dolley, M. *Anglo-Norman Ireland* (Gill & Macmillan, Dublin, 1972)

Frame, R. *Colonial Ireland, 1169–1369* (Dublin, 1981)

Graham, Frank *Castles of Northumberland* (F. Graham, 1976)

Harbison, P. *Guide to National and Historic Monuments of Ireland* (Dublin 1992)

Harvey, John *English Medieval Architects: a Biographical Dictionary* (1954)

Healy, J.N. *Castles of County Cork* (Cork, 1988)

History of the King's Works, vols, i, ii, iii (HMSO, 1963–)

Johnson, D. *Irish Castles* (1980)

Keen, Maurice *Pelican History of Mediaeval Europe* (Penguin, 1969)

King, D.J. Cathcart *Castellarium Anglicanum* (New York, 1983, 2 vols)

Kinross, John *Discovering Castles in England and Wales* (Shire Publications, 1973)

Knoop, D. and Jones, G.P. *The Mediaeval Mason* (Manchester, 1933)

Leask, H.G. *Irish Castles and Castellated Houses* (Dundalk, 1986 edn)

Lloyd, Sir Edward *History of Wales from the Earliest Times to the Edwardian Conquest* (1939, 2 vols)

Lydon, J. *Ireland in the Later Middle Ages* (Dublin, 1980 edn)

Lydon, J. *Lordship of Ireland in the Middle Ages* (Dublin, 1972)

MacGibbon, D. and Ross, T. *The Castellated and Domestic Architecture of Scotland* (1887–92, 5 vols)

McKenzie, W.M. *The Mediaeval Castle in Scotland* (1927)

McKisack, May *The Fourteenth Century* (Oxford, 1959)

Manning, C. *Irish Field Monuments* (Dublin, 1985)

Nicholls, K. *Gaelic and Gaelicised Ireland in the Middle Ages* (Dublin, 1982 edn)

Oman, Sir Charles *A History of the Art of War in the Middle Ages* (Cornell University edn, 1960)

Orpen, G.H. *Ireland under the Normans, 1169–1333* (Oxford, 1911–20)

Otway-Ruthven, A. *A History of Mediaeval Ireland* (London, 1968)

Parker, J.H. *Domestic Architecture of the Middle Ages* (1859)

Poole, A. Lane *From Domesday Book to Magna Carta* (Oxford, 1955)

Powicke, Sir Maurice *King Henry III and the Lord Edward* (Oxford, 1947, 2 vols)

Renn, D.F. *Norman Castles in Britain* (J. Baker, 1973 edn)

Ritchie, R.L. Grahame *Normans in Scotland* (Edinburgh, 1954)

Round, J.H. *Geoffrey de Mandeville* (1892)

Salter, M. *Castles and Strongholds of Ireland* (Malvern, 1993)

Salter, M. *Scottish Castles* (Shire Publications, 1985)

Salzman, L.F. *Building in England down to 1540* (Oxford, 1952)

Simpson, Prof. W.D. *Castles in Britain* (London, 1966)

Simpson, Prof. W.D. *Castles in England and Wales* (Batsford, 1969)

Sorrell, Alan *British Castles* (Batsford, 1973)

Southern, R.W. *Making of the Middle Ages* (Hutchinson, 1953)

Stenton, Sir Frank *The Bayeux Tapestry* (London, 1965)

Stenton, Sir Frank *English Society in the Early Middle Ages* (Penguin, 1951)

Thompson, A. Hamilton *Military Architecture in England during the Middle Ages* (Oxford, 1912)

Toy, Sidney *Castles of Great Britain* (London, 1953)

Viollet le Duc, E. *Military Architecture* (tr. Oxford, 1879)

See also:

The county inventories published by the Royal Commission on Historical Monuments (England); RCAM (Wales), RCAHM (Scotland), and various archaeological surveys of counties of Ireland, including Co. Down, 1966; Co. Donegal, 1983; Co. Louth, 1991. Victoria County Histories of all counties concerned; Sites and Documents Record, 1984 onwards, from Office of Public Works, Dublin.

Academic journals, etc:

Journals other than county archaeological and/or historical journals etc (which should themselves be read) include *Château Gaillard*; *Archaeological Journal*; *English Historical Review*; *Mediaeval Archaeology*; *Antiquity*; Recent Archaeological Excavations in Britain series; *Archaeologia*; *Antiquaries Journal*; *Archaeological Review*; *Archaeology in Wales*; Bulletin of Board of Celtic Studies; Journal of the British Archaeological Association; Bulletin of the Institute of Archaeology; *Scottish Historical Review*; Transactions of the Society of Antiquaries of Scotland; Journal of Irish Archaeology; Proceedings of the Royal Irish Academy; Transactions of the Royal Irish Academy; Journal of the Royal Society of Antiquaries of Ireland; Ulster Journal of Archaeology; Irish Archaeological Research Forum; Irish Historical Studies; Archaeology Ireland; Bulletin of the Group for Study of Irish Historic Settlement.

Index

The index is divided into two parts: Castles, and Names and Subjects. The castles in the index are those mentioned in the introductory chapters (pp. 7–115) and the Introduction to the Gazetteer (pp. 116–18). All of them (except a few foreign castles) have gazetteer entries as well. For some castles, page numbers of gazetteer entries are also given to guide the reader to particular points of interest (eg Bedford, which includes a description of the 1224 siege). Page numbers in *italics* denote illustrations (photographs and drawings) and plans.

CASTLES

Aberdour, 85, *85*, 238; interesting history, 238
Aberystwyth, 40, 60, 61, 62, 63, 66, 114, 118, 297–8, *298*; 'jerry-building' at, 298; recruitment of workforce from England, 298
Abinger, excavations, 119
Adare, 91, 92, *192*, *193*
Affleck, 78, 79, 80, 83, 238–9, *239*; L-plan tower-house (detailed description), 238–9
Alnwick, 69, *69*, 71, 107
Amisfield (7 storeys), 239, *240*
Appleby, 25, 120, *120*
Ardglass (Jordan's), 101, 193
Ardtermon, 102
Arundel, 18; Henry II's garden at, *106*, 107
Ashby de la Zouch, 29, *29*, 110; 15th-century rectangular great tower, 121
Askeaton, 95, 194, *194*
Athenry, 102, 194–5, *195*; early great tower built in 3 phases, 194–5; restored, 194–5
Athlone, 87, 92, 102, 195, *195*
Athlumney, 102, 195
Audley's, 98
Aughnanure, 100, *100*, 103, 196
Aydon, 30, 69, 121

Baconsthorpe, 37, 121; built without permission, 121
Baginbun, 88, 196
Balgonie, *241*, 242
Ballinasloe, 88
Ballintober, Irish copy? of Roscommon, 93, *94*, 196
Ballyloughan, 95
Ballymalis, 100
Ballymoon, 93, 197, *197*, *198*; never completed or occupied, 197
Ballymote, 93, 102, 197–8

198
Ballynahow, 101, 198
Ballyvaghan, 99
Balvenie, *242*, 242–3; once a Douglas castle, 243
Bamburgh, 25, 28, 58, *68*, 69, 71, 121–2, *122*
Bampton (Oxon), 122; quadrangular castle earlier than normal, 122
Barnard, 112, 122–3; round great tower with forebuilding, 122–3, *122*, *123*
Barnwell, 32, 123–4, *124*
Bass of Inverurie, *73*, 243; 12th-century motte, 243
Beal Boru, 91
Beaumaris, 40, *40*, 49, 50, *51*, 60, 61, 62, 63, 66, 78, 109, 114, 298; never attacked, 298; never completed even after 35 years, 298
Bedford, 18, 33, 46, 55, 104, 124; round great tower, 124, *124*; siege, 41–2, 43, 124
Beeston, 32, 49, 125, *125*; well dug 112.8 m (370 ft) down, 125
Belsay, 30, 69, 125–6
Berkeley, 21, 31, 46, 126
Berkhamsted, 17, *19*, 21, 31, 52, 55, 126; motte castle with later conversion to stone, 126
Berwick, 57, 113, 127
Bewcastle, 113
Blarney, 95, *96*, 199; one of largest great towers in Ireland, 199
Bodiam, 32, *55*, 59, 108, *109*, 109–10, 127–8; water defences, 54–5
Bolingbroke, 112, 128, *128*
Bolton, 32, *33*, 108, *109*, 110, 128; built by John Lewyn (builder of Dunstanburgh, qv.), 128
Borthwick, 59, *59*, 79, 81, 82, 107, 244, *244*; most impressive great tower in Scotland, 244; siege, 244

Bothal, 69, 128, *128*
Bothwell, 75, 77, 244–5, *245*; French influence, 75; sieges, 245; slighted, 245
Bowes, 24, 30, 129
Braemar, 245, *245*; L-plan tower-house inside star barmkin, 245
Bramber, 18, 24, 129
Brecon, 67
Bristol, 21, 25
Bronllys, 30
Brough, 22, 23, 26, 130, *130*
Brougham, 26, 46, 130, *131*
Builth, 36, 40, 60, 62, 63, 299; Llywelyn the Last killed nearby (1282), 299; wages on siteworks, 299
Buncrana, 95, 98
Bunratty, 95, *96*, 199–200, *200*; one of the largest great towers in Ireland, 199; restored, 200
Burnchurch, 98, 200
Burncourt, 101, *102*, 200, *200*
Burt, 101, 200; Z-plan, *101*
Bywell, 69, 132–3

Caerlaverock, 49, 59, 64, *76*, 77–8, 83, 245–6, *246*; concentric, 49; doubts on origins, 77; huge gatehouse, 247; restored, 15th century, 247; slighted, 247
Caernarfon, 32, 34, 40, 46, 60, 62, 63, 64, *65*, 66, 106, 114, 300, *300*; design details, 300; masonry like walls of Constantinople, 300
Caerphilly (first concentric castle built from scratch in UK), 49, *49*, 50, *50*, 52–4, 66, 78, 300–1; detailed design history, 300–1
Cahir, 52, 95, *97*, 102, 200–1, *201*; barbican, 201; finely restored, 201; gatehouse converted to great tower, 201
Caister, 59, 110, 132, *132*; details of building costs

survive, 133; mason overcharges for work, 133
Caldicot, 301, *301*; 14th-century gatehouse with garderobe towers, 301
Cambridge, 18, 19, 116, 118
Canterbury, 24, *133*
Cardiff, 31, 67, 112, *113*, 302; 12-sided shell enclosure on motte, 302
Carew, 302, *302*; spur bases to towers, 302
Carisbrooke, 15, 18, 25, 31, 112, 113, 134
Carlingford, 90, 92, *201*, 201–2, *202*
Carlisle, 69, 71, 72, 112, 113
Carlow, 87, *87*, 97, 202, *202*; see also Ferns, Lea, Terryglass
Carreg Cennen, 108, 303, *303*; building details, 303
Carrick, 89
Carrickfergus, *88*, 90, 91, 102, 108, *203*; first stone castle in Ireland, 202
Carrigafoyle, 95
Carrigaphooca, 98, 115, 203; no windows, only loops, 203
Carrigogunnel, 95, *95*, 102, 203–4
Castell-y-Bere, 40, 60, *65*, 67, 303; Welsh built, 303
Castle Acre, 31–2, *32*; excavations, 134
Castle Campbell, 248, *248*; building details, 248
Castlecarra, 204, *204*
Castle Fraser, 249, *249*; 'luggies' in wall, 247; rectangular tower castle converted to Z-plan, 249
Castleknock, 91, 205, *205*
Castle Matrix, 99, 226
Castlemore Barrett, 91
Castle Roche, 93, 205–6, *206*; great tower, 205
Castletobin, 91
Castleventry, 91
Cawdor, 250, *250*; palace built round earlier great tower, 250
Château Gaillard, 7, 43

Chepstow, 22, 52; building details, 303–4; first great tower in UK (1067–71), *22*, 23, 67, 303–4, *304*; Marten's Tower, 304
Chester, 113, 115, *135*
Chilham, 28, *136*
Chillingham, 69
Chipchase, 30, 69, 70
Chirk, 60, 304
Cilgerran, 67, 304, *304*, *305*
Clara, 97, *97*, 98; floor beams survive, 206
Claregalway, 98
Claypotts, 55, *81*, 83, 84, 101, 250–1; gun-ports at chest level, 250; Z-plan, *250*
Clifford's Tower (York), 15, *16*, 74, 137, *137*; quatrefoil plan of great tower, 137
Clonmacnois, 21, *90*, 91; great tower on motte, 206
Clonony, 206–7, *207*
Clough, 15, 21, 90, 91, 207, *207*; small tower built later on motte, 207
Clun, great tower on side of motte, 137
Cockermouth, 69
Coity, 304–5, *305*
Colchester (earliest great tower in England), 22, 23, *23*, 24, 26, 30, 35, 38, 137, *138*
Collooney, 88
Comlongon, 59, 79, *79*, 81, 82, 251; one of the largest great towers in Scotland, 251
Compton, 112
Conisbrough, 26, 38, 47, 112, *112*, 138; unusual design of great tower, 138
Conwy, 10, 32, 40, 52, 60, 62, 63, 64, *64*, 66, 112, 114, 306, *306*; costs of building, 306; Edward I trapped in castle by rising waters outside, 306
Coppinger's, 101, 207–8, *208*
Corbridge, Vicar's Pele, 69, 71

Corfe, 24, 26, *39*, 40, 115, 139, *139*; King John's 'gloriette', 139

Corgarff, 59, 251, 252; tower-house inside star barmkin, 251

Craigie, 253, *253*; hall-tower type, 253

Craigievar, *80*, 83, 85, *253*, 253–4; stepped L-plan, 253; storeys, 254

Craigmillar, 254, *254*; location for plot against Darnley, Mary Queen of Scots' husband, 254; L-plan tower with later extensions, 254

Criccieth, 40, 60, 67, *306*, 306–7; part Welsh built, part English, 306–7

Crichton, 79, *255*, 255–6, *256*; castle of several phases, 255–6; siege, 256

Dartmouth, 111, *111*, 140; wages for building work, 140

Degannwy, 67, 307, *307*; Welsh built, with 2 mottes, 307

Denbigh, 53, 60, 66, 115, 307, *307*; complex triangular gatehouse, 51, 307, *307*

Derryhivenny, 99, 208, *208*

Devizes, 115

Dinefwr, 308, *308*

Dirleton, *74*, 75, 257–8, *258*; cluster of towers, 257

Doe, 102, 209, *209*

Dolbadarn, 67, 308, *309*; round great tower, 308; Welsh built, 308

Dolforwyn, 67, 308

Dolwyddelan, 40, 60, *66*, 67, 308–9, *309*; birthplace of Llywelyn the Great, 308; Welsh built, 308,

Donegal, 101, 102, *209*, 209–10

Donnington, 8, *114*, 141; siege, 114, 115

Donore, 100, *100*; £10 castle?, 210

Doune, *258*, 258–9; powerful enclosure with strong front mass, 258

Doune of Invernochty, 73, *75*, 76–7, 259

Dover, 17, 18, 25, 26, 27, 38, 39, 40, 44, 46, 47, *47*, 48, 49, 52, 106, 107, 112, 113, 115, 141–3, *142*; becomes concentric, 53–4; detailed description, 141–3; motte built in 8 days, 141–3; siege, 43, 142

Downpatrick, *90*, 91

Drogheda, 210; St Lawrence's Gate (13th century), 210

Dromore, 15, 90

Drum, *76*, 78, 79, 259; early great tower, first-floor entrance, 259

Dryslwyn, 309; besieged and undermined, 44, 309; Welsh built, 309

Dublin, 89, 92, 210; brief building history, 210

Duffield, 28, 44, *143*

Duffus, 73, 74; cf. Clonmacnois, 260; great tower on motte collapses, 74, 260, *260*

Dumbarton, 58, *260*, 260–1, *261*

Dunamase, 92, *92*, 210, 212, *212*; great tower with 2 cross-walls, 212

Dundrum, 92, *92*, 212, *212*; large early 13th-century round great tower, 212; short life of, 212

Dunguaire, *211*, 212–13

Dunluce, 213, *213*

Dunmahon, 101

Dunmoe, 213, *214*

Dunnottar, 262, *262*; major 20th-century restoration, 262

Dunsoghly, 95, 214, *214*; original timber roof, 214

Dunstaffnage, 75, 263, *263*; quadrangular stone enclosure, 263

Dunstanburgh, 10, 34, 50, *53*, *143*; gatehouse converted to great tower, 144

Durham, 18, 24, 69, 71, 144; chapel crypt, 144

Edinburgh, 57, *83*, 84, 264; history, 264; sieges, 264

Edlingham, 69, 71

Edzell, famous garden at, 264, *265*

Elcho, 81, 83, 265, *265*

Elphinstone, 59, 79, 82, 266, *266*; once had massive tower like Comlongon, 266

Ely, 18

Enniskillen, 214–15, *215*; water-gate, 215

Etal, 69

Ewloe, 67, *67*, 309, *309*; Welsh built in several phases, 309

Exeter, 145; early Norman gate-tower, 49, 145

Eynsford, 21, 23, 32, 33, *146*; early stone enclosure, 145

Farnham, 21, 31, *146*, 146–7; base of great tower in

motte, 146; motte encased in stone, 146

Featherstone, 69

Ferns, 87, 88, 91, *215*, 215–16; *see also* Carlow, Lea, Terryglass

Fiddaun, 95, 216, *216*; well-preserved bawn, 216

Flint, 36, 40, 50, 60, 62, *62*, 63, 66, 309, *310*; cylindrical great tower, 310

Ford, 69

Fotheringay, 113

Framlingham, 10, 32, *32*, 33, 44, 49, *147*, 147–8; enclosure castle, (with 13 towers)

Fyvie, 268, *268*, 269

Glanworth, 93, 216–17, *217*

Glenbuchat, *82*, 84, 269, *269*; Z-plan with square towers, 269

Gleninagh, 100, 101, 217, *217*

Glenogra, 95

Gloucester, 25, 35, 106, *148*

Goodrich, 25, 26, 34, *34*, 38, 64, 108, 148, *149*; barbican, 52

Granagh, 218, *218*

Greencastle (Donegal), 218, *218*

Greencastle (Down), 3, 93, 219, *219*; great tower cross-walls added later, 219

Grosmont, 310, *310*, *311*

Guildford, 21, 25, 26, *149*; great tower on side of motte, 149

Hallaton, 15

Hanley, 40

Harbottle, 113

Harlech, *26*, 37, 40, 49, 50, 60, 61, 62, 63, 64, 66, 86, *311*, 311–12; attacked by Madog ap Llywelyn, 311; concentric, 311; costs, 311; design, 311; Welsh parliament at, 312

Harry Avery's, 95

Hastings, 13, 14, 16, *17*, 18, 150; built with components brought from Normandy, 150

Haughley, motte over 24.4 m (80 ft) tall, 150

Haughton, 71

Hawarden, 60

Hawick, 15, 19, 20, 73, 270

Hedingham, 24, 25, 26–7, 30, 37, *37*, 105, *105*, 150; flying arch cross-wall, *105*, 150

Helmsley, 151, *151*; great tower with D-end, 151

Hen Domen, 15, 312; major

excavations, 312

Hereford, 16, 18

Hermitage, 270–1, *271*; Douglas castle for centuries, 271; massive tower-house of several periods, 270

Herstmonceux, brick built, 110, 151–2

Hertford, 112, *152*

Hever, 152, *153*

Holt, 60, 312

Hope, 40, 60, 62, 63

Horston, 40

Hunterston, *271*, 271–2

Huntingdon, 153

Huntingtower, 272, *272*; scene of Ruthven Raid (1582), 272

Huntly, 272–3, *273*

Husterknupp, 12, *13*, 52

Hylton, 154; residential gatehouse-tower, 154

Ightermurragh, 219, *220*; cruciform plan, 219

Innischonnel, 273, *274*

Inverlochy, 33, 75, 275, *275*

Kanturk (unfinished), 101, *117*, 200, 220

Kenilworth, 25, 26, 40, 44, 46, 52, 54, *54*, 112, 154; siege, 54; water defences, 54

Kidwelly, 49, *51*, 312–13, *313*; near-concentric plan, 313

Kiessimul, 75, 276, *276*; early stone enclosure on rock, 276

Kilbeg, 91

Kilchurn, 276, *276*

Kilclief, 101, *101*

Kilcoy, 84, 276, *277*; Z-plan, 276, *277*

Kildrummy, *74*, 75, 277, *277*; influence of French design, 77

Kilkenny, 92, 221, *221*; brief history, 221

Kirby Muxloe, 59

Knaresborough, 40

Knockgraffon, *89*, 91, 118, 222

Krak des Chevaliers, *48*

Lancaster, 40, 104, 112, 155, 156; massive gatehouse, 155

Laugharne, 67, 313

Launceston, 31, 156

Lea, 50, 87, 93, *94*, 222–3, *223*; first great tower, 222; twin-towered gatehouse converted to (second) great tower, 223; *see also* Carlow, Ferns, Terryglass

Leeds, *157*, 158

Leicester, 112, 157

Leslie (one of last tower-

houses built in Scotland), 85, 279

Lewes, 15, 17, 18, 19, 158, *158*; 2 mottes, 158

Limerick (King John's), 92, 102, *223*, *224*; discovery of 13th-century great hall, 223, 224; enclosure courtyard level raised, 224; excavations, 223, 224

Lincoln, 18, 19, 20, *158*, *159*; 2 mottes, 158

Linlithgow, 38, 64, *84*, 85, 279–80; associated with Scottish royal family, 279–80; castle of several periods, 279; fortress-palace, 279

Lisclogher, 101, 225

Lisdoonvarna, 100

Llandovery, 67, 313

Llanstephan, 49, 50, 314, *314*; large gatehouse of late 13th century (cf. Tonbridge), 314

Llawhaden, 314

Loch Doon, 280, *280*; pulled down and re-erected elsewhere, 280

Loch Leven, 77, 79, *280*, 280–1; one of first Scottish tower-houses, 280

Longthorpe Tower, 159; medieval wall paintings, 159

Longtown, 30

Lorrha, 90

Loughmoe, 101, *225*, 225–6

Louth, 91

Ludgershall, 106, 160

Ludlow, 24, 34, *34*, 50, *160*; round chapel, 160

Lumphanan, Peel of, 76, 285

Mallow, 102, 226, *226*

Manorbier, 315, *315*; enclosure with flanking towers, 315; home of Giraldus Cambrensis, 315

Manorhamilton, 102

Marlborough, 106, 161

Maxstoke, 110, 161

Maynooth, 92, *93*, 223; great tower, 223; traces of forebuilding, 227

Menzies, 282, *282*

Middleham, 26, 37, 106, 112, 161, *162*; substantial great tower, with special garderobe turrets, 161

Midmar, 84, 85; Z-plan, 283

Mingary, 75, 283, *283*

Monea, 102, *103*, 227, *227*

Monkstown (Cork), 101, *103*, 227

Monmouth, 67, 315–16

Montacute, 19, *19*

Montgomery, 67, 316

Naas, 15, 91
Narrow Water, 98, 99, *99*, 228
Neidpath, 284, *284*
Nenagh, *91*, 92, 102, *228*, 228–9; greatest round tower in Ireland, 228–9; restoration work, 229; traces of forebuilding, 228
Newark, 163; death of King John at, 163
New Buckenham, very early round great tower, 24, *29*, 29–30, 164
Newcastle upon Tyne, 18, 21, 26, 39, *39*, 46, 69, 71, 164; great tower built by same mason as Dover, 164
Newport (Gwent), water-gate, 112, 317, *317*
Newtown (Clare), 97; on spur base, 101, 229
Nobber, 15, 91
Noltland, 59, *59*, 83, 84 284, *284*; over 70 gun-ports, 284; Z-plan, 284
Norham, 24, 40, 69, 71, *71*, 72, 113, 164–5
Norwich, 17, 18, 20, 24, 25, 26, 30, *165*; 19th-century rebuild of great tower, 165
Nottingham, tunnel at, 11, 166
Nunney, 115, 166, *166*

Oakham, Norman hall at, 166
Odiham, 28, 29, 40, 166, *166*
Ogmore, 24, 318, *318*
Okehampton, 166–7, *167*
Old Dundas, 79, 285
Old Sherborne, 109, 180
Ongar, 17, 167
Orford, 26, 30, 35, 38, 39; details of costs, 167–8; unique design, 28, *28*, 167–8, *168*; unusual square great tower, 168
Oxford, 19, 37, 168; unusual square great tower, 168

Pallas, 99, 229
Parke's (Leitrim), 102, 229–30, *230*
Pembroke, 30, 67, 112, *118*, 318, *319*; large round great tower, built by William Marshal, 318
Penhow, 107, *319*
Penrice, *320*
Pevensey (first castle raised in England), 14, 16, 22, 40, 112, 113, 170
Peveril, 22, 23, *169*, 170
Pickering, 31, 112, *170*, 171
Pleshey, 15, 17, 171
Pontefract, 111, 113, *115*, 171, *171*; discussion of great tower shape, 171; siege, 115
Portchester, 24, *25*, 112, 113, 171–2, *172*

Portumna, 101, 102, 230–1; major restoration, 231; unusual oval well-head, 231
Prudhoe, 30, *30*, 69, 71, 172–3

Quin (Clare), 93, 231; ruins absorbed by later friary, 231

Raby, 69, 173
Radnor, 67
Raglan, 8, 29, 59, 107, 110, *110*, 115, *320*, 320–1; Great Tower of Gwent, 320, *320*; hexagonal plan of most buildings, 320; siege (Civil War), 321
Raphoe, 101, *102*, 231; remains of cross-wall, 231
Rathfarnham, 101
Rathmacknee, 97, 100, 231, *232*
Rathmullen, 90
Ravenscraig (built for artillery), *58*, 59, 83, 286–7, *287*; artillery platform, 286–7
Restormel, 31, *31*, 32, 173–4; fine example of shell enclosure, *173*, 173–4
Rhuddlan, 36, 40, 60, 62, *62*, 63, 66, 78; 114, 321, *321*; concentric, 49, 321; types of stone used, 321; waterworks, 321
Richmond, 22, 23, *24*, 26, 28, 32, 37, 108, 112, 174, *174*
Rinndoun, 91, 93, 232
Rising, 24, 25, 26, *27*, 30, 38, 134–5, *135*
Rochester, 18, 22, 23, 25, 26, 27, 28, 34, *36*, 37, *174*, 174–5; arcaded cross-wall, 28, *28*; siege, 34, 43
Rockingham, 49, *52*, 175
Roodstown, 101, 232
Roscommon, 86, *87*, 93, 233, *233*; built prior to Harlech (qv.), 86, 233
Roscrea, 93, 102, 233, *234*; gatehouse-tower converted to great tower, 233; major restorations, 233; tower returned to original form, 233, *234*
Rothesay, 32, *32*, 52, 76, *287*, 287–8; shell enclosure with 4 round towers, 287
Roxburgh, James II of Scotland killed at siege, 57
Roy, 75
Ruthin, 40, 60, 62, 63, 114, 322–3

St Andrews, *44*, 288–9, *289*; besieged and undermined, 44, *44*; history and buildings, 288–9

St Briavels, 49, 175
St Michael's Mount, 175, *176–7*, 178
Sandal, 112, *178*, 178–80, *179*; barbican, 52; b. like Goodrich but much earlier, 179; excavations, *178*, 178–9, *179*; 16th-century drawing of, *178*
Saumur, drawing of, *10*
Scalloway, 289, *289*
Scarborough, 26, 35, 40, 112, 180; fine barbican, 180
Scotstarvit Tower, 290, *290*; L-plan, 290
Shanid, 91, 92, 233–4; multangular tower inside shell enclosure, 233–4
Shirburn, 110, 180
Shrewsbury, 18, 181
Shrule, 100, 234; splayed-out walls of tower-house, 234
Sizergh, 69, 181
Skenfrith, 30, *322*, 322–3, *323*
Skipness, 75, 290
Skipsea, *19*, 52, 181
Skipton, 49, 181
Slade, 99
Southampton, 40, 181–2
South Mymms, 182; excavations, 182
Stafford, 182; recent major excavations and restoration work, 182
Stirling (fortress-palace), *82*, 84, 290–1; siege, 43, 56–7
Stokesay, *183*, 192–3
Swansea, arcading at, 323
Sween (first stone castle in Scotland), 26, 74, *74*, *291*, 291–2
Swords (Dublin), 93, 235, *235*; building details, 235
Synone, 101

Tantallon, *292*, 292–3; Douglas castle, 293; sieges, 293
Tattershall, 110, *110*, 183–4; brick built, 183; building accounts survive, 183
Termon, 98, 101, 235
Terryglass, 87, 92, 235, 235–6; see also Carlow, Ferns, Lea
Thetford, 15, 17, 19, 21, 184
Thornbury, 32, 109, 184
Threave, 57, 79, *79*, 83, 293–4; artillery wall, *293*; Douglas built, 293; Mons Meg at, 57
Tickhill (11-sided great tower), 28, 112, *184*, 184–5
Tioram, 75, 294, *294*
Tolquhon, 7, 59, 83, 84, 85, 294, *294*; gun-ports, 294

Tonbridge, 10, 38, 49, 50, *52*, 112, 185, *185*; great gatehouse-tower similar to Caerphilly, 185
Totnes, 21, 31, 185–6, *186*
Tower of London, 17, 22–3, 24, 30, 38, *48*, 49, 64, 106, 107, 108, 112, 113, 115, *186*, 186–7; becomes concentric, 49
Trematon, 46
Tretower, 30, 31, *31*, 38, 323, *323*; shell enclosure with later round tower inside, 323
Trim, 8, 90, 91, 92, *236*, 236–7; greatest Norman castle in Ireland, 236; unusual rectilinear-plan great tower, similar to Warkworth, 236–7
Tuam, 82
Tutbury, 112, 113, 187

Urquhart, *295*, 295–6, *296*; history of many centuries, 295–6
Urr, Mote of, 73, 283

Wallingford, 17
Wark, 113
Warkworth, 46, 69, *70*, 71, *188*, 188–9; fishtail loop, 46; great tower, 188–9
Warwick, 45, 52, 112, *189*; machicolation, 45, 189
Waterford, 237; early 13th-century large round tower (Reginald's), 237
White Castle, 324, *324*; building design and details, 324
Winchester, 17, 18, *104*, 105, 106, 190; great hall, 190
Windsor, 6, 18, 19, *19*, 107, 109, 112, 113, 115, 190–1
Worcester, 191

York (Baile Hill), 18, 19, 20

NAMES AND SUBJECTS

Aiofa, daughter of Diarmait of Leinster, 88, 89
Alexander II of Scotland, 72, 77
Anglo-Saxons: had no castles themselves, 16–17; pressed into building castles, 16, 18, 20
artillery: in sieges, 8; platform at Ravenscraig, 59; wall at Threave, 83

Bacon, Roger, and gunpowder, 56

ballista, 42
barbican, 52, *53*; *and see* Cahir, Goodrich, Sandal
bartizan, Scottish and Irish feature, 99
battering ram, 42, *42*
battlements, *see* crenellation
Bayeux Tapestry, 13, 16, *17*
belfry, 43, *43*
Bell family of masons, 81
Borthwick, Lord, defies Cromwell, 59, 82
brick for castles, 11, 110; *and see* Caister, Tattershall
Bruce, Edward, brother of Robert I, 94
burh-bot, 18

Caen stone for castles, 10–11
cannon, types, *56*, 57–8
castelwerke, 18
castle: as symbol of authority, 12; basic types, 9–11, 22–6; changing roles, 11– 15; concentric, 47–9; definition of, 9, 12; 'fighting finish' (Civil War), 114–15; first (Pevensey), 16; history and purpose, 9, 12; illegal (adulterine), 14, 21; number of, 12, 17; pay for work at, 24, 36, 62, 64, 140; roles, 12, 14, 15; siting, 18; stone castles, 10, 15, Ch. 3 *passim*; ten pound (£10) castles (Ireland), 100–1; timber and earth castles, 13, Ch. 2 *passim*; William I's earliest castles, 16–17
castle-building, 19–21, 37, Ch. 4 *passim*; control of, 13–14, 17, 73; costs, 38–40, 60, 62; domestic features, 38; employment in Wales, late 13th century, 61, 62; labour recruitment, 36; licensing, 14, 33, 81, 109, 285; materials, 36–8; preparing site, 36–8; problems, 35; stone building, 35–40 *passim*; timber castles from prefabricated parts, 20, 150; time taken: stone, 22, 35, timber, 20
chapels in castles, 38–9, 50, 107; *and see* Dover, Ludlow, Tower of London
Charles the Bald, King of France, first to control castle-building, 14
concentric castles, *see* castle
Constantinople: siege, 57; walls, 47, 300
crenellation, *33*, 46
Cromwell, Lord, builder of Tattershall, 110

Cromwell, Oliver, Lord Protector of England, Scotland and Ireland (1653–8), 59, 95, 101, 102, 115
cross-wall, types, 28, *28*; *and see* Hedingham, Rochester

d'Albini, William, Earl of Sussex (New Buckenham, Rising), 30
Dalyngrygge, Sir Edward, builder of Bodiam, 109
David I of Scotland, 72
d'Avranches, Hugh, Earl of Chester, 67
de Clare, Gilbert, Lord of Glamorgan, 66, 300
de Clare, Richard FitzGilbert, known as Strongbow, invades Ireland, 88, 89
de Lacy, Hugh, 89, 92
de Montfort, Simon, Earl of Leicester, 54, 300
Diarmait MacMurchada, King of Leinster, 88, 89
ditching, *see* earthworks
Douglas family (Scotland), 78
drawbridge, 46, *46*

earthworks, 19, 20, 21, 32, 90
Edward, Black Prince, 95
Edward the Confessor (1042–66), 14, 16
Edward I of England (1272–1307), 36, 40, 54, 56, 60, 63–4, 67, 77, 108, 118, 300, 306, 309, 311, 312
Edward II of England (1307–27), 40, 94, 301
Edward III of England (1327–77), 40, 57, 77, 95
Edward VI of England, (1547–53), 112
Edwardian castles in Wales, 60–6 *passim*
Elizabeth I of England (1558–1603), 101, 112, 113
enclosure castle: as type, 10, 14, 32–4, *and see under* castle; early stone enclosures in Ireland, 92–3; earth enclosures in Ireland, 21, 90

Fastolf, Sir John, builds Caister, 110
feudalism, 11–14, 15, 16; *and see* Ch. 10 (Ireland)
fireplaces, *38*

FitzOsbern, William, Earl of Hereford, 23, 67, 303
forebuilding, types, 26–7; *and see* Barnard, Dover, Nenagh, Rochester

gardens, *see* Arundel, Edzell
garderobes (latrines), 26, *26*, 106, 301
gatehouse, 49
gatehouse-tower, 49; converted to great tower, 50; *and see* Cahir, Dunstanburgh, Lea Ludlow, Roscrea
Giraldus Cambrensis (Gerald of Wales), chronicler of Anglo-Norman settlement in Ireland, 89–90, 315
Glyndwr, Owain, Welsh patriot, attacks many castles taking several in efforts to drive English out of Wales (early 15th century), 301, 302, 303, 307, 311–12, 313, 314, 323, 324
great tower (*magna turris*), 9, 10, 25, 26; features in and out, 25–8; group of one type in Ireland (13th century), 87 (cf. Ferns, Lea etc); other early Irish great towers, 91–2; steady progression from rectangular to round theory exploded, 7, 28–30, 92
Greek Fire, 42–3, 47, 57
gun-ports, 58–9; *and see* Caister, Noltland, Raglan, Tolquhon etc
gunpowder, effect on development of castles, 7–8, 56–9, 83 (Scotland)

hand-guns, 57–8, *58*
Harold II of England, 14, 16
Hastings, battle of, 13, 16, *17*
Henry I of England (1100-35), 13, 24, 35, 43, 302
Henry II of England (1154–89), 21, 38, 40, 48–9, 67, 72, 88, 89, 91, 107
Henry III of England (1216–72), 41, 46, 49, 54, 67, 72, 106, 300, 307
Henry VI of England (1422–61), 100
Henry VII of England (1485–1509), 111, 112

Henry VIII of England (1509–47), 111, 112
Hereward the Wake, 14, 18
hoarding (wooden), 44, *44*

James II of Scotland: commissions Ravenscraig, 83; killed by cannon at siege of Roxburgh, 57
James II of England (VII of Scotland), 57, 95, 102
James III of Scotland, 58
James V of Scotland, 58, 82, 85
James VI of Scotland, 82, 101, 114
James of St George, Master, 24, 37, 56, 63–4, 66, 78, 86, 298, 299, 306, 307, 311, 321, 322
John, King of England (1199–1216), 29, 38, 39, 40, 43, 54, 67, 89, 106

knights, 11, 14

Leland, John, 16th-century antiquary, 112
Llywelyn the Great, Prince of all Wales, 67, 302, 303, 306, 307, 308
Llywelyn the Last, Prince of Wales (died 1282), 299, 300–1, 307, 308, 309, 320
loops, types, *46*, 46–7, *47*
L-plan tower-house (type of castle), 81
luggies (Scottish castles) 79, 249, 255

machicolation: British, *45*; Irish, *45*, 98–100, *99*, *100*
Madog ap Llywelyn: attacks Caernarfon, 63, 300, 306, Harlech, 311
mangonel, *41*, 42
maps: British mottes, *17*; impressment of labour to build castles in Wales, *61*; Irish mottes, *18*
Marshal, William, Earl of Pembroke, 92, 304, 318
Mary I of England (1553–8), 112
Mary, Queen of Scots, 82, 113
mining (undermining) of castles, 43, *43*, 44, *44*; *and see* Dover, Rochester, St Andrews
Mons Meg, cannon in

Scotland, 57; at Dumbarton, 58; at Norham, 164; at Threave, 57
Montgomery, Roger de, 67
motte castles, 10, 13, 15, *15*; basic plan, 18–19; construction, 10, 21 (Thetford); in Ireland, 90–1; in Scotland, 73; m. towers, horizontal or vertical beams, 20; numbers of, 17; siting, 18; sizes, 17
Muirchertach MacLochlainn, *ard rí* (Ireland), 88
mural passage, 26, *26*
murder hole, 44–5, *45*

pele tower (type of castle), 68–72
Philip Augustus, King of France, 43
portcullis, 46, *46*
put-log holes, 37, 38

quadrangular castles, 109–10 (eg. Bodiam)

Richard of Wolviston, master mason, 24
Richard I of England (1189–99), 7, 38
Richard II of England, (1377–99), 72
Richard III of England, (1483–5), 11
Robert of Beverley, master mason, 64
Robert the Devil, Duke of Normandy, 13, 14
Robert I (Bruce) of Scotland, 68, 72, 77, 78, 94, 115
Ruadrí Ua Conchobair, 88

shell enclosure, (type of castle), 30–2 (eg. Restormel, Rothesay, Tretower)
siege engines, *see* mangonel, trebuchet
sieges, Ch. 5 *passim*
slighting of castles: Bruce policy in Scotland, 77; Cromwell's after Civil War, especially Ireland, 115
spur bases, 38 (cf. Goodrich, Newtown)
staircases in great towers, 27–8
star-shaped barmkin, 251
Stephen, King of England

(1135–54), 21, 24
stepped L-plan tower-house, *83*, *85*, *253*
stone, types for building, 10, 11, 150
stronghouse (Ireland), 101–2

Thomas, Sir William ap, builder of Raglan, 110
Tigernán Ua Ruairk, King of Bréifne, 88
Toirrdelbach Ua Conchobair, King of Connacht and *ard rí*, 87
tower-house (Scottish and Irish type of castle), 78–84; Ireland, 93, 95–100; Scotland, *78*
trebuchet, 42, *42*

vassals, 11, 13
vaulting (Irish tower-houses), 98, *98*
Vikings, 13, 14, 20; raids, 11, 12

walls of castle enclosures, gatehouses, towers etc, 44
Warwick, Richard Nevill, Earl of, the Kingmaker, 58, 72, 112
water defences, 52; *and see* Caerphilly, Kenilworth, Skipsea
wells, at Beeston, Dover, Portumna
Welsh-built castles, 66–7
whitewashing of towers, 38
William, Duke of Normandy, and King of England (1066–87), 11, 12, 13, 14, 22, 32, 87, 90, 106; builds first castles in England, 13, 15, 16, 17, 20, 22; introduces feudal order, 14, 16, 18, 20
William the Lion, King of Scotland, 72
William II of England (1087–1100), 23, 32, 71, 106
William III of England, Scotland and Ireland (1689–1702), 95, 102
windows in towers, 26–7

yett, 77

Z-plan castles (Scotland and Ireland), 83–4, 101